Oh! 1001 Homemade Jello Recipes

(Oh! 1001 Homemade Jello Recipes - Volume 1)

Ellen Grubbs

Content

CHAPTER 1: GELATIN DESSERT RECIPES 14

1. Apricot Angel Dessert 14
2. Apricot Delight 14
3. April Fools Berry Soda 15
4. Banana Anna Surprise 15
5. Bavarian Cream Bonnet 16
6. Berry Applesauce Gelatin 16
7. Berry Cream Dessert 17
8. Bing Cherry Amaretti Fool 17
9. Blackberry Cloud Parfaits 18
10. Body Cubes 18
11. Broken Glass Dessert 19
12. Broken Glass Torte 19
13. California Cranberry Torte 20
14. Carrot Pineapple Gelatin Salad 20
15. Cherry Chiffon Gelatin 21
16. Cherry Chocolate Parfaits 21
17. Cherry Cinnamon Dessert Ring 22
18. Cherry Gelatin Flowers 22
19. Cherry Gelatin Salad 23
20. Cherry Gelatin Supreme 23
21. Cherry Mincemeat Mold 24
22. Cherry Rice Fluff 24
23. Chocolate Bavarian With Strawberry Cream 25
24. Chocolate Lime Dessert 25
25. Chocolate Party Cake 26
26. Chocolate Quivers 27
27. Christmas Gelatin Cutouts 27
28. Contest Winning Blueberry Cream Dessert 27
29. Contest Winning Raspberry Ribbon Pie ...28
30. Contest Winning Strawberry Pretzel Dessert 29
31. Cool Coffee Gels 29
32. Cool Mandarin Dessert 30
33. Cool And Creamy Raspberry Delight 30
34. Cottage Cheese Gelatin Mold 31
35. Cran Raspberry Gelatin Dessert 31
36. Cranberry Cream 31
37. Cranberry Jell O Mold 32
38. Cranberry Parfaits 32
39. Cranberry Raspberry Gelatin Salad 33
40. Cranbrosia Gelatin Mold 33
41. Creamy Citrus Mousse 34
42. Creamy Fruit Medley 34
43. Creamy Gelatin Dessert 35
44. Creamy Strawberry Dessert 35
45. Dark Chocolate Panna Cotta 36
46. Dinosaur Eggs 37
47. Easy Cranberry Chiffon Pie 37
48. Edible Juice 38
49. Eggnog Bavarian 38
50. Eggnog Gelatin Mold 39
51. Espresso Panna Cotta 39
52. Fluffy Lemon Dessert 40
53. Fluffy Lemon Squares 40
54. Fluffy Lemonade Gelatin 41
55. Fluffy Orange Gelatin Pie 41
56. Fluffy Rice Dessert 42
57. French Cream With Sugared Grapes 42
58. Frosted Fruit Gelatin 43
59. Frosted Fruit Gelatin Dessert 43
60. Frozen Peach Shortcake Squares 44
61. Fruited Cranberry Gelatin Salad 44
62. Gelatin Banana Split 44
63. Gelatin Game Chips 45
64. Gelatin Parfaits 45
65. Gelatin Torte 46
66. Glitter Gelatin Torte 46
67. Grape Bavarian 47
68. Halloween Gelatin Cutouts 48
69. Ice Blue Igloo And Penguins 48
70. Iced Tea Parfaits 49
71. Icy Blue Parfaits 49
72. Jeweled Gelatin Torte 50
73. Kiwi Lime Gelatin 50
74. Ladyfinger Lemon Dessert 51
75. Layered Cranberry Dessert 51
76. Layered Pudding Dessert 52
77. Lemon Chiffon Dessert 52
78. Lemon Cloud Desserts 53
79. Lemon Fluff Dessert 53
80. Lemon Panna Cotta With Berries 54
81. Lemon Torte With Fresh Berries 54
82. Lemonade Cheesecake Parfaits 55
83. Lemony Tropic Layered Dessert 56
84. Light Christmas Cake 56
85. Light Lemon Fluff Dessert 57

86.	Light Lemon Pie	57
87.	Light Strawberry Gelatin Pie	58
88.	Lime Chiffon Dessert	58
89.	Lime Fluff	59
90.	Lucky Lime Salad	59
91.	Luscious Lime Angel Squares	60
92.	Make Ahead Shortcake	60
93.	Makeover Blueberry Whipped Topping Dessert	61
94.	Makeover Strawberry Pretzel Dessert	61
95.	Mandarin Orange Cream Pie	62
96.	Maple Cream Fluff	63
97.	Maple Syrup Cream	63
98.	Marvelous Melon	63
99.	Mini Orange Gelatin Molds	64
100.	Mocha Parfait Dessert	64
101.	Molded Margaritas	65
102.	Molded Raspberry Gelatin	65
103.	Mom's Gelatin Fruit Salad	66
104.	No Bake Strawberry Dessert	66
105.	Orange Bavarian	67
106.	Orange Blossom Gelatin	67
107.	Orange Charlotte	68
108.	Orange Cream Cheesecake	68
109.	Orange Cream Dessert	69
110.	Orange Lime Gelatin Ring	69
111.	Orange Pineapple Dessert	70
112.	Orange Whip	70
113.	Panna Cotta With Mixed Berries	71
114.	Panna Cotta With Papaya Coulis	71
115.	Pastel Torte	72
116.	Peach Delight	73
117.	Peach Gelatin Dessert	73
118.	Peach Topped Cake	74
119.	Peaches & Cream Dessert	74
120.	Peaches 'n' Cream Gelatin Dessert	75
121.	Peachy Cream Pie	75
122.	Pear Gelatin Salad	76
123.	Peppermint Charlotte	76
124.	Pineapple Delight	77
125.	Pineapple Lime Gelatin	78
126.	Pink Bonnet Gelatin	78
127.	Pink Cloud	79
128.	Potluck Cherry Compote	79
129.	Pretzel Jell O Dessert	79
130.	Pretzel Strawberry Dessert	80
131.	Prism Cake	81
132.	Pumpkin Mousse Pie With Gingersnap Crust	81
133.	Raspberry Bavarian Cake	82
134.	Raspberry Cream	83
135.	Raspberry Cream Gelatin	83
136.	Raspberry Delight	83
137.	Raspberry Gelatin Dessert	84
138.	Raspberry Gelatin Ring	84
139.	Raspberry Icebox Dessert	85
140.	Raspberry Squares	85
141.	Raspberry Whip	86
142.	Red 'n' Green Gelatin	87
143.	Red Raspberry Mousse Dessert	87
144.	Refreshing Cranberry Ice	88
145.	Refreshing Strawberry Pie	88
146.	Rhubarb Rumble	89
147.	Rhubarb Shortbread Squares	89
148.	Rhubarb Strawberry Torte	90
149.	Russian Cream	90
150.	Russian Cream Dessert	91
151.	Russian Creme	91
152.	Russian Creme Heart	92
153.	Sangria Gelatin Dessert	92
154.	Spiced Peach Pie	93
155.	Spiced Tea Delight	93
156.	Stained Glass Gelatin	94
157.	Strawberry Angel Dessert	95
158.	Strawberry Banana Cups	95
159.	Strawberry Banana Delight	96
160.	Strawberry Banana Dessert	96
161.	Strawberry Cloud	96
162.	Strawberry Cream Dessert	97
163.	Strawberry Dessert	97
164.	Strawberry Fluff	98
165.	Strawberry Gelatin Dessert	98
166.	Strawberry Graham Dessert	99
167.	Strawberry Lemon Bavarian	99
168.	Strawberry Malted Mousse Cups	100
169.	Strawberry Rice Dessert	100
170.	Sugarless Licorice Stars	101
171.	Sunny Peaches & Cream Pie	102
172.	Swedish Creme	102
173.	Swedish Rice Ring	103
174.	Sweetheart Mousse	103
175.	Tangy Citrus Gelatin Cups	104
176.	Tart Orange Gelatin Salad	104
177.	Triple Orange Fluff	105

178. Tropical Island Dessert 105
179. Tropical Rainbow Dessert 106
180. Tuxedo Cream Dessert 106
181. Valentine Cutouts 107
182. Watermelon Gelatin Cups 107
183. Watermelon Gelatin Dessert....................108
184. Watermelon Slices..................................108
185. White Chocolate Panna Cotta With
Espresso Syrup 109
186. White Chocolate Terrine With Caramel
Sauce 109
187. Wiggly Pumpkins 110
188. Winner's Trophy Dessert........................110

CHAPTER 2: JELLO CAKE RECIPES......111

189. Berry Cheesecake Dessert.......................111
190. Berry Dream Cake 112
191. Best Rhubarb Pudding Cake 112
192. Blackberry Cake.....................................113
193. Blueberry Pudding Cake 113
194. Brown Sugar Pudding Cake....................114
195. Cake With Pineapple Pudding 114
196. Caramel Pudding Cake 115
197. Cherry Dream Cake 115
198. Cherry Pudding Cake 116
199. Chocolate Malt Pudding Cake 116
200. Chocolate Pudding Cake.........................117
201. Chocolate Pudding Cake Cups 117
202. Chocolate Pudding Cakes 118
203. Chocolate Covered Cherry Pudding Cake
118
204. Chocolate Pecan Pudding Cakes 119
205. Contest Winning Raspberry Chocolate
Torte120
206. Cranberry Orange Cake 120
207. Date Pudding Cake 121
208. Date Pudding Cake Loaf..........................121
209. Double Chocolate Pudding Cake 122
210. Elvis' Pudding Cake.................................123
211. Favorite Lemon Cheesecake Dessert.......123
212. Flag Cake..124
213. Flower Garden Cupcakes 124
214. Fluffy Lemon Pudding Cake 125
215. Frosted Blackberry Cake..........................125
216. Frozen Mini Berry Trifles 126
217. Fudge Pudding Cake.................................126
218. Gingerbread Pudding Cake 127

219. Glazed Lemon Flute Cake 127
220. Golden Lemon Cake 128
221. Grandma Pietz's Cranberry Cake Pudding
129
222. Halloween Poke Cake 129
223. Hawaiian Sunset Cake 130
224. Healthy Hot Fudge Pudding Cake 130
225. Healthy Lemon Cake 131
226. Hot Fudge Pudding Cake 131
227. Lemon Berry Cake 132
228. Lemon Blueberry Cheesecake..................133
229. Lemon Cake..133
230. Lemon Cheesecake Pies 134
231. Lemon Pudding Cake 134
232. Lemon Pudding Cake Cups......................135
233. Lime Pudding Cakes 135
234. Makeover Strawberry Cake......................136
235. Mamaw Emily's Strawberry Cake 136
236. Mardi Gras Cupcakes 137
237. Marmalade Pudding Cakes 138
238. Midsummer Sponge Cake.........................138
239. Mocha Pudding Cakes 139
240. No Bake Blueberry Cheesecake................139
241. No Bake Cheesecake 140
242. No Bake Cheesecake Pie...........................141
243. No Bake Cherry Cheesecake 141
244. No Bake Chocolate Cheesecake 142
245. No Bake Chocolate Chip Cannoli
Cheesecake 142
246. No Bake Lemon Cheesecake 143
247. No Bake Lemon Cheesecake Pie...............143
248. No Bake Lime Cheesecake 144
249. No Bake Oreo Cheesecake.........................144
250. No Bake Pumpkin Cheesecake..................145
251. No Bake Strawberry Cheesecake Pie 146
252. Old Fashioned Rhubarb Pudding Cake...146
253. Orange Angel Food Cake Dessert 147
254. Orange Cream Cake 147
255. Orange Dream Torte 148
256. Orange Lemon Cake 148
257. Ozark Pudding Cake.................................149
258. Peach Angel Dessert.................................149
259. Peach Melba Mountain 150
260. Persimmon Pudding Cake 151
261. Pineapple Pudding Cake 151
262. Pineapple Upside Down Cake 152
263. Pistachio Pudding Cake 153

264. Pool Party Cake 153
265. Pudding Pound Cake Dessert 154
266. Pudding Filled Butterfly Cupcakes...........155
267. Pudding Filled Devil's Food Cake............155
268. Rainbow Layer Cake 156
269. Raspberry Angel Cake 157
270. Raspberry Cake 157
271. Raspberry Lemon Cake 158
272. Red, White & Blueberry Poke Cake 158
273. Rhubarb Pudding Cake 159
274. Rice Pudding Cake..............................160
275. Rich Chocolate Pudding Cake 160
276. Rosemary & Thyme Lemon Pudding Cakes 161
277. Slow Cooker Apple Pudding Cake...........162
278. Spiced Pudding Cake.............................162
279. Strawberry Bavarian Torte.........................163
280. Strawberry Cake 163
281. Strawberry Cheesecake Torte....................164
282. Strawberry Heart Cake 165
283. Strawberry Poke Cake 165
284. Strawberry Rhubarb Torte 166
285. Strawberry Schaum Torte 166
286. Strawberry Shortcake Dessert...................167
287. Strawberry Sunshine Cake 167
288. Strawberry Banana Pudding Cake 168
289. Strawberry Rhubarb Upside Down Cake169
290. Sugarplum Pudding Cake.......................169
291. Sunny Coconut Cake 170
292. Sunny Orange Layer Cake 170
293. Triple Berry No Bake Cheesecake...........171
294. Upside Down Berry Cake 172
295. Upside Down Strawberry Shortcake........172
296. Watermelon Cake..............................173
297. Wave Your Flag Cheesecake...................173
298. Wearing O' Green Cake........................174

CHAPTER 3: JELLO PUDDING RECIPES

....175

299. "S'more, Please" Trifle 175
300. Ambrosia Pudding.............................175
301. Angel Lush...Make It Your Way! 176
302. Apple Spice Cake Trifle 176
303. Aunt Ruth's Famous Butterscotch
Cheesecake 177
304. Banana Butterfinger Pudding....................177
305. Banana Cheesecake Pie 178

306. Banana Chocolate Coconut Pie 179
307. Banana Chocolate Cream Pie....................179
308. Banana Chocolate Parfaits.......................180
309. Banana Cream Brownie Dessert...............180
310. Banana Cream Cheesecake 181
311. Banana Cream Parfait..........................182
312. Banana Flip Cake 182
313. Banana Graham Dessert.........................183
314. Banana Ice Cream 183
315. Banana Pudding Dessert........................184
316. Banana Pudding Parfaits........................184
317. Banana Split Cheesecake 185
318. Banana Split Icebox Cake 185
319. Banana Split Pie...............................186
320. Banana Split Pudding 186
321. Banana And Nut Cake 187
322. Banana Berry Pie 187
323. Berry Cookie Torte 188
324. Berry, Lemon And Doughnut Hole Trifle
188
325. Berry Glazed Chocolate Cake 189
326. Berry Marshmallow Trifle.......................189
327. Birthday Cake Freezer Pops 190
328. Black Forest Dream Dessert 190
329. Black Forest Mousse 191
330. Black Forest Parfaits...........................191
331. Blarney Stones 192
332. Blueberry Cheesecake Ice Cream 192
333. Blueberry Lemon Crepes 193
334. Blueberry Peach Trifle..........................194
335. Boston Cream Pie 194
336. Boston Cream Pie With Chocolate Glaze
195
337. Brownie Mocha Trifle 196
338. Brownie Toffee Trifle 196
339. Budapest Roll..................................197
340. Butter Ball Chiffons............................197
341. Butter Crunch Pudding 198
342. Butterfinger Cookie Bars 198
343. Buttermilk Fruit Topping 199
344. Butterscotch Apple Treat 199
345. Butterscotch Bliss Layered Dessert.........200
346. Butterscotch Bones............................200
347. Butterscotch Gingerbread Men 201
348. Butterscotch Pecan Cookies....................201
349. Butterscotch Pudding Parfaits 202
350. Butterscotch Pudding Torte....................202

351. Butterscotch Pumpkin Mousse 203
352. Butterscotch Pumpkin Pie 203
353. Butterscotch Pumpkin Puffs 204
354. Butterscotch Swirl Cake 204
355. Butterscotch Toffee Cheesecake Bars 205
356. Cake With Lemon Sauce 206
357. Calgary Nanaimo Bars 206
358. Candied Orange Chocolate Cake 207
359. Candy Bar Brownie Trifle 207
360. Candy Bar Freezer Dessert 208
361. Cappuccino Chocolate Pie 208
362. Cappuccino Mousse Trifle 209
363. Cappuccino Parfaits 209
364. Cappuccino Trifle 210
365. Caramel Apple Trifle Delight 210
366. Caramel Banana Ice Cream Pie 211
367. Caramel Pecan Delight 211
368. Caribbean Coconut Rum Cake 212
369. Cheery Cherry Parfaits 213
370. Cheesecake Strawberry Pie 213
371. Cherry Angel Delight 214
372. Cherry Angel Dessert 214
373. Cherry Cream Trifle 214
374. Cherry Crunch Ice Cream 215
375. Cherry Pistachio Bread 215
376. Cherry Rice Dessert 216
377. Cherry Trifle 217
378. Chewy Chocolate Chip Cookies 217
379. Chilly Peanut Butter Pie 218
380. Choco Scotch Marble Cake 218
381. Chocolate & Peanut Butter Pudding Pie
With Bananas 219
382. Chocolate Berry Parfaits 219
383. Chocolate Bundt Cake 220
384. Chocolate Cherry Dessert 220
385. Chocolate Cherry Trifle 221
386. Chocolate Chip Cake 221
387. Chocolate Chip Cookie Delight 222
388. Chocolate Chip Cookie Dessert 222
389. Chocolate Chip Cookie Pizza 223
390. Chocolate Chip Cupcakes 223
391. Chocolate Chip Oatmeal Cookies 224
392. Chocolate Chip Snack Cake 224
393. Chocolate Coconut Bundt Cake 225
394. Chocolate Cream Cheese Pie 226
395. Chocolate Cream Pudding Dessert 226
396. Chocolate Creme Cakes 227
397. Chocolate Delight Dessert 227
398. Chocolate Dream Dessert 228
399. Chocolate Eclair Dessert 228
400. Chocolate Eclair Graham Dessert 229
401. Chocolate Eclair Squares 229
402. Chocolate Espresso Lava Cake 230
403. Chocolate Fudge Mousse 230
404. Chocolate Hazelnut Parfaits 231
405. Chocolate Ice Cream Pie 231
406. Chocolate Lover's Eclairs 231
407. Chocolate Mallow Pie 232
408. Chocolate Mint Cream Cake 233
409. Chocolate Mint Delight 233
410. Chocolate Mint Eclair Dessert 234
411. Chocolate Mint Freeze 234
412. Chocolate Mint Parfaits 235
413. Chocolate Mousse 235
414. Chocolate Mousse Frosting 236
415. Chocolate Nut Candies 236
416. Chocolate Peanut Butter Pie 237
417. Chocolate Peanut Torte 237
418. Chocolate Peppermint Ice Cream Dessert
238
419. Chocolate Pineapple Trifle 238
420. Chocolate Pudding Pizza 239
421. Chocolate Swirl Delight 240
422. Chocolate Torte With Raspberry Filling .240
423. Chocolate Trifle 241
424. Chocolate Cherry Mousse Delight 241
425. Christmas Gingerbread Trifle 242
426. Christmas Trifle 242
427. Cinnamon Apple Coffee Cake 243
428. Cocoa Chocolate Chip Cookies 243
429. Coconut Angel Squares 244
430. Coconut Banana Chocolate Cream Pie ...244
431. Coconut Cream Dessert 245
432. Coconut Cream Pie 245
433. Coconut Crunch Delight 246
434. Coconut Peach Pie 246
435. Coconut Pineapple Pops 247
436. Coconut Pistachio Pie 247
437. Coconut Poppy Seed Bundt Cake 248
438. Coconut Raspberry Trifle 248
439. Coconut Supreme Torte 249
440. Coconut Trifle 249
441. Coffee Cream Tortilla Cups 250
442. Coffee Nut Torte 250

443. Cookie Pudding Pots.................................251
444. Cool Chocolate Mousse..........................251
445. Country Poppy Seed Cake......................252
446. Country Style Vanilla Ice Cream.............252
447. Cran Orange Delight..............................253
448. Cranberry Bliss Cookies.........................254
449. Cranberry Ice Cream Pie........................254
450. Cream Puff Dessert................................255
451. Cream Puff Monsters..............................255
452. Cream Puff Swans..................................256
453. Cream Filled Strawberries.......................257
454. Creamy Banana Berry Pie.......................257
455. Creamy Cappuccino Mousse....................258
456. Creamy Chocolate Cake Roll...................258
457. Creamy Coconut Dessert.........................259
458. Creamy Cranberry Ice Cream Pie.............260
459. Creamy Mango Loaf Cake........................260
460. Creamy Peach Pudding...........................260
461. Creamy Pineapple Cake..........................261
462. Creamy Rhubarb Dessert.........................261
463. Crisp Butter Pecan Cookies.....................262
464. Crunchy Chocolate Pudding Squares.......262
465. Dark Chocolate Carrot Cake....................263
466. Decadent Nanaimo Bars..........................264
467. Delightful Brownies................................264
468. Deluxe Chocolate Pudding......................265
469. Dirt Dessert..265
470. Double Berry Lemon Dessert...................266
471. Double Chocolate Bundt Cakes...............266
472. Double Chocolate Pie.............................267
473. Double Frosted Brownies.........................267
474. Double Chocolate Cream Roll..................268
475. Double Decker Banana Cups....................269
476. Double Layer Pumpkin Pie......................269
477. Doughnut Parfaits..................................270
478. Down South Sweet Tea Cake...................270
479. Dr Pepper Cake.....................................271
480. Dreamy Creamy Peanut Butter Pie..........271
481. Easy Banana Cream Pie..........................272
482. Easy Boston Cream Cake.........................273
483. Easy Chocolate Pound Cake....................273
484. Easy Chocolate Rice Pudding..................274
485. Easy Grasshopper Pie.............................274
486. Easy Pineapple Coconut Cake.................274
487. Easy Pistachio Bundt Cake......................275
488. Easy Strawberry Napoleons.....................275
489. Easy Trifle For Two................................276

490. Easy Vanilla Ice Cream...........................277
491. Eclair Torte...277
492. Eggnog Banana Cream Pies.....................278
493. Eggnog Ladyfinger Dessert......................278
494. Eggnog Pudding.....................................279
495. Eggnog Tube Cake.................................279
496. Elegant Eggnog Dessert..........................280
497. English Trifle...280
498. Fancy Mousse Towers.............................281
499. Festive Apricot Tart................................281
500. Flowerpot Dirt Cake...............................282
501. Fluffy Chocolate Mousse Frosting...........282
502. French Vanilla Cream Puffs.....................283
503. Frosted Butter Cutouts...........................283
504. Frosted Cinnamon Rolls.........................284
505. Frosty Coffee Pie...................................284
506. Frosty Peanut Butter Cups......................285
507. Frosty Pistachio Delight..........................285
508. Frozen Cranberry Pie With Candied
Almonds...286
509. Frozen Lemon Pie..................................287
510. Frozen Mousse Brownie Sandwiches.......287
511. Frozen Pistachio Dessert With Raspberry
Sauce..288
512. Fruit 'n' Pudding Dessert.........................288
513. Fruit Fluff..289
514. Fruit Topped Almond Cream...................289
515. Fruity Angel Food Trifle.........................290
516. Fruity Hazelnut Trifle.............................290
517. Fudgy Almond Pops...............................291
518. Fudgy Chocolate Dessert........................291
519. Fudgy Raspberry Torte...........................292
520. Fudgy White Chocolate Pudding Pie.......292
521. Gift Box Wedding Cake..........................293
522. Gingerbread Pumpkin Trifle....................294
523. Gingerbread Trifle..................................295
524. Gingersnap Ice Cream Torte...................295
525. Gingersnap Pumpkin Pie........................296
526. Glazed Lemon Cake...............................296
527. Golden Chocolate Cake..........................297
528. Golden Pound Cake...............................297
529. Gooey Butterscotch Bars.........................298
530. Graham Cracker Banana Split Dessert.....298
531. Graham Cracker Butterscotch Pie...........299
532. Grandma's Chewy Oatmeal Cookies........299
533. Grandma's English Trifle........................300
534. Hawaiian Cake......................................300

535. Hawaiian Dessert 301
536. Hawaiian Wedding Cake 301
537. Holiday Cheesecake Pie 302
538. Holiday English Trifles 302
539. Holiday Fig Torte 303
540. Homemade Chocolate Easter Eggs 303
541. Honey Gingerbread Trifle 304
542. Ice Cream Pudding 305
543. Irish Creme Chocolate Trifle 305
544. Island Swim Dessert 306
545. Layered Banana Chocolate Pudding 307
546. Layered Brownie Dessert 307
547. Layered Candy Cane Dessert 308
548. Layered Carrot Cake 308
549. Layered Chocolate Peanut Butter Pie 309
550. Layered Chocolate Pudding Dessert 309
551. Layered Ice Box Dessert 310
552. Layered Lemon Pies 311
553. Lemon Bundt Cake 311
554. Lemon Butterfly Cupcakes 312
555. Lemon Cream Cheese Pie 313
556. Lemon Cream Torte 313
557. Lemon Custard Cake 314
558. Lemon Delight Trifle 314
559. Lemon Poppy Seed Cake 315
560. Lemon Pudding Dessert 315
561. Lemon Rice Pudding 316
562. Lemon Slice Sugar Cookies 316
563. Light Lemon Cake 317
564. Lighter Boston Cream Pie 317
565. Low Fat Strawberry Cream Dessert 318
566. Low Fat Vanilla Pudding 319
567. Luscious Apple Trifle 319
568. Macadamia Chip Cookies 319
569. Makeover Cherry Almond Mousse Pie ...320
570. Makeover Coconut Supreme Torte 321
571. Makeover Toffee Crunch Dessert 321
572. Mandarin Orange Cake 322
573. Milky Way Ice Cream 322
574. Mini Coffee Cakes 323
575. Mini Rum Cakes 323
576. Mint Cake 324
577. Mocha Angel Food Torte 324
578. Mocha Java Pie With Kahlua Cream 325
579. Mocha Parfaits 325
580. Mom's Chocolate Chip Cookies 326
581. Moon Cake 326

582. Napoleon Cremes 327
583. No Bake Pineapple Sour Cream Pie 327
584. Nutty Butterscotch Bites 328
585. Old Fashioned Banana Cream Pie 329
586. On The Green Cake 329
587. Orange Creme Squares 330
588. Orange Pineapple Torte 330
589. Paradise Parfaits 331
590. Patriotic Dessert 331
591. Patriotic Trifle 332
592. Pay Dirt Cake 332
593. Peach Ice Cream 333
594. Peach Pudding 333
595. Peanut Butter Brownie Trifle 334
596. Peanut Butter Chocolate Dessert 334
597. Peanut Butter Chocolate Pie 335
598. Peanut Butter Chocolate Pudding 335
599. Peanut Butter Chocolate Tarts 336
600. Peanut Butter Icebox Dessert 336
601. Peanut Butter Puddingwiches 337
602. Peanut Butter Tarts 337
603. Peanut Pudding Dessert 338
604. Pecan Butterscotch Cookies 339
605. Pecan Chip Tube Cake 339
606. Pilgrim Pudding 340
607. Pina Colada Bundt Cake 340
608. Pineapple Angel Food Torte 341
609. Pineapple Coconut Pie 341
610. Pineapple Fluff Pie 341
611. Pineapple Icebox Dessert 342
612. Pineapple Orange Cake 342
613. Pineapple Orange Trifle 343
614. Pineapple Pudding 343
615. Pistachio Bundt Cake 344
616. Pistachio Cheesecake 344
617. Pistachio Cherry Squares 345
618. Pistachio Coconut Cake 345
619. Pistachio Cookie Dessert 346
620. Pistachio Cookies 346
621. Pistachio Cream Dessert 347
622. Pistachio Fluff 347
623. Pistachio Ice Cream Dessert 348
624. Pistachio Pudding Parfaits 348
625. Pistachio Pudding Tarts 349
626. Pistachio Puffs 349
627. Pistachio And Coconut Cake 350
628. Possum Pie 350

629. Puddin' Cones...................................351
630. Pudding Pumpkin Pie....................351
631. Pudding Sugar Cookies 352
632. Pudding Topped Fruit Salad 352
633. Pumpkin Bundt Cake 353
634. Pumpkin Charlotte.........................353
635. Pumpkin Chiffon Pie......................354
636. Pumpkin Chip Cream Pie 355
637. Pumpkin Cream Trifle 355
638. Pumpkin Crunch Parfaits 356
639. Pumpkin Gingersnap Dessert.................356
640. Pumpkin Layered Angel Cake.........357
641. Pumpkin Mousse............................357
642. Pumpkin Pie Dessert 358
643. Pumpkin Pudding 358
644. Pumpkin Pudding Dessert..............359
645. Pumpkin Pudding Desserts 359
646. Pumpkin Spice Cake.......................360
647. Pumpkin Spiced Pudding...............360
648. Pumpkin Trifle 361
649. Punch Bowl Cake...........................361
650. Punch Bowl Trifle..........................362
651. Quick Apple Cream Pie 362
652. Quick Chocolate Mousse................363
653. Quick Coconut Cream Pie..............363
654. Quick Creamy Banana Pie 363
655. Quick Dirt Cake 364
656. Quick Icebox Sandwiches...............364
657. Quick Peanut Butter Pudding.................365
658. Quick Rice Pudding........................365
659. Raisin Butterscotch Pie 366
660. Raspberry Brownie Dessert.............366
661. Raspberry Chocolate Trifle.............367
662. Raspberry Cream Cake....................367
663. Raspberry Cream Trifle...................368
664. Raspberry Mousse Pie 368
665. Raspberry Peach Delight 369
666. Raspberry Pudding Parfaits 369
667. Raspberry Trifle..............................370
668. Raspberry Vanilla Pudding Parfaits.........370
669. Rave Review Coconut Cake 371
670. Rawhide's Whiskey Cake.................371
671. Red, White And Blueberry Pie..................372
672. Rich Chocolate Cream Bars 372
673. Rich Peach Ice Cream 373
674. Rocky Road Freezer Pie...................373
675. Root Beer Float Pie 374

676. S'more Parfaits................................374
677. Sacher Torte Cookies 375
678. Salted Butterscotch & Pecan No Bakes ..375
679. Shortcut Shortcake..........................376
680. Shortcut Strawberry Vanilla Dessert........376
681. Six Fruit Trifle 377
682. Skinny Mint Chip Ice Cream....................377
683. Slow Cooker Chocolate Lava Cake..........378
684. Snappy Pumpkin Dessert............................378
685. Snowflake Bar Cookies 379
686. Southern Chocolate Torte 379
687. Special Chocolate Ice Cream....................380
688. Spiced Sherry Cake 381
689. St. Patrick's Day Cupcakes 381
690. St. Patrick's Day Pistachio Cupcakes 382
691. Stars And Stripes Torte....................382
692. Strawberries 'n' Cream Trifle....................383
693. Strawberry Banana Trifle 383
694. Strawberry Bliss.............................384
695. Strawberry Cheesecake Pie 384
696. Strawberry Ice Cream Dessert 385
697. Strawberry Lemon Trifle.................385
698. Strawberry Peach Trifle..................386
699. Strawberry Raspberry Trifle 386
700. Strawberry Shortcake Trifle............387
701. Strawberry Sorbet Sensation 387
702. Strawberry Swirl Mousse Tarts 388
703. Strawberry Trifle 388
704. Strawberry Banana Graham Pudding 389
705. Strudel Pudding Dessert 389
706. Sugar Free Pineapple Pie 390
707. Sugar Free Pumpkin Chiffon Pie.............390
708. Sugar Free Chocolate Eclairs 390
709. Sugarless Rice Pudding...................391
710. Swedish Cream 392
711. Sweetheart Trifle 392
712. Tempting Caramel Apple Pudding With
Gingersnap Crust 393
713. Tiny Tim Trifle...............................393
714. Tiramisu Parfaits 394
715. Toasted Pecan Pudding...................395
716. Toffee Brownie Trifle 395
717. Toffee Cream Pie 396
718. Toffee Ice Cream Dessert 396
719. Triple Fudge Brownies....................397
720. Triple Layer Mud Pie......................397
721. Triple Chocolate Cake With Raspberry

Sauce 398

722. Tropical Fruit Cream Pie 398
723. Tropical Meringue Tarts 399
724. Two Layer Silk Pie 399
725. Vanilla Chocolate Chip Cake 400
726. Vanilla Cream Puffs................................400
727. Vanilla Fruit Dessert...............................401
728. Vanilla Pudding Dessert..........................401
729. Very Berry Cream Pie.............................402
730. Very Berry Parfaits.................................402
731. Walnut Carrot Bundt Cake 403
732. Watergate Cake......................................404
733. Wedding Swan Cream Puffs.....................404
734. Whipped Chocolate Dessert 405
735. White Chocolate Berry Parfaits 405
736. White Chocolate Pie 406
737. White Chocolate Tarts 406

CHAPTER 4: JELLO SALAD RECIPES...407

738. 7 Layer Gelatin Salad..............................407
739. Angler's Gelatin Delight 407
740. Apple Cherry Salad 408
741. Apple Cider Gelatin Salad 408
742. Apple Cider Salad...................................409
743. Apple Cranberry Delight 409
744. Apple Cinnamon Gelatin.........................410
745. Applesauce Gelatin Squares 410
746. Applesauce Berry Gelatin Mold...............411
747. Applesauce Raspberry Gelatin Mold 411
748. Apricot Aspic..411
749. Apricot Gelatin Mold.............................412
750. Apricot Gelatin Salad 412
751. Apricot Orange Gelatin Salad 413
752. Asian Veggie Gelatin 413
753. Beet Salad 414
754. Berry Gelatin Mold................................414
755. Berry Gelatin Ring 415
756. Best Rosy Rhubarb Mold........................415
757. Best Rosy Rhubarb Salad........................416
758. Blueberry Gelatin Salad..........................416
759. Blueberry Raspberry Gelatin 417
760. Broken Glass Gelatin 417
761. Buttermilk Orange Salad.........................418
762. Cabbage Cucumber Gelatin Cups 418
763. Cherry Coke Salad.................................419
764. Cherry Cola Salad..................................419
765. Cherry Cranberry Salad 419

766. Cherry Gelatin Fruit Salad........................420
767. Cherry Gelatin Salad With Bananas.........420
768. Cherry Gelatin Squares 421
769. Cherry Pineapple Salad...........................421
770. Cherry Ribbon Salad...............................422
771. Christmas Cranberry Salad 422
772. Christmas Gelatin Ring............................423
773. Christmas Ribbon Salad..........................423
774. Christmas Wreath Salad 424
775. Chunky Cranberry Salad 424
776. Cider Cranberry Salad 425
777. Cinnamon Apple Salad............................425
778. Cinnamon Gelatin Salad 426
779. Circus Peanut Gelatin.............................426
780. Citrus Chiffon Salad 426
781. Citrus Gelatin Salad 427
782. Cool Cucumber Salad.............................428
783. Cool Lime Salad 428
784. Cottage Cheese Fluff..............................428
785. Cran Blueberry Mold 429
786. Cran Orange Gelatin Salad 429
787. Cran Raspberry Gelatin...........................430
788. Cran Raspberry Gelatin Salad 430
789. Cran Raspberry Sherbet Mold.................430
790. Cranberry Cherry Salad 431
791. Cranberry Delight 431
792. Cranberry Eggnog Salad 432
793. Cranberry Fruit Mold.............................432
794. Cranberry Gelatin Mold..........................433
795. Cranberry Gelatin Salad 433
796. Cranberry Gelatin Salad Mold 434
797. Cranberry Gelatin Squares.......................434
798. Cranberry Luncheon Salad 435
799. Cranberry Mousse Salad..........................436
800. Cranberry Pecan Salad............................436
801. Cranberry Relish Salad 437
802. Cranberry Salad 437
803. Cranberry Salad Mold.............................437
804. Cranberry Turkey Salad...........................438
805. Cranberry Waldorf Gelatin......................438
806. Cranberry Eggnog Gelatin Salad 439
807. Cranberry Pineapple Gelatin Mold 439
808. Cranberry/Orange Molded Salad............440
809. Creamy 'n' Fruity Gelatin Salad 440
810. Creamy Blueberry Gelatin Salad..............441
811. Creamy Citrus Salad...............................441
812. Creamy Cranberry Gelatin.......................442

813. Creamy Cranberry Pineapple Gelatin 442
814. Creamy Fruit Mold 443
815. Creamy Orange Fluff................................443
816. Creamy Orange Gelatin 444
817. Creamy Orange Salad 444
818. Crisp Cranberry Gelatin..........................444
819. Cucumber & Grapefruit Mold.................445
820. Eggnog Molded Salad 445
821. Festive Cranberry Relish Salad.................446
822. Festive Fruit Gelatin................................446
823. Flavorful Cranberry Gelatin Mold 447
824. Fluffy Cranberry Delight 447
825. Fluffy Cranberry Mousse 448
826. Fluffy Lime Salad 448
827. Fluffy Raspberry Salad 449
828. For Goodness Sakes Salad........................449
829. Fourth Of July Jell O 450
830. Frankenstein Salads 450
831. Frosted Cranberry Gelatin Salad 451
832. Frosted Cranberry Salad..........................451
833. Frosted Fruit Gelatin Salad 452
834. Frosted Gelatin Salad 452
835. Frosted Orange Salad 453
836. Frosted Pineapple Lemon Gelatin 453
837. Frosted Strawberry Salad 454
838. Fruit Parfaits 455
839. Fruit Filled Raspberry Ring 455
840. Fruit Packed Gelatin Salad 456
841. Fruited Cranberry Gelatin 456
842. Fruited Cranberry Salad 457
843. Fruited Gelatin Salad 457
844. Fruited Lemon Gelatin Salad 458
845. Fruity Gelatin Salad 458
846. Fruity Lime Salad Mold...........................459
847. Fruity Orange Gelatin 459
848. Fruity Strawberry Gelatin Salad 460
849. Gelatin Christmas Ornaments 460
850. Gelatin Fruit Salad 460
851. Gelatin Ring With Cream Cheese Balls...461
852. Ginger Pear Gelatin 461
853. Gingered Lime Gelatin 462
854. Golden Gelatin Salad 462
855. Golden Glow Gelatin Mold 463
856. Golden Glow Salad..................................463
857. Grandma's Gelatin Fruit Salad................463
858. Grandmother's Orange Salad...................464
859. Grapefruit Gelatin...................................465

860. Grapefruit Gelatin Molds 465
861. Green Flop Jell O 465
862. Guacamole Mousse With Salsa................466
863. Hidden Pear Salad...................................467
864. Holiday Cranberry Gelatin Salad 467
865. Holiday Cranberry Salad 468
866. Holiday Gelatin Mold..............................468
867. Holiday Gelatin Salad..............................469
868. Holiday Ribbon Gelatin 469
869. Igloo Salad..470
870. Jazzy Gelatin 470
871. Jiggly Applesauce 471
872. Layered Berry Gelatin Salad 471
873. Layered Christmas Gelatin 472
874. Layered Cranberry Gelatin Salad 472
875. Layered Gelatin Salad 473
876. Layered Orange Gelatin...........................473
877. Lime Chiffon Jell O 474
878. Lime Delight..474
879. Lime Gelatin Salad 475
880. Lime Pear Salad 475
881. Lime Sherbet Molded Salad.....................476
882. Lime Strawberry Surprise.........................476
883. Lime Pear Gelatin Bells 476
884. Luau Centerpiece 477
885. Luncheon Mold.......................................478
886. Makeover Fluffy Lime Salad 478
887. Mango Delight Gelatin Mold...................479
888. Mango Gelatin Salad................................479
889. Marshmallow Lime Salad.........................480
890. Mini Molded Salads 480
891. Minty Lime Gelatin.................................481
892. Missouri Peach And Applesauce Salad....481
893. Molded Asparagus Salad 481
894. Molded Cherry Pineapple Salad..............482
895. Molded Cranberry Fruit Salad.................483
896. Molded Cranberry Gelatin Salad 483
897. Molded Cranberry Nut Salad 484
898. Molded Cranberry Salad 484
899. Molded Cranberry Orange Salad 485
900. Molded Egg Salad 485
901. Molded Lime Salad 486
902. Molded Peach Gelatin 486
903. Molded Rhubarb Salad............................487
904. Molded Strawberry Salad 487
905. Molded Vegetable Salad...........................487
906. Mom's Orange Spice Gelatin 488

907. Orange Buttermilk Gelatin Salad............488
908. Orange Buttermilk Gelatin Salad Mold...489
909. Orange Buttermilk Salad............489
910. Orange Gelatin Cups............490
911. Orange Gelatin Salad............490
912. Overnight Fruit Cup............490
913. Pastel Gelatin Salad............491
914. Patriotic Gelatin Salad............491
915. Peach Bavarian............492
916. Peach Gelatin Salad............492
917. Peach Cranberry Gelatin Salad............493
918. Peaches 'n' Cream Salad............493
919. Peachy Applesauce Salad............494
920. Pear Lime Gelatin............494
921. Pear Lime Gelatin Salad............495
922. Picnic Potato Squares Salad............495
923. Pina Colada Molded Salad............496
924. Pineapple Citrus Gelatin Salad............496
925. Pineapple Gelatin Salad............497
926. Pineapple Lime Molds............497
927. Pineapple Blueberry Gelatin Salad............498
928. Pineapple Lime Gelatin Mold............498
929. Pomegranate Gelatin............499
930. Pomegranate Cranberry Salad............499
931. Pretty Gelatin Molds............500
932. Quick Cran Raspberry Gelatin............500
933. Quick Cranberry Gelatin Salad............500
934. Rainbow Gelatin............501
935. Rainbow Gelatin Cubes............501
936. Rainbow Gelatin Salad............502
937. Raspberry Congealed Salad............502
938. Raspberry Cranberry Gelatin Salad............503
939. Raspberry Gelatin Jewels............503
940. Raspberry Gelatin Salad............504
941. Raspberry Luscious Gelatin Salad............504
942. Raspberry Pineapple Gelatin Salad............505
943. Red, White 'n' Blue Salad............505
944. Red, White And Blueberry Salad............506
945. Red Hot Gelatin Salad............506
946. Red Hot Molded Hearts............507
947. Red White And Blue Berry Delight............507
948. Refreshing Rhubarb Salad............508
949. Rhubarb Berry Delight Salad............508
950. Rhubarb Pear Gelatin............509
951. Rhubarb Salad............509
952. Rhubarb Strawberry Gelatin Molds............510
953. Rosey Raspberry Salad............510

954. Rosy Rhubarb Mold............510
955. Rosy Rhubarb Salad............511
956. Ruby Apple Salad............511
957. Ruby Gelatin Salad............512
958. Ruby Red Raspberry Salad............512
959. Ruby Red Beet Salad............513
960. Sailboat Salads............513
961. School Colors Salad............514
962. Seaside Gelatin Salad............514
963. Seven Layer Gelatin Salad............515
964. Simple Lime Gelatin Salad............515
965. Six Layer Gelatin Salad............516
966. Slimy Red Goop Salad............516
967. Snow White Salad............517
968. Snowy Raspberry Gelatin Mold............517
969. Sparkling Gelatin Salad............518
970. Sparkling Rhubarb Salad............518
971. Special Strawberry Salad............519
972. Spiced Cranberry Gelatin Mold............519
973. Spiced Cranberry Chutney Gelatin Salad 520
974. Spiced Orange Gelatin Salad............521
975. Spiced Peach Salad............521
976. Spicy Citrus Gelatin Mold............522
977. Spinach Salad Ring............522
978. Spring Rhubarb Salad............523
979. Springtime Luncheon Salad............523
980. Strawberry Apple Salad............524
981. Strawberry Bavarian Salad............524
982. Strawberry Gelatin Salad............525
983. Strawberry Banana Gelatin Salad............525
984. Strawberry Rhubarb Gelatin............526
985. Sugar Free Cranberry Gelatin Salad............526
986. Summertime Strawberry Gelatin Salad....527
987. Sunshine Gelatin Mold............527
988. Sunshine Gelatin Salad............528
989. Sunshine State Salad............529
990. Sweetheart Jell O Salad............529
991. Tangy Cucumber Gelatin............530
992. Tangy Lemon Gelatin............530
993. Tart Cherry Salad............530
994. Thanksgiving Cranberry Gelatin............531
995. Three Layer Fruit Salad............531
996. Three Layer Gelatin Salad............532
997. Three Ring Mold............532
998. Triple Cranberry Salad Mold............533
999. Waldorf Orange Cinnamon Holiday Mold 533

1000. Waldorf Salad Mold 534
1001. Whipped Cream Gelatin Mosaic 534

INDEX **536**
CONCLUSION **541**

Chapter 1: Gelatin Dessert Recipes

***

1. Apricot Angel Dessert

Serving: 12 servings. | Prep: 10mins | Cook: 10mins | Ready in:

Ingredients

- 1 prepared angel food cake (8 to 10 ounces), cubed
- 1 can (15-1/4 ounces) apricot halves, drained and diced
- Sugar substitute equivalent to 1/2 cup sugar
- 3 tablespoons cornstarch
- 3 cups apricot nectar
- 1 package (.3 ounces) sugar-free orange gelatin
- 1 carton (8 ounces) frozen reduced-fat whipped topping, thawed

Direction

- In an unoiled 13x9 inches dish, put cake cubes; put apricots on top. Combine apricot nectar, cornstarch and sugar substitute in a large saucepan until they become smooth. Boil; cook while stirring until thickened, for 2 mins. Discard from heat. Then stir in the gelatin until it has dissolved.
- Pour over apricot and cake. Let chill with a cover until the gelatin has set, about 3 hours. Spread with the whipped topping. Place the leftovers in the refrigerator.

Nutrition Information

- Calories: 202 calories
- Total Fat: 3g fat (2g saturated fat)
- Sodium: 187mg sodium
- Fiber: 1g fiber)
- Total Carbohydrate: 44g carbohydrate (0 sugars
- Cholesterol: 0 cholesterol
- Protein: 3g protein. Diabetic Exchanges: 2 fruit

2. Apricot Delight

Serving: 8 servings. | Prep: 15mins | Cook: 0mins | Ready in:

Ingredients

- 2 cans (5-1/2 ounces each) apricot nectar, divided
- 1 package (.3 ounces) sugar-free orange gelatin
- 1 package (1 ounce) sugar-free instant vanilla pudding mix
- 2/3 cup nonfat dry milk powder
- 1 carton (8 ounces) frozen reduced-fat whipped topping, thawed
- 5 cups cubed angel food cake
- 1 can (15 ounces) reduced-sugar apricot halves, drained and sliced

Direction

- Add 1 cup of apricot nectar to a microwave-safe bowl and microwave for 50-60 seconds on high until hot. Drizzle gelatin over hot nectar and whisk for approximately 5 minutes until the gelatin dissolves completely. Put aside to cool.
- Mix the remaining apricot nectar with an enough amount of water in a big bowl to measure one and a quarter cups. Stir in milk powder and pudding mix for 1-2 minutes. Stir in cooled gelatin and fold in whipped topping and cake.
- Spread over an 11x7-inch dish. Put the dish into a refrigerator for 2-4 hrs. Use apricot slices to garnish.

Nutrition Information

- Calories: 178 calories
- Total Carbohydrate: 31g carbohydrate (0 sugars
- Cholesterol: 1mg cholesterol
- Protein: 4g protein. Diabetic Exchanges: 1 starch
- Total Fat: 3g fat (3g saturated fat)
- Sodium: 303mg sodium
- Fiber: 1g fiber)

3. April Fools Berry Soda

Serving: 6 servings | Prep: 10mins | Cook: 0mins |Ready in:

Ingredients

- 2 packages (3 ounces each) strawberry gelatin
- 3/4 cup sliced fresh strawberries
- 3/4 cup fresh raspberries
- 3/4 cup fresh blueberries

Direction

- Follow the directions of the package to prepare gelatin. Put into a refrigerator for approximately 2 hrs until partially set. Whisk in berries. Add to 6 soda or tall drink glasses. Insert straws into the glasses, one for each glass. Put into a refrigerator until set.

Nutrition Information

- Calories: 76 calories
- Fiber: 2g fiber)
- Total Carbohydrate: 18g carbohydrate (16g sugars
- Cholesterol: 0 cholesterol
- Protein: 2g protein.
- Total Fat: 0 fat (0 saturated fat)
- Sodium: 33mg sodium

4. Banana Anna Surprise

Serving: 4 servings. | Prep: 20mins | Cook: 0mins |Ready in:

Ingredients

- 1 package (.3 ounce) sugar-free strawberry gelatin
- 3/4 cup boiling water
- 1/2 cup cold water
- 3/4 cup ice cubes
- 2 medium firm bananas, sliced
- 4 ounces fat-free cream cheese, cubed
- 1/2 cup fat-free whipped topping
- 1 teaspoon grated lemon peel

Direction

- Dissolve gelatin in a large bowl with boiling water. Mix ice cubes and cold water; put into the gelatin. Mix till thickened slightly; remove any unmelted ice. Put in bananas. Transfer half of the gelatin mixture into 4 dessert glasses. Place in the refrigerator till firm, 30 minutes.
- Mix lemon peel, whipped topping and cream cheese together in a blender; process with a cover till smooth. Transfer into the glasses. Transfer the remaining gelatin over the top. Place in the refrigerator till firm, 3 hours.

Nutrition Information

- Calories: 103 calories
- Total Carbohydrate: 19g carbohydrate (0 sugars
- Cholesterol: 3mg cholesterol
- Protein: 6g protein. Diabetic Exchanges: 1 lean meat
- Total Fat: 0 fat (0 saturated fat)
- Sodium: 202mg sodium
- Fiber: 1g fiber)

5. Bavarian Cream Bonnet

Serving: 8 servings. | Prep: 30mins | Cook: 0mins | Ready in:

Ingredients

- 1/2 cup sugar
- 1 envelope unflavored gelatin
- 1/4 teaspoon salt
- 2-1/4 cups milk
- 4 egg yolks, lightly beaten
- 1 teaspoon vanilla extract
- 1 cup heavy whipping cream, whipped
- 1 green fruit roll-up
- Blueberries, strawberry halves, peach slices and kiwifruit wedges

Direction

- Combine salt, gelatin and sugar in a large saucepan. Whisk in egg yolks and milk. Allow to stand for one min. Boil over medium heat; cook while stirring until the mixture has thick enough to coat the metal spoon, about 12 mins.
- Discard from heat. Place the pan in a bowl of the ice water to cool quickly; stir about 2 mins. Stir in the vanilla. Pour into a large bowl; then press the plastic wrap onto the surface. Place in the refrigerator until thickened but not set, 60 to 90 mins.
- Fold in the whipped cream. Place in a 9 inches round pan lined with the plastic wrap and coated with the cooking spray. Refrigerate until firm, covered.
- Invert onto the serving platter. Discard plastic wrap. Cut the fruit roll-up into the strips (the width equal to the Bavarian cream height). Wrap around the bonnet with fruit roll strips, then tie into a bowl. Decorate with the fruit.

Nutrition Information

- Calories:

- Protein:
- Total Fat:
- Sodium:
- Fiber:
- Total Carbohydrate:
- Cholesterol:

6. Berry Applesauce Gelatin

Serving: 8 servings. | Prep: 10mins | Cook: 0mins | Ready in:

Ingredients

- 1 package (6 ounces) strawberry gelatin
- 1 cup boiling water
- 2 cups frozen unsweetened strawberries
- 2 cups applesauce
- 2 tablespoons lemon juice

Direction

- Dissolve gelatin in a bowl with boiling water. Stir in strawberries until separated and thawed. Put in lemon juice and applesauce, then blend well. Transfer into a 7-inch x11-inch pan and refrigerate until set.

Nutrition Information

- Calories: 48 calories
- Sodium: 48mg sodium
- Fiber: 0 fiber)
- Total Carbohydrate: 11g carbohydrate (0 sugars
- Cholesterol: 0 cholesterol
- Protein: 1g protein. Diabetic Exchanges: 1 fruit.
- Total Fat: 0 fat (0 saturated fat)

7. Berry Cream Dessert

Serving: 16 servings. | Prep: 10mins | Cook: 0mins | Ready in:

Ingredients

- 1 package (3 ounces) strawberry gelatin
- 1 package (3 ounces) raspberry gelatin
- 2 cups boiling water
- 2 cups cold water
- 1 cup (8 ounces) strawberry yogurt
- 1 cup (8 ounces) raspberry yogurt
- 2 cups sliced fresh or frozen unsweetened strawberries
- 1 carton (12 ounces) frozen whipped topping, thawed
- Additional fresh strawberries, optional

Direction

- Dissolve raspberry and strawberry gelatin in a large bowl of the boiling water. Then stir in raspberry and strawberry yogurt and cold water until they are blended. Let chill for 60 mins or until syrupy.
- Fold in whipped topping and strawberries. Place into the individual dishes by spoon. Let chill for 4 hours or until firm. If desired, enjoy with fresh berries.

Nutrition Information

- Calories: 95 calories
- Protein: 2g protein. Diabetic Exchanges: 1 fruit
- Total Fat: 3g fat (3g saturated fat)
- Sodium: 46mg sodium
- Fiber: 1g fiber)
- Total Carbohydrate: 13g carbohydrate (0 sugars
- Cholesterol: 2mg cholesterol

8. Bing Cherry Amaretti Fool

Serving: 8 servings. | Prep: 30mins | Cook: 0mins | Ready in:

Ingredients

- 1 envelope unflavored gelatin
- 1/3 cup cold water
- 1 cup (8 ounces) sour cream
- 1/2 cup sugar
- 1 tablespoon lemon juice
- 1/2 teaspoon almond extract
- 1/2 teaspoon vanilla extract
- 2 cups coarsely chopped fresh Bing or other dark sweet cherries, divided
- 1 cup heavy whipping cream
- 1 cup coarsely crushed amaretti cookies (about 16 cookies)
- Optional toppings: fresh mint leaves, halved Bing cherries and additional crushed amaretti cookies

Direction

- Drizzle gelatin over cold water in a small saucepan; allow it to stand for 1 minute. Then heat and whisk over low heat until gelatin is fully melted. Allow it to stand for 5 minutes.
- In a blender, combine gelatin mixture, 1 cup cherries, extracts, lemon juice, sugar, and sour cream; then cover and blend until cherries are pureed. Place into a large bowl.
- Whisk cream in a small bowl until soft peaks form. Take out 1/2 cup whipped cream; set aside for the topping. Slowly fold the rest of the whipped cream into cherry mixture. Add in the rest of chopped berries and crushed cookies then fold. Split mixture among 8 dessert dishes. Keep in the refrigerator for at least 2 hours.
- Serve with toppings and whipped cream if preferred.

Nutrition Information

- Calories:

- Fiber:
- Total Carbohydrate:
- Cholesterol:
- Protein:
- Total Fat:
- Sodium:

- Total Carbohydrate: 17g carbohydrate (10g sugars
- Cholesterol: 1mg cholesterol
- Protein: 2g protein. Diabetic Exchanges: 1/2 starch
- Total Fat: 4g fat (3g saturated fat)

9. Blackberry Cloud Parfaits

Serving: 8 servings. | Prep: 30mins | Cook: 0mins | Ready in:

Ingredients

- 1 package (.3 ounce) sugar-free raspberry gelatin
- 1 cup boiling water
- 1/2 cup cold water
- 1 carton (8 ounces) frozen reduced-fat whipped topping, thawed, divided
- 3 cups blackberries, divided
- 1 carton (6 ounces) blackberry yogurt

Direction

- Melt gelatin in boiling water in a large bowl. Mix in cold water. Refrigerate for about 40 minutes, covered, until syrupy.
- Reserve 8 teaspoons whipped topping and 8 blackberries for decorating.
- Add and fold in the rest of whipped topping and yogurt into gelatin.
- Split half of the gelatin mixture among 8 dessert dishes or parfait glasses. Then layer with the rest of blackberries and gelatin mixture. Keep in the refrigerator, covered, until set. Decorate with reserved whipped topping and berries.

Nutrition Information

- Calories: 115 calories
- Sodium: 37mg sodium
- Fiber: 3g fiber)

10. Body Cubes

Serving: 2 dozen. | Prep: 20mins | Cook: 0mins | Ready in:

Ingredients

- 2 envelopes unflavored gelatin
- 1 cup cold prepared limeade
- 2 cups boiling prepared limeade
- 24 gummy body parts

Direction

- Drizzle gelatin over cold limeade and let it sit for a minute. Pour in boiling limeade and whisk until the gelatin dissolves completely.
- Add the mixture to ice cube trays then put into a refrigerator until soft-set, for half an hour. Press a gummy candy into each cube and put into the refrigerator until firm.

Nutrition Information

- Calories: 16 calories
- Sodium: 2mg sodium
- Fiber: 0 fiber)
- Total Carbohydrate: 3g carbohydrate (3g sugars
- Cholesterol: 0 cholesterol
- Protein: 0 protein.
- Total Fat: 0 fat (0 saturated fat)

11. Broken Glass Dessert

Serving: 12-16 servings. | Prep: 30mins | Cook: 0mins | Ready in:

Ingredients

- 1-1/2 cups graham cracker crumbs
- 1/2 cup sugar
- 1/2 cup butter, melted
- 1 package (3 ounces) lime gelatin
- 1 package (3 ounces) strawberry gelatin
- 1 package (3 ounces) orange gelatin
- 4-1/2 cups boiling water, divided
- 1 envelope unflavored gelatin
- 1/4 cup cold water
- 1 cup pineapple juice
- 1 carton (8 ounces) frozen whipped topping, thawed

Direction

- Soften the unflavored gelatin for 5 mins in a small bowl of cold water. Boil pineapple juice in a small saucepan. Stir in the unflavored gelatin until it has dissolved. Pour into large bowl. Put aside until thickened slightly.
- In the meantime, combine butter, sugar and crumbs; press into an oiled 13-inch x 9-inch dish. Chill. Combine one and a half cups of boiling water and lime gelatin; stir until the gelatin dissolves. Transfer to a buttered loaf pan, about 8x4 inches. Let chill until very firm.
- Do the same process with orange and strawberry gelatins. Fold the whipped topping gently into the pineapple juice mixture in large bowl. Dice into 1-inch cubes once flavored gelatins have firm; fold into the whipped topping mixture gently. Add over the crust by spoon. Let chill at least 120 mins.

Nutrition Information

- Calories:
- Sodium:
- Fiber:
- Total Carbohydrate:

- Cholesterol:
- Protein:
- Total Fat:

12. Broken Glass Torte

Serving: 12-15 servings. | Prep: 35mins | Cook: 0mins | Ready in:

Ingredients

- 1 package (3 ounces) orange gelatin
- 4-1/2 cups boiling water, divided
- 1 package (3 ounces) lime gelatin
- 1 package (3 ounces) raspberry gelatin
- 1 envelope unflavored gelatin
- 1/4 cup cold water
- 1/4 cup lemon juice
- 1-1/2 cups graham cracker crumbs
- 3 tablespoons sugar
- 1/4 cup butter, melted
- 2 cups heavy whipping cream

Direction

- Mix orange gelatin in 1-1/2 cups boiling water in a small bowl to dissolve. Add to an 8-in. square dish sprayed with cooking spray. Chill until firm. Keep working with lime gelatin and raspberry gelatin, putting each in a separate 8-in. square pan.
- Mix unflavored gelatin with cold water in a saucepan; let sit for a minute. Put in lemon juice. Cook over low heat, mixing until dissolved. Take off from the heat; let cool.
- Mix the sugar and graham cracker crumbs in a bowl; mix in butter. Save half cup for topping. Push leftover crumb mixture into a 13-in. x 9-in. pan sprayed with cooking spray; put aside.
- Slice the raspberry, lime and orange gelatins into 1-in. cubes. Whip cream in a big bowl until stiff. Fold in unflavored gelatin mixture, fold in flavored gelatin cubes. Move to greased dish. Scatter with saved crumb mixture. Cover and chill for two hours or until firm.

Nutrition Information

- Calories: 246 calories
- Protein: 3g protein.
- Total Fat: 16g fat (9g saturated fat)
- Sodium: 133mg sodium
- Fiber: 0 fiber)
- Total Carbohydrate: 25g carbohydrate (20g sugars
- Cholesterol: 52mg cholesterol

13. California Cranberry Torte

Serving: 12-16 servings. | Prep: 30mins | Cook: 60mins | Ready in:

Ingredients

- 6 large egg whites
- Pinch salt
- 1/4 teaspoon cream of tartar
- 1-1/2 cups sugar
- 1 teaspoon vanilla extract
- 1 can (14 ounces) jellied cranberry sauce
- 2 tablespoons raspberry gelatin powder
- 1-1/2 cups heavy whipping cream
- 2 tablespoons confectioners' sugar
- Fresh cranberries or raspberries for garnish, optional

Direction

- Stand egg whites for 30 minutes at room temperature; line parchment paper on baking sheets. On paper, draw 3 8-inch circles; put aside.
- Beat cream of tartar, salt and egg whites on medium speed till soft peaks form in big bowl; 2 tbsp. at a time, add sugar slowly. Beat till stiff peaks form then add vanilla.
- Insert 1/2-in. round pastry tip #A1 in heavy-duty plastic bag/pastry bag; use meringue to fill bag. Pipe meringue in spiral pattern, beginning in middle of every circle on prepped sheets, till circle is filled completely. Bake for 1 hour at 250°. Turn oven off; dry meringue in oven with door closed for 1 hour.
- Meanwhile, melt cranberry sauce in saucepan on medium heat. Add gelatin powder; mix till melted. Cool. Beat confectioner's sugar and cream in a chilled big bowl; into cranberry mixture, fold 1 cup.
- Assemble: To hold meringue in place, put 1 tbsp. whipped cream in the middle of a serving platter. Put meringue shell over; spread 1/3 cranberry mixture over. Repeat with leftover cranberry mixture and meringue.
- Frost torte sides with reserved whipped cream; you can use pastry bag to decorate torte edges if desired. Refrigerate for 6 hours or overnight. Before serving, garnish with mint and berries; refrigerate leftovers.

Nutrition Information

- Calories: 207 calories
- Total Carbohydrate: 33g carbohydrate (28g sugars
- Cholesterol: 31mg cholesterol
- Protein: 2g protein.
- Total Fat: 8g fat (5g saturated fat)
- Sodium: 48mg sodium
- Fiber: 0 fiber)

14. Carrot Pineapple Gelatin Salad

Serving: 4 servings. | Prep: 15mins | Cook: 0mins | Ready in:

Ingredients

- 1 can (8 ounces) unsweetened crushed pineapple
- 1 package (.3 ounce) sugar-free lemon gelatin
- 1 cup boiling water
- 1/2 cup cold water
- 1 teaspoon white vinegar

- 1/8 teaspoon salt
- 2 medium carrots, grated

Direction

- Drain pineapple, saving 1/2 cup juice; put the juice and pineapple aside. Dissolve gelatin in a bowl of boiling water. Mix in the saved juice, salt, vinegar, and cold water. Refrigerate for about 45 minutes until partly thickened. Mix in the saved pineapple and carrots. Add to an oil-coated 3-cup mold. Refrigerate until firm. Remove the mold and enjoy.

Nutrition Information

- Calories: 59 calories
- Total Fat: 0 fat (0 saturated fat)
- Sodium: 158mg sodium
- Fiber: 2g fiber)
- Total Carbohydrate: 12g carbohydrate (0 sugars
- Cholesterol: 0 cholesterol
- Protein: 1g protein. Diabetic Exchanges: 1 vegetable

cold water and stir. Place in the refrigerator for 60 mins or until set partially. Mix in the cherries. Transfer to a 7-cup mold coated with the cooking spray. Place in the refrigerator until firm, about 60 mins.

- Dissolve the remaining gelatin in a small bowl of the remaining boiling water. Then stir in the remaining cold water. Place in the refrigerator for 60 mins or until set partially. Fold in the whipped topping; and spread over top carefully. Place in the refrigerator until firm, about 4 hours. Unmold onto a serving platter.

Nutrition Information

- Calories: 163 calories
- Protein: 2g protein. Diabetic Exchanges: 2 starch.
- Total Fat: 3g fat (3g saturated fat)
- Sodium: 50mg sodium
- Fiber: 1g fiber)
- Total Carbohydrate: 32g carbohydrate (29g sugars
- Cholesterol: 0 cholesterol

15. Cherry Chiffon Gelatin

Serving: 8 servings. | Prep: 10mins | Cook: 0mins | Ready in:

Ingredients

- 2 packages (3 ounces each) cherry gelatin, divided
- 1-1/2 cups boiling water, divided
- 2 cups cold water, divided
- 1 can (15 ounces) pitted dark sweet cherries, drained
- 2 cups whipped topping

Direction

- Dissolve one gelatin package in a large bowl of 3/4 cup of boiling water. Put in one cup of the

16. Cherry Chocolate Parfaits

Serving: 4 servings. | Prep: 15mins | Cook: 0mins | Ready in:

Ingredients

- 1 package (.3 ounce) sugar-free cherry gelatin
- 1 cup boiling water
- 1/2 cup reduced-fat sour cream
- 1/4 teaspoon almond extract
- 1/2 cup diet lemon-lime soda
- 8 reduced-fat Oreo cookies, crushed
- 1/4 cup reduced-fat whipped topping

Direction

- Dissolve gelatin in boiling water in a small bowl. Take 1/2 cup to another bowl; mix in extract and sour cream. Split among 4 parfait glasses or dessert dishes. Keep in the refrigerator for approximately 35 minutes, until firm. Add soda and stir into the rest of the gelatin; refrigerate, covered, until partly set.

- To arrange, over cherry layer, scatter half of the cookies. Place soda mixture and the rest of the cookies on top. Keep in the refrigerator until firm. Dollop with whipped topping just before serving.

Nutrition Information

- Calories: 146 calories
- Fiber: 1g fiber)
- Total Carbohydrate: 20g carbohydrate (12g sugars
- Cholesterol: 10mg cholesterol
- Protein: 4g protein. Diabetic Exchanges: 1 starch
- Total Fat: 5g fat (3g saturated fat)
- Sodium: 207mg sodium

17. Cherry Cinnamon Dessert Ring

Serving: 20 servings. | Prep: 25mins | Cook: 0mins | Ready in:

Ingredients

- 3 cups fresh or frozen pitted dark sweet cherries
- 3-1/4 cups water, divided
- 1 cup sugar
- 2 cinnamon sticks
- 1 teaspoons almond extract
- 2 envelopes unflavored gelatin
- Sweetened whipped cream

Direction

- Combine cinnamon, sugar, 3 cups of water and cherries together in a saucepan. Boil the mixture; lower the heat; simmer with a cover for 15 minutes. Take away from the heat. Mix

in extract. Set aside. Put the remaining water into a saucepan. Sprinkle gelatin over; allow to sit for 1 minute. Heat till dissolved. Combine into the cherry mixture; stir properly. Refrigerate while stirring occasionally to evenly distribute the cherries, till the mixture starts to thicken. Spoon into a 5 1/2-cup ring mold. Place in the refrigerator for around 3-4 hours, or till set. Turn onto a serving platter. Serve accompanied with whipped cream.

Nutrition Information

- Calories:
- Cholesterol:
- Protein:
- Total Fat:
- Sodium:
- Fiber:
- Total Carbohydrate:

18. Cherry Gelatin Flowers

Serving: about 1 dozen. | Prep: 15mins | Cook: 0mins | Ready in:

Ingredients

- 2-1/2 cups white grape juice
- 4 packages (3 ounces each) cherry gelatin
- Seedless red or green grapes, halved, optional

Direction

- Bring grape juice in a small saucepan to a boil. In a bowl, add gelatin and mix in juice until gelatin has dissolved. Transfer into a 13"x9" dish that coated with cooking spray. Chill until set.
- Cut gelatin into flower shapes with cookie cutters, then put in the center of each flower with a grape half, if you want.

Nutrition Information

- Calories: 38 calories
- Protein: 1g protein.
- Total Fat: 0 fat (0 saturated fat)
- Sodium: 13mg sodium
- Fiber: 0 fiber)
- Total Carbohydrate: 9g carbohydrate (9g sugars
- Cholesterol: 0 cholesterol

19. Cherry Gelatin Salad

Serving: 8 | Prep: 5mins | Cook: 5mins | Ready in:

Ingredients

- 1 (21 ounce) can cherry pie filling
- 1 (8 ounce) can crushed pineapple, undrained
- 2 (3 ounce) packages cherry-flavored gelatin mix
- 2 cups boiling water

Direction

- Stir gelatin mix, cherry pie filling and pineapple, into the boiling water until the gelatin dissolves. Transfer to the glass baking dish. Place in the refrigerator for at least 120 mins or until set.

Nutrition Information

- Calories: 179 calories;
- Total Fat: 0.1
- Sodium: 111
- Total Carbohydrate: 43.4
- Cholesterol: 0
- Protein: 2.3

20. Cherry Gelatin Supreme

Serving: 12 servings. | Prep: 20mins | Cook: 0mins | Ready in:

Ingredients

- 2 cups water, divided
- 1 package (3 ounces) cherry gelatin
- 1 can (21 ounces) cherry pie filling
- 1 package (3 ounces) lemon gelatin
- 3 ounces cream cheese, softened
- 1/3 cup mayonnaise
- 1 can (8 ounces) crushed pineapple, undrained
- 1 cup miniature marshmallows
- 1/2 cup heavy whipping cream, whipped
- 2 tablespoons chopped pecans

Direction

- Boil 1 cup of water in a big saucepan. Whisk in cheery gelatin until dissolves. Whisk in pie filling. Add to an 11x7-inch dish. Cover and chill until set, for 2 hrs.
- Boil the remaining water in a small saucepan. Whisk in lemon gelatin until dissolves. Beat the mayonnaise and cream cheese in a small bowl until smooth. Whisk in pineapple and the lemon gelatin. Cover and chill in a refrigerator for 45 minutes.
- Add the whipped cream and the marshmallows to the mixture and fold. Scoop over the cheery layer and drizzle pecans on top. Cover and put into a refrigerator until set, 2 hrs.

Nutrition Information

- Calories: 248 calories
- Protein: 2g protein.
- Total Fat: 12g fat (5g saturated fat)
- Sodium: 101mg sodium
- Fiber: 1g fiber)
- Total Carbohydrate: 34g carbohydrate (31g sugars
- Cholesterol: 24mg cholesterol

21. Cherry Mincemeat Mold

Serving: 8 servings. | Prep: 15mins | Cook: 0mins | Ready in:

Ingredients

- 1 can (15 ounces) pitted dark sweet cherries
- 2 packages (3 ounces each) cherry gelatin
- 2 cups boiling water
- 2 tablespoons lemon juice
- 1/2 cup chopped tart apple
- 1/2 cup prepared mincemeat
- 1/2 cup chopped walnuts

Direction

- Strain cherries, reserving the juice in a 2-cup measuring cup; put in enough water to measure 1 1/2 cups. Divide the cherries in half and set aside.
- Dissolve gelatin in a large bowl with boiling water. Mix in the cherry juice mixture and lemon juice. Place in the refrigerator till partially set. Stir in cherries, walnuts, mincemeat and apple. Transfer into a 6-cup ring mold oiled with cooking spray. Place in the refrigerator till firm. Unmold onto a serving plate.

Nutrition Information

- Calories: 190 calories
- Sodium: 55mg sodium
- Fiber: 2g fiber)
- Total Carbohydrate: 36g carbohydrate (33g sugars
- Cholesterol: 0 cholesterol
- Protein: 4g protein.
- Total Fat: 5g fat (0 saturated fat)

22. Cherry Rice Fluff

Serving: 6 servings. | Prep: 25mins | Cook: 0mins | Ready in:

Ingredients

- 1-1/2 cups cooked rice
- 1 teaspoon butter, softened
- 1/4 teaspoon salt
- 1 cup milk, divided
- 1 package (3 ounces) cherry gelatin
- 1-1/2 cups boiling water
- 1/4 teaspoon almond extract
- 1/2 cup heavy whipping cream
- 2 tablespoons sugar
- 1 can (16 ounces) pitted tart cherries
- 1 tablespoon cornstarch
- 1/4 teaspoon almond extract

Direction

- Combine a half cup of milk, salt, butter and rice in a bowl. Allow to stand. Combine boiling water and gelatin in a bowl; stir until the gelatin dissolves. Stir in remaining milk and almond extract. Let chill until set partially.
- Beat the cream in a small bowl with sugar until it forms the soft peaks. Drain the cherries; for glaze, saving juice. Fold whipped cream, cherries and rice mixture into gelatin. Scoop into a 6-cup mold coated with the cooking spray. Let chill until set, about 4 hours.
- For glaze, combine reserved cherry juice and cornstarch in a small saucepan until they become smooth. Boil. Cook while stirring until thickened, about one min. Discard from heat. Mix in the extract. Let chill. Unmold; drizzle glaze over to serve.

Nutrition Information

- Calories: 524 calories
- Sodium: 459mg sodium
- Fiber: 1g fiber)
- Total Carbohydrate: 44g carbohydrate (31g sugars

- Cholesterol: 111mg cholesterol
- Protein: 4g protein.
- Total Fat: 38g fat (24g saturated fat)

23. Chocolate Bavarian With Strawberry Cream

Serving: 10 servings. | Prep: 20mins | Cook: 5mins | Ready in:

Ingredients

- 1 package (10 ounces) frozen sweetened sliced strawberries, thawed
- 2 envelopes unflavored gelatin
- 1 cup (6 ounces) semisweet chocolate chips
- 1/2 cup sugar
- 2-1/4 cups 2% milk, divided
- 1 teaspoon vanilla extract
- 1 cup heavy whipping cream
- CREAM:
- 1 cup heavy whipping cream
- 2 tablespoons confectioners' sugar
- 1 teaspoon vanilla extract
- 2 drops red food coloring, optional

Direction

- Drain strawberries and reserve its' syrup. Put the strawberries in the fridge. Add enough cold water to syrup to have a 3/4 cup. Sprinkle gelatin on top of the syrup mixture and let it stand for a minute.
- Mix together the half a cup of milk, sugar and chocolate chips in a big saucepan. Cook and stir the mixture over low heat until chips melt. Add the gelatin mixture; cook while stirring for additional 1 minute or until gelatin has dissolved.
- Take the mixture off from heat; stir in the remaining milk and vanilla. Pour the mixture into a big bowl. Keep inside the fridge for about 40 minutes until partly set.
- Beat the cream in a small bowl, until it reaches soft peaks stage; fold it in the chocolate

mixture. Move to a 6-cup ring mold greased with cooking spray. Keep inside the fridge for about 2 hours until firm.
- To make the cream, put the saved strawberries in a food processor; process with cover until pureed. Beat the cream in a small bowl until it starts to get thick. Add the vanilla, confectioners' sugar and food coloring if preferred; beat until it reaches soft peaks stage. Fold in the strawberry puree.
- Before serving, unmold the Bavarian on a serving plate. Scoop strawberry cream into the middle and on top of the ring.

Nutrition Information

- Calories: 356 calories
- Total Fat: 24g fat (15g saturated fat)
- Sodium: 46mg sodium
- Fiber: 2g fiber)
- Total Carbohydrate: 33g carbohydrate (30g sugars
- Cholesterol: 71mg cholesterol
- Protein: 5g protein.

24. Chocolate Lime Dessert

Serving: | Prep: 30mins | Cook: 0mins | Ready in:

Ingredients

- 1 package (3 ounces) lime gelatin
- 1-3/4 cups boiling water
- 2 cups crushed chocolate wafers
- 6 tablespoons butter, melted
- 1/4 cup lime juice
- 2 teaspoons lemon juice
- 1 cup sugar
- 1 can (12 ounces) evaporated milk
- Pots o' Gold

Direction

- Dissolve gelatin in a small bowl with boiling water. Place in the refrigerator for around 1 1/2 hours, or till partially set. Mix butter and wafer crumbs together in a bowl; press into a 13x9-in. dish. Set aside.
- Using an electric mixer, beat gelatin till foamy. Put in lemon and lime juices. Slowly put in sugar, beating till dissolved. Gradually put in milk while beating; stir properly. Transfer over the prepared crust. Place in the refrigerator till set. Use Pots o' Gold for garnish if you want.

Nutrition Information

- Calories:
- Sodium:
- Fiber:
- Total Carbohydrate:
- Cholesterol:
- Protein:
- Total Fat:

25. Chocolate Party Cake

Serving: 10-12 servings. | Prep: 35mins | Cook: 0mins | Ready in:

Ingredients

- 1 envelope unflavored gelatin
- 2 tablespoons cold water
- 2 ounces unsweetened chocolate
- 1/2 cup sugar
- 1/2 cup hot water
- 4 egg yolks, lightly beaten
- 1 teaspoon vanilla extract
- 2 cups heavy whipping cream, whipped
- 1/2 cup chopped almonds, toasted
- 1 prepared angel food cake (8 to 10 ounces)
- FROSTING:
- 1 cup heavy whipping cream
- 1 tablespoon confectioners' sugar
- 1 teaspoon vanilla extract
- 1/2 cup chopped almonds, toasted

Direction

- Sprinkle gelatin on top of cold water in a small saucepan; allow to sit for 1 minute. Cook while stirring over low heat till the gelatin is dissolved completely; set aside.
- Place a heavy saucepan over low heat; cook while stirring hot water, sugar and chocolate till the chocolate is melted. Take away from the heat. Mix a small amount of hot chocolate mixture into egg yolks; turn all back to the pan, stirring constantly. Cook while stirring over low heat till a thermometer registers 160°. Take away from the heat. Mix in vanilla and the gelatin mixture till smooth. Allow to cool to room temperature. Stir in whipped cream. Mix in almonds.
- Cut the cake into cubes with a serrated knife. Spread 1/3 of the cubes into a 10-in. removable-bottom tube pan coated with grease. Top with 1/3 of the chocolate mixture. Repeat the layers twice. Tap the pan on a work surface so the chocolate mixture fills in spaces. Refrigerate with a cover for 8 hours or overnight.
- To make frosting, beat cream in a bowl till it starts to thicken. Put in vanilla and confectioners' sugar; beat till the mixture forms stiff peaks. Run a knife carefully around the edge of the pan to loosen. Invert the cake onto a serving plate; take the pan away. Frost the sides and top of the cake. Sprinkle almonds on top. Place in the refrigerator for storage.

Nutrition Information

- Calories:
- Total Carbohydrate:
- Cholesterol:
- Protein:
- Total Fat:
- Sodium:
- Fiber:

26. Chocolate Quivers

Serving: about 1 dozen. | Prep: 15mins | Cook: 0mins | Ready in:

Ingredients

- 2 envelopes unflavored gelatin
- 2 cups milk, divided
- 1/2 cup instant chocolate drink mix
- 1/4 cup sugar

Direction

- Dissolve gelatin in a bowl with 1 cup of milk. Place a small saucepan on medium-high heat, mix in the remaining milk, sugar and drink mix; boil while stirring till the sugar and chocolate are dissolved. Put into the gelatin mixture; stir properly. Transfer into an 8-in. square pan. Allow to cool for 30 minutes at room temperature. Refrigerate with a cover for around 5 hours, or till firm (do not freeze). Use a cookie cutter or a knife to cut.

Nutrition Information

- Calories:
- Cholesterol:
- Protein:
- Total Fat:
- Sodium:
- Fiber:
- Total Carbohydrate:

27. Christmas Gelatin Cutouts

Serving: 4 dozen. | Prep: 60mins | Cook: 0mins | Ready in:

Ingredients

- 2 packages (6 ounces each) strawberry gelatin
- 5 cups boiling water, divided
- 2 packages (6 ounces each) lime gelatin
- 2 cups cold milk
- 2 packages (3.4 ounces each) instant vanilla pudding mix

Direction

- In 2 1/2 cups of boiling water, dissolve strawberry gelatin in a big bowl. Dissolve lime gelatin in leftover boiling water in another bowl; put aside both for 30 minutes.
- Whisk pudding mixes and milk for 1 minute till smooth in a big bowl. Put 1/2 pudding into each gelatin bowl quickly; whisk till blended well.
- Put in 2 13x9-in. dishes coated in cooking spray; chill till set for 3 hours. Use 2-in. Christmas cookie cutters to cut.

Nutrition Information

- Calories: 40 calories
- Protein: 1g protein.
- Total Fat: 0 fat (0 saturated fat)
- Sodium: 49mg sodium
- Fiber: 0 fiber)
- Total Carbohydrate: 8g carbohydrate (8g sugars
- Cholesterol: 1mg cholesterol

28. Contest Winning Blueberry Cream Dessert

Serving: 9 servings. | Prep: 20mins | Cook: 0mins | Ready in:

Ingredients

- 1 cup (8 ounces) sour cream
- 3/4 cup (6 ounces) blueberry yogurt
- 1 envelope unflavored gelatin
- 3/4 cup cold water
- 3/4 cup sugar, divided
- 1/2 teaspoon vanilla extract
- 1-1/4 cups graham cracker crumbs

- 6 tablespoons butter, melted
- 1 cup fresh blueberries
- 1/2 cup heavy whipping cream, whipped

Direction

- Mix sour cream with yogurt in a small bowl; put aside. Scatter gelatin on top of cold water in a small saucepan; let sit for a minute. Put in half cup sugar. Cook and mix over low heat until dissolved fully.
- Take off from the heat; mix in sour cream mixture and vanilla until combined. Add to a big bowl. Refrigerate until set partially.
- In the meantime, mix the butter, graham cracker crumbs and remaining sugar in a small bowl; put aside a quarter cup for garnishing. Push the leftover crumb mixture into an ungreased 8-in. square pan; put aside.
- Mix blueberries into gelatin mixture; fold in whipped cream. Scoop into crust. Scatter with saved crumb mixture. Refrigerate until firm. Chill leftovers.

Nutrition Information

- Calories: 288 calories
- Sodium: 175mg sodium
- Fiber: 1g fiber)
- Total Carbohydrate: 33g carbohydrate (25g sugars
- Cholesterol: 48mg cholesterol
- Protein: 3g protein.
- Total Fat: 16g fat (10g saturated fat)

29. Contest Winning Raspberry Ribbon Pie

Serving: 8 servings. | Prep: 15mins | Cook: 10mins | Ready in:

Ingredients

- 1 cup crushed vanilla wafers (about 30 wafers)

- 1/4 cup butter, melted
- 1 package (3 ounces) raspberry gelatin
- 1 cup boiling water
- 1/4 cup sugar
- 1 cup fresh raspberries
- 1 tablespoon lemon juice
- 3 ounces cream cheese, softened
- 1/3 cup confectioners' sugar
- 1 teaspoon vanilla extract
- Pinch salt
- 1 cup heavy whipping cream
- Additional whipped cream and fresh raspberries

Direction

- Combine butter and wafer crumbs in a small bowl; press up sides and onto bottom of an unoiled 9-in. pie plate. Bake for 10 mins at 350°, until golden brown.
- Dissolve the gelatin in a bowl of boiling water. Put in lemon juice, raspberries and sugar. Place in the refrigerator for 1-1/2 hours or until partially set.
- Beat confectioners' sugar and cream cheese in a bowl until smooth. Put in salt and vanilla. Beat the whipping cream in another bowl until it forms stiff peaks. Fold into the cream cheese mixture. Spread bottom of the crust with 3/4 cup mixture.
- Spread the top with 3/4 cup of the raspberry mixture; repeat these layers. Place in the refrigerator 8 hours or up to overnight. Garnish the pie with the additional berries and whipped cream. Place the leftovers in refrigerator.

Nutrition Information

- Calories: 345 calories
- Total Fat: 23g fat (13g saturated fat)
- Sodium: 189mg sodium
- Fiber: 1g fiber)
- Total Carbohydrate: 34g carbohydrate (27g sugars
- Cholesterol: 69mg cholesterol

- Protein: 3g protein.

- Fiber: 2g fiber)

30. Contest Winning Strawberry Pretzel Dessert

Serving: 2 servings. | Prep: 15mins | Cook: 0mins | Ready in:

Ingredients

- 1/3 cup crushed pretzels
- 2 tablespoons butter, softened
- 2 ounces cream cheese, softened
- 1/4 cup sugar
- 3/4 cup whipped topping
- 2 tablespoons plus 1-1/2 teaspoons strawberry gelatin powder
- 1/2 cup boiling water
- 1 cup sliced fresh strawberries

Direction

- Mix pretzels with butter in a big bowl. Push onto the bottom of 2 10-oz. greased custard cups. Bake for 6-8 minutes at 375° or until firm. Let cool on a wire rack.
- Mix cream cheese with sugar in a small bowl until smooth. Fold in whipped topping. Scoop on top of crust. Chill for half an hour.
- In the meantime, mix gelatin with boiling water in a small bowl to dissolve. Cover and chill for 20 minutes or until thickened slightly. Fold in strawberries. Scoop over filling carefully. Cover and chill for at least 3 hours.

Nutrition Information

- Calories: 516 calories
- Total Carbohydrate: 64g carbohydrate (47g sugars
- Cholesterol: 62mg cholesterol
- Protein: 6g protein.
- Total Fat: 27g fat (18g saturated fat)
- Sodium: 458mg sodium

31. Cool Coffee Gels

Serving: 4 servings. | Prep: 20mins | Cook: 0mins | Ready in:

Ingredients

- 1 envelope unflavored gelatin
- 1/4 cup cold water
- 1-1/2 cups hot brewed coffee
- 1/4 cup plus 2 tablespoons sugar, divided
- 1/2 cup heavy whipping cream
- Instant espresso powder and chocolate-covered coffee beans, optional

Direction

- Drizzle gelatin over cold water in a small saucepan and let it sit for a minute. Whisk in a quarter cup of sugar and coffee. Heat over low heat and whisk until the gelatin completely dissolves.
- Add the mixture to four 4-ounce custard cups or Irish coffee mugs. Cover and chill until set.
- Beat the cream in a big bowl until it starts thickening. Put in the remaining sugar and beat until stiff peaks form. Serve with gelatin. You can decorate with coffee beans and espresso powder if you want.

Nutrition Information

- Calories: 182 calories
- Sodium: 17mg sodium
- Fiber: 0 fiber)
- Total Carbohydrate: 20g carbohydrate (19g sugars
- Cholesterol: 41mg cholesterol
- Protein: 2g protein.
- Total Fat: 11g fat (7g saturated fat)

32. Cool Mandarin Dessert

Serving: 10 servings. | Prep: 20mins | Cook: 0mins | Ready in:

Ingredients

- 1 can (11 ounces) mandarin oranges
- 2 packages (.3 ounce each) sugar-free orange gelatin
- 2 cups boiling water
- 1 pint orange sherbet, softened
- Fresh mint, optional

Direction

- Drain the oranges, saving juice. Pour enough water into juice to measure one cup. Place the oranges in the refrigerator.
- Dissolve gelatin in large bowl of boiling water. Mix in the reserved juice. Put in sherbet, stir until it has dissolved. Place in the refrigerator until thickened, about 60 mins.
- For garnish, keep ten orange segments refrigerated. Fold the remaining oranges into the gelatin mixture; refrigerate overnight, covered. If desired, decorate with mint and reserved oranges. Then serve.

Nutrition Information

- Calories: 134 calories
- Sodium: 462mg sodium
- Fiber: 1g fiber)
- Total Carbohydrate: 15g carbohydrate (0 sugars
- Cholesterol: 2mg cholesterol
- Protein: 7g protein. Diabetic Exchanges: 1 starch
- Total Fat: 1g fat (1g saturated fat)

33. Cool And Creamy Raspberry Delight

Serving: 12 servings. | Prep: 20mins | Cook: 20mins | Ready in:

Ingredients

- 2-1/4 cups all-purpose flour
- 2 tablespoons sugar
- 3/4 cup cold butter, cubed
- FILLING:
- 1 package (8 ounces) cream cheese, softened
- 1 cup confectioners' sugar
- 1 teaspoon vanilla extract
- 1/4 teaspoon salt
- 2 cups whipped topping
- TOPPING:
- 2 cups boiling water
- 2 packages (3 ounces each) raspberry gelatin
- 2 packages (10 ounces each) frozen sweetened raspberries or sliced strawberries
- Additional whipped topping, optional

Direction

- Set oven to 300° to preheat. Combine flour with sugar in a big bowl; stir in butter until crumbly. Push onto bottom of an ungreased 13x9-in. dish. Bake 20-25 minutes until firm, (crust won't brown). Let cool completely on a wire rack.
- Whip first 4 filling ingredients until smooth. Fold in whipped topping; put evenly on top of crust.
- To make topping, pour boiling water to gelatin; mix 2 minutes to dissolve completely. Put in raspberries; mix until combined. Chill for 20 minutes, until mixture starts to thicken. Scoop over filling. Chill until set. Enjoy with more whipped topping, if wanted.

Nutrition Information

- Calories: 435 calories
- Total Fat: 20g fat (13g saturated fat)
- Sodium: 233mg sodium

- Fiber: 3g fiber)
- Total Carbohydrate: 58g carbohydrate (38g sugars
- Cholesterol: 50mg cholesterol
- Protein: 5g protein.

34. Cottage Cheese Gelatin Mold

Serving: 6 servings. | Prep: 15mins | Cook: 0mins | Ready in:

Ingredients

- 1 package (.3 ounce) sugar-free gelatin flavor of your choice
- 1-1/2 cups boiling water
- 1-3/4 cups fat-free cottage cheese
- 1-1/2 cups reduced-fat whipped topping

Direction

- Dissolve gelatin in a bowl with boiling water. In a food processor or a blender, process cottage cheese till smooth. Mix into the gelatin. Place in the refrigerator till partially set. Stir in whipped topping. Transfer into a 3-cup mold oiled with cooking spray. Place in the refrigerator till set.

Nutrition Information

- Calories: 92 calories
- Cholesterol: 6mg cholesterol
- Protein: 9g protein. Diabetic Exchanges: 1 lean meat
- Total Fat: 2g fat (2g saturated fat)
- Sodium: 256mg sodium
- Fiber: 0 fiber)
- Total Carbohydrate: 6g carbohydrate (0 sugars

35. Cran Raspberry Gelatin Dessert

Serving: 12 servings. | Prep: 10mins | Cook: 0mins | Ready in:

Ingredients

- 2 packages (3 ounces each) raspberry gelatin
- 2 cups boiling water
- 1 can (14 ounces) jellied cranberry sauce
- 1 package (10 ounces) frozen sweetened raspberries
- 1 tablespoon lemon juice
- 1 cup (8 ounces) sour cream
- 1 carton (8 ounces) frozen whipped topping, thawed

Direction

- Dissolve gelatin in large bowl of boiling water. Put in lemon juice, raspberries and cranberry sauce; beat until combined on low speed. Transfer to a 3-quart serving dish. Place in the refrigerator until set, about 8 hours.
- In a large bowl, put sour cream; fold in the whipped topping. Then spread over the gelatin. Serve.

Nutrition Information

- Calories: 197 calories
- Protein: 1g protein.
- Total Fat: 7g fat (5g saturated fat)
- Sodium: 34mg sodium
- Fiber: 2g fiber)
- Total Carbohydrate: 31g carbohydrate (23g sugars
- Cholesterol: 13mg cholesterol

36. Cranberry Cream

Serving: 8-10 servings. | Prep: 10mins | Cook: 5mins | Ready in:

Ingredients

- 2-1/2 cups orange juice, divided
- 1 can (14 ounces) jellied cranberry sauce
- 2 packages (3 ounces each) raspberry gelatin
- 1-1/2 cups heavy whipping cream
- 1 to 2 medium navel oranges, peeled and sectioned
- 1/4 cup fresh or frozen cranberries, thawed
- Corn syrup and sugar

Direction

- Mix the gelatin, cranberry sauce, and 3/4 cup of orange juice in a saucepan. Mash and cook the mixture on medium-low heat until the gelatin dissolves. Whisk in the remaining orange juice. Then refrigerate for approximately two and a half hours until the mixture starts thickening.
- Beat the cream until soft peaks form then pour into the gelatin mixture and fold. Add the mixture to an 8-cup serving bowl and put into a refrigerator until firm. Use oranges to garnish. Spread the corn syrup over the cranberries with a brush and drizzle sugar on top. Then place on top of oranges.

Nutrition Information

- Calories: 282 calories
- Fiber: 1g fiber)
- Total Carbohydrate: 40g carbohydrate (33g sugars
- Cholesterol: 49mg cholesterol
- Protein: 3g protein.
- Total Fat: 13g fat (8g saturated fat)
- Sodium: 62mg sodium

37. Cranberry Jell O Mold

Serving: 8-10 servings. | Prep: 10mins | Cook: 0mins | Ready in:

Ingredients

- 1 package (6 ounces) strawberry or 6 ounces lemon gelatin
- 3 cups boiling water
- 1 can (14 ounces) whole-berry cranberry sauce
- 1 can (8 ounces) crushed pineapple, undrained
- 1 cup chopped pecans
- Sour cream, optional

Direction

- In large bowl, dissolve gelatin in water. Stir in pineapple and cranberry sauce. Refrigerate, covered, until thickened slightly, about 60 mins. Mix in nuts. Transfer to a 1-1/2-quart gelatin mold coated with the cooking spray. Place in the refrigerator until set. Then unmold onto the serving platter. If desired, enjoy with the sour cream.

Nutrition Information

- Calories: 222 calories
- Sodium: 49mg sodium
- Fiber: 2g fiber)
- Total Carbohydrate: 37g carbohydrate (29g sugars
- Cholesterol: 0 cholesterol
- Protein: 3g protein.
- Total Fat: 9g fat (1g saturated fat)

38. Cranberry Parfaits

Serving: 6 | Prep: 20mins | Cook: 5mins | Ready in:

Ingredients

- 3 tablespoons unsalted butter
- 3 tablespoons sugar
- 1/2 cup graham cracker crumbs
- 1 (14 ounce) can low-fat sweetened condensed milk
- 1/2 cup cranberry sauce
- 1 cup cold whipping cream

Direction

- Melt butter over medium heat in a pan. Add in sugar, cooking until bubbles appear, for about 1 minute. Make crumbs out of graham cracker and stir into pan until the color darkens, for 3 minutes. Transfer to plate and let cool.
- Mix together cranberry sauce and condensed milk in a mixing bowl using a hand mixer until the mixture is thick. Beat the whipping cream in another bowl using an electric mixer until firm peaks appear. Fold whipped cream into the cranberry mixture.
- Prepare 6 eight ounce wine glasses or goblets and layer a quarter cup cranberry mixture into each wine glass. Top with a layer of 1 tbsp. crumbs and do layering once more. Keep refrigerated 1-4 hours.

Nutrition Information

- Calories: 581 calories;
- Total Fat: 24.7
- Sodium: 158
- Total Carbohydrate: 75.5
- Cholesterol: 81
- Protein: 8.4

39. Cranberry Raspberry Gelatin Salad

Serving: 8 servings. | Prep: 10mins | Cook: 0mins | Ready in:

Ingredients

- 2 packages (.3 ounce each) sugar-free raspberry gelatin
- 1-3/4 cups reduced-calorie reduced-sugar cranberry-raspberry juice, divided
- 1 can (14 ounces) whole-berry cranberry sauce
- 1 can (20 ounces) crushed pineapple, undrained
- 2-1/2 cups frozen unsweetened raspberries, thawed
- 1 cup (8 ounces) reduced-fat sour cream
- 2 tablespoons brown sugar
- 1 cup reduced-fat whipped topping

Direction

- Add 1 cup of boiling cranberry juice and gelatin to a big bowl and stir until dissolved. Whisk in cranberry sauce and break up the mixture. Whisk in the remaining cranberry juice until combined. Cover and put into a refrigerator for approximately 1-1/4 hrs until partially set.
- Add raspberries and pineapple to the mixture and fold. Move to an 11x7-inch dish greased with cooking spray. Put into a refrigerator until firm. Mix the brown sugar and sour cream in a bowl until blended. Add whipped topping and fold. Pour over the gelatin mixture and serve instantly.

Nutrition Information

- Calories: 148 calories
- Sodium: 28mg sodium
- Fiber: 2g fiber)
- Total Carbohydrate: 30g carbohydrate (0 sugars
- Cholesterol: 7mg cholesterol
- Protein: 2g protein. Diabetic Exchanges: 1 starch
- Total Fat: 2g fat (2g saturated fat)

40. Cranbrosia Gelatin Mold

Serving: 10-12 servings. | Prep: 20mins | Cook: 10mins | Ready in:

Ingredients

- 2 cups fresh or frozen cranberries, coarsely ground
- 1 cup sugar

- 1 can (11 ounces) mandarin oranges
- 1 can (8 ounces) sliced pineapple
- 2 envelopes unflavored gelatin
- 1 cup (8 ounces) sour cream
- 1 cup heavy whipping cream
- 2 tablespoons confectioners' sugar

Direction

- Combine sugar and cranberries in a bowl. Allow to stand, stirring occasionally, until sugar dissolves, about half an hour. Drain the juice from pineapple and oranges, saving 3/4 cup of juice. Cut the pineapple into the small pieces. Put the fruit aside.
- Sprinkle the reserved juice in a small saucepan with gelatin; allow to stand for one min. Over low heat, cook while stirring for 2 mins or until the gelatin dissolves. Put into cranberry mixture; mix in pineapple and oranges. Fold in the sour cream.
- Beat cream in a small bowl until it starts to thicken. Put in confectioners' sugar; then beat until it forms the soft peaks. Fold into the fruit mixture. Transfer to 12 individual molds or a 6-cup ring mold coated with the cooking spray lightly. Place in the refrigerator until set. Unmold. Then serve.

Nutrition Information

- Calories: 215 calories
- Protein: 2g protein.
- Total Fat: 11g fat (7g saturated fat)
- Sodium: 23mg sodium
- Fiber: 1g fiber)
- Total Carbohydrate: 28g carbohydrate (26g sugars
- Cholesterol: 41mg cholesterol

41. Creamy Citrus Mousse

Serving: 6 servings. | Prep: 15mins | Cook: 0mins | Ready in:

Ingredients

- 2 tablespoons lime juice
- 2 tablespoons sugar
- 1 package (3 ounces) lime gelatin
- 1 cup boiling water
- 1/3 cup cold water
- 2 cups whipped topping
- 1/2 cup sweetened condensed milk
- 1 tablespoon grated lime zest, optional
- 2 teaspoons orange extract
- Maraschino cherries, optional
- Additional grated lime zest, optional

Direction

- Dip 6 individual dessert dishes' rims in lime juice then in sugar; put aside. Melt gelatin in boiling water in bowl; mix cold water in. Refrigerate for 30 minutes till slightly thickened. Meanwhile, mix orange extra, lime zest (optional), milk and whipped topping; fold into gelatin. Put in dessert dishes using spoon; refrigerate till firm or for 1 hour. If desired, garnish with lime zest and cherries just before serving.

Nutrition Information

- Calories: 225 calories
- Total Carbohydrate: 36g carbohydrate (33g sugars
- Cholesterol: 9mg cholesterol
- Protein: 3g protein.
- Total Fat: 6g fat (5g saturated fat)
- Sodium: 65mg sodium
- Fiber: 0 fiber)

42. Creamy Fruit Medley

Serving: 6 servings. | Prep: 10mins | Cook: 0mins | Ready in:

Ingredients

- 1 carton (16 ounces) frozen whipped topping, thawed
- 1 package (3 ounces) orange gelatin
- 1 can (20 ounces) crushed pineapple, drained
- 1 can (11 ounces) mandarin oranges, drained
- 2 cups miniature marshmallows
- 1/2 cup chopped pecans, optional

Direction

- Set aside 1 cup whipped topping. In a big bowl, add the remaining topping, then sprinkle with gelatin and stir until blended. Fold in marshmallows, oranges, pineapple and pecans if wanted. Decorate with reserved topping.

Nutrition Information

- Calories: 403 calories
- Protein: 2g protein.
- Total Fat: 13g fat (13g saturated fat)
- Sodium: 44mg sodium
- Fiber: 1g fiber)
- Total Carbohydrate: 66g carbohydrate (50g sugars
- Cholesterol: 0 cholesterol

43. Creamy Gelatin Dessert

Serving: 16-20 servings. | Prep: 20mins | Cook: 0mins | Ready in:

Ingredients

- 1 package (6 ounces) lemon gelatin
- 2 cups boiling water
- 2 cups miniature marshmallows
- 4 large ripe bananas, cut into 1/4-inch slices
- 1 can (20 ounces) crushed pineapple
- 2 cups cold water
- 1/2 cup sugar
- 2 tablespoons all-purpose flour
- 2 tablespoons butter

- 1 cup heavy whipping cream
- 1/2 cup chopped walnuts

Direction

- Sprinkle boiling water with gelatin. Discard from heat and stir for 5 mins or until the gelatin is dissolved completely. Stir in the marshmallows until it has melted. Mix in bananas. Then drain pineapple, saving juice. Put cold water and pineapple into gelatin mixture.
- Transfer to a 13x9 inches pan. Let chill until set. Combine flour and sugar in a small saucepan. Stir in the reserved pineapple juice gradually. Put in butter. Boil. Cook while stirring for 2 mins. Discard from heat; let cool for 35 to 40 mins to room temperature.
- Beat cream in a small bowl until it forms the firm peaks; fold into the pineapple juice mixture. Then spread over the gelatin mixture. Sprinkle nuts over. Let chill for 60-120 mins.

Nutrition Information

- Calories: 186 calories
- Sodium: 38mg sodium
- Fiber: 1g fiber)
- Total Carbohydrate: 30g carbohydrate (26g sugars
- Cholesterol: 19mg cholesterol
- Protein: 2g protein.
- Total Fat: 7g fat (4g saturated fat)

44. Creamy Strawberry Dessert

Serving: 15 servings. | Prep: 25mins | Cook: 0mins | Ready in:

Ingredients

- 1-1/2 cups crushed vanilla wafers (about 45 wafers)
- 1/2 cup sugar
- 1/2 cup packed brown sugar

- 1/2 cup butter, melted
- 2 packages (3 ounces each) strawberry gelatin
- 1 cup boiling water
- 2 packages (10 ounces each) frozen sweetened sliced strawberries, thawed
- 1 can (14 ounces) sweetened condensed milk
- 1 carton (12 ounces) frozen whipped topping, thawed

Direction

- Mix the wafer crumbs, butter and sugars in a big bowl. Then press into a coated 13x9-inch dish. Cover and put into a refrigerator for half an hour.
- Drizzle gelatin over boiling water. Take away from heat and whisk for approximately 5 minutes until the gelatin dissolves completely. Move to a big bowl and whisk in milk and strawberries. Put in to a refrigerator until partially set, for half an hour.
- Add whipped topping into strawberries mixture and fold. Pour over the prepared crust. Put into a refrigerator until set, for 2 hrs. Slice into squares.

Nutrition Information

- Calories:
- Fiber:
- Total Carbohydrate:
- Cholesterol:
- Protein:
- Total Fat:
- Sodium:

45. Dark Chocolate Panna Cotta

Serving: 8 servings. | Prep: 25mins | Cook: 10mins | Ready in:

Ingredients

- 1 can (14 ounces) whole-berry cranberry sauce
- 5 tablespoons raspberry liqueur, divided

- 1 envelope unflavored gelatin
- 1 cup cold 2% milk
- 4 ounces 53% cacao dark baking chocolate, chopped
- 1-1/2 cups heavy whipping cream
- 1/2 cup sugar
- 1/8 teaspoon salt
- 2 teaspoons vanilla extract
- Fresh raspberries and mint leaves, optional

Direction

- In a food processor, add cranberry sauce; cover and blend until pureed. Drain and remove pulp. Mix in 3 tablespoons liqueur; put aside.
- Scatter gelatin on top of milk in a small bowl; let sit for a minute. In the meantime, put chocolate in a separate small bowl. Heat up salt, sugar and cream just to a boil in a small saucepan. Add over chocolate; mix until smooth.
- Mix a bit of chocolate mixture into gelatin mixture until dissolved. Mix in vanilla and a cup cranberry puree. Add into 8 6-oz. custard cups. Cover and chill for 8 hours or overnight.
- Mix the leftover cranberry puree with liqueur in a small bowl; cover and chill until enjoying.
- Unmold onto serving platters. Enjoy with sauce and top with mint and raspberries (optional).

Nutrition Information

- Calories: 397 calories
- Total Fat: 22g fat (14g saturated fat)
- Sodium: 81mg sodium
- Fiber: 2g fiber)
- Total Carbohydrate: 45g carbohydrate (36g sugars
- Cholesterol: 63mg cholesterol
- Protein: 4g protein.

46. Dinosaur Eggs

Serving: 4 | Prep: 20mins | Cook: 10mins | Ready in:

Ingredients

- Mustard Sauce:
- 1/4 cup coarse-grain mustard
- 1/4 cup Greek yogurt
- 1 teaspoon garlic powder
- 1 pinch cayenne pepper
- Eggs:
- 2 eggs, beaten
- 2 cups instant mashed potato flakes
- 4 hard-boiled eggs, peeled
- 1 (15 ounce) can HORMEL® Mary Kitchen® Corned Beef Hash
- 2 quarts vegetable oil for frying

Direction

- In a small bowl, combine cayenne pepper, garlic powder, Greek yogurt and whole grain mustard together till well-blended.
- In a shallow dish, place 2 beaten eggs; in a separate shallow dish, place potato flakes.
- Separate corned beef hash into 4 portions. Roll the corned beef hash around each egg till the egg is encased completely.
- Roll the encased eggs into the beaten egg; coat with the mashed potato flakes till well-covered.
- In a large saucepan or a deep-fryer, heat oil to 375°F (190°C).
- Drop 2 eggs into the hot oil; fry for 3-5 minutes, or till browned. Using a slotted spoon, take away and place on a plate lined with paper towel. Repeat with the remaining 2 eggs.
- Cut the eggs lengthwise; serve accompanied with mustard sauce.

Nutrition Information

- Calories: 784 calories;
- Total Carbohydrate: 34
- Cholesterol: 333
- Protein: 19.9
- Total Fat: 63.2
- Sodium: 702

47. Easy Cranberry Chiffon Pie

Serving: 10 servings. | Prep: 20mins | Cook: 5mins | Ready in:

Ingredients

- 1-1/2 cups reduced-calorie reduced-sugar cranberry juice
- 1 package (.6 ounce) sugar-free raspberry gelatin
- 1 can (14 ounces) jellied cranberry sauce
- 1 carton (8 ounces) frozen reduced-fat whipped topping, thawed, divided
- 1 extra-servings-size graham cracker crust (9 ounces)
- 10 fresh raspberries

Direction

- Microwave cranberry juice for 2-3 minutes on high or until boiling in a microwaveable bowl; put in gelatin and mix until dissolved. Cover and chill for 45 to 60 minutes or until thickened slightly.
- Whip cranberry sauce in a big bowl for 1-2 minutes or until smooth. Whip in gelatin mixture gradually. Chill, covered, for 45 minutes or until thickened.
- Chill 10 tablespoons whipped topping for topping. Mix 1/2 of the leftover whipped topping into cranberry mixture; fold in leftover whipped topping. Put filling evenly into shell. Cover and chill for 8 hours or overnight.
- Slice into slices; garnish each with a raspberry and a tablespoon whipped topping.

Nutrition Information

- Calories: 256 calories

- Total Fat: 9g fat (4g saturated fat)
- Sodium: 194mg sodium
- Fiber: 1g fiber)
- Total Carbohydrate: 40g carbohydrate (27g sugars
- Cholesterol: 0 cholesterol
- Protein: 2g protein. Diabetic Exchanges: 2-1/2 starch

48. Edible Juice

Serving: 4 servings. | Prep: 5mins | Cook: 5mins |Ready in:

Ingredients

- 2 envelope unflavored gelatin
- 4 cups orange juice, divided
- 4 teaspoons sugar
- 4 drinking straws

Direction

- Sprinkle the gelatin over one cup of juice in small bowl; allow to stand for one min.
- Boil remaining juice and sugar in large saucepan. Stir in the gelatin mixture. Over low heat, cook while stirring until the gelatin is dissolved completely. Transfer to 4 glasses and insert the straws. Refrigerate, covered, until firm.

Nutrition Information

- Calories: 138 calories
- Total Fat: 0 fat (0 saturated fat)
- Sodium: 7mg sodium
- Fiber: 0 fiber)
- Total Carbohydrate: 30g carbohydrate (26g sugars
- Cholesterol: 0 cholesterol
- Protein: 4g protein.

49. Eggnog Bavarian

Serving: 12 servings (1 cup sauce). | Prep: 30mins | Cook: 5mins |Ready in:

Ingredients

- 3 envelopes unflavored gelatin
- 4 cups eggnog, divided
- 1/2 cup 2% milk
- 1 tablespoon rum extract
- 1/8 teaspoon salt
- 2 cups heavy whipping cream
- 1 cup finely chopped walnuts
- RASPBERRY-CURRANT SAUCE:
- 1 package (10 ounces) frozen sweetened raspberries, thawed
- 1/2 cup red currant jelly
- 1 tablespoon cornstarch
- 2 tablespoons cold water

Direction

- Scatter gelatin over a cup eggnog with milk in a small saucepan; let sit for a minute. Cook over low heat, mixing until dissolved completely. Add to a big bowl; mix in the leftover eggnog, salt and extract. Let sit for 10 minutes.
- Whip cream in a big bowl until forming stiff peaks. Fold walnuts and cream into gelatin mixture. Add to an 8-cup ring mold greased with cooking spray; chill for 2 hours or until set.
- Mash and drain raspberries, saving juice. Remove seeds. Add to a small saucepan; mix in jelly. Heat up to a boil. Mix cornstarch with water until smooth. Mix into the pan gradually. Heat up to a boil; cook and mix for a minute or until thickened. Let cool to room temperature. Enjoy with gelatin.

Nutrition Information

- Calories: 377 calories
- Cholesterol: 105mg cholesterol
- Protein: 9g protein.

- Total Fat: 27g fat (13g saturated fat)
- Sodium: 94mg sodium
- Fiber: 2g fiber)
- Total Carbohydrate: 26g carbohydrate (17g sugars

50. Eggnog Gelatin Mold

Serving: 8-10 servings (2 cups sauce). | Prep: 5mins | Cook: 10mins |Ready in:

Ingredients

- 3 envelopes unflavored gelatin
- 3/4 cup cold water
- 4 cups eggnog, divided
- 1/4 cup sugar
- 1/4 teaspoon ground nutmeg
- 1 cup heavy whipping cream, whipped
- CRAN-APPLE COMPOTE:
- 3/4 cup sugar
- 1/3 cup water
- 1 cup fresh or frozen cranberries
- 1 teaspoon unflavored gelatin
- 3 tablespoons cold water
- 1 cup chopped peeled apple
- 1/3 cup chopped walnuts

Direction

- Place cold water in a large saucepan; sprinkle gelatin over; allow to sit for 1 minute. Mix in nutmeg, sugar and 1 cup of eggnog. Cook over medium-low heat till the sugar and gelatin are dissolved while stirring sometimes. Put in the remaining eggnog.
- Place in the refrigerator for around 1 hour, or till thickened slightly. Stir in cream. Transfer into a 7-cup mold oiled with cooking spray. Place in the refrigerator till firm, at least 4 hours.
- Meanwhile, to make compote, stir water and sugar together in a saucepan. Boil the mixture; stir till the sugar is dissolved. Put in cranberries; boil while stirring occasionally for

5 minutes. Sprinkle gelatin over cold water; allow to sit for 1 minute. Mix into the cranberry mixture till the gelatin is dissolved.
- Take away from the heat; mix in walnuts and apple. Transfer into a bowl; place in the refrigerator for at least 2 hours. Serve accompanied with the eggnog gelatin.

Nutrition Information

- Calories: 300 calories
- Cholesterol: 76mg cholesterol
- Protein: 7g protein.
- Total Fat: 14g fat (7g saturated fat)
- Sodium: 64mg sodium
- Fiber: 1g fiber)
- Total Carbohydrate: 37g carbohydrate (36g sugars

51. Espresso Panna Cotta

Serving: 6 servings. | Prep: 15mins | Cook: 10mins |Ready in:

Ingredients

- 1 envelope unflavored gelatin
- 1 cup milk
- 3 cups heavy whipping cream
- 1/2 cup sugar
- 2 tablespoons instant espresso powder or instant coffee granules
- 1/8 teaspoon salt
- Dark and white chocolate curls

Direction

- Add milk to a small saucepan and drizzle gelatin over the milk. Let it sit for a minute. Heat over low heat and whisk until the gelatin completely dissolves. Whisk in salt, espresso powder, sugar and cream. Cook while stirring until the sugar dissolves. Take away from heat.

- Add the mixture to 6 dessert dishes. Cover and put into a refrigerator for an hour, whisk every 20 minutes.
- Chill for a minimum of 5 more hours until set. Decorate with chocolate curls then serve.

Nutrition Information

- Calories: 533 calories
- Protein: 6g protein.
- Total Fat: 48g fat (30g saturated fat)
- Sodium: 115mg sodium
- Fiber: 1g fiber)
- Total Carbohydrate: 24g carbohydrate (19g sugars
- Cholesterol: 167mg cholesterol

52. Fluffy Lemon Dessert

Serving: 10 servings. | Prep: 20mins | Cook: 0mins | Ready in:

Ingredients

- 1 can (12 ounces) evaporated milk
- 1 package (3 ounces) lemon gelatin
- 1 cup sugar
- 1-3/4 cups boiling water
- 1/4 cup lemon juice
- 3/4 cup whipped topping
- 1 medium lemon, sliced
- 10 mint sprigs

Direction

- Add milk to a small bowl and put the mixer beaters in the bowl. Cover and put into a refrigerator until chilled, for at least 2 hrs. At the same time, add water, sugar and gelatin to a big bowl and stir until dissolves. Whisk in lemon juice. Cover and chill for approximately one and a half hours until syrupy.
- Whisk the gelatin until tiny bubbles form. Beat chilled milk until soft peaks form and put in

gelatin and fold. Add to serving plates and put into a refrigerator for a minimum of 3 hrs or overnight.
- Add whipped topping, mint, and lemon on top to garnish. Keep the leftovers in a refrigerator.

Nutrition Information

- Calories: 153 calories
- Sodium: 52mg sodium
- Fiber: 0 fiber)
- Total Carbohydrate: 31g carbohydrate (30g sugars
- Cholesterol: 11mg cholesterol
- Protein: 3g protein.
- Total Fat: 2g fat (2g saturated fat)

53. Fluffy Lemon Squares

Serving: 12 servings. | Prep: 25mins | Cook: 0mins | Ready in:

Ingredients

- 1-1/2 cups crushed vanilla wafers (about 45 wafers)
- 1/3 cup chopped pecans
- 6 tablespoons butter, melted
- 1/2 cup heavy whipping cream
- 2 packages (3 ounces each) lemon gelatin
- 1-1/4 cups boiling water
- 1 package (3.4 ounces) instant lemon pudding mix
- 1 pint lemon sherbet, softened

Direction

- Combine butter, pecans and wafer crumbs in a small bowl. For topping, put a quarter cup aside. Press the remaining crumb mixture into an unoiled dish, about 11x7 inches. Place in the refrigerator for half an hour.
- In the meantime, beat cream in a small bowl until it forms the stiff peaks. Put aside.

Dissolve gelatin in a large bowl of boiling water. Put in pudding mix; then beat for 2 mins on low speed. Put in sherbet; then beat for one min on low until soft-set. Then fold in the whipped cream.

- Spread over the crust; top with the reserved crumb mixture. Let chill until set, about 60 mins. Place the leftovers in the refrigerator.

Nutrition Information

- Calories: 285 calories
- Sodium: 231mg sodium
- Fiber: 2g fiber)
- Total Carbohydrate: 39g carbohydrate (30g sugars
- Cholesterol: 31mg cholesterol
- Protein: 3g protein.
- Total Fat: 14g fat (7g saturated fat)

54. Fluffy Lemonade Gelatin

Serving: 20-24 servings. | Prep: 10mins | Cook: 0mins | Ready in:

Ingredients

- 5 packages (3 ounces each) lemon gelatin
- 6 cups boiling water
- 1 can (12 ounces) frozen lemonade concentrate
- 1 carton (12 ounces) frozen whipped topping, thawed

Direction

- Dissolve gelatin with boiling water in a big bowl; mix in lemonade to dissolve. Refrigerate about 2 hours until firm partially.
- Beat in whipped topping. Add into 2 13-in. x 9-in. pans. Refrigerate until set.

Nutrition Information

- Calories: 78 calories

- Protein: 0 protein.
- Total Fat: 2g fat (2g saturated fat)
- Sodium: 9mg sodium
- Fiber: 0 fiber)
- Total Carbohydrate: 13g carbohydrate (11g sugars
- Cholesterol: 0 cholesterol

55. Fluffy Orange Gelatin Pie

Serving: 8 servings. | Prep: 15mins | Cook: 0mins | Ready in:

Ingredients

- 1 can (15 ounces) mandarin oranges
- 1 package (3 ounces) orange gelatin
- 1 can (5 ounces) evaporated milk, chilled
- 1 reduced-fat graham cracker crust (8 inches)
- 1 medium navel orange, sliced

Direction

- Drain the liquid from the oranges to measuring cup. Put enough water to measure one cup; put the oranges aside. Add liquid to the saucepan; boil. Whisk in gelatin till dissolved.
- Move into big bowl; add the mixer beaters into the bowl. Keep covered and refrigerated till the mixture is syrupy.
- Put in the milk. Beat on high speed till almost doubled. Fold in the mandarin oranges. Add to the crust. Keep in the refrigerator till becoming set, 2 to 3 hours. Use the slices of the orange to decorate.

Nutrition Information

- Calories: 202 calories
- Protein: 4g protein. Diabetic Exchanges: 1-1/2 starch
- Total Fat: 4g fat (2g saturated fat)
- Sodium: 140mg sodium

- Fiber: 1g fiber)
- Total Carbohydrate: 37g carbohydrate (0 sugars
- Cholesterol: 6mg cholesterol

56. Fluffy Rice Dessert

Serving: 10 servings. | Prep: 10mins | Cook: 0mins | Ready in:

Ingredients

- 1 package (.3 ounces) sugar-free cherry gelatin
- 1 cup boiling water
- 1 can (20 ounces) unsweetened crushed pineapple
- 1-1/2 cups hot cooked rice
- 1 cup reduced-fat whipped topping

Direction

- Dissolve gelatin in a bowl of boiling water. Drain the pineapple, saving juice; put aside the pineapple. Pour juice into gelatin; mix in rice. Let chill the mixture until it started to thicken. Then fold in pineapple and whipped topping. Let chill for 60 mins.

Nutrition Information

- Calories: 79 calories
- Sodium: 19mg sodium
- Fiber: 0 fiber)
- Total Carbohydrate: 16g carbohydrate (0 sugars
- Cholesterol: 0 cholesterol
- Protein: 1g protein. Diabetic Exchanges: 1/2 starch
- Total Fat: 1g fat (0 saturated fat)

57. French Cream With Sugared Grapes

Serving: 6 servings. | Prep: 20mins | Cook: 0mins | Ready in:

Ingredients

- 1 cup (8 ounces) sour cream
- 1 cup heavy whipping cream
- 3/4 cup sugar
- 1 envelope unflavored gelatin
- 1/4 cup cold water
- 1 package (8 ounces) cream cheese, softened
- 1 teaspoon vanilla extract
- Seedless green and red grapes
- Additional sugar

Direction

- Combine cream and sour cream in large saucepan until blended well. Stir in sugar gradually. Over medium heat, cook while stirring just until sugar dissolves and mixture is warm. Discard from heat.
- Sprinkle the cold water in a small microwave-safe bowl with gelatin; allow to stand for one min. Microwave, uncovered, for 40 secs on high. Stir; allow to stand until the gelatin is dissolved completely, about one min. Stir into the sour cream mixture.
- Beat the cream cheese in small bowl until fluffy and light. Put in vanilla and gelatin cream mixture gradually until just combined. Transfer to a 4-cup mold coated with the cooking spray. Let chill until set, at least 4 hours.
- Submerge grapes into the water; then shake excess moisture off; dip in the sugar, coat by turning. Unmold dessert onto the serving platter; arrange sugared grapes around.

Nutrition Information

- Calories: 451 calories
- Fiber: 0 fiber)

- Total Carbohydrate: 28g carbohydrate (27g sugars
- Cholesterol: 123mg cholesterol
- Protein: 6g protein.
- Total Fat: 35g fat (22g saturated fat)
- Sodium: 150mg sodium

- Sodium: 123mg sodium
- Fiber: 2g fiber)
- Total Carbohydrate: 44g carbohydrate (39g sugars
- Cholesterol: 50mg cholesterol

58. Frosted Fruit Gelatin

Serving: 8 servings. | Prep: 15mins | Cook: 0mins | Ready in:

Ingredients

- 2 packages (3 ounces each) raspberry gelatin
- 2 cups boiling water
- 1 can (8 ounces) crushed pineapple
- 1-1/2 cups fresh blueberries
- 3 to 4 medium firm banana, sliced
- 1 package (8 ounces) cream cheese, softened
- 1 cup (8 ounces) sour cream
- 1/2 cup sugar
- 1/2 cup chopped walnuts

Direction

- Dissolve gelatin in large bowl of boiling water. Drain the pineapple, saving juice in 1 measuring cup. Pour enough water into juice to measure one cup; stir into the gelatin mixture. Mix in blueberries and pineapple.
- In a 13x9 inches dish, put bananas. Add the gelatin mixture over the bananas. Refrigerate, covered, until firm.
- Beat sugar, sour cream and cream cheese in a small bowl until they become smooth. Then spread over the gelatin. Refrigerate until serving, covered. Sprinkle walnuts over.

Nutrition Information

- Calories: 368 calories
- Protein: 7g protein.
- Total Fat: 19g fat (10g saturated fat)

59. Frosted Fruit Gelatin Dessert

Serving: 9 servings. | Prep: 20mins | Cook: 10mins | Ready in:

Ingredients

- 2 envelopes unflavored gelatin
- 1/3 cup cold water
- 2 cups plus 2 tablespoons cranberry juice, divided
- 3/4 cup orange juice
- 1 can (20 ounces) unsweetened pineapple tidbits, drained
- 1-1/2 cups sliced firm bananas
- 2 tablespoons sugar
- 1 cup (8 ounces) fat-free plain yogurt

Direction

- Measure 1-1/8 teaspoons of the gelatin. Put aside for topping. Sprinkle the cold water in a small saucepan with remaining gelatin; allow to stand for one min. Over low heat, cook while stirring until the gelatin is dissolved completely. Discard from heat; then stir in 2 cups of orange juice and cranberry juice.
- In the 8 inches square dish coated with the cooking spray, put bananas and pineapple. Add the juice mixture over the fruit. Refrigerate, covered, until firm, about 45 to 60 mins.
- For topping, sprinkle remaining cranberry juice in a small saucepan with the reserved gelatin; allow to stand for one min. Stir in sugar. Over low heat, cook while stirring until dissolved completely. Put yogurt into a bowl; mix in the cranberry mixture. Then spread

over the gelatin. Refrigerate at least 120 mins, covered.

Nutrition Information

- Calories: 114 calories
- Protein: 3g protein. Diabetic Exchanges: 1-1/2 fruit.
- Total Fat: 0 fat (0 saturated fat)
- Sodium: 25mg sodium
- Fiber: 1g fiber)
- Total Carbohydrate: 29g carbohydrate (25g sugars
- Cholesterol: 1mg cholesterol

60. Frozen Peach Shortcake Squares

Serving: 12 | Prep: | Cook: |Ready in:

Ingredients

- 1 (8 ounce) tub COOL WHIP Whipped Topping, thawed
- 1 pint vanilla ice cream, softened
- 1 pkg. (4 serving size) JELL-O Brand Peach Flavor Gelatin (unprepared)
- 4 cups pound cake cubes
- 1/4 cup raspberry preserves
- 12 small peach slices
- 12 raspberries

Direction

- Mix dry gelatin, ice cream and whipped topping till well blended in a big bowl. Mix cake cubes in; put in a square 8-inch pan.
- Freeze till firm for 3 hours.
- Drizzle raspberry preserves on. Cut to squares; put 1 raspberry and 1 peach slice on each square. Keep leftover dessert in the freezer.

Nutrition Information

61. Fruited Cranberry Gelatin Salad

Serving: 6 servings. | Prep: 10mins | Cook: 0mins | Ready in:

Ingredients

- 1 package (6 ounces) orange gelatin
- 1 can (14 ounces) whole-berry cranberry sauce
- 1 can (8 ounces) crushed pineapple, undrained
- 1 can (12 ounces) ginger ale

Direction

- Cook cranberry sauce and gelatin together in a big saucepan on moderate heat until gelatin has dissolved. Take away from the heat then stir in ginger ale and pineapple until mixed.
- Transfer into a 1 1/2-quart serving bowl, then refrigerate until set and stir after an hour and a half.

Nutrition Information

- Calories: 253 calories
- Fiber: 1g fiber)
- Total Carbohydrate: 63g carbohydrate (53g sugars
- Cholesterol: 0 cholesterol
- Protein: 3g protein.
- Total Fat: 0 fat (0 saturated fat)
- Sodium: 85mg sodium

62. Gelatin Banana Split

Serving: 6 servings. | Prep: 15mins | Cook: 0mins | Ready in:

Ingredients

- 2 packages (3 ounces each) strawberry gelatin
- 2 cups boiling water
- 1 cup cold water

- 6 medium firm bananas
- Whipped cream in a can
- Chopped nuts, optional

Direction

- Dissolve gelatin in boiling water in a small bowl. Mix in cold water. Transfer into a 13x9-inch dish. Keep in the refrigerator for 2 hours or until firm. Slice gelatin into 1/2-inch cubes. Just before serving, divide bananas in half lengthwise. Then put two pieces per serving dish. Place nuts, whipped cream, and gelatin cubes on top, if preferred.

Nutrition Information

- Calories: 245 calories
- Sodium: 76mg sodium
- Fiber: 3g fiber)
- Total Carbohydrate: 44g carbohydrate (38g sugars
- Cholesterol: 25mg cholesterol
- Protein: 4g protein.
- Total Fat: 8g fat (5g saturated fat)

63. Gelatin Game Chips

Serving: 9 dozen. | Prep: 30mins | Cook: 0mins | Ready in:

Ingredients

- 1/2 cup milk
- 1/2 cup sugar
- 3 envelopes unflavored gelatin
- 3/4 cup cold water
- 1-1/2 teaspoons vanilla extract
- 2 cups (16 ounces) sour cream
- 5 cups lemon-lime soda
- 4 packages (3 ounces each) berry blue gelatin
- 4 packages (3 ounces each) raspberry gelatin

Direction

- Cook milk with sugar in a saucepan over low heat until dissolved. Soak unflavored gelatin in water to soften; stir into the milk mix until dissolved. Take off from heat; put in vanilla. Let cool to lukewarm; combine in sour cream. Add to a 13-in. x 9-in. pan. Refrigerate until firm.
- Heat up the soda to a boil in a saucepan. Add blue gelatin to bowl; mix in 2-1/2 cups of soda until gelatin has dissolved. Add to another 13-in. x 9-in. pan. Keep working in the same manner with raspberry gelatin and leftover soda. Chill until firm. Cut red, blue and white gelatin into rounds with a 1-1/2-in. round cookie cutter. Scatter or stack on a serving platter.

Nutrition Information

- Calories:
- Sodium:
- Fiber:
- Total Carbohydrate:
- Cholesterol:
- Protein:
- Total Fat:

64. Gelatin Parfaits

Serving: 6 servings. | Prep: 15mins | Cook: 0mins | Ready in:

Ingredients

- 1 package (3 ounces) lemon gelatin
- 1 package (3 ounces) orange gelatin
- 3 cups cubed pound cake (1-inch cubes)
- 2-1/4 cups whipped topping
- 2 tablespoons sugar
- 1/8 teaspoon ground cinnamon
- 6 maraschino cherries with stems

Direction

- Prepare the gelatins individually based on the package directions. Transfer onto individual 9x5-inch pans that are not greased. Store in the refrigerator until set. Slice into 1-inch cubes. Layer 1/4 cup cake cubes, 1/3cup cubed orange gelatin, 3 tablespoons whipped topping, 1/3 cup cubed lemon gelatin, 1/4 cup cake cubes, and 3 tablespoons whipped topping in each of six 1-1/2-cup parfait glasses or dessert dishes. Mix cinnamon and sugar; dust over whipped topping. Put a cherry on top.

Nutrition Information

- Calories: 299 calories
- Protein: 4g protein.
- Total Fat: 9g fat (7g saturated fat)
- Sodium: 156mg sodium
- Fiber: 0 fiber)
- Total Carbohydrate: 50g carbohydrate (42g sugars
- Cholesterol: 36mg cholesterol

65. Gelatin Torte

Serving: 8 servings. | Prep: 30mins | Cook: 30mins | Ready in:

Ingredients

- 3 eggs, separated
- 1 cup sugar, divided
- 1 can (8 ounces) crushed pineapple, drained
- 1 cup graham cracker crumbs (about 16 squares)
- 1/2 teaspoon baking powder
- 1/4 cup chopped pecans
- 1 package (6 ounces) cherry gelatin
- 2 cups boiling water
- 1-1/2 cups cold water
- 3 medium firm bananas, sliced
- 1 cup heavy whipping cream
- 3 tablespoons confectioners' sugar

- Maraschino cherries, optional

Direction

- Beat 1/2 cup sugar and egg yolks till lemon colored and thick in bowl; mix pineapple in. Mix baking powder and cracker crumbs; mix into pineapple mixture. Add pecans; put aside. Beat egg whites till foamy in a bowl; beat leftover sugar in slowly till soft peaks form. Fold into pineapple mixture; put in 9-in. ungreased springform pan. Bake for 30 minutes at 350° till lightly touching top makes it spring back. Cool on a wire rack. (Do not remove sides of pan.), Dissolve gelatin in boiling
- Mix cold water in; refrigerate for 40 minutes till mixture starts to thicken. Mix bananas in; put on cooled cake layer. Refrigerate for 2 hours till firm.
- Beat sugar and cream till soft peaks form in bowl; spoon/pipe on gelatin layer. Run knife around pan edge to loosen before serving; remove pan sides. If desired, garnish with cherries.

Nutrition Information

- Calories: 443 calories
- Protein: 7g protein.
- Total Fat: 17g fat (8g saturated fat)
- Sodium: 173mg sodium
- Fiber: 2g fiber)
- Total Carbohydrate: 71g carbohydrate (60g sugars
- Cholesterol: 120mg cholesterol

66. Glitter Gelatin Torte

Serving: 12-14 servings. | Prep: 35mins | Cook: 0mins | Ready in:

Ingredients

- 1-1/2 cups graham cracker crumbs (about 24 squares)
- 1/3 cup plus 1/4 cup sugar, divided
- 1/2 cup butter, melted
- 1 package (3 ounces) strawberry gelatin
- 3 cups boiling water, divided
- 1-1/4 cups cold water, divided
- 1 package (3 ounces) lime gelatin
- 1 package (3 ounces) lemon gelatin
- 1 can (8 ounces) crushed pineapple, drained
- 3 tablespoons lemon juice
- Dash salt
- 1-1/2 cups heavy whipping cream, whipped
- 1/4 cup chopped walnuts

Direction

- Combine butter, 1/3 cup of sugar and cracker crumbs in a bowl; press 2 inches up the sides and onto the bottom of an oiled 9 inches springform pan. Place in the refrigerator.
- Dissolve strawberry gelatin in small bowl with one cup of the boiling water; then stir in half cup of the cold water. Transfer to an 8 inches square dish coated with the cooking spray. Let chill until firm. Do the same process with the lime gelatin, putting into another 8 inches square dish.
- Dissolve remaining sugar and lemon gelatin in a large bowl of the remaining boiling water. Put in remaining cold water, salt, lemon juice and pineapple. Place in the refrigerator for 60 mins or until set partially. Beat for 2 mins, until foamy on medium speed.
- Cut lime gelatin and strawberry into 1/2 inches cubes. Put a quarter cup of each aside for decorating. Fold the remaining cubes into the lemon gelatin, followed by the whipped cream. Put into crust by spoon. Top with the reserved gelatin cubes and walnuts. Refrigerate at least 6 hours, covered. Discard the pan sides. Cut into the wedges.

Nutrition Information

- Calories: 306 calories

- Total Carbohydrate: 35g carbohydrate (28g sugars
- Cholesterol: 52mg cholesterol
- Protein: 3g protein.
- Total Fat: 18g fat (10g saturated fat)
- Sodium: 182mg sodium
- Fiber: 1g fiber)

67. Grape Bavarian

Serving: 4 servings. | Prep: 10mins | Cook: 0mins | Ready in:

Ingredients

- 1 packages (3 ounces) lemon gelatin
- 3/4 cup boiling water
- 1 cup Concord grape juice
- 1-3/4 cups whipped topping

Direction

- Dissolve gelatin in a bowl of boiling water; then stir in the grape juice. Let chill until thickened slightly. Then gently fold in the whipped topping. Transfer to dessert glasses or a greased 4-cup mold. Let chill until set.

Nutrition Information

- Calories: 202 calories
- Fiber: 0 fiber)
- Total Carbohydrate: 34g carbohydrate (30g sugars
- Cholesterol: 0 cholesterol
- Protein: 2g protein.
- Total Fat: 5g fat (5g saturated fat)
- Sodium: 52mg sodium

68. Halloween Gelatin Cutouts

Serving: 4 dozen. | Prep: 60mins | Cook: 0mins | Ready in:

Ingredients

- 4 packages (3 ounces each) orange gelatin
- 5 cups boiling water, divided
- 4 packages (3 ounces each) grape gelatin
- 2 cups cold milk
- 2 packages (3.4 ounces each) instant vanilla pudding mix

Direction

- Dissolve the orange gelatin in a large bowl with two and a half cups boiling water. Dissolve the grape gelatin in another bowl with the remaining boiling water; put aside both for half an hour.
- Whisk pudding mixes and milk in large bowl for one min until or they become smooth. Pour 1/2 pudding quickly into each gelatin bowl; whisk until blended well. Transfer to 2 dishes (13x9 inches) coated with the cooking spray. Let chill until set, about 3 hours. Using 2 inches Halloween cookie cutters to cut.

Nutrition Information

- Calories: 27 calories
- Sodium: 41mg sodium
- Fiber: 0 fiber)
- Total Carbohydrate: 5g carbohydrate (5g sugars
- Cholesterol: 1mg cholesterol
- Protein: 1g protein.
- Total Fat: 0 fat (0 saturated fat)

69. Ice Blue Igloo And Penguins

Serving: 12-16 servings. | Prep: 30mins | Cook: 0mins | Ready in:

Ingredients

- 6 envelopes unflavored gelatin
- 1-1/2 cups cold water
- 4 packages (3 ounces each) berry blue gelatin
- 7 cups boiling water
- 1 package (8 ounces) cream cheese, softened
- 6 tablespoons butter, softened
- 1-1/2 cups confectioners' sugar
- 2 large black gumdrops
- 2 large orange gumdrops
- Colored sprinkles
- 1/2 cup sweetened shredded coconut
- 6-ounce custard cup
- #7 round pastry tip
- Pastry or plastic bag

Direction

- Into a bowl, add unflavored gelatin and cold water, letting sit a minute to soften. Mix blue gelatin with boiling water in a big bowl to dissolve. Mix in unflavored gelatin mixture until dissolved. Add to a 6-oz. custard cup and a 2-qt. bowl sprayed with cooking spray. Chill for 4 hours or overnight.
- Whip confectioners' sugar, butter and cream cheese in a bowl. Add to a pastry or plastic bag. Snip a small hole in corner of bag and put in the pastry tip.
- For Penguins: Cut black gumdrops lengthwise in half. For eyes, pipe 2 dots of cream cheese mixture on the sugared side of each black gumdrop. For the chest, pipe a line from the middle of each black gumdrop to the bottom.
- Slice 2 1/4-in. thick circles from each orange gumdrop. Chop a small triangle from the edge of each orange circle and put aside. To make white chest lined up with cutout notch, put a black gumdrop on each orange circle. To make beaks, chop a 1/4-in. piece from the tip of each triangle and put over each penguin's chest. Put in sprinkles for buttons and eyes. Put penguins aside, to make Igloo: Unmold gelatin in the bowl onto a 12-in. round serving platter for igloo. Unmold gelatin in custard cup onto a cutting board for igloo's doorway. Chop a 1/4-

in. slice from 2 opposite sides of entrance dome. Position one cut side against igloo, leaving the other cut side to serve as the "entrance". Just before serving, draw cream cheese mixture on igloo to form an ice block pattern. Starting at the base of igloo and leaving entrance plain for now, draw a straight line surround bottom of big dome, spacing them 1-in apart. Create ice blocks by drawing vertical lines 1-1/2 in. apart, alternating their position from 1 row to the next.

- Outline the door by piping around cut-off area on igloo's entrance. Create ice blocks on small dome the same as for big dome.
- Spread leftover cream cheese mixture on serving platter around igloo and scatter with coconut. Randomly add penguins around igloo.

Nutrition Information

- Calories:
- Fiber:
- Total Carbohydrate:
- Cholesterol:
- Protein:
- Total Fat:
- Sodium:

---

70. Iced Tea Parfaits

Serving: 4 servings. | Prep: 15mins | Cook: 0mins | Ready in:

Ingredients

- 2 cups water
- 3 tea bags
- 1 package (3 ounces) lemon gelatin
- 4 maraschino cherries
- 1-1/2 cups whipped topping, divided
- 4 lemon slices

Direction

- Place water in a small saucepan then boil. Separate from the heat; put in tea bags. Steep for 5 minutes, covered. Discard the tea bags. Mix gelatin into tea until fully dissolved. Slightly cool.
- Into every four glasses of parfait, put 1/4 cup gelatin mixture. In each glass, put a cherry; keep in the refrigerator for about 1 hour until set yet not firm. Place the rest of the gelatin mixture to a small bowl; keep in the refrigerator for 1 hour or until set to soft.
- Whip gelatin mixture for 2 to 3 minutes or until smooth. Mix in 1/2 cup whipped topping; scoop into parfait glasses. Keep in the refrigerator for at least 2 hours. Just before serving, put the rest of whipped topping on top and decorate with lemon slices.

Nutrition Information

- Calories: 162 calories
- Total Carbohydrate: 27g carbohydrate (24g sugars
- Cholesterol: 0 cholesterol
- Protein: 2g protein. Diabetic Exchanges: 1-1/2 starch
- Total Fat: 5g fat (5g saturated fat)
- Sodium: 48mg sodium
- Fiber: 0 fiber)

---

71. Icy Blue Parfaits

Serving: 4 servings. | Prep: 20mins | Cook: 0mins | Ready in:

Ingredients

- 3 ounces cream cheese, softened
- 1 carton (8 ounces) frozen whipped topping, thawed
- 1 package (14 ounces) blue gelatin snack cups or 1-1/3 cups cubed blue gelatin
- 1 cup fresh or frozen blueberries

Direction

- Whisk cream cheese in a big bowl until smooth. Mix in whipped topping. Take gelatin out from snack cups and slice into 1/2 inch cubes.
- Layer 1/2 of the cream cheese mixture into 4 parfait glasses or dessert bowls, add gelatin and place blueberries. Repeat layering once again. Keep refrigerated just until serving.

Nutrition Information

- Calories: 613 calories
- Fiber: 1g fiber)
- Total Carbohydrate: 104g carbohydrate (96g sugars
- Cholesterol: 23mg cholesterol
- Protein: 11g protein.
- Total Fat: 17g fat (14g saturated fat)
- Sodium: 289mg sodium

72. Jeweled Gelatin Torte

Serving: 10-12 servings. | Prep: 25mins | Cook: 0mins | Ready in:

Ingredients

- 1 package (3 ounces) cherry gelatin
- 3 cups boiling water, divided
- 2 cups cold water, divided
- 1 package (3 ounces) lime gelatin
- 1 package (3 ounces) orange gelatin
- 1 cup pineapple juice
- 1 package (3 ounces) lemon gelatin
- 1/4 cup sugar
- 36 ladyfingers
- 1 carton (8 ounces) frozen whipped topping, thawed
- Citrus slices and fresh mint, optional

Direction

- Place 1 cup of boiling water in a small bowl, dissolve in cherry gelatin; mix in 1/2 cup of cold water. Transfer into a 9x5-in. loaf pan greased with cooking spray. Repeat with orange and lime gelatin, using two more loaf pans. Place in the refrigerator for around 1 1/2 hours, or till firm.
- Boil pineapple juice in a small saucepan. Mix in sugar and lemon gelatin till dissolved. Mix in the remaining cold water. Place in the refrigerator for around 45 minutes, or till syrupy. Meanwhile, use ladyfingers to line the bottom and sides of a 9-in. springform pan; set aside.
- Cut the orange, lime and cherry gelatin into 1/2-in. cubes. Transfer the lemon gelatin mixture into a large bowl; stir in whipped topping. Fold in the gelatin cubes gently. Transfer into the prepared pan. Place in the refrigerator till set. Use mint and citrus for garnish if you want.

Nutrition Information

- Calories: 304 calories
- Sodium: 113mg sodium
- Fiber: 0 fiber)
- Total Carbohydrate: 55g carbohydrate (47g sugars
- Cholesterol: 120mg cholesterol
- Protein: 6g protein.
- Total Fat: 6g fat (4g saturated fat)

73. Kiwi Lime Gelatin

Serving: 8 servings. | Prep: 15mins | Cook: 0mins | Ready in:

Ingredients

- 6 kiwifruit, peeled, sliced and quartered
- 1 cup dry white wine or diet lemon-lime soda
- 2 packages (3 ounces each) lime gelatin
- 3 cups diet lemon-lime soda, chilled

- 2 tablespoons orange juice
- 1 can (11 ounces) mandarin oranges, drained

Direction

- Heat up kiwi with wine or soda to a boil in a saucepan. Cook over medium heat, mixing sometimes, for 5 minutes. Put in gelatin; mix until dissolved. Mix in orange juice and chilled soda. Chill until set partially.
- Fold in oranges. Add to a six-cup mold sprayed with cooking spray. Chill 8 hours or overnight until set.

Nutrition Information

- Calories: 81 calories
- Total Fat: 0 fat (0 saturated fat)
- Sodium: 31mg sodium
- Fiber: 2g fiber)
- Total Carbohydrate: 16g carbohydrate (0 sugars
- Cholesterol: 0 cholesterol
- Protein: 1g protein. Diabetic Exchanges: 1 fruit.

74. Ladyfinger Lemon Dessert

Serving: 10 servings. | Prep: 15mins | Cook: 0mins | Ready in:

Ingredients

- 1 can (12 ounces) evaporated milk
- 1 package (3 ounces) ladyfingers, split
- 1 package (3 ounces) lemon gelatin
- 1 cup boiling orange juice
- 1/2 cup sugar
- 1/3 cup lemon juice
- 2 teaspoons grated lemon peel
- 1 cup reduced-fat whipped topping

Direction

- Add milk into a small metal bowl; add in mixer beaters. Refrigerate with a cover for at least 2 hours or overnight. Use ladyfingers to line the sides of a 9-in. springform pan; set aside.
- Dissolve gelatin in a large bowl with orange juice. Mix in lemon peel, juice and sugar; let cool to room temperature.
- Beat chilled milk till it forms soft peaks; stir into the gelatin mixture. Transfer into the prepared pan. Place in the refrigerator till firm, at least 3 hours. Spread with whipped topping. Remove the sides of the pan. Place any leftovers in the refrigerator.

Nutrition Information

- Calories: 221 calories
- Sodium: 100mg sodium
- Fiber: 0 fiber)
- Total Carbohydrate: 40g carbohydrate (0 sugars
- Cholesterol: 98mg cholesterol
- Protein: 6g protein. Diabetic Exchanges: 1-1/2 starch
- Total Fat: 5g fat (2g saturated fat)

75. Layered Cranberry Dessert

Serving: 12 servings. | Prep: 25mins | Cook: 0mins | Ready in:

Ingredients

- 2 packages (3 ounces each) cranberry gelatin
- 1-1/2 cups boiling water
- 1 can (14 ounces) whole-berry cranberry sauce
- 1-1/2 cups cold water
- 1-1/2 cups graham cracker crumbs
- 1/2 cup sugar, divided
- 1/2 cup butter, melted
- 1 package (8 ounces) cream cheese, softened
- 1 carton (16 ounces) frozen whipped topping, thawed, divided

- 1 can (15 ounces) mandarin oranges, drained

Direction

- Place boiling water in a large bowl, dissolve in gelatin. Mix in cold water and cranberry sauce till well-blended. Place in the refrigerator till partially set, 45 minutes.
- Meanwhile, mix butter, 1/4 cup of sugar and cracker crumbs together in a small bowl. Press into an ungreased 13x9-in. dish. Place in the refrigerator till set.
- Beat the remaining sugar and cream cheese in a large bowl, till smooth. Stir in half of the whipped topping. Spread the filling over the crust.
- Stir oranges into the gelatin mixture; transfer over the cream cheese layer. Place in the refrigerator till firm, 4 hours. Cut into squares; dollop with the remaining whipped topping.

Nutrition Information

- Calories: 416 calories
- Fiber: 1g fiber)
- Total Carbohydrate: 51g carbohydrate (35g sugars
- Cholesterol: 41mg cholesterol
- Protein: 3g protein.
- Total Fat: 22g fat (15g saturated fat)
- Sodium: 223mg sodium

76. Layered Pudding Dessert

Serving: 9 servings. | Prep: 20mins | Cook: 0mins | Ready in:

Ingredients

- 1 cup crushed vanilla wafers (about 30 wafers), divided
- 1 package (3 ounces) cook-and-serve vanilla pudding mix
- 2 medium ripe bananas, divided
- 1 package (3 ounces) strawberry gelatin

- 1 cup whipped topping

Direction

- Spread in bottom of the oiled 8 inches square pan with 1/2 crushed wafers. Prepare the pudding mix following the package instructions; scoop the hot pudding over crumbs. Slice 1 banana; arrange over the pudding. Add the remaining crumbs over top. Let chill for 60 mins. In the meantime, prepare the gelatin following the package instructions; let chill until set partially, about half an hour. Pour over the crumbs. Slice remaining banana; arrange over the gelatin. Spread over all with whipped topping. Let chill for 120 mins.

Nutrition Information

- Calories:
- Sodium:
- Fiber:
- Total Carbohydrate:
- Cholesterol:
- Protein:
- Total Fat:

77. Lemon Chiffon Dessert

Serving: 6 servings. | Prep: 20mins | Cook: 0mins | Ready in:

Ingredients

- 2 envelopes unflavored gelatin
- 1-1/4 cups cold water, divided
- 1-1/3 cups nonfat dry milk powder
- 2-1/2 teaspoons Crystal Light lemonade drink mix
- 3 to 4 drops yellow food coloring, optional
- 1/8 teaspoon salt
- 3/4 cup 1% cottage cheese
- 1 cup reduced-fat whipped topping
- 1 tablespoon graham cracker crumbs

Direction

- Scatter gelatin on top of half cup cold water in a small saucepan; let sit for a minute. Cook and mix over low heat until dissolved completely; put aside.
- Mix the food coloring (optional), drink mix, milk and salt in a bowl; whip on high speed until combined. In a blender or food processor, put the cottage cheese and leftover water; cover and blend until smooth. Put in gelatin and milk mixture; cover and blend until thickened.
- Scoop into 6 6-oz. custard cups. Cover and chill for an hour. Spread whipped topping over; garnish with cracker crumbs.

Nutrition Information

- Calories: 81 calories
- Protein: 7g protein. Diabetic Exchanges: 1 lean meat
- Total Fat: 2g fat (2g saturated fat)
- Sodium: 202mg sodium
- Fiber: 0 fiber)
- Total Carbohydrate: 7g carbohydrate (0 sugars
- Cholesterol: 2mg cholesterol

78. Lemon Cloud Desserts

Serving: 8 servings. | Prep: 20mins | Cook: 0mins | Ready in:

Ingredients

- 2 packages (.3 ounce each) sugar-free lemon gelatin
- 2 cups boiling water
- 2 cups diet lemon-lime soda
- 1/4 cup lemon juice
- 1 carton (8 ounces) frozen reduced-fat whipped topping, thawed
- 1/4 teaspoon yellow food coloring, optional
- 3/4 cup fresh blueberries

- 3/4 cup sliced fresh strawberries
- 2 medium kiwifruit, peeled and sliced

Direction

- Dissolve gelatin in a large bowl of boiling water. Then stir in lemon juice and soda. Refrigerate, covered, until set, about 120 mins.
- Put in the whipped topping; beat for 4 to 5 mins on high speed, until they become smooth. If desired, mix in the food coloring. Put 3/4 cup of mixture into each of 8 dessert dishes. Place in the refrigerator until set. Place kiwi and berries on top. Then serve.

Nutrition Information

- Calories: 97 calories
- Protein: 2g protein. Diabetic Exchanges: 1/2 starch
- Total Fat: 3g fat (3g saturated fat)
- Sodium: 58mg sodium
- Fiber: 1g fiber)
- Total Carbohydrate: 13g carbohydrate (8g sugars
- Cholesterol: 0 cholesterol

79. Lemon Fluff Dessert

Serving: 12 servings. | Prep: 25mins | Cook: 0mins | Ready in:

Ingredients

- 1 can (12 ounces) evaporated milk
- 1 package (3 ounces) lemon gelatin
- 1 cup sugar
- 1-1/3 cups boiling water
- 1/4 cup lemon juice
- 1-3/4 cups graham cracker crumbs
- 5 tablespoons butter, melted

Direction

- Add milk to a small metal bowl and place the mixer beaters in the bowl. Cover and put into a refrigerator for a minimum of 2 hours.
- At the same time, add sugar, gelatin and boiling water to a big bowl and stir until dissolved. Whisk in lemon juice. Then cover and put into a refrigerator for approximately one and a half hours until syrupy.
- Mix the butter and crumbs in a small bowl then put aside 2 tbsp. for decoration. Press the remaining crumbs onto the bottom of a 13x9-inch dish. Beat the cold milk until soft peaks form. Beat the gelatin mixture until tiny bubbles form. Add milk to gelatin mixture and fold. Add the mixture to the prepared dish. Drizzle reserved crumbs over the mixture. Then cover and put into a refrigerator until set. Slice into squares.

Nutrition Information

- Calories: 221 calories
- Sodium: 151mg sodium
- Fiber: 0 fiber)
- Total Carbohydrate: 35g carbohydrate (29g sugars
- Cholesterol: 22mg cholesterol
- Protein: 3g protein. Diabetic Exchanges: 2 starch
- Total Fat: 8g fat (5g saturated fat)

80. Lemon Panna Cotta With Berries

Serving: 7 servings. | Prep: 20mins | Cook: 5mins | Ready in:

Ingredients

- 1 envelope unflavored gelatin
- 1-1/3 cups half-and-half cream
- 2 cups heavy whipping cream
- 1/3 cup honey
- 1 teaspoon grated lemon peel

- Dash salt
- 2/3 cup each fresh blackberries, blueberries and raspberries
- 2 tablespoons sugar
- 2 tablespoons lemon juice
- 1 tablespoon Amaretto, optional

Direction

- Sprinkle gelatin over half-and-half in a small saucepan; let sit for one minute. Heat gelatin over low heat, stirring until completely dissolved. Mix in salt, lemon peel, honey and the whipping cream. Cook while stirring until blended. Add to seven 6-oz. ramekins or custard cups.
- Refrigerate with a cover until set, about at least 5 hours. In a small bowl, mix together Amaretto (if preferred), lemon juice, sugar and the berries. Refrigerate with a cover for at least 30 minutes. Unmold panna cotta onto dessert plates; enjoy with berry mixture.

Nutrition Information

- Calories: 382 calories
- Sodium: 73mg sodium
- Fiber: 2g fiber)
- Total Carbohydrate: 25g carbohydrate (21g sugars
- Cholesterol: 116mg cholesterol
- Protein: 4g protein.
- Total Fat: 30g fat (19g saturated fat)

81. Lemon Torte With Fresh Berries

Serving: 12 servings. | Prep: 20mins | Cook: 0mins | Ready in:

Ingredients

- 1 package (3 ounces) lemon gelatin
- 1/2 cup boiling water
- 1/3 cup thawed lemonade concentrate
- 1 can (12 ounces) evaporated milk

- 3 cups angel food cake cubes
- 3 cups fresh raspberries or sliced strawberries
- 1 tablespoon sugar

Direction

- Melt gelatin in boiling water in big bowl; mix milk and lemonade concentrate in. Cover; refrigerate it for 1-2 hours.
- Put cake cubes in 9-in. springform pan coated in cooking spray. Beat gelatin mixture for 5 minutes on medium speed or till fluffy; put on cake cubes. Cover; chill till firm or for 4 hours. Mix sugar and berries in small bowl; chill for 2 hours.
- Before serving, run knife around pan edge carefully to loosen; remove pan sides. Put berry mixture on torte; refrigerate leftovers.

Nutrition Information

- Calories: 124 calories
- Total Carbohydrate: 24g carbohydrate (20g sugars
- Cholesterol: 9mg cholesterol
- Protein: 3g protein.
- Total Fat: 2g fat (1g saturated fat)
- Sodium: 127mg sodium
- Fiber: 2g fiber)

82. Lemonade Cheesecake Parfaits

Serving: 6 parfaits. | Prep: 35mins | Cook: 5mins | Ready in:

Ingredients

- 2 whole graham crackers, crushed
- 1 cup half-and-half cream
- 1-3/4 cups sugar, divided
- 2 tablespoons lemon juice, divided
- 2 envelopes unflavored gelatin
- 1 package (8 ounces) cream cheese, softened
- 3 teaspoons grated lemon peel, divided

- 1 teaspoon vanilla extract
- 1-1/4 cups cold water
- 1 tablespoon grenadine syrup
- Dash salt

Direction

- Split graham crackers among six dessert dishes. Mix in a small saucepan the 1 tablespoon lemon juice, 1 cup sugar and cream. Drizzle 1 envelope of gelatin over cream mixture; allow it to stand for 1 minute or until softened.
- Then heat over low heat, whisking until sugar and gelatin are fully melted. Whisk cream cheese in a large bowl until smooth. Mix in gelatin mixture. Mix in vanilla and 1 teaspoon lemon peel. Transfer into glasses over graham crackers, about 1/2 cup in each. Keep in the refrigerator, covered, until firm.
- Mix in a small saucepan the remaining lemon juice and sugar, salt, grenadine and water. Drizzle the remaining gelatin over water mixture; allow it to stand for 1 minute. Then heat over low heat, whisking until sugar and gelatin are fully melted. Put 2 tablespoons mixture into each parfait glass.
- Keep in the refrigerator, covered, until firm.
- Keep the remaining grenadine mixture in the refrigerator for about 30 minutes, until syrupy. Whisk using a hand mixer until frothy. Split among glasses. Store in the refrigerator, covered, until firm. Decorate with remaining lemon peel.

Nutrition Information

- Calories: 449 calories
- Cholesterol: 62mg cholesterol
- Protein: 7g protein.
- Total Fat: 18g fat (11g saturated fat)
- Sodium: 193mg sodium
- Fiber: 0 fiber)
- Total Carbohydrate: 67g carbohydrate (62g sugars

83. Lemony Tropic Layered Dessert

*Serving: 15 servings. | Prep: 35mins | Cook: 25mins
| Ready in:*

Ingredients

- 1 cup all-purpose flour
- 1/2 cup chopped walnuts, toasted
- 1/4 cup packed brown sugar
- 1/2 cup cold butter, cubed
- FILLING/TOPPING:
- 2 cans (8 ounces each) crushed pineapple
- 2 packages (3 ounces each) lemon gelatin
- 1 cup boiling water
- 2 cups cold water
- 4 medium firm bananas, chopped
- 1 cup miniature marshmallows
- 1/2 cup sugar
- 2 tablespoons all-purpose flour
- 2 eggs, lightly beaten
- 1/2 cup heavy whipping cream, whipped

Direction

- Mix the brown sugar, walnuts and flour in a small bowl; slice in butter until mixture forms coarse crumbs. Push into a greased 13-in. x 9-in. baking pan. Bake for 12-15 minutes at 350° or until golden brown. Let cool on a wire rack.
- To make filling, strain pineapple, saving juice for garnishing. Put pineapple aside. Mix gelatin in boiling water in a big bowl to dissolve; mix in cold water. Chill about 1 hour until thickened,
- Fold in the saved pineapple, marshmallows and bananas. Scoop on top of crust. Chill about 45 minutes until firm.
- To make topping, mix saved pineapple juice and water just enough to measure 1 cup. Mix pineapple juice mixture, flour and sugar in a small saucepan until smooth. Cook and mix over medium heat until bubbly and thickened. Turn down heat; cook and mix 2 minutes more. Take off from the heat.
- Mix a small amount of hot mixture into eggs. Put back all to the pan, mixing continuously. Heat up to a gentle boil; cook and mix 2 minutes more. Add to a small bowl; let cool completely. Fold in whipped cream. Spread on top of gelatin layer. Chill until cooled.

Nutrition Information

- Calories: 279 calories
- Cholesterol: 50mg cholesterol
- Protein: 5g protein.
- Total Fat: 11g fat (5g saturated fat)
- Sodium: 83mg sodium
- Fiber: 2g fiber)
- Total Carbohydrate: 44g carbohydrate (32g sugars

84. Light Christmas Cake

*Serving: 16 servings. | Prep: 15mins | Cook: 0mins
| Ready in:*

Ingredients

- 1 package (.3 ounce) sugar-free raspberry gelatin
- 2-1/2 cups unsweetened applesauce, divided
- 1 package (.3 ounce) sugar-free lime gelatin
- 21 whole graham crackers, divided
- 1 carton (8 ounces) frozen reduced-fat whipped topping, thawed

Direction

- Mix 1-1/4 cups applesauce and the raspberry gelatin in bowl. Mix the rest of applesauce and the lime gelatin in a separate bowl.
- On serving plate, put 3 graham crackers next to each other. Top with 1/3 of raspberry applesauce to cover. Put on 3 additional crackers and 1/3 of lime applesauce. Redo the piling two more times; put the rest of the crackers on top.

- With whipped topping, ice surface and sides. Chill overnight. Slice into half-inch pieces.

Nutrition Information

- Calories: 95 calories
- Sodium: 97mg sodium
- Fiber: 0 fiber)
- Total Carbohydrate: 15g carbohydrate (0 sugars
- Cholesterol: 0 cholesterol
- Protein: 1g protein. Diabetic Exchanges: 1/2 starch
- Total Fat: 3g fat (0 saturated fat)

85. Light Lemon Fluff Dessert

Serving: 20 servings. | Prep: 15mins | Cook: 0mins | Ready in:

Ingredients

- 1 can (12 ounces) evaporated milk
- 1-1/2 cups graham cracker crumbs
- 1/3 cup butter, melted
- 1 package (.3 ounce) sugar-free lemon gelatin
- 1 cup boiling water
- 3 tablespoons lemon juice
- 1 package (8 ounces) reduced-fat cream cheese
- 3/4 cup sugar
- 1 teaspoon vanilla extract

Direction

- Add milk into a big metal bowl; put mixer beaters in the bowl. Cover and chill for no less than 2 hours.
- Mix graham cracker crumbs with butter in a small bowl; put aside a tablespoon for garnishing. Push leftover crumb mixture into a 13-in. x 9-in. baking pan. Refrigerate until set.
- In the meantime, mix gelatin in boiling water in a small bowl to dissolve. Mix in lemon juice; let cool.

- Whip the vanilla, sugar and cream cheese in a separate bowl until smooth. Put in gelatin mixture and stir well. Whip evaporated milk until forming soft peaks; fold into cream cheese mixture. Add on top of crust. Scatter with saved crumbs. Chill for no less than 2 hours prior to serving. Chill leftovers.

Nutrition Information

- Calories: 135 calories
- Sodium: 136mg sodium
- Fiber: 0 fiber)
- Total Carbohydrate: 15g carbohydrate (12g sugars
- Cholesterol: 21mg cholesterol
- Protein: 3g protein. Diabetic Exchanges: 1 starch
- Total Fat: 7g fat (4g saturated fat)

86. Light Lemon Pie

Serving: 8 servings. | Prep: 20mins | Cook: 0mins | Ready in:

Ingredients

- 1 package (.3 ounces) sugar-free lemon gelatin
- 1/2 cup boiling water
- 3/4 cup cold water
- Sugar substitute equivalent to 3 tablespoons plus 1 teaspoon sugar
- 1 cup (8 ounces) 1% cottage cheese
- 1 carton (8 ounces) frozen reduced-fat whipped topping, thawed
- 1 reduced-fat graham cracker crust (8 inches)
- 1/2 cup 100% strawberry spreadable fruit
- 8 large strawberries, halved

Direction

- Dissolve gelatin in boiling water in a large bowl. Mix in sugar substitute and cold water. Refrigerate till partially set.

- Strain cottage cheese in a fine strainer. Put the cottage cheese in a blender; process with a cover till smooth. Move into a bowl; mix in gelatin mixture. Fold in whipped topping.
- Transfer into the crust. Keep in a refrigerator till set. Cut into slices just before serving; garnish each with 2 strawberry halves and 1 tablespoon of spreadable fruit.

Nutrition Information

- Calories: 216 calories
- Fiber: 1g fiber)
- Total Carbohydrate: 31g carbohydrate (0 sugars
- Cholesterol: 4mg cholesterol
- Protein: 5g protein. Diabetic Exchanges: 1-1/2 fat
- Total Fat: 7g fat (5g saturated fat)
- Sodium: 213mg sodium

87. Light Strawberry Gelatin Pie

Serving: 8 servings. | Prep: 20mins | Cook: 0mins | Ready in:

Ingredients

- 2 pints fresh strawberries, hulled
- 2 tablespoons cornstarch
- 1-1/2 cups cold water
- 1 package (.3 ounce) sugar-free strawberry gelatin
- 3 tablespoons sugar
- 1 reduced-fat graham cracker crust (8 inches)
- 2 cups reduced-fat whipped topping

Direction

- Set the four whole berries aside for garnish. Cut the remaining strawberries; set aside. Mix water and cornstarch together in a large saucepan, till smooth. Boil the mixture; cook while stirring till thickened, 2 minutes.

- Take away from the heat; mix in sugar and gelatin till dissolved. Mix in the sliced strawberries. Transfer into the crust. Refrigerate with a cover till firm, 2 hours.
- Cut the reserved strawberries in half. Use a berry half and whipped topping for garnish each serving.

Nutrition Information

- Calories: 197 calories
- Fiber: 2g fiber)
- Total Carbohydrate: 33g carbohydrate (0 sugars
- Cholesterol: 0 cholesterol
- Protein: 2g protein. Diabetic Exchanges: 1 starch
- Total Fat: 5g fat (3g saturated fat)
- Sodium: 125mg sodium

88. Lime Chiffon Dessert

Serving: 12-15 servings. | Prep: 20mins | Cook: 0mins | Ready in:

Ingredients

- 1-1/2 cups crushed graham crackers (about 24 squares)
- 1/3 cup sugar
- 1/2 cup butter, melted
- FILLING:
- 1 package (3 ounces) lime gelatin
- 1 cup boiling water
- 2 packages (one 8 ounces, one 3 ounces) cream cheese, softened
- 1 cup sugar
- 1 teaspoon vanilla extract
- 1 carton (16 ounces) frozen whipped topping, thawed

Direction

- Mix the first 3 ingredients then put aside 2 tbsp. for topping. Press the remaining crumbs onto the bottom of an uncoated 13x9-inch dish then put aside. Add boiling water and gelatin to a small bowl and stir until dissolved then put aside to cool.
- Beat the sugar and cream cheese in a big bowl until smooth. Add vanilla and beat. Put in gelatin in a slow stream until blended. Put in whipped topping and fold. Scoop the mixture over the crust and drizzle the reserves crumbs on top. Cover and put into a refrigerator until set, for 3 hrs.

Nutrition Information

- Calories: 336 calories
- Sodium: 187mg sodium
- Fiber: 0 fiber)
- Total Carbohydrate: 36g carbohydrate (27g sugars
- Cholesterol: 39mg cholesterol
- Protein: 3g protein.
- Total Fat: 19g fat (14g saturated fat)

89. Lime Fluff

Serving: 9 | Prep: 5mins | Cook: |Ready in:

Ingredients

- 1 (6 ounce) package lime flavored Jell-O® mix
- 1 (8 ounce) container frozen whipped topping, thawed
- 1 (20 ounce) can crushed pineapple with juice
- 1 (16 ounce) container sour cream
- 1 (16 ounce) package miniature marshmallows
- 1 cup chopped pecans

Direction

- Mix pecans, marshmallows, sour cream, pineapple with juice, whipped topping and gelatin in a big bowl. Cover then chill in the fridge for a minimum of an hour. Serve while cold.

Nutrition Information

- Calories: 532 calories;
- Total Fat: 24.4
- Sodium: 152
- Total Carbohydrate: 75.9
- Cholesterol: 22
- Protein: 5.7

90. Lucky Lime Salad

Serving: 9 servings. | Prep: 20mins | Cook: 0mins | Ready in:

Ingredients

- 1 package (3 ounces) lime gelatin
- 1 cup boiling water
- 1/2 cup cold water
- 3 ounces cream cheese, softened
- 1/4 teaspoon lemon juice
- 2 cups whipped topping
- 1 can (8 ounces) crushed pineapple, drained
- SHAMROCKS:
- 1 package (6 ounces) lime gelatin
- 2-1/2 cups boiling water

Direction

- Dissolve gelatin in a small bowl with boiling water; mix in cold water. Keep chilled till thickened slightly. Meanwhile, beat whipped topping, lemon juice and cream cheese together in a small bowl till smooth; mix into the gelatin. Stir in pineapple.
- Transfer into a 9-in. square dish coated with grease. Place in the refrigerator for around 3 hours, or till set.
- For shamrocks, dissolve gelatin in boiling water. Transfer into an 11x7-in. pan coated

with grease. Place in the refrigerator for around 3 hours, or till set.
- Cut the plain gelatin into 9 shamrocks with a 2-in. shamrock-shaped cutter. Cut the gelatin mixture into 9 squares; place a gelatin shamrock on top of each.

Nutrition Information

- Calories: 200 calories
- Total Carbohydrate: 33g carbohydrate (31g sugars
- Cholesterol: 10mg cholesterol
- Protein: 3g protein.
- Total Fat: 6g fat (5g saturated fat)
- Sodium: 93mg sodium
- Fiber: 0 fiber)

91. Luscious Lime Angel Squares

Serving: 15 servings. | Prep: 15mins | Cook: 0mins | Ready in:

Ingredients

- 1 package (.3 ounce) sugar-free lime gelatin
- 1 cup boiling water
- 1 prepared angel food cake (8 inches), cut into 1-inch cubes
- 1 package (8 ounces) reduced-fat cream cheese, cubed
- 1/2 cup sugar
- 2 teaspoons lemon juice
- 1-1/2 teaspoons grated lemon peel
- 1 carton (8 ounces) reduced-fat whipped topping, thawed, divided

Direction

- Add boiling water and gelatin to a small bowl and stir until dissolves. Put into a refrigerator for approximately 35 minutes until the mixture just starts thickening. Arrange the cake cubes in a 13x9-inch dish greased with cooking spray and put aside.

- Beat the cream cheese in a small bowl until smooth. Whisk in lemon peel, lemon juice, and the sugar. Put in the gelatin mixture and whisk until blended. Put in one and a half cups of whipped topping and fold.
- Spread over the cake top until completely covered. Put into a refrigerator until firm, at least 2 hrs. Slice into squares and add the remaining whipped topping on top.

Nutrition Information

- Calories: 139 calories
- Protein: 3g protein. Diabetic Exchanges: 1-1/2 starch
- Total Fat: 4g fat (3g saturated fat)
- Sodium: 145mg sodium
- Fiber: 0 fiber)
- Total Carbohydrate: 21g carbohydrate (0 sugars
- Cholesterol: 8mg cholesterol

92. Make Ahead Shortcake

Serving: 12 servings. | Prep: 15mins | Cook: 0mins | Ready in:

Ingredients

- 1 loaf loaf-shaped angel food cake (10-1/2 ounces), cut into 1/2-inch slices
- 1/2 cup cold 2% milk
- 1 package (5.1 ounces) instant vanilla pudding mix
- 1 pint vanilla ice cream, softened
- 1 package (6 ounces) strawberry gelatin
- 1 cup boiling water
- 2 packages (10 ounces each) frozen sweetened sliced strawberries
- Sliced fresh strawberries, optional

Direction

- In 1 layer, put cake slices in 13x9-in. ungreased dish. Beat pudding mix and milk till thick for 2 minutes in big bowl. Beat ice cream in; put on cake. Chill.

- Meanwhile, melt gelatin in boiling water in big bowl; mix frozen strawberries in. Chill till partially set.
- Put on pudding mixture; chill till firm. If desired, garnish with fresh strawberries.

Nutrition Information

- Calories: 256 calories
- Protein: 4g protein.
- Total Fat: 3g fat (2g saturated fat)
- Sodium: 411mg sodium
- Fiber: 1g fiber)
- Total Carbohydrate: 56g carbohydrate (37g sugars
- Cholesterol: 11mg cholesterol

93. Makeover Blueberry Whipped Topping Dessert

Serving: 20 servings. | Prep: 30mins | Cook: 0mins | Ready in:

Ingredients

- 1 cup all-purpose flour
- 3/4 cup finely chopped pecans
- 6 tablespoons butter, melted
- 1 envelope unflavored gelatin
- 1/2 cup cold water
- 2 packages (8 ounces each) fat-free cream cheese
- 2 cups confectioners' sugar
- 1 carton (8 ounces) frozen reduced-fat whipped topping, thawed
- 1 can (21 ounces) blueberry pie filling

Direction

- Mix together the butter, pecans and flour in a small bowl, then press onto the bottom of a cooking spray coated 13x9-inch baking dish.

Let it bake for 10 minutes at 350 degrees. Allow to cool on a wire rack.

- In the meantime, sprinkle the gelatin on cold water in a small saucepan and allow it to stand for a minute. Heat on low heat, mixing until the gelatin is fully dissolved. Take away from heat, then put aside.
- Beat the confectioners' sugar and cream cheese in a big bowl until smooth. Beat in the gelatin mixture until combined. Fold in whipped topping, then pour it on top of the crust. Scoop the pie filling on top. Put cover on and let it chill in the fridge for a minimum of 4 hours or until firm. Chill the leftovers in the fridge.

Nutrition Information

- Calories: 232 calories
- Total Fat: 8g fat (4g saturated fat)
- Sodium: 152mg sodium
- Fiber: 1g fiber)
- Total Carbohydrate: 36g carbohydrate (24g sugars
- Cholesterol: 11mg cholesterol
- Protein: 5g protein.

94. Makeover Strawberry Pretzel Dessert

Serving: 18 servings. | Prep: 30mins | Cook: 0mins | Ready in:

Ingredients

- 2 cups crushed pretzels (8 ounces)
- 3/4 cup butter, melted
- 3 tablespoons plus 1/2 cup sugar, divided
- 1 package (8 ounces) reduced-fat cream cheese
- Sugar substitute equivalent to 1/2 cup sugar
- 1 carton (8 ounces) frozen reduced-fat whipped topping, thawed
- 1 can (20 ounces) unsweetened crushed pineapple

- 2 packages (.3 ounce each) sugar-free strawberry gelatin
- 2 packages (10 ounces each) frozen sliced sweetened strawberries, thawed

Direction

- Mix together 3 tbsp. sugar, butter and pretzels in a big bowl, then press into a cooking spray coated 13x9-inch baking dish. Let it bake for 18 to 20 minutes at 400 degrees until set. Allow it to cool on a wire rack.
- Beat the leftover sugar, sugar substitute and cream cheese in a big bowl until smooth. Fold in the whipped topping, then spread it on top of the cooled crust. Let chill in the fridge.
- Drain the pineapple and save the juice, then put the pineapple aside. If needed, pour water into pineapple juice to measure one cup and pour it into a saucepan; boil. Pour into a big bowl, then mix in gelatin until it dissolves.
- Drain the strawberries, saving juice, then put the strawberries aside. If needed, pour water into the strawberry juice to measure 1 1/2 cups, then mix into the gelatin mixture. Let chill in the fridge until partly set.
- Mix in strawberries and reserved pineapple, then spoon on top of the filling carefully. Put cover on and let it chill in the fridge for 3 to 4 hours or until firm.

Nutrition Information

- Calories: 244 calories
- Protein: 3g protein.
- Total Fat: 12g fat (8g saturated fat)
- Sodium: 262mg sodium
- Fiber: 1g fiber)
- Total Carbohydrate: 34g carbohydrate (21g sugars
- Cholesterol: 29mg cholesterol

95. Mandarin Orange Cream Pie

Serving: 6-8 servings. | Prep: 10mins | Cook: 0mins | Ready in:

Ingredients

- 1 package (3 ounces) orange or sparkling mandarin orange gelatin
- 1/2 cup boiling water
- 1-1/4 cups cold club soda
- 1 graham cracker crust (9 inches)
- 1/2 cup whipped topping
- 1 can (11 ounces) mandarin oranges, well drained

Direction

- Dissolve gelatin in a bowl of boiling water. Stir in the soda. Put half cup aside at room temperature. Place the remaining gelatin mixture in refrigerator until thickened slightly, about 20 mins; put into the crust. Place in the refrigerator until set, about half an hour.
- Whisk the whipped topping into the reserved gelatin mixture. Put into the crust slowly. Top with orange segments; lightly press down. Place in the refrigerator until firm, about at least 3 hours.

Nutrition Information

- Calories: 180 calories
- Fiber: 1g fiber)
- Total Carbohydrate: 30g carbohydrate (26g sugars
- Cholesterol: 0 cholesterol
- Protein: 2g protein.
- Total Fat: 6g fat (2g saturated fat)
- Sodium: 156mg sodium

96. Maple Cream Fluff

Serving: 12-15 servings. | Prep: 25mins | Cook: 5mins | Ready in:

Ingredients

- 2 envelopes unflavored gelatin
- 1/2 cup cold water
- 1 cup maple syrup
- 2 cups milk
- 1 cup heavy whipping cream
- 1 cup chopped pecans, toasted, divided
- 2 cups vanilla wafer crumbs (about 60 wafers), divided

Direction

- Soften gelatin in large saucepan of cold water; allow to stand for one min. Cook while stirring over low heat for 4 mins or until gelatin dissolves (avoid boiling). Discard from the heat; stir in syrup slowly. Place pan into ice water and whisk in the milk. Keep on whisking for 10 mins or until thickened. Discard pan from the ice bath. Put aside.
- Beat cream in a bowl until it forms the stiff peaks. Fold in maple mixture and 3/4 cup of pecans. Sprinkle a 13x9 inches dish with one cup of the wafer crumbs; add maple mixture over top. Sprinkle with the remaining wafer crumbs and pecans.
- Let chill with a cover for at least 6 hours or overnight. Place any leftovers in refrigerator.

Nutrition Information

- Calories:
- Protein:
- Total Fat:
- Sodium:
- Fiber:
- Total Carbohydrate:
- Cholesterol:

97. Maple Syrup Cream

Serving: 8 servings. | Prep: 20mins | Cook: 5mins | Ready in:

Ingredients

- 1 tablespoon unflavored gelatin
- 1/4 cup cold water
- 1/2 cup milk
- 2/3 cup maple syrup
- 1/8 teaspoon salt
- 2 cups heavy whipping cream
- Additional maple syrup

Direction

- Sprinkle the cold water in small bowl with gelatin; allow to stand for one min. Gently boil milk in a small saucepan; stir in the gelatin mixture until it has dissolved. Discard from heat; mix in salt and syrup. Refrigerate, covered, until partially set, about 45 mins.
- Beat cream in large bowl until it forms the stiff peaks; fold into the gelatin mixture. Spoon into 8 individual serving dishes. Refrigerate at least 4 hours, covered, until set. Drizzle more maple syrup over. Then serve.

Nutrition Information

- Calories: 185 calories
- Fiber: 0 fiber)
- Total Carbohydrate: 19g carbohydrate (17g sugars
- Cholesterol: 42mg cholesterol
- Protein: 2g protein.
- Total Fat: 12g fat (7g saturated fat)
- Sodium: 58mg sodium

98. Marvelous Melon

Serving: 6 servings. | Prep: 15mins | Cook: 0mins | Ready in:

Ingredients

- 1 large cantaloupe
- 1 package (3 ounces) strawberry banana gelatin
- 1 cup boiling water
- 1/2 cup unsweetened applesauce
- 1 cup sliced fresh strawberries

Direction

- Halve the melon lengthwise from the bud to stem end; remove seeds. Thinly slice off the bottom of each half so the melon can sit level; pat dry.
- Dissolve gelatin in a large bowl of boiling water. Mix in strawberries and applesauce. Transfer to the melon halves (reserve all the remaining gelatin mixture for later use or remove).
- Cover in the plastic wrap. Place in the refrigerator overnight. Slice each half of melon into 3 wedges. Then serve immediately.

Nutrition Information

- Calories: 72 calories
- Total Carbohydrate: 17g carbohydrate (0 sugars
- Cholesterol: 0 cholesterol
- Protein: 2g protein. Diabetic Exchanges: 1 fruit.
- Total Fat: 0 fat (0 saturated fat)
- Sodium: 21mg sodium
- Fiber: 2g fiber)

99. Mini Orange Gelatin Molds

Serving: 2 servings. | Prep: 20mins | Cook: 0mins | Ready in:

Ingredients

- 3 tablespoons plus 1 teaspoon orange gelatin
- 1/3 cup boiling water
- 1/2 cup cold water
- 1 can (11 ounces) mandarin oranges, drained
- 3 ounces cream cheese, softened
- 1/2 cup whipped topping, divided

Direction

- Mix gelatin in boiling water in a small bowl to dissolve. Mix in cold water. At room temperature, put aside 3 tablespoons gelatin mixture. Chill, covered, leftover gelatin mixture for half an hour or until set partially.
- Put aside 6 mandarin oranges for topping and pat dry. Fold the leftover oranges into prepared gelatin. Split between 2 individual fluted tube pans sprayed with cooking spray; cover and chill for half an hour or until set.
- Whip the saved gelatin, 1/4 cup whipped topping and cream cheese in a small bowl until smooth. Spread on top of gelatin molds carefully. Chill for an hour or until firm. Flip molds onto a dish; top with leftover whipped topping and saved oranges.

Nutrition Information

- Calories: 224 calories
- Total Fat: 11g fat (8g saturated fat)
- Sodium: 235mg sodium
- Fiber: 0 fiber)
- Total Carbohydrate: 22g carbohydrate (20g sugars
- Cholesterol: 30mg cholesterol
- Protein: 6g protein.

100.   Mocha Parfait Dessert

Serving: 8-10 servings. | Prep: 45mins | Cook: 25mins | Ready in:

Ingredients

- 1 package (9 ounces) devil's food cake mix
- 1 envelope unflavored gelatin
- 1 cup milk, divided

- 1/2 cup sugar
- 4 teaspoons instant coffee granules
- 1/8 teaspoon salt
- 1 cup heavy whipping cream
- 3/4 cup chopped walnuts, toasted, divided

Direction

- Ready and bake cake based on the package directions, using a round baking pan that is 9-inch. Let it cool for 10 minutes prior to taking out from the pan to a wire rack to fully cool.
- Drizzle gelatin over 1/4 cup milk in a small bowl; allow it to stand for 1 minute. Mix in a small saucepan the remaining milk, salt, coffee granules, and sugar. Whisk and cook until bubbles appear around the edge of the pan. Stir in gelatin mixture; whisk until dissolved. Put to a bowl. Keep in the refrigerator for about 1-1/4 hours or until slightly thickened.
- Whisk cream into a chilled bowl until it forms soft peaks. Add in whipped cream and 1/2 cup walnuts, then fold into gelatin mixture.
- Use waxed paper to line the bottom of a 9-inch round pan that is greased. Place the gelatin mixture into pan; cautiously put the cooled cake layer on top. Keep in the refrigerator for at least 3 hours.
- Turn dessert upside down onto a serving platter, just prior to serving; cautiously take off waxed paper. Decorate with remaining walnuts.

Nutrition Information

- Calories:
- Fiber:
- Total Carbohydrate:
- Cholesterol:
- Protein:
- Total Fat:
- Sodium:

101.　　Molded Margaritas

Serving: 4 servings. | Prep: 15mins | Cook: 0mins | Ready in:

Ingredients

- 2 packages (3 ounces each) lime gelatin
- 2 cups boiling water
- 1/2 cup thawed nonalcoholic margarita mix or limeade concentrate
- 1/2 cup tequila

Direction

- Dissolve gelatin in a small bowl with boiling water. Mix in tequila and margarita mix. Transfer into 4 margarita glasses. Place in the refrigerator till set, 4 hours. Use a fork to stir gently before serving if you want.

Nutrition Information

- Calories: 264 calories
- Protein: 4g protein.
- Total Fat: 0 fat (0 saturated fat)
- Sodium: 97mg sodium
- Fiber: 0 fiber)
- Total Carbohydrate: 49g carbohydrate (48g sugars
- Cholesterol: 0 cholesterol

102.　　Molded Raspberry Gelatin

Serving: 12 servings. | Prep: 20mins | Cook: 0mins | Ready in:

Ingredients

- 2 packages (3 ounces each) raspberry gelatin
- 1 cup boiling water
- 2 cups vanilla ice cream, softened
- 1 cup orange juice
- 2 medium bananas, chopped

- 2 cans (8 ounces each) unsweetened crushed pineapple, drained

Direction

- Dissolve gelatin in a small bowl of boiling water. Stir in orange juice and ice cream until they are blended. Then fold in pineapple and bananas. Spoon into a 6-cup mold coated with the cooking spray. Refrigerate until firm, covered. Unmold the gelatin onto the serving platter.

Nutrition Information

- Calories: 145 calories
- Protein: 3g protein.
- Total Fat: 3g fat (2g saturated fat)
- Sodium: 50mg sodium
- Fiber: 1g fiber)
- Total Carbohydrate: 30g carbohydrate (25g sugars
- Cholesterol: 10mg cholesterol

---

103. Mom's Gelatin Fruit Salad

Serving: 12 servings. | Prep: 15mins | Cook: 10mins | Ready in:

Ingredients

- 2 envelopes unflavored gelatin
- 1/2 cup cold water
- 2 cups sugar
- 2 cups orange juice
- 1/2 cup lemon juice
- 6 medium oranges, peeled and sectioned
- 1 cup green grapes, halved
- 12 maraschino cherries, halved
- 1/2 cup chopped dates, optional

Direction

- Sprinkle gelatin over cold water in a small saucepan, then allow to stand for 1 minute. Heat and stir on low heat until gelatin is dissolved thoroughly. Stir in lemon juice, orange juice and sugar, then cook and stir until sugar has dissolved, about 6 to 8 minutes.
- Turn to a bowl, then chill with a cover for 1 1/2 hours, until thickened a little bit. Stir in fruit then transfer into a 2-quarter serving bowl or 6-cup ring mold greased with cooking spray. Chill until firm. Unmold onto a serving plate if using a ring mold.

Nutrition Information

- Calories:
- Protein:
- Total Fat:
- Sodium:
- Fiber:
- Total Carbohydrate:
- Cholesterol:

---

104. No Bake Strawberry Dessert

Serving: 20 servings. | Prep: 20mins | Cook: 0mins | Ready in:

Ingredients

- 1 loaf (10-1/2 ounces) angel food cake, cut into 1-inch cubes
- 2 packages (.3 ounce each) sugar-free strawberry gelatin
- 2 cups boiling water
- 1 package (20 ounces) frozen unsweetened whole strawberries, thawed
- 2 cups cold 1% milk
- 1 package (1 ounce) sugar-free instant vanilla pudding mix
- 1 carton (8 ounces) frozen reduced-fat whipped topping, thawed

- Chopped fresh strawberries, optional

Direction

- In a 13"x9" dish, put one single layer of cake cubes. Dissolve gelatin in boiling water in a bowl, then stir in strawberries. Pour the mixture over cake and press cake down gently. Chill for an hour, until set.
- Whisk together pudding mix and milk in a big bowl about 2 minutes. Allow to stand until soft-set, about 2 minutes.
- Scoop over gelatin layer then spread with whipped topping. Chill until serving. Use chopped fresh strawberries to decorate if you want.

Nutrition Information

- Calories: 92 calories
- Protein: 2g protein. Diabetic Exchanges: 1 starch.
- Total Fat: 2g fat (1g saturated fat)
- Sodium: 172mg sodium
- Fiber: 1g fiber)
- Total Carbohydrate: 16g carbohydrate (0 sugars
- Cholesterol: 2mg cholesterol

105.   Orange Bavarian

Serving: 12-14 servings. | Prep: 15mins | Cook: 0mins | Ready in:

Ingredients

- 3 packages (3 ounces each) orange gelatin
- 2-1/4 cups boiling water
- 1 cup sour cream
- 1 quart orange sherbet, softened
- 1 can (11 ounces) mandarin oranges, drained and halved
- Red and green grapes, optional

Direction

- Stir the gelatin with water until dissolves. Whisk in sour cream until smooth. Whisk in sherbet until melted. Refrigerate until partially set. Put in oranges and fold. Then move the mixture to a 7-cup ring mold greased with cooking spray. Cover and put into a refrigerator overnight or 8 hrs. Unmold the gelatin and place on a platter then serve. You can fill the middle with grapes if you want.

Nutrition Information

- Calories: 126 calories
- Sodium: 43mg sodium
- Fiber: 0 fiber)
- Total Carbohydrate: 22g carbohydrate (20g sugars
- Cholesterol: 13mg cholesterol
- Protein: 2g protein.
- Total Fat: 4g fat (2g saturated fat)

106.   Orange Blossom Gelatin

Serving: 2 servings. | Prep: 5mins | Cook: 0mins | Ready in:

Ingredients

- 1 package (3 ounces) orange gelatin
- 1/2 cup boiling water
- 1/3 cup orange yogurt

Direction

- Dissolve gelatin in a small bowl with boiling water. Let cool to room temperature; blend in yogurt. Distribute between 2 dessert dishes. Chill with a cover till firm, 4 hours.

Nutrition Information

- Calories: 195 calories
- Fiber: 0 fiber)

- Total Carbohydrate: 44g carbohydrate (44g sugars
- Cholesterol: 2mg cholesterol
- Protein: 5g protein.
- Total Fat: 0 fat (0 saturated fat)
- Sodium: 118mg sodium

107. Orange Charlotte

Serving: 10-12 servings. | Prep: 30mins | Cook: 0mins | Ready in:

Ingredients

- 3 envelopes unflavored gelatin
- 3/4 cup cold water
- 3/4 cup boiling water
- 1-1/2 cups orange juice
- 2 tablespoons lemon juice
- 1-1/2 teaspoons grated orange zest
- 1-1/2 cups sugar, divided
- 2-1/2 cups heavy whipping cream
- 1/2 cup mandarin oranges
- 3 maraschino cherries

Direction

- Mix the cold water with gelatin in a big bowl and let it sit for 10 minutes. Put in boiling water and stir until dissolved. Add 3/4 cup of sugar, orange zest, and juice. Place the bowl in ice water until it becomes syrupy, stir occasionally. At the same time, whip the cream until soft peaks form. Put in remaining sugar in a slow stream and beat till the stiff peaks form.
- Once the gelatin mixture starts thickening, fold in whipped cream. Lightly grease a 9-inch springform pan with cooking spray. Add the mixture to the pan and keep inside a refrigerator overnight.
- Run a knife around the edges of pan to loosen the cake before serving. Take off the sides of pan and add cherries and oranges on top to garnish.

Nutrition Information

- Calories: 297 calories
- Fiber: 0 fiber)
- Total Carbohydrate: 32g carbohydrate (31g sugars
- Cholesterol: 68mg cholesterol
- Protein: 3g protein.
- Total Fat: 18g fat (11g saturated fat)
- Sodium: 23mg sodium

108. Orange Cream Cheesecake

Serving: 10-12 servings. | Prep: 25mins | Cook: 0mins | Ready in:

Ingredients

- 2 cups graham cracker crumbs
- 1 teaspoon ground cinnamon
- 1 teaspoon grated orange zest
- 1/2 cup butter, melted
- FILLING:
- 1 package (3 ounces) orange gelatin
- 3 packages (8 ounces each) cream cheese, softened
- 1-1/4 cups sugar
- 1 can (5 ounces) evaporated milk
- 1/3 cup thawed orange juice concentrate
- 1 teaspoon lemon juice
- 1 teaspoon vanilla extract
- 1 envelope unflavored gelatin
- 2 tablespoons cold water
- 2 tablespoons boiling water
- 1 carton (8 ounces) frozen whipped topping, thawed
- TOPPING:
- 2 cups whipped topping
- 1/4 cup sugar
- Citrus fruits and lemon balm, optional

Direction

- Mix butter, orange zest, cinnamon and cracker crumbs in a big bowl; press on bottom of 10-in. greased springform pan. Refrigerate it for 30 minutes.
- Follow package directions to prep orange gelatin; put 1/2 cup aside in room temperature. Chill leftover gelatin for 40-60 minutes till slightly thick.
- Beat sugar and cream cheese till smooth in a big bowl; beat in vanilla, lemon juice, orange juice concentrate and milk. Beat for 2 minutes at medium high speed.
- Sprinkle unflavored gelatin on cold water in a small bowl; stand for 2 minutes. Mix in boiling water till gelatin is fully dissolved. Mix into room-temperature orange gelatin; mix into cream cheese mixture. Fold in whipped topping; put in crust.
- Topping: Beat sugar and whipped topping in a big bowl; beat in the refrigerated orange gelatin. It'll be thin. Chill it for 30 minutes. Put on filling gently; it'll be full. Refrigerate it for 8 hours – overnight. Remove pan sides. If desired, garnish with lemon balm and fruit.

Nutrition Information

- Calories: 433 calories
- Cholesterol: 45mg cholesterol
- Protein: 5g protein.
- Total Fat: 22g fat (15g saturated fat)
- Sodium: 248mg sodium
- Fiber: 1g fiber)
- Total Carbohydrate: 54g carbohydrate (41g sugars

109.　　　Orange Cream Dessert

Serving: 12-15 servings. | Prep: 15mins | Cook: 0mins | Ready in:

Ingredients

- 2 cups cream-filled chocolate sandwich cookie crumbs
- 1/3 cup butter, melted
- 1 package (6 ounces) orange or lime gelatin
- 2 cups boiling water
- 1 quart vanilla ice cream, softened

Direction

- Mix cookie crumbs with butter in a big bowl; put aside a quarter cup for garnishing. Push leftover crumb mixture into a greased 13-in. x 9-in. pan. Dissolve gelatin in water in a separate bowl; cover and chill for 10 minutes.
- Mix in ice cream until smooth. Add on top of crust. Scatter with saved crumb mixture. Refrigerate until set.

Nutrition Information

- Calories: 244 calories
- Sodium: 196mg sodium
- Fiber: 1g fiber)
- Total Carbohydrate: 32g carbohydrate (23g sugars
- Cholesterol: 26mg cholesterol
- Protein: 3g protein.
- Total Fat: 12g fat (6g saturated fat)

110.　　　Orange Lime Gelatin Ring

Serving: 10 servings. | Prep: 40mins | Cook: 0mins | Ready in:

Ingredients

- 1 can (11 ounces) mandarin oranges, drained
- 1 can (20 ounces) crushed pineapple, undrained
- 2 tablespoons lemon juice
- 1 package (3 ounces) lime gelatin
- 1 package (8 ounces) reduced-fat cream cheese, cubed

- Lettuce leaves
- 2 cups seedless red grapes

Direction

- Place oranges in the bottom of a 9-in. ring mold greased with cooking spray. Freeze, covered, for 30 minutes. In the meantime, strain pineapple, saving a cup juice (remove any leftover juice or save for other uses); put pineapple aside.
- Heat up lemon juice and saved pineapple juice to a boil in a saucepan. Take off from the heat; let cool for 10 minutes. Add into a blender or food processor. Put in gelatin powder; cover and blend for half a minute or until dissolved. Put in cream cheese; cover and blend for a minute or until smooth.
- Mix in pineapple. Put into ring mold. Cover and chill for 8 hours or until set. Unmold onto a serving plate lined with lettuce. Put grapes in the center.

Nutrition Information

- Calories: 158 calories
- Total Carbohydrate: 25g carbohydrate (0 sugars
- Cholesterol: 16mg cholesterol
- Protein: 4g protein. Diabetic Exchanges: 1 fruit
- Total Fat: 5g fat (3g saturated fat)
- Sodium: 126mg sodium
- Fiber: 1g fiber)

111.   Orange Pineapple Dessert

Serving: 18 servings. | Prep: 10mins | Cook: 0mins | Ready in:

Ingredients

- 2 packages (.3 ounce each) sugar-free orange gelatin

- 2 cups boiling water
- 16 ice cubes (about 3 cups)
- 1 can (20 ounces) unsweetened crushed pineapple, drained
- 1 can (11 ounces) mandarin oranges, drained and cut into pieces
- 1 cup (8 ounces) fat-free sour cream
- 1 carton (12 ounces) frozen reduced-fat whipped topping, thawed
- 1 prepared angel food cake (8 to 10 ounces), cut into 1-inch cubes

Direction

- Add boiling water and gelatin to a bowl and stir until dissolved. Put in ice cubes and whisk until a bit thickened. Take away any unmelted ice cubes. Whisk in oranges and pineapple then sour cream until combined. Put in whipped topping and cake cubes and fold until well coated. Scoop the mixture into an uncoated 13x9-inch dish. Cover and put into a refrigerator till serving.

Nutrition Information

- Calories: 0g saturated fat (0 sugars.

112.   Orange Whip

Serving: 6 servings. | Prep: 10mins | Cook: 0mins | Ready in:

Ingredients

- 1 envelope unflavored gelatin
- 1/3 cup sugar
- 1/8 teaspoon salt
- 1-3/4 cups hot orange juice (150°)
- 3/4 cup whipped topping

Direction

- In the bowl, mix salt, sugar and gelatin; pour in the orange juice and whisk till the gelatin is dissolved. Keep chilled for roughly 1.5 hours, till becoming thick a bit. Whip on low speed till becoming fluffy and light. Pour into the dessert plates; keep chilled till becoming firm. Add a dollop of whipped topping on top.

Nutrition Information

- Calories: 104 calories
- Sodium: 52mg sodium
- Fiber: 0 fiber)
- Total Carbohydrate: 21g carbohydrate (18g sugars
- Cholesterol: 0 cholesterol
- Protein: 1g protein.
- Total Fat: 2g fat (2g saturated fat)

113. Panna Cotta With Mixed Berries

Serving: 6 servings. | Prep: 10mins | Cook: 20mins | Ready in:

Ingredients

- 1 envelope unflavored gelatin
- 3 cups whole milk
- 1/3 cup sugar
- 1/2 teaspoon almond extract
- 1 cup water
- Sugar substitute equivalent to 1/2 cup sugar
- 2 cups frozen unsweetened mixed berries
- 1/2 cup port wine or grape juice
- 1/2 cup fresh raspberries
- 1/2 cup fresh blueberries

Direction

- Sprinkle gelatin over a small saucepan of milk, allow to sit for 1 minute. Turn the heat to low, whisking until the gelatin has fully melted. Mix in sugar until melted. Mix in extract.
- Add to 6 greased custard cups or 6-oz. ramekins. Put a cover on and chill until set.

- In the meantime, boil sugar substitute and water in a small saucepan. Add juice or wine and frozen berries; boil again. Lower the heat and simmer without a cover for 5 minutes. Mash and drain the berries, saving the juice. Remove the seeds.
- Put the juice back into the pan, boil it. Lower the heat and simmer without a cover until the sauce has decreased to 3/4 cup, about 5-10 minutes. Remove to a bowl, put a cover on and chill until cold.
- Remove the panna cotta onto dessert dishes. Enjoy with fresh berries and sauce.

Nutrition Information

- Calories: 174 calories
- Sodium: 64mg sodium
- Fiber: 2g fiber)
- Total Carbohydrate: 27g carbohydrate (21g sugars
- Cholesterol: 17mg cholesterol
- Protein: 6g protein. Diabetic Exchanges: 1 starch
- Total Fat: 4g fat (3g saturated fat)

114. Panna Cotta With Papaya Coulis

Serving: 4 servings. | Prep: 15mins | Cook: 5mins | Ready in:

Ingredients

- 2-1/2 teaspoons unflavored gelatin
- 1/4 cup 2% milk
- 2 cups heavy whipping cream
- 1/4 cup sugar
- 1 teaspoon vanilla extract
- PAPAYA COULIS:
- 2 cups coarsely chopped papaya
- 2 to 3 tablespoons lime juice
- 1 tablespoon sugar
- Fresh raspberries and fresh mint leaves

Direction

- Sprinkle gelatin over milk in a small bowl; allow to sit for 5 minutes. Meanwhile, mix sugar and cream together in a small saucepan; cook while stirring over medium heat till the sugar is dissolved. Put in vanilla and the gelatin mixture, stirring till the gelatin is dissolved completely.
- Distribute the mixture among 4 dessert dishes. Refrigerate with a cover till set, 2 hours.
- For coulis, in a food processor, place sugar, lime juice and papaya; process till smooth, scraping down the sides of the bowl as necessary. Remove into a small bowl. Cover and refrigerate till cold.
- To serve, spoon the papaya coulis over panna cotta. Place mint and raspberries over the top.

Nutrition Information

- Calories: 524 calories
- Sodium: 62mg sodium
- Fiber: 1g fiber)
- Total Carbohydrate: 28g carbohydrate (26g sugars
- Cholesterol: 166mg cholesterol
- Protein: 5g protein.
- Total Fat: 45g fat (28g saturated fat)

---

115.   Pastel Torte

Serving: 9 servings. | Prep: 50mins | Cook: 15mins | Ready in:

Ingredients

- 1/2 cup butter, softened
- 1/2 cup packed brown sugar
- 2 egg yolks
- 1-1/2 cups all-purpose flour
- 1 teaspoon baking powder
- TOPPING:
- 3/4 cup sugar

- 2 envelopes unflavored gelatin
- Pinch salt
- 1 cup cold water
- 1 cup confectioners' sugar
- 1 teaspoon baking powder
- 1/2 teaspoon almond extract
- 2 drops green food coloring
- 2 drops red food coloring
- 1/4 cup sweetened shredded coconut, toasted

Direction

- Cream brown sugar and butter in bowl; one by one, beat egg yolks in. Mix baking powder and flour; add to creamed mixture. Press in 9-in. square greased baking pan; bake for 15-20 minutes at 325° or till light brown then cool.
- Mix salt, gelatin and sugar in saucepan; mix water in. Stand for a minute; mix and cook on medium heat till it boils. Lower heat; simmer, occasionally mixing, for 10 minutes. Take off heat; put in bowl. Add confectioners' sugar; beat for about 12 minutes on high till creamy white and thick. Add extract and baking powder; divide to 3 even portions. Add red food coloring to 1 portion and green food coloring to another; stir well. Leave 3rd portion white. Put green mixture on crust; chill 3 minutes. Put white mixture over; chill 3 minutes. Put pink mixture over; sprinkle coconut. Cover; refrigerate till set or for 1 hour.

Nutrition Information

- Calories: 360 calories
- Total Fat: 12g fat (7g saturated fat)
- Sodium: 225mg sodium
- Fiber: 1g fiber)
- Total Carbohydrate: 59g carbohydrate (42g sugars
- Cholesterol: 75mg cholesterol
- Protein: 4g protein.

116. Peach Delight

Serving: 15 servings. | Prep: 25mins | Cook: 15mins | Ready in:

Ingredients

- 1/4 cup butter, softened
- 1/2 cup sugar
- 1 cup all-purpose flour
- 1/4 cup chopped walnuts
- FILLING:
- 1 package (8 ounces) reduced-fat cream cheese
- 3/4 cup confectioners' sugar
- 1 carton (8 ounces) frozen reduced-fat whipped topping, thawed, divided
- 7 medium peaches, thinly sliced
- GLAZE:
- 3 tablespoons cornstarch
- 2 cups water
- 1 package (.3 ounce) sugar-free lemon gelatin

Direction

- Cream sugar and butter till fluffy and light in a small bowl. Add flour slowly; mixture will be crumbly. Mix in walnuts. Press into 13x9-in. baking dish that's coated with cooking spray. Bake it at 350° till lightly browned for 14-16 minutes. Allow to cool on a wire rack.
- Filling: Beat confectioners' sugar and cream cheese till smooth in a big bowl. Fold in 1/2 whipped topping. Spread on crust carefully. Put peaches over.
- Glaze: Mix water and cornstarch till smooth in a small saucepan. Boil; mix and cook till thick for 2 minutes. Mix in gelatin slowly till dissolved. Cool to room temperature. Put on top of peaches. Cover; refrigerate till firm. Dollop with leftover whipped topping.

Nutrition Information

- Calories: 225 calories
- Fiber: 1g fiber)
- Total Carbohydrate: 32g carbohydrate (20g sugars

- Cholesterol: 19mg cholesterol
- Protein: 4g protein. Diabetic Exchanges: 2 starch
- Total Fat: 9g fat (6g saturated fat)
- Sodium: 109mg sodium

117. Peach Gelatin Dessert

Serving: 12-14 servings. | Prep: 15mins | Cook: 0mins | Ready in:

Ingredients

- 1 can (20 ounces) unsweetened crushed pineapple, undrained
- 1 cup water
- 1 package (6 ounces) peach or orange gelatin
- 4 tablespoons sugar, divided
- 2 cups chopped peeled fresh peaches
- 1 cup buttermilk
- 1 carton (12 ounces) frozen whipped topping, thawed

Direction

- Combine 2 tablespoons of sugar, gelatin powder, water and pineapple in a large saucepan. Over medium heat, cook while stirring mixture until just comes to a boil. Transfer to a large bowl. Place in the refrigerator until the mixture starts to thicken, about 45 mins.
- Combine remaining sugar, buttermilk and peaches in a large bowl; fold in the whipped topping, followed by the gelatin mixture. Transfer to an unoiled 13x 9 inches dish. Place in the refrigerator until firm.

Nutrition Information

- Calories: 167 calories
- Total Fat: 4g fat (4g saturated fat)
- Sodium: 46mg sodium
- Fiber: 1g fiber)

- Total Carbohydrate: 29g carbohydrate (25g sugars
- Cholesterol: 1mg cholesterol
- Protein: 2g protein.

118. Peach Topped Cake

Serving: 12 servings. | Prep: 20mins | Cook: 10mins | Ready in:

Ingredients

- 2 tablespoons butter, softened
- 1/2 cup sugar
- 1 large egg
- 1/2 teaspoon vanilla extract
- 3/4 cup cake flour
- 3/4 teaspoon baking powder
- 1/4 teaspoon salt
- 1/4 cup fat-free milk
- TOPPING:
- 1 envelope unflavored gelatin
- 1-3/4 cups cold water, divided
- 1/4 cup sugar
- 1 envelope sugar-free orange soft drink mix
- 2 medium ripe peaches, thinly sliced or 1 can (15 ounces) sliced peaches
- 1/2 cup reduced-fat whipped topping

Direction

- Beat sugar and butter in a small bowl until crumbly. Then beat in vanilla and egg. Combine salt, baking powder and flour. Put alternately with the milk into the sugar mixture.
- Spread into a springform pan (about 9 inches) coated with the cooking spray. Bake at 350° until the toothpick inserted in middle comes out clean, about 10 to 15 mins. Place on wire rack to cool.
- Sprinkle half cup of cold water in a small saucepan with gelatin. Allow to stand for one min. Stir in soft drink mix and sugar. Over low heat, cook while stirring until the gelatin

dissolves. Pour into the large bowl; then stir in the remaining cold water. Place in the refrigerator for 90 mins or until set partially.
- Line foil on the outside of the springform pan. Top the cake with peaches. Pour the gelatin over the peaches. Let chill overnight. Discard the pan sides and foil, then serve. Decorate with the whipped topping. Place the leftovers in the refrigerator.

Nutrition Information

- Calories: 121 calories
- Cholesterol: 23mg cholesterol
- Protein: 2g protein. Diabetic Exchanges: 1-1/2 starch
- Total Fat: 3g fat (2g saturated fat)
- Sodium: 103mg sodium
- Fiber: 0 fiber)
- Total Carbohydrate: 22g carbohydrate (15g sugars

119. Peaches & Cream Dessert

Serving: 15 servings. | Prep: 20mins | Cook: 10mins | Ready in:

Ingredients

- 1 package (16 ounces) pecan shortbread cookies, crushed
- 1/2 cup butter, melted
- 1 cup sugar
- 1 package (3 ounces) peach gelatin
- 2 tablespoons cornstarch
- 1 can (12 ounces) lemon-lime soda
- 1 package (8 ounces) cream cheese, softened
- 1 cup confectioners' sugar
- 1 carton (8 ounces) frozen whipped topping, thawed
- 6 cups fresh or frozen sliced peeled peaches, thawed
- 1/3 cup unsweetened pineapple juice

Direction

- Mix the butter and cookies crumbs in a small bowl then press onto the bottom of an ungreased 13x9-inch dish.
- Mix the cornstarch, gelatin, and the sugar in a small saucepan and whisk in soda until smooth. Bring the mixture to a boil. Cook while stirring until the mixture is a bit thickened, 5-7 minutes. Let it cool to room temperature while stirring occasionally.
- At the same time, beat the confectioners' sugar and cream cheese in a big bowl until smooth. Put in whipped topping and continue beating until blended. Pour over the crust. Mix together the pineapple juice and peaches. Place over the cream cheese layer. Spread the gelatin mixture over the cake top. Cover and keep in a refrigerator overnight.

Nutrition Information

- Calories: 446 calories
- Total Fat: 21g fat (12g saturated fat)
- Sodium: 241mg sodium
- Fiber: 2g fiber)
- Total Carbohydrate: 60g carbohydrate (36g sugars
- Cholesterol: 39mg cholesterol
- Protein: 4g protein.

---

120.   Peaches 'n' Cream Gelatin Dessert

Serving: 12-15 servings. | Prep: 20mins | Cook: 0mins | Ready in:

Ingredients

- 1-1/3 cups graham cracker crumbs (about 22 squares)
- 1/4 cup sugar
- 1/3 cup butter, melted
- TOPPING:

- 1 package (8 ounces) cream cheese, softened
- 1/4 cup sugar
- 1/4 cup milk
- 1 carton (8 ounces) frozen whipped topping, thawed
- 1 can (15-1/4 ounces) sliced peaches, drained
- 1 package (3 ounces) peach or orange gelatin
- 3/4 cup boiling water
- 1-1/4 cups cold water

Direction

- Combine butter, sugar and crumbs in a small bowl. Press into a 13x 9 inches dish. Beat sugar and cream cheese until they become smooth in a large bowl. Pour in milk gradually. Then fold in whipped topping and spread over the crust.
- Halve the peach slices lengthwise; place on top. Dissolve gelatin in a small bowl of the boiling water; then mix in cold water. Place in the refrigerator until thickened slightly, about 90 mins.
- Spoon gelatin gently over peaches. Let chill until set. Slice into the squares.

Nutrition Information

- Calories:
- Protein:
- Total Fat:
- Sodium:
- Fiber:
- Total Carbohydrate:
- Cholesterol:

---

121.   Peachy Cream Pie

Serving: 8 servings. | Prep: 25mins | Cook: 0mins | Ready in:

Ingredients

- 3/4 cup sugar

- 5 teaspoons cornstarch
- 1-1/2 cups cold water
- 1 package (3 ounces) peach, apricot or orange gelatin
- 1-1/2 cups frozen unsweetened peach slices, thawed
- 3 ounces cream cheese, softened
- 3 tablespoons confectioners' sugar
- 1 tablespoon whole milk
- 1-1/2 cups whipped topping
- 1 extra-servings-size graham cracker crust (9 ounces)

Direction

- Mix sugar with cornstarch in a big saucepan. Mix in water until smooth. Heat up to a boil; cook and mix for 1-2 minutes or until thickened. Take off from the heat; mix in gelatin until dissolved. Put in peaches. Chill about 20 minutes until thickened slightly,
- Whip the milk, confectioners' sugar and cream cheese in a big bowl until smooth. Fold in whipped topping. Scoop into pie crust. Scoop gelatin mixture on top of cream cheese layer. Chill about 3 hours until firm.

Nutrition Information

- Calories: 376 calories
- Fiber: 1g fiber)
- Total Carbohydrate: 60g carbohydrate (50g sugars
- Cholesterol: 12mg cholesterol
- Protein: 3g protein.
- Total Fat: 14g fat (6g saturated fat)
- Sodium: 239mg sodium

- 1 can (15 ounces) reduced-sugar sliced pears
- 1 package (.6 ounce) sugar-free lime gelatin or 2 packages (.3 ounce each) sugar-free lime gelatin
- 2 cups boiling water
- 3/4 cup (6 ounces) fat-free reduced-sugar vanilla yogurt
- 1/4 cup cold water

Direction

- Strain pears; reserve 1/2 cup of the liquid. Dissolve gelatin in a bowl with boiling water. Put yogurt into a bowl. Slowly whisk in 1 cup of the gelatin mixture till blended. Pour into an 8-in. square dish oiled with cooking spray. Refrigerate with a cover till almost set, 1 hour.
- Combine the reserved liquid and cold water into the remaining gelatin mixture (do not refrigerate). Distribute the pears on the gelatin-yogurt mixture. Spoon the remaining gelatin mixture carefully over the pears. Refrigerate with a cover till firm, around 2 hours.

Nutrition Information

- Calories: 61 calories
- Protein: 2g protein. Diabetic Exchanges: 1 fruit.
- Total Fat: 0 fat (0 saturated fat)
- Sodium: 90mg sodium
- Fiber: 1g fiber)
- Total Carbohydrate: 11g carbohydrate (0 sugars
- Cholesterol: 1mg cholesterol

122.   Pear Gelatin Salad

Serving: 6 servings. | Prep: 10mins | Cook: 0mins | Ready in:

Ingredients

123.   Peppermint Charlotte

Serving: 10-12 servings. | Prep: 10mins | Cook: 15mins | Ready in:

Ingredients

- 2 envelopes unflavored gelatin

- 3-1/2 cups milk
- 1/2 cup sugar
- 1/8 teaspoon salt
- 5 egg yolks, beaten
- 1/2 cup finely crushed peppermint candy
- 8 drops red food coloring
- 1-1/2 cups heavy whipping cream, whipped
- 12 ladyfingers, split

Direction

- Soften gelatin in a saucepan with milk for 1 minute. Mix in salt and sugar. Cook while stirring over medium-low heat till the gelatin is dissolved, 5 minutes. Take away from the heat.
- Combine a small amount of the hot mixture into egg yolks. Turn all back to the pan. Cook while stirring over low heat till the mixture reaches 160° (do not boil), or is slightly thickened to coat the back of a metal spoon. Take away from the heat. Put in food coloring and candy; mix till the candy is dissolved.
- Place in the refrigerator for around 30 minutes, stirring occasionally, till the mixture starts to thicken. Stir in whipped cream. Arrange ladyfinger halves around a 9-in. springform pan coated with grease. Transfer the mixture into the center of the pan. Chill with a cover for 4 hours or overnight. Run a knife carefully around the edge of the pan to loosen just before serving; remove the sides.

Nutrition Information

- Calories: 262 calories
- Total Fat: 17g fat (9g saturated fat)
- Sodium: 94mg sodium
- Fiber: 0 fiber)
- Total Carbohydrate: 23g carbohydrate (19g sugars
- Cholesterol: 179mg cholesterol
- Protein: 6g protein.

124.   Pineapple Delight

Serving: 12 servings. | Prep: 25mins | Cook: 0mins | Ready in:

Ingredients

- 1 cup reduced-fat graham cracker crumbs (about 5 whole crackers)
- 3 tablespoons butter, melted
- 1 package (.3 ounce) sugar-free lemon gelatin
- 1 cup boiling water
- 3 cups (24 ounces) 1% cottage cheese
- Sugar substitute equivalent to 7 teaspoons sugar
- 2 teaspoons cornstarch
- 1 tablespoon water
- 1 can (8 ounces) unsweetened crushed pineapple, undrained

Direction

- Combine butter and cracker crumbs in a bowl. Press into an unoiled 9 inches square dish. Place in the refrigerator until firm.
- Combine water and gelatin in a bowl; stir until it has dissolved. Let cool to the room temperature. Combine sugar substitute and cottage cheese in a blender; process, covered, until they become smooth. Put in gelatin mixture slowly; blend until they become smooth. Transfer to the crust. Place in the refrigerator until firm.
- In the meantime, combine water and cornstarch in a saucepan until they become smooth. Put in pineapple. Boil. Cook while stirring until thickened, about 2 mins. Let cool to the room temperature. Then spread over the layer of gelatin. Place in the refrigerator for at least 60 mins. Then serve.

Nutrition Information

- Calories: 105 calories
- Protein: 8g protein. Diabetic Exchanges: 1 lean meat
- Total Fat: 4g fat (0 saturated fat)

- Sodium: 307mg sodium
- Fiber: 0 fiber)
- Total Carbohydrate: 9g carbohydrate (0 sugars
- Cholesterol: 5mg cholesterol

- Protein: 3g protein.
- Total Fat: 16g fat (7g saturated fat)
- Sodium: 52mg sodium
- Fiber: 1g fiber)

125. Pineapple Lime Gelatin

*Serving: 12 servings. | Prep: 15mins | Cook: 0mins
| Ready in:*

Ingredients

- 2 cups boiling water, divided
- 1 package (3 ounces) lime gelatin
- 16 large marshmallows
- 3 ounces cream cheese, softened
- 1 can (8 ounces) unsweetened crushed pineapple, undrained
- 1 cup heavy whipping cream, whipped
- 1 cup chopped pecans
- 2 to 3 drops green food coloring, optional

Direction

- Add gelatin and 1 cup of boiling water to a bowl and whisk until completely dissolves, for 2 minutes. Mix the remaining water and marshmallows in a small saucepan. Cook while stirring occasionally over low heat until combined. Whisk into the gelatin and put into a refrigerator until partially set.
- Whisk cream cheese in a big bowl until smooth. Whisk in pineapple. Add pecans, whipped cream and gelatin mixture and fold. You can also add food colorings if you want. Add to a 6-cup mold grease with cooking spray. Cover and put into a refrigerator until set. Unmold and transfer to a serving plate.

Nutrition Information

- Calories: 223 calories
- Total Carbohydrate: 19g carbohydrate (16g sugars
- Cholesterol: 30mg cholesterol

126. Pink Bonnet Gelatin

*Serving: 12 servings. | Prep: 20mins | Cook: 0mins
| Ready in:*

Ingredients

- 1 cup ginger ale
- 1 package (3 ounces) strawberry or cherry gelatin
- 1 can (15 ounces) fruit cocktail, drained
- 1-1/2 cups cooked rice, chilled
- 1 carton (12 ounces) whipped topping
- 2 red Fruit by the Foot fruit rolls
- 1 cup sliced fresh strawberries
- Silk flowers, optional

Direction

- Heat up ginger ale to a boil in a small saucepan. Take off from the heat; mix in gelatin to dissolve. Cover and chill for an hour or until set partially. Mix in fruit cocktail and rice. Fold in whipped topping. Scoop two cups mixture into a 9-in. pie pan lined with plastic wrap.
- Scoop leftover mixture into a 1-qt. round-bottomed bowl lined using plastic wrap. Cover and chill for 4 hours or until firmed. Flip gelatin from bowl over. Cover fruit rolls around the hat and tie into a bow. Top with strawberries and silk flowers (optional).

Nutrition Information

- Calories: 99 calories
- Cholesterol: 0 cholesterol
- Protein: 1g protein. Diabetic Exchanges: 1 fruit
- Total Fat: 3g fat (3g saturated fat)

- Sodium: 6mg sodium
- Fiber: 0 fiber)
- Total Carbohydrate: 15g carbohydrate (0 sugars

127. Pink Cloud

Serving: 12 | Prep: 10mins | Cook: |Ready in:

Ingredients

- 1 (3 ounce) package raspberry flavored gelatin (such as Jell-O®)
- 1 (16 ounce) package frozen whipped topping, thawed
- 1 (16 ounce) package large curd cottage cheese
- 1 (20 ounce) can crushed pineapple, drained

Direction

- In a big bowl, mix together pineapple, cottage cheese, whipped topping and gelatin. Stir till evenly pink. Chill till ready to serve.

Nutrition Information

- Calories: 212 calories;
- Total Fat: 11.2
- Sodium: 179
- Total Carbohydrate: 23.3
- Cholesterol: 6
- Protein: 5.9

128. Potluck Cherry Compote

Serving: 24 servings. | Prep: 10mins | Cook: 0mins | Ready in:

Ingredients

- 2 packages (3 ounces each) cherry gelatin
- 2 cups boiling water

- 1 package (10 ounces) frozen sweetened sliced strawberries
- 1 can (21 ounces) cherry pie filling
- 1 can (20 ounces) pineapple chunks, drained
- 1 can (15 ounces) pear halves, drained and cut into chunks
- 3 medium firm bananas, sliced
- 2 medium navel oranges, peeled, sectioned and chopped
- 2 medium tart apples, peeled and chopped
- 1 cup fresh or frozen blackberries, thawed

Direction

- Dissolve gelatin in boiling water in a large bowl. Mix in the strawberries until thawed. Mix in the rest of the ingredients. Move to a 4-qt. serving bowl. Refrigerate with a cover for 3 to 4 hours before serving.

Nutrition Information

- Calories: 102 calories
- Sodium: 15mg sodium
- Fiber: 2g fiber)
- Total Carbohydrate: 26g carbohydrate (22g sugars
- Cholesterol: 0 cholesterol
- Protein: 1g protein.
- Total Fat: 0 fat (0 saturated fat)

129. Pretzel Jell O Dessert

Serving: 12 servings. | Prep: 30mins | Cook: 0mins | Ready in:

Ingredients

- 2 cups crushed pretzels
- 3/4 cup butter, melted
- 2 tablespoons sugar
- FILLING:
- 1 package (8 ounces) cream cheese, softened
- 1 cup sugar

- 1 carton (8 ounces) frozen whipped topping, thawed
- TOPPING:
- 2 packages (3 ounces each) strawberry gelatin
- 2 cups boiling water
- 1/2 cup cold water
- Fresh strawberries and additional whipped topping, optional

Direction

- Set the oven at 350° to preheat. Mix sugar, melted butter, and crushed pretzels; press onto the bottom of an ungreased 13x9-in. baking dish. Then bake for around 10 minutes. Let cool completely.
- To make the filling: Beat sugar and cream cheese until smooth. Add whipped topping, stir and spread over the crust. Cover and chill in the fridge until cold.
- Dissolve gelatin in a small bowl of boiling water. Stir in cold water; chill until set partially. Carefully pour over the filling. Cover and chill for 4-6 hours, until firm.
- Slice into squares. Serve with additional whipped topping and strawberries if desired.

Nutrition Information

- Calories: 401 calories
- Sodium: 401mg sodium
- Fiber: 1g fiber)
- Total Carbohydrate: 48g carbohydrate (37g sugars
- Cholesterol: 50mg cholesterol
- Protein: 4g protein.
- Total Fat: 22g fat (14g saturated fat)

130. Pretzel Strawberry Dessert

Serving: 18 servings. | Prep: 30mins | Cook: 0mins | Ready in:

Ingredients

- 2-2/3 cups crushed pretzels (10 ounces)
- 1 cup butter, melted
- 1 package (8 ounces) cream cheese, softened
- 1 cup sugar
- 1 carton (8 ounces) frozen whipped topping, thawed
- 1 can (20 ounces) crushed pineapple
- 2 packages (3 ounces each) strawberry gelatin
- 2 packages (10 ounces each) frozen sliced sweetened strawberries, thawed

Direction

- Combine butter and pretzels in a bowl. Press onto the bottom of an oiled baking dish, about 13x9 inches. Bake at 350° until set, about 8 to 10 mins. Place on wire rack to cool. Beat sugar and cream cheese in a bowl until they become smooth. Then fold in the whipped topping and spread over the cooled crust. Place in the refrigerator until chilled.
- Drain the pineapple, saving the juice; put pineapple aside. If necessary, pour water into pineapple juice to measure one cup; mix into the gelatin mixture. Place in the refrigerator until set partially. Mix in the strawberries and reserved pineapple. Spoon over the filling carefully. Refrigerate, covered, until firm, about 3 to 4 hours.

Nutrition Information

- Calories: 363 calories
- Protein: 4g protein.
- Total Fat: 18g fat (11g saturated fat)
- Sodium: 592mg sodium
- Fiber: 1g fiber)
- Total Carbohydrate: 49g carbohydrate (0 sugars
- Cholesterol: 41mg cholesterol

Serving: 10-12 servings. | Prep: 30mins | Cook: 10mins
| Ready in:

Ingredients

- 1 package (3 ounces) orange gelatin
- 3 cups boiling water, divided
- 2 cups cold water, divided
- 1 package (3 ounces) cherry gelatin
- 1 package (3 ounces) lime gelatin
- 1 cup unsweetened pineapple juice
- 1/2 cup sugar, divided
- 1 envelope unflavored gelatin
- 1 package (3 ounces) lemon gelatin
- 2 cups graham cracker crumbs
- 1/2 cup butter, melted
- 2 cups heavy whipping cream

Direction

- Add 1 cup of boiling water and orange gelatin to a small bowl and stir until dissolve. Whisk in half a cup of cold water. Coat an ice cube tray with cooking spray then pour the liquid into the prepared tray. Repeat the process with lime and cherry gelatins. Pour into 2 different ice cube trays. Put into a refrigerator for approximately one and a half hour until firm.
- Mix a quarter cup of sugar and pineapple juice in a small saucepan. Drizzle unflavored gelatin on top and let it sit for a minute. Cook while stirring until the mixture reaches a boil. Take away from heat and whisk in lemon gelatin until dissolved. Whisk in the remaining cold water and move to a big bowl. Put into a refrigerator until syrupy, 30-40 minutes.
- Mix the remaining sugar with cracker crumbs then whisk in butter. Press onto the bottom and 2 inch up the sides of a greased 9 inch springform pan. Arrange on a baking sheet. Bake for 8-10 minutes at 350° until set. Transfer to a wire rack to cool.
- Take the gelatin cubes out of the ice cube trays. Add cream to a big bowl and whisk until stiff peaks form. Gently fold into the lemon gelatin mixture. Then add gelatin cubes and fold.

Scoop the crust over the gelatin and keep in a refrigerator overnight or 8 hours.

Nutrition Information

- Calories:
- Cholesterol:
- Protein:
- Total Fat:
- Sodium:
- Fiber:
- Total Carbohydrate:

Serving: 8 servings. | Prep: 35mins | Cook: 10mins
| Ready in:

Ingredients

- 1-1/2 cups finely crushed gingersnap cookies (about 30 cookies)
- 1 cup finely chopped pecans, toasted
- 1/3 cup butter, melted
- 1 envelope unflavored gelatin
- 1/4 cup cold water
- 1/2 cup packed brown sugar
- 1/2 cup half-and-half cream
- 3 large egg yolks
- 1 can (15 ounces) solid-pack pumpkin
- 2 teaspoons pumpkin pie spice
- 2 cups whipped topping
- 1/4 cup butterscotch-caramel ice cream topping
- 1/2 cup chopped pecans, toasted

Direction

- Prepare the oven by preheating to 350°F. Combine chopped pecans and crushed cookies in a small bowl; mix in butter. Then push onto the bottom and up sides of a 9-inch deep-dish pie plate that is not greased. Bake in the preheated oven for 10 to 12 minutes or until lightly browned. Let it cool on a wire rack.

- Drizzle gelatin over cold water in a microwave-safe bowl; allow it to stand for 1 minute. Place in a microwave for 30 to 40 seconds on high. Whisk and allow it to stand for 1 minute or until gelatin is fully melted.
- Beat egg yolks, cream and brown sugar in a large saucepan until combined. Then cook over low heat until a thermometer registers at least 160°F, whisking constantly. (Avoid from boiling.) Separate from the heat; mix in gelatin mixture, pumpkin and pie spice. Let it fully cool.
- Add in whipped topping then fold. Put into crust; store in the refrigerator until set. Sprinkle with ice cream topping; dust with pecans.

Nutrition Information

- Calories: 516 calories
- Sodium: 227mg sodium
- Fiber: 4g fiber)
- Total Carbohydrate: 53g carbohydrate (28g sugars
- Cholesterol: 98mg cholesterol
- Protein: 7g protein.
- Total Fat: 32g fat (12g saturated fat)

133. Raspberry Bavarian Cake

Serving: 16 servings. | Prep: 20mins | Cook: 0mins | Ready in:

Ingredients

- 5 packages (12 ounces each) frozen unsweetened raspberries, thawed
- 2 cups confectioners' sugar
- 2 envelopes unflavored gelatin
- 1/3 cup plus 1/2 cup cold water, divided
- 38 ladyfingers, split
- 2 tablespoons seedless raspberry jam

- 1 teaspoon water
- 1 carton (12 ounces) frozen reduced-fat whipped topping, thawed, divided

Direction

- Mix confectioners' sugar and raspberries together in a big saucepan. Boil it. Lower the heat and simmer until bubbly and the sugar melts, whisking sometimes, about 5-10 minutes. Mash and drain the raspberries, saving the syrup. Remove the seeds and put aside.
- Sprinkle over a small saucepan of 1/3 cup cold water with gelatin; allow to sit for 1 minute. Turn the heat to low, mixing until the gelatin has fully melted. Mix in raspberry juice and the leftover cold water. Put a cover on and chill until partially thickened, about 1 1/2-2 hours, whisking sometimes.
- In the meantime, use ladyfingers to line the sides and bottom of a 9-inch springform pan. Mix together water and raspberry jam in a small bowl; spread this mixture over ladyfingers lining pan's bottom. Fold into the raspberry mixture with 3 3/4 cups whipped topping. Add to the prepared pan. Put a cover on and chill until firm, about a minimum of 3 hours. Use the leftover whipped topping to garnish.

Nutrition Information

- Calories: 223 calories
- Fiber: 3g fiber)
- Total Carbohydrate: 46g carbohydrate (29g sugars
- Cholesterol: 35mg cholesterol
- Protein: 4g protein.
- Total Fat: 3g fat (3g saturated fat)
- Sodium: 121mg sodium

Serving: 2 servings. | Prep: 10mins | Cook: 0mins | Ready in:

Ingredients

- 1 package (3 ounces) raspberry gelatin
- 1/2 cup boiling water
- 1 package (10 ounces) frozen sweetened raspberries
- 1 cup vanilla ice cream, softened
- Whipped cream

Direction

- Dissolve the gelatin in a bowl with boiling water, then stir in ice cream and raspberries until mixed. Scoop into 2 dessert dishes then cover and chill for a minimum of an hour. Use whipped cream to decorate.

Nutrition Information

- Calories: 433 calories
- Fiber: 6g fiber)
- Total Carbohydrate: 89g carbohydrate (79g sugars
- Cholesterol: 29mg cholesterol
- Protein: 7g protein.
- Total Fat: 7g fat (4g saturated fat)
- Sodium: 151mg sodium

Serving: 10 servings. | Prep: 15mins | Cook: 0mins | Ready in:

Ingredients

- 1 package (10 ounces) frozen sweetened raspberries, thawed
- 1 package (3 ounces) raspberry gelatin
- 1 cup boiling water
- 1 tablespoon lemon juice

- 1 can (5 ounces) fat-free evaporated milk, chilled

Direction

- Strain the raspberries and save the syrup. Put the berries aside. Add boiling water and gelatin to a bowl and stir until dissolved. Whisk in the reserved raspberry syrup and lemon juice. Put into a refrigerator until partially set. Put in milk and whisk for approximately 4 minutes on high speed until thickened. Put in the reserved raspberries and fold. Add to a 2 quart bowl. Put into a refrigerator until set.

Nutrition Information

- Calories: 72 calories
- Total Carbohydrate: 17g carbohydrate (0 sugars
- Cholesterol: 1mg cholesterol
- Protein: 2g protein. Diabetic Exchanges: 1 fruit.
- Total Fat: 0 fat (0 saturated fat)
- Sodium: 36mg sodium
- Fiber: 1g fiber)

Serving: 12-16 servings. | Prep: 25mins | Cook: 0mins | Ready in:

Ingredients

- 2 cups fiinely crushed pretzels
- 2 tablespoons sugar
- 1/3 cup chopped pecans
- 3/4 cup butter, softened
- FILLING:
- 1 package (8 ounces) cream cheese, softened
- 3/4 cup sugar
- 1 carton (8 ounces) frozen whipped topping, thawed
- 1 package (6 ounces) raspberry gelatin

- 2 cups boiling water
- 2 packages (10 ounces each) frozen unsweetened raspberries

Direction

- Combine butter, pecans, sugar and the pretzels together in a large bowl. Press the mixture into an ungreased 13x9-in. baking pan. Put in oven and bake at 350° until lightly browned, 10 minutes; cool.
- Beat cream cheese and sugar until smooth in a large bowl. Fold in whipped topping, then spread over crust. In boiling water, dissolve gelatin in a large bowl. Mix in frozen raspberries until the gelatin is nearly set. Spread over filling. Chill for a few hours or overnight.

Nutrition Information

- Calories: 312 calories
- Protein: 4g protein.
- Total Fat: 18g fat (11g saturated fat)
- Sodium: 316mg sodium
- Fiber: 1g fiber)
- Total Carbohydrate: 34g carbohydrate (23g sugars
- Cholesterol: 39mg cholesterol

---

137. Raspberry Gelatin Dessert

Serving: 8 servings. | Prep: 10mins | Cook: 10mins | Ready in:

Ingredients

- 1 package (.3 ounce) sugar-free raspberry gelatin
- 1 cup boiling water
- 1 package (.8 ounce) sugar-free cook-and-serve vanilla pudding mix
- 1 cup cold water

- 1 package (12 ounces) frozen unsweetened raspberries, thawed

Direction

- Dissolve gelatin in a large bowl of boiling water. Put aside. Combine raspberries, water and pudding mix in a small saucepan. Over medium heat, boil, stirring constantly. Cook while stirring until thickened, about 1 to 2 mins more.
- Discard from heat; mix in the reserved gelatin mixture. Transfer to an 8 inches square dish coated with the cooking spray. Refrigerate, covered, 8 hours or overnight.

Nutrition Information

- Calories: 33 calories
- Total Fat: 0 fat (0 saturated fat)
- Sodium: 78mg sodium
- Fiber: 1g fiber)
- Total Carbohydrate: 6g carbohydrate (2g sugars
- Cholesterol: 0 cholesterol
- Protein: 1g protein. Diabetic Exchanges: 1/2 fruit.

---

138. Raspberry Gelatin Ring

Serving: 12 servings. | Prep: 20mins | Cook: 0mins | Ready in:

Ingredients

- 2 packages (3 ounces each) raspberry gelatin
- 1-1/2 cups boiling water
- 2 packages (10 ounces each) frozen sweetened raspberries, thawed and drained
- 2 cans (8 ounces each) crushed pineapple, undrained
- 1/4 teaspoon salt
- 1 package (8 ounces) cream cheese, softened
- 1/2 cup sour cream

Direction

- Dissolve the gelatin in a bowl of water. Mix in salt, pineapple and raspberries. Transfer 1/2 to an 8-cup ring mold coated with the cooking spray. Place in the refrigerator until firm, about half an hour. Allow the remaining gelatin mixture to stand at room temperature.
- Beat sour cream and cream cheese in a bowl until they become smooth. Spread the mold with gelatin carefully; add the remaining gelatin mixture over top. Place in the refrigerator until firm, about 6 hours.

Nutrition Information

- Calories: 173 calories
- Total Carbohydrate: 22g carbohydrate (20g sugars
- Cholesterol: 27mg cholesterol
- Protein: 3g protein.
- Total Fat: 8g fat (5g saturated fat)
- Sodium: 143mg sodium
- Fiber: 1g fiber)

139.   Raspberry Icebox Dessert

Serving: 12-15 servings. | Prep: 20mins | Cook: 0mins | Ready in:

Ingredients

- 2 packages (3 ounces each) raspberry gelatin
- 2 cups boiling water
- 3 cups fresh or frozen raspberries
- 2 cups graham cracker crumbs (about 32 squares)
- 1/4 cup packed brown sugar
- 1/2 cup butter, melted
- 1-1/2 cups cold milk
- 1 package (3.4 ounces) instant vanilla pudding mix
- 1 package (8 ounces) cream cheese, softened

Direction

- Mix water and gelatin in a large bowl; mix till the gelatin is dissolved. Stir in raspberries. Place in the refrigerator till syrupy, 1 hour.
- Combine butter, brown sugar and cracker crumbs together in a small bowl. Press into a 13x9-in. dish coated with grease.
- Whisk pudding mix and milk in a large bowl for 2 minutes. Allow to sit till soft-set, 2 minutes.
- Beat cream cheese in another bowl, till smooth. Slowly put in pudding. Spread over the crust. Transfer the gelatin mixture on top. Keep chilled till set. Place any leftovers in the refrigerator.

Nutrition Information

- Calories: 239 calories
- Sodium: 291mg sodium
- Fiber: 2g fiber)
- Total Carbohydrate: 27g carbohydrate (18g sugars
- Cholesterol: 36mg cholesterol
- Protein: 4g protein.
- Total Fat: 13g fat (8g saturated fat)

140.   Raspberry Squares

Serving: 9 | Prep: | Cook: 25mins | Ready in:

Ingredients

- 1 cup white whole-wheat flour or all-purpose flour
- ⅓ cup confectioners' sugar
- 3 tablespoons cornstarch
- ¼ teaspoon salt
- 3 tablespoons canola oil
- 2 tablespoons butter, softened
- 3 cups raspberries, fresh or frozen (not thawed), plus more for garnish
- ⅓ cup water

- 2 tablespoons lemon juice or lime juice
- 2 large eggs
- ⅓ cup granulated sugar
- 3 tablespoons cornstarch
- ⅛ teaspoon salt
- Confectioners' sugar for garnish

Direction

- Prepare the oven by preheating to 350°F. Get an 8 in.square baking pan and use foil to line the pan and use cooking spray to generously coat it.
- To ready the crust: in a medium bowl, combine together 1/4 teaspoon salt, cornstarch, confectioner's sugar, and flour. Stir in butter and oil; mix into the flour mixture until equally combined using your fingertips. The mixture should be a bit crumbly. Into the prepared pan, Press the dough firmly. Bake for 15 to 20 minutes until barely starting to brown in color around the edges.
- To ready the filling; In the meantime, in a medium sauce pan, mix together the water and raspberries. Cook for 4 to 6 minutes over high heat, regularly stirring, until the fruit is almost broken down and very soft. Into a medium bowl place through a fine mesh sieve, pushing on the solids to extract all the liquid. Then put the drained juice into a glass measuring cup. You will be needing 1 cup drained juice; get rid of any excess or you can add a bit of water if you are short. Mix in lemon or lime juice.
- In a medium bowl, mix together the 1/8 teaspoon salt, cornstarch, and granulated sugar until mixed well. Add in the eggs. Mix in the juice mixture. Place the filling on top of the crust.
- Bake for 15 to 20 minutes until just set. (The middle should still be a bit jiggly – as it cools it will firm up.)
- At a room temperature, let it cool for about 1 1/2 hours in the pan on a wire rack. Using the edges of the foil, slowly lift out of the pan all in one piece. Slice into nine squares. Use fresh raspberries to garnish and sprinkle with

confectioners' sugar, if you want, prior to serving.

Nutrition Information

- Calories: 207 calories;
- Total Carbohydrate: 31
- Protein: 4
- Total Fat: 8
- Sodium: 114
- Cholesterol: 48
- Sugar: 13
- Saturated Fat: 2
- Fiber: 3

141. Raspberry Whip

Serving: 6 servings. | Prep: 15mins | Cook: 0mins | Ready in:

Ingredients

- 1 package (.3 ounce) sugar-free raspberry gelatin
- 1 cup boiling water
- 2/3 cup cold water
- 1 cup (8 ounces) vanilla yogurt
- 1 cup fresh or frozen unsweetened raspberries, drained, divided

Direction

- Dissolve gelatin in a bowl of boiling water. Stir in the cold water. Refrigerate for 30 to 45 mins, covered, until set partially. Put in yogurt. Beat for 2 to 3 mins on medium speed until foamy and light. Place in the refrigerator for 15 mins.
- Portion 2/3 cup of raspberries into 6 dessert dishes. Add about a half cup of gelatin mixture and the remaining raspberries over top each. Place in the refrigerator until enjoying.

Nutrition Information

- Calories: 48 calories
- Protein: 3g protein. Diabetic Exchanges: 1/2 reduced-fat milk.
- Total Fat: 1g fat (0 saturated fat)
- Sodium: 65mg sodium
- Fiber: 1g fiber)
- Total Carbohydrate: 8g carbohydrate (0 sugars
- Cholesterol: 2mg cholesterol

142. Red 'n' Green Gelatin

Serving: 8 servings. | Prep: 20mins | Cook: 0mins | Ready in:

Ingredients

- 1 package (3 ounces) lime gelatin
- 2 cups boiling water, divided
- 1 can (8 ounces) crushed pineapple, undrained
- 2 cups large marshmallows
- 1 package (3 ounces) cherry gelatin
- 1 cup cherry pie filling

Direction

- Mix lime gelatin with a cup boiling water in a small bowl to dissolve. Let sit for 2 minutes. Mix in pineapple. Add to an 11x7-in. pan. Put marshmallows on top. Chill, covered, until firm.
- Mix cherry gelatin in leftover boiling water in a small bowl. Let sit for 2 minutes. Mix in pie filling; add on top of marshmallows. Cover and chill until firm.

Nutrition Information

- Calories:
- Fiber:
- Total Carbohydrate:
- Cholesterol:
- Protein:
- Total Fat:
- Sodium:

143. Red Raspberry Mousse Dessert

Serving: 12 servings. | Prep: 10mins | Cook: 0mins | Ready in:

Ingredients

- 2 packages (3 ounces each) raspberry gelatin
- 1-3/4 cups boiling water
- 2 packages (10 ounces each) frozen sweetened raspberries, thawed
- 2 cups heavy whipping cream, whipped
- 23 ladyfingers
- Fresh mint, and raspberries and additional whipped cream, optional

Direction

- Melt gelatin in boiling water in big bowl; mix raspberries in. Refrigerate till thickened partially; fold whipped cream in.
- Put ladyfingers around sides of 9-in. ungreased springform pan, rounded side out; put raspberry mixture in pan carefully. Cover; refrigerate till firm. Garnish with whipped cream, raspberries and mint (optional).

Nutrition Information

- Calories: 314 calories
- Sodium: 79mg sodium
- Fiber: 2g fiber)
- Total Carbohydrate: 38g carbohydrate (32g sugars
- Cholesterol: 131mg cholesterol
- Protein: 5g protein.
- Total Fat: 17g fat (10g saturated fat)

144. Refreshing Cranberry Ice

Serving: 7 cups. | Prep: 20mins | Cook: 03hours00mins | Ready in:

Ingredients

- 4 cups fresh or frozen cranberries
- 3 cups water
- 1-1/8 teaspoons unflavored gelatin
- 1 cup cold water
- 2-1/2 cups sugar
- 1 cup orange juice
- 1/4 cup lemon juice
- 1/2 cup heavy whipping cream

Direction

- Boil water and cranberries in a large saucepan. Lower the heat to medium and cook, uncovered, until berries pop. Discard from heat.
- Sprinkle the cold water in a bowl with gelatin; allow to stand 5 mins. In the meantime, strain the cranberries into a large bowl through the food mill, remove skin and seeds. Put in softened gelatin, lemon juice, orange juice and sugar; stir until the gelatin dissolves. Mix in cream. Transfer to a 13-inch x 9-inch dish. Freeze, covered, until firm, about 3 to 4 hours.

Nutrition Information

- Calories: 191 calories
- Total Carbohydrate: 42g carbohydrate (0 sugars
- Cholesterol: 12mg cholesterol
- Protein: 1g protein.
- Total Fat: 3g fat (2g saturated fat)
- Sodium: 4mg sodium
- Fiber: 1g fiber)

145. Refreshing Strawberry Pie

Serving: 6-8 servings. | Prep: 30mins | Cook: 0mins | Ready in:

Ingredients

- 1 unbaked pastry shell (9 inches)
- 3/4 cup sugar
- 2 tablespoons cornstarch
- 1 cup water
- 1 package (3 ounces) strawberry gelatin
- 4 cups sliced fresh strawberries
- Fresh mint, optional

Direction

- Using a double thickness of heavy-duty foil, line an unpricked pastry shell. Bake for 8 minutes at 450°. Take the foil away; bake for 5 more minutes. Place on a wire rack to cool.
- Mix water, cornstarch and sugar in a small saucepan till smooth. Boil the mixture; cook while stirring till thickened, or for 2 minutes. Take away from the heat; mix in gelatin till dissolved. Place in the refrigerator till slightly cooled, or for 15-20 minutes.
- Meanwhile, spread strawberries into the crust. Transfer over the berries with the gelatin mixture. Keep in the refrigerator till set. Use mint for garnish if you want.

Nutrition Information

- Calories: 264 calories
- Sodium: 125mg sodium
- Fiber: 2g fiber)
- Total Carbohydrate: 49g carbohydrate (32g sugars
- Cholesterol: 5mg cholesterol
- Protein: 2g protein.
- Total Fat: 7g fat (3g saturated fat)

146. Rhubarb Rumble

Serving: 8 servings. | Prep: 15mins | Cook: 0mins | Ready in:

Ingredients

- 3 cups chopped rhubarb
- 1 package (.3 ounce) sugar-free strawberry gelatin
- 1-1/2 cups cold skim milk
- 1 package (1 ounce) instant sugar-free vanilla pudding mix
- 1 reduced-fat graham cracker crust (8 inches)

Direction

- Arrange rhubarb in a microwave-safe bowl; microwave, covered, for 6 to 8 minutes on high power, stirring every 2 minutes, until rhubarb is tender. Mix in gelatin until dissolved; allow to cool completely.
- Beat pudding mix and milk on low speed in a bowl for 2 minutes. Fold into rhubarb mixture. Spread over the crust. Chill, covered, until firm.

Nutrition Information

- Calories: 134 calories
- Protein: 3g protein. Diabetic Exchanges: 1 starch
- Total Fat: 3g fat (0 saturated fat)
- Sodium: 160mg sodium
- Fiber: 0 fiber)
- Total Carbohydrate: 23g carbohydrate (0 sugars
- Cholesterol: 1mg cholesterol

147. Rhubarb Shortbread Squares

Serving: 9 servings. | Prep: 30mins | Cook: 15mins | Ready in:

Ingredients

- 1 cup all-purpose flour
- 2 tablespoons sugar
- 1/4 teaspoon salt
- 1/2 cup cold butter, cubed
- FILLING:
- 4 cups diced fresh or frozen rhubarb
- 1-1/4 cups sugar
- 1/4 cup water
- 1/8 teaspoon salt
- 2 envelopes unflavored gelatin
- 1/3 cup cold water
- 4 to 6 drops red food coloring, optional
- 1 cup heavy whipping cream, whipped

Direction

- Combine salt, sugar and flour in a bowl; cut in the butter until it is crumbly. Then press into an oiled 8-inch square baking dish. Bake for 15 to 20 mins at 350°, until lightly browned the edges. Place on wire rack to cool.
- Boil salt, water, sugar and rhubarb in a saucepan. Lower the heat and simmer, uncovered, stirring occasionally, until rhubarb becomes tender, about 8 to 10 mins. Sprinkle cold water with gelatin in a small bowl; allow to stand for one min. Stir into the rhubarb mixture. Cook while stirring until the gelatin dissolves. If desired, stir in the food coloring. Refrigerate, covered, for 120 mins or until cooled.
- Fold in the whipped cream. Then spread over the crust. Refrigerate, covered, until set, about 3 hours. Cut into squares.

Nutrition Information

- Calories: 366 calories
- Sodium: 217mg sodium
- Fiber: 1g fiber)
- Total Carbohydrate: 44g carbohydrate (32g sugars
- Cholesterol: 63mg cholesterol
- Protein: 4g protein.
- Total Fat: 20g fat (12g saturated fat)

148. Rhubarb Strawberry Torte

Serving: 12 servings. | Prep: 40mins | Cook: 0mins | Ready in:

Ingredients

- 6 cups chopped fresh or frozen rhubarb
- 1 cup water
- 3/4 cup sugar, divided
- 2 packages (3 ounces each) strawberry gelatin
- 1 teaspoon vanilla extract
- 4-1/2 teaspoons cornstarch
- 1 tablespoon cold water
- 4 drops red food coloring, optional
- 2 cups heavy whipping cream, whipped
- 24 ladyfingers, split
- Fresh strawberries and additional whipped cream

Direction

- Boil 1/2 cup sugar, water and rhubarb in a big saucepan. Lower heat; simmer for 6-8 minutes, uncovered, till rhubarb is tender. Slightly cool; set 1 cup rhubarb liquid aside for glaze. Put leftover liquid and rhubarb in food processor/blender; process, covered, till pureed.
- Put back in saucepan; boil. Mix gelatin in till melted; mix vanilla in. Cover; chill till slightly thick for 1 hour.
- Meanwhile, for glaze: Boil leftover sugar and reserved rhubarb liquid in a small saucepan. Mix cold water and cornstarch till smooth in a small bowl; whisk into boiling mixture. Mix and cook till thick; take off from heat. If desired, mix food coloring in. Cover; refrigerate overnight.
- Fold whipped cream slowly into rhubarb mixture; put 17 split ladyfingers on the bottom then 26 around 9-in. ungreased springform pan edge. Spread 1/2 rhubarb mixture into the pan. Put leftover ladyfingers on rhubarb mixture; spread leftover rhubarb mixture carefully. Cover; chill overnight. Spread glaze over the top carefully; remove pan sides. Garnish with whipped cream and strawberries.

Nutrition Information

- Calories: 305 calories
- Fiber: 1g fiber)
- Total Carbohydrate: 39g carbohydrate (31g sugars
- Cholesterol: 84mg cholesterol
- Protein: 4g protein.
- Total Fat: 16g fat (9g saturated fat)
- Sodium: 149mg sodium

149. Russian Cream

Serving: 4 servings. | Prep: 20mins | Cook: 0mins | Ready in:

Ingredients

- 1 envelope unflavored gelatin
- 1/2 cup cold water
- 1 cup heavy whipping cream
- 3/4 cup sugar
- 1 cup (8 ounces) sour cream
- 1/2 teaspoon vanilla extract
- 1 package (10 ounces) frozen sweetened raspberries, thawed
- Fresh raspberries and mint sprigs, optional

Direction

- Scatter gelatin on top of cold water in a small saucepan; let sit for a minute. Heat up to a boil; cook and mix until dissolved. Take off from the heat; put aside.
- Heat whipping cream with sugar in a separate saucepan over medium heat until dissolved and mixture is lukewarm. Take off from the heat; mix in gelatin mixture until dissolved

completely. Cover and chill for half an hour or until thickened slightly.

- Mix in vanilla and sour cream. Put a scant 1/4 cupful of cream mixture in each of 4 parfait glasses; garnish each with a rounded tablespoonful of raspberries on top. Keep layering. Put on each with scant 1/4 cup of cream mixture.
- Cover and chill for 3 hours or until firm. Top with mint and fresh raspberries (optional) just before serving.

Nutrition Information

- Calories: 544 calories
- Cholesterol: 119mg cholesterol
- Protein: 5g protein.
- Total Fat: 32g fat (20g saturated fat)
- Sodium: 46mg sodium
- Fiber: 3g fiber)
- Total Carbohydrate: 60g carbohydrate (55g sugars

150.   Russian Cream Dessert

Serving: 8 servings. | Prep: 20mins | Cook: 0mins | Ready in:

Ingredients

- 3/4 cup sugar
- 1 envelope (1 tablespoon) unflavored gelatin
- 1/2 cup cold water
- 1 cup heavy whipping cream
- 1-1/2 cups sour cream
- 1 teaspoon vanilla extract
- 4 to 5 cups fresh fruit (bite-size pieces)

Direction

- Combine gelatin and sugar in saucepan. Stir in the water. Allow to stand 5 mins. Boil, stirring constantly. Discard from the heat; mix in the whipping cream.

- Combine vanilla and sour cream in a bowl. Gradually put into the hot mixture; then mix until they become smooth. Transfer to a 4-cup mold or bowl. Let chill with a cover for 4 hours or overnight. Serve over fruit.

Nutrition Information

- Calories: 306 calories
- Total Carbohydrate: 31g carbohydrate (29g sugars
- Cholesterol: 71mg cholesterol
- Protein: 3g protein.
- Total Fat: 19g fat (12g saturated fat)
- Sodium: 39mg sodium
- Fiber: 1g fiber)

151.   Russian Creme

Serving: 10-12 servings. | Prep: 20mins | Cook: 0mins | Ready in:

Ingredients

- CREME:
- 1 cup sugar
- 2-1/4 cups water
- 2 envelopes unflavored gelatin
- 1-1/2 cups sour cream
- 1-1/2 teaspoons vanilla extract
- 1-1/2 cups heavy whipping cream, whipped
- TOPPING:
- 1 package (10 ounces) frozen raspberries
- 1 package (4-3/4 ounces) raspberry-flavored Danish Dessert

Direction

- Dissolve gelatin and sugar in water on low heat. Take away from the stove; stir in the vanilla and sour cream until it gets smooth. Allow the mixture to chill until lightly thickened (like unbeaten egg whites). Using wire whisk, fold in whipped cream until well combined. Pour into 6-cup ring mold coated with grease; let them chill until set. For topping, strain raspberries, keeping the juice. Following package instructions for pudding, prepare dessert mix, using reserved raspberry juice as part of liquid. Allow the topping to chill; fold in the raspberries. Transfer the molded cream onto the glass serving plate to serve (with minimum of 1 in. bigger than mold). In a small bowl, put the raspberry topping in middle of mold. Guests can serve themselves with a slice of crème pudding and put topping over it using spoon.

Nutrition Information

- Calories: 238 calories
- Cholesterol: 40mg cholesterol
- Protein: 3g protein.
- Total Fat: 11g fat (7g saturated fat)
- Sodium: 23mg sodium
- Fiber: 1g fiber)
- Total Carbohydrate: 31g carbohydrate (27g sugars

152.   Russian Creme Heart

Serving: 14-16 servings. | Prep: 15mins | Cook: 0mins | Ready in:

Ingredients

- 2-3/4 cups cold water
- 1-1/2 cups sugar
- 2 envelopes unflavored gelatin
- 1-3/4 cups sour cream
- 1 tablespoon vanilla extract
- 8 to 10 drops yellow liquid food coloring, optional
- 1-3/4 cups whipped topping
- Assorted fruit, optional

Direction

- Combine gelatin, sugar and water in a 2-quart saucepan; allow to stand for one min. Over medium-low heat, cook while stirring until sugar and gelatin are dissolved completely; Discard from heat. Blend in sour cream, vanilla and if desired, food coloring, using a wire whisk. Let chill for half an hour or until thickened slightly. Blend in the whipped topping. Transfer to an oiled 8-cup heart-shaped mold. Let chill for at least 6 hours or until firm. Unmold onto the platter. If desired, decorate with fruit.

Nutrition Information

- Calories:
- Sodium:
- Fiber:
- Total Carbohydrate:
- Cholesterol:
- Protein:
- Total Fat:

153.   Sangria Gelatin Dessert

Serving: 6 servings. | Prep: 15mins | Cook: 0mins | Ready in:

Ingredients

- 1 package (.3 ounce) sugar-free lemon gelatin
- 1 package (.3 ounce) sugar-free raspberry gelatin
- 1-1/2 cups boiling water
- 1 cup cold water
- 1 cup white wine
- 1 can (11 ounces) mandarin oranges, drained
- 1 cup fresh raspberries
- 1 cup green grapes, halved

Direction

- Add boiling water and gelatins to a big bowl and stir until dissolve. Let it sit for 10 minutes. Whisk in the wine and cold water then put into a refrigerator until partially set, 45 minutes.

- Add grapes, raspberries and oranges and fold. Pour 1 cup of the mixture into each of 6 big wine glasses. Put into a refrigerator until set, 4 hrs.

Nutrition Information

- Calories: 95 calories
- Sodium: 83mg sodium
- Fiber: 2g fiber)
- Total Carbohydrate: 13g carbohydrate (10g sugars
- Cholesterol: 0 cholesterol
- Protein: 2g protein. Diabetic Exchanges: 1 fruit.
- Total Fat: 0 fat (0 saturated fat)

---

154.   Spiced Peach Pie

Serving: 6-8 servings. | Prep: 20mins | Cook: 0mins | Ready in:

Ingredients

- 1 can (15 ounces) sliced peaches
- 2 tablespoons brown sugar
- 1/4 teaspoon ground ginger
- 1 cinnamon stick (3 inches)
- 1 package (3 ounces) peach or orange gelatin
- 4 ounces cream cheese, softened
- 2 tablespoons butter, softened
- 1/8 teaspoon ground nutmeg
- 1 pastry shell (9 inches), baked
- 1 carton (8 ounces) frozen whipped topping, thawed
- Fresh mint, optional

Direction

- Strain the syrup from peaches into a 2-cup measuring cup. Put in enough water to

measure 1 1/3 cups. Chop the peaches; set aside.

- Mix cinnamon stick, ginger, brown sugar and syrup together in a large saucepan. Boil the mixture. Lower the heat; cook while stirring for 5 minutes. Take away from the heat.
- Discard the cinnamon stick. Mix in gelation till dissolved. Put in the peaches. Chill in a refrigerator for a round 40 minutes, till partially set.
- Beat nutmeg, butter and cream cheese in a large bowl, till smooth. Spread up the sides and over the bottom of the baked crust. Pour the gelatin mixture on top of the cream cheese layer.
- Chill till serving. Spread whipped topping over. Serve together with mint if you want.

Nutrition Information

- Calories: 367 calories
- Cholesterol: 28mg cholesterol
- Protein: 3g protein.
- Total Fat: 20g fat (13g saturated fat)
- Sodium: 201mg sodium
- Fiber: 0 fiber)
- Total Carbohydrate: 42g carbohydrate (27g sugars

---

155.   Spiced Tea Delight

Serving: 6 servings. | Prep: 20mins | Cook: 5mins | Ready in:

Ingredients

- 3 cups water
- 4 ginger-flavored herbal tea bags
- 4 green tea bags
- 3 envelopes unflavored gelatin
- 3/4 cup cold water
- 1 cup heavy whipping cream
- 1/2 cup honey
- 2 tablespoons brown sugar

- 1/2 teaspoon ground cinnamon
- 1/4 teaspoon ground cloves
- Additional ground cinnamon, optional

Direction

- Boil water in large saucepan. Put in tea bags. Steep, covered, for 3 to 5 mins.
- In the meantime, sprinkle the cold water in a small saucepan with gelatin; allow to stand for one min. Over low heat, heat while stirring until the gelatin is dissolved completely. Stir into the tea mixture. Remove tea bags.
- Mix in cloves, cinnamon, brown sugar, honey and cream. Portion among 6 dessert dishes or transfer to a 5-cup mold coated with the cooking spray. Refrigerate, covered, until set. If desired, sprinkle with more cinnamon.

Nutrition Information

- Calories: 253 calories
- Sodium: 25mg sodium
- Fiber: 0 fiber)
- Total Carbohydrate: 29g carbohydrate (28g sugars
- Cholesterol: 54mg cholesterol
- Protein: 4g protein.
- Total Fat: 15g fat (9g saturated fat)

156. Stained Glass Gelatin

Serving: 15 servings. | Prep: 25mins | Cook: 0mins | Ready in:

Ingredients

- 2 packages (3 ounces each) lime gelatin
- 6 cups boiling water, divided
- 2 packages (3 ounces each) orange gelatin
- 2 envelopes unflavored gelatin
- 1/3 cup cold water
- 1-1/2 cups white grape juice
- 1 carton (12 ounces) frozen whipped topping, thawed

Direction

- Dissolve lime gelatin in a bowl with 3 cups of boiling water. Transfer to an 8 inches square dish coated with the cooking spray. Dissolve orange gelatin in another bowl with the remaining boiling water. Transfer to another 8 inches square dish coated with the cooking spray. Place in the refrigerator until very firm, about 4 hours.
- Sprinkle the cold water in a small saucepan with unflavored gelatin; allow to stand for one min. Put in grape juice. Over low heat, heat while stirring until the gelatin is dissolved completely. Transfer to a large bowl. Place in the refrigerator until thickened slightly, about 45 mins. Fold in the whipped topping.
- Cut orange gelatin into 1-inch cubes and green gelatin into 1/2 inches cubes. For garnish, put 8 to 10 cubes of each color aside. Put 2 cups of the whipped topping mixture into a bowl; then fold in the remaining green cubes. Then spread in a 13-inch x 9-inch dish coated with the cooking spray. Then fold the remaining orange cubes into the remaining whipped topping mixture and spread over the bottom layer. Top with the reserved orange and green gelatin cubes. Place in the refrigerator until set, about 120 mins. Divide into squares.

Nutrition Information

- Calories: 122 calories
- Protein: 2g protein.
- Total Fat: 4g fat (4g saturated fat)
- Sodium: 29mg sodium
- Fiber: 0 fiber)
- Total Carbohydrate: 18g carbohydrate (16g sugars
- Cholesterol: 0 cholesterol

157. Strawberry Angel Dessert

Serving: 16 servings | Prep: 20mins | Cook: |Ready in:

Ingredients

- 2 cups boiling water
- 2 pkg. (3 oz. each) JELL-O Strawberry Flavor Gelatin
- 1 cup cold water
- 2 cups strawberries, divided
- 1 tub (8 oz.) COOL WHIP Whipped Topping, thawed
- 1 pkg. (10 oz.) prepared angel food cake, cut into 3/4-inch cubes

Direction

- 1. In large bowl, pour boiling water into the gelatin mixes; stir until dissolved completely, about 2 mins. Stir in the cold water. Place in the refrigerator until thickened slightly, about 60 mins.
- 2. In the meantime, slice enough strawberries, measuring half cup; chop the remaining strawberries coarsely. Place in the refrigerator till ready to use.
- 3. Using mixer, beat gelatin for 6 mins on high speed, until foamy. Put in the COOL WHIP; beat until they are just blended on low speed. Stir in chopped strawberries and cake cubes.
- 4. Transfer by spoon to 9-in. springform pan.
- 5. Place in the refrigerator until firm, about 3 hours.
- 6. Loosen the dessert by running a knife around the pan rim. Discard the rim. Arrange the sliced strawberries on top of dessert. Then serve.

Nutrition Information

- Calories: 140
- Saturated Fat: 3 g
- Sodium: 190 mg
- Fiber: 0.6438 g
- Cholesterol: 0 mg
- Total Carbohydrate: 25 g

- Total Fat: 4 g
- Sugar: 13 g
- Protein: 2 g

158. Strawberry Banana Cups

Serving: 2 servings. | Prep: 15mins | Cook: 0mins | Ready in:

Ingredients

- 1-1/2 teaspoons sugar-free strawberry gelatin powder
- 1/2 cup boiling water
- 1/2 cup unsweetened apple juice
- 3 strawberries, sliced
- 1 small firm banana, cut into 1/4-inch slices
- 2 strawberries, halved for garnish

Direction

- Stir boiling water with gelatin until dissolved. Whisk in apple juice and put into a refrigerator for half an hour. Arrange sliced strawberries in the bottom of two 10-ounce custard cups or 2 individual serving dishes. Add banana to the gelatin mixture and whisk. Spread over the strawberries then put into a refrigerator until firm, for a minimum of 2 hrs. Use strawberries halves to garnish.

Nutrition Information

- Calories: 107 calories
- Cholesterol: 0 cholesterol
- Protein: 1g protein. Diabetic Exchanges: 2 fruit.
- Total Fat: 1g fat (1g saturated fat)
- Sodium: 5mg sodium
- Fiber: 3g fiber)
- Total Carbohydrate: 27g carbohydrate (0 sugars

159. Strawberry Banana Delight

Serving: 4 servings. | Prep: 15mins | Cook: 0mins | Ready in:

Ingredients

- 1 package (.3 ounce) sugar-free strawberry gelatin
- 1 cup boiling water
- 6 ice cubes
- 2 medium ripe bananas, cut into chunks
- 4 tablespoons whipped topping
- 4 fresh strawberries

Direction

- Dissolve gelatin in a small bowl of boiling water. Let cool about 10 mins. Pour enough water into the ice cubes to measure one cup. Combine ice mixture and gelatin in a blender; process for one min, covered, until the ice cubes dissolve. Put in bananas and process until they are blended, about 1 to 2 mins more.
- Transfer to 4 dessert dishes. Place in the refrigerator until set, at least half an hour. Place one tablespoon of whipped topping and 1 strawberry on top each for garnish.

Nutrition Information

- Calories: 78 calories
- Fiber: 2g fiber)
- Total Carbohydrate: 16g carbohydrate (12g sugars
- Cholesterol: 0 cholesterol
- Protein: 2g protein. Diabetic Exchanges: 1 fruit.
- Total Fat: 1g fat (1g saturated fat)
- Sodium: 48mg sodium

160. Strawberry Banana Dessert

Serving: 16 servings. | Prep: 15mins | Cook: 0mins | Ready in:

Ingredients

- 3 medium firm bananas, sliced
- 1 prepared angel food cake (8 to 10 ounces), cut into 1-inch cubes
- 1 pint fresh strawberries, halved
- 1 package (.6 ounce) sugar-free strawberry gelatin
- 2 cups boiling water
- 1-1/2 cups cold water
- 1 carton (8 ounces) reduced-fat whipped topping, thawed

Direction

- In a 13x9 inches dish coated with the cooking spray, layer slices of banana then the cake cubes. Top the cake with strawberries and gently press down.
- Dissolve gelatin in a small bowl of boiling water; mix in the cold water. Add over the strawberries. Place in the refrigerator until set, about 3 hours. Frost with the whipped topping.

Nutrition Information

- Calories: 0g sugar total.

161. Strawberry Cloud

Serving: 6-8 servings. | Prep: 20mins | Cook: 0mins | Ready in:

Ingredients

- 1 package (3 ounces) strawberry gelatin
- 1 package (3 ounces) cook-and-serve vanilla pudding mix

- 2-1/2 cups water
- 1 carton (8 ounces) frozen whipped topping, thawed

Direction

- Cook while stirring the water, pudding mix, and gelatin in a saucepan over medium heat for approximately 15 minutes until the mixture boils. Let it cool until partially set. Put in whipped topping and fold. Scoop the mixture into parfait glasses or individual dishes or a bowl. Put into a refrigerator until ready to serve.

Nutrition Information

- Calories: 156 calories
- Protein: 1g protein.
- Total Fat: 5g fat (5g saturated fat)
- Sodium: 89mg sodium
- Fiber: 0 fiber)
- Total Carbohydrate: 25g carbohydrate (20g sugars
- Cholesterol: 0 cholesterol

162.   Strawberry Cream Dessert

Serving: 12 servings, 2/3 cup each | Prep: 15mins | Cook: | Ready in:

Ingredients

- 1 pkg. (3 oz.) soft ladyfingers, split
- 2 cups strawberries, divided
- 1-3/4 cups boiling water
- 2 pkg. (1 oz. each) JELL-O Strawberry Flavor Sugar Free Gelatin
- 2 cups ice cubes
- 1 tub (8 oz.) COOL WHIP LITE Whipped Topping, thawed

Direction

- Cut off 3/4 inch from ends of ladyfingers; put ends on bottom of 9-inch springform pan. Place leftover ladyfingers standing around side of pan, cut sides facing in. Save 2 strawberries for topping; mash leftover strawberries.
- In a big bowl, pour boiling water to gelatin mixes; mix 2 min. until dissolved completely. Put in ice cubes; mix until melted. Put in mashed strawberries and COOL WHIP; gently mix using whisk until combined. Chill 10 min. or until thick enough to mound. Scoop into pan.
- Chill 3 hours or until set. Take off side of pan. Top dessert with saved strawberries.

Nutrition Information

- Calories: 90
- Total Fat: 3 g
- Sodium: 120 mg
- Cholesterol: 25 mg
- Protein: 3 g
- Sugar: 9 g
- Total Carbohydrate: 12 g
- Saturated Fat: 2.5 g
- Fiber: 1 g

163.   Strawberry Dessert

Serving: 24 servings. | Prep: 15mins | Cook: 0mins | Ready in:

Ingredients

- 1 loaf-shaped angel food cake (10-1/2 ounces), cubed
- 1 package (1 ounce) sugar-free instant vanilla pudding mix
- 1 cup cold fat-free milk
- 2 cups sugar-free low-fat vanilla ice cream, softened
- 1 package (.3 ounce) sugar-free strawberry gelatin

- 1 cup boiling water
- 1 cup cold water
- 1 package (20 ounces) frozen unsweetened strawberries, partially thawed and sliced

Direction

- In a 13x9 inches dish, place cake. Whisk milk and pudding mix in a bowl for 90 seconds. Put in ice cream and whisk for one min. Pour over the cake; let chill.
- In the boiling water, dissolve gelatin. Put in strawberries and cold water; stir until set partially. Scoop over the pudding layer. Let chill overnight with a cover.

Nutrition Information

- Calories: 62 calories
- Sodium: 142mg sodium
- Fiber: 0 fiber)
- Total Carbohydrate: 14g carbohydrate (0 sugars
- Cholesterol: 0 cholesterol
- Protein: 3g protein. Diabetic Exchanges: 1 starch.
- Total Fat: 0 fat (0 saturated fat)

164. Strawberry Fluff

Serving: 9 | Prep: | Cook: | Ready in:

Ingredients

- 2 (3 ounce) packages strawberry flavored Jell-O®
- 1 (16 ounce) package cottage cheese
- 1 (8 ounce) container frozen whipped topping, thawed
- 1 (20 ounce) can crushed pineapple, drained

Direction

- Mix together the pineapple, whipped topping, cottage cheese and gelatin mix in a mixing

bowl. Combine well, place in refrigerator until chilled and serve.

Nutrition Information

- Calories: 236 calories;
- Total Fat: 8.6
- Sodium: 285
- Total Carbohydrate: 33
- Cholesterol: 7
- Protein: 8.5

165. Strawberry Gelatin Dessert

Serving: 9 servings. | Prep: 40mins | Cook: 0mins | Ready in:

Ingredients

- 1 cup graham cracker crumbs
- 1 tablespoon sugar
- 2 tablespoons butter, melted
- 2 cups sliced fresh strawberries
- 2 tablespoons sugar
- 1 package (.3 ounce) sugar-free strawberry gelatin
- 1 cup boiling water
- 4 cups miniature marshmallows
- 1/2 cup fat-free milk
- 1 carton (8 ounces) reduced-fat whipped topping

Direction

- Mix the butter, sugar and cracker crumbs in a bowl. Then press into a greased 9-inch square baking dish. Bake at 350° until golden brown, 10 minutes. Transfer to a wire rack to cool.
- In a small bowl, mix the sugar and strawberries then let it sit for 20 minutes. Add water and gelatin to a different bowl then stir until dissolve. Strain the berries and save the juices. Put in an enough amount of water to

the juice to measure 1 cup. Whisk the juice mixture and berries into the gelatin. Put into a refrigerator until partially set.

- At the same time, in a saucepan, mix the milk with marshmallow. Cook while stirring on low heat until smooth and blended. Let it cool for 15 minutes, until it reaches room temperature. Fold in whipped topping and then the gelatin mixture. Spread over the prepared crust. Put into a refrigerator until firm, 4 hours.

Nutrition Information

- Calories: 243 calories
- Protein: 2g protein. Diabetic Exchanges: 2 starch
- Total Fat: 7g fat (5g saturated fat)
- Sodium: 150mg sodium
- Fiber: 1g fiber)
- Total Carbohydrate: 41g carbohydrate (0 sugars
- Cholesterol: 7mg cholesterol

---

166. Strawberry Graham Dessert

Serving: 9 servings. | Prep: 15mins | Cook: 10mins | Ready in:

Ingredients

- 1 cup graham cracker crumbs (about 16 squares)
- 2 tablespoons butter, melted
- 1 package (3 ounces) strawberry gelatin
- 1 cup boiling water
- 2 packages (10 ounces each) frozen sweetened sliced strawberries, thawed
- 1 tablespoon lemon juice
- 4 ounces cream cheese, softened
- 1/2 cup confectioners' sugar
- 1 teaspoon vanilla extract
- Dash salt

- 1 cup heavy whipping cream, whipped
- Fresh strawberries and mint, optional

Direction

- Mix butter and cracker crumbs in a small bowl; set 1 tablespoon of the mixture aside for the topping. Press the remaining crumb mixture into an 8-in. square baking dish coated with grease. Bake at 325° till golden brown, 10-14 minutes. Let cool on a wire rack.
- Dissolve gelatin in a large bowl with boiling water; mix in lemon juice and strawberries. Place in the refrigerator for around 1 1/2 hours, or till partially set.
- Beat salt, vanilla, sugar and cream cheese together in a small bowl, till smooth. Stir in whipped cream. Spread half over the cooled crust. Refrigerate the remaining cream mixture, covered.
- Transfer the gelatin mixture over the filling, place in the refrigerator till firm. Transfer the remaining cream mixture on top. Sprinkle the reserved crumb mixture over. Place in the refrigerator for overnight. Use mint and fresh berries for garnish if you want.

Nutrition Information

- Calories: 262 calories
- Protein: 3g protein.
- Total Fat: 13g fat (8g saturated fat)
- Sodium: 164mg sodium
- Fiber: 1g fiber)
- Total Carbohydrate: 36g carbohydrate (29g sugars
- Cholesterol: 39mg cholesterol

---

167. Strawberry Lemon Bavarian

Serving: 6 servings. | Prep: 20mins | Cook: 5mins | Ready in:

Ingredients

- 1 envelope unflavored gelatin
- 3/4 cup cold water
- 1/2 cup thawed lemonade concentrate
- 1 package (10 ounces) frozen sweetened sliced strawberries, thawed
- 1-1/2 teaspoons sugar
- 1 cup heavy whipping cream, whipped
- Fresh strawberries and additional whipped cream, optional

Direction

- Sprinkle cold water in small saucepan with the gelatin; allow to stand for one min. Over low heat, heat while stirring until the gelatin is dissolved completely. Discard from heat; mix in sugar, strawberries and lemonade concentrate.
- Put into a large bowl; refrigerate, covered, for 50 mins or until set partially.
- Fold in the whipped cream. Spoon onto 6 dessert dishes. Refrigerate, covered, until firm, about 120 mins. If desired, decorate with more whipped cream and fresh berries.

Nutrition Information

- Calories: 166 calories
- Sodium: 12mg sodium
- Fiber: 1g fiber)
- Total Carbohydrate: 25g carbohydrate (23g sugars
- Cholesterol: 27mg cholesterol
- Protein: 2g protein.
- Total Fat: 7g fat (5g saturated fat)

168. Strawberry Malted Mousse Cups

Serving: 6 servings. | Prep: 15mins | Cook: 5mins | Ready in:

Ingredients

- 1 package (3 ounces) strawberry gelatin
- 1 tablespoon cornstarch
- 1 cup water
- 1/4 cup malted milk powder
- 1 cup refrigerated French vanilla nondairy creamer
- 1 carton (8 ounces) frozen whipped topping, thawed, divided
- Fresh strawberries and mint, optional

Direction

- Combine water, cornstarch and gelatin in a small saucepan until they become smooth. Boil; cook while stirring the mixture until clear, about 3 to 5 mins. Discard from heat; let cool about 5 mins.
- Combine creamer and malted milk powder in small bowl; stir into the gelatin mixture. Then stir in two cups of the whipped topping. Transfer to 6 dessert dishes by spoon. Let chill until set.
- Dollop with the remaining whipped topping just before serving. If desired, decorate with mint and berries.

Nutrition Information

- Calories:
- Sodium:
- Fiber:
- Total Carbohydrate:
- Cholesterol:
- Protein:
- Total Fat:

169. Strawberry Rice Dessert

Serving: 6 servings. | Prep: 20mins | Cook: 30mins | Ready in:

Ingredients

- 1/2 cup uncooked long grain rice
- 1-3/4 cups cold milk, divided
- 1/2 teaspoon salt
- 1 package unflavored gelatin
- 1/2 cup sugar
- 1 cup heavy whipping cream, whipped
- FILLING:
- 2 packages (10 ounces each) frozen sweetened sliced strawberries, thawed
- 2 tablespoons cornstarch
- 1 tablespoon lemon juice

Direction

- Combine salt, 1 1/2 cups of milk and rice together in a saucepan. Boil while stirring frequently over medium heat. Lower the heat; simmer with a cover till the rice is tender and the liquid is absorbed, 20 minutes.
- Place the remaining milk in a microwave-safe bowl, sprinkle gelatin over; allow to sit for 1 minute. Mix in sugar. Microwave for 45 seconds on high; stir. Allow to sit till the sugar and gelatin are dissolved completely, 1 minute. Combine into the hot rice. Remove into a bowl. Place in the refrigerator for around 1 hour, or till chilled. Fold in whipped cream. Scoop the mixture into a 5-cup ring mold greased with cooking spray. Place in the refrigerator till firm, at least 2 hours.
- Meanwhile, strain strawberries, reserving 1 cup of juice. Combine the reserved strawberry juice and cornstarch together in a saucepan till smooth. Boil the mixture; cook while stirring till thickened, 2 minutes. Take away from the heat; mix in lemon juice. Allow to cool for 10 minutes. Put in the strawberries; stir properly to coat. Place in the refrigerator till chilled. Invert the rice mold onto a serving platter; unmold. Fill the strawberry mixture into the center. Use mint for garnish if you like.

Nutrition Information

- Calories: 293 calories
- Protein: 5g protein.
- Total Fat: 10g fat (6g saturated fat)

- Sodium: 244mg sodium
- Fiber: 1g fiber)
- Total Carbohydrate: 48g carbohydrate (32g sugars
- Cholesterol: 37mg cholesterol

170.   Sugarless Licorice Stars

Serving: 7-9 dozen. | Prep: 15mins | Cook: 0mins |Ready in:

Ingredients

- 2 envelopes unflavored gelatin
- 4 cups diet cherry soda, divided
- 3 packages (.3 ounce each) sugar-free cherry gelatin
- 2 teaspoons anise flavoring

Direction

- Place 1/2 cup of soda in a large bowl, soften in gelatin. Boil the remaining soda in a small saucepan. Take away from the heat; put into the gelatin mixture; stir properly. Mix in the flavored gelatin till dissolved. Put in anise.
- Skim foam if necessary. Transfer into a 13x9-in. pan. Keep chilled till firm. Cut into 1-in. squares with any holiday cutters or a small star-shaped one. Place in the refrigerator for storage.

Nutrition Information

- Calories: 3 calories
- Total Fat: 0 fat (0 saturated fat)
- Sodium: 7mg sodium
- Fiber: 0 fiber)
- Total Carbohydrate: 0 carbohydrate (0 sugars
- Cholesterol: 0 cholesterol
- Protein: 0 protein.

171. Sunny Peaches & Cream Pie

Serving: 8 servings. | Prep: 25mins | Cook: 5mins | Ready in:

Ingredients

- 1-1/4 cups graham cracker crumbs
- 1/4 cup sugar
- 6 tablespoons margarine, melted
- FILLING:
- 4 ounces cream cheese, softened
- 1/2 cup confectioners' sugar
- 1/2 cup frozen whipped topping, thawed
- TOPPING:
- 1 package (3 ounces) peach gelatin
- 1 package (3 ounces) cook-and-serve vanilla pudding mix
- 1-1/4 cups water
- 2 cups sliced peeled fresh peaches or canned sliced peaches

Direction

- Combine cracker crumbs with sugar in a small bowl; mix in margarine. Push up the sides and onto the bottom of an ungreased 9-in. pie pan. Bake for 6-8 minutes at 375° or until browned lightly. Let cool completely on a wire rack.
- To make filling, combine cream cheese with confectioners' sugar in a small bowl until mixed. Fold in whipped topping. Put over crust carefully; chill until firm.
- To make topping, stir gelatin with pudding mix in a small saucepan; mix in water. Heat up just to a boil over medium-low heat, mixing continuously; take off from the heat. Let cool 5 minutes.
- Place peach slices on top of filling. Scoop gelatin mixture on top of peaches. Chill for 4 hours or until cooled.

Nutrition Information

- Calories: 351 calories
- Protein: 3g protein.
- Total Fat: 16g fat (6g saturated fat)
- Sodium: 306mg sodium
- Fiber: 1g fiber)
- Total Carbohydrate: 48g carbohydrate (39g sugars
- Cholesterol: 14mg cholesterol

172. Swedish Creme

Serving: 8 servings. | Prep: 15mins | Cook: 5mins | Ready in:

Ingredients

- 2 cups heavy whipping cream
- 1 cup plus 2 teaspoons sugar, divided
- 1 envelope unflavored gelatin
- 1 teaspoon vanilla extract
- 1 teaspoon almond extract
- 2 cups sour cream
- 1 cup fresh or frozen raspberries

Direction

- Mix cream and a cup sugar in a big saucepan; cook and mix over low heat until a thermometer registers 160° (don't let it boil). Mix in gelatin until dissolved completely.
- Take off from heat; mix in extracts. Let cool 10 minutes. Stir in sour cream. Add to eight 8 dessert dishes. Chill no less than an hour.
- Crush raspberries lightly just before serving; mix in leftover sugar gently. Scoop over tops.

Nutrition Information

- Calories: 440 calories
- Total Carbohydrate: 32g carbohydrate (30g sugars
- Cholesterol: 122mg cholesterol
- Protein: 4g protein.
- Total Fat: 32g fat (21g saturated fat)
- Sodium: 55mg sodium
- Fiber: 1g fiber)

173. Swedish Rice Ring

Serving: 12 servings. | Prep: 15mins | Cook: 20mins | Ready in:

Ingredients

- 2 envelopes unflavored gelatin
- 1/4 cup cold water
- 3 cups whole milk
- 1/2 cup uncooked long-grain rice
- 1/2 cup sugar
- 1/2 teaspoon salt
- 1 cup heavy whipping cream
- Fresh or thawed frozen sweetened strawberries

Direction

- Place cold water in a small bowl; sprinkle gelatin over; set aside. Mix salt, sugar, rice and milk in a small, heavy saucepan; boil while stirring sometimes. Lower the heat; simmer with a cover till the rice is tender, 15-20 minutes. Take away from the heat; mix in the gelatin mixture till dissolved completely. Refrigerate with a cover till partially set.
- Beat cream in a bowl, till it forms stiff peaks. Stir into the chilled rice mixture. Transfer into a 6-cup ring mold oiled with cooking spray; place in the refrigerator for around 3 hours, or till firm. Unmold onto a serving platter. Serve coupled with strawberries.

Nutrition Information

- Calories: 170 calories
- Sodium: 139mg sodium
- Fiber: 0 fiber)
- Total Carbohydrate: 18g carbohydrate (12g sugars
- Cholesterol: 35mg cholesterol
- Protein: 4g protein.
- Total Fat: 9g fat (6g saturated fat)

174. Sweetheart Mousse

Serving: 10-12 servings. | Prep: 30mins | Cook: 0mins | Ready in:

Ingredients

- 2 packages (3 ounces each) cook-and-serve vanilla pudding mix
- 5 cups whole milk, divided
- 1 package (6 ounces) cherry gelatin
- 2 packages (8 ounces each) cream cheese, softened
- Whipped cream and maraschino cherries, optional

Direction

- Follow package directions to cook 4 cups milk and pudding mix in saucepan; take off heat. Sprinkle gelatin; mix till melted completely then cool for 10 minutes.
- Beat leftover milk and cream cheese till smooth in bowl. Add gelatin mixture slowly; stir well. Put in oiled solo molds; refrigerate overnight then unmold; if desired, garnish with cherries and whipped cream.

Nutrition Information

- Calories: 247 calories
- Total Carbohydrate: 29g carbohydrate (27g sugars
- Cholesterol: 42mg cholesterol
- Protein: 7g protein.
- Total Fat: 12g fat (8g saturated fat)
- Sodium: 218mg sodium
- Fiber: 0 fiber)

175. Tangy Citrus Gelatin Cups

Serving: 9 servings. | Prep: 20mins | Cook: 0mins | Ready in:

Ingredients

- 3 cups orange juice, divided
- 1/2 cup unsweetened grapefruit juice
- 2 packages (.3 ounce each) sugar-free orange gelatin
- 1 can (8 ounces) unsweetened crushed pineapple
- 1 envelope whipped topping mix (Dream Whip)
- 1/2 cup fat-free milk
- 1/2 teaspoon vanilla extract

Direction

- Refrigerate 2 cups orange juice. Heat up grapefruit juice and leftover orange juice to a boil in a saucepan or microwave. Mix in gelatin to dissolve. Mix in chilled orange juice. Strain pineapple, saving juice; put pineapple aside. Mix pineapple juice into gelatin mixture. Chill about an hour until set partially. Fold in saved pineapple. Whip vanilla, milk and whipped topping mix in a bowl on low speed until combined. Whip on high for 4 minutes or until hold soft peaks. Fold into gelatin mixture. Split between individual serving plates. Chill about 2 hours until firm.

Nutrition Information

- Calories: 93 calories
- Protein: 2g protein. Diabetic Exchanges: 1 fruit.
- Total Fat: 1g fat (1g saturated fat)
- Sodium: 16mg sodium
- Fiber: 0 fiber)
- Total Carbohydrate: 18g carbohydrate (0 sugars
- Cholesterol: 0 cholesterol

176. Tart Orange Gelatin Salad

Serving: 12 servings. | Prep: 15mins | Cook: 0mins | Ready in:

Ingredients

- 2 packages (.3 ounce each) sugar-free orange gelatin
- Sugar substitute equivalent to 3 tablespoons sugar
- 2 cups boiling water
- 1 can (6 ounces) frozen orange juice concentrate, thawed
- 1 cup cold water
- 1 can (20 ounces) unsweetened pineapple tidbits, drained
- 1 can (11 ounces) mandarin oranges, drained
- 1 cup cold fat-free milk
- 1 package (1 ounce) sugar-free instant vanilla pudding mix
- 1 teaspoon grated lemon peel
- 2 cups reduced-fat whipped topping

Direction

- Dissolve sugar substitute and gelatin in a big bowl with boiling water. Stir in cold water and orange juice concentrate. Put in oranges and pineapple and mix well. Transfer into a 13x9-in dish and chill until set.
- Whisk pudding mix and milk together in a big bowl for 2 minutes. Put in lemon peel, then combine well. Allow to stand until soft-set, about 2 minutes. Fold in whipped topping and pour over gelatin. Chill until set.

Nutrition Information

- Calories: 99 calories
- Sodium: 149mg sodium
- Fiber: 1g fiber)
- Total Carbohydrate: 18g carbohydrate (0 sugars

- Cholesterol: 0 cholesterol
- Protein: 2g protein. Diabetic Exchanges: 1/2 starch
- Total Fat: 1g fat (1g saturated fat)

177. Triple Orange Fluff

Serving: 15 servings. | Prep: 15mins | Cook: 0mins | Ready in:

Ingredients

- 1 package (.3 ounce) sugar-free orange gelatin
- 1 cup boiling water
- 1 pint orange sherbet, softened
- 1 carton (8 ounces) frozen reduced-fat whipped topping, thawed
- 1 prepared angel food cake (8 to 10 ounces), cut into 1-inch pieces
- 1 can (15 ounces) mandarin oranges, drained

Direction

- Dissolve the gelatin powder in a large bowl of boiling water. Mix in sherbet. Place in the refrigerator until set partially. Fold in the whipped topping. Put the cake pieces into a 13x9 inches dish. Top the cake with oranges. Top with the gelatin mixture. Refrigerate, covered, until firm, about 4 hours.

Nutrition Information

- Calories: 0g sugar total.

178. Tropical Island Dessert

Serving: 12-16 servings. | Prep: 30mins | Cook: 0mins | Ready in:

Ingredients

- 3 packages (3 ounces each) berry blue gelatin
- 2 cups boiling water
- 2-1/2 cups cold water
- 4 tablespoons fish-shaped gummy candies, divided
- 2 cups cold milk
- 1 package (3.4 ounces) instant vanilla pudding mix
- 1 medium lime
- 2 cinnamon sticks
- 1 round wooden toothpick
- 2 tablespoons graham cracker crumbs
- 6 whole allspice
- 1 disposable cup (2-ounce size)
- Fresh blueberries and additional gummy candies, optional

Direction

- Dissolve gelatin in boiling water in a bowl. Mix in cold water. Add into a 6-cup ring mold greased with cooking spray. Put in 2 tablespoons of gummy candies. Allow to chill for 60 mins. Mix in the rest of candies. Allow to chill until set, about 1-2 hours.
- Whisk pudding and milk together in a bowl. Cover up and let chill until ready to use.
- To create palm tree leaves, cut lime into two; remove and throw away the pulp. On a cutting board, arrange lime halves with cut side down. Sketch five leaves with a pencil from bottom up to top on each half. Cut out the leaves, leaving the middle intact; create little cuts to form a palm leaf look. To make tree bases, place the disposable cup upside down; make two small slits in the bottom. For tree trunks, put a cinnamon stick in each slits. Break toothpick into two. Add the pointed ends into the middle of lime halves; add the broken ends into cinnamon sticks.
- Unmold the gelatin to place on a serving platter of 12 inches. Put cup in the middle of gelatin ring. With a spoon, add vanilla pudding over cup, filling middle of the ring. For sand, sprinkle with graham cracker crumbs. For coconuts, arrange allspice at the tree bases (remove the allspice before serving).

If desired, garnish with more gummy fish and blueberries.

Nutrition Information

- Calories: 78 calories
- Sodium: 118mg sodium
- Fiber: 0 fiber)
- Total Carbohydrate: 16g carbohydrate (14g sugars
- Cholesterol: 4mg cholesterol
- Protein: 2g protein.
- Total Fat: 1g fat (1g saturated fat)

179. Tropical Rainbow Dessert

Serving: 12 servings. | Prep: 30mins | Cook: 0mins | Ready in:

Ingredients

- 2 packages (3 ounces each) strawberry gelatin, divided
- 5 cups boiling water, divided
- 5 cups cold water, divided
- 1 can (15 ounces) cream of coconut, divided
- 2 packages (3 ounces each) orange gelatin, divided
- 2 packages (3 ounces each) pineapple gelatin, divided
- 2 packages (3 ounces each) lime gelatin, divided

Direction

- In 3/4-cup of boiling water, dissolve a strawberry gelatin package in small bowl. Mix in 3/4-cup of cold water. Distribute between a dozen dessert dishes and chill till firm, or put into one 3-quart gelatin mold greased using cooking spray and chill for 20 to 25 minutes till set yet not firm.

- In half-cup of boiling water, dissolve the leftover strawberry gelatin package in small bowl. Put in scant half cup cream of coconut and half cup of cold water; mix. Scoop on the initial layer. Refrigerate for 20 to 25 minutes till set yet not firm.
- Redo six times, alternate the plain gelatin layers and the creamy gelatin layers. Refrigerate every layer till set yet not firm prior to scooping the next layer over. Chill for 4 hours to overnight. Remove mold to serving platter.

Nutrition Information

- Calories: 345 calories
- Total Fat: 6g fat (5g saturated fat)
- Sodium: 148mg sodium
- Fiber: 0 fiber)
- Total Carbohydrate: 71g carbohydrate (71g sugars
- Cholesterol: 0 cholesterol
- Protein: 5g protein.

180. Tuxedo Cream Dessert

Serving: 6-8 servings. | Prep: 40mins | Cook: 0mins | Ready in:

Ingredients

- 1-3/4 teaspoons unflavored gelatin
- 2 tablespoons cold water
- 1-1/2 cups heavy whipping cream, divided
- 3/4 cup semisweet chocolate chips
- VANILLA LAYER:
- 1-3/4 teaspoons unflavored gelatin
- 2 tablespoons cold water
- 1-2/3 cups heavy whipping cream, divided
- 1/4 cup sugar
- 2 teaspoons vanilla extract
- STRAWBERRY SAUCE:
- 2 cups sliced fresh strawberries
- 2 to 3 tablespoons sugar

Direction

- Scatter gelatin on top of cold water in a small bowl; let sit for a minute. Heat up 1 cup cream to a simmer in a small saucepan. Mix half a cup into gelatin mixture until gelatin is dissolved completely. Mix chocolate chips into leftover warm cream until melted. Mix in gelatin mixture and leftover cream.
- Add to an 8x4-in. loaf pan greased with cooking spray. Chill, covered, for 30 minutes or until set.
- To make vanilla layer, scatter gelatin over cold water in a small bowl; let sit for a minute. Heat up a cup cream and sugar to a simmer in a small saucepan. Mix in gelatin mixture until dissolved completely. Mix in vanilla and leftover cream. Scoop on top of chocolate layer. Chill, covered, for no less than 2 hours or until set.
- To make sauce, blend strawberries with sugar in a blender. Add to a bowl; cover and chill until serving.
- Unmold dessert and slice into slices just before serving. Enjoy with strawberry sauce.

Nutrition Information

- Calories: 455 calories
- Protein: 4g protein.
- Total Fat: 40g fat (25g saturated fat)
- Sodium: 40mg sodium
- Fiber: 2g fiber)
- Total Carbohydrate: 25g carbohydrate (23g sugars
- Cholesterol: 129mg cholesterol

181.　　Valentine Cutouts

Serving: 8-10 servings. | Prep: 45mins | Cook: 0mins | Ready in:

Ingredients

- 2 packages (6 ounces each) cherry or raspberry gelatin
- 2-1/2 cups boiling water
- 1 cup cold milk
- 1 package (3.4 ounces) instant vanilla pudding mix

Direction

- Dissolve gelatin in a bowl with water; set aside for 30 minutes. Whisk pudding mix and milk in a small bowl for around 1 minute, or till smooth. Transfer quickly into the gelatin; whisk till well-blended. Transfer into a greased 13x9-in. dish. Keep chilled till set. Use a heart-shaped cookie cutter to cut or cut into cubes.

Nutrition Information

- Calories: 113 calories
- Total Carbohydrate: 25g carbohydrate (23g sugars
- Cholesterol: 3mg cholesterol
- Protein: 2g protein.
- Total Fat: 1g fat (1g saturated fat)
- Sodium: 187mg sodium
- Fiber: 0 fiber)

182.　　Watermelon Gelatin Cups

Serving: 8 servings. | Prep: 15mins | Cook: 0mins | Ready in:

Ingredients

- 1 package (3 ounces) watermelon gelatin
- 1 cup boiling water
- 1 cup cold water
- 4 large limes
- 1/4 cup miniature chocolate chips

Direction

- Dissolve the gelatin in the boiling water in a small bowl. Add in cold water and stir. Store in the fridge until thicken slightly, for an hour.
- In the meantime, halve the limes along the length. To release the pulp from the shell, cut the membrane at each end using a sharp knife or small scissors. Remove the pulp and membrane from the shell with your fingertips. Reserve the pulp for other use or discard.
- Fold the chocolate chips into the gelatin; then scoop in lime shells. Store in the fridge until set completely, for 2 hours.

Nutrition Information

- Calories: 75 calories
- Sodium: 25mg sodium
- Fiber: 1g fiber)
- Total Carbohydrate: 16g carbohydrate (12g sugars
- Cholesterol: 0 cholesterol
- Protein: 1g protein.
- Total Fat: 2g fat (1g saturated fat)

183. Watermelon Gelatin Dessert

Serving: 12-15 servings. | Prep: 30mins | Cook: 0mins | Ready in:

Ingredients

- 2 packages (3 ounces each) lime gelatin
- 6 cups boiling water, divided
- 1 package (3 ounces) watermelon gelatin
- 1 package (3 ounces) strawberry gelatin
- 2 envelopes unflavored gelatin
- 1/3 cup cold water
- 1-1/2 cups white grape juice
- 1 carton (12 ounces) frozen whipped topping, thawed, divided

Direction

- Dissolve the lime gelatin in 3 cups of boiling water in a large bowl. Pour in an 8-inch square dish greased using cooking spray. Mix strawberry and watermelon gelatins in a different large bowl; add in the rest of boiling water and stir until the gelatin dissolves. Then pour in a different 8-inch square dish coated in cooking spray. Store both dishes in the fridge until the gelatin becomes very firm.
- In the meantime, dust cold water with unflavored gelatin; allow to stand for a minute. Boil grape juice in a small saucepan; add in softened unflavored gelatin and stir. Stir on low heat until the gelatin dissolves. Pour in a large bowl; then store in the fridge until thicken slightly, for 45 minutes. Fold in 2 cups of the whipped topping gently.
- Slice the red gelatin into 1-inch cubes and green gelatin into 1/2-inch cubes. In a large bowl, put 2 cups of the whipped topping mixture; then fold in the green gelatin. Scatter in a 13-by 9-inch dish sprayed with cooking spray. Fold the red gelatin into the rest of whipped topping; scatter on top of the green gelatin layer. Store in the fridge until; set, for 2 hours. Slice into squares.

Nutrition Information

- Calories:
- Total Fat:
- Sodium:
- Fiber:
- Total Carbohydrate:
- Cholesterol:
- Protein:

184. Watermelon Slices

Serving: 16-20 servings. | Prep: 10mins | Cook: 0mins | Ready in:

Ingredients

- 1 package (3 ounces) lime gelatin
- 2 packages (6 ounces each) cherry gelatin
- 2 cups boiling water
- 1 pint vanilla ice cream, softened
- 1/4 cup miniature semisweet chocolate chips

Direction

- Following the package directions, prepare lime gelatin properly. Transfer into a 13x9-in. dish coated with grease; keep chilled till firm slightly.
- Dissolve cherry gelatin in a bowl with boiling water. Stir in ice cream; stir till smooth. Transfer over the lime layer. Sprinkle chocolate chips over; keep chilled till firm. Cut into triangles and serve chilled.

Nutrition Information

- Calories:
- Protein:
- Total Fat:
- Sodium:
- Fiber:
- Total Carbohydrate:
- Cholesterol:

Direction

- Mix the milk, sugar and cream in a small saucepan. Scatter with gelatin; let sit for a minute. Cook over low heat, mixing until gelatin and sugar are dissolved completely. Mix in chocolate until melted.
- Add to 8 4-oz. ramekins greased with cooking spray. Cover and chill for no less than 5 hours or until firm.
- Mix espresso with sugar in a small saucepan. Heat up to a boil; cook until liquid is reducing to a syrup consistency and remains about 1/4 cup. Unmold panna cotta onto dessert platters; sprinkle 1-1/2 teaspoons syrup on each serving.

Nutrition Information

- Calories: 480 calories
- Protein: 4g protein.
- Total Fat: 35g fat (22g saturated fat)
- Sodium: 66mg sodium
- Fiber: 0 fiber)
- Total Carbohydrate: 38g carbohydrate (36g sugars
- Cholesterol: 108mg cholesterol

185. White Chocolate Panna Cotta With Espresso Syrup

Serving: 8 servings. | Prep: 15mins | Cook: 15mins | Ready in:

Ingredients

- 2-1/2 cups heavy whipping cream
- 2/3 cup sugar
- 2/3 cup 2% milk
- 1 envelope unflavored gelatin
- 6 ounces white baking chocolate, chopped
- ESPRESSO SYRUP:
- 3/4 cup brewed espresso
- 1/4 cup sugar

186. White Chocolate Terrine With Caramel Sauce

Serving: 10 servings (1-2/3 cups sauce). | Prep: 20mins | Cook: 25mins | Ready in:

Ingredients

- 2 teaspoons unflavored gelatin
- 1/3 cup bourbon
- 12 ounces white baking chocolate, chopped
- 1/4 cup butter, cubed
- 1-1/2 cups heavy whipping cream, divided
- 1/2 cup chopped pecans
- CARAMEL SAUCE:
- 1/2 cup sugar

- 1 cup butter, cubed
- 1/2 cup heavy whipping cream

Direction

- Use plastic wrap to line an 8x4-in. loaf pan; set aside. Sprinkle gelatin over the top of bourbon and set aside.
- Melt butter and chocolate in a metal bowl or a double boiler over hot water; stir till smooth. Put in the gelatin mixture and 1 cup of cream; mix till the gelatin is dissolved completely. Take away from the heat; let cool slightly. Mix in pecans; refrigerate with a cover for 20 minutes.
- Beat the remaining cream in a small bowl, till it forms stiff peaks. Stir into the cooled chocolate mixture; pour into the prepared pan. Refrigerate with a cover for at least 4 hours or overnight.
- For sauce, spread sugar in a large, heavy saucepan; cook over medium-low heat, without stirring, till it starts to melt. Drag the melted sugar gently to the center of the pan so the sugar melts evenly. Cook for around 25 minutes, without stirring, till the melted sugar becomes a medium amber color. Slowly mix in cream and butter.
- Use plastic wrap to lift terrine; take away from the pan. Remove the plastic. Cut the terrine into 10 slices; serve accompanied with the sauce. Place any leftovers in the refrigerator.

Nutrition Information

- Calories:
- Total Fat:
- Sodium:
- Fiber:
- Total Carbohydrate:
- Cholesterol:
- Protein:

187. Wiggly Pumpkins

Serving: 14-16 servings. | Prep: 45mins | Cook: 0mins | Ready in:

Ingredients

- 2 packages (6 ounces each) orange gelatin
- 2-1/2 cups boiling water
- 1 cup cold milk
- 1 package (3.4 ounces) instant vanilla pudding mix
- Candy corn
- Black licorice and/or gumdrops

Direction

- Mix gelatin in water to dissolve; put aside for half an hour. Stir milk with pudding mix about a minute until smooth. Add to gelatin rapidly; beat until well combined. Add to a greased 13x9-in. dish. Refrigerate until firm. Slice into circles or use a pumpkin-shaped cookie cutter. Place candy eyes and mouths just before serving.

Nutrition Information

- Calories: 71 calories
- Fiber: 0 fiber)
- Total Carbohydrate: 16g carbohydrate (14g sugars
- Cholesterol: 2mg cholesterol
- Protein: 1g protein.
- Total Fat: 1g fat (0 saturated fat)
- Sodium: 117mg sodium

188. Winner's Trophy Dessert

Serving: 8-10 servings. | Prep: 15mins | Cook: 0mins | Ready in:

Ingredients

- 1 package (3 ounces) lemon gelatin

- 2 cups boiling water, divided
- 2 cups vanilla ice cream, softened
- 1 package (3 ounces) orange gelatin
- 1 cup cold water
- 1 can (11 ounces) mandarin oranges, drained

Direction

- Dissolve the lemon gelatin in a bowl with one cup of boiling water. Whisk in the ice cream until they are blended. Transfer to stemmed glasses, about 4-oz.; chill until set, about 120 mins.
- In the remaining boiling water, dissolve the orange gelatin. Stir in oranges and cold water. Chill until set partially, about 120 mins. Spread over lemon layer. Chill until set, about 120 mins.

Nutrition Information

- Calories: 134 calories
- Fiber: 0 fiber)
- Total Carbohydrate: 26g carbohydrate (24g sugars
- Cholesterol: 12mg cholesterol
- Protein: 3g protein.
- Total Fat: 3g fat (2g saturated fat)
- Sodium: 62mg sodium

Chapter 2: Jello Cake Recipes

***

189. Berry Cheesecake Dessert

Serving: 12-15 servings. | Prep: 45mins | Cook: 40mins | Ready in:

Ingredients

- 2-1/4 cups graham cracker crumbs
- 1/2 cup butter, melted
- 2 packages (8 ounces each) cream cheese, softened
- 1 cup sugar
- 3 eggs
- 2 cups (16 ounces) sour cream
- 1 package (3 ounces) strawberry gelatin
- 1 cup boiling water
- 3/4 cup cold water
- 1 quart fresh strawberries, sliced

Direction

- Combine butter and cracker crumbs in a small bowl. Press 1-inch up sides and onto bottom of an oiled 13x9 inches baking dish. Beat sugar and cream cheese in large bowl until they become smooth. Put in eggs and beat until they are just combined on low speed. Put into crust.
- Bake at 350° until middle has almost set, about 30 to 35 mins. Spread the top with the sour cream carefully. Bake for 10 more mins. Place on wire rack to cool.
- In the meantime, dissolve gelatin in a small bowl of boiling water. Stir in the cold water. Place in the refrigerator until thickened yet set, about 45 mins.
- Pour 1/3 gelatin carefully over layer of sour cream. Top gelatin with strawberries; add the remaining gelatin over the berries. Refrigerate, covered, until set, about 4 hours.

Nutrition Information

- Calories: 319 calories
- Sodium: 224mg sodium
- Fiber: 1g fiber)
- Total Carbohydrate: 32g carbohydrate (23g sugars
- Cholesterol: 96mg cholesterol
- Protein: 5g protein.
- Total Fat: 19g fat (11g saturated fat)

190.   Berry Dream Cake

Serving: 15 servings. | Prep: 15mins | Cook: 30mins
| Ready in:

Ingredients

- 1 package white cake mix (regular size)
- 1-1/2 cups boiling water
- 1 package (3 ounces) cherry gelatin
- 1 package (8 ounces) cream cheese, softened
- 2 cups whipped topping
- 4 cups fresh strawberries, coarsely chopped

Direction

- Prepare and bake the cake mix batter following the package instructions, using an oiled 13x9-inch baking pan.
- Put the boiling water into the gelatin in a small bowl. Dissolve completely by stirring for 2 mins. Allow the cake to cool on a wire rack for 3 to 5 mins. Pierce the holes in top of the cake with a wooden skewer to within 1 inch of the edge, gently twisting skewer to create the slightly larger holes. Pour the gelatin over the cake gradually, filling each hole carefully. Let cool for 15 mins. Place in the refrigerator, covered, for half an hour.
- Beat the cream cheese in a large bowl until fluffy. Then fold in the whipped topping. Spread over cake carefully. Place the strawberries on top. Place in the refrigerator, covered, for at least 2 hours before enjoying.

Nutrition Information

- Calories: 306 calories
- Sodium: 315mg sodium
- Fiber: 1g fiber)
- Total Carbohydrate: 37g carbohydrate (22g sugars
- Cholesterol: 54mg cholesterol
- Protein: 5g protein.
- Total Fat: 16g fat (6g saturated fat)

191.   Best Rhubarb Pudding Cake

Serving: 9 servings. | Prep: 15mins | Cook: 55mins
| Ready in:

Ingredients

- 3 to 4 cups diced fresh or frozen rhubarb
- 1 cup all-purpose flour
- 3/4 cup sugar
- 1/3 cup milk
- 3 tablespoons butter, melted
- 1 teaspoon baking powder
- 1/4 teaspoon salt
- 1/4 teaspoon vanilla extract
- TOPPING:
- 1 cup sugar
- 1 tablespoon cornstarch
- 1 cup boiling water
- 1/2 teaspoon ground cinnamon

Direction

- In an oil-coated 8-inch square baking pan, put rhubarb. Combine vanilla, salt, baking powder, butter, milk, sugar, and flour in a small bowl (the mixture should be stiff). Spread over the rhubarb. To prepare the topping, mix together cornstarch and sugar. Sprinkle over the dough. Add water to all without whisking. Sprinkle over the top with cinnamon. Bake at 350° until the pudding tests have done, about 55-65 minutes.

Nutrition Information

- Calories: 253 calories
- Total Fat: 4g fat (3g saturated fat)
- Sodium: 155mg sodium
- Fiber: 1g fiber)
- Total Carbohydrate: 53g carbohydrate (39g sugars

- Cholesterol: 11mg cholesterol
- Protein: 2g protein.

---

192. Blackberry Cake

Serving: 12-16 servings. | Prep: 20mins | Cook: 25mins | Ready in:

Ingredients

- 1 package white cake mix (regular size)
- 1 package (3 ounces) raspberry or black cherry gelatin
- 1 cup canola oil
- 1/2 cup milk
- 4 eggs
- 1 cup fresh or frozen blackberries
- 1 cup sweetened shredded coconut
- 1 cup chopped pecans
- ICING:
- 1/2 cup butter, softened
- 3-3/4 cups confectioners' sugar
- 4 to 5 tablespoons milk
- 1/2 cup fresh or frozen blackberries, crushed
- 1/2 cup sweetened shredded coconut
- 1/2 cup chopped pecans

Direction

- Mix together milk, oil, gelatin and the cake mix in a large bowl, until blended. Crack in eggs, one at a time, beating well after each addition. Mix in the pecans, coconut and blackberries. Pour the mixture into three greased 9-in. round baking pans.
- Put into oven and bake at 350° for 25 to 30 minutes, until a toothpick inserted in the center comes out clean. Allow to cool for 10 minutes before transferring to wire racks to cool completely.
- To make icing, beat butter in a small bowl. Put in sugar and milk; beat until the icing gets expected consistency. Mix in the pecans, coconut and blackberries. Spread between

layers, over the top and sides of cake with icing.

Nutrition Information

- Calories: 590 calories
- Total Fat: 35g fat (10g saturated fat)
- Sodium: 320mg sodium
- Fiber: 3g fiber)
- Total Carbohydrate: 66g carbohydrate (50g sugars
- Cholesterol: 70mg cholesterol
- Protein: 5g protein.

---

193. Blueberry Pudding Cake

Serving: Makes 6 to 8 breakfast or dessert servings | Prep: 15mins | Cook: 50mins | Ready in:

Ingredients

- 1/3 cup plus 1/2 cup sugar
- 1/4 cup water
- 1 tablespoon fresh lemon juice
- 1 teaspoon cornstarch
- 10 oz blueberries (2 cups)
- 1 cup all-purpose flour
- 1 3/4 teaspoons baking powder
- 1 teaspoon salt
- 1 large egg
- 1/2 cup whole milk
- 1 stick (1/2 cup) unsalted butter, melted and cooled slightly
- 1 teaspoon vanilla

Direction

- Preparation: Place an oven rack in the middle position; preheat the oven to 375°F. Coat a 9-in square baking pan with butter.
- In a small saucepan, mix cornstarch, lemon juice, water and 1/3 cup of sugar; combine in blueberries. Simmer while stirring occasionally for 3 minutes. Take away from the heat.

- In a medium bowl, whisk the remaining 1/2 cup of sugar together with salt, baking powder and flour.
- In a large bowl, whisk vanilla, butter, milk and egg; include in the flour mixture; whisk till just combined.
- Using a spoon, transfer the batter into the baking pan, arranging evenly; transfer the blueberry mixture evenly over the batter (the berries will sink). Bake for 25-30 minutes, till a knife comes out clean when inserted into the center of the cake portion. Allow to cool for 5 minutes in the pan on a rack.
- Note: You can make the cake 1 day ahead and let it cool completely; uncover; then, use foil to wrap and keep at room temperature.

Nutrition Information

- Calories: 376
- Saturated Fat: 10 g(52%)
- Sodium: 373 mg(16%)
- Fiber: 2 g(7%)
- Total Carbohydrate: 53 g(18%)
- Cholesterol: 74 mg(25%)
- Protein: 4 g(9%)
- Total Fat: 17 g(26%)

194. Brown Sugar Pudding Cake

Serving: 6-8 servings. | Prep: 20mins | Cook: 40mins | Ready in:

Ingredients

- SAUCE:
- 1 cup packed brown sugar
- 1 tablespoon all-purpose flour
- 2 tablespoons butter, melted
- 1/4 teaspoon salt
- 2 cups boiling water
- PUDDING:
- 2 tablespoons butter, melted

- 1/2 cup packed brown sugar
- 1 cup all-purpose flour
- 1 teaspoon baking powder
- 1/2 teaspoon salt
- 1/2 cup chopped nuts
- 1/2 cup milk

Direction

- Combine all sauce ingredients in a small bowl. Transfer to a 1-1/2-quart baking dish. Put aside.
- Beat sugar and butter in large bowl for pudding. Combine nuts, salt, baking powder and flour; gradually put into the butter mixture alternately with the milk. Transfer to baking dish by spoon. Bake at 350° until a knife inserted in middle comes out clean, about 40 to 45 mins.

Nutrition Information

- Calories: 323 calories
- Protein: 4g protein.
- Total Fat: 11g fat (4g saturated fat)
- Sodium: 353mg sodium
- Fiber: 1g fiber)
- Total Carbohydrate: 54g carbohydrate (41g sugars
- Cholesterol: 17mg cholesterol

195. Cake With Pineapple Pudding

Serving: 6 servings. | Prep: 10mins | Cook: 0mins | Ready in:

Ingredients

- 2 cups cold 2% milk
- 1 package (3.4 ounces) instant French vanilla pudding mix
- 1 can (8 ounces) unsweetened crushed pineapple, drained

- 1 cup whipped topping
- 6 slices angel food cake

Direction

- For 2 minutes, beat the pudding mix and milk in a big bowl and leave it standing until it becomes soft-set for 2 minutes. Mix the whipped topping and pineapple in then keep refrigerated until ready to serve. Enjoy with cake..

Nutrition Information

- Calories: 236 calories
- Fiber: 1g fiber)
- Total Carbohydrate: 43g carbohydrate (21g sugars
- Cholesterol: 8mg cholesterol
- Protein: 4g protein.
- Total Fat: 5g fat (4g saturated fat)
- Sodium: 470mg sodium

196.   Caramel Pudding Cake

Serving: 9 servings. | Prep: 10mins | Cook: 40mins | Ready in:

Ingredients

- 1/2 cup butter, softened
- 1/2 cup sugar
- 1-1/2 cups all-purpose flour
- 1 teaspoon baking powder
- 1/2 teaspoon salt
- 1/2 cup milk
- 1/2 cup raisins
- 1 cup packed brown sugar
- 2 cups cold water

Direction

- Cream the sugar and butter in a small bowl until fluffy and light. Mix the baking powder, flour, and salt; add the flour mixture into the

cream, adding milk. Stir until smooth and add raisins.
- Grease a square 8-inch baking pan and pour in the batter. Mix the brown sugar with the cold water and pour the mixture over batter. Bake for 40 minutes at 350 degrees; the cake should turn golden brown. Serve warm.

Nutrition Information

- Calories: 332 calories
- Protein: 3g protein.
- Total Fat: 11g fat (7g saturated fat)
- Sodium: 296mg sodium
- Fiber: 1g fiber)
- Total Carbohydrate: 58g carbohydrate (41g sugars
- Cholesterol: 29mg cholesterol

197.   Cherry Dream Cake

Serving: 20 servings. | Prep: 15mins | Cook: 30mins | Ready in:

Ingredients

- 1 package white cake mix (regular size)
- 1 package (3 ounces) cherry gelatin
- 1-1/2 cups boiling water
- 1 package (8 ounces) cream cheese, softened
- 2 cups whipped topping
- 1 can (21 ounces) cherry pie filling

Direction

- Following the package directions, prepare cake mix properly, using a 13x9-in. baking pan coated with grease. Bake at 350° till a toothpick comes out clean, 30-35 minutes.
- Dissolve gelatin in boiling water. Let the cake cool for 3-5 minutes on a wire rack. Use a wooden skewer or a meat fork to poke holes in the cake; slowly transfer the gelatin over the cake. Let cool for 15 minutes. Refrigerate with a cover for 30 minutes.

- Beat cream cheese in a large bowl, till fluffy. Stir in whipped topping. Spread carefully over the cake. Transfer the pie filling on top. Refrigerate with a cover before serving, at least 2 hours.

Nutrition Information

- Calories: 164 calories
- Protein: 3g protein. Diabetic Exchanges: 1-1/2 starch
- Total Fat: 4g fat (1g saturated fat)
- Sodium: 251mg sodium
- Fiber: 0 fiber)
- Total Carbohydrate: 28g carbohydrate (0 sugars
- Cholesterol: 1mg cholesterol

---

198. Cherry Pudding Cake

Serving: 12 servings. | Prep: 10mins | Cook: 40mins | Ready in:

Ingredients

- 2 cups all-purpose flour
- 2-1/2 cups sugar, divided
- 4 teaspoons baking powder
- 1 cup whole milk
- 2 tablespoons canola oil
- 2 cans (14-1/2 ounces each) water-packed pitted tart red cherries, well drained
- 2 to 3 drops red food coloring, optional
- 1/8 teaspoon almond extract
- Whipped cream or ice cream, optional

Direction

- Combine oil, milk, baking powder, one cup sugar and flour in a bowl. Transfer to an oiled shallow 3-quart baking dish. Combine remaining sugar, extract, cherries and if desired, food coloring in a bowl; scoop over the batter.

- Bake at 375° until inserted toothpick in the cake portion comes out clean, about 40 to 45 mins. Enjoy warm with the ice cream or whipped cream if desired.

Nutrition Information

- Calories: 296 calories
- Protein: 3g protein.
- Total Fat: 3g fat (1g saturated fat)
- Sodium: 147mg sodium
- Fiber: 1g fiber)
- Total Carbohydrate: 65g carbohydrate (48g sugars
- Cholesterol: 3mg cholesterol

---

199. Chocolate Malt Pudding Cake

Serving: 8 servings. | Prep: 25mins | Cook: 02hours00mins | Ready in:

Ingredients

- 1/2 cup 2% milk
- 2 tablespoons canola oil
- 1/2 teaspoon almond extract
- 1 cup all-purpose flour
- 1/2 cup packed brown sugar
- 2 tablespoons baking cocoa
- 1-1/2 teaspoons baking powder
- 1/2 cup coarsely chopped malted milk balls
- 1/2 cup semisweet chocolate chips
- 3/4 cup sugar
- 1/4 cup malted milk powder
- 1-1/4 cups boiling water
- 4 ounces cream cheese, softened and cubed
- Vanilla ice cream and sliced almonds

Direction

- Mix extract, oil and milk in a large bowl. Mix together baking powder, cocoa, brown sugar and flour; slowly beat into the milk mixture till well-blended. Mix in chocolate chips and milk balls.

- Transfer into a 3-qt. slow cooker coated with grease. Mix milk powder and sugar in a small bowl; mix in cream cheese and water. Pour over the batter (do not combine).
- Cook with a cover on high till a toothpick turns out clean when inserted into the center, about 2-3 hours. Turn off the heat. Allow to sit for 15 minutes. Accompany with ice cream and sprinkle almonds on top to serve.

Nutrition Information

- Calories: 430 calories
- Sodium: 167mg sodium
- Fiber: 2g fiber)
- Total Carbohydrate: 67g carbohydrate (50g sugars
- Cholesterol: 19mg cholesterol
- Protein: 6g protein.
- Total Fat: 17g fat (8g saturated fat)

200.   Chocolate Pudding Cake

Serving: | Prep: 10mins | Cook: 50mins | Ready in:

Ingredients

- 1 1/4 cups Sugar
- 1 cup Flour
- 1/2 cup Cocoa (Hersheys)
- 2 teaspoons Baking Powder
- 1/4 teaspoon Salt
- 1/2 cup Milk
- 1/3 cup Butter (melted)
- 1 1/2 teaspoons Vanilla Extract
- 1/2 cup Brown Sugar (packed)
- 1 1/4 cups Water (hot)
- 1 cup Cool Whip (optional topping)

Direction

- Preparation

- 1. Heat oven beforehand to 350°F. Combine baking powder, salt, 1/4 cup cocoa, 3/4 cup granulated sugar and flour. Mix in vanilla, butter and milk; beat till smooth.
- 2. Spread batter into 9-inch ungreased square baking pan. Mix together the leftover 1/2 cup granulated sugar, brown sugar and the reserved 1/4 cup cocoa; evenly sprinkle them over the batter. Pour hot water atop; don't stir.
- 3. Bake until center is almost set, for about 35 to 40 minutes. Take out of the oven; let sit for 15 minutes. Serve it in dessert dishes, spoon sauce from the pan's bottom over top. Garnish with whipped topping, if you wish. Make 9 (1/2 cup) servings.

Nutrition Information

201.   Chocolate Pudding Cake Cups

Serving: 2 servings. | Prep: 10mins | Cook: 25mins | Ready in:

Ingredients

- 1/2 cup biscuit/baking mix
- 2 tablespoons sugar
- 2 teaspoons baking cocoa
- 3 tablespoons milk
- 1/2 teaspoon vanilla extract
- TOPPING:
- 3 tablespoons brown sugar
- 1 tablespoon baking cocoa
- 1/2 cup boiling water
- Ice cream or whipped cream, optional

Direction

- Mix cocoa, sugar, and baking mix together in a small bowl. Mix in vanilla and milk. Add to 2 greased 8-10-oz. custard cups.

- To prepare the topping: In a bowl, mix together cocoa and brown sugar. Mix in boiling water. Pour on the batter. Bake at 350° until a toothpick will come out clean when you insert it into the middle of the cake layer, about 25 minutes. Put whipped cream or ice cream on top if you want.

Nutrition Information

- Calories: 277 calories
- Sodium: 397mg sodium
- Fiber: 1g fiber)
- Total Carbohydrate: 55g carbohydrate (34g sugars
- Cholesterol: 3mg cholesterol
- Protein: 4g protein.
- Total Fat: 6g fat (2g saturated fat)

202.   Chocolate Pudding Cakes

Serving: Serves 6 | Prep: | Cook: |Ready in:

Ingredients

- 1 1/2 cups (3 sticks) butter
- 3/4 cup water
- 12 ounces semisweet chocolate, chopped
- 1 1/2 cups sugar
- 1 1/2 tablespoons instant coffee crystals or granules
- Pinch of salt
- 3 tablespoons dark rum
- 1 1/2 tablespoons vanilla extract
- 6 large eggs
- Vanilla ice cream (optional)

Direction

- Turn the oven to 350°F to preheat. Coat six custard cups or 1 1/4-cup soufflé dishes with butter. In a big, heavy saucepan, mix together 3/4 cup water and butter over high heat. Boil it, whisking to melt the butter. Take away

from heat. Add salt, coffee, sugar, and chocolate; whisk until the mixture is smooth and the chocolate melts. Mix in vanilla and rum. In a big bowl, whisk eggs to mix; slowly stir in the chocolate mixture.

- Distribute the chocolate mixture between the prepared dishes. Bake for 25 minutes until the cake's edge crack a little but 2-inch in the middle is still glossy and tender. Enjoy the cakes warm, put vanilla ice cream on top if you want.

Nutrition Information

- Calories: 972
- Cholesterol: 308 mg(103%)
- Protein: 9 g(18%)
- Total Fat: 68 g(104%)
- Saturated Fat: 41 g(204%)
- Sodium: 134 mg(6%)
- Fiber: 3 g(13%)
- Total Carbohydrate: 88 g(29%)

203.   Chocolate Covered Cherry Pudding Cake

Serving: 8 servings. | Prep: 20mins | Cook: 02hours00mins |Ready in:

Ingredients

- 1/2 cup reduced-fat sour cream
- 2 tablespoons canola oil
- 1 tablespoon butter, melted
- 2 teaspoons vanilla extract
- 1 cup all-purpose flour
- 1/4 cup sugar
- 1/4 cup packed brown sugar
- 3 tablespoons baking cocoa
- 2 teaspoons baking powder
- 1/2 teaspoon ground cinnamon
- 1/8 teaspoon salt
- 1 cup fresh or frozen pitted dark sweet cherries, thawed

- 1 cup fresh or frozen pitted tart cherries, thawed
- 1/3 cup 60% cacao bittersweet chocolate baking chips
- PUDDING:
- 1/2 cup packed brown sugar
- 2 tablespoons baking cocoa
- 1-1/4 cups hot water

Direction

- Beat vanilla, butter, oil and sour cream in a large bowl until they are blended. Combine salt, cinnamon, baking powder, cocoa, sugars and flour. Put into the sour cream mixture until just combined. Mix in chips and cherries. Transfer to a 3-qt. slow cooker coated with the cooking spray.
- Combine cocoa and brown sugar in a small bowl. Stir in the hot water until they are blended. Pour over batter (but don't stir). Cook, covered, on high for 120-150 mins, until set. Allow to stand about 15 mins. Enjoy warm.

Nutrition Information

- Calories: 291 calories
- Cholesterol: 9mg cholesterol
- Protein: 4g protein.
- Total Fat: 9g fat (3g saturated fat)
- Sodium: 167mg sodium
- Fiber: 2g fiber)
- Total Carbohydrate: 51g carbohydrate (35g sugars

204. Chocolate Pecan Pudding Cakes

Serving: 6 servings. | Prep: 15mins | Cook: 25mins | Ready in:

Ingredients

- 1 cup all-purpose flour
- 2/3 cup sugar
- 6 tablespoons baking cocoa, divided
- 2 teaspoons baking powder
- 1/4 teaspoon salt
- 1/2 cup 2% milk
- 1/4 cup butter, melted
- 1 teaspoon vanilla extract
- 1/2 cup coarsely chopped pecans
- 2/3 cup packed brown sugar
- 3/4 cup hot water
- Whipped cream, optional

Direction

- In a large bowl, mix together salt, baking powder, 3 tablespoons of cocoa, sugar and flour. Mix vanilla, butter and milk; mix into the dry ingredients just till well-combined. Mix in pecans. Using a spoon, transfer to six 6-oz. custard cups coated with grease.
- Mix the remaining cocoa and brown sugar; scatter over the batter. Transfer 2 tablespoons of hot water over each cup. Arrange the cups on a baking sheet.
- Bake at 350° till a toothpick comes out clean when inserted into the cake portion, about 25-30 minutes. Allow to cool for 15 minutes on wire racks. Carefully run a knife around the edge of each cup; invert onto dessert plates. Accompany with whipped cream if you want. Serve warm.

Nutrition Information

- Calories: 418 calories
- Sodium: 329mg sodium
- Fiber: 3g fiber)
- Total Carbohydrate: 67g carbohydrate (47g sugars
- Cholesterol: 23mg cholesterol
- Protein: 5g protein.
- Total Fat: 16g fat (6g saturated fat)

205. Contest Winning Raspberry Chocolate Torte

Serving: 12 servings. | Prep: 40mins | Cook: 20mins | Ready in:

Ingredients

- 1 cup butter, softened
- 2 cups sugar
- 4 eggs
- 1 teaspoon vanilla extract
- 1-1/2 cups all-purpose flour
- 1/3 cup baking cocoa
- GLAZE:
- 1/4 cup boiling water
- 4 teaspoons raspberry gelatin
- 2 tablespoons seedless raspberry jam
- TOPPING:
- 2 cups (12 ounces) semisweet chocolate chips
- 2 cartons (8 ounces each) frozen whipped topping, thawed
- 2 cups fresh raspberries

Direction

- Using waxed paper, line a 15x10x1-in. baking pan coated with grease; then grease the paper. Cream sugar and butter in a large bowl until fluffy and light. Put in eggs, one at a time, while beating thoroughly after each addition. Then beat in vanilla. Combine cocoa and flour; beat slowly into the creamed mixture. Move to the prepared pan.
- Bake for 20-25 minutes at 350°, or until a toothpick put in the middle comes out clean. Let it cool for 5 minutes before transferring onto a wire rack upside down to cool thoroughly. Carefully get rid of the waxed paper.
- To make glaze, stir gelatin and water until gelatin gets dissolved. Stir in jam. Evenly brush over bottom of cake. Trim the edges; slice cake into thirds widthwise.
- To make topping, melt chips in a microwave; stir until it gets smooth. Fold in half of whipped topping until combined; fold in the rest of whipped topping (mixture will become thick).
- Put one cake layer onto a serving platter; spread using 3/4 cup topping. Repeat the layers; put the leftover cake on top. Frost and garnish with the leftover topping and raspberries.

Nutrition Information

- Calories: 614 calories
- Protein: 6g protein.
- Total Fat: 32g fat (21g saturated fat)
- Sodium: 138mg sodium
- Fiber: 4g fiber)
- Total Carbohydrate: 79g carbohydrate (58g sugars
- Cholesterol: 111mg cholesterol

206. Cranberry Orange Cake

Serving: 14 servings. | Prep: 30mins | Cook: 25mins | Ready in:

Ingredients

- 1 package yellow cake mix (regular size)
- 1-1/4 cups mayonnaise
- 4 large eggs
- 1/4 cup orange juice
- FILLING:
- 1/3 cup whole-berry cranberry sauce
- 1/4 cup cranberry juice
- 4 teaspoons cranberry gelatin powder
- 1/2 cup whipped topping
- 1/2 teaspoon grated orange zest
- FROSTING:
- 1 package (8 ounces) cream cheese, softened
- 1 jar (7 ounces) marshmallow creme
- 1/8 teaspoon almond extract
- 1-1/2 cups whipped topping

Direction

- Beat orange juice, eggs, mayonnaise and cake mix till well blended in a big bowl; put into 2 9-in. round greased and floured baking pans.
- Bake for 25-30 minutes at 350° till inserted toothpick in middle exits clean. Cool it for 10 minutes. Transfer from pans onto wire racks; fully cool.
- Filling: Boil juice and cranberry sauce in a big saucepan; mix and cook till blended. Mix in gelatin powder till melted. Slightly cool; put into small bowl. Refrigerate till it starts to thicken for 30 minutes. Fold in orange zest and whipped topping.
- Frosting: Beat cream cheese till fluffy in a big bowl. Add extract and marshmallow crème; beat till smooth. Beat in the whipped topping.
- Put 1 cake layer onto serving plate; spread 1/2 filling. Put leftover cake layer over; spread 2 cups of frosting on sides and top of cake. To within 1-in. from edges, spread leftover filling on top of cake. Pipe leftover frosting around cake's edge. Keep in the fridge.

Nutrition Information

- Calories: 460 calories
- Protein: 4g protein.
- Total Fat: 27g fat (9g saturated fat)
- Sodium: 432mg sodium
- Fiber: 0 fiber)
- Total Carbohydrate: 49g carbohydrate (32g sugars
- Cholesterol: 85mg cholesterol

207.   Date Pudding Cake

Serving: 6-8 servings. | Prep: 25mins | Cook: 45mins | Ready in:

Ingredients

- 1-1/2 cups packed brown sugar, divided
- 3 tablespoons butter, divided
- 1 cup all-purpose flour

- 2 teaspoons baking powder
- 1/2 teaspoon salt
- 1/2 teaspoon ground cinnamon
- 1/2 cup chopped dates
- 1/2 cup chopped pecans
- 1/2 cup milk
- 2 cups water
- Whipped cream or ice cream

Direction

- Whip half cup brown sugar with a tablespoon butter in a bowl. Sift cinnamon, baking powder, salt and flour together; put in nuts and dates. Put flour mixture with milk, alternately, into whipped mixture; put aside.
- Mix water with butter and leftover brown sugar in a saucepan. Heat up to a boil; boil 5 minutes. Add to a 9-in. round baking dish. Scoop batter over sauce. Bake for 45 minutes at 350°. Enjoy cold or warm with ice cream or whipped cream.

Nutrition Information

- Calories: 341 calories
- Sodium: 315mg sodium
- Fiber: 2g fiber)
- Total Carbohydrate: 62g carbohydrate (49g sugars
- Cholesterol: 14mg cholesterol
- Protein: 3g protein.
- Total Fat: 10g fat (3g saturated fat)

208.   Date Pudding Cake Loaf

Serving: 12 servings (1-1/3 cups sauce). | Prep: 20mins | Cook: 45mins | Ready in:

Ingredients

- 1 cup finely chopped dates
- 1 cup boiling water
- 4-1/2 teaspoons shortening

- 1 cup sugar
- 1 large egg
- 1 teaspoon vanilla extract
- 1 cup all-purpose flour
- 1 teaspoon baking soda
- 1/2 teaspoon baking powder
- 1 cup chopped walnuts
- VANILLA SAUCE:
- 1/2 cup sugar
- 1/2 cup packed brown sugar
- 1 tablespoon cornstarch
- 1 cup whole milk
- 1 teaspoon butter
- 1 teaspoon vanilla extract

Direction

- In a small bowl, add the dates; pour in boiling water. Allow to sit for 5 minutes. In the meantime, beat sugar and shortening in a small bowl for 2 minutes until it resembles crumbs. Put in vanilla and egg; stir thoroughly. Mix together baking powder, baking soda and flour; alternately pour into the beaten mixture with water and dates. Fold walnuts into the batter.
- Pour into a 9x5-inch loaf pan coated with grease. Bake in 350-degree oven until a toothpick is clean when pierced into the middle, or about 45 to 55 minutes. Place on a wire rack to cool for 20 minutes.
- Mix together cornstarch and sugars in a small saucepan. Stir in milk, little at a time, until the mixture is smooth. Over medium heat, boil the mixture; cook while stirring until the mixture is thick, or about 2 minutes. Mix in vanilla and butter. Add to cake and serve while still warm.

Nutrition Information

- Calories: 313 calories
- Fiber: 2g fiber)
- Total Carbohydrate: 56g carbohydrate (44g sugars
- Cholesterol: 20mg cholesterol
- Protein: 5g protein.

- Total Fat: 9g fat (1g saturated fat)
- Sodium: 142mg sodium

209.   Double Chocolate Pudding Cake

Serving: 16-20 servings. | Prep: 15mins | Cook: 20mins | Ready in:

Ingredients

- 1 package chocolate cake mix (regular size)
- 1 package (3.4 ounces) instant vanilla pudding mix
- 1 cup chocolate syrup, divided
- 1 carton (12 ounces) frozen whipped topping, thawed
- 1/2 cup chopped pecans

Direction

- Follow instructions on the package to prepare and bake the cake in a greased 13x9-inch baking pan. Place on a wire rack to cool.
- In the meantime, make pudding following the directions on package; transfer to a 13x9-inch dish.
- Tear cake apart into small bits and lightly press down into the pudding. Drizzle 3/4 cup chocolate syrup on top. Frost with whipped topping. Drizzle the rest of chocolate syrup over. Garnish pecans on top. Chill in the refrigerator then serve.

Nutrition Information

- Calories: 235 calories
- Sodium: 238mg sodium
- Fiber: 1g fiber)
- Total Carbohydrate: 39g carbohydrate (26g sugars
- Cholesterol: 0 cholesterol
- Protein: 2g protein.
- Total Fat: 8g fat (4g saturated fat)

210. Elvis' Pudding Cake

Serving: 12 servings. | Prep: 10mins | Cook: 03hours00mins | Ready in:

Ingredients

- 3 cups cold 2% milk
- 1 package (3.4 ounces) instant banana cream pudding mix
- 1 package banana cake mix (regular size)
- 1/2 cup creamy peanut butter
- 2 cups peanut butter chips
- 1 cup chopped dried banana chips

Direction

- Add the pudding mix and milk to a small bowl and stir for 2 minutes. Let it sit for approximately 2 minutes until soft-set. Move to a greased 5 quart slow cooker.
- Follow the directions on the package to prepare the cake mix batter, put in peanut butter then mix. Spread the batter over the pudding. Cover and cook for 3-3 1/2 hrs on low until the toothpick you inserted into the middle comes out with moist crumbs.
- Drizzle peanut butter chips on top then cover and let it sit for 15-20 minutes until partially melted. Add banana chips on top.

Nutrition Information

- Calories: 574 calories
- Fiber: 3g fiber)
- Total Carbohydrate: 67g carbohydrate (44g sugars
- Cholesterol: 57mg cholesterol
- Protein: 14g protein.
- Total Fat: 29g fat (11g saturated fat)
- Sodium: 564mg sodium

211. Favorite Lemon Cheesecake Dessert

Serving: 12 servings (2 cups sauce). | Prep: 25mins | Cook: 30mins | Ready in:

Ingredients

- 2 cups graham cracker crumbs
- 1/4 cup sugar
- 1/2 cup butter, melted
- FILLING:
- 4 packages (8 ounces each) cream cheese, softened
- 1-1/4 cups sugar
- 1 package (3 ounces) lemon gelatin
- 1 teaspoon lemon extract
- 5 eggs, lightly beaten
- LEMON SAUCE:
- 1 package (2.9 ounces) cook-and-serve lemon pudding mix
- 1/4 cup sugar
- 2-1/2 cups cold water

Direction

- Mix butter, sugar and cracker crumbs in a small bowl; press onto bottom and 1-in. up sides of 13x9-in. greased baking dish then refrigerate.
- Beat sugar and cream cheese till smooth in a big bowl. Add lemon extract and dry gelatin; beat for 3 more minutes. Add eggs; beat on low speed till just combined. Pour it into crust.
- Bake it at 325° till center is almost set for 30-40 minutes; cool for 1 hour on wire rack. Cover; refrigerate overnight.
- Mix sugar and pudding mix in a small saucepan; mix in water slowly. Mix and cook on medium heat till it boils. Mix and cook till thickened for 1-2 more minutes. Pour into bowl. Use waxed paper to cover surface; refrigerate till chilled. Serve it with dessert.

Nutrition Information

- Calories: 585 calories

- Cholesterol: 191mg cholesterol
- Protein: 10g protein.
- Total Fat: 37g fat (22g saturated fat)
- Sodium: 442mg sodium
- Fiber: 0 fiber)
- Total Carbohydrate: 54g carbohydrate (43g sugars

212.　　　Flag Cake

Serving: 20 | Prep: 30mins | Cook: | Ready in:

Ingredients

- 1 (10.75 ounce) loaf prepared pound cake, sliced
- 4 cups mixed berry fruit juice
- 4 teaspoons agar-agar powder
- 1 cup sliced fresh strawberries
- 1 cup fresh blueberries
- 1 pint heavy cream
- 1/4 cup honey
- 1/3 cup fresh blueberries
- 3 cups fresh strawberries, halved

Direction

- Cover the bottom of a 9x13-inch pan with cake slices. Pour the fruit juice to a saucepan and scatter the agar-agar over the juice; let soak for 15 minutes. Heat the juice to simmer and stir until the agar-agar is dissolved. Take the pan away from the heat and allow to sit until the juice starts to thicken. Blend 1 cup of blueberries and 1 cup of sliced strawberries into the slightly thickened juice. Spread the fruit and juice mixture over the pound cake slices and allow to sit until the juice is set.
- Whip the heavy cream in a large bowl until foamy and about to form peaks. Whisk in honey until stiff peaks form. Pour the whipped cream over the cake. Spread the blueberries over the whipped cream to make the stars of the flag. Arrange the strawberry halves on the whipped cream to form the stripes of a flag.

Nutrition Information

- Calories: 195 calories;
- Total Fat: 11.9
- Sodium: 72
- Total Carbohydrate: 21.7
- Cholesterol: 66
- Protein: 1.6

213.　　　Flower Garden Cupcakes

Serving: 24 servings | Prep: 15mins | Cook: | Ready in:

Ingredients

- 1 pkg. (2-layer size) white cake mix
- 1 cup boiling water
- 1 pkg. (3 oz.) JELL-O Strawberry Flavor Gelatin
- 1 tub (8 oz.) COOL WHIP Whipped Topping, thawed
- food colorings (assorted colors)
- suggested decorations: JET-PUFFED Marshmallows, colored sugar, small hard candies, BAKER'S ANGEL FLAKE Coconut, JET-PUFFED BUNNY MALLOWS Marshmallows, vanilla wafers, JET-PUFFED Miniature Marshmallows

Direction

- 1. Follow the directions on the package to prepare the cake batter and bake 24 cakes. Let the cakes cool in pans for 10 minutes. Then use a fork to piece the tops.
- 2. Stir the gelatin with boiling water in a small bowl for 2 minutes until completely dissolved. Scoop the mixture over the cupcakes. Put into a refrigerator for half an hour. You can tint the cool whip with food coloring if you want then spread over the cakes.
- 3. You can decorate the cupcakes your ways.

Nutrition Information

- Calories: 180
- Saturated Fat: 2 g
- Fiber: 0 g
- Protein: 2 g
- Total Fat: 4 g
- Sodium: 180 mg
- Sugar: 23 g
- Total Carbohydrate: 33 g
- Cholesterol: 0 mg

---

214. Fluffy Lemon Pudding Cake

Serving: 6 servings. | Prep: 20mins | Cook: 40mins | Ready in:

Ingredients

- 4-1/2 teaspoons butter, softened
- 1 cup sugar
- 1/3 cup lemon juice
- 1 egg yolk
- 3 tablespoons all-purpose flour
- 2 teaspoons grated lemon peel
- 1/4 teaspoon salt
- 1 cup fat-free milk
- 3 egg whites

Direction

- Beat sugar and butter in a big bowl until mixture resembles coarse crumbs. Whisk in salt, lemon peel, lemon juice, flour, and egg yolk until well combined. Whisk in milk in a slow stream. Beat the egg whites in a different big bowl until stiff peaks form then slowly fold into the lemon mixture.
- Add the mixture to an ungreased 1 quart baking dish. Arrange the dish in a 13x9 inch baking dish. Add 1 inch of boiling water to the bigger baking dish.
- Bake for 40-45 minutes at 325° until the top becomes golden and the knife you inserted

into the middle comes out clean. Serve while still warm.

Nutrition Information

- Calories: 205 calories
- Total Carbohydrate: 40g carbohydrate (35g sugars
- Cholesterol: 44mg cholesterol
- Protein: 4g protein. Diabetic Exchanges: 2-1/2 starch.
- Total Fat: 4g fat (2g saturated fat)
- Sodium: 178mg sodium
- Fiber: 0 fiber)

---

215. Frosted Blackberry Cake

Serving: 20 servings. | Prep: 15mins | Cook: 35mins | Ready in:

Ingredients

- 1 package yellow cake mix (regular size)
- 1 package (1 ounce) sugar-free instant vanilla pudding mix
- 1 package (.3 ounce) sugar-free raspberry gelatin
- 2 eggs
- 1/3 cup egg substitute
- 1 jar (10 ounces) seedless blackberry spreadable fruit
- 1/2 cup unsweetened applesauce
- 1/4 cup canola oil
- ICING:
- 1/4 cup butter, softened
- 3 cups confectioners' sugar
- 3 tablespoons fat-free milk

Direction

- Mix gelatin, pudding mix, and cake mix together in a big bowl. Whisk oil, applesauce, spreadable fruit, egg substitute, and eggs together in a small bowl. Mix into the dry ingredients until just moisten.

- Add to a 15x10x1-inch baking pan greased using cooking spray. Bake at 350° until a toothpick will come out clean when you insert it into the middle, about 30-40 minutes. Put on a wire rack to cool.
- Mix the icing ingredients together in a small bowl until smooth. Put on the cooled cake and spread.

Nutrition Information

- Calories: 272 calories
- Total Fat: 8g fat (3g saturated fat)
- Sodium: 270mg sodium
- Fiber: 1g fiber)
- Total Carbohydrate: 48g carbohydrate (35g sugars
- Cholesterol: 27mg cholesterol
- Protein: 3g protein.

216.   Frozen Mini Berry Trifles

Serving: 24 servings. | Prep: 30mins | Cook: 0mins | Ready in:

Ingredients

- 1 package (12 ounces) frozen unsweetened mixed berries, thawed
- 1 cup boiling water
- 1 package (3 ounces) cherry gelatin
- 2 cups butter pecan ice cream, softened if necessary
- 1 loaf (16 ounces) frozen pound cake, thawed and cut into 1/2-inch cubes
- Whipped topping

Direction

- Process berries till pureed, covered, in blended. Mix gelatin and boiling water to completely melt for 2 minutes in small bowl.

- Mix pureed berries and ice cream in till blended; fold cake cubes in. Fill 24 muffin cups to 2/3 full. Freeze till firm for 4 hours, covered.
- 10 minutes before serving, remove from freeze. Run knife around cup sides carefully to loosen; invert them onto serving plates. Serve it with whipped topping.

Nutrition Information

- Calories:
- Total Carbohydrate:
- Cholesterol:
- Protein:
- Total Fat:
- Sodium:
- Fiber:

217.   Fudge Pudding Cake

Serving: 9 servings. | Prep: 15mins | Cook: 30mins | Ready in:

Ingredients

- 3/4 cup sugar
- 1 tablespoon butter, softened
- 1/2 cup milk
- 1 cup all-purpose flour
- 2 tablespoons baking cocoa
- 1 teaspoon baking powder
- 1/4 teaspoon salt
- 1/2 cup chopped walnuts
- TOPPING:
- 1/2 cup sugar
- 1/2 cup packed brown sugar
- 1/4 cup baking cocoa
- 1-1/4 cup boiling water
- Ice cream, optional

Direction

- Beat milk, butter and sugar in a bowl. Mix salt, baking powder, cocoa and flour together; whisk into the sugar mixture. Put in walnuts. Transfer to a 9" square baking pan coated with cooking spray. Mix coca and sugars together to make topping, then add onto the batter. Put all over with water. Do not whisk. Bake for half an hour at 350 degrees. Allow to cool for 10 minutes. Drizzle a little fudge sauce onto each serving, then add ice cream on top as preferred.

Nutrition Information

- Calories: 276 calories
- Cholesterol: 5mg cholesterol
- Protein: 4g protein.
- Total Fat: 6g fat (1g saturated fat)
- Sodium: 135mg sodium
- Fiber: 1g fiber)
- Total Carbohydrate: 54g carbohydrate (40g sugars

---

218. Gingerbread Pudding Cake

Serving: 8 servings. | Prep: 20mins | Cook: 02hours00mins | Ready in:

Ingredients

- 1/2 cup molasses
- 1 cup water
- 1/4 cup butter, softened
- 1/4 cup sugar
- 1 large egg white
- 1 teaspoon vanilla extract
- 1-1/4 cups all-purpose flour
- 3/4 teaspoon baking soda
- 1/4 teaspoon salt
- 1/2 teaspoon ground cinnamon
- 1/2 teaspoon ground ginger
- 1/4 teaspoon ground allspice
- 1/8 teaspoon ground nutmeg

- 1/2 cup chopped pecans
- 6 tablespoons brown sugar
- 3/4 cup hot water
- 2/3 cup butter, melted
- Sweetened whipped cream, optional

Direction

- Mix one cup of the water and molasses. Cream sugar and softened butter until fluffy and light; beat in vanilla and egg white. Whisk spices, salt, baking soda and flour together in another bowl. Put into the creamed mixture alternately with the molasses mixture, beating well before adding the next. Fold in the pecans.
- Transfer to an oiled 3-quart slow cooker. Dust the brown sugar over. Stir melted butter and hot water; pour over batter (but don't stir).
- Cover and cook on high for 2 to 2-1/2 hours or until toothpick inserted in middle comes out clean. Turn the slow cooker off; allow to stand for 15 mins. Enjoy with the whipped cream if desired.

Nutrition Information

- Calories: 431 calories
- Protein: 3g protein.
- Total Fat: 26g fat (14g saturated fat)
- Sodium: 377mg sodium
- Fiber: 1g fiber)
- Total Carbohydrate: 48g carbohydrate (32g sugars
- Cholesterol: 56mg cholesterol

---

219. Glazed Lemon Flute Cake

Serving: 12-16 servings. | Prep: 15mins | Cook: 40mins | Ready in:

Ingredients

- 1 package yellow cake mix (regular size)
- 1 package (3 ounces) lemon gelatin
- 4 eggs
- 2/3 cup water
- 2/3 cup canola oil
- GLAZE:
- 1 cup confectioners' sugar
- 3 tablespoons lemon juice
- 1 teaspoon grated lemon peel

Direction

- Whisk together oil, water, eggs, gelatin and cake mix in a big bowl. On low speed, blend the mixture for 60 seconds. Increase the speed to medium and blend for 2 minutes.
- In a 10-in fluted tube pan already greased and floured, put the batter. Bake at 350 degrees until a toothpick comes out clean when inserted in the cake's center, or about 38 to 42 minutes. Let the cake cool for 10 minutes; take out of the pan and place on a wire rack.
- Mix together ingredients for the glaze, then pour onto the cake while still warm. Allow to cool entirely, then slice the cake.

Nutrition Information

- Calories: 283 calories
- Total Carbohydrate: 38g carbohydrate (26g sugars
- Cholesterol: 53mg cholesterol
- Protein: 4g protein.
- Total Fat: 13g fat (3g saturated fat)
- Sodium: 231mg sodium
- Fiber: 1g fiber)

220.   Golden Lemon Cake

Serving: 8-10 servings. | Prep: 20mins | Cook: 40mins | Ready in:

Ingredients

- 1 package white cake mix (regular size)
- 3/4 cup vegetable oil
- 3/4 cup warm tap water
- 4 large ggs
- 1 package (3 ounces) lemon gelatin
- 1 teaspoon lemon extract
- TANGY CITRUS GLAZE:
- 2/3 cup orange juice
- 3 tablespoons sugar
- 2 tablespoons lemon juice
- 3/4 cup confectioners' sugar

Direction

- To make the cake: In a big bowl, whisk together all the ingredients. On low speed, blend the mixture until moist; increase to medium speed and beat for 2 minutes. Transfer to a 12-cup tube pan already greased and dusted with flour. Bake at 350 degrees until a toothpick comes out clean when inserted in the middle, or about 40 to 50 minutes. Let the cake cool for 10 minutes; remove cake and transfer to a wire rack.
- To make the glaze: Mix all the ingredients in a saucepan, then boil; simmer for 5 minutes. Let cool for no less than 10 minutes. Put a platter below a wire rack. Poke holes in the cake's top with a toothpick; glaze the top and sides of the cake. Let cool entirely, then slice the cake.

Nutrition Information

- Calories: 484 calories
- Total Carbohydrate: 63g carbohydrate (43g sugars
- Cholesterol: 85mg cholesterol
- Protein: 5g protein.
- Total Fat: 23g fat (4g saturated fat)
- Sodium: 373mg sodium
- Fiber: 1g fiber)

221. Grandma Pietz's Cranberry Cake Pudding

Serving: 15 servings (2 cups sauce). | Prep: 30mins | Cook: 20mins | Ready in:

Ingredients

- 3 tablespoons butter, softened
- 1 cup sugar
- 1 large egg
- 2 cups all-purpose flour
- 2 teaspoons baking powder
- Dash salt
- 1 cup 2% milk
- 2 cups fresh or frozen cranberries, thawed
- SAUCE:
- 2 cups packed brown sugar
- 1 cup water
- 1/2 cup sugar
- 3 tablespoons butter
- 1/4 teaspoon vanilla extract

Direction

- Set oven to 350 degrees and start preheating. Coat a 13x9-inch baking pan with grease.
- Beat sugar and butter in a big bowl until forming crumbs. Mix in egg. Stir salt, baking powder and flour in a separate bowl. Pour flour mixture alternately with milk into the butter mixture, beating thoroughly between additions. Chop cranberries into coarse pieces (optional). Fold cranberries into the mixture.
- Pour batter into the greased pan. Bake until a toothpick comes out clean when pierced into the middle, about 20 to 25 minutes.
- Mix together butter, sugar, water and brown sugar in a big saucepan; over medium heat, boil the mixture, whisking continuously until the sugar dissolves. Cook and whisk until the mixture becomes a little thick; mix in vanilla. Serve with cake while still warm.

Nutrition Information

- Calories: 311 calories

- Protein: 3g protein.
- Total Fat: 5g fat (3g saturated fat)
- Sodium: 125mg sodium
- Fiber: 1g fiber)
- Total Carbohydrate: 64g carbohydrate (50g sugars
- Cholesterol: 26mg cholesterol

222. Halloween Poke Cake

Serving: 16 servings | Prep: 20mins | Cook: | Ready in:

Ingredients

- 1 pkg. (2-layer size) white cake mix
- 1 cup boiling water
- 1 pkg. (3 oz.) JELL-O Orange Flavor Gelatin
- 1/2 cup cold water
- 1 tub (8 oz.) COOL WHIP Whipped Topping, thawed
- 1/2 tsp. yellow food coloring
- 1/4 tsp. red food coloring
- 3 Tbsp. Halloween sprinkles

Direction

- 1. Prepare the cake batter. Then bake in 13x9-in. pan following the package directions. Allow the cake to cool in pan for 15 mins. Using large fork, pierce cake at 1/2-in. intervals.
- 2. Pour boiling water into the gelatin mix in the small bowl and stir until dissolved completely, about 2 mins. Mix in the cold water; then pour over the cake. Place in the refrigerator for 3 hours.
- 3. Tint food colorings to the COOL WHIP; spread over the cake. Place in the refrigerator for 60 mins. Decorate with the sprinkles. Then serve immediately.

Nutrition Information

- Calories: 220

- Fiber: 0 g
- Protein: 2 g
- Total Fat: 8 g
- Saturated Fat: 4 g
- Sodium: 230 mg
- Sugar: 22 g
- Total Carbohydrate: 34 g
- Cholesterol: 0 mg

223. Hawaiian Sunset Cake

Serving: 12-16 servings. | Prep: 20mins | Cook: 25mins | Ready in:

Ingredients

- 1 package white or orange cake mix (regular size)
- 1-1/2 cups milk
- 1 package (3.4 ounces) instant vanilla pudding mix
- 1 package (3 ounces) orange gelatin
- 4 large eggs
- 1/2 cup canola oil
- FILLING:
- 1 can (20 ounces) crushed pineapple, drained
- 2 cups sugar
- 3-1/2 cups sweetened shredded coconut (about 10 ounces)
- 1 cup (8 ounces) sour cream
- 1 carton (8 ounces) frozen whipped topping, thawed
- Additional coconut, toasted, optional

Direction

- Mix the first 6 ingredients in a big bowl; whip for 30 seconds on low speed. Whip on medium for 2 minutes.
- Add to 3 greased and floured 9-in. round baking trays. Bake for 25-30 minutes at 350° or until a toothpick inserted exists clean. Let cool for 10 minutes prior to taking out from pans to wire racks to cool completely.

- Mix the sour cream, 3-1/2 cups coconut, sugar and pineapple in a big bowl. Put aside a cup for topping. Put a cake on a serving platter; garnish with 1/3 of the leftover pineapple mixture. Keep layering twice.
- Fold whipped topping into the saved pineapple mixture. Put on top and sides of cake. Scatter with toasted coconut (optional). Chill until serving.

Nutrition Information

- Calories: 548 calories
- Sodium: 384mg sodium
- Fiber: 2g fiber)
- Total Carbohydrate: 80g carbohydrate (61g sugars
- Cholesterol: 66mg cholesterol
- Protein: 5g protein.
- Total Fat: 23g fat (12g saturated fat)

224. Healthy Hot Fudge Pudding Cake

Serving: 9 servings. | Prep: 15mins | Cook: 30mins | Ready in:

Ingredients

- 1 cup all-purpose flour
- 1 cup sugar, divided
- 3 tablespoons plus 1/4 cup baking cocoa, divided
- 2 teaspoons baking powder
- 1/4 teaspoon salt
- 1/2 cup fat-free milk
- 1/3 cup prune baby food
- 1-1/2 teaspoons vanilla extract
- 1/4 cup plus 2 tablespoons packed brown sugar
- 1-1/4 cups boiling water

Direction

- Mix together the salt, 3/4 cup sugar, 3 tablespoons cocoa, baking powder and flour in a large bowl. Combine the vanilla, baby food and milk in a different bowl. Stir them into the dry ingredients just till moisten. Spread it out into an 8-inch square baking dish sprayed using cooking spray.
- Mix together the brown sugar, remaining sugar and cocoa; sprinkle on top of the batter. Add water on top carefully (do not stir). Bake, with no cover, until top is set and edges pull away from the dish's sides, at 350° for 28-32 minutes. Serve while warm.

Nutrition Information

- Calories: 196 calories
- Total Fat: 1g fat (0 saturated fat)
- Sodium: 164mg sodium
- Fiber: 1g fiber)
- Total Carbohydrate: 46g carbohydrate (33g sugars
- Cholesterol: 0 cholesterol
- Protein: 3g protein.

---

225. Healthy Lemon Cake

Serving: 14 servings. | Prep: 15mins | Cook: 35mins | Ready in:

Ingredients

- 1 package yellow cake mix (regular size)
- 1 package (.3 ounce) sugar-free lemon gelatin
- 3/4 cup egg substitute
- 1 can (5-1/2 ounces) apricot nectar
- 1/2 cup unsweetened applesauce
- 2 tablespoons canola oil
- 1 teaspoon lemon extract
- GLAZE:
- 1 cup confectioners' sugar
- 1/4 cup lemon juice

Direction

- Combine the first 7 ingredients in a large bowl. Beat for 2 mins on medium speed. Coat cooking spray over a 10 inches fluted tube pan, dust flour over; put in batter.
- Bake for 35 to 40 mins at 350°, until the toothpick inserted in center comes out clean. Let cool 10 mins. Then remove to a wire rack. Poke the holes in cake with a wooden skewer or meat fork.
- Put 2 tablespoons of confectioners' sugar aside. Combine lemon juice and remaining confectioners' sugar in a small bowl. Pour over the warm cake gradually. Let cool completely. Then dust the reserved confectioners' sugar over.

Nutrition Information

- Calories: 227 calories
- Fiber: 1g fiber)
- Total Carbohydrate: 41g carbohydrate (27g sugars
- Cholesterol: 0 cholesterol
- Protein: 3g protein. Diabetic Exchanges: 2-1/2 starch
- Total Fat: 5g fat (1g saturated fat)
- Sodium: 274mg sodium

---

226. Hot Fudge Pudding Cake

Serving: 9 | Prep: 15mins | Cook: 45mins | Ready in:

Ingredients

- 1 cup all-purpose flour
- 2 teaspoons baking powder
- 3/4 cup white sugar
- 2 tablespoons unsweetened cocoa powder
- 1/4 teaspoon salt
- 1/2 cup milk
- 2 tablespoons butter, melted
- 1 cup chopped walnuts
- 1/4 cup unsweetened cocoa powder
- 1 cup packed brown sugar

- 1 3/4 cups hot water

Direction

- Set oven to preheat at 350°F (175°C).
- Grease a baking pan, 9x9-inch in size.
- Whisk the salt, baking powder, white sugar, 2 tablespoon cocoa powder, and flour together in a large bowl.
- Stir milk and butter into the mix till smooth.
- Fold walnuts into the mixture until just incorporated.
- Evenly spread the batter into the prepared baking pan.
- Mix together brown sugar and 1/4 cup cocoa in a small bowl; sprinkle the mixture over the batter.
- Add hot water over the batter.
- In the preheated oven, bake until the cake's center is nearly set, for about 45 minutes. During baking, the hot water, cocoa, and brown sugar will combine together to create a chocolate sauce then settles to bottom of cake.
- Best served while warm.

Nutrition Information

- Calories: 333 calories;
- Total Carbohydrate: 55.9
- Cholesterol: 8
- Protein: 4.7
- Total Fat: 12.1
- Sodium: 206

227. Lemon Berry Cake

Serving: 16 servings | Prep: 30mins | Cook: | Ready in:

Ingredients

- 1 pkg. (8 oz.) PHILADELPHIA Cream Cheese, softened
- 1 cup butter, softened
- 2-1/2 cups granulated sugar
- 3 Tbsp. lemon juice, divided
- 6 eggs
- 3 cups flour
- 2 cups raspberries, divided
- 3 cups powdered sugar
- 1 Tbsp. water
- 1/2 cup blueberries

Direction

- Line parchment paper in a 9-inch springform pan; coat with cooking spray. In large bowl with mixer, beat butter and cream cheese until mixed. Put in granulated sugar; beat until fluffy and light. Blend in 1 tablespoon lemon juice. Put in egg, individually, beating well after adding egg. Slowly beat in flour until mixed. Put in 1 cup raspberries and fold; spread into prepared pan.
- Bake until a clean toothpick comes out after inserted in the center, about 1 hour 45 minutes. Let cool in pan for 10 minutes. Take out of rim; cool entirely.
- In medium bowl, mix water, the rest of lemon juice and powdered sugar. (Glaze should have a thick consistency). Sprinkle glaze over top of cake, let it run down sides. Add the rest of blueberries and raspberries on top.

Nutrition Information

- Calories: 480
- Saturated Fat: 11 g
- Sodium: 170 mg
- Fiber: 2 g
- Sugar: 53 g
- Protein: 6 g
- Total Carbohydrate: 75 g
- Cholesterol: 120 mg
- Total Fat: 18 g

228. Lemon Blueberry Cheesecake

Serving: 12 servings. | Prep: 30mins | Cook: 0mins | Ready in:

Ingredients

- 1 package (3 ounces) lemon gelatin
- 1 cup boiling water
- 1 cup graham cracker crumbs
- 2 tablespoons butter, melted
- 1 tablespoon canola oil
- 3 cups (24 ounces) fat-free cottage cheese
- 1/4 cup sugar
- TOPPING:
- 2 tablespoons sugar
- 1-1/2 teaspoons cornstarch
- 1/4 cup water
- 1-1/3 cups fresh or frozen blueberries, divided
- 1 teaspoon lemon juice

Direction

- Dissolve gelatin in boiling water in a large bowl. Let cool. In a small bowl, mix oil, butter, and crumbs. Press onto the bottom of a 9-inch springform pan. Let chill.
- In a blender, blend, covered, sugar and cottage cheese until smooth. While blending, slowly put in cooled gelatin. Transfer into crust; cover and leave in the refrigerator overnight.
- To make the topping, in a small saucepan, mix cornstarch and sugar; slowly whisk in water until smooth. Put in 1 cup of blueberries. Heat to a boil; cook and stir for 2 minutes, until thick. Blend in lemon juice; let cool slightly.
- Place on a blender; blend, covered, until smooth. Leave in the refrigerator until chilled.
- Carefully use a knife to run around the edge of pan to loosen the cheesecake; remove the sides of the pan. Spread over the top with the blueberry mixture. Scatter with remaining blueberries. Leave the leftover in the refrigerator.

Nutrition Information

- Calories: 171 calories
- Protein: 8g protein. Diabetic Exchanges: 1-1/2 starch
- Total Fat: 4g fat (1g saturated fat)
- Sodium: 352mg sodium
- Fiber: 1g fiber)
- Total Carbohydrate: 27g carbohydrate (0 sugars
- Cholesterol: 8mg cholesterol

229. Lemon Cake

Serving: 20 | Prep: 15mins | Cook: 28mins | Ready in:

Ingredients

- 1 (18.25 ounce) package yellow cake mix
- 1 (3.4 ounce) package instant lemon pudding mix
- 1 3/4 cups water
- 3 egg whites
- 3/4 cup nonfat milk
- 1/2 teaspoon lemon extract
- 1 (1 ounce) package instant sugar-free vanilla pudding mix
- 1 (8 ounce) container frozen light whipped topping, thawed

Direction

- Preheat an oven to 175°C/350°F. Spray nonstick cooking spray on a 10x15-in. pan.
- Mix pudding mix and cake mix in a big bowl. Add egg whites and water; beat for 1 minute on low speed. Put speed on high; beat for 4 minutes. Put batter in prepped 10x15-in. pan.
- In the preheated oven, bake till an inserted toothpick in middle of cake exits clean for 25-30 minutes; fully cool.
- Beat vanilla pudding mix, lemon extract and milk for 2 minutes on low in a big bowl; fold in whipped topping then spread on cooled cake. Keep cake in the fridge.

Nutrition Information

- Calories: 159 calories;
- Sodium: 310
- Total Carbohydrate: 30
- Cholesterol: < 1
- Protein: 2
- Total Fat: 3.1

Nutrition Information

- Calories: 214 calories
- Sodium: 190mg sodium
- Fiber: 0 fiber)
- Total Carbohydrate: 29g carbohydrate (24g sugars
- Cholesterol: 15mg cholesterol
- Protein: 3g protein.
- Total Fat: 10g fat (4g saturated fat)

230. Lemon Cheesecake Pies

Serving: 4 pies (8 slices each). | Prep: 30mins | Cook: 0mins | Ready in:

Ingredients

- 1 can (12 ounces) evaporated milk
- 2 packages (3 ounces each) lemon gelatin
- 2 cups boiling water
- 1 package (8 ounces) cream cheese, cubed
- 1 tablespoon lemon juice
- 1 cup sugar
- 4 graham cracker crusts (9 inches)
- TOPPING:
- 1 cup graham cracker crumbs
- 1/4 cup butter, melted
- 2 tablespoons sugar

Direction

- Add milk to a big metal bowl. Cover and chill for a minimum of 2 hrs.
- Add boiling water and gelatin to a big bowl and stir until dissolves. Let it cool for 10 minutes. Put in lemon juice and cream cheese and beat until combined. Put aside.
- Whisk the chilled milk until soft peaks form. Slowly put in sugar and whisk in gelatin mixture. Spread over the crusts.
- Mix the topping ingredients and drizzle over pies. Put into a refrigerator until set, for 4 hrs.

231. Lemon Pudding Cake

Serving: Makes 6 servings | Prep: | Cook: | Ready in:

Ingredients

- 2 large lemons
- 1/4 cup all-purpose flour
- Rounded 1/4 teaspoon salt
- 3/4 cup plus 2 tablespoons sugar
- 3 large eggs, separated
- 1 1/3 cups whole milk

Direction

- Set oven to 350°F and start preheating.
- Delicately grate 1 tablespoon zest from lemons, then squeeze one quarter cup plus 2 tablespoons juice.
- In a large bowl, whisk a half cup plus 2 tablespoons sugar, salt, and flour together. In a small bowl, whisk together juice, zest, milk, and yolks and add to flour mixture, whisking until fully blended.
- In another large bowl, beat whites using an electric mixer until they hold soft peaks. Beat in leftover 1/4 cup sugar, a little at a time, and keep beating until whites hold glossy, stiff peaks. Whisk about 1/4 of whites into batter to lighten, then fold in leftover whites gently but thoroughly (batter will be thin).
- Pour into a 1 1/2-quart ceramic gratin or other shallow baking dish greased with butter and

bake in a hot water bath for 45 to 50 minutes until golden and puffed.

- Move to a rack. Serve at room temperature or warm.

Nutrition Information

- Calories: 208
- Cholesterol: 98 mg(33%)
- Protein: 6 g(11%)
- Total Fat: 4 g(7%)
- Saturated Fat: 2 g(9%)
- Sodium: 157 mg(7%)
- Fiber: 1 g(3%)
- Total Carbohydrate: 38 g(13%)

232. Lemon Pudding Cake Cups

Serving: 2 servings. | Prep: 10mins | Cook: 35mins | Ready in:

Ingredients

- 1/3 cup sugar
- 2 tablespoons all-purpose flour
- 1-1/2 teaspoons grated lemon peel
- 1/8 teaspoon salt
- 1/2 cup 2% milk
- 1 egg yolk, lightly beaten
- 2 tablespoons lemon juice
- 1 egg white

Direction

- Mix the first 7 ingredients in a small bowl. Whip egg white until forming stiff peaks in a separate small bowl. Fold into lemon mixture gently.
- Add to two ungreased 6-oz. ramekins or custard tins. Put in a shallow baking pan; pour 1 in. of hot water into dish.
- Bake at 350° for 35-40 minutes, uncovered, or until a thermometer register 170°. Let cool for

10 minutes in water bath before moving cups carefully to a wire rack. Serve warm or chill.

Nutrition Information

- Calories: 230 calories
- Fiber: 0 fiber)
- Total Carbohydrate: 44g carbohydrate (36g sugars
- Cholesterol: 111mg cholesterol
- Protein: 6g protein.
- Total Fat: 4g fat (2g saturated fat)
- Sodium: 210mg sodium

233. Lime Pudding Cakes

Serving: 6 servings. | Prep: 20mins | Cook: 40mins | Ready in:

Ingredients

- 2 tablespoons butter, softened
- 1-1/2 cups sugar
- 1/3 cup all-purpose flour
- 1/4 teaspoon salt
- 1/2 cup lime or lemon juice
- 1 teaspoon grated lime or lemon peel
- 3 large eggs, separated
- 1-1/4 cups 2% milk

Direction

- Beat the sugar and butter in a small bowl until mixture resembles coarse crumbs. Put in lime peel, lime juice, salt, and the flour and stir well. Put in milk and egg yolks and beat until smooth. Beat the egg whites in a different bowl until stiff peaks form. Slowly fold into the batter.
- Add the batter to 6 ungreased 6-ounce custard cups. Arrange the cups in a big baking pan and add 1 inch of boiling water to the pan.
- Bake without covering for 40-45 minutes at 325° until the top becomes golden and the knife you inserted into the middle comes out

clean. Serve while it is still warm or at room temperature.

Nutrition Information

- Calories: 324 calories
- Sodium: 181mg sodium
- Fiber: 0 fiber)
- Total Carbohydrate: 60g carbohydrate (53g sugars
- Cholesterol: 121mg cholesterol
- Protein: 6g protein.
- Total Fat: 8g fat (4g saturated fat)

234. Makeover Strawberry Cake

Serving: 16 servings. | Prep: 20mins | Cook: 20mins | Ready in:

Ingredients

- 1 package white cake mix (regular size)
- 1 package (.3 ounce) sugar-free strawberry gelatin
- 4 egg whites
- 1/3 cup canola oil
- 1 cup frozen unsweetened strawberries, thawed
- 1/2 cup water
- ICING:
- 1/3 cup butter, softened
- 2-1/3 cups confectioners' sugar

Direction

- Use waxed paper to line two 9-inch round baking pans. Use cooking spray to coat the pans and sprinkle flour on top, then put aside. Mix together the gelatin and cake mix in a big bowl, then add oil and egg whites and beat until well combined.
- Mash the strawberries in their juice in a small bowl, then reserve 3 tbsp. for icing. Add

leftover berries and water into the batter, then stir well.

- Pour it into the prepped pans. Let bake for 20 to 25 minutes at 350 degrees, until an inserted toothpick in the middle exits clean. Allow it to cool for 10 minutes prior to taking out from the pans to the wire racks to fully cool.
- To make icing, mix together the reserved strawberries and butter in a small bowl. Slowly beat in the confectioners' sugar until it becomes fluffy and light. On a serving platter, put 1 cake layer, then put 1/2 of the icing on top. Redo the layers.

Nutrition Information

- Calories: 287 calories
- Sodium: 264mg sodium
- Fiber: 0 fiber)
- Total Carbohydrate: 44g carbohydrate (31g sugars
- Cholesterol: 10mg cholesterol
- Protein: 3g protein.
- Total Fat: 11g fat (4g saturated fat)

235. Mamaw Emily's Strawberry Cake

Serving: 12 servings. | Prep: 15mins | Cook: 25mins | Ready in:

Ingredients

- 1 package white cake mix (regular size)
- 1 package (3 ounces) strawberry gelatin
- 3 tablespoons sugar
- 3 tablespoons all-purpose flour
- 1 cup water
- 1/2 cup canola oil
- 2 large eggs
- 1 cup finely chopped strawberries
- FROSTING:
- 1/2 cup butter, softened
- 1/2 cup crushed strawberries

- 4-1/2 to 5 cups confectioners' sugar

Direction

- Start preheating the oven to 350°. Line the parchment papers onto the bottom of 2 greased 8-inch round baking pans then grease the paper.
- Mix the flour, sugar, gelatin and the cake mix in a big bowl. Put in eggs, oil, and water. Beat for half a minute in low speed. Beat for 2 minutes in medium speed. Add chopped strawberries and fold. Pour into the prepared pans.
- Bake until the toothpick you inserted into the middle comes out clean, 25-30 minutes. Let cool in pans for 10 minutes then transfer from pans to wire racks to cool completely. Discard the paper.
- To make the frosting, beat the butter in a small bowl until creamy. Add crushed strawberries and beat. Slowly whisk in an enough amount of the confectioners' sugar until you reach the consistency you want. Spread the frosting between layer and the sides and cover the top of the cake.

Nutrition Information

- Calories: 532 calories
- Protein: 4g protein.
- Total Fat: 21g fat (7g saturated fat)
- Sodium: 340mg sodium
- Fiber: 1g fiber)
- Total Carbohydrate: 85g carbohydrate (69g sugars
- Cholesterol: 51mg cholesterol

---

236. Mardi Gras Cupcakes

Serving: 2 dozen. | Prep: 25mins | Cook: 20mins | Ready in:

Ingredients

- 1 package white cake mix (regular size)
- 1 cup (8 ounces) sour cream
- 2/3 cup canola oil
- 1/3 cup sugar
- 4 large eggs
- 3 tablespoons each lemon, lime and grape gelatin powder
- 1 can (16 ounces) cream cheese frosting
- Purple, green and yellow sprinkles

Direction

- Combine eggs, sugar, oil, sour cream and cake mix together in a large bowl; beat for 30 seconds on low speed. Beat for 2 minutes on medium. Evenly distribute among 3 bowls.
- Mix one flavor of gelatin powder into each bowl till well-blended. Fill a scant 2 tablespoons of each flavored batter into muffin cups lined with paper.
- Bake at 350° till a toothpick comes out clean when inserted into the center, 18-22 minutes. Allow to cool for 10 minutes; take away from pans and let cool completely on wire racks. Use cream cheese frosting to frost. Decorate with sprinkles.

Nutrition Information

- Calories: 301 calories
- Total Fat: 15g fat (4g saturated fat)
- Sodium: 218mg sodium
- Fiber: 0 fiber)
- Total Carbohydrate: 38g carbohydrate (30g sugars
- Cholesterol: 42mg cholesterol
- Protein: 3g protein.

---

237. Marmalade Pudding Cakes

Serving: 8 servings. | Prep: 20mins | Cook: 25mins | Ready in:

Ingredients

- 2 tablespoons butter, softened
- 3/4 cup sugar, divided
- 1/4 cup all-purpose flour
- 4 large eggs, separated
- 1 cup 2% milk
- 1/4 cup orange juice
- 1/4 cup lemon juice, divided
- 1-1/2 teaspoons grated orange zest
- 1/3 cup orange marmalade, warmed

Direction

- Beat half a cup of sugar and butter in a small bowl until mixture resembles coarse crumbs. Whisk in egg yolks and flour until smooth. Whisk in milk, orange juice, 2 tbsp. of lemon juice and orange zest in a slow stream.
- In a different small bowl, put in egg whites and whisk on high speed until soft peaks form. Put in the remaining sugar and whisk until stiff peaks form. Gently fold into the orange mixture.
- Thoroughly coat eight 6-ounce custard cups with cooking spray and pour in the batter. Arrange the cups in two 13x9-inch baking pans and pour 1 inch of boiling water to the pans.
- Bake at 325° until tops of the cakes are golden brown and the knife you inserted into the cakes comes out clean, 25-30 minutes. Run a knife around the edges and gently transfer cakes to dessert plates.
- Mix the remaining lemon juice with the marmalade and sprinkle over the cakes while they are still warm.

Nutrition Information

- Calories: 201 calories
- Cholesterol: 116mg cholesterol
- Protein: 5g protein. Diabetic Exchanges: 2 starch
- Total Fat: 6g fat (3g saturated fat)
- Sodium: 78mg sodium
- Fiber: 0 fiber)

- Total Carbohydrate: 34g carbohydrate (29g sugars

238.   Midsummer Sponge Cake

Serving: 10-12 servings. | Prep: 40mins | Cook: 20mins | Ready in:

Ingredients

- 4 eggs
- 1-1/4 cups sugar
- 1-1/4 cups all-purpose flour
- 2 teaspoons baking powder
- 1/2 cup water
- 1-1/2 cups cold milk
- 1/2 teaspoon vanilla extract
- 1 package (3.4 ounces) instant vanilla pudding mix
- 2 cups whipped topping
- 3 tablespoons lemon gelatin
- 1/2 cup boiling water
- 10 to 12 ribbons with small charms attached
- Assorted fresh fruit

Direction

- Beat eggs in a large bowl till fluffy and light. Slowly beat in sugar till lemon-colored and light. Mix baking powder and flour together; put into the egg mixture together with water, alternately, beating just till smooth. Transfer into a 10-in. springform pan coated with grease and flour.
- Bake at 375° till the cake springs back when touched lightly, 20-25 minutes. Let cool for 1 hour on a wire rack.
- Run a knife carefully around the edge of the pan; remove the sides. Invert onto a wire rack. Take the bottom of the pan away; invert the cake so the top is up. To make the filling, whisk pudding mix, vanilla and milk together in a large bowl till thickened, 2 minutes; keep chilled for 10 minutes. Stir in whipped topping.

- To make glaze, dissolve gelatin in boiling water. Put in enough cold water to measure 1 cup. Keep chilled till thickened slightly, 15 minutes.
- Cut cake horizontally in half. Arrange the bottom layer on a serving plate. Tuck charms under the edge of the cake. Spread over the cake layer with the filling; place fruit and the second cake layer on top. Drizzle with glaze. Keep chilled till serving.

Nutrition Information

- Calories: 261 calories
- Total Fat: 5g fat (3g saturated fat)
- Sodium: 233mg sodium
- Fiber: 0 fiber)
- Total Carbohydrate: 49g carbohydrate (35g sugars
- Cholesterol: 75mg cholesterol
- Protein: 5g protein.

239. Mocha Pudding Cakes

Serving: 2 servings. | Prep: 15mins | Cook: 15mins | Ready in:

Ingredients

- 1/4 cup all-purpose flour
- 3 tablespoons sugar
- 1-1/2 teaspoons baking cocoa
- 1/2 teaspoon baking powder
- 1/8 teaspoon salt
- 3 tablespoons 2% milk
- 1-1/2 teaspoons butter, melted
- 1/4 teaspoon vanilla extract
- TOPPING:
- 2 tablespoons brown sugar
- 1-1/2 teaspoons baking cocoa
- 3 tablespoons hot brewed coffee
- 1 tablespoon hot water
- Whipped topping, optional

Direction

- Combine salt, baking powder, cocoa, sugar and flour together in a small bowl. Mix in vanilla, butter and milk till smooth. Transfer into two 4-oz ramekins greased with cooking spray.
- Mix cocoa and brown sugar; sprinkle over the batter. Mix water and coffee; transfer over the topping. Bake at 350° till a knife comes out clean when inserted into the center, 15-20 minutes. Serve at room temperature or warm, accompanied with whipped topping if you want.

Nutrition Information

- Calories: 227 calories
- Total Carbohydrate: 47g carbohydrate (33g sugars
- Cholesterol: 9mg cholesterol
- Protein: 3g protein.
- Total Fat: 4g fat (2g saturated fat)
- Sodium: 294mg sodium
- Fiber: 1g fiber)

240. No Bake Blueberry Cheesecake

Serving: 4 servings. | Prep: 25mins | Cook: 0mins | Ready in:

Ingredients

- 3/4 cup crushed vanilla wafers (about 22 wafers)
- 2 tablespoons butter, melted
- FILLING:
- 1-1/4 teaspoons unflavored gelatin
- 2 tablespoons cold water
- 1 package (8 ounces) cream cheese, softened
- 1-1/2 teaspoons lemon juice
- 1/2 teaspoon grated lemon zest
- 1 cup marshmallow creme

- 1-1/2 cups whipped topping
- 1 cup fresh or frozen blueberries

Direction

- Mix butter and wafer crumbs together in a small bowl. In a 6-in. springform pan coated with cooking spray, press the mixture onto the bottom; put aside.
- In a small saucepan filled with cold water, sprinkle with gelatin; allow to sit for 1 minute. Heat over low heat, stirring till the gelatin is dissolved completely; allow to cool.
- In a small bowl, add cream cheese; slowly beat in gelatin mixture till smooth. Put in lemon zest and lemon juice. Beat in marshmallow crème; and then fold in whipped topping.
- In a food processor, puree the blueberries; fold into cream cheese mixture. Use a spoon to add the mixture over crust. Cover up and cool in the fridge overnight. Discard sides of pan.

Nutrition Information

- Calories: 523 calories
- Protein: 6g protein.
- Total Fat: 34g fat (21g saturated fat)
- Sodium: 318mg sodium
- Fiber: 1g fiber)
- Total Carbohydrate: 49g carbohydrate (32g sugars
- Cholesterol: 79mg cholesterol

241. No Bake Cheesecake

Serving: | Prep: | Cook: | Ready in:

Ingredients

- 20 sheets Graham crackers
- 2 tablespoons packed brown sugar
- 3/4 stick unsalted butter, melted
- 450 grams cream cheese, at room temperature
- 1 can sweetened condensed milk

- 2 tablespoons freshly squeezed lemon juice
- 1 tablespoon vanilla extract

Direction

- Preparation:
- Create the crust: In a food processor fitted with the blade attachment, put the salt, sugar and graham crackers and pulse into an equal crumb, about 10 pulses. Add in the butter and blend to combine. The mixture should come together in your hand when squeezed.
- Push down the crust into the pan; place the crust mixture into a 9-inch springform pan. Push down the crumbs equally over the bottom and 1 inch up the sides of pan, using a heavy-bottomed cup as necessary to press the mixture into the pan.
- Crust chilling: place in the refrigerator for 10 minutes. In the meantime, make the filling.
- Create the filling: In a large bowl, put the cream cheese and use an electric mixer to beat on medium speed until turn smooth. Put in the vanilla, lemon juice and sweetened condensed milk and keep on beating for about 2 minutes until fully smooth.
- Chill the filling: place the filling into the crust and use an offset spatula to smooth the top. Put in the refrigerator for at least 4 hours, but ideally overnight. Take from the pan and serve: prior serving, take the sides of the springform pan. Slice the cheesecake using a long, thin knife dipped in hot water then dried.

Nutrition Information

242. No Bake Cheesecake Pie

Serving: 8 servings. | Prep: 15mins | Cook: 0mins | Ready in:

Ingredients

- 1 cup white baking chips
- 2 packages (8 ounces each) cream cheese, cubed
- 1 carton (8 ounces) frozen whipped topping, thawed
- 1 graham cracker crust (9 inches)
- 1/3 cup English toffee bits or almond brickle chips

Direction

- Melt chips in a microwave-safe bowl; stir until they become smooth. Mix in the cream cheese until they become smooth. Then fold in the whipped topping. Transfer to the crust.
- Refrigerate overnight, covered, until set. Sprinkle toffee bits over. Then serve.

Nutrition Information

- Calories: 450 calories
- Sodium: 281mg sodium
- Fiber: 0 fiber)
- Total Carbohydrate: 39g carbohydrate (20g sugars
- Cholesterol: 39mg cholesterol
- Protein: 4g protein.
- Total Fat: 30g fat (18g saturated fat)

---

243. No Bake Cherry Cheesecake

Serving: 12 | Prep: | Cook: 40mins | Ready in:

Ingredients

- 4 cups halved pitted sour or sweet cherries, fresh or frozen (thawed, drained; see Tips)
- ¾ cup granulated sugar, divided
- ¼ cup plus 4 teaspoons water, divided
- 2 tablespoons cornstarch
- Half a 14-ounce box graham crackers, preferably whole-wheat
- ½ cup chopped walnuts, toasted (see Tips)

- ⅓ cup canola oil
- 2 8-ounce packages reduced-fat cream cheese (Neufchâtel), softened
- 2 cups nonfat plain or vanilla Greek yogurt
- 6 tablespoons confectioners' sugar
- 1 teaspoon vanilla extract

Direction

- In a large saucepan, bring 1/4 cup water, 1/2 cup sugar, and cherries to a boil. Mix 4 teaspoons water and cornstarch then mix into the cherry mixture; bring back to a boil. Lower the heat to medium and cook for about 1 minute until the liquid appears syrupy and thickens. Take away from the heat.
- Place graham crackers in a food processor and pulse until finely ground. Put in walnuts and process until finely chopped. Place into a bowl; mix in the rest 1/4 cup sugar. Dot with oil and whisk to mix. Transfer to a 9x13-inch baking dish and press into the bottom.
- In a medium bowl, use an electric mixer to whisk vanilla, confectioner's sugar, yogurt and cream cheese until smooth, dragging down the sides as needed. Put over the crust and spread. Scoop the cherry mixture over the top. Keep in the refrigerator, covered, for about 3 hours, until cold.

Nutrition Information

- Calories: 349 calories;
- Saturated Fat: 4
- Protein: 9
- Total Fat: 17
- Sodium: 228
- Fiber: 2
- Cholesterol: 20
- Total Carbohydrate: 42
- Sugar: 29

244. No Bake Chocolate Cheesecake

Serving: 8-10 servings. | Prep: 50mins | Cook: 0mins | Ready in:

Ingredients

- 1 envelope unflavored gelatin
- 1 cup cold milk
- 4 Milky Way candy bars (2.05 ounces each), sliced
- 1-1/2 cups finely crushed chocolate wafers
- 1/4 cup butter, melted
- 2 packages (8 ounces each) cream cheese, softened
- 2 tablespoons sugar
- 1 teaspoon vanilla extract
- 1 cup heavy whipping cream
- Whipped topping and fresh raspberries or fresh strawberries

Direction

- Bloom the gelatin in a big sauce pan by mixing it with milk; set aside for 1 minute. Add the candy bars. Stir until they are melted, and the gelatin is dissolved for about 5 minutes. Then cool for 45 minutes or until room temperature.
- In another bowl, combine wafer crumbs and butter. Grease a 9-inch springform pan, then pour and press the wafer mixture on it to form a crust; set aside.
- Beat the sugar, cream cheese and vanilla in a separate large bowl until smooth. Then add the cream and chocolates mixture. Beat for 4 minutes on high speed. Transfer the mixture onto the prepared crust. Cover and let sit in the refrigerator for at least 8 hours or overnight.
- Slowly run a knife around the edge of the pan to loosen up the sides; unlock and remove the side of the pan. Garnish and serve with whipped topping and berries.

Nutrition Information

- Calories: 327 calories
- Protein: 5g protein.
- Total Fat: 25g fat (15g saturated fat)
- Sodium: 247mg sodium
- Fiber: 1g fiber)
- Total Carbohydrate: 21g carbohydrate (8g sugars
- Cholesterol: 74mg cholesterol

245. No Bake Chocolate Chip Cannoli Cheesecake

Serving: 8 servings. | Prep: 25mins | Cook: 0mins | Ready in:

Ingredients

- 1 package (4 ounces) cannoli shells
- 1/2 cup sugar
- 1/2 cup graham cracker crumbs
- 1/3 cup butter, melted
- FILLING:
- 2 packages (8 ounces each) cream cheese, softened
- 1 cup confectioners' sugar
- 1/2 teaspoon grated orange zest
- 1/4 teaspoon ground cinnamon
- 3/4 cup part-skim ricotta cheese
- 1 teaspoon vanilla extract
- 1/2 teaspoon rum extract
- 1/2 cup miniature semisweet chocolate chips
- Chopped pistachios, optional

Direction

- In a food processor, process cannoli shells until it forms coarse crumbs. Mix in cracker crumbs, sugar and melted butter; Process just until combined. Press down the mixture onto the bottom and sides of a greased 9-in. pie plate. Chill until firm for about 1 hour.
- Combine the first four filling ingredients, beat until combined. Mix in extracts and ricotta cheese. Add in chocolate chips. Spread into crust.

- Cover and place in the refrigerator for about 4 hours until set. Garnish with pistachios if desired.

Nutrition Information

- Calories: 548 calories
- Total Carbohydrate: 51g carbohydrate (38g sugars
- Cholesterol: 88mg cholesterol
- Protein: 8g protein.
- Total Fat: 36g fat (20g saturated fat)
- Sodium: 292mg sodium
- Fiber: 1g fiber)

---

246.   No Bake Lemon Cheesecake

Serving: 8 servings | Prep: 15mins | Cook: | Ready in:

Ingredients

- 1 pkg. (3.4 oz.) JELL-O Lemon Flavor Instant Pudding
- 1-1/4 cups cold milk
- 2 pkg. (8 oz. each) PHILADELPHIA Cream Cheese , softened
- 2 Tbsp. sugar
- 1 tsp. lemon juice
- 1 cup thawed COOL WHIP Whipped Topping
- 1   ready-to-use shortbread pie crust (6 oz.)

Direction

- 1. In medium bowl, beat the milk and pudding mix using whisk for 2 minutes.
- 2. In a large bowl with mixer, beat the lemon juice, sugar and cream cheese until mixed. Put in the pudding gradually, beating well after every addition. Mix in the COOL WHIP gently. Spoon into the crust.
- 3. Refrigerate for 4 hours.

Nutrition Information

- Calories: 400
- Fiber: 0 g
- Sugar: 23 g
- Cholesterol: 80 mg
- Total Carbohydrate: 35 g
- Protein: 6 g
- Total Fat: 26 g
- Saturated Fat: 17 g
- Sodium: 480 mg

---

247.   No Bake Lemon Cheesecake Pie

Serving: 8 servings. | Prep: 20mins | Cook: 0mins | Ready in:

Ingredients

- 2 tablespoons graham cracker crumbs, divided
- 1 package (.3 ounce) sugar-free lemon gelatin
- 2/3 cup boiling water
- 1 package (8 ounces) reduced-fat cream cheese, cubed
- 1 cup (8 ounces) 1% cottage cheese
- 2 cups reduced-fat whipped topping

Direction

- Use cooking spray to coat sides and bottom of 9-in. pie plate. Sprinkle 1 tbsp. cracker crumbs; put aside.
- Dissolve gelatin in boiling water in a small bowl; slightly cool. Put into blender. Add cottage cheese and cream cheese; cover. Process till smooth. Pour into big bowl. Fold in the whipped topping. Put in prepped pie plate; top with leftover cracker crumbs. Cover; refrigerate till set.

Nutrition Information

- Calories: 141 calories
- Fiber: 0 fiber)

- Total Carbohydrate: 9g carbohydrate (4g sugars
- Cholesterol: 21mg cholesterol
- Protein: 7g protein. Diabetic Exchanges: 1-1/2 fat
- Total Fat: 8g fat (6g saturated fat)
- Sodium: 272mg sodium

248.   No Bake Lime Cheesecake

Serving: 12 servings. | Prep: 30mins | Cook: 0mins | Ready in:

Ingredients

- 3 cups graham cracker crumbs
- 2/3 cup sugar
- 2/3 cup butter, melted
- FILLING:
- 2 envelopes unflavored gelatin
- 1 cup lime juice
- 1/4 cup cold water
- 1-1/2 cups sugar
- 5 large eggs, lightly beaten
- 2 teaspoons grated lime zest
- 2 packages (8 ounces each) cream cheese, softened
- 1/2 cup butter, softened
- 1/2 cup heavy whipping cream

Direction

- Mix butter, sugar and graham cracker crumbs in a big bowl; press onto bottom and 2-in. up sides of 9-in. greased springform pan. Cover; refrigerate for at least 30 minutes.
- Sprinkle gelatin over cold water and lime juice in a small saucepan; allow to stand for 1 minute. Mix in lime zest, eggs and sugar; mix and cook on medium heat till it reaches 160°. Take off heat.
- Beat butter and cream cheese till fluffy in a big bowl; beat in gelatin mixture slowly. Cover;

refrigerate, occasionally mixing, till partially set for 45 minutes.
- Beat cream till stiff peaks form in a small bowl; fold into lime mixture. Scoop into crust; cover. Refrigerate till set for 3-4 hours. Remove sides of pan just before serving; refrigerate leftovers.

Nutrition Information

- Calories: 590 calories
- Total Carbohydrate: 56g carbohydrate (44g sugars
- Cholesterol: 190mg cholesterol
- Protein: 8g protein.
- Total Fat: 39g fat (23g saturated fat)
- Sodium: 400mg sodium
- Fiber: 1g fiber)

249.   No Bake Oreo Cheesecake

Serving: 8 servings. | Prep: 40mins | Cook: 0mins | Ready in:

Ingredients

- 24 Oreo cookies, crushed
- 6 tablespoons butter, melted
- FILLING:
- 1 envelope unflavored gelatin
- 1/4 cup cold water
- 1 package (8 ounces) cream cheese, softened
- 1/2 cup sugar
- 3/4 cup 2% milk
- 1 cup whipped topping
- 10 Oreo cookies, coarsely chopped

Direction

- Mix together in a small bowl the butter and crushed cookies. Then push onto bottom of a 9-inch springform pan that is greased. Place inside the refrigerator until ready to use. Drizzle gelatin over cold water in a small saucepan; for 1 minutes let it stand. Stir and heat on low until gelatin fully melts. Let it stand for 5 minutes. Beat sugar and cream cheese in a large bowl until turns smooth; slowly mix in milk. Add in gelatin mixture. Fold in chopped cookies and whipped topping. Place on top of crust. Place inside the refrigerator overnight, covered. Use a knife to loosen sides of cheesecake; detach rim from pan.

Nutrition Information

- Calories: 499 calories
- Protein: 7g protein.
- Total Fat: 30g fat (16g saturated fat)
- Sodium: 374mg sodium
- Fiber: 1g fiber)
- Total Carbohydrate: 53g carbohydrate (37g sugars
- Cholesterol: 53mg cholesterol

250.   No Bake Pumpkin Cheesecake

Serving: 14 | Prep: 30mins | Cook: | Ready in:

Ingredients

- Graham Cracker Crust
- ¾ cup finely crushed graham crackers
- 3 tablespoons canola oil
- 2 tablespoons sugar (see Tips)
- Cheesecake
- 1 (.25 ounce) envelope unflavored gelatin
- ¼ cup water
- ½ (8 ounce) container light cream cheese
- 1 (15 ounce) can pumpkin
- 2 tablespoons sugar (see Tips)
- 1 teaspoon ground cinnamon
- Frozen light whipped dessert topping, thawed (optional)

- Ground cinnamon, chopped toasted pecans, and/or pomegranate seeds (optional; see Tips) (optional)

Direction

- For graham cracker crust: Set the oven to 350°F and start preheating. Combine 2 tablespoons sugar, canola oil and crushed graham crackers in a small bowl. Mix well. Spread in bottom of an 8- or 9-inch springform pan evenly; press onto bottom firmly. Bake for 5 minutes. Rest on a wire rack.
- For cheesecake: Stir water and gelatin together in a small saucepan; allow to rest for 5 minutes to soften. Cook while stirring over low heat until gelatin is dissolved; put aside to cool slightly.
- Using an electric mixer, whisk cream cheese until smooth on medium speed in a large bowl. Add gelatin mixture, a teaspoon cinnamon, sugar and pumpkin; whisk until mixed well. Fold in 3/4 container of dessert topping. Fill mixture into crust in a springform pan. Keep in the fridge, covered, until set or for 4-24 hours.
- Loosen the cheesecake from the side of the springform pan with a table knife or a thin metal spatula. If preferred, remove the cheesecake from the bottom of pan with a wide spatula and transfer to a serving plate. Cut into wedges to serve. If preferred, place additional whipped topping on top. Decorate with chopped pecans, additional cinnamon and/or pomegranate seeds if preferred.

Nutrition Information

- Calories: 150 calories;
- Sodium: 144
- Fiber: 1
- Sugar: 7
- Total Fat: 8
- Saturated Fat: 4
- Cholesterol: 11
- Total Carbohydrate: 14
- Protein: 5

251. No Bake Strawberry Cheesecake Pie

Serving: 6-8 servings. | Prep: 25mins | Cook: 0mins | Ready in:

Ingredients

- 4 ounces cream cheese, softened
- 1/4 cup sugar
- 1/2 cup sour cream
- 1 teaspoon vanilla extract
- 1-3/4 cups whipped topping
- 1 cup strawberry glaze
- 1 graham cracker crust (9 inches)
- 2 pints fresh strawberries, thinly sliced
- Fresh mint and additional strawberries, optional

Direction

- Beat sugar and cream cheese until smooth in a small bowl. Stir in vanilla and sour cream until they are blended. Then fold in the whipped topping.
- Spread over the bottom of crust with 1/2 glaze, then layer with the strawberries. Add the remaining glaze on top. Scoop over the top with the cream cheese mixture. Place in the refrigerator until set, or about 2 to 4 hours. If desired, garnish with more berries and mint.

Nutrition Information

- Calories: 317 calories
- Total Fat: 16g fat (9g saturated fat)
- Sodium: 199mg sodium
- Fiber: 2g fiber)
- Total Carbohydrate: 39g carbohydrate (31g sugars
- Cholesterol: 26mg cholesterol
- Protein: 3g protein.

252. Old Fashioned Rhubarb Pudding Cake

Serving: 9 servings. | Prep: 30mins | Cook: 30mins | Ready in:

Ingredients

- 4 cups diced fresh or frozen rhubarb
- 1-1/2 cups sugar, divided
- 1/4 cup shortening
- 1 egg
- 1/2 teaspoon vanilla extract
- 1 cup all-purpose flour
- 2 teaspoons baking powder
- 1/4 teaspoon salt
- 1/2 cup milk

Direction

- Prepare the oven by preheating to 350 degrees F. Combine together in a large saucepan 1 cup sugar and rhubarb. Cook for 12-15 minutes on medium heat or until rhubarb is soft.
- In the meantime, cream left sugar and shortening in a small bowl until fluffy and light in weight; mix in vanilla and egg. Mix together in a bowl the salt, baking powder and flour; add into the creamed mixture alternately with milk. Whisk well until combined.
- Then place into a 9-inch baking dish that is greased. Put rhubarb mixture on top of batter. Place inside the preheated oven for 30-35 minutes or until used toothpick inserted in the middle comes out clean. Let it cool on wire rack.

Nutrition Information

- Calories: 257 calories
- Sodium: 171mg sodium
- Fiber: 1g fiber)
- Total Carbohydrate: 47g carbohydrate (35g sugars
- Cholesterol: 25mg cholesterol

- Protein: 3g protein.
- Total Fat: 7g fat (2g saturated fat)

253. Orange Angel Food Cake Dessert

Serving: 15 servings. | Prep: 30mins | Cook: 30mins | Ready in:

Ingredients

- 1 package (16 ounces) angel food cake mix
- 1 package (.3 ounce) sugar-free orange gelatin
- 3/4 cup boiling water
- 1/2 cup cold water
- 1-1/2 cups cold fat-free milk
- 1 package (1 ounce) sugar-free instant vanilla pudding mix
- 1 teaspoon orange extract
- 1 carton (8 ounces) frozen reduced-fat whipped topping, thawed
- 1 small navel orange, halved and sliced
- 1/2 cup sliced almonds, toasted

Direction

- Prepare, bake the cake following the package instructions, using an unoiled tube pan, about 10 inches. Invert the tube pan immediately; let cool completely.
- Dissolve gelatin in a small bowl of boiling water; then stir in the cold water. Put aside. Slice the cake into 2-inch slices. Place on an unoiled 13x9 inches dish. Poke holes into cake, using a meat fork, about 2 inches apart. Pour gelatin slowly over cake. Let chill until set.
- Whisk pudding mix and milk for 2 mins in large bowl. Whisk in the extract. Allow to stand until soft-set, about 2 mins. Then fold in the whipped topping and spread over the cake. Decorate with almonds and orange slices. Refrigerate, covered, until serving.

Nutrition Information

- Calories: 184 calories
- Cholesterol: 1mg cholesterol
- Protein: 5g protein. Diabetic Exchanges: 2 starch
- Total Fat: 3g fat (2g saturated fat)
- Sodium: 285mg sodium
- Fiber: 1g fiber)
- Total Carbohydrate: 32g carbohydrate (0 sugars

254. Orange Cream Cake

Serving: 12-15 servings. | Prep: 20mins | Cook: 25mins | Ready in:

Ingredients

- 1 package lemon cake mix (regular size)
- 1 envelope unsweetened orange Kool-Aid mix
- 1 cup water
- 3 eggs
- 1/3 cup vegetable oil
- 2 packages (3 ounces each) orange gelatin, divided
- 1 cup boiling water
- 1 cup cold water
- 1 cup cold milk
- 1 teaspoon vanilla extract
- 1 pacakge (3.4 ounces) instant vanilla pudding mix
- 1 carton (8 ounces) frozen whipped topping, thawed

Direction

- Mix the oil, eggs, water, Kool-Air mix and the cake mix in a big bowl. Beat for half a minute on low speed. Then beat for 2 minutes on medium speed.
- Pour the batter into an ungreased 13x9-inch baking pan. Bake at 350° until the toothpick you inserted into the middle of the cake comes out clean, 25-30 minutes. Poke holes in cake with a wooden skewer or a meat fork. Transfer to a wire rack to cool for half an hour.

- At the same time, add boiling water and one package of gelatin to a big bowl and stir until dissolve. Whisk in cold water and spread the mixture over the cake. Cover and put into a refrigerator for 2 hrs.
- Mix the remaining gelatin, pudding mix, vanilla, and the milk in a big bowl. Whisk the mixture for 2 minutes on low. Let it sit for 5 minutes then add whipped topping and fold. Frost the cake and keep the leftovers in the refrigerator.

Nutrition Information

- Calories:
- Protein:
- Total Fat:
- Sodium:
- Fiber:
- Total Carbohydrate:
- Cholesterol:

---

255. Orange Dream Torte

Serving: 12 servings. | Prep: 20mins | Cook: 0mins | Ready in:

Ingredients

- 1 package (3 ounces) orange gelatin
- 2/3 cup boiling water
- 1/2 cup cold water
- 1 carton (16 ounces) frozen whipped topping, thawed, divided
- 1 package (8 ounces) cream cheese, softened
- 1/4 cup sugar
- 1/4 cup milk
- 1/4 cup graham cracker crumbs
- 1 package (3 ounces) ladyfingers, split
- 1 can (11 ounces) mandarin oranges, drained

Direction

- Melt gelatin in boiling water in big bowl; mix cold water in. Cover; refrigerate till syrupy for 30 minutes.
- Fold 3 cups whipped topping in; put aside. Beat sugar and cream cheese till smooth in a small bowl; beat milk in slowly. Fold leftover whipped topping in.
- Grease the bottom of a 9-in. springform pan; sprinkle with cracker crumbs. Put ladyfingers around pan edges; put 1 1/2 cups orange mixture aside. Alternately spoon leftover orange mixture and cream cheese mixture in pan; spread leftover orange mixture over the top. Refrigerate till set for 1 hour.
- Remove pan sides; garnish with mandarin oranges.

Nutrition Information

- Calories: 193 calories
- Fiber: 0 fiber)
- Total Carbohydrate: 21g carbohydrate (0 sugars
- Cholesterol: 39mg cholesterol
- Protein: 4g protein. Diabetic Exchanges: 2 fat
- Total Fat: 9g fat (7g saturated fat)
- Sodium: 120mg sodium

---

256. Orange Lemon Cake

Serving: 12 servings. | Prep: 15mins | Cook: 35mins | Ready in:

Ingredients

- 1 package lemon cake mix (regular size)
- 1 package (3 ounces) orange gelatin
- 2/3 cup water
- 2/3 cup canola oil
- 4 eggs
- ICING:
- 1 cup confectioners' sugar
- 3 to 4 teaspoons orange juice

Direction

- Mix together eggs, oil, water, gelatin and cake mix in a big bowl; on low speed, beat the mixture for half a minute. Increase to medium speed and blend for 2 minutes. Grease and flour a fluted a tube pan of 10 inches, then put in the batter.
- Bake at 350 degrees until an inserted toothpick is clean when pulled out of the middle, about 35 to 40 minutes. Allow the cake to cool in pan for 10 minutes; transfer to a wire rack and let cool entirely.
- Mix together confectioners' sugar and enough orange juice until reaching wanted consistency. Glaze over the cake.

Nutrition Information

- Calories: 370 calories
- Sodium: 320mg sodium
- Fiber: 0 fiber)
- Total Carbohydrate: 51g carbohydrate (36g sugars
- Cholesterol: 71mg cholesterol
- Protein: 4g protein.
- Total Fat: 17g fat (3g saturated fat)

257.   Ozark Pudding Cake

Serving: 6 servings. | Prep: 15mins | Cook: 20mins | Ready in:

Ingredients

- 2 tablespoons all-purpose flour
- 1-1/4 teaspoons baking powder
- 1/8 teaspoon salt
- 1 egg
- 3/4 cup sugar
- 1 teaspoon vanilla extract
- 1 cup chopped peeled apple
- 1/2 cup chopped walnuts or pecans
- Whipped cream or vanilla ice cream, optional

Direction

- Set the oven to 350° for preheating. Coat a 9 inches deep-dish pie plate with oil.
- Mix salt, baking powder and flour in a small bowl. Beat sugar and egg in another bowl until lemon-colored and thick. Stir in the vanilla, followed by the flour mixture. Then fold in walnuts and apple.
- Put into prepared pie plate. Bake until golden brown, about 20 to 25 mins. (When the cake is removed from oven, it will puff up and fall). While it's still warm, loosen sides from the pie plate with a knife.
- Enjoy warm. Add whipped cream over top, if desired.

Nutrition Information

- Calories:
- Cholesterol:
- Protein:
- Total Fat:
- Sodium:
- Fiber:
- Total Carbohydrate:

258.   Peach Angel Dessert

Serving: 15 servings. | Prep: 20mins | Cook: 0mins | Ready in:

Ingredients

- 3/4 cup sugar
- 2 tablespoons cornstarch
- 1 cup water
- 2 tablespoons corn syrup
- 1/4 cup peach, apricot or orange gelatin powder
- 1 loaf-shaped angel food cake (10-1/2 ounces)
- 1 package (8 ounces) reduced-fat cream cheese
- 2/3 cup confectioners' sugar
- 2 tablespoons fat-free milk

- 1 carton (8 ounces) frozen reduced-fat whipped topping, thawed
- 3 cups sliced peeled fresh or frozen unsweetened sliced peaches, thawed

Direction

- Combine cornstarch and sugar in small saucepan. Whisk in corn syrup and water gradually until they become smooth. Boil. Cook while stirring until thickened, about 1 to 2 mins. Discard from heat; mix in the gelatin until it has dissolved. Let cool to the room temperature, stirring occasionally.
- Slice angel food cake into 9 pieces. Line slices on an unoiled 13x9 inches dish. Put aside. Beat confectioners' sugar and cream cheese in a large bowl until they become smooth. Beat in milk gradually.
- For garnish, put aside 1/3 cup of the whipped topping. Fold the remaining whipped topping into the cream cheese mixture; then spread over the cake. Place peaches on top. Pour the gelatin mixture over the peaches.
- Refrigerate at least 4 hours, covered. Cut into the squares. Place one teaspoon reserved whipped topping on top of each piece. Place the leftovers in refrigerator.

Nutrition Information

- Calories: 215 calories
- Sodium: 157mg sodium
- Fiber: 1g fiber)
- Total Carbohydrate: 40g carbohydrate (0 sugars
- Cholesterol: 9mg cholesterol
- Protein: 3g protein.
- Total Fat: 4g fat (3g saturated fat)

259.   Peach Melba Mountain

Serving: 12-14 servings. | Prep: 30mins | Cook: 35mins | Ready in:

Ingredients

- 1 package (16 ounces) angel food cake mix
- 1 package (3 ounces) peach or orange gelatin
- 1 cup boiling water
- 1 package (8 ounces) cream cheese, softened
- 1 teaspoon almond extract
- 1 carton (12 ounces) frozen whipped topping, thawed
- 1 cup sliced almonds, toasted, divided
- 3 cups sliced peeled fresh peaches
- 3 cups fresh raspberries

Direction

- Prepare and bake the cake following the package instructions with an unoiled 10-in. tube pan. Invert the pan immediately. Let cool completely for 60 mins.
- In the meantime, dissolve the gelatin in a small bowl in boiling water. Then cool. Beat extract and cream cheese in a large bowl, until fluffy. Beat in the gelatin gradually. Fold in 3/4 cup of the almonds and the whipped topping. Place in the refrigerator, covered, for half an hour.
- Run a knife around center tube and side of the pan. Discard the cake.
- Divide the cake into 3 horizontal layers. Arrange the bottom layer on the serving plate; spread with 1/3 cream mixture. Add one cup raspberries and one cup peaches on top. Repeat the layers. Top with the remaining almonds. Let chill for at least half an hour before enjoying. Place the leftovers in refrigerator.

Nutrition Information

- Calories: 336 calories
- Sodium: 301mg sodium
- Fiber: 3g fiber)
- Total Carbohydrate: 47g carbohydrate (35g sugars
- Cholesterol: 18mg cholesterol
- Protein: 7g protein.
- Total Fat: 13g fat (8g saturated fat)

260. Persimmon Pudding Cake

Serving: 12 | Prep: | Cook: | Ready in:

Ingredients

- 3/4 cup white sugar
- 1 cup all-purpose flour
- 1 cup persimmon pulp
- 1 teaspoon baking soda
- 1/2 teaspoon baking powder
- 1/2 teaspoon salt
- 1/2 cup raisins
- 1/2 cup chopped walnuts
- 1/2 cup milk

Direction

- Heat oven to 175 degrees C/350 degrees F. Grease a 9-10-inch bundt pan lightly.
- Mix baking soda and persimmon pulp. Mix in milk, chopped nuts, raisins, salt, baking powder, flour and salt. Stir until combined. Put batter in prepared pan.
- Bake at 175 degrees C/350 degrees F for an hour. Serve with vanilla ice cream or lemon sauce while warm.

Nutrition Information

- Calories: 166 calories;
- Total Fat: 3.6
- Sodium: 227
- Total Carbohydrate: 33
- Cholesterol: < 1
- Protein: 2.5

261. Pineapple Pudding Cake

Serving: 12 | Prep: 30mins | Cook: 30mins | Ready in:

Ingredients

- 1 (3.5 ounce) package instant vanilla pudding mix
- 2 cups milk
- 1 (8 ounce) can crushed pineapple, drained
- 1/2 cup shortening
- 1 1/2 cups white sugar
- 2 eggs
- 2 1/4 cups cake flour
- 2 1/2 teaspoons baking powder
- 1 teaspoon salt
- 1 cup milk
- 1 (8 ounce) container frozen whipped topping, thawed

Direction

- Preheat the oven to 375°F (190°C). Set two nine-inch round cake pans; grease and flour the pans.
- Prepare a pudding using milk, according to the package instructions. Set aside two tablespoons of the pudding, placing the rest in the refrigerator. Once chilled, take off the pudding from the refrigerator, and mix in the pineapple.
- In a large bowl, cream the sugar and shortening, using an electric mixer for 15 minutes on medium speed. Mix in two tablespoons of the reserved vanilla pudding. Beat in the eggs one at a time and combine well after each egg.
- In a separate bowl, combine and sift cake flour, salt and baking powder. Add dry ingredients to the creamed mixture, alternately with a cup of milk. Blend after each addition. Equally divide the batter between the prepared pans.
- Bake for about 20 to 25 minutes, or until having the top springing back when lightly touched. Cool the baking pans on a rack. Then remove the cakes from the baking pans.

- Once the cake layers have cooled completely, top with the pudding mixture on one layer to desired thickness. You may have some left overs. Top with the second layer. Ice the cake with the whipped topping. Refrigerate until ready for serving.

Nutrition Information

- Calories: 413 calories;
- Cholesterol: 36
- Protein: 5.6
- Total Fat: 15.6
- Sodium: 455
- Total Carbohydrate: 63.9

---

262.   Pineapple Upside Down Cake

Serving: 8 | Prep: | Cook: 30mins | Ready in:

Ingredients

- Topping
- 1 tablespoon butter
- 1 tablespoon dark corn syrup
- ½ cup packed light brown sugar
- 1 small pineapple
- 2 tablespoons chopped pecans, or walnuts
- Cake
- ½ cup pecans, or walnuts
- ⅔ cup cake flour
- 1 teaspoon baking powder
- ¼ teaspoon salt
- ¼ teaspoon ground nutmeg
- 2 large egg whites
- ⅔ cup packed light brown sugar, divided
- 2 large eggs
- 1 tablespoon dark rum
- 1 teaspoon vanilla extract

Direction

- Making the topping: Set an oven to preheat to 375 degrees F. Oil a 10-inch cast iron frying pan lightly.
- In the frying pan, heat the corn syrup and butter on medium heat, mixing, until the butter has melted. Take it out of the heat, then sprinkle 1/2 cup of brown sugar on top of the mixture.
- Take off the skin, slice it in quarter and core the pineapple. Slice across into 1/4-inch pieces. Lay out the pineapple on the sugar using the biggest, most uniform slices in slightly overlapping circles. Set aside leftover pineapple for later use. Sprinkle 2 tbsp. of walnuts or pecans around the pineapple, then put aside.
- Making the cake: In a pie pan, spread 1/2 cup pecans or walnuts and let it bake for 5-7 minutes, until it becomes aromatic. Allow it to cool.
- In a food processor, mix together the nutmeg, salt, baking powder, flour and toasted nuts, then process until the nut become coarsely ground.
- In a big bowl, beat the egg whites on medium-high speed using an electric mixer, until it forms soft peaks. Slowly add 1/3 cup of brown sugar and beat it until it becomes glossy and stiff (this will take up to five minutes).
- In a separate bowl, beat the leftover 1/3 cup of brown sugar, vanilla, rum and whole eggs for about 5 minutes on medium-high speed using a mixer, until it becomes pale and thick.
- Whisk 1/4 of the beaten egg whites into the whole-egg mixture and gently fold in half the nut mixture, then the leftover whites, followed by the leftover nut mixture. Spread the batter on top of the pineapple.
- Let the cake bake for 30-35 minutes until an inserted skewer in the middle exits clean and the top bounces back once lightly touched. Allow it to cool in the pan for 10 minutes on a wire rack. Loosen the edges and turn it upside down onto a cake plate and replace any topping that was stuck into the frying pan.

Allow it to cool for 20 more minutes. Serve it at room temperature or warm.

Nutrition Information

- Calories: 327 calories;
- Total Fat: 9
- Cholesterol: 50
- Fiber: 3
- Total Carbohydrate: 59
- Sugar: 45
- Protein: 5
- Saturated Fat: 2
- Sodium: 169

- 4. Right before serving, scatter sugar on top of the cake.

Nutrition Information

- Calories: 230
- Total Fat: 7 g
- Total Carbohydrate: 38 g
- Cholesterol: 60 mg
- Protein: 3 g
- Saturated Fat: 1.5 g
- Sodium: 400 mg
- Fiber: 0 g
- Sugar: 26 g

263. Pistachio Pudding Cake

Serving: 12 servings | Prep: 20mins | Cook: | Ready in:

Ingredients

- 1 pkg. (2-layer size) yellow cake mix
- 1 pkg. (3.4 oz.) JELL-O Pistachio Flavor Instant Pudding
- 4 eggs
- 1-1/4 cups water
- 1/4 cup oil
- 1/2 tsp. almond extract
- 7 drops green food coloring
- 2 Tbsp. powdered sugar

Direction

- 1. Using a mixer, beat together all of the ingredients (except sugar) until combined.
- 2. Grease and flour a 10-inch tube pan or 12-cup fluted tube pan and pour in batter.
- 3. Bake until an inserted toothpick is clean when coming out of the cake middle, about 50-55 minutes. Allow to cool for 10 minutes inside the pan. Use a knife to loosen the cake from the pan's sides. Turn out onto a wire rack and carefully take out the pan. Allow to cool fully.

264. Pool Party Cake

Serving: 12-16 servings. | Prep: 45mins | Cook: 25mins | Ready in:

Ingredients

- 1 package white cake mix (regular size)
- 1 package (3 ounces) berry blue gelatin
- 3/4 cup boiling water
- 1/2 cup cold water
- Ice cubes
- 1 package (8 ounces) cream cheese, softened
- 1/4 cup butter, softened
- 1 teaspoon vanilla extract
- 1/8 teaspoon salt
- 4 cups confectioners' sugar
- 1 piece red shoestring licorice
- 14 Swedish Fish candies
- 5 Peachie-O's candies
- 5 Necco wafer candies, divided
- 2 Air Head candies
- 8 Runts candies
- 1 lollipop stick
- 2 Now and Later candies
- 1 stick spearmint chewing gum
- 1 Life Savers Gummy
- 98 Smarties candies
- 1 Sour Brite Octopus candy

Direction

- Coat two 9-in. round baking pans with grease; use waxed paper to line the pans; grease and flour the paper. Following the package directions, prepare cake batter properly. Transfer into the prepared pans. Bake at 350° till a toothpick comes out clean, 21-26 minutes. Let cool for 10 minutes; take away from the pans and let cool completely on wire racks.
- Dissolve gelatin in a small bowl with boiling water. Transfer cold water into a 2-cup measuring cup; put in enough ice cubes to measure 1 1/4 cups. Put into the gelatin; mix till thickened slightly. Discard any remaining ice. Place in the refrigerator till soft-set, 30 minutes.
- For frosting, beat butter and cream cheese in a large bowl, till smooth. Put in salt and vanilla. Beat in confectioners' sugar till fluffy and smooth. Set 2 tablespoons of the frosting aside for decorating. Lay one cake on a plastic or glass board. Frost the top of the cake with 2/3 cup of the frosting.
- For pool, in the center of the second cake, cut a 5-in. circle (1-in. deep) (reserve the removed cake for another use). Place over the frosted cake. Gradually transfer gelatin into the circle. Frost the sides and top of the cake.
- For ladder, slice licorice into two 4-in. pieces; press gently into the frosting, 1 1/4 in. apart, looping the top ends for handles. Slice three 1 1/4-in. pieces of the licorice for ladle steps; press into the frosting. Use Peachie-O's and Swedish Fish to decorate the sides of the cake.
- For pool steps, attach four wafer candies to board with a small amount of the reserved frosting. Trim two Air Head candies; form into chair shapes; attach Runts to the chairs for legs with the frosting. For table, attach the remaining wafer candy to a lollipop stick; push into the cake. Arrange the chairs on the board and cake.
- For diving board, spread the frosting between two Now and Later candies; attach gum to the top of the candies with the frosting. Slice Life Saver Gummy in half; attach to the sides of the gum. Place on the cake.
- Distribute Smarties on the cake for pool tile. Lay a line of the Smarties on the gelatin to make a buoy rope. Arrange octopus candy in the pool. Place in the refrigerator till the gelatin is set, 1-2 hours.

Nutrition Information

- Calories: 431 calories
- Sodium: 321mg sodium
- Fiber: 0 fiber)
- Total Carbohydrate: 70g carbohydrate (55g sugars
- Cholesterol: 23mg cholesterol
- Protein: 4g protein.
- Total Fat: 16g fat (6g saturated fat)

---

265.   Pudding Pound Cake Dessert

Serving: 9 servings. | Prep: 30mins | Cook: 0mins | Ready in:

Ingredients

- 1 frozen pound cake (10-3/4 ounces), thawed
- 3 cups cold milk
- 2 packages (3.9 ounces each) instant chocolate pudding mix
- 3 cups whipped topping
- 1/2 cup chopped walnuts
- 3/4 cup chopped Oreo cookies

Direction

- Cut the cake horizontally into 4 parts; in an 8 inches square dish, arrange 2 pieces side by side. Whisk pudding mixes and milk in large bowl for 2 mins. Allow to stand until soft-set, about 2 mins. Then fold in the whipped topping.

- Spoon 1/2 over the cake; top with half cup of cookies and walnuts. Layer with the remaining cake and the pudding mixture, then the cookies (the dish will be full). Place in the refrigerator until enjoying.

Nutrition Information

- Calories: 365 calories
- Total Carbohydrate: 43g carbohydrate (27g sugars
- Cholesterol: 59mg cholesterol
- Protein: 7g protein.
- Total Fat: 18g fat (9g saturated fat)
- Sodium: 393mg sodium
- Fiber: 1g fiber)

266.   Pudding Filled Butterfly Cupcakes

Serving: 2 dozen. | Prep: 30mins | Cook: 20mins | Ready in:

Ingredients

- 1 package chocolate cake mix (regular size)
- 1 cup cold milk
- 1 package (3.9 ounces) instant chocolate pudding mix
- 1 carton (8 ounces) frozen whipped topping, thawed
- Pastel sprinkles
- Black shoestring licorice, cut into 2-inch pieces

Direction

- Follow the package instructions to prepare and bake the cake mix for the cupcakes. Let them cool completely before slicing the top fourth of each cupcake off. Divide the slices in half; put aside.
- Whisk the pudding mix with milk in a large bowl for 2 minutes until thick. Fold in the

whipped topping. Drizzle 2 tbsp. of the pudding mixture over each of the cupcakes.
- Put 2 reserved cupcake halves into the pudding mixture, arranging the rounded edges together for the wings. Press the sprinkles gently into the wings. The cupcakes must be moist enough so that the candy will stick. Insert 2 pieces of licorice into each cupcake for the antennae.

Nutrition Information

- Calories:
- Sodium:
- Fiber:
- Total Carbohydrate:
- Cholesterol:
- Protein:
- Total Fat:

267.   Pudding Filled Devil's Food Cake

Serving: 12 servings. | Prep: 50mins | Cook: 30mins | Ready in:

Ingredients

- 4 large egg whites
- 1/2 cup butter, softened
- 1-3/4 cups sugar
- 1 teaspoon vanilla extract
- 2 cups all-purpose flour
- 1/2 cup baking cocoa
- 1/2 teaspoon baking soda
- 1/4 teaspoon salt
- 1 cup water
- PUDDING:
- 1 cup sugar
- 1/4 cup all-purpose flour
- 1/2 teaspoon salt
- 2 cups 2% milk
- 2 large egg yolks, beaten
- 3 ounces unsweetened chocolate, chopped

- 1 tablespoon butter
- 1 teaspoon vanilla extract
- FROSTING:
- 1 cup sugar
- 3 large egg whites
- 3 tablespoons cold water
- 2 tablespoons light corn syrup
- 1/2 teaspoon cream of tartar
- 1/8 teaspoon salt
- 1 teaspoon vanilla extract

Direction

- Stand egg whites for 30 minutes in a big bowl at room temperature. Meanwhile, cream sugar and butter till fluffy and light in a big bowl; beat in vanilla. Mix salt, baking soda, cocoa and flour. Alternately with water, add to creamed mixture; beat well after each.
- Beat egg whites till stiff peaks form with clean beaters; fold into batter. Put in 13x9-in. greased baking pan; bake it at 350° till inserted toothpick in middle exits clean for 30-35 minutes. On wire rack, cool.
- Pudding: Mix salt, flour and sugar in a big heavy saucepan; mix in milk till smooth. Mix and cook on medium high heat till bubbly and thick. Lower heat to low; mix and cook for 2 minutes. Take off heat.
- Mix small hot mixture amount into egg yolks; put all back in pan, constantly mixing. Gently boil; mix and cook for 2 minutes. Take off heat; mix in chocolate till smooth. Mix in vanilla and butter. Cool, occasionally mixing, to room temperature. Spread on cake.
- Mix salt, cream of tartar, corn syrup, water, egg whites and sugar in a big heavy saucepan on low heat; beat on low speed with a hand mixer for 1 minute. Beat on low speed on low heat for 8-10 minutes till frosting reaches 160°.
- Put in big bowl; add vanilla. Beat at high for 7 minutes till stiff peaks form. Spread on cake; keep refrigerated.

Nutrition Information

- Calories: 495 calories

- Total Fat: 14g fat (8g saturated fat)
- Sodium: 342mg sodium
- Fiber: 2g fiber)
- Total Carbohydrate: 88g carbohydrate (66g sugars
- Cholesterol: 60mg cholesterol
- Protein: 8g protein.

268. Rainbow Layer Cake

Serving: | Prep: | Cook: | Ready in:

Ingredients

- 2 pkg. (2-layer size each) white cake mix es, divided
- 3 Tbsp. (1/2 of 3-oz. pkg.) each JELL-O Raspberry Flavor Gelatin, Orange Flavor Gelatin, Lime Flavor Gelatin and Berry Blue Flavor Gelatin, divided
- 2/3 cup BREAKSTONE'S or KNUDSEN Sour Cream
- 2/3 cup powdered sugar
- 1 tub (8 oz.) COOL WHIP Whipped Topping, thawed

Direction

- Set the oven to 350 degrees F. Coat 2 9-in. round pans with grease and flour, then use parchment to cover the bottoms. Following package directions to prepare cake batter from 1 pkg. of cake mix. Transfer each 1/2 of the batter into a separate bowls. Put in batter in one bowl with dry raspberry gelatin mix then combine well. Stir into leftover batter with dry orange gelatin mix. Transfer into the prepped pans.
- Bake until a toothpick stuck in the centers exits clean, about 28-30 minutes. Allow cakes to cool in pans about 15 minutes. Transfer from pans to wire racks and allow to cool thoroughly.
- Do same process with leftover dry gelatin mixes and cake mix, then stir in COOL WHIP

gently. Stack on plate with cake layers while spreading on each cake with 1/3 cup of COOLWHIP prior to covering with the following layer. Use leftover COOLWHIP mixture to frost top as well as side of cake, then chill for 2 hours.

Nutrition Information

- Calories: 280
- Total Carbohydrate: 44 g
- Fiber: 0 g
- Protein: 3 g
- Sodium: 310 mg
- Cholesterol: 5 mg
- Total Fat: 10 g
- Saturated Fat: 4 g
- Sugar: 28 g

---

269.   Raspberry Angel Cake

Serving: 16 | Prep: 20mins | Cook: | Ready in:

Ingredients

- 3 cups boiling water
- 2 (3 ounce) packages JELL-O Raspberry Flavor Gelatin
- 1 (12 ounce) package frozen red raspberries (do not thaw)
- 1 (7.5 ounce) package round angel food cake, cut into 21 thin slices
- 1 cup thawed COOL WHIP Whipped Topping

Direction

- In a medium bowl, add boiling water to gelatin mixes; mix for 2 minutes until fully dissolved. Add in raspberries; mix until melted. Transfer into a 9-inch round pan that is coated with cooking spray.
- Assemble the slices of cake in concentric circles over gelatin, overlapping the slices as needed to fully coat the gelatin.

- Place inside the refrigerator for 3 hours or until the gelatin becomes solid. Transfer onto a plate; put Cool Whip on top.

Nutrition Information

- Calories: 55 calories;
- Cholesterol: 0
- Protein: 1.1
- Total Fat: 0.8
- Sodium: 101
- Total Carbohydrate: 10.7

---

270.   Raspberry Cake

Serving: 12 | Prep: 20mins | Cook: | Ready in:

Ingredients

- Nonstick cooking spray
- 1 cup fresh or frozen raspberries
- 1 cup all-purpose flour
- 1 cup sugar
- 1 teaspoon baking powder
- ¼ cup margarine or butter, melted
- ½ cup refrigerated or frozen egg product, thawed
- 2 teaspoons vanilla
- 1 (8 ounce) container plain fat-free yogurt
- 2 tablespoons all-purpose flour
- 1½ teaspoons finely shredded lemon peel

Direction

- Spray nonstick coating on a 9-inch springform pan. Put aside. If using, thaw the frozen raspberries for 15 mins at room temperature. Then drain the thawed berries.
- Combine baking powder and half cup sugar and 1 cup of the flour in a medium bowl. Put in one teaspoon vanilla, melted butter or margarine and a quarter cup egg product, then stir until combined. Spread the mixture onto

bottom of the prepared pan. Then top with raspberries.

- Combine remaining one teaspoon of vanilla, lemon peel, 2 tablespoons of the flour, the remaining quarter cup of the egg product, the remaining half cup of sugar and yogurt in a medium mixing bowl. Mix until smooth then transfer over the berries.
- Bake for 35 mins at 350°F in the oven, until the middle sets when gently shaken. Place the pan on a wire rack to cool about 15 mins. Loosen and discard the sides of pan, then cool completely. Chill with a cover for 2- 24 hours. Enjoy!

Nutrition Information

- Calories: 164 calories;
- Fiber: 1
- Total Carbohydrate: 28
- Cholesterol: 1
- Protein: 4
- Total Fat: 4
- Saturated Fat: 1
- Sodium: 107

271.   Raspberry Lemon Cake

Serving: 12 | Prep: 25mins | Cook: 25mins | Ready in:

Ingredients

- cooking spray
- 2 tablespoons all-purpose flour
- 1 (15.25 ounce) package white cake mix (such as Duncan Hines®)
- 1 cup water
- 3 egg whites
- 1/4 cup vegetable oil
- 1 (16 ounce) can vanilla frosting
- 1 (8 ounce) container frozen whipped topping, thawed
- 2 lemons, peels grated
- 1 (6 ounce) container fresh raspberries

Direction

- Turn on the oven and preheat it to 350°F (175°C). Spray two eight inch baking pans with cooking spray; lightly sprinkle the sides and bottoms with the flour.
- Combine egg whites, cake mix, oil, and water in a large bowl. Stir the mixture making it well mixed. Pour the batter evenly between two baking pans.
- Bake for 25 to 30 minutes in the preheated oven; check if center-placed toothpick exits clean. Cool off the cake layers on a wire racks directly in pans, about 15 minutes. Take off the cake layers from the pans and allow them to cool completely for about 30 minutes.
- Mix together whipped topping, vanilla frosting, and grated lemon peel in a bowl.
- Put the first cake layer on a serving dish, spread half the frosting over it and top with raspberries. Cover with the second cake layer. Use the remaining frosting to top the cake.

Nutrition Information

- Calories: 419 calories;
- Total Carbohydrate: 59.6
- Cholesterol: 0
- Protein: 2.8
- Total Fat: 19.1
- Sodium: 333

272.   Red, White & Blueberry Poke Cake

Serving: 12 servings. | Prep: 40mins | Cook: 25mins | Ready in:

Ingredients

- 1 package white cake mix (regular size)
- 1-1/4 cups water
- 2 eggs
- 1/4 cup canola oil

- STRAWBERRY GELATIN:
- 1 cup fresh strawberries
- 2/3 cup sugar
- 1/4 cup water
- 2-1/4 teaspoons strawberry gelatin
- BLUEBERRY GELATIN:
- 3/4 cup fresh blueberries
- 1/2 cup water
- 4-1/2 teaspoons sugar
- 4-1/2 teaspoons berry blue gelatin
- FROSTING AND FILLING:
- 2-1/2 cups heavy whipping cream
- 1/3 cup confectioners' sugar

Direction

- Set oven to 350° to preheat. Line bottoms of two 9-in. round baking dishes using parchment or waxed paper; spray paper with cooking spray. Mix oil, eggs, water and cake mix in a big bowl; whip on low speed half a minute. Whip on medium 2 minutes.
- Turn to lined pans. Bake 25-30 minutes or until a toothpick inserted exists clean. Let cool completely in pans on wire racks.
- To make strawberry gelatin, mix water, sugar and strawberries in a small saucepan; heat up to a boil. Turn down heat; simmer with no cover, 2-3 minutes or until berries soften. Drain into a small bowl, lightly pushing berries; remove pulp. Add gelatin to syrup, mixing until completely dissolved. Let cool to room temperature. Keep working as the same process to make blueberry gelatin.
- Pierce tops of cakes to within 1 inch of edge with a wooden skewer; gently twist skewer to form slightly bigger holes. Add cooled strawberry mixture on top of one cake gradually, be careful to fill each hole. Keep working with blueberry mixture and leftover cake. Cover and chill overnight.
- Whip cream in a big bowl until it starts to thicken. Put in confectioners' sugar; whip until forming soft peaks.
- Draw a knife around sides of pans to separate cakes from pan. Take out strawberry cake

from pan; discard paper. Put cake on a serving platter. Spread a cup whipped cream over.
- Take out blueberry cake from pan; discard paper. Put cake on top of whipped cream layer. Put on top and sides with leftover cream. Chill at least 1 hour prior to serving.

Nutrition Information

- Calories: 477 calories
- Sodium: 328mg sodium
- Fiber: 0 fiber)
- Total Carbohydrate: 55g carbohydrate (38g sugars
- Cholesterol: 100mg cholesterol
- Protein: 4g protein.
- Total Fat: 28g fat (13g saturated fat)

273.   Rhubarb Pudding Cake

Serving: 12 | Prep: | Cook: | Ready in:

Ingredients

- 1 cup chopped rhubarb
- 1 cup white sugar
- 6 drops red food coloring
- 1 (3.5 ounce) package instant vanilla pudding mix
- 1 (9 ounce) package yellow cake mix
- 1/4 cup confectioners' sugar for dusting

Direction

- Preheat an oven to 175°C (350°F).
- Mix food coloring, white sugar and chopped fresh rhubarb; put aside.
- Follow package directions to prepare vanilla pudding mix; transfer finished vanilla pudding in 1 9-in. square ungreased baking dish. Scoop rhubarb mixture over vanilla pudding.
- Follow package directions to prepare the cake

mix; evenly pour over vanilla pudding and rhubarb.

- Bake till cake tests done for 50 minutes at 175°C (350°F); allow to sit for 10 minutes in pan. Turn onto serving dish; dust using confectioners' sugar. Best served while warm.

Nutrition Information

- Calories: 198 calories;
- Sodium: 256
- Total Carbohydrate: 43.7
- Cholesterol: < 1
- Protein: 1
- Total Fat: 2.5

---

274. Rice Pudding Cake

Serving: 12-16 servings. | Prep: 45mins | Cook: 55mins | Ready in:

Ingredients

- 5 large eggs, separated
- 1/2 cup raisins
- Boiling water
- 1 cup uncooked long grain rice
- Water
- 4 cups milk
- 3/4 cup butter, softened
- 1 cup sugar
- 2 tablespoons grated orange zest
- 2 tablespoons graham cracker crumbs
- Confectioners' sugar

Direction

- Add the egg whites into a small bowl; let sit for 30 minutes at room temperature.
- In the meantime, cover the raisins with boiling water in a small bowl. Let them sit for 5 minutes; drain the liquid and put aside. Cover the rice with water in a large saucepan. Heat until boiling. Drain the liquid; add milk into

the rice. Heat until boiling. Lower the heat; simmer, covered, until rice is tender, or for 15-20 minutes; put aside.

- Cream butter and sugar together in a large bowl till fluffy and light. Beat egg yolks into the mixture. Add in the orange zest, raisins and rice mixture. Beat egg whites till stiff; fold them into the batter. Use a spoon to transfer the batter into a greased 10-in. tube pan. Sprinkle it with crumbs.
- Bake until an inserted toothpick in the middle exits clean, at 350° or for 55-60 minutes. Flip the pan right away; let cool thoroughly for about 1 hour.
- Run a knife around the pan's side and center tube. Take the cake out to a serving plate. Sprinkle with confectioners' sugar. Serve either warm or chilled.

Nutrition Information

- Calories: 244 calories
- Fiber: 0 fiber)
- Total Carbohydrate: 29g carbohydrate (18g sugars
- Cholesterol: 98mg cholesterol
- Protein: 5g protein.
- Total Fat: 12g fat (7g saturated fat)
- Sodium: 142mg sodium

---

275. Rich Chocolate Pudding Cake

Serving: 9 servings. | Prep: 15mins | Cook: 30mins | Ready in:

Ingredients

- 1/2 cup sugar
- Sugar substitute equivalent to 1/4 cup sugar
- 2 tablespoons butter, melted
- 1 teaspoon vanilla extract
- 1 cup all-purpose flour
- 2 tablespoons baking cocoa

- 2 teaspoons baking powder
- 1/8 teaspoon salt
- 1/2 cup fat-free milk
- TOPPING:
- 1/2 cup packed brown sugar
- 1/4 cup sugar
- Sugar substitute equivalent to 1/4 cup sugar
- 2 tablespoons baking cocoa
- 1 cup cold water
- 3 cups fat-free vanilla ice cream

Direction

- Whisk vanilla, butter, sugar substitute, and sugar together in a big bowl. Mix together salt, baking powder, cocoa, and flour; add to the sugar mixture alternately with milk. Add to an 8-inch square baking dish that is coated with cooking spray and spread.
- To prepare the topping, mix cocoa, sugar substitute, and sugars together in a small bowl. Sprinkle over the batter. Drizzle the topping with water. Bake at 350° for 37-42 minutes until the edges shrink from the sides of the dish and the top has set. Enjoy warm with ice cream.

Nutrition Information

- Calories: 261 calories
- Sodium: 203mg sodium
- Fiber: 1g fiber)
- Total Carbohydrate: 55g carbohydrate (40g sugars
- Cholesterol: 7mg cholesterol
- Protein: 4g protein.
- Total Fat: 3g fat (2g saturated fat)

276. Rosemary & Thyme Lemon Pudding Cakes

Serving: 6 servings. | Prep: 30mins | Cook: 20mins | Ready in:

Ingredients

- 3 large eggs
- 2 tablespoons butter, melted, divided
- 7 tablespoons sugar, divided
- 1 cup unsweetened vanilla almond milk
- 2 teaspoons dried rosemary, crushed
- 2 teaspoons dried thyme
- 1/4 cup all-purpose flour
- 3 teaspoons grated lemon zest
- 1/4 cup lemon juice
- 1 tablespoon coarse sugar

Direction

- Split the eggs; at a room temperature, let it stand for 30 minutes. Brush lightly with 1 tablespoon melted butter the inside of six 6 oz ramekins or custard cups. Sprinkle with 1/2 teaspoon sugar each. Prepare the oven by preheating to 350°F. Combine the herbs and milk in a small sauce pan; make it boil. Instantly remove from heat; then let it stand for 10 minutes. Drain milk through a fine mesh strainer; get rid of herbs. In a large bowl put 2 tablespoons sugar and flour; mix in the strained milk, remaining melted butter, lemon juice, lemon zest and yolks. In another bowl, whisk egg whites until foamy on medium speed. 1 tablespoon at a time, slowly add remaining 4 tablespoons sugar, whisking on high speed after every addition until sugar melted. Keep on whisking until forms a stiff glossy peaks; add slowly into flour mixture. Split among ramekins. Place inside the preheated oven and bake for 17 to 20 minutes until tops spring back when touched lightly. (Cakes will drop slightly). Drizzle with coarse sugar; let it cool on a wire rack for five minutes. Serve hot

Nutrition Information

- Calories: 165 calories
- Cholesterol: 103mg cholesterol
- Protein: 4g protein. Diabetic Exchanges: 1-1/2 starch

- Total Fat: 7g fat (3g saturated fat)
- Sodium: 97mg sodium
- Fiber: 1g fiber)
- Total Carbohydrate: 23g carbohydrate (17g sugars

277. Slow Cooker Apple Pudding Cake

Serving: 10 servings. | Prep: 15mins | Cook: 02hours00mins | Ready in:

Ingredients

- 2 cups all-purpose flour
- 2/3 cup plus 1/4 cup sugar, divided
- 3 teaspoons baking powder
- 1 teaspoon salt
- 1/2 cup cold butter
- 1 cup 2% milk
- 2 medium tart apples, peeled and chopped
- 1-1/2 cups orange juice
- 1/2 cup honey
- 2 tablespoons butter, melted
- 1 teaspoon ground cinnamon
- 1-1/3 cups sour cream
- 1/4 cup confectioners' sugar

Direction

- Combine salt, baking powder, 2/3 cup of sugar and flour together in a small bowl. Cut in butter till the mixture resembles coarse crumbs. Mix in milk just till moistened. Spread onto the bottom of a 4- or 5-qt. slow cooker coated with grease; sprinkle apples over the top of the batter.
- Mix the remaining sugar, cinnamon, melted butter, honey and orange juice together in a small bowl; transfer over the apples. Cook with a cover on high till the apples become tender, 2-3 hours.
- Mix confectioners' sugar and sour cream in a small bowl. Serve accompanied with warm pudding cake.

Nutrition Information

- Calories: 431 calories
- Total Fat: 17g fat (11g saturated fat)
- Sodium: 461mg sodium
- Fiber: 1g fiber)
- Total Carbohydrate: 64g carbohydrate (44g sugars
- Cholesterol: 53mg cholesterol
- Protein: 5g protein.

278. Spiced Pudding Cake

Serving: 15 servings. | Prep: 25mins | Cook: 35mins | Ready in:

Ingredients

- 1/2 cup butter, softened
- 1/2 cup sugar
- 1 egg
- 1 cup molasses
- 2-1/2 cups all-purpose flour
- 1-1/2 teaspoons baking soda
- 1-1/2 teaspoons ground cinnamon
- 1-1/4 teaspoons ground ginger
- 1/2 teaspoon ground allspice
- 1/4 teaspoon ground nutmeg
- 1/4 teaspoon salt
- 2-1/2 cups water, divided
- 2/3 cup packed brown sugar
- 1/4 cup butter, cubed
- Whipped cream and ground cinnamon, optional

Direction

- Cream sugar and butter in large bowl until fluffy and light. Put in egg and beat well. Then beat in the molasses. Mix salt, spices, baking soda and flour. Put into creamed mixture alternately with one cup of the water, beating well before adding the next.

- Place in an unoiled baking pan, about 13x9 inches; sprinkle brown sugar over. Heat remaining water and butter in microwave, until the butter melts; pour over the batter carefully.
- Bake at 350° until the toothpick inserted in middle comes out clean, about 35 to 40 mins. Place on a wire rack to cool. Enjoy warm. If desired, decorate with cinnamon and whipped cream.

Nutrition Information

- Calories: 287 calories
- Total Carbohydrate: 48g carbohydrate (28g sugars
- Cholesterol: 38mg cholesterol
- Protein: 3g protein.
- Total Fat: 10g fat (6g saturated fat)
- Sodium: 247mg sodium
- Fiber: 1g fiber)

279. Strawberry Bavarian Torte

Serving: 10-12 servings | Prep: 15mins | Cook: 0mins | Ready in:

Ingredients

- 1 package (6 ounces) strawberry gelatin
- 1 cup boiling water
- 2 quarts fresh strawberries, sliced
- 1/2 pint heavy whipping cream, whipped
- 1 sponge cake, cut into cubes
- Additional whipped cream
- Whole strawberries for garnish

Direction

- Melt gelatin in water in bowl. Add berries; let partially thicken. Fold whipped cream in. Fold cake cubes in; mix till coated well. Spread in greased springform pan. Cover; chill

overnight. Take out of pan; put on torte plate. Frost using whipped cream; garnish with berries.

Nutrition Information

- Calories: 258 calories
- Sodium: 133mg sodium
- Fiber: 2g fiber)
- Total Carbohydrate: 43g carbohydrate (34g sugars
- Cholesterol: 66mg cholesterol
- Protein: 4g protein.
- Total Fat: 9g fat (5g saturated fat)

280. Strawberry Cake

Serving: | Prep: | Cook: | Ready in:

Ingredients

- 1 cup Butter Softened
- 1 1/2 cups Sugar
- 3 ounces Strawberry-Flavored Gelatin
- 4 pieces Eggs, room temperature
- 2 1/2 cups All-Purpose Flour
- 2 1/2 teaspoons Baking Powder
- 1 cup Milk, Whole, room temperature
- 1/2 cup Strawberries, frozen, pureed
- 1 tablespoon Vanilla Extract

Direction

- Preparation
- A few hours before preparing the batter, take butter, milk and eggs away from the refrigerator.
- Set the oven at 350° and start preheating.
- Coat two 9-in. round pans with grease and flour.
- Mix strawberry gelatin, sugar and butter in a large bowl. Combine on medium speed, till fluffy and light.

- Separate eggs; include egg yolks into the batter and stir properly.
- Before stirring into the batter, vigorously whip the eggs till it forms soft peaks.
- Sift flour; measure and place into a separate bowl.
- Mix the sifted flour with baking powder.
- Include the flour mixture alternately with milk into the batter, stirring well after each addition.
- Make a strawberries purée with a blender from frozen strawberries. Include a bit of water till smooth.
- Include 1/2 cup of the purée into the batter with vanilla; stir properly.
- Transfer the batter into the prepared pans.
- Bake till a toothpick comes out clean, 25-30 minutes.
- Allow to cool for a minimum of 10 minutes on wire racks, then take away from the pans; cool completely before frosting.
- Prepare strawberry cake frosting or use your favorite frosting.

Nutrition Information

---

281.   Strawberry Cheesecake Torte

Serving: 12 servings. | Prep: 30mins | Cook: 25mins | Ready in:

Ingredients

- 1 package (16 ounces) angel food cake mix
- 1 tablespoon confectioners' sugar
- 1 package (.3 ounce) sugar-free strawberry gelatin
- 1/2 cup boiling water
- 1/4 cup seedless strawberry jam
- 1 package (8 ounces) reduced-fat cream cheese, cubed
- 1/3 cup fat-free milk

- 2 tablespoons lemon juice
- 3 cups reduced-fat whipped topping
- 1 package (3.4 ounces) instant cheesecake or vanilla pudding mix
- 1 cup sliced fresh strawberries
- 1 kiwifruit, peeled, halved and sliced
- 1-1/2 teaspoons grated lemon peel

Direction

- Use ungreased parchment paper to line a 15x10x1-in. baking pan. Following the package instructions, prepare cake mix properly. Evenly spread the batter into the prepared pan. Bake at 350° till the top slightly turns brown, or for 24-26 minutes. Sprinkle sugar over a baking sheet lined with waxed paper. Invert the cake onto the baking sheet immediately. Peel off the parchment paper gently; allow to cool completely.
- In boiling water, dissolve gelatin. Mix in jam till melted. Poke the cake, using a fork, at 1/2-in. intervals. Use the gelatin mixture to brush; chill for 10 minutes.
- Beat lemon juice, milk and cream cheese in a bowl, till smooth. Beat in pudding mix and whipped topping. Reserve 1 cup. In the corner of a plastic bag or pastry, cut a small hole; insert a large star tip. Fill the pudding mixture into the bag.
- Trim the edges of the cake. Cut into three equal rectangles widthwise; arrange one on a serving plate. In the center, spread 1/2 cup of the reserved pudding mixture. Pipe the mixture around the top edge of the cake. Repeat the layer. Place the third cake layer on top. Pipe the pudding mixture along the top edges. Fill fruit into the center. Sprinkle lemon peel over. Place in the refrigerator for storage.

Nutrition Information

- Calories: 284 calories
- Total Fat: 6g fat (4g saturated fat)
- Sodium: 427mg sodium
- Fiber: 1g fiber)

- Total Carbohydrate: 51g carbohydrate (0 sugars
- Cholesterol: 11mg cholesterol
- Protein: 6g protein.

282. Strawberry Heart Cake

Serving: 12-16 servings. | Prep: 30mins | Cook: 30mins | Ready in:

Ingredients

- 1 package white cake mix (regular size)
- 1 package (3 ounces) strawberry gelatin
- 3 tablespoons all-purpose flour
- 1/3 cup vegetable oil
- 4 large eggs
- 1 package (10 ounces) frozen sweetened sliced strawberries, thawed
- 1/2 cup cold water
- 1/2 cup butter, softened
- 5 to 5-1/2 cups confectioners' sugar
- Red-hot candies, optional

Direction

- Combine flour, gelatin and cake mix in a bowl. Beat in eggs and oil. Drain strawberries; for frosting, saving half cup of syrup. Put water and berries into batter and mix well. Separate the batter between 2 waxed paper-lined 8 inches baking pans, 1 round and 1 square.
- Bake at 350° for 35 to 40 mins (round) and 30 to 35 mins (square) or until the cake tests done. Let cool about 10 mins. Take off from the pans; let cool completely on wire racks.
- Combine reserved syrup and butter in small bowl. Put in sugar gradually; beat for 2 mins or until fluffy and light. On the 20x15 inches covered board, arrange the square cake diagonally. Halve the round cake.
- Frost the cut sides; arrange the frosted sides against top 2 sides of the square cake, shaping a heart. Then frost top and sides of the cake. If desired, decorate with red-hots.

Nutrition Information

- Calories: 430 calories
- Total Fat: 15g fat (5g saturated fat)
- Sodium: 291mg sodium
- Fiber: 1g fiber)
- Total Carbohydrate: 72g carbohydrate (57g sugars
- Cholesterol: 68mg cholesterol
- Protein: 4g protein.

283. Strawberry Poke Cake

Serving: Makes 24 servings. | Prep: 30mins | Cook: | Ready in:

Ingredients

- 1 pkg. (2-layer size) white cake mix
- 2 cups boiling water
- 2 pkg. (3 oz. each) JELL-O Strawberry Flavor Sugar Free Gelatin
- 4 cups sliced strawberries, mashed
- 1 tub (8 oz.) COOL WHIP LITE Whipped Topping, thawed

Direction

- Prepare the cake batter and bake following the directions on the package for 13x9-inch pan. Let the cake cool in pan for 15 min. Using the large fork, pierce cake at 1/2-in. intervals.
- Pour the boiling water into gelatin mixes and stir until completely dissolved, about 2 mins. Mix in the strawberries then spoon over the cake. Place in the refrigerator for 120 mins.
- Frost with the COOL WHIP. Place in the refrigerator for 60 mins.

Nutrition Information

- Calories: 130
- Sugar: 13 g

- Total Carbohydrate: 22 g
- Cholesterol: 0 mg
- Protein: 2 g
- Saturated Fat: 1.5 g
- Sodium: 170 mg
- Fiber: 1 g
- Total Fat: 3.5 g

284. Strawberry Rhubarb Torte

Serving: 4 servings. | Prep: 40mins | Cook: 0mins | Ready in:

Ingredients

- 2 cups sliced fresh or frozen rhubarb
- 1/3 cup water
- 2 tablespoons plus 4-1/2 teaspoons sugar, divided
- 3 tablespoons plus 1 teaspoon strawberry gelatin
- 2/3 cup heavy whipping cream
- 1/4 teaspoon vanilla extract
- 14 ladyfingers, split
- 1 teaspoon cornstarch
- 1 teaspoon cold water
- 1/2 cup sliced fresh strawberries

Direction

- Boil 2 tablespoons of sugar, water and rhubarb in a small saucepan. Lower the heat; simmer without a cover until rhubarb is softened, or for 6 to 8 minutes. Allow to cool slightly. Refrigerate, covered, a third cup of rhubarb liquid to make glaze.
- Bring the rest of liquid and rhubarb into a blender; process, covered, until it turns into a puree. Bring back into the saucepan. Boil; whisk in gelatin until dissolved. Leave in the fridge for a minimum period of 15 minutes or until thickened slightly.
- In the meantime, beat cream until it starts to thicken in a big bowl. Put in vanilla; beat until

it forms stiff peaks. Fold whipped cream into the rhubarb mixture.
- Place 1/2 of ladyfingers onto an unoiled 6" springform pan. Spread 1/2 of rhubarb mixture into the pan. Place the rest of ladyfingers onto rhubarb mixture, then carefully spread the rest of rhubarb mixture on top. Leave in the fridge for 8 hours or overnight.
- Pour rhubarb liquid reserved earlier into a small saucepan; whisk in the rest of the sugar. Boil. Mix water and cornstarch together until smooth. Slowly mix into the pan. Boil; cook, while stirring, until thick or for 2 minutes. Spread atop rhubarb layer. Place strawberry slices onto the glaze. Discard pan's sides.

Nutrition Information

- Calories: 334 calories
- Cholesterol: 106mg cholesterol
- Protein: 5g protein.
- Total Fat: 16g fat (10g saturated fat)
- Sodium: 218mg sodium
- Fiber: 2g fiber)
- Total Carbohydrate: 44g carbohydrate (32g sugars

285. Strawberry Schaum Torte

Serving: 12 servings. | Prep: 25mins | Cook: 45mins | Ready in:

Ingredients

- 6 large egg whites
- 2 teaspoons water
- 2 teaspoons white vinegar
- 2 teaspoons vanilla extract
- 1 teaspoon baking powder
- 1/4 teaspoon salt
- 2 cups sugar
- FILLING:
- 1 package (3 ounces) strawberry gelatin

- 1/2 cup boiling water
- 1 cup fresh or frozen sliced strawberries
- 1 teaspoon lemon juice
- Dash salt
- 1-1/2 cups whipped cream

Direction

- Put egg whites in big bowl; stand for 30 minutes at room temperature. Add salt, baking powder, vanilla, vinegar and water; beat at medium speed till soft peaks form. 2 tbsp. at a time, beat sugar in slowly on high till sugar melts and stiff glossy peaks form.
- Evenly spread in 13x9-in. greased baking pan; bake for 45 minutes at 300°. Turn oven off; don't open door. Dry crust overnight in oven.
- Filling: Melt gelatin in boiling water in bowl. Mix salt, lemon juice and strawberries in (it will quickly thicken); fold cream in. Spread on crust; keep in fridge.

Nutrition Information

- Calories: 0

286.　　Strawberry Shortcake Dessert

Serving: 8 servings | Prep: 10mins | Cook: | Ready in:

Ingredients

- 8　graham cracker s, broken in half (16 squares)
- 8　JET-PUFFED Marshmallow s
- 2 Tbsp.　white and chocolate chunk cookie (2-inch) , divided
- 4 large fresh strawberries , each cut into 6 slices

Direction

- Put chocolate chips and marshmallows on top of 8 graham squares. On microwaveable plate, put 4 topped squares.
- Microwave for 15 to 20 seconds on HIGH till marshmallows puff. Put 3 strawberry slices every top and one of the leftover graham squares; gently press together to set.
- Redo with the rest of topped graham squares.

Nutrition Information

- Calories: 100
- Total Fat: 2 g
- Protein: 1 g
- Saturated Fat: 0.5 g
- Sodium: 90 mg
- Fiber: 1 g
- Sugar: 11 g
- Total Carbohydrate: 20 g
- Cholesterol: 0 mg

287.　　Strawberry Sunshine Cake

Serving: 12-16 servings. | Prep: 30mins | Cook: 50mins | Ready in:

Ingredients

- 1 cup egg whites (about 7)
- 5 egg yolks
- 1-1/2 cups sugar, divided
- 2 tablespoons water
- 1/2 teaspoon each almond, lemon and vanilla extract
- 1 cup all-purpose flour
- 1/2 teaspoon cream of tartar
- 1/2 teaspoon salt
- FILLING:
- 1 package (3 ounces) strawberry gelatin
- 1 cup boiling water
- 1/2 cup ice water
- 1 pint fresh strawberries, sliced
- 1 carton (8 ounces) frozen whipped topping, thawed, divided

- Additional strawberries

Direction

- Allow egg whites to sit for 30 minutes. Beat egg yolks in a large bowl, on high speed till lemon-colored and thick, or for 5 minutes. Slowly beat in 1/2 cup of sugar. Mix in extracts and water. Sift flour twice; slowly put into the yolk mixture; combine properly. (The batter should be very thick.)
- In a large bowl, beat salt, cream of tartar and egg whites with clean beaters till the mixture forms soft peaks. Slowly put in the remaining sugar, 1 tablespoon at a time, beating till it forms stiff peaks; set aside. Fold into the egg yolk mixture just till well blended.
- Using a spoon, transfer into an ungreased 10-in. tube pan. Using a knife, cut through the batter to discard any air pockets; smooth the top. Bake for 50-55 minutes at 325°, or till the cake springs back when touched slightly. Invert a pan immediately; allow to cool completely.
- Dissolve gelatin into boiling water in a large bowl. Put in ice water; mix. Place the bowl in ice water till thickened slightly, or around 5 minutes. Fold in 1/2 cup of whipped topping and strawberries.
- Run a knife around the side and center tube of the pan. Split into 3 layers horizontally; move the bottom layer onto a serving plate. Spread half of the gelatin mixture over. Repeat. Place the remaining cake layer on top. Frost the sides and top with the remaining whipped topping. Use strawberries for garnish. Keep any leftovers in refrigerator.

Nutrition Information

- Calories: 193 calories
- Sodium: 114mg sodium
- Fiber: 1g fiber)
- Total Carbohydrate: 34g carbohydrate (26g sugars
- Cholesterol: 66mg cholesterol
- Protein: 4g protein.

- Total Fat: 4g fat (3g saturated fat)

---

288. Strawberry Banana Pudding Cake

Serving: 10 servings. | Prep: 15mins | Cook: 03hours30mins | Ready in:

Ingredients

- 1 package strawberry cake mix (regular size)
- 1 package (3.4 ounces) instant banana cream pudding mix
- 2 cups plain Greek yogurt
- 4 large eggs
- 1 cup water
- 3/4 cup canola oil
- 2 tablespoons minced fresh basil
- 1 cup white baking chips
- Optional toppings: vanilla ice cream, sliced bananas, sliced strawberries and fresh basil

Direction

- Combine first 6 ingredients in a large bowl; beat for half a minute on low speed. Beat for 2 mins on medium; mix in basil. Place to an oiled 5-qt. slow cooker. Cook, covered, on low for 3-1/2 to 4 hours or until the edges of the cake turn golden brown (the middle will be moist).
- Discard the slow cooker insert; top cake with a sprinkle of the baking chips. Allow the cake to stand, uncovered, 10 mins prior to serving. Enjoy with the toppings as preferred.

Nutrition Information

- Calories: 373 calories
- Cholesterol: 90mg cholesterol
- Protein: 5g protein.
- Total Fat: 29g fat (8g saturated fat)
- Sodium: 239mg sodium
- Fiber: 0 fiber)

- Total Carbohydrate: 23g carbohydrate (21g sugars

289. Strawberry Rhubarb Upside Down Cake

Serving: 10 | Prep: | Cook: 30mins | Ready in:

Ingredients

- 1 cup sliced fresh rhubarb
- ¾ cup orange juice, preferably fresh-squeezed, divided
- 3 tablespoons granulated sugar
- 2½ cups sliced strawberries
- 3 large eggs
- ⅔ cup extra-virgin olive oil
- ¾ cup packed light brown sugar
- 1 tablespoon freshly grated orange zest
- 2 teaspoons vanilla extract
- 1½ cups white whole-wheat flour or all-purpose flour
- 2 teaspoons baking powder
- ½ teaspoon salt

Direction

- Start preheating the oven at 350°F. Liberally grease a 9-inch round cake pan with olive oil.
- Mix granulated sugar, 1/4 cup of orange juice, and rhubarb in a medium bowl and allow to stand for 20 minutes, combining from time to time. Put in strawberries; stir to mix. Scatter the fruit mixture into the greased pan.
- Blend the leftover 1/2 cup of orange juice, vanilla, orange zest, brown sugar, oil, and eggs in a large bowl. Blend salt, baking powder, and flour in a medium bowl. Slowly combine the dry ingredients into the wet ingredients. Don't overmix. Scoop the cake batter on top of the fruit mixture.
- Bake for 40 to 50 minutes until a toothpick comes out dry when inserted into the center of the cake layer.

- Trace a knife around the outside of the pan and shake it slightly to loosen the base. Turn the cake over onto a serving plate and take off the pan. Allow the cake to cool at room temperature for about 2 hours then serve.

Nutrition Information

- Calories: 321 calories;
- Saturated Fat: 3
- Fiber: 3
- Cholesterol: 56
- Sugar: 24
- Protein: 5
- Sodium: 241
- Total Carbohydrate: 40
- Total Fat: 17

290. Sugarplum Pudding Cake

Serving: 6 servings. | Prep: 20mins | Cook: 30mins | Ready in:

Ingredients

- 1/4 cup butter, softened
- 1/2 cup sugar
- 1 egg
- 3/4 cup all-purpose flour
- 3/4 teaspoon baking soda
- 3/4 teaspoon ground cinnamon
- 1/4 teaspoon ground nutmeg
- 3/4 cup buttermilk
- 3/4 cup chopped pitted dried plums
- 1/2 cup chopped walnuts
- COCONUT TOPPING:
- 2 tablespoons butter
- 1/3 cup sugar
- 2 tablespoons buttermilk
- 1/2 cup sweetened shredded coconut
- 1/4 teaspoon vanilla extract

Direction

- Cream sugar and butter in a small bowl; beat in egg. Mix nutmeg, cinnamon, baking soda and flour; alternately with buttermilk, add to creamed mixture. Beat till just combined. Fold in walnuts and plums.
- Put into 9x5-inch loaf pan coated in cooking spray; bake it at 350° till inserted toothpick exits clean for 30-35 minutes.
- Meanwhile, melt butter in a small saucepan; mix in buttermilk and sugar. Boil. Lower heat; simmer for 1 minute, uncovered. Mix in vanilla and coconut. Spread topping on cake immediately when removed from oven; serve warm.

Nutrition Information

- Calories: 450 calories
- Sodium: 345mg sodium
- Fiber: 2g fiber)
- Total Carbohydrate: 60g carbohydrate (38g sugars
- Cholesterol: 68mg cholesterol
- Protein: 7g protein.
- Total Fat: 21g fat (10g saturated fat)

291. Sunny Coconut Cake

Serving: 12-16 servings. | Prep: 20mins | Cook: 30mins | Ready in:

Ingredients

- 2 cups sour cream
- 2 cups sugar
- 1/4 cup orange juice
- 1 package (14 ounces) sweetened shredded coconut
- 1 package yellow cake mix (regular size)
- 1 package (3 ounces) orange gelatin
- 1 cup water
- 1/3 cup vegetable oil
- 2 large eggs
- 1 cup heavy whipping cream
- 1 can (11 ounces) mandarin oranges, well drained

Direction

- Mix the orange juice, sugar, and the sour cream in a small bowl. Add coconut and whisk. Cover and put into a refrigerator. Mix well the eggs, oil, water, gelatin, and he cake mix in a big bowl.
- Grease and then flour two 9 inch round baking pans then add the mixture to the prepared pans. Bake for 30-35 minutes at 350° until the toothpick you inserted into the middle comes out clean. Let cool for 10 minutes then transfer from pans to wire racks to cool completely.
- Divide each cake into 2 layers horizontally. Put aside 1 cup of the coconut filling then spread the remaining between cake layers. Put into a refrigerator. Beat cream in a chilled big bowl until stiff peaks form then add to the reserved filling and fold. Spread over the sides and top of the cake. Use oranges to garnish and keep in the refrigerator.

Nutrition Information

- Calories: 550 calories
- Sodium: 310mg sodium
- Fiber: 2g fiber)
- Total Carbohydrate: 72g carbohydrate (56g sugars
- Cholesterol: 67mg cholesterol
- Protein: 5g protein.
- Total Fat: 27g fat (17g saturated fat)

292. Sunny Orange Layer Cake

Serving: 14 servings. | Prep: 45mins | Cook: 25mins | Ready in:

Ingredients

- 2/3 cup shortening
- 1-1/2 cups sugar
- 3 large eggs
- 1 tablespoon grated orange zest
- 2-1/2 cups cake flour
- 1 package (3 ounces) orange gelatin
- 2-1/2 teaspoons baking powder
- 1 teaspoon salt
- 3/4 cup orange juice
- 1/3 cup 2% milk
- FROSTING:
- 1 package (8 ounces) cream cheese, softened
- 1/2 cup butter, softened
- 1-1/2 cups confectioners' sugar
- 2 tablespoons orange gelatin powder
- 2 teaspoons vanilla extract

Direction

- Cream sugar and shortening till fluffy and light in a big bowl. One by one, add eggs; beat well after each. Beat in orange zest. Mix salt, baking powder, gelatin and flour. Alternately with milk and orange juice, add to creamed mixture; beat well after each.
- Put into 2 9-in. round greased and floured baking pans; bake for 25-30 minutes at 350° till inserted toothpick in middle exits clean. Cool it for 10 minutes. Transfer from pans onto wire racks; fully cool.
- Beat butter and cream cheese till fluffy and light in a big bowl; beat in vanilla, gelatin powder and confectioners' sugar till blended.
- Put 1 cake layer onto serving plate; spread frosting. Put leftover cake layer over; frost sides and top of cake. Keep refrigerated.

Nutrition Information

- Calories: 475 calories
- Total Fat: 23g fat (10g saturated fat)
- Sodium: 370mg sodium
- Fiber: 0 fiber)
- Total Carbohydrate: 63g carbohydrate (42g sugars
- Cholesterol: 81mg cholesterol

- Protein: 6g protein.

293.　　Triple Berry No Bake Cheesecake

Serving: 12 servings (3-1/3 cups topping). | Prep: 20mins | Cook: 0mins | Ready in:

Ingredients

- 1-1/2 cups graham cracker crumbs
- 1/3 cup packed brown sugar
- 1/2 teaspoon ground cinnamon
- 1/3 cup butter, melted
- FILLING:
- 2 packages (8 ounces each) cream cheese, softened
- 1/3 cup sugar
- 2 teaspoons lemon juice
- 2 cups heavy whipping cream
- TOPPING:
- 2 cups sliced fresh strawberries
- 1 cup fresh blueberries
- 1 cup fresh raspberries
- 2 tablespoons sugar

Direction

- Combine together in a small bowl the cinnamon, brown sugar, and mix cracker crumbs; add in butter. Then push onto bottom and 1 inch up side of a springform pan that is 9 inch and ungreased. Place inside the refrigerator for 30 minutes. Beat in a large bowl the lemon juice, sugar and cream cheese until it becomes smooth. Slowly add the cream; mix until stiff peaks are formed. Move to the prepared crust. Place inside the refrigerator overnight, covered. Slowly toss berries with sugar in a bowl. Let it stand for 15 to 30 minutes or until juices are out from berries. Loosen the side of cheesecake from pan using a knife; then take away from rim. Present the cheesecake with toppings.

Nutrition Information

- Calories: 432 calories
- Protein: 5g protein.
- Total Fat: 34g fat (21g saturated fat)
- Sodium: 229mg sodium
- Fiber: 2g fiber)
- Total Carbohydrate: 29g carbohydrate (20g sugars
- Cholesterol: 109mg cholesterol

294. Upside Down Berry Cake

Serving: 15 servings. | Prep: 20mins | Cook: 30mins | Ready in:

Ingredients

- 1/2 cup chopped walnuts
- 1 cup fresh or frozen blueberries
- 1 cup fresh or frozen raspberries, halved
- 1 cup sliced fresh strawberries
- 1/4 cup sugar
- 1 package (3 ounces) raspberry gelatin
- 1 package yellow cake mix (regular size)
- 2 large eggs
- 1-1/4 cups water
- 2 tablespoons canola oil
- 1-1/2 cups miniature marshmallows

Direction

- In a well-greased baking pan of 13x9 inches, layer in order the walnuts and berries; sprinkle with gelatin and sugar. Mix oil, water, eggs and cake mix together in a large bowl; beat for half a minute on low speed. Keep beating for 2 minutes on medium. Fold in marshmallows. Add over top.
- Bake in the oven at 350° until a toothpick put in the middle goes out clean, about 35-40 minutes. Allow to cool for 5 minutes before flipping onto a serving platter. Keep the leftovers in the fridge.

Nutrition Information

- Calories: 276 calories
- Protein: 3g protein.
- Total Fat: 7g fat (2g saturated fat)
- Sodium: 249mg sodium
- Fiber: 1g fiber)
- Total Carbohydrate: 51g carbohydrate (36g sugars
- Cholesterol: 28mg cholesterol

295. Upside Down Strawberry Shortcake

Serving: 12-16 servings. | Prep: 20mins | Cook: 45mins | Ready in:

Ingredients

- 1 cup miniature marshmallows
- 2 packages (10 ounces each) frozen sweetened sliced strawberries
- 1 package (3 ounces) strawberry gelatin
- 1/2 cup shortening
- 1-1/2 cups sugar
- 3 eggs
- 1 teaspoon vanilla extract
- 2-1/4 cups all-purpose flour
- 3 teaspoons baking powder
- 1/2 teaspoon salt
- 1 cup 2% milk
- Fresh strawberries and whipped cream

Direction

- Evenly sprinkle marshmallows in 13x9-in. greased baking dish; put aside. Mix gelatin powder and strawberries in small bowl; put aside.
- Cream sugar and shortening till fluffy and light in big bowl. One by one, add eggs, beating well after every addition; beat vanilla in. Mix salt, baking powder and flour. Alternately with milk, add to creamed mixture, beating well after every addition.

- Put batter on marshmallows; evenly put strawberry mixture on batter. Bake for 45-50 minutes at 350° till an inserted toothpick in middle exits clean. On wire rack, cool. Cut to squares. Garnish with whipped cream and strawberries.

Nutrition Information

- Calories: 272 calories
- Cholesterol: 42mg cholesterol
- Protein: 4g protein.
- Total Fat: 8g fat (2g saturated fat)
- Sodium: 183mg sodium
- Fiber: 1g fiber)
- Total Carbohydrate: 47g carbohydrate (32g sugars

296.   Watermelon Cake

Serving: 12 servings. | Prep: 20mins | Cook: 30mins | Ready in:

Ingredients

- 1 package white cake mix (regular size)
- 1 package (3 ounces) watermelon gelatin
- 1-1/4 cups water
- 2 eggs
- 1/4 cup canola oil
- 2-1/2 cups prepared vanilla or cream cheese frosting, divided
- Red and green gel food coloring
- Chocolate chips

Direction

- Mix oil, eggs, water, gelatin, and cake mix in a large bowl; whisk for half a minute at low speed. Whisk for 2 minutes at medium speed.
- Add into 2 greased and floured 9-inch round baking pans. Bake at 350 degrees until a toothpick comes out clean when inserted into the center, for 30-35 minutes. Let cool for 10

minutes, then transfer from the pans onto wire racks to cool entirely.
- Put 2 tablespoons of the frosting aside for garnish. In a bowl, put 1 1/4 cups of the frosting; color red. Color the rest of frosting green.
- On a serving plate, arrange a cake layer. Smear with 1/2 cup of the red frosting leaving 1/4 inch border from the edges. Add the second cake on top. Frost the top with the rest of red frosting to within 3/4 inch of edges. Frost the sides and top edge of cake using green frosting.
- Cut 1/4-inch hole in the corner of plastic or pastry bag. Add the saved white frosting in the bag. Pipe around the top edge of the cake where the pink and green frosting meet. Insert inverted chocolate chips in the cake top for seeds.

Nutrition Information

- Calories:
- Total Fat:
- Sodium:
- Fiber:
- Total Carbohydrate:
- Cholesterol:
- Protein:

297.   Wave Your Flag Cheesecake

Serving: 20 | Prep: 20mins | Cook: 5mins | Ready in:

Ingredients

- 1 quart strawberries, divided
- 1 1/2 cups boiling water
- 2 pkg. (4 serving size) JELL-O Brand Strawberry Flavor Gelatin
- Ice cubes
- 1 cup cold water

- 1 (10.75 ounce) loaf pound cake, cut into 10 slices
- 1 1/3 cups blueberries, divided
- 2 (8 ounce) packages PHILADELPHIA Cream Cheese, softened
- 1/4 cup sugar
- 1 (8 ounce) tub COOL WHIP Whipped Topping, thawed

Direction

- Slice 1 cup of strawberries; put aside. Halve the leftover 3 cups of strawberries; put aside. In a large bowl, stir boiling water into dry gelatin mixes until dissolved completely, at least 2 minutes. Put enough ice into cold the water to measure 2 cups. Pour into gelatin; stir until ice melts completely. Cool in the fridge for 5 minutes or until gelatin is thickened slightly to the consistency of unbeaten egg whites).
- In the meantime, line cake slices on the bottom of a 13x9-inch dish. Put in strawberries slices and 1 cup of blueberries to thickened gelatin; gently stir. Use a spoon to add over cake slices. Keep in the fridge for 4 hours, or until set.
- In a large bowl, beat sugar and cream cheese together with electric mixer or wire whisk until well combined; stir gently into whipped topping. Spread the mixture over the gelatin. Place strawberry halves on cream cheese mixture to simulate the flag stripes. Place the remaining 1/3 cup blueberries over the cream cheese mixture to form the stars. Keep any leftovers in fridge.

Nutrition Information

298.　　　Wearing O' Green Cake

Serving: 15 servings. | Prep: 25mins | Cook: 30mins | Ready in:

Ingredients

- 1 package white cake mix (regular size)
- 2 packages (3 ounces each) lime gelatin
- 1 cup boiling water
- 1/2 cup cold water
- TOPPING:
- 1 cup cold milk
- 1 package (3.4 ounces) instant vanilla pudding mix
- 1 carton (8 ounces) frozen whipped topping, thawed
- Green sprinkles

Direction

- Follow package directions to prep and bake cake using 13x9-in. greased baking dish; cool for 1 hour on wire rack. Dissolve gelatin in boiling water in a small bowl; mix in cold water. Put aside.
- Poke holes into cooled cake, 2-in. apart, with a wooden skewer/meat fork. Put gelatin on cake slowly. Cover; refrigerate.
- Whisk pudding mix and milk till thick for 2 minutes in a big bowl; fold in the whipped topping. Spread on cake; decorate using sprinkles. Cover; refrigerate till serving.

Nutrition Information

- Calories: 303 calories
- Sodium: 328mg sodium
- Fiber: 1g fiber)
- Total Carbohydrate: 48g carbohydrate (33g sugars
- Cholesterol: 39mg cholesterol
- Protein: 4g protein.
- Total Fat: 11g fat (4g saturated fat)

Chapter 3: Jello Pudding Recipes

***

299.   "S'more, Please" Trifle

Serving: 16 servings. | Prep: 25mins | Cook: 30mins | Ready in:

Ingredients

- 1 package chocolate cake mix (regular size)
- 1 can (12 ounces) diet lemon-lime soda
- 2-1/2 cups plus 2 tablespoons fat-free milk, divided
- 2 packages (1.4 ounces each) sugar-free instant chocolate pudding mix
- 1 carton (8 ounces) frozen fat-free whipped topping, thawed
- 1/2 cup dark chocolate chips
- 10 whole reduced-fat graham crackers, divided
- 1 jar (7 ounces) marshmallow creme
- Grated chocolate, optional

Direction

- Beat soda and cake mix for 30 seconds at a low speed in a big bowl; beat for 2 minutes on medium. Put into a 13x9-in. baking pan coated in cooking spray; bake for 30-35 minutes at 350° till inserted toothpick in the middle exits clean. Completely cool on a wire rack.
- Meanwhile, whisk pudding mix and 2 1/2 cups milk for 2 minutes in a big bowl; stand till soft set for 2 minutes. Fold whipped topping in; put aside. Melt leftover milk and chocolate chips in a microwave; mix till smooth. Crush 5 crackers coarsely; put aside. Slice cake into 1-in. cubes.
- Layer 1/2 of cake cubes, marshmallow crème, chocolate mixture, crushed crackers and pudding in a 3-qt. trifle bowl/glass bowl; repeat layers. Before serving, refrigerate for at least 1 hour. Crush leftover crackers coarsely before serving; sprinkle on top. If desired, garnish with grated chocolate.

Nutrition Information

- Calories: 300 calories
- Sodium: 463mg sodium
- Fiber: 2g fiber)
- Total Carbohydrate: 59g carbohydrate (34g sugars
- Cholesterol: 1mg cholesterol
- Protein: 4g protein.
- Total Fat: 6g fat (3g saturated fat)

300.   Ambrosia Pudding

Serving: 4 | Prep: 20mins | Cook: | Ready in:

Ingredients

- 1 (3.4 ounce) package instant vanilla pudding mix
- 2 cups cold milk
- 1/4 cup honey
- 2 teaspoons grated orange peel
- 1/4 teaspoon vanilla extract
- 1 cup whipping cream, whipped
- 1 banana, sliced
- 1 (11 ounce) can mandarin orange sections, drained
- 1/4 cup shredded coconut
- 1/4 cup sliced almonds

Direction

- Combine milk and pudding in a bowl following package instructions. Stir in orange peel, honey and vanilla. Fold in the whipped cream. In single dessert trays, layer 1/2 of the pudding, followed by banana slices, orange wedges, then coconut and almonds. Repeat the layers once more. Chill in refrigerator.

Nutrition Information

301. Angel Lush...Make It Your Way!

Serving: 12 servings. | *Prep: 15mins* | *Cook: 0mins* | *Ready in:*

Ingredients

- 1 can (20 ounces) unsweetened crushed pineapple, undrained
- 1 package (3.4 ounces) JELL-O® Vanilla Flavor Instant Pudding
- 1 cup thawed Cool Whip® Whipped Topping
- 1 prepared angel food cake or 12 individual round sponge cakes
- Mixed fresh berries

Direction

- Combine pudding mix and pineapple in a small bowl and beat together until well mixed. Incorporate whipped topping by folding in. Keep inside refrigerator and chill until assembly.
- Split the cake into three horizontal slices to fill the angel food cake. Place and apply filling on the layers. Use berries as topping.
- The individual sponge cakes are filled by scooping the filling with a spoon, and berries are added on top.
- Make parfaits by layering angel food cake shaped into cubes, filling, and 2 cups of berries in 12 individual dessert glasses.

Nutrition Information

- Calories:
- Total Carbohydrate:
- Cholesterol:
- Protein:
- Total Fat:
- Sodium:
- Fiber:

302. Apple Spice Cake Trifle

Serving: 20-24 servings. | *Prep: 30mins* | *Cook: 35mins* | *Ready in:*

Ingredients

- 1 package spice cake mix (regular size)
- 1-1/4 cups cinnamon applesauce
- 3 eggs
- 1/3 cup canola oil
- 1 can (21 ounces) apple pie filling
- 1 tablespoon butter
- 7 teaspoons ground cinnamon, divided
- 3 cups cold milk
- 1 package (5.1 ounces) instant vanilla pudding mix
- 1 envelope whipped topping mix (Dream Whip)
- 1 carton (12 ounces) frozen whipped topping, thawed
- 1/2 cup chopped walnuts
- 1/4 cup English toffee bits or almond brickle chips

Direction

- Beat oil, eggs, applesauce and cake mix for 2 minutes on medium speed in big bowl; put in 13x9-in. greased baking pan.
- Bake for 35-40 minutes at 350° or till inserted toothpick in middle exits clean; on wire rack, cool.
- Mix and cook 1 tsp. cinnamon, butter and pie filling till butter melts and blended well in small saucepan; cool.
- Beat leftover cinnamon, topping mix, pudding mix and milk on high, for about 5 minutes, till thickened in big bowl; put aside. Spread 1/3 whipped topping in 6-qt. trifle bowl.
- Cut cake to cubes; put 1/2 on topping. Top using 1/2 fruit mixture, walnuts then pudding mixture; repeat layers. Spread leftover whipped topping; sprinkle toffee bits. Cover; chill for a minimum of 2 hours.

Nutrition Information

- Calories: 288 calories
- Total Fat: 13g fat (6g saturated fat)
- Sodium: 303mg sodium
- Fiber: 1g fiber)
- Total Carbohydrate: 39g carbohydrate (27g sugars
- Cholesterol: 38mg cholesterol
- Protein: 4g protein.

303. Aunt Ruth's Famous Butterscotch Cheesecake

Serving: 12 servings. | Prep: 30mins | Cook: 01hours05mins | Ready in:

Ingredients

- 1-1/2 cups graham cracker crumbs
- 1/3 cup packed brown sugar
- 1/3 cup butter, melted
- 1 can (14 ounces) sweetened condensed milk
- 3/4 cup cold 2% milk
- 1 package (3.4 ounces) instant butterscotch pudding mix
- 3 packages (8 ounces each) cream cheese, softened
- 1 teaspoon vanilla extract
- 3 large eggs, lightly beaten
- Whipped cream and crushed butterscotch candies, optional

Direction

- Place an oiled 9-inch springform pan on a double-thickness of heavy-duty foil (around 18-inch square). Wrap securely foil around the pan. Mix sugar and cracker crumbs together in a small bowl; mix in butter. Press the mixture onto bottom of the prepared pan. Lay the pan on a baking sheet. Bake 10 minutes at 325 degrees. Place on wire rack to cool.
- Whisk pudding mix and milks in a small bowl, about 2 minutes. Allow to stand until soft-set, about 2 minutes.

- At the same time, beat cream cheese in a big bowl until smooth. Whisk in vanilla and pudding. Put in eggs and whisk at low speed just until blended. Pour over crust. Arrange the springform pan in a big baking pan; pour in 1 inch of hot water to larger pan.
- Bake 65-75 minutes at 325 degrees until top appears dull and center is almost set. Take springform pan out of water bath. Allow to cool on wire rack 10 minutes.
- Run a knife following the edge of the pan carefully to loosen; let cool 1 hour more. Chill in the fridge overnight. If wanted, use whipped cream and butterscotch candies to garnish.

Nutrition Information

- Calories: 473 calories
- Protein: 10g protein.
- Total Fat: 30g fat (18g saturated fat)
- Sodium: 460mg sodium
- Fiber: 0 fiber)
- Total Carbohydrate: 42g carbohydrate (34g sugars
- Cholesterol: 141mg cholesterol

304. Banana Butterfinger Pudding

Serving: 4-6 servings. | Prep: 15mins | Cook: 0mins | Ready in:

Ingredients

- 1 cup cold milk
- 1 package (3.4 ounces) instant banana pudding mix
- 3 Butterfinger candy bars (2.1 ounces each), crushed
- 1 carton (8 ounces) frozen whipped topping, thawed
- 3 medium firm bananas, sliced

Direction

- Beat pudding mix and milk till thick for 2 minutes in a big bowl; for topping, put 1/3 cup crushed candy aside. Fold leftover candy, bananas and whipped topping into pudding.
- Put into serving dishes; chill till serving. Sprinkle reserved candy right before serving.

Nutrition Information

- Calories: 290 calories
- Total Fat: 10g fat (8g saturated fat)
- Sodium: 265mg sodium
- Fiber: 2g fiber)
- Total Carbohydrate: 45g carbohydrate (33g sugars
- Cholesterol: 6mg cholesterol
- Protein: 3g protein.

305.   Banana Cheesecake Pie

Serving: 8 servings. | Prep: 25mins | Cook: 0mins | Ready in:

Ingredients

- 1 package (11.1 ounces) no-bake home-style cheesecake mix
- 1/2 cup crushed vanilla wafers (about 15 wafers)
- 2 tablespoons sugar
- 1/2 cup cold butter, cubed
- 1 cup 2% milk plus 1-1/2 cups 2% milk, divided
- 1 package (3.4 ounces) instant banana cream pudding mix
- 2 medium bananas, cut into 1/4-in. slices
- 1 cup whipped topping
- 1/4 cup chopped pecans, toasted

Direction

- Combine sugar, wafers and contents of the crust mix in large bowl; cut in butter until coarse crumbs resemble. Press up sides and onto bottom of an unoiled 9 inches deep-dish pie plate.
- Beat contents of the filling mix and one cup of milk in large bowl on low speed until they are blended. Beat for 3 mins on medium, until they become smooth (the filling should become thick). Transfer to crust by spoon. Let chill for half an hour.
- In the meantime, whisk pudding mix and remaining milk in small bowl for 2 mins. Allow to stand until soft-set, about 2 mins (the pudding should become stiff). Place banana slices onto filling. Spread pudding over, followed by the whipped topping. Top with the pecans. Let chill at least 60 mins. Then serve.

Nutrition Information

- Calories: 468 calories
- Sodium: 594mg sodium
- Fiber: 2g fiber)
- Total Carbohydrate: 64g carbohydrate (43g sugars
- Cholesterol: 38mg cholesterol
- Protein: 5g protein.
- Total Fat: 22g fat (12g saturated fat)

306.   Banana Chocolate Coconut Pie

Serving: 6-8 servings. | Prep: 30mins | Cook: 0mins | Ready in:

Ingredients

- 1-1/2 teaspoons plus 2 tablespoons butter, divided
- 1/3 cup plus 1-1/2 cups sweetened shredded coconut, divded
- 2 ounces unsweetened chocolate
- 2/3 cup confectioners' sugar
- 2 tablespoons milk

- FILLING:
- 2 medium bananas, cut into 1/4-inch slices
- 1-3/4 cups cold milk
- 1 package (3.9 ounces) instant chocolate pudding mix

Direction

- Use 1 1/2 teaspoons butter to grease a 9-inch pie plate. Scatter 1/3 cup coconut over the buttered pie plate; put to one side.
- Melt the remaining butter and chocolate in a heavy saucepan or microwave oven; whisk until no lumps remain.
- Whisk milk and confectioners' sugar together; mix into chocolate mixture. Mix in the rest of coconut. Gently pat mixture onto the bottom and around the sides of the prepared pie plate. Chill for 1 hour or until set.
- Place bananas over the crust. Beat pudding mix and cold milk for 2 minutes in a mixing bowl; allow to sit until soft-set, about 2 minutes.
- Spread pudding mixture over bananas. Refrigerate for 3 hours prior to serving. Chill leftovers in the fridge.

Nutrition Information

- Calories: 307 calories
- Protein: 3g protein.
- Total Fat: 15g fat (11g saturated fat)
- Sodium: 325mg sodium
- Fiber: 3g fiber)
- Total Carbohydrate: 43g carbohydrate (34g sugars
- Cholesterol: 17mg cholesterol

---

307. Banana Chocolate Cream Pie

Serving: 4 servings. | Prep: 15mins | Cook: 15mins | Ready in:

Ingredients

- 1 sheet refrigerated pie pastry
- 3/4 cup plus 2 tablespoons 2% milk
- 1/3 cup instant chocolate pudding mix
- 1/4 cup English toffee bits or almond brickle chips
- 1 small ripe banana, sliced
- 3/4 cup whipped topping

Direction

- Slice the pastry sheet into halves. Repackage one half and refrigerate for a different use. Roll out the remaining half on a lightly floured surface into an 8-in. circle. Transfer it into a 7-in. pie plate; flute the edges.
- Use a double thickness heavy-duty foil to line the unpricked pastry shell. Bake for 8 minutes at 450°. Take off the foil; bake for another 5 minutes. Let it cool down on a wire rack.
- Whisk together milk and pudding mix in a small bowl for 2 minutes. Let sit until soft set for 2 minutes. Sprinkle toffee bits onto the crust; layer with the banana and pudding. Spread the whipped topping on top. Chill in the refrigerator for at least 1 hour before serving. For storage, keep leftovers in the refrigerator.

Nutrition Information

- Calories: 339 calories
- Fiber: 1g fiber)
- Total Carbohydrate: 47g carbohydrate (27g sugars
- Cholesterol: 14mg cholesterol
- Protein: 3g protein.
- Total Fat: 16g fat (8g saturated fat)
- Sodium: 416mg sodium

308. Banana Chocolate Parfaits

Serving: 8 servings. | Prep: 20mins | Cook: 0mins | Ready in:

Ingredients

- 3 medium bananas, sliced
- 1/4 cup lemon juice
- 2 cups cold fat-free milk
- 1 package (1.4 ounces) sugar-free instant chocolate pudding mix
- 1 cup (8 ounces) reduced-fat sour cream
- 1-1/2 cups reduced-fat whipped topping
- 8 chocolate wafers, crushed

Direction

- Mix lemon juice and bananas in a small bowl; allow it to stand for 5 minutes. Combine pudding mix and milk in a separate bowl for 2 minutes. Keep for 5 minutes in the refrigerator. Mix in sour cream.
- Strain bananas. In each eight parfait glasses, put half of the banana slices; then layer with chocolate wafer crumbs, whipped topping, pudding mixture, and the rest of banana slices. Keep in the refrigerator until serving time.

Nutrition Information

- Calories: 183 calories
- Fiber: 2g fiber)
- Total Carbohydrate: 27g carbohydrate (15g sugars
- Cholesterol: 11mg cholesterol
- Protein: 5g protein. Diabetic Exchanges: 1 starch
- Total Fat: 6g fat (5g saturated fat)
- Sodium: 236mg sodium

309. Banana Cream Brownie Dessert

Serving: 12-15 servings. | Prep: 20mins | Cook: 30mins | Ready in:

Ingredients

- 1 package fudge brownie mix (13x9-inch pan size)
- 1 cup (6 ounces) semisweet chocolate chips, divided
- 3/4 cup dry roasted peanuts, chopped, divided
- 3 medium firm bananas
- 1-2/3 cups cold milk
- 2 packages (5.1 ounces each) instant vanilla pudding mix
- 1 carton (8 ounces) frozen whipped topping, thawed

Direction

- Prepare brownie batter as instructed on the package for fudge like brownies. Mix in 1/4 cup of peanuts and 1/2 cup of chocolate chips. Spread into a 13x9-in. greased baking pan. Bake at 350° until a toothpick comes out clean after being inserted into the middle, for 28-30 minutes. Let cool on a wire rack.
- Cut the bananas; layer over brownies in one layer. Sprinkle 1/4 cup of peanuts and 1/4 cup of chips on top.
- In a large bowl, beat together milk and pudding mixes for 2 minutes on low speed. Fold in the whipped topping. Spread on top. Sprinkle with the rest of the chips and peanuts. Chill in refrigerator until serving.

Nutrition Information

- Calories: 479 calories
- Total Carbohydrate: 66g carbohydrate (46g sugars
- Cholesterol: 29mg cholesterol
- Protein: 6g protein.
- Total Fat: 23g fat (8g saturated fat)

- Sodium: 349mg sodium
- Fiber: 3g fiber)

310. Banana Cream Cheesecake

Serving: 12 | Prep: 35mins | Cook: 1hours | Ready in:

Ingredients

- Crust:
- 1 1/4 cups vanilla wafer crumbs
- 1/2 cup ground walnuts
- 5 tablespoons butter, melted
- Filling:
- 4 (8 ounce) packages cream cheese, room temperature
- 1 1/8 cups white sugar
- 3 tablespoons all-purpose flour
- 4 eggs
- 1 cup sour cream
- 2 ripe bananas, mashed
- 1/4 cup banana liqueur
- 1 1/2 teaspoons vanilla extract
- Topping:
- 1 1/2 teaspoons unflavored gelatin
- 3 tablespoons cold water
- 1 cup milk
- 1/3 cup white sugar
- 4 egg yolks
- 2 teaspoons vanilla extract
- 1 1/2 cups heavy cream, chilled
- 12 vanilla wafer cookies

Direction

- Preheat the oven to 175 ° C (350 ° F). Grease a 9-inch springform pan sides. Blend the melted butter, ground walnuts and vanilla wafer crumbs together in a medium bowl. Pat onto the bottom of the prepared pan.
- Mix the cream cheese in a big bowl to soften. Blend flour and 1 1/8 cups of sugar; mix into cream cheese until smooth. Mix in the eggs,

one by one, stirring until well mixed after each addition. Mix in the 1 1/2 teaspoons vanilla, banana liqueur, mashed banana and sour cream. Pour onto the crust in the springform pan.
- Use the aluminum foil to cover the bottom of the outside of cheesecake pan to keep water from the water bath from seeping in. In a bigger pan, position the springform pan. Position the entire thing in the preheated oven then fill hot water into the outer pan.
- Bake in the preheated oven for 45 minutes. Turn off the oven after the time is up, but leave the door closed. Leave the cheesecake for an hour in the unopened oven. Prior to removing from water bath, run a knife around the cake's outer edge to prevent it from shrinking away from the middle and cracking. Allow to cool to room temperature, then refrigerate for minimum of 3 hours or overnight until chilled.
- Dust the unflavored gelatin on cold water in a small bowl then put aside until soft. Heat the milk over medium-low heat in a small saucepan till hot but not boiling. In the meantime, stir egg yolks and 1/3 cup sugar together until frothy and smooth. Stir about 1/3 the hot milk into the egg yolk blend, and pour the yolk blend into the pan with the rest of the milk. Cook over low heat, constantly mixing using a spatula, ensuring the blend will not burn on the bottom until it is thick enough to coat a metal spoon's back. Take away from the heat. Mix the softened gelatin into the hot pastry cream, until dissolved and then mix in the vanilla. Put into a bowl, then position a plastic wrap sheet directly on the surface then refrigerate for 1 hour until cooled.
- Whip the heavy cream just past soft peaks after pastry cream is cooled. Mix to soften the pastry cream and fold in the whipped cream. Put the vanilla wafers over the cooled cheesecake and spread vanilla cream all over the top. Chill until you serve. Prior to removing the sides for a cleaner look, run a wet knife around the cake's outer edge.

Nutrition Information

- Calories: 790 calories;
- Sodium: 388
- Total Carbohydrate: 56
- Cholesterol: 276
- Protein: 13
- Total Fat: 57.5

---

311. Banana Cream Parfait

Serving: 4 servings. | Prep: 25mins | Cook: 0mins
| Ready in:

Ingredients

- 1 package (3-1/2 ounces) instant banana pudding mix
- 2 cups cold milk
- 1/2 cup graham cracker crumbs
- 2 medium ripe bananas, sliced
- Whipped cream
- 4 maraschino cherries, optional

Direction

- Prepare the pudding based on the package directions, with 2 cups cold milk. Into each four parfait or dessert glasses, scatter 1 tablespoon graham crackers crumbs. Put 1/4 cup prepared pudding and half of the banana slices on top of crumbs. Continue layers of crumbs, pudding, and banana slices. Decorate each dessert with whipped cream and a cherry if preferred.

Nutrition Information

- Calories: 263 calories
- Sodium: 471mg sodium
- Fiber: 2g fiber)
- Total Carbohydrate: 50g carbohydrate (36g sugars
- Cholesterol: 17mg cholesterol
- Protein: 5g protein.

- Total Fat: 5g fat (3g saturated fat)

---

312. Banana Flip Cake

Serving: 16 servings. | Prep: 30mins | Cook: 30mins
| Ready in:

Ingredients

- 1 package yellow cake mix (regular size)
- 1 package (3.4 ounces) instant banana or vanilla pudding mix
- 1-1/2 cups 2% milk
- 4 eggs
- FROSTING:
- 1/3 cup all-purpose flour
- 1 cup 2% milk
- 1/2 cup butter, softened
- 1/2 cup shortening
- 1 cup sugar
- 1-1/2 teaspoons vanilla extract
- 2 tablespoons confectioners' sugar

Direction

- Use waxed paper to line 2 15"x10"x1" baking pans coated with grease, then grease the paper and put aside.
- Mix together eggs, milk, pudding mix and cake mix in a big bowl, then beat on low speed about half a minute. Continue to beat on medium about 2 minutes.
- Spread the batter into prepped pans and bake at 350 degrees until a toothpick exits clean after being inserted into the center, about 12 to 15 minutes. Allow to cool about 5 minutes prior to inverting on wire racks to cool thoroughly. Peel off waxed paper gently.
- In the meantime, whisk together milk and flour in a small saucepan until smooth. Bring mixture to a boil, then cook and stir until thickened, about 2 minutes. Take away from the heat, then place on a cover and allow to cool to room temperature.

- Cream together sugar, shortening and butter in the bowl of a heavy-duty stand mixer until fluffy and light. Beat in vanilla. Put in milk mixture and beat on high until fluffy, about 10 to 15 minutes.
- Put on a big cutting board with one cake and spread frosting over top. Put leftover cake on top and sprinkle with more confectioners' sugar. Cut cake into slices and chill leftovers.

Nutrition Information

- Calories: 355 calories
- Sodium: 372mg sodium
- Fiber: 0 fiber)
- Total Carbohydrate: 49g carbohydrate (35g sugars
- Cholesterol: 71mg cholesterol
- Protein: 4g protein.
- Total Fat: 16g fat (7g saturated fat)

313. Banana Graham Dessert

Serving: 9 servings. | Prep: 20mins | Cook: 0mins | Ready in:

Ingredients

- 1 package (1.5 ounces) instant sugar-free vanilla pudding mix
- 2-3/4 cups fat-free milk
- 1 cup fat-free sour cream
- 12 whole reduced-fat graham crackers
- 2 large firm bananas, sliced

Direction

- Beat milk and pudding mix for 2 minutes on low speed in bowl; fold sour cream in. stand for 5 minutes. Layer 1/3 graham crackers, bananas then pudding mixture in 3-qt. bowl; repeat layers twice then refrigerate.

Nutrition Information

- Calories: 114 calories
- Cholesterol: 4mg cholesterol
- Protein: 5g protein. Diabetic Exchanges: 1-1/2 starch.
- Total Fat: 1g fat (0 saturated fat)
- Sodium: 141mg sodium
- Fiber: 0 fiber)
- Total Carbohydrate: 22g carbohydrate (0 sugars

314. Banana Ice Cream

Serving: 8 | Prep: 5mins | Cook: 40mins | Ready in:

Ingredients

- 2 cups skim milk
- 1/2 (12 fluid ounce) can evaporated milk
- 1/2 cup white sugar
- 1 teaspoon vanilla extract
- 2 bananas, mashed
- 1/2 cup golden raisins (optional)

Direction

- Mix vanilla, sugar, evaporated milk and skim milk in a medium bowl; put into an ice cream maker. Follow manufacturer's instructions to freeze.
- Add raisins and bananas once ice cream is finished freezing; let them mix in. Put into freezer container; freeze overnight to improve texture before serving.

Nutrition Information

- Calories: 160 calories;
- Sodium: 52
- Total Carbohydrate: 32.9
- Cholesterol: 8
- Protein: 4.3
- Total Fat: 2

315. Banana Pudding Dessert

Serving: 6-8 servings. | Prep: 15mins | Cook: 0mins | Ready in:

Ingredients

- 1 package (3.4 ounces) instant vanilla pudding mix
- 1-1/4 cups cold water
- 1 can (14 ounces) sweetened condensed milk
- 2 cups whipped topping
- 24 to 32 vanilla wafers
- 3 large firm bananas, sliced

Direction

- Beat milk, water and pudding mix for 2 minutes on low speed in a big bowl; chill for 5 minutes then fold in whipped topping.
- Layer wafers, pudding, bananas then more pudding in individual dessert dishes; top each using a wafer then chill till serving.

Nutrition Information

- Calories: 354 calories
- Fiber: 1g fiber)
- Total Carbohydrate: 63g carbohydrate (52g sugars
- Cholesterol: 18mg cholesterol
- Protein: 5g protein.
- Total Fat: 10g fat (6g saturated fat)
- Sodium: 271mg sodium

316. Banana Pudding Parfaits

Serving: 4 servings | Prep: 15mins | Cook: | Ready in:

Ingredients

- 24 vanilla wafers , divided

- 1 pkg. (3.4 oz.) JELL-O Banana Cream Flavor Instant Pudding
- 2 cups cold milk
- 3/4 cup thawed COOL WHIP Whipped Topping
- 1 banana , cut into 20 slices

Direction

- 1. Mash 20 wafers to make coarse crumbs. In a medium bowl, combine milk and pudding mix using a whisk for 2 minutes. Mix in COOL WHIP.
- 2. Set aside 4 slices of banana for decorating. Then layer half of the wafer crumbs and the rest of bananas evenly in 4 dessert dishes; continue layering.
- 3. Keep in the refrigerator for 15 minutes. Place the rest of the wafers and reserved banana slices on top just prior to serving.

Nutrition Information

- Calories: 320
- Saturated Fat: 5 g
- Cholesterol: 15 mg
- Protein: 6 g
- Total Fat: 9 g
- Sugar: 39 g
- Total Carbohydrate: 55 g
- Sodium: 510 mg
- Fiber: 1 g

317. Banana Split Cheesecake

Serving: 18 | Prep: | Cook: | Ready in:

Ingredients

- 2 1/2 cups graham cracker crumbs
- 3/4 cup melted butter
- 4 cups confectioners' sugar
- 2 (8 ounce) packages cream cheese
- 1 (8 ounce) can crushed pineapple, drained

- 3 medium bananas, quartered
- 1 (12 ounce) container frozen whipped topping, thawed
- 8 maraschino cherries, halved
- 1/4 cup chocolate syrup
- 1/2 cup pecan halves

Direction

- Combine melted margarine or butter with graham crackers; press mixture into the bottom of a 9x12-inch pan.
- Beat cream cheese with confectioners' sugar until smooth. Spread over graham cracker layer. Arrange bananas and crushed pineapple over the cream cheese. Top with a spreading layer of whipped topping. Garnish on top with maraschino cherry halves. Drizzle over the top with chocolate syrup and scatter with pecans. Refrigerate for a minimum of 4 hours prior to serving.

Nutrition Information

- Calories: 428 calories;
- Cholesterol: 48
- Protein: 3.6
- Total Fat: 24.6
- Sodium: 207
- Total Carbohydrate: 50.9

318.   Banana Split Icebox Cake

Serving: 10 servings. | Prep: 30mins | Cook: 0mins | Ready in:

Ingredients

- 1 carton (16 ounces) frozen whipped topping, thawed
- 1 cup (8 ounces) sour cream
- 1 package (3.4 ounces) instant vanilla pudding mix
- 1 can (8 ounces) crushed pineapple, drained
- 24 whole graham crackers

- 2 medium bananas, sliced
- Toppings: chocolate syrup, halved fresh strawberries and additional banana slices

Direction

- Combine pudding mix, sour cream, and whipped topping in a large mixing bowl until incorporated. Mix in pineapple. Snip a small hole in a corner of a food-safe plastic bag or in the tip of a pastry bag. Pour pudding mixture into the bag.
- Place 4 crackers in a rectangle on a flat serving plate. Squeeze about 1 cup of pudding mixture over cracker layer; place about 1/4 cup banana slices over pudding mixture. Repeat layering process 5 more times. Cover and chill overnight.
- Top cake with more banana slices, strawberries, and chocolate syrup right before serving.

Nutrition Information

- Calories: 405 calories
- Protein: 4g protein.
- Total Fat: 15g fat (11g saturated fat)
- Sodium: 372mg sodium
- Fiber: 2g fiber)
- Total Carbohydrate: 60g carbohydrate (30g sugars
- Cholesterol: 16mg cholesterol

319.   Banana Split Pie

Serving: 22 | Prep: 30mins | Cook: | Ready in:

Ingredients

- 1 cup margarine, softened
- 2 eggs
- 2 cups confectioners' sugar
- 2 (9 inch) prepared graham cracker crusts
- 5 bananas, sliced

- 1 (15 ounce) can crushed pineapple, drained with juice reserved
- 1 (16 ounce) container frozen whipped topping, thawed
- 1 (4 ounce) jar maraschino cherries
- 1/2 cup pecans

Direction

- Cream confectioners' sugar, eggs and margarine together in a medium bowl; whisk 15 minutes. Evenly spread into graham cracker crusts.
- Arrange banana slices atop the sugar mixture in each crust; arrange pineapple over banana. With a spoon, spread a small amount of reserved juice over fruit. Arrange whipped topping over fruit using the spoon; garnish with pecans and cherries. Allow to chill, then serve.

Nutrition Information

- Calories: 339 calories;
- Total Carbohydrate: 39.1
- Cholesterol: 17
- Protein: 2.3
- Total Fat: 20.4
- Sodium: 217

320.   Banana Split Pudding

Serving: 6-8 servings. | Prep: 10mins | Cook: 0mins | Ready in:

Ingredients

- 3 cups cold 2% milk
- 1 package (5.1 ounces) instant vanilla pudding mix
- 1 medium firm banana, sliced
- 1 cup sliced fresh strawberries
- 1 can (8 ounces) crushed pineapple, drained
- 1 carton (8 ounces) frozen whipped topping, thawed

- 1/4 cup chocolate syrup
- 1/4 cup chopped pecans
- Additional sliced strawberries and bananas, optional

Direction

- Whisk pudding mix and milk for 2 minutes in a big bowl; set till soft set for 2 minutes. Add pineapple, strawberries and banana.
- Put into a big serving bowl; dollop using whipped topping. Drizzle chocolate syrup; sprinkle pecans. If desired, top with extra bananas and strawberries.

Nutrition Information

- Calories: 291 calories
- Protein: 4g protein.
- Total Fat: 11g fat (7g saturated fat)
- Sodium: 305mg sodium
- Fiber: 2g fiber)
- Total Carbohydrate: 43g carbohydrate (34g sugars
- Cholesterol: 12mg cholesterol

321.   Banana And Nut Cake

Serving: 12 servings. | Prep: 10mins | Cook: 50mins | Ready in:

Ingredients

- 1 package yellow cake mix (regular size)
- 1 package (3.4 ounces) instant banana cream pudding mix
- 1 cup water
- 3 eggs
- 1/4 cup vegetable oil
- 1-1/2 cups mashed ripe bananas (about 2 medium)
- 3/4 cup chopped walnuts
- Confectioners' sugar, optional

Direction

- Beat first 5 ingredients for 30 seconds on low speed in a big bowl; beat for 2 minutes on medium. Beat in bananas; mix in nuts.
- Put into 13x9-in. greased baking pan; bake it at 350° till inserted toothpick in middle exits clean for 30-35 minutes. Cool on the wire rack. If desired, dust with confectioners' sugar.

Nutrition Information

- Calories: 341 calories
- Protein: 6g protein.
- Total Fat: 14g fat (3g saturated fat)
- Sodium: 399mg sodium
- Fiber: 2g fiber)
- Total Carbohydrate: 49g carbohydrate (30g sugars
- Cholesterol: 53mg cholesterol

322.   Banana Berry Pie

Serving: 8 servings. | Prep: 30mins | Cook: 0mins | Ready in:

Ingredients

- 1-1/4 cups graham cracker crumbs
- 5 tablespoons butter, melted
- 2 tablespoons sugar
- 1 teaspoon ground ginger
- FILLING:
- 3/4 cup sugar
- 2 tablespoons plus 3/4 teaspoon cornstarch
- 1 tablespoon strawberry gelatin
- 3/4 cup cold water
- 2 cups sliced fresh strawberries, divided
- 1 can (14 ounces) sweetened condensed milk
- 1 package (8 ounces) reduced-fat cream cheese
- 1/4 cup cold 2% milk
- 1 package (3.4 ounces) instant banana cream pudding mix

Direction

- Combine ginger, sugar, butter and graham cracker crumbs. Press up sides and onto bottom of an unoiled 9-in. pie plate. Bake for 8 to 10 mins at 350°, or until lightly browned. Place on wire rack to cool.
- To make filling, combine gelatin, sugar and cornstarch in a small saucepan. Mix in the water until smooth. Boil; cook while stirring until thickened, or about 2 mins. Slightly cool. Place one cup of the strawberries over the crust. Add the gelatin mixture over the strawberries. Place in the refrigerator until set, or about 120 mins.
- Beat pudding mix, milk, cream cheese and sweetened condensed milk in a large bowl for one minute. Spread the mixture over top of the pie. Place in the refrigerator until set, or about 120 mins. Add the remaining strawberries for garnish. Place the leftovers in refrigerator.

Nutrition Information

- Calories: 508 calories
- Protein: 9g protein.
- Total Fat: 19g fat (12g saturated fat)
- Sodium: 495mg sodium
- Fiber: 1g fiber)
- Total Carbohydrate: 78g carbohydrate (67g sugars
- Cholesterol: 56mg cholesterol

323.   Berry Cookie Torte

Serving: 8 servings. | Prep: 45mins | Cook: 9mins | Ready in:

Ingredients

- 1 tube (18 ounces) refrigerated sugar cookie dough
- 1 package (8 ounces) cream cheese, softened
- 1/2 cup confectioners' sugar
- 1 cup cold milk

- 1 package (3.4 ounces) instant vanilla pudding mix
- 2 cups whipped topping, divided
- 1 cup fresh blueberries
- 1 cup fresh raspberries
- 8 miniature Milano cookies

Direction

- Separate the dough into three parts. Cover up and chill two portions. Roll one portion into a circle of 9 inches with the thickness of about 1/8 inch on a floured surface.
- Remove to a clean and dry baking sheet. Bake at 350° until lightly browned, about 7-9 minutes. Let cool for 2 minutes; transfer carefully to a wire rack for cooling. Repeat two more time.
- Beat confectioners' sugar and cream cheese together in a large bowl until smooth. Whisk pudding mix and milk in a large bowl for 2 minutes; beat into the cream cheese mixture. Fold in 1 cup of whipped topping. Cover up and allow to chill for at least 15 minutes.
- On a serving plate, add one cookie layer. Place the 3/4 cup pudding mixture, 1/3 cup each blueberries and raspberries on top. Repeat. Add the remaining cookie layer on top; spread with 1/2 cup of pudding mixture.
- Pipe the rest of pudding mixture and whipped topping on top. Garnish with the remaining berries and cookies.

Nutrition Information

- Calories: 564 calories
- Protein: 6g protein.
- Total Fat: 29g fat (14g saturated fat)
- Sodium: 550mg sodium
- Fiber: 2g fiber)
- Total Carbohydrate: 70g carbohydrate (40g sugars
- Cholesterol: 55mg cholesterol

---

324.   Berry, Lemon And Doughnut Hole Trifle

Serving: 10 servings. | Prep: 25mins | Cook: 0mins | Ready in:

Ingredients

- 2 cups cold 2% milk
- 1 package (3.4 ounces) instant lemon pudding mix
- 1 carton (8 ounces) frozen whipped topping, thawed and divided
- 16 to 32 plain doughnut holes
- 3 cups fresh strawberries, halved
- 2 cups fresh blueberries

Direction

- Whisk pudding mix and milk for 2 minutes; stand till soft set or for 2 minutes. Fold 2 1/2 cups whipped topping in; put aside.
- Put 1/2 doughnut holes in 3-qt. trifle bowl; spread 1/2 pudding mixture on top. Top using 1/2 blueberries and strawberries; repeat layers. Put leftover whipped topping over; chill till serving.

Nutrition Information

- Calories:
- Total Carbohydrate:
- Cholesterol:
- Protein:
- Total Fat:
- Sodium:
- Fiber:

---

325.   Berry Glazed Chocolate Cake

Serving: 12 servings. | Prep: 15mins | Cook: 45mins | Ready in:

Ingredients

- 1 package devil's food cake mix (regular size)
- 1 package (3.9 ounces) instant chocolate pudding mix
- 4 large eggs
- 3/4 cup water
- 1/2 cup apple juice
- 1/2 cup canola oil
- 1 teaspoon rum extract
- 1 cup (6 ounces) semisweet chocolate chips
- RASPBERRY GLAZE:
- 1/4 cup seedless raspberry jam
- 2 tablespoons apple juice
- 1/2 teaspoon rum extract
- CHOCOLATE ICING:
- 2 tablespoons baking cocoa
- 1/4 cup heavy whipping cream
- 2 tablespoons butter, melted
- 1 cup confectioners' sugar
- 1 teaspoon vanilla extract

Direction

- Mix the first 7 ingredients in a large bowl; whisk for half a minute at low speed. Whisk for 2 minutes at medium speed. Add chocolate chips and stir.
- Pour into a floured and greased 10-inch fluted tube pan. Bake at 350 degrees until a toothpick comes out clean when inserted into the center, for 45-50 minutes. Let cool for 10 minutes, then transfer from the pan onto a wire rack to completely cool.
- Mix the glaze ingredients in a small saucepan. Stir and cook on low until smooth. Brush over the cake. Allow to stand until set, 10 minutes.
- In a small saucepan, arrange cocoa. Stir in butter and cream until they are smooth. Stir and cook on low heat until thickened, 2 minutes. Remove from the heat; then stir in vanilla and confectioners' sugar until smooth. Let cool slightly; drizzle on the cake. Allow to stand until it is set.

Nutrition Information

- Calories: 470 calories
- Protein: 5g protein.
- Total Fat: 23g fat (8g saturated fat)
- Sodium: 511mg sodium
- Fiber: 2g fiber)
- Total Carbohydrate: 63g carbohydrate (42g sugars
- Cholesterol: 83mg cholesterol

326.   Berry Marshmallow Trifle

Serving: 10 servings. | Prep: 25mins | Cook: 0mins | Ready in:

Ingredients

- 1-3/4 cups cold fat-free milk
- 1 package (1 ounce) sugar-free instant vanilla pudding mix
- 1 carton (8 ounces) frozen fat-free whipped topping, thawed, divided
- 1 loaf (10-3/4 ounces) frozen reduced-fat pound cake, thawed and cut into 1-inch cubes
- 3 cups fresh strawberries, halved
- 2 cups miniature marshmallows
- 3 tablespoons sliced almonds

Direction

- Whisk pudding mix and milk for 2 minutes in small bowl; stand till soft set for 2 minutes. Fold 2 1/2 cups whipped topping in; put aside.
- Put 1/2 cake cubes in 3-qt. trifle bowl; put 1/2 reserved pudding mixture over. Put 1/2 strawberries then marshmallows over; repeat layers. Top with leftover whipped topping; sprinkle almonds. Chill; serve.

Nutrition Information

- Calories: 230 calories
- Total Carbohydrate: 40g carbohydrate (23g sugars

- Cholesterol: 18mg cholesterol
- Protein: 4g protein.
- Total Fat: 6g fat (1g saturated fat)
- Sodium: 298mg sodium
- Fiber: 2g fiber)

- Protein: 1g protein. Diabetic Exchanges: 1-1/2 starch
- Total Fat: 7g fat (3g saturated fat)
- Sodium: 96mg sodium
- Fiber: 0 fiber)
- Total Carbohydrate: 23g carbohydrate (15g sugars
- Cholesterol: 4mg cholesterol

---

327.   Birthday Cake Freezer Pops

Serving: 1-1/2 dozen. | Prep: 25mins | Cook: 0mins | Ready in:

Ingredients

- 2/3 cup sprinkles, divided
- 18 disposable plastic or paper cups (3 ounces each)
- 2 cups cold 2% milk
- 1 package (3.4 ounces) instant vanilla pudding mix
- 1 carton (8 ounces) frozen whipped topping, thawed
- 2 cups crushed vanilla wafers (about 60 wafers)
- 18 wooden pop sticks

Direction

- In each cup, spoon 1 teaspoon sprinkles.
- Whisk pudding mix and milk for 2 minutes in a big bowl. Let stand for 2 minutes till soft-set. Mix leftover sprinkles, crushed wafers and whipped topping in.
- Cut 1-in. hole in tip of pastry bag/corner of food-safe plastic bag. Use pudding mixture to fill bag. Pipe in prepped cups. Put foil on top of cups. Insert pop sticks through the foil.
- Freeze for 4 hours till firm. Let stand for 5 minutes at room temperature. Gently remove pops.

Nutrition Information

- Calories: 161 calories

---

328.   Black Forest Dream Dessert

Serving: 12 servings. | Prep: 30mins | Cook: 15mins | Ready in:

Ingredients

- 1 cup all-purpose flour
- 2 tablespoons sugar
- 1/2 cup cold butter, cubed
- 1/2 cup sweetened shredded coconut
- 1/2 cup chopped walnuts, toasted
- 1 package (8 ounces) cream cheese, softened
- 1 cup confectioners' sugar
- 1 carton (8 ounces) frozen whipped topping, thawed, divided
- 1 can (21 ounces) cherry pie filling
- 1-1/2 cups semisweet chocolate chips
- 2-1/2 cups cold milk
- 2 packages (3.4 ounces each) instant vanilla pudding mix
- Chocolate curls, optional

Direction

- Mix sugar and flour together in a large bowl; cut butter into the flour mixture until crumbly. Mix in walnuts and coconut. Press into an unoiled 13x9-inch baking dish. Bake for 15 to 18 minutes at 350° or until light brown. Allow to cool on a wire rack.
- Beat cream cheese with confectioners' sugar in a small bowl until smooth. Add 1 cup of whipped topping; fold gently. Spread all over

the crust. Add pie filling over the top; chill, covered.

- Melt chocolate chips in a microwave, whisk until smooth. Stir pudding mixes and milk for 2 minutes in a large bowl. Allow to rest until soft-set, or for 2 minutes. Stir a small amount of pudding into melted chocolate. Pour everything back into the pudding, stirring continuously. Transfer mixture over cherry filling. Refrigerate until firm, or for 2 hours.
- Spread over the dessert with remaining whipped topping just before serving. If desired, garnish on top with chocolate curls.

Nutrition Information

- Calories: 540 calories
- Sodium: 293mg sodium
- Fiber: 2g fiber)
- Total Carbohydrate: 64g carbohydrate (47g sugars
- Cholesterol: 48mg cholesterol
- Protein: 7g protein.
- Total Fat: 30g fat (18g saturated fat)

329. Black Forest Mousse

Serving: 8 servings. | Prep: 5mins | Cook: 10mins | Ready in:

Ingredients

- 2 cups cold 2% milk
- 1 package (3.9 ounces) instant chocolate pudding mix
- 1 can (21 ounces) cherry pie filling
- 2 cups whipped topping

Direction

- Beat pudding mix and milk till smooth for 2 minutes in big bowl; stand till thick for 2 minutes. Mix pie filling in; fold whipped topping in gently. Put in solo dessert dishes; refrigerate till serving.

Nutrition Information

- Calories: 222 calories
- Protein: 2g protein.
- Total Fat: 5g fat (4g saturated fat)
- Sodium: 247mg sodium
- Fiber: 1g fiber)
- Total Carbohydrate: 40g carbohydrate (32g sugars
- Cholesterol: 8mg cholesterol

330. Black Forest Parfaits

Serving: 6 servings. | Prep: 10mins | Cook: 0mins | Ready in:

Ingredients

- 2 cups cold 2% milk
- 1 package (3.9 ounces) instant chocolate pudding mix
- 1 can (21 ounces) cherry pie filling, divided
- 2 cups whipped topping, divided
- 6 maraschino cherries with stems, optional

Direction

- Beat pudding mix and milk for 2 minutes in a large bowl. Allow it to stand for 2 minutes or until set to soft. Mix in 1 cup pie filling; slightly fold in 1 cup whipped topping.
- Into six tall cups or glasses, put half of the pudding mixture. Place the rest of the pie filling, pudding mixture, and whipped topping on top. Decorate with cherries if preferred.

Nutrition Information

- Calories: 296 calories
- Sodium: 330mg sodium
- Fiber: 1g fiber)

- Total Carbohydrate: 53g carbohydrate (43g sugars
- Cholesterol: 11mg cholesterol
- Protein: 3g protein.
- Total Fat: 7g fat (6g saturated fat)

331. Blarney Stones

Serving: 25 dozen. | Prep: 15mins | Cook: 10mins | Ready in:

Ingredients

- 1 cup butter, softened
- 3/4 cup packed brown sugar
- 1/4 cup sugar
- 1 package (3.4 ounces) instant pistachio pudding mix
- 1/2 teaspoon vanilla extract
- 1/2 teaspoon almond extract
- 2 eggs
- Green food coloring, optional
- 2-1/2 cups all-purpose flour
- 1 teaspoon baking soda
- 1 package (10 to 11 ounces) butterscotch chips
- 1 cup chopped walnuts

Direction

- Beat extracts, pudding mix, sugars and butter in a large bowl until fluffy and light. Put in eggs, one by one, beating thoroughly between additions. If preferred, add several drops of green coloring. Mix baking soda and flour together; slowly bring into the creamed mixture. Mix in nuts and chips (batter is supposed to be firm). Refrigerate, covered, for a few hours. Form into 1/2" balls; arrange onto unoiled baking sheets, keeping a 2"-distance away from each other.
- Bake for 8 minutes at 350 degrees. Move to wire racks to cool.

Nutrition Information

- Calories:
- Sodium:
- Fiber:
- Total Carbohydrate:
- Cholesterol:
- Protein:
- Total Fat:

332. Blueberry Cheesecake Ice Cream

Serving: 16 | Prep: 25mins | Cook: 20mins | Ready in:

Ingredients

- 1/2 cup white sugar
- 1 tablespoon cornstarch
- 1/2 cup water
- 1 1/4 cups blueberries
- 1 tablespoon lemon juice
- 2 1/4 cups graham cracker crumbs
- 2 tablespoons white sugar
- 1/2 teaspoon ground cinnamon
- 1/2 cup butter, melted
- 1 1/2 cups white sugar
- 1 (3.5 ounce) package instant vanilla pudding mix
- 4 cups heavy whipping cream
- 2 cups milk
- 2 teaspoons vanilla extract

Direction

- Combine 1/2 cup of sugar and cornstarch in a small saucepan; gradually mix in water until smooth. Mix in lemon juice and blueberries; let it come to a boil. Decrease heat to low and simmer with no cover for about 5 minutes, until slightly thickened. Cover up and keep in the fridge for about half an hour, until chilled.
- Set the oven to 350°F (175°C), and start preheating.
- In a large bowl, mix cinnamon, 2 tablespoons of sugar and graham cracker crumbs together;

mix in butter. Pat into a clean and dry baking pan of 10x15 inches.

- Bake crust in the prepared oven for 10-15 minutes, until lightly browned. Let cool completely on a wire rack; and then crumble crust.
- In a large bowl, whisk vanilla extract, milk, whipping cream, pudding mix and 1 1/2 cups sugar together. Fill the vanilla mixture into ice cream freezer cylinder 2/3 full. Allow to freeze following manufacturer's instructions; cool the remaining mixture in the fridge until ready to freeze. Whisk the rest of the mixture before adding in cylinder to remove the lumps.
- In a large bowl, layer ice cream, graham cracker mixture, and blueberry sauce and repeat layers two more times; swirl to blend. Freeze till ready to serve.

Nutrition Information

- Calories: 459 calories;
- Total Fat: 29.6
- Sodium: 239
- Total Carbohydrate: 46.5
- Cholesterol: 99
- Protein: 3.1

333.   Blueberry Lemon Crepes

Serving: 6 servings. | Prep: 30mins | Cook: 0mins | Ready in:

Ingredients

- CREPES:
- 1/2 cup biscuit/baking mix
- 6 tablespoons milk
- 1 large egg
- FILLING:
- 3 ounces cream cheese, softened
- 1-1/2 cups half-and-half cream
- 1 tablespoon lemon juice

- 1 package (3.4 ounces) instant lemon pudding mix
- TOPPING:
- 1 cup blueberry pie filling

Direction

- Mix together in a large bowl the egg, milk and biscuit mix. Refrigerate for 1 hour, covered. Place a 8-inches non-stick skillet on the stove and turn on to medium heat, lightly grease the pan; put 2 tablespoons of batter into the middle of pan. Raise and slant pan to equally coat the bottom. Let cook until top turns dry; roll and cook for 15-20 seconds more. Put on a wire rack. Redo with left batter, grease skillet as necessary. When chilled, pile crepes with a paper towels or waxed papers in between. (You may make the crepes in advance and place inside the refrigerator, covered tightly, and use when needed). For filling, beat together in a large bowl the pudding mix, lemon juice, cream and cheese and mix until well combined. Place inside the refrigerator for 30 minutes. Scoop pudding mixture about 2 tablespoons onto each crepe; rotate. Put left pudding mixture on top; use blueberry pie filling for garnishing.

Nutrition Information

- Calories: 302 calories
- Cholesterol: 83mg cholesterol
- Protein: 6g protein.
- Total Fat: 14g fat (8g saturated fat)
- Sodium: 440mg sodium
- Fiber: 1g fiber)
- Total Carbohydrate: 38g carbohydrate (26g sugars

334.   Blueberry Peach Trifle

Serving: 20 servings. | Prep: 15mins | Cook: 0mins | Ready in:

Ingredients

- 1 can (14 ounces) sweetened condensed milk
- 1-1/2 cups cold water
- 2 teaspoons grated lemon zest
- 1 package (3.4 ounces) instant vanilla pudding mix
- 2 cups heavy whipping cream, whipped
- 4 cups cubed pound cake (3/4-inch cubes)
- 2-1/2 cups chopped peeled peaches
- 2 cups fresh or frozen unsweetened blueberries, thawed

Direction

- Mix lemon zest, water and condensed milk in big bowl; whisk pudding mix in. Chill for 5 minutes.
- Fold whipped cream in; put 2 cups pudding mixture in 4-qt. glass serving bowl. Put 1/2 cake cubes, all peaches, 1/2 leftover pudding mixture, leftover cake cubes then blueberries over. Within 1-in. of bowl edge, spread leftover pudding mixture; chill for 4 hours minimum.

Nutrition Information

- Calories: 239 calories
- Fiber: 1g fiber)
- Total Carbohydrate: 28g carbohydrate (23g sugars
- Cholesterol: 61mg cholesterol
- Protein: 3g protein.
- Total Fat: 13g fat (8g saturated fat)
- Sodium: 160mg sodium

335. Boston Cream Pie

Serving: | Prep: | Cook: | Ready in:

Ingredients

- 1 1/2 sticks (3/4 cup) unsalted, butter, softened
- 1 1/4 cups sugar
- 1 teaspoon vanilla
- 2 large eggs
- 2 cups cake flour (not self-rising)
- 2 1/2 teaspoons double-acting baking powder
- 1/2 teaspoon salt
- 3/4 cup milk
- 3 tablespoons cornstarch
- 1/3 cup sugar
- 1 cup milk
- 3 large eggs
- 1/2 cup heavy cream
- 1/4 teaspoon salt
- 1 vanilla bean, split lengthwise
- 3 tablespoons unsalted butter
- 6 ounces fine-quality bittersweet chocolate (not unsweetened), broken into pieces
- 3 tablespoons water
- 2 tablespoons unsalted butter
- 1 1/2 tablespoons light corn syrup
- 1/4 teaspoon salt
- seasonal fruit and blossoms (non-toxic only) for garnish

Direction

- Preparation: Make the cake: Set oven to 350°F to preheat. Coat a 9 1/2-inch springform pan with butter and flour. Use an electric mixer to cream vanilla, sugar and the butter together in a bowl until fluffy and light and crack in each egg at a time, beating well between additions. Sift the salt, baking powder and flour together into another bowl and beat the mixture alternately with the milk into the butter mixture in batches, starting and finishing with the flour mixture. Put the batter into the buttered springform pan and bake the cake in the center of the oven until a tester comes out clean, 50 to 55 minutes. Let it cool in the pan on a rack.
- Make the custard: Mix together the milk, the sugar and the cornstarch in a saucepan put in the eggs, the salt, and the cream, then whisk until smooth. Take out the seeds from the vanilla bean, putting the pod aside for another use, then put them into the cream mixture, and

bring the custard to a boil on moderate heat, constantly whisking. Boil while whisking the custard for 2 minutes, then take away the pan from the heat, and blend in the butter. Let the custard cool down completely while whisking occasionally.

- Make the glaze: Melt the chocolate together with the salt, corn syrup, butter and water in a metal bowl set over a saucepan of lightly simmering water; keep stirring until glaze is smooth, and take the bowl away from the pan.

- Take out the cake from the pan, use a long serrated knife to halve it horizontally, and place the bottom half on a plate with cut side up. Add the custard on top of the bottom half, spreading the custard to the edge; place the other cake half on the custard with cut side down, and pour over the cake with the glaze, spreading the glaze to the edge and allowing it to drip down the side. The Boston cream pie can be made 1 day in advance and kept with a loose cover and chilled. Use the fruit and the blossoms to garnish the pie.

Nutrition Information

- Calories: 300
- Saturated Fat: 10 g(49%)
- Sodium: 195 mg(8%)
- Fiber: 1 g(3%)
- Total Carbohydrate: 36 g(12%)
- Cholesterol: 83 mg(28%)
- Protein: 4 g(8%)
- Total Fat: 17 g(25%)

---

336. Boston Cream Pie With Chocolate Glaze

Serving: 12 servings. | Prep: 10mins | Cook: 30mins | Ready in:

Ingredients

- 1 package yellow cake mix (regular size)

- 1-1/2 cups cold whole milk
- 1 package (3.4 ounces) instant vanilla pudding mix
- 2 ounces unsweetened chocolate
- 2 tablespoons butter
- 1 cup confectioners' sugar
- 1/2 teaspoon vanilla extract
- 2 to 3 tablespoons hot water

Direction

- Follow the package directions to prepare the cake mix batter properly. Transfer into two 9-in. round baking pans coated with grease and flour.
- Bake at 350° till a toothpick turns out clean when inserted into the center, about 28-33 minutes. Allow to cool for 1 minute; take away from the pans and allow to cool completely on wire racks.
- Whisk pudding mix and milk in a small bowl for 2 minutes. Allow to sit till soft-set, about 2 minutes. Refrigerate with a cover.
- Melt butter and chocolate in a microwave; stir till smooth. Mix in vanilla, confectioners' sugar, and enough water to attain a thick glaze; set aside.
- On a serving plate, place one cake layer; spread pudding over. Place the second cake layer on top. Spoon the chocolate glaze over the top, letting the glaze drip down the sides of the cake. Place in the refrigerator till serving.

Nutrition Information

- Calories: 397 calories
- Cholesterol: 55mg cholesterol
- Protein: 4g protein.
- Total Fat: 17g fat (5g saturated fat)
- Sodium: 409mg sodium
- Fiber: 2g fiber)
- Total Carbohydrate: 57g carbohydrate (37g sugars

337. Brownie Mocha Trifle

Serving: 12 servings. | Prep: 15mins | Cook: 25mins | Ready in:

Ingredients

- 1 package fudge brownie mix (8-inch-square pan size)
- 1-3/4 cups cold 2% milk
- 2 packages (3.4 ounces each) instant vanilla pudding mix
- 1/4 cup cold brewed coffee
- 2 cups whipped topping
- 1 Heath candy bar (1.4 ounces), crushed

Direction

- Follow package directions to prep and bake brownie batter; cool. Slice to 1-in. pieces.
- Beat pudding mixes and milk for 2 minutes till thick in big bowl; mix coffee in. Fold whipped topping in.
- Layer 1/3 brown pieces, pudding mixture then crushed candy bar in 2-qt. glass bowl/trifle bowl; repeat layers twice. Chill till serving.

Nutrition Information

- Calories: 344 calories
- Total Fat: 14g fat (5g saturated fat)
- Sodium: 404mg sodium
- Fiber: 1g fiber)
- Total Carbohydrate: 51g carbohydrate (36g sugars
- Cholesterol: 22mg cholesterol
- Protein: 4g protein.

338. Brownie Toffee Trifle

Serving: 10-12 servings. | Prep: 45mins | Cook: 0mins | Ready in:

Ingredients

- 1 package fudge brownie mix (13-in. x 9-in. pan size)
- 4 teaspoons instant coffee granules
- 1/4 cup warm water
- 1-3/4 cups cold milk
- 1 package (3.4 ounces) instant vanilla pudding mix
- 2 cups whipped topping
- 1 package (11 ounces) vanilla or white baking chips
- 3 Heath candy bars (1.55 ounces each), chopped

Direction

- Follow package directions to prepare and bake brownies. Cool; slice into 3/4-in. cubes.
- Melt coffee granules in warm water. Beat pudding mix and milk for 2 minutes on low speed in a big bowl; beat coffee mixture in. Fold whipped topping in.
- Layer 1/2 brownie cubes, candy bars, vanilla chips and pudding in a 3-qt. trifle glass/bowl; repeat layers. Cover; refrigerate for 1 hour minimum before serving.

Nutrition Information

- Calories: 440 calories
- Sodium: 345mg sodium
- Fiber: 1g fiber)
- Total Carbohydrate: 66g carbohydrate (35g sugars
- Cholesterol: 12mg cholesterol
- Protein: 5g protein.
- Total Fat: 18g fat (10g saturated fat)

339. Budapest Roll

Serving: 12 servings. | Prep: 25mins | Cook: 20mins | Ready in:

Ingredients

- 6 large egg whites
- 2/3 cup finely ground hazelnuts
- 6 tablespoons instant vanilla pudding mix
- 1-1/3 cups sugar
- FILLING:
- 1-1/3 cups heavy whipping cream
- 1 tablespoon sugar
- 1/2 teaspoon vanilla extract
- 1 can (11 ounces) mandarin oranges, drained
- 1 ounce bittersweet chocolate, chopped

Direction

- Let egg whites sit for half an hour at room temperature. At the same time, mix the pudding mix and nuts. Line parchment paper onto a 15x10-inch baking pan.
- Set the oven at 350° to preheat. Whisk the egg whites on medium speed until foamy. Slowly put in 1 tbsp. of sugar at a time, whisking on high after each addition until the sugar dissolves. Keep beating until stiff glossy peaks form. Fold in nut mixture.
- Spread the meringue over the prepared pan or pipe in long strips until the whole pan is covered. Bake for approximately 20 minutes until dry and set. Let cool completely. Use parchment paper to cover the meringue; put a different baking pan on top. Flip the pans. Take away the top pan and gently remove the parchment paper from meringue.
- Beat the cream until it starts to thicken. Put in vanilla and sugar and beat until stiff peaks form. Pour the cream over the meringue and add oranges on top; beginning with a long side, roll up jelly-roll style, removing the paper while rolling.
- Melt the chocolate in a microwave on high, whisk occasionally. Sprinkle the meringue roll with melted chocolate.

Nutrition Information

- Calories: 256 calories
- Protein: 3g protein.
- Total Fat: 13g fat (7g saturated fat)
- Sodium: 68mg sodium

- Fiber: 1g fiber)
- Total Carbohydrate: 33g carbohydrate (31g sugars
- Cholesterol: 37mg cholesterol

---

340.   Butter Ball Chiffons

Serving: 5 dozen. | Prep: 15mins | Cook: 15mins | Ready in:

Ingredients

- 1 cup butter, softened
- 1/4 cup confectioners' sugar
- 1 package (3.4 ounces) instant lemon pudding mix
- 2 teaspoons water
- 1 teaspoon vanilla extract
- 2 cups all-purpose flour
- 1 cup chopped pecans or walnuts
- 2 Heath candy bars (1.4 ounces each), chopped

Direction

- Start preheating the oven to 325°. Cream the confectioners' sugar and butter in a small bowl until fluffy and light. Whisk in vanilla, water and pudding mix. Put in flour gradually. Whisk in chopped candy bars and nuts.
- Roll the mixture into 1-inch balls. Arrange 2 inches apart on ungreased baking sheets. Bake until lightly browned, 12-15 minutes. Let cool for 3 min., then transfer to wire racks.

Nutrition Information

- Calories: 141 calories
- Protein: 1g protein.
- Total Fat: 10g fat (4g saturated fat)
- Sodium: 107mg sodium
- Fiber: 1g fiber)
- Total Carbohydrate: 13g carbohydrate (5g sugars
- Cholesterol: 17mg cholesterol

341.   Butter Crunch Pudding

Serving: 4 servings. | Prep: 30mins | Cook: 0mins | Ready in:

Ingredients

- 1 cup all-purpose flour
- 1/2 cup sweetened shredded coconut
- 1/4 cup packed brown sugar
- 1/2 cup cold butter, cubed
- 2 cups cold milk
- 1 package (3.4 ounces) instant lemon pudding mix or flavor of your choice

Direction

- Combine brown sugar, coconut, and flour in a large mixing bowl. Cut butter into mixture until crumbly. Distribute mixture over the bottom of a 15x10x1-inch baking pan. Bake for 15 minutes at 375°, stirring one time. Allow to cool briefly.
- In the meantime, whisk pudding mix and milk together in a separate large bowl for 2 minutes. Allow mixture to sit until soft-set, about 2 minutes. Refrigerate for 5 minutes.
- Transfer half of the crumbs to each of four dessert bowls. Top with pudding and the rest of crumb mixture.

Nutrition Information

- Calories: 586 calories
- Sodium: 617mg sodium
- Fiber: 1g fiber)
- Total Carbohydrate: 72g carbohydrate (42g sugars
- Cholesterol: 78mg cholesterol
- Protein: 8g protein.
- Total Fat: 31g fat (20g saturated fat)

342.   Butterfinger Cookie Bars

Serving: 3 dozen. | Prep: 20mins | Cook: 25mins | Ready in:

Ingredients

- 1 package dark chocolate cake mix (regular size)
- 1 cup all-purpose flour
- 1 package (3.9 ounces) instant chocolate pudding mix
- 1 tablespoon baking cocoa
- 1/2 cup 2% milk
- 1/3 cup canola oil
- 1/3 cup butter, melted
- 2 large eggs, divided use
- 6 Butterfinger candy bars (2.1 ounces each), divided
- 1-1/2 cups chunky peanut butter
- 1 teaspoon vanilla extract
- 1-1/2 cups semisweet chocolate chips, divided

Direction

- Set oven to preheat at 350°. In a large bowl, combine cocoa, pudding mix, flour and cake mix. In another bowl, whisk 1 egg, butter, oil and milk until incorporated. Put into dry ingredients; mix until just moistened. Pat half of the mixture into a 15x10x1-in. greased baking pan. Bake for 10 minutes.
- In the meantime, chop up two candy bars. Mix remaining egg, vanilla and peanut butter into the reserved cake mix mixture. Fold in 1 cup chocolate chips and chopped bars.
- Chop three more candy bars; sprinkle on top of the warm crust and gently push down. Cover using the cake mix mixture; firmly push down using a metal spatula. Crush the leftover candy bar; sprinkle remaining chocolate chips and crushed bar on top.
- Bake 25-30 minutes or until tested done using a toothpick. Allow to cool on a wire rack. Slice into bars. Keep in an airtight container.

Nutrition Information

- Calories: 305 calories
- Protein: 5g protein.
- Total Fat: 16g fat (6g saturated fat)
- Sodium: 284mg sodium
- Fiber: 2g fiber)
- Total Carbohydrate: 39g carbohydrate (22g sugars
- Cholesterol: 16mg cholesterol

343. Buttermilk Fruit Topping

Serving: about 4-1/2 cups. | Prep: 5mins | Cook: 0mins | Ready in:

Ingredients

- 1-1/2 cups cold buttermilk
- 1 package (3.4 ounces) instant vanilla pudding mix
- 1 carton (8 ounces) frozen whipped topping, thawed
- Fresh fruit

Direction

- Stir pudding mix and buttermilk together in a bowl. Beat for 2 minutes over low speed. Fold whipped topping into the mixture. Refrigerate for 60 minutes. Serve on top of the fruit.

Nutrition Information

- Calories: 22 calories
- Total Fat: 1g fat (0 saturated fat)
- Sodium: 43mg sodium
- Fiber: 0 fiber)
- Total Carbohydrate: 3g carbohydrate (0 sugars
- Cholesterol: 0 cholesterol
- Protein: 0 protein.

344. Butterscotch Apple Treat

Serving: 6-8 servings. | Prep: 10mins | Cook: 0mins | Ready in:

Ingredients

- 3 cups diced red apples
- 1 cup miniature marshmallows
- 1 cup peanuts
- 1 can (8 ounces) crushed pineapple, drained
- 1/3 cup raisins, optional
- 1 carton (8 ounces) frozen whipped topping, thawed
- 1 package (3.4 ounces) instant butterscotch pudding

Direction

- Mix the pineapple, peanuts, marshmallows, apples and raisins, if you want, in a big bowl. Mix the dry pudding mix with the whipped topping; fold into the fruit mixture and stir well. Chill until serving.

Nutrition Information

- Calories: 291 calories
- Total Carbohydrate: 37g carbohydrate (25g sugars
- Cholesterol: 0 cholesterol
- Protein: 5g protein.
- Total Fat: 14g fat (6g saturated fat)
- Sodium: 269mg sodium
- Fiber: 3g fiber)

345. Butterscotch Bliss Layered Dessert

Serving: 24 servings. | Prep: 20mins | Cook: 0mins | Ready in:

Ingredients

- 1-1/2 cups graham cracker crumbs

- Sugar substitute equivalent to 1/2 cup sugar, divided
- 6 tablespoons butter, melted
- 2 packages (8 ounces each) reduced-fat cream cheese
- 3 cups cold fat-free milk, divided
- 2 packages (1 ounce each) sugar-free instant butterscotch pudding mix
- 1 carton (8 ounces) frozen reduced-fat whipped topping, thawed
- 1/2 teaspoon rum extract

Direction

- Mix butter, 1/2 sugar substitute and cracker crumbs in a small bowl; press into 13x9-in. dish coated in cooking spray.
- Beat leftover sugar substitute, 1/4 cup milk and cream cheese till smooth in a small bowl; spread on crust.
- Whisk pudding mix and leftover milk for 2 minutes in another bowl; allow to stand till soft set for 2 minutes. Spread on cream cheese layer gently. Mix extract and whipped topping; spread on top. Refrigerate for 4 hours minimum.

Nutrition Information

- Calories: 136 calories
- Sodium: 245mg sodium
- Fiber: 0 fiber)
- Total Carbohydrate: 12g carbohydrate (5g sugars
- Cholesterol: 21mg cholesterol
- Protein: 3g protein. Diabetic Exchanges: 1 starch
- Total Fat: 8g fat (6g saturated fat)

---
346.   Butterscotch Bones

Serving: 1-1/2 dozen. | Prep: 30mins | Cook: 10mins | Ready in:

Ingredients

- 1 package (10 ounces) miniature marshmallows
- 3 tablespoons butter
- 3 tablespoons instant butterscotch pudding mix
- 6 cups crisp rice cereal
- 1/2 cup butterscotch chips
- 1/2 cup vanilla or white chips
- 1 teaspoon shortening

Direction

- Combine butter and marshmallows in a large saucepan. Cook over medium-low heat, stirring, until melted. Turn off the heat; whisk in pudding mix until incorporated. Fold in cereal. Pat mixture into a greased 15x10x1-inch pan. Chill in the fridge for half an hour.
- Cut out shapes with a 3-inch bone-shaped cookie cutter. Heat shortening, butterscotch and vanilla chips in a shallow microwaveable dish at 50% powder until melted; whisk until smooth.
- Immerse bottoms of bones into melted butterscotch mixture; arrange on foil. Arrange some of the mixture in a heavy-duty resealable plastic bag, if desired. Snip a tiny hole in the corner of the bag and pipe decoratively over bones. Allow to sit until set. Gently peel off the foil.

Nutrition Information

- Calories: 114 calories
- Total Carbohydrate: 20g carbohydrate (9g sugars
- Cholesterol: 4mg cholesterol
- Protein: 1g protein. Diabetic Exchanges: 1 starch
- Total Fat: 4g fat (3g saturated fat)
- Sodium: 98mg sodium
- Fiber: 0 fiber)

347.   Butterscotch Gingerbread Men

Serving: 1-1/2 dozen. | Prep: 20mins | Cook: 10mins | Ready in:

Ingredients

- 1/2 cup butter, softened
- 1/2 cup packed brown sugar
- 1 package (3.4 ounces) instant butterscotch pudding mix
- 1 egg
- 1-1/2 cups all-purpose flour
- 1-1/2 teaspoons ground ginger
- 1/2 teaspoon baking soda
- 1/2 teaspoon ground cinnamon
- FROSTING:
- 2 cups confectioners' sugar
- 3 tablespoons milk

Direction

- Whisk the brown sugar, pudding mix, and butter into a small sized bowl until fluffy and light. Stir in the egg. Mix together the ginger, cinnamon, flour, and baking soda. Slowly pour into the butter mixture, stirring well to combine. Keep in the refrigerator while covered, overnight.
- Roll the dough out into 1/8-inch thick on a lightly floured working surface. Using 5-inches gingerbread man cutter, cut out shapes. Put on the ungreased baking pans, 1-inch apart. On 350° heat, bake until edges turn golden, 8 to 10 minutes. Transfer onto wire racks; cool.
- Mix together the milk and confectioner's sugar until the mixture is smooth. Use frosting to decorate the cookies as preferred.

Nutrition Information

- Calories: 183 calories
- Total Fat: 6g fat (3g saturated fat)
- Sodium: 177mg sodium
- Fiber: 0 fiber)

- Total Carbohydrate: 32g carbohydrate (23g sugars
- Cholesterol: 26mg cholesterol
- Protein: 2g protein.

348.   Butterscotch Pecan Cookies

Serving: 18 | Prep: | Cook: | Ready in:

Ingredients

- 1 (18.25 ounce) package butter cake mix
- 1 (3.4 ounce) package instant butterscotch pudding mix
- 1/4 cup all-purpose flour
- 3/4 cup vegetable oil
- 1 egg
- 1 cup chopped pecans
- 1 cup butterscotch chips

Direction

- Set oven to 175°C (350°F) and start preheating. Coat cookie sheets with grease.
- Combine flour, instant pudding and cake mix in a medium bowl. Put in egg and oil; stir until fully incorporated. Mix in butterscotch chips and pecans. The texture will resemble crumbs.
- Using a small ice cream scoop or a tablespoon, scoop dough into balls of cookie. Arrange onto greased cookie sheets, placing each 2 inches away from others. Bake at 175°C (350°F) until beginning to brown on the edges, about 10-12 minutes. Cool for two minutes, then turn out onto wire racks and finish cooling.

Nutrition Information

- Calories: 318 calories;
- Total Fat: 18.5
- Sodium: 275
- Total Carbohydrate: 36.2
- Cholesterol: 10

- Protein: 1.7

349. Butterscotch Pudding Parfaits

Serving: 6 servings. | Prep: 10mins | Cook: 0mins | Ready in:

Ingredients

- 2 cups cold fat-free milk
- 1 package (1 ounce) sugar-free instant butterscotch pudding mix
- 18 vanilla wafers, coarsely crushed
- 1 carton (8 ounces) frozen reduced-fat whipped topping, thawed

Direction

- Beat pudding mix and milk in a large bowl for 2 minutes. Allow it to stand for 2 minutes or until soft-set.
- Alter layers of whipped topping, wafer crumbs, and pudding in six parfait glasses. Keep in the refrigerator until serving time.

Nutrition Information

- Calories:
- Cholesterol:
- Protein:
- Total Fat:
- Sodium:
- Fiber:
- Total Carbohydrate:

350. Butterscotch Pudding Torte

Serving: 15 servings. | Prep: 15mins | Cook: 0mins | Ready in:

Ingredients

- 1 package (16 ounces) cream-filled vanilla sandwich cookies, crushed
- 1/2 cup butter, melted
- 1 package (8 ounces) cream cheese, softened
- 1 cup confectioners' sugar
- 1 carton (12 ounces) frozen whipped topping, thawed, divided
- 2-1/2 cups cold 2% milk
- 2 packages (3.4 ounces each) instant butterscotch pudding mix

Direction

- For topping, put 1 cup cookie crumbs aside. Mix butter and leftover cookie crumbs in a small bowl; press into 13x9-in. greased dish. Beat confectioners' sugar and cream cheese till smooth in a big bowl; fold in 1 1/2 cups of whipped topping. Spread on crust.
- Whisk pudding mix and milk for 2 minutes in a small bowl; stand till soft set for 2 minutes. Put over the cream cheese layer. Put leftover whipped toppings over; sprinkle reserved crumbs. Cover; refrigerate for a minimum of 2 hours.

Nutrition Information

- Calories: 413 calories
- Cholesterol: 36mg cholesterol
- Protein: 4g protein.
- Total Fat: 22g fat (12g saturated fat)
- Sodium: 414mg sodium
- Fiber: 0 fiber)
- Total Carbohydrate: 49g carbohydrate (33g sugars

351. Butterscotch Pumpkin Mousse

Serving: 4 servings. | Prep: 15mins | Cook: 0mins | Ready in:

Ingredients

- 1-1/2 cups cold fat-free milk
- 1 package (1 ounce) sugar-free instant butterscotch pudding mix
- 1/2 cup canned pumpkin
- 1/2 teaspoon ground cinnamon
- 1/4 teaspoon ground ginger
- 1/4 teaspoon ground allspice
- 1 cup fat-free whipped topping, divided

Direction

- Whisk pudding mix and milk for 2 minutes in big bowl; stand till soft set for 2 minutes. Mix allspice, ginger, cinnamon and pumpkin; fold into pudding then fold 1/2 cup whipped topping in.
- Put in solo serving dishes; refrigerate till serving. Use leftover whipped topping to garnish.

Nutrition Information

- Calories: 95 calories
- Fiber: 1g fiber)
- Total Carbohydrate: 19g carbohydrate (8g sugars
- Cholesterol: 2mg cholesterol
- Protein: 4g protein. Diabetic Exchanges: 1/2 starch
- Total Fat: 0 fat (0 saturated fat)
- Sodium: 351mg sodium

---

352. Butterscotch Pumpkin Pie

Serving: 8 servings. | Prep: 30mins | Cook: 0mins | Ready in:

Ingredients

- 1 cup graham cracker crumbs
- 1/4 cup butter, melted
- FILLING:

- 1 cup fat-free milk
- 1 package (1 ounce) sugar-free instant butterscotch pudding mix
- 1 cup canned pumpkin
- 1 teaspoon ground cinnamon
- 1/2 teaspoon ground nutmeg
- TOPPING:
- 1 cup reduced-fat whipped topping
- 1 teaspoon vanilla extract

Direction

- Mix butter and cracker crumbs in a small bowl; put onto the base of a 9-inch pie plate. Let bake for 10 minutes at 350°; allow to cool.
- For the filling, beat pudding mix and milk in a small bowl for 2 minutes; the mixture will be thick. Mix in nutmeg, cinnamon and pumpkin till incorporated.
- Put into the crust. Refrigerate for a minimum of 2 hours. Mix the topping ingredients; serve along with pie.

Nutrition Information

- Calories: 148 calories
- Protein: 3g protein. Diabetic Exchanges: 2-1/2 fat
- Total Fat: 9g fat (0 saturated fat)
- Sodium: 203mg sodium
- Fiber: 0 fiber)
- Total Carbohydrate: 17g carbohydrate (0 sugars
- Cholesterol: 1mg cholesterol

---

353. Butterscotch Pumpkin Puffs

Serving: 5 dozen. | Prep: 35mins | Cook: 35mins | Ready in:

Ingredients

- 2 packages (3.4 ounces each) instant butterscotch pudding mix
- 1 can (12 ounces) evaporated milk
- 1/2 teaspoon ground cinnamon
- 1/4 teaspoon ground ginger
- 1 cup canned pumpkin
- 1 cup whipped topping, optional
- CREAM PUFFS:
- 1-1/2 cups water
- 3/4 cup butter, cubed
- 1/2 teaspoon salt
- 1-1/2 cups all-purpose flour
- 6 eggs
- 1/3 cup confectioners' sugar
- 1/3 cup semisweet chocolate chips, melted

Direction

- Mix the spices, milk, and pudding mix in a bowl and beat for half a minute on medium speed. You can whisk in whipped topping and pumpkin if you want. Chill for an hour or overnight.
- Mix the salt, butter and water in a medium saucepan; bring the mixture to a boil. Lower the heat to low; put in all of the flour at once and whisk until a smooth ball forms. Take away from heat and put in 1 egg at a time, use an electric mixer to whisk well after each addition. Keep beating until the mixture becomes shiny and smooth. Drop the batter by tablespoonfuls, 2 inches apart, onto greased baking sheets.
- Bake for 10 minutes at 400°. Lower the heat to 350° and bake for 25 minutes more until golden brown. Take out of the oven; turn off the oven. Slice a slit halfway through each puff and put back into the oven for half an hour while the oven door is open. Transfer to a wire rack to cool. Just before serving, scoop approximately 1 tbsp. of the filling into each puff. Sprinkle with confectioners' sugar and drizzle melted chocolate on top.

Nutrition Information

- Calories: 60 calories

- Cholesterol: 29mg cholesterol
- Protein: 1g protein.
- Total Fat: 3g fat (2g saturated fat)
- Sodium: 80mg sodium
- Fiber: 0 fiber)
- Total Carbohydrate: 6g carbohydrate (3g sugars

---

354.   Butterscotch Swirl Cake

Serving: 12 servings. | Prep: 30mins | Cook: 01hours05mins | Ready in:

Ingredients

- 1 cup butter, softened
- 2 cups sugar
- 6 eggs
- 3 teaspoons rum extract
- 1 teaspoon vanilla extract
- 3 cups all-purpose flour
- 1 teaspoon baking soda
- 1 teaspoon baking powder
- 1 cup (8 ounces) sour cream
- 1 package (3.4 ounces) instant butterscotch pudding mix
- 3/4 cup butterscotch ice cream topping
- BUTTERSCOTCH GLAZE:
- 1/4 cup butter, cubed
- 1/4 cup packed brown sugar
- 2 tablespoons 2% milk
- 1 cup confectioners' sugar
- 1 teaspoon vanilla extract
- 1/4 cup chopped pecans

Direction

- Preheat an oven to 350°. Cream sugar and butter till fluffy and light in a big bowl. One by one, add 5 eggs; beat well after each. Mix in extracts. Mix baking powder, baking soda and flour; alternately with sour cream, add to creamed mixture slowly, beating well after each.

- Put 2 cups batter into another big bowl; beat in leftover egg, butterscotch topping and pudding mix till blended well. Put 1/2 plain batter into 10-in. fluted greased and floured tube pan. Put 1/2 butterscotch batter over; to swirl, cut through using a knife. Repeat layers; swirl.
- Bake till inserted toothpick in middle exits clean for 65-70 minutes; cool for 10 minutes. Transfer from pan onto wire rack; fully cool.
- Glaze: Boil milk, brown sugar and butter in a small saucepan; take off heat. Add vanilla and confectioners' sugar; beat till creamy and smooth. Drizzle on cake; sprinkle pecans.

Nutrition Information

- Calories: 650 calories
- Fiber: 1g fiber)
- Total Carbohydrate: 94g carbohydrate (67g sugars
- Cholesterol: 171mg cholesterol
- Protein: 8g protein.
- Total Fat: 27g fat (15g saturated fat)
- Sodium: 573mg sodium

---

355. Butterscotch Toffee Cheesecake Bars

Serving: 2 dozen. | Prep: 15mins | Cook: 30mins | Ready in:

Ingredients

- 1 package yellow cake mix (regular size)
- 1 package (3.4 ounces) instant butterscotch pudding mix
- 1/3 cup canola oil
- 2 large eggs, divided use
- 1 package (8 ounces) cream cheese, softened
- 1/3 cup sugar
- 1 cup brickle toffee bits, divided
- 1/2 cup butterscotch chips

Direction

- Set oven to 350 degrees and start preheating. Mix together 1 egg, oil, pudding mix and cake mix in a big bowl until mixture forms crumbs. Set aside a cup of mixture for topping. Pat the rest into an ungreased baking pan (13x9 inches). Bake in the preheated oven for 10 minutes. Place on a wire rack until completely cool.
- Whisk sugar and cream cheese in a small bowl until smooth. Pour in remaining eggs; on low speed, beat mixture until incorporated. Fold in half cup toffee bits. Pour onto crust. Garnish with saved crumb mixture. Bake until filling is set, about 15 to 20 minutes.
- Garnish with the rest of toffee bits and butterscotch chips. Continue baking for another minute. Place on a wire rack for an hour to cool. Chill in the refrigerator for 2 hours. Slice into bars.

Nutrition Information

- Calories: 257 calories
- Sodium: 297mg sodium
- Fiber: 0 fiber)
- Total Carbohydrate: 34g carbohydrate (22g sugars
- Cholesterol: 31mg cholesterol
- Protein: 2g protein.
- Total Fat: 13g fat (6g saturated fat)

---

356. Cake With Lemon Sauce

Serving: 4 servings. | Prep: 10mins | Cook: 0mins | Ready in:

Ingredients

- 3 ounces cream cheese, softened
- 1-3/4 cups cold whole milk
- 1 package (3.4 ounces) instant lemon pudding mix

- 4 slices pound cake or angel food cake
- Fresh raspberries, optional

Direction

- Beat the cream cheese in a small bowl until it has a smooth consistency. Mix in pudding mix and milk and continue beating until consistency is thickened and smooth. Consume with cake. Decorate with raspberries if preferred.

Nutrition Information

- Calories: 502 calories
- Fiber: 1g fiber)
- Total Carbohydrate: 66g carbohydrate (45g sugars
- Cholesterol: 79mg cholesterol
- Protein: 9g protein.
- Total Fat: 24g fat (10g saturated fat)
- Sodium: 688mg sodium

---

357. Calgary Nanaimo Bars

Serving: 3-1/2 dozen. | Prep: 20mins | Cook: 5mins | Ready in:

Ingredients

- 1/4 cup sugar
- 1/4 cup baking cocoa
- 3/4 cup butter, cubed
- 2 large eggs, beaten
- 2 cups graham cracker crumbs
- 1 cup sweetened shredded coconut
- 1/2 cup chopped almonds, optional
- FILLING:
- 2 cups confectioners' sugar
- 2 tablespoons instant vanilla pudding mix
- 1/4 cup butter, melted
- 3 tablespoons 2% milk
- GLAZE:
- 3 ounces semisweet chocolate, chopped

- 1 tablespoon butter

Direction

- Use foil to line an 8-inch baking pan that's square, allowing ends to overlap over sides by an inch. In a big, heavy saucepan, mix the cocoa and sugar; put butter. Stir and cook on medium-low heat until the butter melts. Beat a small amount of the hot mixture into the eggs. Put all back in the pan, beating constantly. Mix and cook until mixture achieves 160°F. Take off heat.
- Mix in coconut, cracker crumbs, and if you want, almonds. Then press in prepared pan. Keep in the refrigerator for 30 minutes or until it has set.
- To make filling, in a small bowl mix the milk, butter, pudding mix, and confectioner's sugar until it turns smooth; then spread on crust.
- Dissolve butter and chocolate in a microwave; whisk until smooth. Spread on top. Keep in the refrigerator until it has set. Take bars out of the pan using foil. Get rid of foil; slice into bars.

Nutrition Information

- Calories: 116 calories
- Total Carbohydrate: 14g carbohydrate (11g sugars
- Cholesterol: 21mg cholesterol
- Protein: 1g protein.
- Total Fat: 7g fat (4g saturated fat)
- Sodium: 72mg sodium
- Fiber: 0 fiber)

---

358. Candied Orange Chocolate Cake

Serving: 12 servings. | Prep: 25mins | Cook: 45mins | Ready in:

Ingredients

- 1/3 cup sliced almonds
- 1 package devil's food cake mix (regular size)
- 1 package (3.9 ounces) instant chocolate pudding mix
- 3 large eggs
- 1-1/4 cups milk
- 1/2 cup canola oil
- 1 teaspoon orange extract
- 1 cup chopped orange candy slices
- ORANGE GLAZE:
- 3/4 cup confectioners' sugar
- 2 tablespoons butter
- 2 tablespoons orange juice

Direction

- In a fluted tube pan of 10 inches already greased and dusted with flour, scatter almonds and put aside. Mix together extract, oil, milk, eggs, pudding mix and cake mix in a big bowl; on low speed, blend the mixture for half a minute. Increase the speed to medium and beat for 2 minutes. Fold orange slices into batter.
- Transfer to the cake pan. Bake at 350 degrees until a toothpick comes out clean when pierced into the middle of the cake, about 45 to 50 minutes. Let the cake cool for 10 minutes, then transfer from pan to a wire rack and cool entirely.
- Boil ingredients for the glaze in a small saucepan. Boil the mixture, stirring often, about 60 seconds. Take away from the heat and let it cool for 5 minutes. Glaze the cake.

Nutrition Information

- Calories:
- Protein:
- Total Fat:
- Sodium:
- Fiber:
- Total Carbohydrate:
- Cholesterol:

359.   Candy Bar Brownie Trifle

Serving: 16 servings. | Prep: 20mins | Cook: 30mins | Ready in:

Ingredients

- 1 package fudge brownie mix (13-inch x 9-inch pan size)
- 1 package (3.9 ounces) instant chocolate pudding mix
- 1 package (11-1/2 ounces) miniature Snickers candy bars, refrigerated
- 1 carton (8 ounces) frozen whipped topping, thawed
- 1 jar (12 ounces) caramel ice cream topping

Direction

- Follow package directions to prep and bake brownies; on wire rack, cool. Follow package directions to prep pudding. Crush candy bars; put aside.
- Cut brownies to 1-in. cubes. Put 1/2 cubes in big glass serving bowl/3-qt. trifle bowl; lightly press down. Put 1/2 whipped topping, crushed candy bars, caramel topping and pudding over. Repeat layers. Cover; refrigerate till serving.

Nutrition Information

- Calories: 444 calories
- Protein: 6g protein.
- Total Fat: 19g fat (6g saturated fat)
- Sodium: 378mg sodium
- Fiber: 2g fiber)
- Total Carbohydrate: 65g carbohydrate (35g sugars
- Cholesterol: 33mg cholesterol

360. Candy Bar Freezer Dessert

Serving: 12-15 servings. | Prep: 20mins | Cook: 0mins | Ready in:

Ingredients

- 2 cups graham cracker crumbs
- 1 cup crushed saltines (about 30 crackers)
- 1/2 cup butter, melted
- 2 cups cold 2% milk
- 2 packages (3.4 ounces each) instant vanilla pudding mix
- 4 cups butter pecan ice cream, softened
- 1 carton (8 ounces) frozen whipped topping, thawed
- 1 Butterfinger candy bar (2.1 ounces), chopped

Direction

- Mix cracker crumbs and butter together in a large mixing bowl. Press 3/4 of the mixture into an ungreased 13x9-inch dish. Chill, covered.
- Stir pudding mixes and milk for 2 minutes in a large mixing bowl until mixture becomes thick. Mix in ice cream until incorporated. Spoon mixture into crust, spreading evenly. Top pudding layer with whipped topping.
- Mix the remaining crumb mixture and chopped candy bar together in a small mixing bowl; scatter over whipped topping. Freeze, covered, for a minimum of 2 hours.

Nutrition Information

- Calories: 320 calories
- Total Fat: 19g fat (10g saturated fat)
- Sodium: 375mg sodium
- Fiber: 1g fiber)
- Total Carbohydrate: 34g carbohydrate (19g sugars
- Cholesterol: 34mg cholesterol
- Protein: 5g protein.

361. Cappuccino Chocolate Pie

Serving: 6-8 servings. | Prep: 15mins | Cook: 10mins | Ready in:

Ingredients

- 1 cup (6 ounces) semisweet chocolate chips
- 1/3 cup heavy whipping cream
- 1 tablespoon light corn syrup
- 1/2 teaspoon vanilla extract
- Dash salt
- 1 graham cracker crust (10 inches)
- 1 cup chopped pecans
- 4 ounces cream cheese, softened
- 1-1/2 cups milk
- 2 tablespoons brewed coffee
- 2 packages (3.4 ounces each) instant vanilla pudding mix
- 2 tablespoons instant coffee granules
- 1 carton (8 ounces) frozen whipped topping, thawed, divided

Direction

- Melt together the salt, cream, corn syrup, vanilla and chocolate chips in a saucepan on low heat; stir till smooth. Spoon the mixture into the crust. Sprinkle pecans on top.
- Beat cream cheese in a large bowl till smooth. Add milk and brewed coffee into the mixture slowly; combine thoroughly. Add pudding mixes and instant coffee into this mixture; beat till smooth. Fold 1-1/2 cups whipped topping into the mixture. Spoon it onto the pecans. Spread the rest of the whipped topping over the filling. Chill in the refrigerator for no less than 3 hours before serving.

Nutrition Information

- Calories: 554 calories
- Total Carbohydrate: 52g carbohydrate (39g sugars

- Cholesterol: 35mg cholesterol
- Protein: 6g protein.
- Total Fat: 37g fat (17g saturated fat)
- Sodium: 384mg sodium
- Fiber: 3g fiber)

- Total Carbohydrate: 20g carbohydrate (13g sugars
- Cholesterol: 26mg cholesterol
- Protein: 2g protein.
- Total Fat: 8g fat (6g saturated fat)
- Sodium: 139mg sodium

362. Cappuccino Mousse Trifle

Serving: 16-20 servings. | Prep: 35mins | Cook: 0mins | Ready in:

Ingredients

- 2-1/2 cups cold milk
- 1/3 cup instant coffee granules
- 2 packages (3.4 ounces each) instant vanilla pudding mix
- 1 carton (16 ounces) frozen whipped topping, thawed, divided
- 2 loaves (10-3/4 ounces each) frozen pound cake, thawed and cubed
- 1 ounce semisweet chocolate, grated
- 1/4 teaspoon ground cinnamon

Direction

- Mix coffee granules and milk till melted in big bowl. Take 1 cup; put aside. Add pudding mixes into leftover milk mixture; beat for 2 minutes on low speed till thick. Fold 1/2 whipped topping in.
- Put 1/3 cake cubes in trifle/4-qt. serving bowl. Layer 1/3 leftover milk mixture and pudding mixture then 1/4 grated chocolate. Repeat layers 2 times. Garnish using chocolate and leftover whipped topping. Sprinkle cinnamon. Cover; refrigerate till serving.

Nutrition Information

- Calories: 166 calories
- Fiber: 0 fiber)

363. Cappuccino Parfaits

Serving: Makes 6 servings. | Prep: 15mins | Cook: | Ready in:

Ingredients

- 24 NILLA Wafers , divided
- 1/4 cup
- 1 Tbsp. hot water
- 2 cups cold milk
- 1 pkg. (4-serving size) JELL-O Vanilla Flavor Instant Pudding
- 1-1/2 cups thawed COOL WHIP Whipped Topping , divided

Direction

- Coarsely chop 18 of the wafers; reserve. Reserve the rest of the 6 wafers for decorating.
- In a medium bowl with hot water, add flavored instant coffee to dissolve. Slowly stir in milk until well combined. Mix in dry pudding mix. Use a wire whisk to beat for 2 minutes or until well incorporated. Slightly mix in 1 cup of the whipped topping.
- Into 6 dessert dishes, equally scoop half of the pudding mixture; scatter with the chopped wafers. Place the rest of the pudding mixture on top. Keep in the refrigerator for at least 1hour or until ready to serve. Put the rest of 1/2 cup whipped topping and 6 reserved wafers on top just before serving.

Nutrition Information

- Calories: 250
- Total Fat: 9 g

- Sodium: 360 mg
- Fiber: 0 g
- Sugar: 28 g
- Total Carbohydrate: 39 g
- Saturated Fat: 5 g
- Cholesterol: 5 mg
- Protein: 4 g

- Total Carbohydrate: 34g carbohydrate (21g sugars
- Cholesterol: 2mg cholesterol
- Protein: 6g protein. Diabetic Exchanges: 2 starch
- Total Fat: 3g fat (2g saturated fat)
- Sodium: 342mg sodium
- Fiber: 0 fiber)

364.   Cappuccino Trifle

Serving: 12 servings. | Prep: 30mins | Cook: 0mins | Ready in:

Ingredients

- 1 package (8 ounces) fat-free cream cheese
- 1/2 cup cold strong brewed coffee
- 1-1/2 cups cold fat-free milk
- 1 package (3.4 ounces) instant vanilla pudding mix
- 1 teaspoon ground cinnamon
- 1 carton (8 ounces) frozen reduced-fat whipped topping, thawed
- 1 package (13.6 ounces) fat-free pound cake, cut into 1/2-inch cubes

Direction

- Beat cream cheese till softened in big bowl; beat coffee in slowly. Whisk cinnamon, pudding mix and milk for 2 minutes in small bowl; stand for 5 minutes. Mix into cream cheese mixture.
- Put 1/4 cup whipped topping aside; fold leftover whipped topping into the pudding mixture. Layer 1/3 of the pound cake cubes then 1/3 pudding mixture in 2 1/2-qt. serving bowl; repeat layers 2 times. Garnish using leftover whipped topping; refrigerate till serving.

Nutrition Information

- Calories: 193 calories

365.   Caramel Apple Trifle Delight

Serving: 24 servings (2/3 cup each). | Prep: 25mins | Cook: 0mins | Ready in:

Ingredients

- 4 cups cold milk
- 2 packages (3.4 ounces each) instant vanilla pudding mix
- 2 cans (21 ounces each) apple pie filling
- 1 cup English toffee bits
- 1/2 cup packed brown sugar
- 1 teaspoon ground cinnamon
- 1 loaf (16 ounces) frozen pound cake, thawed and cut into 1-inch cubes
- 1-1/4 cups caramel ice cream topping
- 1-1/2 cups heavy whipping cream, whipped
- 1/2 cup finely chopped walnuts, toasted
- Additional caramel ice cream topping

Direction

- Whisk pudding mixes and milk for 2 minutes in big bowl; stand till soft set or for 2 minutes. Mix cinnamon, brown sugar, toffee bits and pie filling in another bowl.
- Layer 1/2 cake cubes, walnuts, whipped cream, ice cream topping, apple mixture and pudding in glass bowl/4-qt. trifle bowl; repeat layers. Drizzle extra ice cream topping; chill till serving.

Nutrition Information

- Calories: 361 calories
- Protein: 4g protein.
- Total Fat: 15g fat (7g saturated fat)
- Sodium: 350mg sodium
- Fiber: 1g fiber)
- Total Carbohydrate: 56g carbohydrate (33g sugars
- Cholesterol: 55mg cholesterol

- Fiber: 0 fiber)
- Total Carbohydrate: 68g carbohydrate (45g sugars
- Cholesterol: 34mg cholesterol
- Protein: 5g protein.
- Total Fat: 17g fat (10g saturated fat)

---

366.   Caramel Banana Ice Cream Pie

Serving: 8 servings. | Prep: 20mins | Cook: 0mins | Ready in:

Ingredients

- 1/4 cup plus 1 tablespoon caramel ice cream topping, divided
- 1 graham cracker crust (9 inches)
- 1 cup cold 2% milk
- 2 packages (3.4 ounces each) instant banana cream pudding mix
- 1 quart vanilla ice cream, softened
- 1-3/4 cups whipped topping
- 1 English toffee candy bar (1.4 ounces), chopped

Direction

- Into crust, spread 1/4 cup of caramel topping. Beat pudding mix and milk for 2 minutes on low speed in a big bowl. Put ice cream then mix well.
- Into prepped crust, spoon it on. Put whipped topping on. Drizzle leftover caramel topping on. Sprinkle chopped candy bar on top.
- Freeze till firm for 2 hours, covered. 15 minutes before serving, remove from freezer.

Nutrition Information

- Calories: 442 calories
- Sodium: 597mg sodium

---

367.   Caramel Pecan Delight

Serving: 12-15 servings. | Prep: 30mins | Cook: 0mins | Ready in:

Ingredients

- 1 package (16 ounces) pecan shortbread cookies
- 1/2 cup butter, melted
- 2 packages (8 ounces each) cream cheese, softened
- 1 jar (12 ounces) caramel ice cream topping, divided
- 1-1/2 cups cold milk
- 1 package (5.1 ounces) instant vanilla pudding mix
- 3/4 cup chopped pecans

Direction

- Mix the butter and cookie crumbs together in a big bowl until the texture is crumbly. Push the cookie crumb mixture evenly into the bottom of a 13x9-inch baking dish that is greased. Put it in a preheated 375° oven and let it bake for 10 minutes. Put the baked crust onto a wire rack and let it cool down.
- Whisk 1/2 cup of caramel topping and cream cheese together in a big bowl until it is smooth in consistency. Beat the dry pudding mix and milk together in a small bowl for 2 minutes. Allow it to set for 2 minutes or until the mixture has softly set; add it into the cream cheese mixture and fold. Spread it evenly on top of the cooled down baked crust. Top it off with pecans.

- Cover the baking dish and keep it in the fridge for not less than 6 hours or until the filling mixture has set. Slice it into square shapes and drizzle the remaining caramel topping on top.

Nutrition Information

- Calories: 408 calories
- Protein: 5g protein.
- Total Fat: 24g fat (10g saturated fat)
- Sodium: 471mg sodium
- Fiber: 1g fiber)
- Total Carbohydrate: 46g carbohydrate (24g sugars
- Cholesterol: 43mg cholesterol

368. Caribbean Coconut Rum Cake

Serving: 12 servings. | Prep: 25mins | Cook: 60mins | Ready in:

Ingredients

- 1/2 cup unsalted butter, softened
- 1-1/2 cups sugar
- 4 large eggs
- 1 teaspoon coconut extract
- 3/4 cup amber rum
- 3/4 cup whole milk
- 1-3/4 cups all-purpose flour
- 1 package (3.4 ounces) instant vanilla pudding mix
- 1/4 cup cornstarch
- 2 teaspoons baking powder
- 1 teaspoon salt
- SYRUP:
- 1/2 cup unsalted butter, melted
- 1/2 cup water
- 1/2 cup sugar
- Dash salt
- 1/2 cup amber rum
- 1 teaspoon coconut extract

Direction

- Preheat an oven to 325°F. Cream sugar and butter till fluffy and light. One by one, add eggs; beat well after each. Beat in extract. Mix milk and rum in a small bowl. Whisk salt, baking powder, cornstarch, pudding mix and flour in a big bowl. Alternately with rum mixture, add to creamed mixture; beat well after every addition.
- Put into 10-in. greased then floured fluted tube pan; bake for 1 hour till inserted toothpick in middle exits clean. Cool for 10 minutes. Briefly remove from pan to avoid sticking; put in pan. On wire rack, cool.
- For syrup: Meanwhile, heat salt, sugar, water and butter in a small saucepan on medium heat. Boil, constantly mixing. Take off heat; add extract and rum.
- Poke holes in cake using small skewer. Put syrup on cake slowly till absorbed; cover. Stand overnight.

Nutrition Information

- Calories: 461 calories
- Total Carbohydrate: 58g carbohydrate (41g sugars
- Cholesterol: 104mg cholesterol
- Protein: 5g protein.
- Total Fat: 18g fat (10g saturated fat)
- Sodium: 823mg sodium
- Fiber: 1g fiber)

369. Cheery Cherry Parfaits

Serving: 4 servings. | Prep: 10mins | Cook: 0mins | Ready in:

Ingredients

- 2 cups whole milk
- 1 package (3.3 ounces) instant white chocolate pudding mix

- 8 date oatmeal cookies, coarsely crumbled
- 1 cup cherry pie filling

Direction

- Beat milk and pudding mix for 2 minutes in a small bowl. Allow it to stand for 2 minutes or until soft-set. In each of 4 parfait glasses, put 1/4 cup pudding.
- Then layer each with 1/3 cup cookie crumbs and 1/4 cup pie filling. Put the rest of the pudding and cookie crumbs on top. Keep in the refrigerator for 1 hour prior to serving.

Nutrition Information

- Calories: 335 calories
- Total Fat: 6g fat (2g saturated fat)
- Sodium: 551mg sodium
- Fiber: 2g fiber)
- Total Carbohydrate: 68g carbohydrate (46g sugars
- Cholesterol: 7mg cholesterol
- Protein: 3g protein.

370.   Cheesecake Strawberry Pie

Serving: 8 servings. | Prep: 10mins | Cook: 0mins | Ready in:

Ingredients

- 2 cups sliced fresh strawberries
- 1/4 cup chopped almonds, toasted
- 1 tablespoon sugar
- 1 reduced-fat graham cracker crust (8 inches)
- 1 package (8 ounces) fat-free cream cheese, softened
- 2 cups cold fat-free milk, divided
- 1 package (1 ounce) sugar-free instant vanilla pudding mix

Direction

- Combine sugar, almonds and strawberries in a bowl. Transfer to the crust. Beat the cream cheese in a bowl until smooth. Pour in half a cup milk gradually. Put in pudding mix and the remaining milk. Beat until blended, about one minute; add over the strawberries. Place in the refrigerator, covered, until set, about 120 mins.

Nutrition Information

- Calories:
- Total Fat:
- Sodium:
- Fiber:
- Total Carbohydrate:
- Cholesterol:
- Protein:

371.   Cherry Angel Delight

Serving: 9 servings. | Prep: 20mins | Cook: 0mins | Ready in:

Ingredients

- 1 prepared angel food cake (8 to 10 ounces)
- 1 can (21 ounces) cherry pie filling
- 1 package (3.4 ounces) instant vanilla pudding mix
- 1-1/2 cups cold whole milk
- 1 cup sour cream

Direction

- Cut cake into 1/2-in. pieces and create 8 cups measurement from it. In a 9-in. square baking dish, put the half of the cake cubes. Prepare a pie filling. Scoop out 1/3 cup of the filling and set aside. Using the remaining pie filling, pour it over the cake and spread evenly. Put the remaining half of the cake cubes on top. Mix the sour cream, pudding mix and milk then spoon the mixture over the cake. Put a cake cover and keep it chilled. Serve the cake by cutting it into squares and by topping it with reserved cherries.

Nutrition Information

- Calories:
- Sodium:
- Fiber:
- Total Carbohydrate:
- Cholesterol:
- Protein:
- Total Fat:

372. Cherry Angel Dessert

Serving: 15 servings. | Prep: 10mins | Cook: 0mins | Ready in:

Ingredients

- 1 prepared angel food cake (8 to 10 ounces), cut into 1-inch cubes
- 1 can (20 ounces) reduced-sugar cherry pie filling
- 1-1/3 cups cold fat-free milk
- 1 package (1 ounce) sugar-free instant vanilla pudding mix
- 1/2 cup reduced-fat sour cream
- 1 carton (8 ounces) frozen reduced-fat whipped topping, thawed

Direction

- Arrange cake cubes in an ungreased 13x9-inch dish; pour pie filling over to cover.
- Beat pudding mix and milk together in a mixing bowl for 2 minutes. Fold in sour cream. Gently smear over pie filling; spread whipped topping on top.
- Chill, covered, for a minimum of 1 day prior to serving. Chill leftovers in the fridge.

Nutrition Information

- Calories: 0g sugar total.

373. Cherry Cream Trifle

Serving: 25-30 servings. | Prep: 25mins | Cook: 40mins | Ready in:

Ingredients

- 1 package yellow cake mix (regular size)
- 2 packages (3.4 ounces each) instant vanilla pudding mix
- 2 cans (21 ounces each) cherry pie filling
- 2 cans (20 ounces each) crushed pineapple, drained
- 2 cartons (16 ounces each) frozen whipped topping, thawed
- 2 cups chopped pecans

Direction

- Follow package directions to prep and bake cake with 13x9-in. pan; on wire rack, cool. Meanwhile, follow package directions to prep pudding.
- Cut cake to 1 1/2-in. cubes; put 1/3 cubes in 8-qt. punch bowl. Put 1/3 pie filling, pudding, pineapple, whipped topping then pecans over; repeat layers 2 times. Cover; refrigerate till serving.

Nutrition Information

- Calories: 195 calories
- Total Fat: 12g fat (4g saturated fat)
- Sodium: 71mg sodium
- Fiber: 1g fiber)
- Total Carbohydrate: 18g carbohydrate (14g sugars
- Cholesterol: 26mg cholesterol
- Protein: 3g protein.

374.   Cherry Crunch Ice Cream

Serving: 2-1/2 quarts. | Prep: 25mins | Cook: 20mins | Ready in:

Ingredients

- 6 large eggs
- 2 cups sugar
- 2 cups milk
- 1 package (3.4 ounces) instant vanilla pudding mix
- 4 cups heavy whipping cream
- 1 teaspoon vanilla extract
- Dash salt
- 1 cup old-fashioned oats
- 1/2 cup all-purpose flour
- 1/2 cup packed brown sugar
- 1/2 teaspoon ground cinnamon
- 1/3 cup cold butter
- 1 can (21 ounces) cherry pie filling

Direction

- Whisk milk, sugar and eggs in large saucepan until combined. Over low heat, cook while stirring until the mixture coats the metal spoon back and reaches 160°. Take away from heat; let cool. Beat in salt, vanilla, cream and pudding mix. Place in the refrigerator, covered, for 8 hours up to overnight.
- Combine cinnamon, brown sugar, flour and oats in a bowl. Cut in the butter until forming coarse crumbs. Spread into an unoiled baking pan, about 15x10x1-inch size. Bake at 350° until golden brown, about 10 to 15 mins. Place on wire rack to cool.
- Stir the pie filling into the cream mixture. Fill 2/3 full cylinder of the ice cream freezer; freeze following the manufacturer's instructions. Place the remaining mixture in refrigerator until it is ready to freeze.
- Remove from the ice cream freezer then stir 1 oat mixture portion into each batch. Place into the freezer container. Freeze, covered, at least 4 hours. Then serve.

Nutrition Information

- Calories: 405 calories
- Sodium: 163mg sodium
- Fiber: 1g fiber)
- Total Carbohydrate: 46g carbohydrate (38g sugars
- Cholesterol: 140mg cholesterol
- Protein: 5g protein.
- Total Fat: 23g fat (14g saturated fat)

375.   Cherry Pistachio Bread

Serving: 2 loaves (16 slices each). | Prep: 15mins | Cook: 40mins | Ready in:

Ingredients

- 1 package yellow cake mix (regular size)
- 1 package (3.4 ounces) instant pistachio pudding mix
- 4 large eggs
- 1 cup (8 ounces) sour cream
- 1/4 cup canola oil
- 2 tablespoons water
- 4 drops green food coloring, optional
- 3/4 cup halved maraschino cherries
- 1/2 cup chopped pecans
- 1/4 cup sugar
- 1 teaspoon ground cinnamon

Direction

- Mix pudding mixes and cake together in a large mixing bowl. Combine water, oil, sour cream, eggs, and food coloring (if using); beat into dry ingredients until incorporated and thick. Fold in pecans and cherries.
- Mix cinnamon and sugar together; scatter 1 tablespoon of sugar mixture over the bottom and up the sides of two greased 8x4-inch loaf pans. Pour in batter; scatter with the rest of cinnamon-sugar.
- Bake for 40 to 50 minutes at 350° until a toothpick comes out clean from the center.

Allow to cool in pans for 10 minutes before transferring to wire racks.

Nutrition Information

- Calories:
- Sodium:
- Fiber:
- Total Carbohydrate:
- Cholesterol:
- Protein:
- Total Fat:

---

376. Cherry Rice Dessert

Serving: 16-20 servings. | Prep: 20mins | Cook: 0mins | Ready in:

Ingredients

- 3 cups cooked long grain rice
- 1/2 cup chopped pecans
- 1 package (8 ounces) cream cheese, softened, divided
- 1 can (21 ounces) cherry or strawberry pie filling
- 1 cup confectioners' sugar
- 1 carton (12 ounces) frozen whipped topping, thawed, divided
- 1-1/2 cups cold milk
- 1/2 teaspoon coconut extract
- 1 package (3.4 ounces) instant vanilla pudding mix
- 1 cup sweetened shredded coconut, toasted

Direction

- Mix the pecans, 1/3 of the cream cheese and the rice in a big bowl. Pour into a greased 13x9-inch dish. Chill for half an hour, then spread the pie filling on top. Chill for 15 minutes.
- Mix the remaining cream cheese and confectioner's sugar in a bowl. Fold 1/2 of the

whipped topping into the mixture; spread over the filling. Chill for half an hour.

- Stir the pudding mix, extract, and the milk for 2 minutes in a bowl. Let it sit until partially set, 2 minutes. Spread over the top, then chill for half an hour. Spread the remaining whipped topping on top and add coconut over.

Nutrition Information

- Calories: 0
- Fiber: 1 g fiber
- Total Carbohydrate: 33 g carbohydrate
- Cholesterol: 15 mg cholesterol
- Protein: 3 g protein.
- Total Fat: 12 g fat (8 g saturated fat)
- Sodium: 110 mg sodium

---

377. Cherry Trifle

Serving: 12-15 servings. | Prep: 20mins | Cook: 0mins | Ready in:

Ingredients

- 2-1/4 cups cold whole milk, divided
- 1 package (3.4 ounces) instant vanilla pudding mix
- 1 envelope whipped topping mix (Dream Whip)
- 1/2 teaspoon vanilla extract
- 1 prepared angel food cake (8 to 10 ounces)
- 2 tablespoon maraschino cherry juice
- 1 can (21 ounces) cherry pie filling
- 3/4 cup chocolate syrup
- 1/2 cup sweetened shredded coconut, toasted
- 1/4 cup sliced almonds, toasted

Direction

- Beat pudding mix and 1 3/4 cups milk for 2 minutes on low speed in a big bowl; stand till soft set for 2 minutes. Beat leftover milk, vanilla and whipped topping mix till stiff peaks form in another big bowl.

- Cut cake into 1/2-in. cubes; put 1/2 in a 3-qt. glass bowl. Sprinkle with 1 tbsp. cherry juice. Put 1/4 cup chocolate syrup, 1/2 pudding and 1/2 pie filling over the top. Repeat layers. Put whipped topping then leftover syrup over; sprinkle with almonds and coconut. Cover; refrigerate for 4 hours minimum.

Nutrition Information

- Calories:
- Protein:
- Total Fat:
- Sodium:
- Fiber:
- Total Carbohydrate:
- Cholesterol:

---

378. Chewy Chocolate Chip Cookies

Serving: Makes 22 | Prep: | Cook: | Ready in:

Ingredients

- 200g (about 14 tablespoons) cold unsalted butter, chopped
- 1 cup (175g) brown sugar
- 3/4 cup (165g) white (granulated) sugar
- 1 teaspoon vanilla extract
- 2 tablespoons milk
- 1 egg
- 2 cups (300g) plain (all-purpose) flour
- 1/4 teaspoon baking powder
- 1/4 teaspoon baking soda
- 1/4 teaspoon table salt
- 300g dark chocolate, chopped

Direction

- Heat oven beforehand to 350°F (180°C).

- Add the butter and both the sugars into an electric mixer's bowl and beat on low speed until just incorporated.
- Raise the speed to medium and beat till pale and creamy, for about 8 minutes, scrape down the bowl's sides.
- Add the egg, milk and vanilla into the bowl and beat till light and fluffy, for about 2 minutes.
- Sift in the salt, baking powder, baking soda, and flour and beat till incorporated.
- Add in the chocolate. Mix to combine.
- Form heaped tablespoon of the mixture into balls and put them onto lightly greased baking trays lined with non-stick baking paper. Bake to a golden brown, for 12–14 minutes.
- Let cool on the trays for about 5 minutes then take out to wire racks to cool.
- Note: Place the balls 2–3cm apart to spread in the oven. When cookies are ready, they should be golden around the edges and the base has an even coloring.

Nutrition Information

- Calories: 260
- Total Carbohydrate: 32 g(11%)
- Cholesterol: 27 mg(9%)
- Protein: 3 g(6%)
- Total Fat: 14 g(21%)
- Saturated Fat: 8 g(41%)
- Sodium: 55 mg(2%)
- Fiber: 2 g(7%)

---

379. Chilly Peanut Butter Pie

Serving: 6-8 servings. | Prep: 15mins | Cook: 0mins | Ready in:

Ingredients

- 1 carton (8 ounces) frozen whipped topping, thawed, divided
- 1 graham cracker crust (9 inches)

- 1/2 cup strawberry jelly or jam
- 1 cup cold milk
- 1 package (3.4 ounces) instant vanilla pudding mix
- 1/2 cup peanut butter

Direction

- Spread the crust bottom with one cup of the whipped topping. Drop tablespoonfuls of jelly onto the topping; carefully spread. Whisk pudding mix and milk in a bowl until thickened. Stir in peanut butter till well mixed. Then fold in remaining whipped topping. Then spread over the jelly.
- Place in the freezer, covered, until firm, about 4 hours. Discard from freezer for 10 mins. Then serve.

Nutrition Information

- Calories: 393 calories
- Protein: 6g protein.
- Total Fat: 19g fat (8g saturated fat)
- Sodium: 381mg sodium
- Fiber: 1g fiber)
- Total Carbohydrate: 49g carbohydrate (37g sugars
- Cholesterol: 4mg cholesterol

---

380. Choco Scotch Marble Cake

Serving: 12 servings. | Prep: 15mins | Cook: 40mins | Ready in:

Ingredients

- 1 package yellow cake mix (regular size)
- 1 package (3.4 ounces) instant butterscotch pudding mix
- 4 eggs
- 1 cup (8 ounces) sour cream
- 1/3 cup canola oil

- 1/2 cup butterscotch chips
- 1 ounce unsweetened chocolate, melted
- FROSTING:
- 1-1/2 cups butterscotch chips, melted
- 1 ounce unsweetened chocolate, melted
- 5 to 6 tablespoons half-and-half cream
- 2 tablespoons finely chopped pecans

Direction

- Mix in a large bowl the oil, sour cream, eggs, pudding mix and cake mix; whisk on low speed for 30 seconds. Whisk on medium for 2 minutes. Split batter in half; mix the butterscotch chips into half and chocolate into the other half.
- Scoop half of the butterscotch batter in a 10-inch fluted tube pan that was greased and floured; put half of the chocolate batter on top. Repeat layers. Slice through batter with a knife to swirl.
- Place in the oven and bake for 40-45 minutes at 350 degrees F or until a toothpick pricked in the middle comes out clean. Let it cool for 10 minutes before taking out from the pan to a wire rack to fully cool.
- To make frosting, mix in a small bowl the chocolate and butterscotch chips. Mix in enough cream until the frosting turns smooth and achieves the desired spreading consistency. Place over the top of a cake and spread. Sprinkle with pecans.

Nutrition Information

- Calories: 439 calories
- Fiber: 2g fiber)
- Total Carbohydrate: 52g carbohydrate (38g sugars
- Cholesterol: 67mg cholesterol
- Protein: 5g protein.
- Total Fat: 23g fat (13g saturated fat)
- Sodium: 347mg sodium

381. Chocolate & Peanut Butter Pudding Pie With Bananas

Serving: 8 servings. | Prep: 25mins | Cook: 10mins | Ready in:

Ingredients

- 1 cup chocolate wafer crumbs (about 20 wafers)
- 1/4 cup butter, melted
- 2 medium firm bananas
- 3/4 cup creamy peanut butter
- 2 ounces semisweet chocolate, chopped
- 2 cups cold 2% milk
- 2 packages (3.4 ounces each) instant vanilla pudding mix
- 2 cups whipped topping, divided
- 2 tablespoons chopped salted peanuts
- Peanut butter cups, optional

Direction

- Mix butter and wafer crumbs in a small bowl; push up the sides and onto the bottom of an ungreased 9-in. pie pan. Bake for 8-10 minutes at 350° or until firm. Let cool completely on a wire rack.
- Chop bananas; put on bottom of shell. Mix chocolate and peanut butter in a microwaveable bowl; melt in a microwave on high for 1 to 1-1/2 minutes or until combined and smooth, mixing every half a minute. Scoop on top of bananas.
- Whip pudding mix and milk in a big bowl for 2 minutes. Let sit for 2 minutes or until soft-set. Fold in a cup whipped topping; spread on top of chocolate mixture. Frost leftover whipped topping over edge. Cover and chill for at least 3 hours.
- Garnish with peanuts prior to serving. Serve with chopped peanut butter cups (optional).

Nutrition Information

- Calories: 507 calories
- Fiber: 3g fiber)
- Total Carbohydrate: 54g carbohydrate (39g sugars
- Cholesterol: 20mg cholesterol
- Protein: 10g protein.
- Total Fat: 28g fat (12g saturated fat)
- Sodium: 418mg sodium

382. Chocolate Berry Parfaits

Serving: 4-6 servings. | Prep: 15mins | Cook: 0mins | Ready in:

Ingredients

- 2 cups cold 2% milk
- 1 package (3.9 ounces) instant chocolate pudding mix
- 1 package (10 ounces) frozen sweetened strawberries, thawed
- 1 cup heavy whipping cream
- 1/4 cup confectioners' sugar
- Sliced fresh strawberries, optional

Direction

- Combine pudding mix and milk for 2 minutes in a large bowl. Allow it to stand for 2 minutes or until set to soft; reserve. Strain strawberries (discard the juice or keep for another use); transfer berries in a blender. Then cover and pulse until smooth; reserve.
- Whisk sugar and cream in a large bowl until stiff peaks form. Slightly fold in strawberry puree. Split half of the chocolate pudding among four or six parfait glasses. Put half of the strawberry mixture on top. Continue layers. Decorate with a slice of strawberry if preferred.

Nutrition Information

- Calories: 317 calories
- Sodium: 329mg sodium
- Fiber: 1g fiber)

- Total Carbohydrate: 39g carbohydrate (33g sugars
- Cholesterol: 65mg cholesterol
- Protein: 4g protein.
- Total Fat: 18g fat (11g saturated fat)

- Protein: 7.4
- Total Fat: 27.2
- Sodium: 265
- Total Carbohydrate: 77
- Cholesterol: 120

383. Chocolate Bundt Cake

Serving: 12 | Prep: 15mins | Cook: 1hours10mins |Ready in:

Ingredients

- 3 cups all-purpose flour
- 1/2 teaspoon baking powder
- 1/2 teaspoon salt
- 1/2 cup unsweetened cocoa powder
- 1 cup butter, softened
- 1/2 cup shortening
- 3 cups white sugar
- 1 teaspoon vanilla extract
- 5 eggs
- 1 cup milk

Direction

- Set the oven at 325°F (165°C) and start preheating. Coat a 10-in. Bundt pan with grease and flour. Sift together cocoa, salt, baking powder and flour. Set aside.
- Cream vanilla, sugar, shortening and butter together in a large bowl till fluffy and light. Put in eggs, one per time, beating properly after each addition. Put in the flour mixture alternately with milk. Stir properly.
- Transfer to the prepared pan. Bake at 325°F (165°C) till a toothpick comes out clean when inserted into the cake, 70 minutes. Allow to cool in the pan for 10 minutes; remove to cool completely on a wire rack.

Nutrition Information

- Calories: 568 calories;

384. Chocolate Cherry Dessert

Serving: 9 servings. | Prep: 30mins | Cook: 0mins | Ready in:

Ingredients

- 26 chocolate wafer cookies, crushed
- 1/4 cup butter, melted
- 1 cup sour cream
- 1 package (3.9 ounces) instant chocolate pudding mix
- 3/4 cup milk
- 1 can (21 ounces) cherry pie filling

Direction

- Mix butter and wafer crumbs together in a bowl, then press into an 8-inch square dish. Put into freezer about 10 minutes.
- Mix together milk, pudding and sour cream in a separate bowl, then beat on low speed about 1 1/2 minutes. Spread mixture over crust and scoop on top with pie filling. Place a cover and chill until ready to serve.

Nutrition Information

- Calories: 302 calories
- Protein: 3g protein.
- Total Fat: 13g fat (7g saturated fat)
- Sodium: 368mg sodium
- Fiber: 1g fiber)
- Total Carbohydrate: 44g carbohydrate (26g sugars
- Cholesterol: 34mg cholesterol

385.   Chocolate Cherry Trifle

Serving: 18 servings. | Prep: 20mins | Cook: 0mins | Ready in:

Ingredients

- 3 cups cold fat-free milk
- 2 packages (1.4 ounces each) sugar-free instant chocolate fudge pudding mix
- 1 prepared angel food cake (8 to 10 ounces), cut into 1-inch cubes
- 2 cans (20 ounces each) reduced-sugar cherry pie filling
- 2 cans (20 ounces each) unsweetened crushed pineapple, drained
- 1 carton (16 ounces) frozen reduced-fat whipped topping, thawed
- 1/4 cup chopped pecans

Direction

- Whisk pudding mixes and milk for 2 minutes in big bowl; stand till soft set or for 2 minutes.
- Put 1/2 cake cubes in glass bowl/4-qt. trifle bowl; top with 1/2 each of: pudding, the pie filling, the pineapple then whipped topping. Repeat the layers; sprinkle pecans then refrigerate leftovers.

Nutrition Information

- Calories: 221 calories
- Fiber: 1g fiber)
- Total Carbohydrate: 41g carbohydrate (29g sugars
- Cholesterol: 1mg cholesterol
- Protein: 3g protein.
- Total Fat: 5g fat (3g saturated fat)
- Sodium: 266mg sodium

386.   Chocolate Chip Cake

Serving: 12 | Prep: | Cook: | Ready in:

Ingredients

- 2/3 cup butter
- 3/4 cup packed brown sugar
- 3/4 cup white sugar
- 3 eggs
- 1 1/2 cups all-purpose flour
- 3/4 cup whole wheat flour
- 2 1/2 teaspoons baking powder
- 1 teaspoon salt
- 1 cup milk
- 1 1/2 teaspoons vanilla extract
- 1 cup semisweet chocolate chips

Direction

- Set oven to 175°C (or 350°F) and begin preheating. Grease 2 9-inch round pans and dust with flour.
- Beat sugars and butter together in a big mixing bowl. Beat eggs into creamed mixture.
- Sift salt, baking powder and flours into a different bowl. Alternately add into creamed mixture with milk. Whisk in vanilla. Coarsely chop chocolate chips, then put into the batter.
- Transfer batter to greased and floured pans; bake until inserted knife into the center comes out clean, about 25-30 minutes. If desired, fill with Butterscotch filling and pour chocolate glaze on top.

Nutrition Information

- Calories: 371 calories;
- Cholesterol: 75
- Protein: 5.6
- Total Fat: 16.4
- Sodium: 400
- Total Carbohydrate: 53.6

387. Chocolate Chip Cookie Delight

Serving: 15 servings. | Prep: 20mins | Cook: 15mins | Ready in:

Ingredients

- 1 tube (16-1/2 ounces) refrigerated chocolate chip cookie dough
- 1 package (8 ounces) cream cheese, softened
- 1 cup confectioners' sugar
- 1 carton (12 ounces) frozen whipped topping, thawed, divided
- 3 cups cold 2% milk
- 1 package (3.9 ounces) instant chocolate pudding mix
- 1 package (3.4 ounces) instant vanilla pudding mix
- Chopped nuts, chocolate curls and miniature semisweet chocolate chips, optional

Direction

- Allow the cookie dough to rest at room temperature for 5 to 10 minutes to become tender. Press it into the ungreased 13x9-inch baking pan. Bake at 350 degrees till it turns golden-brown or for 14 to 16 minutes. Let cool down on the wire rack.
- In the big bowl, whip the confectioners' sugar and cream cheese till smooth. Fold in 1.75 cups of the whipped topping. Spread on the crust.
- In the big bowl, stir the pudding mixes and milk for 2 minutes. Spread on the cream cheese layer. Add the rest of the whipped topping on top. Drizzle with the chocolate curls and nuts if you want.
- Keep covered and refrigerated for 8 hours or overnight till firm.

Nutrition Information

- Calories: 365 calories
- Total Carbohydrate: 47g carbohydrate (22g sugars
- Cholesterol: 29mg cholesterol
- Protein: 4g protein.
- Total Fat: 17g fat (10g saturated fat)
- Sodium: 329mg sodium
- Fiber: 1g fiber)

388. Chocolate Chip Cookie Dessert

Serving: 15 servings. | Prep: 25mins | Cook: 15mins | Ready in:

Ingredients

- 1 tube (16-1/2 ounces) refrigerated chocolate chip cookie dough
- 1/2 cup caramel ice cream topping
- 1/2 cup cold 2% milk
- 1 package (3.4 ounces) instant vanilla pudding mix
- 1 carton (8 ounces) frozen whipped topping, thawed
- 3/4 cup chopped nuts
- 3/4 cup English toffee bits or almond brickle chips
- 3 ounces semisweet chocolate, chopped
- 3 tablespoons butter

Direction

- Allow dough to sit for 5 to 10 minutes at room temperature until softened. Pat dough into an ungreased 13x9-inch baking pan. Bake for 13 to 15 minutes at 350° until golden brown. Let cool entirely on a wire rack.
- Spoon caramel topping into crust, spreading evenly. Whisk pudding mix and milk for 2 minutes in a large mixing bowl until thickened. Fold in toffee bits, nuts, and whipped topping. Distribute over caramel layer. Freeze for 4 hours, covered, or until firm.
- Melt butter and chocolate in a microwave; whisk until smooth. Drizzle chocolate mixture over pudding layer. Slice into squares to serve.

Nutrition Information

- Calories: 345 calories
- Cholesterol: 18mg cholesterol
- Protein: 3g protein.
- Total Fat: 18g fat (8g saturated fat)
- Sodium: 271mg sodium
- Fiber: 1g fiber)
- Total Carbohydrate: 42g carbohydrate (32g sugars

389. Chocolate Chip Cookie Pizza

Serving: 14-16 slices. | Prep: 25mins | Cook: 15mins | Ready in:

Ingredients

- 1 tube (16-1/2 ounces) refrigerated chocolate chip cookie dough
- 1 package (8 ounces) cream cheese, softened
- 1/3 cup sugar
- 2 cups cold half-and-half cream
- 1 package (3.9 ounces) instant chocolate pudding mix
- 1/4 cup chopped pecans or walnuts

Direction

- Place cookie dough into a clean and dry 12-inch pizza pan and press down. Bake for 15-20 minutes at 350° until the dough has a deep golden-brown color. Let it cool for 5 minutes; loosen the crust by running a flexible metal spatula under crust gently. Let it fully cool.
- Beat sugar and cream cheese in a small bowl until they are combined. Spread it on top of the crust. Whip pudding mix and cream for 2 minutes in a big bowl. Allow to sit for 2 minutes or until soft-set. Spread it on top of cream cheese mixture; top with nuts. Keep in the fridge until you serve it.

Nutrition Information

- Calories: 284 calories
- Total Fat: 16g fat (7g saturated fat)
- Sodium: 226mg sodium
- Fiber: 1g fiber)
- Total Carbohydrate: 32g carbohydrate (23g sugars
- Cholesterol: 38mg cholesterol
- Protein: 4g protein.

390. Chocolate Chip Cupcakes

Serving: 2-1/2 dozen. | Prep: 15mins | Cook: 20mins | Ready in:

Ingredients

- 1 package yellow cake mix (regular size)
- 1 package (3.4 ounces) instant vanilla pudding mix
- 1 cup water
- 1/2 cup canola oil
- 4 large eggs
- 1 cup (6 ounces) miniature semisweet chocolate chips
- 1 can (16 ounces) chocolate or vanilla frosting
- Additional miniature semisweet chocolate chips, optional

Direction

- Combine eggs, oil, water, pudding mixes, and cake in a large bowl; beat mixture for half a minute on low speed. Beat for 2 minute on medium speed. Mix in chocolate chips.
- Pour into paper-lined muffin cups to 2/3 full. Bake for 18 to 22 minutes at 375° until a toothpick comes out clean from the center. Allow to cool for 10 minutes before transferring to wire racks to cool entirely. Frost cupcakes. Garnish top with more chips if desired.

Nutrition Information

- Calories: 215 calories
- Cholesterol: 28mg cholesterol
- Protein: 2g protein.
- Total Fat: 10g fat (3g saturated fat)
- Sodium: 199mg sodium
- Fiber: 1g fiber)
- Total Carbohydrate: 30g carbohydrate (21g sugars

---

391. Chocolate Chip Oatmeal Cookies

Serving: 30 | Prep: | Cook: |Ready in:

Ingredients

- 1 cup butter, softened
- 1 1/4 cups packed brown sugar
- 1/2 cup white sugar
- 2 eggs
- 2 tablespoons milk
- 1 teaspoon vanilla extract
- 1 3/4 cups all-purpose flour
- 1 teaspoon baking soda
- 1/2 teaspoon salt
- 2 1/2 cups rolled oats
- 2 cups semisweet chocolate chips
- 1 cup chopped walnuts

Direction

- Set oven to preheat at 190°C (375°F).
- Beat the sugars and margarine together till creamy. Add in the vanilla, milk and eggs; beat well. Add in the salt, baking soda and combined flour; mix thoroughly. Stir in nuts, chocolate chips and oats; mix thoroughly.
- On ungreased cookie sheet, drop rounded tablespoonfuls of the dough. Bake for 9-10 minutes. Let them cool down on cookie sheet for 1 minute; transfer to wire rack.

Nutrition Information

- Calories: 239 calories;
- Sodium: 134
- Total Carbohydrate: 30.2
- Cholesterol: 29
- Protein: 3.2
- Total Fat: 12.9

---

392. Chocolate Chip Snack Cake

Serving: 12-15 servings. | Prep: 15mins | Cook: 45mins | Ready in:

Ingredients

- 1 package yellow cake mix (regular size)
- 1 package (3.4 ounces) instant vanilla pudding mix
- 4 eggs
- 1 cup water
- 1/2 cup canola oil
- 1 package (12 ounces) miniature semisweet chocolate chips
- 4 ounces German sweet chocolate, grated, divided
- Confectioners' sugar

Direction

- Mix together the first 5 ingredients in a big bowl; beat for half a minute over low speed. Switch to medium and beat for another 2 minutes. Whisk in 1/2 of the grated chocolate and chocolate chips.
- Transfer to a greased 13-inch by 9-inch baking pan. Bake at 350 degrees until a toothpick slid into the middle comes out without any batter streaks, about 45 to 50 minutes.
- While cake is still a little warm, sprinkle on the rest of grated chocolate. Let cool down fully. Dust confectioners' sugar on top of the cake.

Nutrition Information

- Calories: 396 calories
- Protein: 5g protein.
- Total Fat: 21g fat (8g saturated fat)
- Sodium: 327mg sodium
- Fiber: 2g fiber)
- Total Carbohydrate: 52g carbohydrate (38g sugars
- Cholesterol: 57mg cholesterol

---

393. Chocolate Coconut Bundt Cake

Serving: 12 servings. | Prep: 15mins | Cook: 50mins | Ready in:

Ingredients

- 1 package chocolate cake mix (regular size)
- 1 package (3.9 ounces) instant chocolate pudding mix
- 4 large eggs
- 3/4 cup vegetable oil
- 3/4 cup water
- 1 teaspoon vanilla extract
- FILLING:
- 2 cups sweetened shredded coconut
- 1/3 cup sweetened condensed milk
- 1/4 teaspoon almond extract
- 1 can (16 ounces) chocolate frosting

Direction

- Mix vanilla, water, oil, eggs, pudding mix, and cake mix together in a big bowl. Whisk for 30 seconds on low speed. Whisk for 2 minutes on medium speed.
- Add 3 cups of mixture to a 10-inch fluted tube pan coated with flour and grease. Mix extract, milk, and coconut together in a small bowl. Drop onto the batter by spoonfuls. Put on the rest of the batter to cover.
- Bake at 350° until a toothpick will come out clean when you insert it into the middle, about

50-60 minutes. Let cool for 10 minutes, and then transfer from the pan to a wire rack to fully cool. Use the chocolate frosting to frost.

Nutrition Information

- Calories: 492 calories
- Cholesterol: 59mg cholesterol
- Protein: 4g protein.
- Total Fat: 26g fat (9g saturated fat)
- Sodium: 452mg sodium
- Fiber: 2g fiber)
- Total Carbohydrate: 63g carbohydrate (45g sugars

---

394. Chocolate Cream Cheese Pie

Serving: 6 servings. | Prep: 25mins | Cook: 0mins | Ready in:

Ingredients

- 3 ounces cream cheese, softened
- 2 tablespoons sugar
- 1-3/4 cups milk, divided
- 2 cups whipped topping, divided
- 1 graham cracker crust (9 inches)
- 1 package (3.9 ounces) instant chocolate pudding mix
- Miniature semisweet chocolate chips, optional

Direction

- Beat 1 tablespoon milk, sugar and cream cheese in a small bowl to form a smooth mixture. Fold a cup of whipped topping into the mixture. Pour into crust and even out.
- Beat remaining milk and pudding mix in a small bowl for 2 minutes. Allow to sit until soft-set, 2 minutes. Spread onto cream cheese layer. Refrigerate to set.
- Top with chocolate chips and remaining

whipped topping (optional) for garnishing purpose right before serving.

Nutrition Information

- Calories: 381 calories
- Total Carbohydrate: 48g carbohydrate (36g sugars
- Cholesterol: 25mg cholesterol
- Protein: 5g protein.
- Total Fat: 19g fat (10g saturated fat)
- Sodium: 511mg sodium
- Fiber: 1g fiber)

---

395. Chocolate Cream Pudding Dessert

Serving: 15 servings. | Prep: 15mins | Cook: 15mins | Ready in:

Ingredients

- 1/4 cup cold butter, cubed
- 1 cup all-purpose flour
- 1 package (8 ounces) reduced-fat cream cheese, softened
- Artificial sweetener equivalent to 2 tablespoons sugar
- 1 carton (8 ounces) frozen reduced-fat whipped topping, thawed, divided
- 1-1/2 cups cold fat-free milk
- 1 package (1/4 ounces) instant sugar-free chocolate pudding mix

Direction

- Cut butter into flour in a small bowl until crumbly. Pat into an 11x7-in. baking dish covered with cooking spray. Bake to a light brown, at 350° for 15-18 minutes. Cool thoroughly.
- Beat cream cheese and sweetener in a large bowl till smooth. Fold half of the whipped

topping into the mixture. Spread on top of the crust carefully.

- In a different large bowl, combine pudding mix and milk together. Beat for 2 minutes on low speed. Let it sit until soft-set, for 2 minutes. Spread on top of the cream cheese. Put the remaining whipped topping on top.

Nutrition Information

- Calories: 134 calories
- Total Fat: 6g fat (0 saturated fat)
- Sodium: 184mg sodium
- Fiber: 0 fiber)
- Total Carbohydrate: 14g carbohydrate (0 sugars
- Cholesterol: 6mg cholesterol
- Protein: 4g protein. Diabetic Exchanges: 1-1/2 fat

---

396. Chocolate Creme Cakes

Serving: 12-18 servings. | Prep: 25mins | Cook: 30mins | Ready in:

Ingredients

- 1 package chocolate cake mix (regular size)
- 1 package (3.9 ounces) instant chocolate pudding mix
- 3/4 cup vegetable oil
- 3/4 cup water
- 4 eggs
- FILLING:
- 3 tablespoons all-purpose flour
- 1 cup milk
- 1/2 cup butter, softened
- 1/2 cup shortening
- 1 cup sugar
- 1 teaspoon vanilla extract

Direction

- Beat eggs, water, oil, pudding and cake mixes together in a big bowl. Transfer to a 13x9" baking pan dusted with flour and coated with cooking spray.
- Bake at 350 degrees until a toothpick slid into the middle comes out with no batter streaks, or for 30 to 35 minutes. Allow to chill for 10 minutes, then flip onto a wire rack to chill thoroughly.
- Mix milk and flour together until no lumps remain in a small saucepan. Boil; cook, while stirring, until thick or for 2 minutes. Let cool.
- Beat vanilla, sugar, shortening and butter together until fluffy and light in a big bowl; whisk in milk mixture for approximately 5 minutes until sugar dissolves.
- Slice cake in half, horizontal layers. Lather the bottom layer with filling, then place top layer on top. Slice cake into serving-size pieces. Store in an airtight container and place in the freezer for 1 month maximum. Take out of the freezer for 1 hour prior to serving.

Nutrition Information

- Calories: 389 calories
- Cholesterol: 63mg cholesterol
- Protein: 3g protein.
- Total Fat: 24g fat (7g saturated fat)
- Sodium: 343mg sodium
- Fiber: 1g fiber)
- Total Carbohydrate: 42g carbohydrate (29g sugars

---

397. Chocolate Delight Dessert

Serving: 12 servings. | Prep: 30mins | Cook: 0mins | Ready in:

Ingredients

- 1 cup crushed saltines
- 1/2 cup graham cracker crumbs

- 1/3 cup butter, melted
- 2 cups milk
- 1 package (3.9 ounces) instant chocolate pudding mix
- 1 package (3.4 ounces) instant vanilla pudding mix
- 1-1/2 quarts cookies and cream ice cream, softened
- 1 carton (12 ounces) frozen whipped topping, thawed
- 3 Heath candy bars (1.4 ounces each), crushed

Direction

- Mix graham cracker crumbs and saltines in a small bowl; mix in butter. Press onto bottom of 13x9-in. greased baking pan; refrigerate for 15 minutes.
- Meanwhile, whisk pudding mixes and milk for 2 minutes in a big bowl; fold in the ice cream. Spread on crust; top using whipped topping. Sprinkle crushed candy bars. Freeze till firm, covered. 30 minutes before serving, remove from freezer.

Nutrition Information

- Calories: 439 calories
- Cholesterol: 44mg cholesterol
- Protein: 5g protein.
- Total Fat: 22g fat (14g saturated fat)
- Sodium: 477mg sodium
- Fiber: 1g fiber)
- Total Carbohydrate: 54g carbohydrate (38g sugars

---

398. Chocolate Dream Dessert

Serving: 12-15 servings. | Prep: 20mins | Cook: 15mins | Ready in:

Ingredients

- CRUST:
- 1 cup all-purpose flour

- 1 cup finely chopped pecans
- 1/2 cup cold butter
- FILLING:
- 1 package (8 ounces) cream cheese, softened
- 1 cup confectioners' sugar
- 1 carton (8 ounces) frozen whipped topping, thawed, divided
- 1 package (3.4 ounces) instant vanilla pudding mix
- 1 package (3.9 ounces) instant chocolate pudding mix
- 3 cups cold whole milk
- 1 chocolate bar, grated

Direction

- Mix together pecans and flour in a bowl, then slice in butter until mixture looks like fine crumbs. Press into a 13-inch x9-inch baking pan.
- Bake at 350 degrees until golden brown, about 15 to 20 minutes. Allow to cool on a wire rack. In a big bowl, put half of the whipped topping, sugar and cream cheese, beating until smooth. Spread mixture over crust.
- Whisk together milk and pudding mixes until soft-set, about 2 minutes. Spread mix over cream cheese mixture and refrigerate until firm. Spread leftover whipped topping over and sprinkle grated chocolate over top. Chill until serving.

Nutrition Information

- Calories: 360 calories
- Sodium: 333mg sodium
- Fiber: 1g fiber)
- Total Carbohydrate: 36g carbohydrate (23g sugars
- Cholesterol: 40mg cholesterol
- Protein: 5g protein.
- Total Fat: 22g fat (12g saturated fat)

399. Chocolate Eclair Dessert

Serving: 12 | Prep: 15mins | Cook: | Ready in:

Ingredients

- 2 individual packages graham crackers
- 2 (3 ounce) packages instant vanilla pudding mix
- 3 cups milk
- 1 (8 ounce) container frozen whipped topping, thawed
- 1 (16 ounce) package prepared chocolate frosting

Direction

- Use graham crackers to line the bottom of a 13"x9" pan.
- Mix together milk and pudding mix in a big bowl, then stir well. Mix into the pudding mixture with whipped topping. Spread over graham cracker layer with a half of the mixture, then put another layer of graham crackers as well as leftover pudding on top.
- Place on overall with the last layer of graham crackers and use chocolate frosting to frost. Chill for a minimum of 2 hours prior to serving to let graham crackers soften.

Nutrition Information

- Calories: 401 calories;
- Total Carbohydrate: 65.6
- Cholesterol: 5
- Protein: 4.2
- Total Fat: 13.7
- Sodium: 481

400. Chocolate Eclair Graham Dessert

Serving: 4 servings. | Prep: 20mins | Cook: 0mins | Ready in:

Ingredients

- 9 graham cracker squares
- 1/2 cup cold 2% milk
- 1/3 cup instant vanilla pudding mix
- 1/2 cup whipped topping
- TOPPING:
- 1/2 ounce semisweet chocolate
- 1-1/2 teaspoons butter
- 2-1/4 teaspoons 2% milk
- 1-1/2 teaspoons light corn syrup
- 1/2 teaspoon vanilla extract
- 1/3 cup confectioners' sugar

Direction

- Halve graham crackers into 18 rectangles. In one unoiled loaf pan, 8x4-inch in size, put 9 rectangles; reserve.
- Whip pudding mix and milk in small bowl for two minutes. Rest for two minutes or till set yet not firm. Fold in the whipped topping. Scatter on top of graham crackers; put the rest of graham crackers on top.
- For the topping, liquify butter and chocolate in a microwavable bowl. Mix in confectioners' sugar, vanilla, corn syrup and milk. Scatter on top of graham crackers. Put on cover and chill overnight.

Nutrition Information

- Calories: 229 calories
- Sodium: 284mg sodium
- Fiber: 0 fiber)
- Total Carbohydrate: 40g carbohydrate (28g sugars
- Cholesterol: 6mg cholesterol
- Protein: 2g protein.
- Total Fat: 7g fat (4g saturated fat)

401.   Chocolate Eclair Squares

Serving: 16 servings. | Prep: 15mins | Cook: 0mins | Ready in:

Ingredients

- 2 cups cold milk
- 2 packages (3.4 ounces each) JELL-O® Vanilla Flavor Instant Pudding
- 1 carton (8 ounces) Cool Whip® Whipped Topping, thawed
- 64 vanilla wafers
- 2 squares (1 ounce each) semisweet chocolate

Direction

- Whisk pudding mix and milk in a big bowl for 2 minutes. Let the mixture sit until soft-set, 2 minutes. Fold whipped topping in the mixture. On the bottom an 8-inch square dish, place 16 wafers and spread one-third of pudding mixture on top. Make layers two more times. Place the rest of wafers on top. Chill, while covered, for 4 hours.
- Right before serving, put chocolate in a microwaveable bowl. Heat chocolate until melted; whisk to smoothen and drizzle on top of wafers. Keep refrigerated to store.

Nutrition Information

- Calories:
- Sodium:
- Fiber:
- Total Carbohydrate:
- Cholesterol:
- Protein:
- Total Fat:

402. Chocolate Espresso Lava Cake

Serving: 16 servings. | Prep: 15mins | Cook: 03hours00mins | Ready in:

Ingredients

- 1 package chocolate fudge cake mix (regular size)
- 1 tablespoon instant espresso powder
- 3 cups 2% milk
- 1 package (3.9 ounces) instant chocolate pudding mix
- 1 cup (6 ounces) semisweet chocolate chips
- 1 cup white baking chips

Direction

- Follow package instructions to prepare cake mix batter, then put in espresso powder before combining. Pour into a 4-quart slow cooker coated with cooking spray.
- Stir pudding mix and milk in a small bowl, 2 minutes. Allow to sit for about 2 minutes until softly set. Pour onto the batter. Cover and cook over low heat until a toothpick slid into the cake portion comes out with wet crumbs attached, or for 3-3 1/2 hours.
- Sprinkle baking chips and chocolate chips onto the cake's surface. Switch off the slow cooker; take out the insert. Uncover and allow to rest for 15 to 30 minutes until chips are tender. Serve while still warm.

Nutrition Information

- Calories: 327 calories
- Cholesterol: 41mg cholesterol
- Protein: 5g protein.
- Total Fat: 15g fat (6g saturated fat)
- Sodium: 317mg sodium
- Fiber: 2g fiber)
- Total Carbohydrate: 45g carbohydrate (29g sugars

403. Chocolate Fudge Mousse

Serving: 6 servings. | Prep: 10mins | Cook: 0mins | Ready in:

Ingredients

- 2 cups cold milk
- 1 package (3.9 ounces) instant chocolate pudding mix
- 1/4 cup hot fudge ice cream topping
- 3 cups whipped topping

Direction

- Beat pudding mix and milk for 2 minutes on low speed in a bowl. Mix fudge topping in; fold whipped topping in. Put in dessert dishes; chill till serving.

Nutrition Information

- Calories: 259 calories
- Cholesterol: 11mg cholesterol
- Protein: 4g protein.
- Total Fat: 10g fat (8g saturated fat)
- Sodium: 329mg sodium
- Fiber: 1g fiber)
- Total Carbohydrate: 36g carbohydrate (25g sugars

404. Chocolate Hazelnut Parfaits

Serving: 8 servings. | Prep: 10mins | Cook: 0mins | Ready in:

Ingredients

- 3 cups cold milk
- 1 cup refrigerated hazelnut nondairy creamer
- 2 packages (3.9 ounces each) instant chocolate pudding mix

- 1 cup crushed shortbread cookies
- 2 cups sliced fresh strawberries
- Whipped cream, optional

Direction

- Combine pudding mixes, creamer, and milk for 2 minutes in a large bowl. Allow it to stand for 2 minutes or until set to soft.
- Into each of 8 parfait glasses, put 1/4 cup pudding; scatter each with 1 tablespoon cookie crumbs. Put strawberries and the rest of pudding and crumbs on top. Keep in the refrigerator for 1 hour before serving. Decorate with whipped cream if preferred.

Nutrition Information

- Calories: 249 calories
- Fiber: 2g fiber)
- Total Carbohydrate: 35g carbohydrate (16g sugars
- Cholesterol: 16mg cholesterol
- Protein: 5g protein.
- Total Fat: 10g fat (4g saturated fat)
- Sodium: 352mg sodium

405. Chocolate Ice Cream Pie

Serving: 2 pies (6-8 servings each). | Prep: 10mins | Cook: 0mins | Ready in:

Ingredients

- 2 quarts vanilla ice cream, melted
- 1 package (5.9 ounces) instant chocolate pudding mix
- 2 graham cracker crusts (10 inches each)
- Whipped topping, optional

Direction

- For 2 minutes, whisk pudding mix and melted ice cream in a big bowl. Put in crusts. Freeze till firm.

- You can freeze pie for a max of 2 months. 10 minutes before serving, remove from freeze. Put whipped topping on top if you want.

Nutrition Information

- Calories: 275 calories
- Protein: 3g protein.
- Total Fat: 13g fat (6g saturated fat)
- Sodium: 329mg sodium
- Fiber: 1g fiber)
- Total Carbohydrate: 39g carbohydrate (29g sugars
- Cholesterol: 29mg cholesterol

406. Chocolate Lover's Eclairs

Serving: 8-9 servings. | Prep: 35mins | Cook: 35mins | Ready in:

Ingredients

- 1/2 cup butter, cubed
- 1 cup water
- 1 cup all-purpose flour
- 1/4 teaspoon salt
- 4 large eggs
- FILLING:
- 2-1/2 cups cold whole milk
- 1 package (5.1 ounces) instant vanilla pudding mix
- 1 cup heavy whipping cream
- 1/4 cup confectioners' sugar
- 1 teaspoon vanilla extract
- CHOCOLATE ICING:
- 2 ounces semisweet chocolate
- 2 tablespoons butter
- 1 cup confectioners' sugar
- 2 to 3 tablespoons hot water

Direction

- Mix in a large saucepan the water and butter. Bring to a rapid boil, mixing until the butter melts. Lower heat; put in salt and flour. Whisk vigorously until mixture leaves the sides of the pan and makes a stiff ball. Separate from heat. Put in eggs, one at a time, whisking well after every addition.

- Using a pastry tube fitting with a #10 or larger tip or a tablespoon, pipe or scoop dough into 4-inch long x 1-1/2-inch wide strips on a greased baking sheet.
- Place in the oven and bake for 15 minutes at 450°F. Lower heat to 325°F and bake for 20 more minutes. Put on a wire rack and cool.
- To make filling, beat pudding mix and milk in a large bowl for 2 minutes. Allow to stand for 2 minutes or until soft-set. Whip cream in a separate large bowl until it forms soft peaks. Mix in vanilla and sugar; fold into pudding. Then fill cooled shells. (Chill left of pudding mixture for another use). To make icing, melt butter and chocolate in a small saucepan over low heat. Mix in sugar. Put in hot water until icing turns smooth and achieves the desired consistency. Slightly cool. Put over eclairs and spread. Let it chill then serve.

Nutrition Information

- Calories: 470 calories
- Fiber: 1g fiber)
- Total Carbohydrate: 48g carbohydrate (34g sugars
- Cholesterol: 174mg cholesterol
- Protein: 7g protein.
- Total Fat: 28g fat (17g saturated fat)
- Sodium: 492mg sodium

407. Chocolate Mallow Pie

Serving: 6-8 servings. | Prep: 20mins | Cook: 0mins | Ready in:

Ingredients

- 1 package (8 ounces) cream cheese, softened

- 2 cups cold 2% milk, divided
- 1 package (3.9 ounces) instant chocolate pudding mix
- 1-1/2 cups miniature marshmallows
- 1 graham cracker crust (9 inches)

Direction

- Beat cream cheese and 1/2 cup milk in a large bowl till smooth. Beat the dry pudding mix and remaining milk into the mix. Fold the marshmallows into the mixture. Pour on top of the crust. Chill in the refrigerator until serving.

Nutrition Information

- Calories: 320 calories
- Cholesterol: 39mg cholesterol
- Protein: 5g protein.
- Total Fat: 17g fat (9g saturated fat)
- Sodium: 444mg sodium
- Fiber: 1g fiber)
- Total Carbohydrate: 37g carbohydrate (28g sugars

408. Chocolate Mint Cream Cake

Serving: 14 servings. | Prep: 30mins | Cook: 20mins | Ready in:

Ingredients

- 1 package white cake mix (regular size)
- 1 cup water
- 1/2 cup canola oil
- 3 large eggs
- 1/2 teaspoon peppermint extract
- 1 cup crushed mint creme Oreo cookies
- TOPPING:
- 2 packages (3.9 ounces each) instant chocolate pudding mix
- 1/3 cup confectioners' sugar

- 1-1/2 cups cold 2% milk
- 1/2 to 1 teaspoon peppermint extract
- 1 carton (12 ounces) frozen whipped topping, thawed
- 1/2 cup crushed mint creme Oreo cookies
- 15 mint Andes candies

Direction

- Combine extract, eggs, oil, water, and cake mix in a large mixing bowl; beat for half a minute on low speed. Raise speed to medium and beat for 2 more minutes. Mix in crushed cookies.
- Divide mixture among 3 greased and floured 9-inch round baking pans. Bake for 18 to 24 minutes at 350°, or until a toothpick comes out clean from the center. Allow to cool in pans for 10 minutes before transferring to wire racks to cool entirely.
- To make topping: Beat extract, milk, confectioners' sugar, and dry pudding mixes together until thickened. Fold in crushed cookies and whipped topping.
- Lay 1 cake layer on a serving plate; smear with topping. Repeat layering process 2 more times. Pipe remaining topping over sides of the cake.
- Cut 8 candies into small pieces; scatter over the center of the cake. Cut the rest of the candies in half; place 1 candy half on top of each serving to garnish. Keep chilled in the fridge.

Nutrition Information

- Calories: 492 calories
- Cholesterol: 48mg cholesterol
- Protein: 5g protein.
- Total Fat: 23g fat (10g saturated fat)
- Sodium: 574mg sodium
- Fiber: 1g fiber)
- Total Carbohydrate: 67g carbohydrate (43g sugars

409.   Chocolate Mint Delight

Serving: 4 servings. | Prep: 15mins | Cook: 0mins | Ready in:

Ingredients

- 1 package (3.9 ounces) instant chocolate pudding mix
- 2 cups cold milk
- 28 miniature cream-filled chocolate sandwich cookies, crushed, divided
- 1/4 cup crushed miniature candy canes or peppermint candy
- Frozen whipped topping, thawed
- Additional miniature candy canes or peppermint candy

Direction

- Make pudding using milk following instructions on the package. Distribute equally into separate dessert dishes.
- Set aside two tablespoons of crushed cookies; scatter the rest of cookies on top of the pudding. Place crushed candy over the top. Put whipped topping on top of candy with a spoon. Scatter the rest of crushed cookies over top. Add more peppermint candies to serve.

Nutrition Information

- Calories:
- Protein:
- Total Fat:
- Sodium:
- Fiber:
- Total Carbohydrate:
- Cholesterol:

410. Chocolate Mint Eclair Dessert

Serving: 15 servings. | Prep: 20mins | Cook: 0mins | Ready in:

Ingredients

- 23 whole chocolate graham crackers
- 3 cups cold fat-free milk
- 2 packages (3.3 to 3.4 ounces each) instant white chocolate or vanilla pudding mix
- 1/2 teaspoon mint or peppermint extract
- 3 to 4 drops green food coloring, optional
- 1 carton (8 ounces) frozen reduced-fat whipped topping, thawed
- CHOCOLATE FROSTING:
- 1 tablespoon butter
- 2 tablespoons baking cocoa
- 2 tablespoons plus 1 teaspoon fat-free milk
- 1 teaspoon vanilla extract
- 1 cup confectioners' sugar

Direction

- Use cooking spray to spray a 13x9-inch dish. Break 5 whole graham crackers into halves, using 6 whole crackers and 3 halves to line the pan's bottom.
- Stir food coloring (optional), extract, pudding mix and milk in a big bowl for 2 minutes (the mixture will have a thick consistency). Fold whipped topping into the mixture.
- Spread 1/2 mixture onto the crackers. Put on top another layer of 6 whole crackers and 3 cracker halves. Spread the rest of pudding mixture and graham crackers on top (leave the rest of cracker halves for later use). Chill while covered for 2 hours.
- To make the frosting, heat butter in a saucepan until melted. Mix in milk and cocoa until combined. Take away from the heat and mix in confectioners' sugar and vanilla until forming a smooth mixture. Frost onto the pudding. Chill while covered overnight.

Nutrition Information

- Calories: 244 calories
- Protein: 4g protein. Diabetic Exchanges: 2 starch
- Total Fat: 7g fat (3g saturated fat)
- Sodium: 296mg sodium
- Fiber: 1g fiber)
- Total Carbohydrate: 41g carbohydrate (0 sugars
- Cholesterol: 3mg cholesterol

411. Chocolate Mint Freeze

Serving: 9 servings. | Prep: 15mins | Cook: 0mins | Ready in:

Ingredients

- 1-1/2 cups cold milk
- 1 package (3.9 ounces) instant chocolate pudding mix
- 1/2 cup miniature semisweet chocolate chips
- 1 cup heavy whipping cream
- 1/4 teaspoon peppermint extract

Direction

- Whisk together pudding mix and milk in a big bowl about 2 minutes, then allow to stand until soft-set, about 2 minutes. Stir in chocolate chips. Beat cream in a small bowl until starts to thicken. Put in peppermint extract and beat until soft peaks form, then fold into the pudding.
- Transfer to an 8-inch ungreased square dish, then cover and freeze until firm, about 2 hours. Take out of the freezer about 15 minutes before cutting.

Nutrition Information

- Calories: 206 calories
- Protein: 2g protein.
- Total Fat: 14g fat (9g saturated fat)

- Sodium: 212mg sodium
- Fiber: 1g fiber)
- Total Carbohydrate: 20g carbohydrate (16g sugars
- Cholesterol: 42mg cholesterol

---

412. Chocolate Mint Parfaits

Serving: 4 servings. | Prep: 15mins | Cook: 0mins | Ready in:

Ingredients

- 2 cups plus 1 tablespoon cold 2% milk, divided
- 1 package (3.9 ounces) instant chocolate pudding mix
- 4 ounces cream cheese, softened
- 1 tablespoon sugar
- 1/4 teaspoon peppermint extract
- 1 cup whipped topping
- Mint Andes candies, optional

Direction

- Beat pudding mix and 2 cups of milk for 2 minutes in a large bowl; reserve. Whisk the rest of the milk, extract, sugar, and cream cheese in a small bowl. Add in whipped topping then fold.
- Into four glasses of parfait, put half of the pudding. Place half of the cream cheese mixture on top. Continue layers. Decorate with candies if preferred.

Nutrition Information

- Calories: 323 calories
- Total Fat: 16g fat (11g saturated fat)
- Sodium: 555mg sodium
- Fiber: 1g fiber)
- Total Carbohydrate: 39g carbohydrate (30g sugars
- Cholesterol: 41mg cholesterol
- Protein: 7g protein.

---

413. Chocolate Mousse

Serving: 6 | Prep: | Cook: 30mins | Ready in:

Ingredients

- 1 teaspoon unflavored gelatin
- 2 tablespoons coffee liqueur, rum or strong brewed coffee
- ¾ cup low-fat milk
- 1 large egg
- 1 cup packed light brown sugar
- ⅔ cup unsweetened cocoa powder, preferably Dutch-process
- 2 ounces bittersweet (not unsweetened) chocolate, chopped
- 2 teaspoons vanilla extract
- 4 large egg whites
- ½ teaspoon cream of tartar
- 3 tablespoons water

Direction

- Sprinkle gelatin on coffee/rum/liqueur in small bowl; let stand for 1 minute till softened.
- Whisk cocoa, 1/4 cup brown sugar, whole egg and milk in medium saucepan till smooth; cook on low heat for 5 minutes till thick, constantly whisking. Take off heat; add softened gelatin mixture, mixing till gelatin melts. Add vanilla and chocolate; mix till chocolate melts. Cool for 30 minutes to room temperature.
- Put 1-in. water to bare simmer in wide saucepan. Mix leftover 3/4 cup brown sugar, water, cream of tartar and egg whites in heatproof bowl big enough to fit above saucepan; put bowl above barely simmering water. Use electric mixer to beat at low speed for 3-5 minutes, constantly moving beaters around, till an instant-read thermometer reads 140°F.
- Put mixer speed on high; beat for 3 1/2

minutes on heat; take bowl off heat. Beat meringue for another 4-5 minutes till cool.

- Whisk 1/4 meringue into chocolate mixture till smooth; fold chocolate mixture back into leftover meringue using rubber spatula till incorporated completely. Put mousse in 6 dessert glasses; chill for 3 hours till set.

Nutrition Information

- Calories: 247 calories;
- Sodium: 67
- Cholesterol: 34
- Protein: 7
- Total Fat: 6
- Saturated Fat: 3
- Fiber: 4
- Total Carbohydrate: 48
- Sugar: 40

---

414. Chocolate Mousse Frosting

Serving: 3-1/2 cups. | Prep: 10mins | Cook: 0mins | Ready in:

Ingredients

- 1 cup cold fat-free milk
- 1 package (1.4 ounces) sugar-free instant chocolate fudge pudding mix
- 1 carton (8 ounces) frozen reduced-fat whipped topping, thawed
- 1 prepared angel food cake

Direction

- Beat in a bowl the pudding mix and milk for 2 minutes on low speed. Add whipped topping and fold. Then frost the cake.

Nutrition Information

- Calories: 56 calories

- Fiber: 0 fiber)
- Total Carbohydrate: 7g carbohydrate (0 sugars
- Cholesterol: 0 cholesterol
- Protein: 1g protein. Diabetic Exchanges: 1/2 starch
- Total Fat: 2g fat (0 saturated fat)
- Sodium: 94mg sodium

---

415. Chocolate Nut Candies

Serving: 12-1/2 dozen. | Prep: 15mins | Cook: 10mins | Ready in:

Ingredients

- 3 cups (18 ounces) semisweet chocolate chips
- 2 cups creamy peanut butter
- 1 cup butter, cubed
- 1/2 cup evaporated milk
- 1/4 cup instant vanilla pudding mix
- 1 teaspoon vanilla extract
- 2 pounds confectioners' sugar
- 3 cups salted peanuts

Direction

- Melt peanut butter and chocolate chips over low heat in a heavy saucepan, whisking frequently. Transfer half of mixture to a buttered 15x10x1-inch pan, then chill. Put the rest of the chocolate mixture aside.
- Bring pudding mix, milk and butter in a separate saucepan to a boil; boil for 1 minute, whisking constantly. Put off the heat; transfer to a large mixing bowl; add vanilla. Slowly mix in sugar. Spread over the layer of chocolate in the pan; put into the fridge to chill.
- Put peanuts into the reserved chocolate mixture; spread over filling. Put into the fridge to chill. Divide into 1x1 1/2-inch bars.

Nutrition Information

- Calories:

- Protein:
- Total Fat:
- Sodium:
- Fiber:
- Total Carbohydrate:
- Cholesterol:

416. Chocolate Peanut Butter Pie

Serving: 16 | Prep: 20mins | Cook: |Ready in:

Ingredients

- 1 cup peanut butter
- 3/4 cup butter
- 3 cups confectioners' sugar
- 2 (8 inch) prepared graham cracker crusts
- 2 cups milk
- 1 (3.9 ounce) package instant chocolate pudding mix
- 1 (8 ounce) container frozen whipped topping, thawed

Direction

- Mix peanut butter and butter in a medium microwaveable bowl. Microwave until soft; stir well. Slowly mix in confectioners' sugar until the mixture forms a soft dough. Spread mixture into 2 pie shells.
- Stir the instant pudding with milk in a small bowl. Put on top of the peanut butter mixture in the shells. Refrigerate until set.
- Decorate pies with whipped topping just before serving.

Nutrition Information

- Calories: 453 calories;
- Total Fat: 26.4
- Sodium: 371
- Total Carbohydrate: 51.1
- Cholesterol: 25

- Protein: 6.4

417. Chocolate Peanut Torte

Serving: 16-20 servings. | Prep: 20mins | Cook: 10mins |Ready in:

Ingredients

- 2 cups crushed vanilla wafers (about 60 wafers)
- 1/3 cup butter, melted
- 1 cup salted peanuts, finely chopped, divided
- 1 package (8 ounces) cream cheese, softened
- 1 cup confectioners' sugar
- 1/2 cup peanut butter
- 4 cups whipped topping, divided
- 3 cups cold milk
- 2 packages (3.9 ounces each) instant chocolate pudding mix
- 1 milk chocolate candy bar (1.55 ounces), grated

Direction

- Combine 2/3 cup peanuts, butter, and wafer crumbs in a large mixing bowl. Pat into an ungreased 13x9-inch baking dish. Bake for 8 to 10 minutes at 350° until lightly brown. Allow to cool.
- Whisk cream cheese with peanut butter and sugar in a large mixing bowl until smooth. Add 2 cups of whipped topping and fold gently. Spread over the baked crust.
- Whisk pudding mixes and milk in a separate large bowl for 2 minutes on low speed. Gently spread over the layer of cream cheese. Chill, covered, for 4 to 6 hours.
- Gently spread the rest of topping over the pudding layer right before serving. Scatter with the remaining peanuts and grated chocolate.

Nutrition Information

- Calories: 314 calories
- Protein: 6g protein.
- Total Fat: 20g fat (9g saturated fat)
- Sodium: 263mg sodium
- Fiber: 1g fiber)
- Total Carbohydrate: 29g carbohydrate (19g sugars
- Cholesterol: 27mg cholesterol

- Calories:
- Sodium:
- Fiber:
- Total Carbohydrate:
- Cholesterol:
- Protein:
- Total Fat:

418. Chocolate Peppermint Ice Cream Dessert

Serving: 12-15 servings. | Prep: 20mins | Cook: 0mins | Ready in:

Ingredients

- 2 cups graham cracker crumbs
- 3/4 cup butter, softened
- 3 tablespoons sugar
- FILLING:
- 1-1/2 cups cold milk
- 2 packages (3.9 ounces each) instant chocolate pudding mix
- 1 quart peppermint ice cream, softened
- 1 carton (8 ounces) frozen whipped topping, thawed

Direction

- Mix the sugar, butter, and cracker crumbs in a bowl. Put aside 3/4 cup for topping. Press the remaining crumb mixture into an ungreased 13x9-inch dish. Stir the pudding mix and milk in a big bowl for 2 minutes (the mixture will thicken). Whisk in ice cream until smooth. Spread over the crust. Refrigerate for a minimum of 1 hour.
- Spread the whipped topping over the pudding and drizzle the reserved crumbs on top. Cover and chill overnight or 6-8 hrs.

Nutrition Information

419. Chocolate Pineapple Trifle

Serving: 10-12 servings. | Prep: 30mins | Cook: 35mins | Ready in:

Ingredients

- 1 package (16 ounces) angel food cake mix
- 1/2 cup sugar
- 2 tablespoons cornstarch
- 4 cups cold milk, divided
- 3 large eggs, lightly beaten
- 1 can (20 ounces) crushed pineapple, drained
- 1 teaspoon vanilla extract
- 1 package (5.9 ounces) instant chocolate pudding mix
- 1/3 cup water
- 2 teaspoons rum extract
- 2 cups heavy whipping cream
- 2 tablespoons confectioners' sugar
- Pineapple chunks and grated chocolate, optional

Direction

- Follow package direction to prep and bake cake; completely cool. Meanwhile, for pineapple pudding: Mix cornstarch and sugar in big saucepan; whisk 2 cups milk in slowly. Boil; mix and cook till thick for 2 minutes. Take off heat. Mix 1/2 cup hot mixture into eggs; put all in pan, constantly mixing. Gently boil; mix and cook for 2 more minutes.
- Take off heat; mix vanilla and pineapple in. Put in bowl; press plastic wrap/waxed paper piece over pudding. Refrigerate till cooled;

don't mix. Meanwhile, whisk pudding mix and leftover milk for 2 minutes; stand till soft set for 2 minutes. Chill.

- Assemble: Slice cooled cake to 1-in. cubes. Put 1/3 cake in 3 1/2-qt. trifle dish. Mix rum extract and water; drizzle 1/3 on cake. Put pineapple pudding, 1/3 cake and 1/3 rum mixture over. Layer using chocolate pudding, leftover cake then rum mixture. Cover; chill.
- Beat cream till it starts to thicken in big bowl before serving. Add confectioners' sugar; beat till stiff peaks form. Spread on cake; if desired, garnish with grated chocolate and pineapple.

Nutrition Information

- Calories: 471 calories
- Protein: 9g protein.
- Total Fat: 19g fat (11g saturated fat)
- Sodium: 556mg sodium
- Fiber: 1g fiber)
- Total Carbohydrate: 68g carbohydrate (56g sugars
- Cholesterol: 119mg cholesterol

420. Chocolate Pudding Pizza

Serving: 12 servings. | Prep: 20mins | Cook: 15mins | Ready in:

Ingredients

- 1 package (17-1/2 ounces) peanut butter cookie mix
- 1 carton (12 ounces) spreadable cream cheese, softened
- 1-3/4 cups cold milk
- 1 package (3.9 ounces) instant chocolate pudding mix
- 1 carton (8 ounces) frozen whipped topping, thawed
- 1/4 cup miniature semisweet chocolate chips

Direction

- Set the oven to 375 degrees to preheat. Follow package directions to prepare cookie mix dough, then press into a 12-inch pizza pan coated with grease. Bake for 15 minutes, until set, then allow to cool.
- Beat cream cheese until smooth, then spread over crust. Beat pudding mix and milk together in a separate bowl on medium speed about 2 minutes, then spread over layer of cream cheese. Chill for 20 minutes, until set. Spread whipped topping over top and sprinkle with chips. Refrigerate about 1 to 2 hours.

Nutrition Information

- Calories: 449 calories
- Sodium: 376mg sodium
- Fiber: 1g fiber)
- Total Carbohydrate: 46g carbohydrate (13g sugars
- Cholesterol: 37mg cholesterol
- Protein: 7g protein.
- Total Fat: 26g fat (12g saturated fat)

421. Chocolate Swirl Delight

Serving: 12 servings. | Prep: 25mins | Cook: 0mins | Ready in:

Ingredients

- 1-1/2 packages (13 ounces each) Swiss cake rolls
- 2-3/4 cups 2% milk
- 2 packages (3.9 ounces each) instant chocolate fudge pudding mix
- 2 cups whipped topping

Direction

- Cut every cake roll to 6 slices; keep broken chocolate coating for topping. Line cake slices on sides and bottom of 9-in. springform pan, completely covering.

- Whisk pudding mixes and milk for 2 minutes; it will be thick. Spread on bottom cake rolls layers; use whipped topping to cover. Sprinkle leftover chocolate pieces; refrigerate for minimum of 2 hours, covered. Serve.

Nutrition Information

- Calories: 331 calories
- Total Fat: 12g fat (5g saturated fat)
- Sodium: 382mg sodium
- Fiber: 1g fiber)
- Total Carbohydrate: 46g carbohydrate (35g sugars
- Cholesterol: 16mg cholesterol
- Protein: 4g protein.

---

422. Chocolate Torte With Raspberry Filling

Serving: 12 servings. | Prep: 15mins | Cook: 25mins | Ready in:

Ingredients

- 1 package chocolate cake mix (regular size)
- 3 ounces cream cheese, softened
- 3/4 cup cold whole milk
- 1 package (3.4 ounces) instant vanilla pudding mix
- 1 carton (8 ounces) frozen whipped topping, thawed
- 2 cups fresh raspberries
- Confectioners' sugar
- Fresh mint and additional raspberries, optional

Direction

- Follow package direction to prepare the cake; put into a 3 9-in. round greased and floured baking pans. Bake for 25-30 minutes at 350° till inserted toothpick in the middle exits clean;

cool for 10 minutes. Transfer from pans onto wire racks; completely cool.
- Beat cream cheese till fluffy in a big bowl. Mix pudding mix and milk; beat into cream cheese till smooth. Fold raspberries and whipped topping in.
- Put 1 cake layer on a serving plate; spread 1/2 filling. Repeat layers. Put leftover cake over; dust with confectioners' sugar. If desired, garnish with raspberries and mint. Keep in the fridge.

Nutrition Information

- Calories:
- Fiber:
- Total Carbohydrate:
- Cholesterol:
- Protein:
- Total Fat:
- Sodium:

---

423. Chocolate Trifle

Serving: 12 | Prep: 30mins | Cook: 25mins | Ready in:

Ingredients

- 1 (19.8 ounce) package brownie mix
- 1 (3.9 ounce) package instant chocolate pudding mix
- 1/2 cup water
- 1 (14 ounce) can sweetened condensed milk
- 1 (8 ounce) container frozen whipped topping, thawed
- 1 (12 ounce) container frozen whipped topping, thawed
- 1 (1.5 ounce) bar chocolate candy

Direction

- Follow package directions to prep brownie mix; completely cool. Cut to 1-in. squares.

- Mix sweetened condensed milk, water and pudding mix till smooth in big bowl; fold 8-oz. whipped topping in till there are no streaks remained.
- Put 1/2 brownies, 1/2 pudding mixture then 1/2 12-oz. whipped topping container in trifle bowl/glass serving dish; repeat layers. Shave chocolate on top layer as garnish. Refrigerate before serving for 8 hours.

Nutrition Information

- Calories: 488 calories;
- Total Carbohydrate: 73.7
- Cholesterol: 12
- Protein: 4.8
- Total Fat: 18.8
- Sodium: 314

---

424. Chocolate Cherry Mousse Delight

Serving: 12 servings. | Prep: 25mins | Cook: 40mins | Ready in:

Ingredients

- 1 jar (10 ounces) maraschino cherries with stems
- 1 package (16 ounces) angel food cake mix
- 2/3 cup semisweet chocolate chips
- 1-1/2 cups cold fat-free milk
- 1 package (1.4 ounces) sugar-free instant chocolate pudding mix
- 1 carton (8 ounces) frozen reduced-fat whipped topping, thawed

Direction

- Drain cherries, reserving the juice; set aside the cherries. Pour enough cold water into the cherry juice to measure 1 1/4 cups. Beat the cherry juice mixture and cake mix on low speed in a large bowl, 30 seconds. Beat for 2 minutes on medium.
- Using a spoon, gently transfer to an ungreased 10-in. tube pan. Using a knife, cut through the batter to discard any air pockets. Bake at 350° on the lowest oven rack till the entire top appears dry and the cake turns dark golden brown, 40-50 minutes. Invert the pan onto a wire rack immediately; allow to cool completely, around 1 hour. Carefully run a knife around the sides of the cake; take away from the pan.
- Melt chocolate chips in a microwave; mix till smooth. Pat the cherries dry with paper towels. Hold the cherries by the stem; dip in the melted chocolate; drip off any excess. Arrange on waxed paper; place in the refrigerator till set.
- Whisk together pudding mix and milk in a large bowl, 2 minutes. Allow to sit till thickened, 15 minutes. Whisk till smooth. Mix in whipped topping. Slice the cake; serve accompanied with the dipped cherries and mousse.

Nutrition Information

- Calories: 280 calories
- Sodium: 392mg sodium
- Fiber: 1g fiber)
- Total Carbohydrate: 54g carbohydrate (0 sugars
- Cholesterol: 1mg cholesterol
- Protein: 5g protein.
- Total Fat: 5g fat (4g saturated fat)

---

425. Christmas Gingerbread Trifle

Serving: 14 servings. | Prep: 15mins | Cook: 30mins | Ready in:

Ingredients

- 1 package (14-1/2 ounces) gingerbread cake/cookie mix
- 2 cups cold 2% milk
- 2 cups cold eggnog
- 2 packages (3.4 ounces each) instant French vanilla pudding mix
- 1 package (5 ounces) gingerbread man cookies
- 1 carton (16 ounces) frozen whipped topping, thawed

Direction

- Follow package directions to prepare cake mix and bake with a square 9-in. baking pan. Completely cool on a wire rack; slice into 1-in. cubes.
- Whisk pudding mix, milk and eggnog for 2 minutes in a big bowl; stand till soft set for 2 minutes.
- Around sides, put 9 cookies in a 4-qt. glass bowl; use 1/3 cake cubes to stand the cookies upright. Top with 1/3 pudding then whipped topping; repeat the layers. Put leftover cake, whipped topping and pudding on top. Refrigerate for 4 hours – overnight, covered.
- Top with leftover cookies before serving.

Nutrition Information

- Calories: 371 calories
- Cholesterol: 37mg cholesterol
- Protein: 5g protein.
- Total Fat: 14g fat (9g saturated fat)
- Sodium: 477mg sodium
- Fiber: 1g fiber)
- Total Carbohydrate: 54g carbohydrate (35g sugars

---

426. Christmas Trifle

Serving: 12 | Prep: 30mins | Cook: 15mins |Ready in:

Ingredients

- 1 (5.9 ounce) package individual jelly-filled roll cakes
- 1/2 cup sherry
- 2 pints fresh raspberries
- 1 tablespoon white sugar, or to taste
- 1 egg
- 2 egg yolks
- 1/2 cup white sugar
- 1/3 cup all-purpose flour
- 2 cups milk
- 1/2 cup half-and-half cream
- 1/2 teaspoon vanilla extract
- 2 tablespoons sherry
- 1 tablespoon butter
- whipped cream (optional)
- fresh raspberries (optional)
- chocolate curls (optional)

Direction

- Cut jellyrolls to 1-in. pieces; line sliced jellyrolls in glass trifle bowl. Drizzle 1/2 cup sherry on jellyroll slices. Toss 1 tbsp. sugar or to taste and raspberries; put on jellyroll slices.
- Whisk 1/2 cup sugar, egg yolks and egg till smooth in bowl; whisk flour in till free of lumps and combined thoroughly. Heat half and half and milk in saucepan on medium heat till milk mixture becomes steaming hot yet not simmering. Whisk 1/4 cup hot milk mixture into egg mixture till smooth; repeat, whisking hot milk in well each time till you whisked in 3/4 cup hot milk mixture. Whisk egg-milk mixture back into steaming milk in saucepan; lower heat to low. Constantly whisking, heat sauce for 3-4 minutes till just at point of simmering, don't boil, and thick. Whisk butter, 2 tbsp. sherry and vanilla extract in; cool sauce for 10 minutes, whisking it often to prevent lumps.
- Put custard on raspberries in trifle bowl; use plastic wrap to cover bowl. Refrigerate for 2 hours till set and well chilled. Garnish with chocolate shavings (optional), extra raspberries and dollops of whipped creamed.

Nutrition Information

- Calories: 279 calories;
- Sodium: 186
- Total Carbohydrate: 43
- Cholesterol: 70
- Protein: 4
- Total Fat: 10.5

---

427.   Cinnamon Apple Coffee Cake

Serving: 9 servings. | Prep: 10mins | Cook: 50mins | Ready in:

Ingredients

- 1 package (9 ounces) yellow cake mix
- 1 package (3.4 ounces) instant vanilla pudding mix
- 2 large eggs
- 1/2 cup sour cream
- 1/4 cup butter, melted
- 2 medium tart apples, peeled and shredded
- 1/2 cup sugar
- 1/4 cup chopped walnuts
- 1 teaspoon ground cinnamon

Direction

- Whip butter, sour cream, eggs, pudding mix and cake mix in a big bowl for 30 seconds on low speed. Whip for 2 minutes on moderate speed.
- Put 1/2 into an oiled 8-inch square baking dish. Put apples on top. Mix cinnamon, nuts and sugar; scatter 1/2 on top of apples. Put the rest of the sugar mixture and batter on top.
- Bake for 50 to 55 minutes at 350° or until a toothpick pricked in the middle comes out clean. Let cool on the wire rack.

Nutrition Information

- Calories: 326 calories

- Fiber: 1g fiber)
- Total Carbohydrate: 48g carbohydrate (35g sugars
- Cholesterol: 56mg cholesterol
- Protein: 4g protein.
- Total Fat: 13g fat (4g saturated fat)
- Sodium: 409mg sodium

---

428.   Cocoa Chocolate Chip Cookies

Serving: about 8-1/2 dozen. | Prep: 30mins | Cook: 10mins | Ready in:

Ingredients

- 2/3 cup butter, softened
- 1/2 cup canola oil
- 1 cup sugar
- 1 cup packed brown sugar
- 2 eggs
- 1 package (3.9 ounces) instant chocolate pudding mix
- 3 tablespoons water
- 3 cups all-purpose flour
- 1 teaspoon baking soda
- 1 teaspoon salt
- 1 package (12 ounces) miniature semisweet chocolate chips

Direction

- In a large bowl, cream together the sugars, oil and butter until fluffy and light. Beat in the eggs. Beat in the water and pudding mix. Combine the salt, baking soda and flour; add to the mixture of chocolate slowly and combine well (the dough will become stiff). Mix in the chocolate chips.
- Roll into balls of 1-in. size. On ungreased baking sheets, place them 2 inches apart from each other. Bake at 350° until set and edges are firm, or 9-11 minutes. Allow to cool for 2 minutes, then transfer to wire racks.

Nutrition Information

- Calories:
- Protein:
- Total Fat:
- Sodium:
- Fiber:
- Total Carbohydrate:
- Cholesterol:

---

429.   Coconut Angel Squares

Serving: 12-15 servings. | Prep: 15mins | Cook: 0mins
| Ready in:

Ingredients

- 1 prepared angel food cake (8 to 10 ounces), cut into 1/2-inch cubes
- 1-1/2 cups cold 2% milk
- 1 teaspoon coconut extract
- 2 packages (3.4 ounces each) instant vanilla pudding mix
- 1 quart vanilla ice cream, softened
- 1 cup sweetened shredded coconut, divided
- 1 carton (8 ounces) frozen whipped topping, thawed

Direction

- In a 13"x9" dish that grease, arrange cake cubes. Whisk together pudding mixes, extract and milk in a big bowl about 2 minutes (the mixture will become thick). Put in 3/4 cup of coconut and ice cream, then beat on low speed until just mixed.
- Scoop over cake cubes and spread whipped topping on top. Toast the leftover coconut and sprinkle over top of cake cubes. Cover and refrigerate for a minimum of an hour, then chill leftovers.

Nutrition Information

- Calories: 0

- Sodium: 338 mg sodium
- Fiber: 1 g fiber
- Total Carbohydrate: 36 g carbohydrate
- Cholesterol: 19 mg cholesterol
- Protein: 4 g protein.
- Total Fat: 9 g fat (6 g saturated fat)

---

430.   Coconut Banana Chocolate Cream Pie

Serving: 8 servings. | Prep: 20mins | Cook: 0mins
| Ready in:

Ingredients

- 1-1/3 cups cold water
- 2/3 cup nonfat dry milk powder
- 1 package (1.4 ounces) sugar-free instant chocolate pudding mix
- 1 cup reduced-fat whipped topping, divided
- 1/2 teaspoon coconut extract, divided
- 2 medium ripe bananas, cut into 1/4-inch slices
- 1 chocolate crumb crust (9 inches)
- 1 tablespoon sweetened shredded coconut, toasted

Direction

- Stir water and milk powder together in a bowl until the powder dissolves. Add pudding mix into the liquid; whisk until thickened, or for 1-2 minutes. Fold 1/4 cup whipped topping and 1/4 teaspoon extract into the mixture. Layer the banana slices into the crust; add the pudding mixture on top. Cover then place in the refrigerator.
- Mix together the extract and rest of the whipped topping; spread on top of the pudding. Sprinkle coconut on top. Refrigerate, covered, for no less than 1 hour before serving.

Nutrition Information

- Calories: 172 calories
- Total Fat: 5g fat (2g saturated fat)
- Sodium: 172mg sodium
- Fiber: 2g fiber)
- Total Carbohydrate: 28g carbohydrate (0 sugars
- Cholesterol: 1mg cholesterol
- Protein: 4g protein. Diabetic Exchanges: 1-1/2 starch

431.   Coconut Cream Dessert

Serving: 12-15 servings. | Prep: 15mins | Cook: 0mins | Ready in:

Ingredients

- 2-1/2 cups crushed butter-flavored crackers (about 68 crackers)
- 1/2 cup plus 2 tablespoons butter, melted
- 1/2 gallon vanilla ice cream, softened
- 1/2 cup cold milk
- 1 teaspoon coconut extract
- 2 packages (3.4 ounces each) instant vanilla pudding mix
- 1 cup sweetened shredded coconut, divided
- 1 carton (8 ounces) frozen whipped topping, thawed

Direction

- In a small bowl, mix butter and cracker crumbs. Press into an ungreased 13x9-inch dish.
- In a large bowl, blend 2/3cup of coconut, pudding mixes, extract, milk, and ice cream until well-combined. Pour over the crust; pour on the top with whipped topping. Toast the coconut left; spread over the top. Cover and let cool in the freezer for up to 2 months.
- Take out from the freezer 15 minutes before enjoying.

Nutrition Information

- Calories: 0
- Protein: 4 g protein.
- Total Fat: 24 g fat (14 g saturated fat)
- Sodium: 350 mg sodium
- Fiber: 1 g fiber
- Total Carbohydrate: 35 g carbohydrate
- Cholesterol: 53 mg cholesterol

432.   Coconut Cream Pie

Serving: 8 | Prep: 25mins | Cook: 30mins | Ready in:

Ingredients

- 1 cup white sugar
- 1/2 cup all-purpose flour
- 1/4 teaspoon salt
- 3 cups milk
- 4 egg yolks
- 3 tablespoons butter
- 1 1/2 teaspoons vanilla extract
- 1 cup flaked coconut
- 1 (9 inch) pie shell, baked

Direction

- In a medium saucepan, mix together salt, flour and sugar over medium heat; slowly mix in milk. Cook and stir over medium heat till bubbly and thick. Decrease heat to low and cook for an additional 2 minutes. Remove pan from the heat.
- Put a strainer on top a clean mixing bowl; put aside.
- Slightly beat egg yolks. Pour slowly a cup of hot custard mixture into yolks, whisking constantly. Put the egg mixture back into the saucepan; then bring the entire mixture to a gentle boil. Cook and stir for 2 minutes before removing from heat. Pour the custard through the strainer immediately.
- Mix coconut, vanilla and butter into the hot mixture. Add hot filling into baked pie crust. Allow to cool and chill in the fridge for about 4 hours, until set.

Nutrition Information

- Calories: 399 calories;
- Total Fat: 18.8
- Sodium: 293
- Total Carbohydrate: 51.1
- Cholesterol: 121
- Protein: 6.9

433.   Coconut Crunch Delight

Serving: 12-16 servings. | Prep: 15mins | Cook: 0mins | Ready in:

Ingredients

- 1/2 cup butter, melted
- 1 cup all-purpose flour
- 1-1/4 cups sweetened shredded coconut
- 1/4 cup packed brown sugar
- 1 cup slivered almonds
- 2-2/3 cups cold milk
- 1/2 teaspoon coconut extract
- 2 packages (3.4 ounces each) instant vanilla pudding mix
- 2 cups whipped topping
- Fresh strawberries, optional

Direction

- Mix the initial 5 ingredients in a big bowl; lightly press into an oiled 13x9-inch baking dish. Bake till golden brown at 350° for 25 minutes to half an hour, mixing after every 10 minutes to make coarse crumbs. Let cool.
- Distribute the mixture of crumb in half; force 1/2 in the same baking pan. Whip pudding mixes, extract and milk for 2 minutes in a big bowl. Rest till soft-set, for 2 minutes.
- Fold in the whipped topping; scoop on crust. Put leftover crumb mixture on top. Place cover and chill overnight. Jazz up with fresh strawberries if wished.

Nutrition Information

- Calories:
- Total Fat:
- Sodium:
- Fiber:
- Total Carbohydrate:
- Cholesterol:
- Protein:

434.   Coconut Peach Pie

Serving: 8 servings. | Prep: 10mins | Cook: 0mins | Ready in:

Ingredients

- 4 cups sliced fresh or frozen peaches, thawed, divided
- 1-3/4 cups cold milk
- 1/2 teaspoon coconut extract
- 1 package (3.4 ounces) instant vanilla pudding mix
- 1/2 cup sweetened shredded coconut
- 1 graham cracker crust (9 inches)
- 1 cup whipped topping
- Additional sliced peaches, optional

Direction

- Use paper towels to pat dry frozen peaches, if using. In a big bowl, whisk the pudding mix, extract and milk for 2 minutes. Allow to stand for 2 minutes or till soft-set. Fold in coconut.
- Line 1/3 of the peaches in crust; add half of the pudding on top. Redo the layers one more time. Refrigerate for a minimum of 3 hours or till serving.
- Top with the rest of peaches. If wished, garnish with extra peaches and whipped topping.

Nutrition Information

- Calories: 0
- Sodium: 273 mg sodium
- Fiber: 2 g fiber
- Total Carbohydrate: 38 g carbohydrate
- Cholesterol: 7 mg cholesterol
- Protein: 3 g protein.
- Total Fat: 10 g fat (5 g saturated fat)

435.   Coconut Pineapple Pops

Serving: 14 servings. | Prep: 10mins | Cook: 0mins | Ready in:

Ingredients

- 1-1/2 cups cold 2% milk
- 1 can (8 ounces) unsweetened crushed pineapple
- 1 can (6 ounces) unsweetened pineapple juice
- 1 teaspoon coconut extract
- 1 package (3.4 ounces) instant vanilla pudding mix
- 14 freezer pop molds or14 paper cups (3 ounces each) and wooden pop sticks

Direction

- Blend pineapple extract and juice, pineapple, and milk in a blender with cover until smooth. Move to a bowl; stir in pudding mix for 2mins.
- Scoop a quarter cup of mixture into each paper cup or mold; add holders on top. Place foil on top then put in sticks through if using cups. Place in the freezer until solid.

Nutrition Information

- Calories: 56 calories
- Cholesterol: 2mg cholesterol
- Protein: 1g protein. Diabetic Exchanges: 1 starch.
- Total Fat: 1g fat (0 saturated fat)
- Sodium: 96mg sodium
- Fiber: 0 fiber)

- Total Carbohydrate: 12g carbohydrate (0 sugars

436.   Coconut Pistachio Pie

Serving: 8 servings. | Prep: 20mins | Cook: 0mins | Ready in:

Ingredients

- 2-1/2 cups sweetened shredded coconut, lightly toasted
- 1/3 cup butter, melted
- 2 cups cold 2% milk
- 2 packages (3.4 ounces each) instant pistachio pudding mix
- 1 cup whipped topping
- 2 tablespoons chopped pistachios, optional

Direction

- Mix butter and coconut in a small bowl; press up sides and bottom of 9-in. greased pie plate; refrigerate till firm for 30 minutes.
- Whisk pudding mixes and milk for 2 minutes in a small bowl; stand till soft set for 2 minutes. Spread crust with 1 1/2 cups.
- Fold whipped topping into leftover pudding; spread on pie. If desired, sprinkle pistachios. Cover; refrigerate for 2 hours.

Nutrition Information

- Calories: 371 calories
- Protein: 3g protein.
- Total Fat: 22g fat (17g saturated fat)
- Sodium: 520mg sodium
- Fiber: 1g fiber)
- Total Carbohydrate: 41g carbohydrate (31g sugars
- Cholesterol: 29mg cholesterol

437. Coconut Poppy Seed Bundt Cake

Serving: 12 servings. | Prep: 15mins | Cook: 50mins | Ready in:

Ingredients

- 1 package yellow cake mix (regular size)
- 1 package (3.4 ounces) instant vanilla pudding mix
- 1 cup water
- 1/2 cup canola oil
- 3 large eggs
- 1/2 teaspoon coconut extract
- 1/2 cup sweetened shredded coconut
- 2 tablespoons poppy seeds
- Confectioners' sugar

Direction

- Mix together extract, eggs, oil, water, dry pudding mix and cake mix in a big bowl; blend for half a minute on low speed. Increase the speed to medium and blend for 2 minutes. Mix poppy seeds and coconut into the mixture.
- Transfer batter to a fluted tube pan of 10 inches already greased and dusted with flour. Bake for 48 to 52 minutes in 350-degree oven, or until a toothpick is clean when coming out of the middle of the cake. Let the cake cool for 10 minutes; transfer to a wire rack and cool fully. Sprinkle confectioners' sugar on top.

Nutrition Information

- Calories: 0
- Protein: 3 g protein.
- Total Fat: 12 g fat (3 g saturated fat)
- Sodium: 296 mg sodium
- Fiber: 1 g fiber
- Total Carbohydrate: 33 g carbohydrate
- Cholesterol: 43 mg cholesterol

438. Coconut Raspberry Trifle

Serving: 12 servings. | Prep: 15mins | Cook: 0mins | Ready in:

Ingredients

- 4 cups cold milk
- 2 packages (3.4 ounces each) instant French vanilla pudding mix
- 1 package (18 ounces) individual raspberry cream-filled cakes
- 3 cups fresh raspberries
- 2 cups whipped topping

Direction

- Whisk pudding mixes and milk for 2 minutes in big bowl; stand till soft set for 2 minutes. Cut every cake to quarters.
- Line bottom of 3 1/2-qt. glass bowl using 1/2 cake pieces. Put 1/2 pudding then 1 cup raspberries on top; repeat layers. Refrigerate till serving.
- Spread whipped topping before serving; sprinkle leftover raspberries.

Nutrition Information

- Calories: 310 calories
- Cholesterol: 18mg cholesterol
- Protein: 4g protein.
- Total Fat: 10g fat (5g saturated fat)
- Sodium: 420mg sodium
- Fiber: 2g fiber)
- Total Carbohydrate: 52g carbohydrate (44g sugars

439. Coconut Supreme Torte

Serving: 16 servings. | Prep: 25mins | Cook: 25mins | Ready in:

Ingredients

- 1 package yellow cake mix (regular size)
- 1-1/3 cups water
- 4 large eggs
- 1 package (3.4 ounces) instant vanilla pudding mix
- 1/2 cup vegetable oil
- 1-1/2 cups sweetened shredded coconut, toasted
- 1 cup chopped walnuts
- FROSTING:
- 1 package (8 ounces) cream cheese, softened
- 2 teaspoons whole milk
- 1 teaspoon vanilla extract
- 3-1/2 cups confectioners' sugar
- 2 cups sweetened shredded coconut, toasted, divided

Direction

- Beat oil, pudding mix, eggs, water and cake mix for 4 minutes at medium speed in a big bowl; scrape bowl sides occasionally. Mix walnuts and coconut in.
- Put into a 3 9-in. round greased and floured baking pans; bake for 23-27 minutes at 350° till inserted toothpick in the middle exits clean. Cool for 10 minutes. Transfer from pans onto wire racks; fully cool.
- Frosting: Beat vanilla, milk and cream cheese till smooth in a big bowl; beat confectioners' sugar in slowly. Mix 1 1/2 cups coconut in.
- Put bottom cake layer on a serving plate; spread with 3/4 cup frosting then repeat layers. Put leftover layer then frosting over; sprinkle with leftover coconut. Keep in the fridge.

Nutrition Information

- Calories: 542 calories
- Sodium: 405mg sodium
- Fiber: 2g fiber)
- Total Carbohydrate: 69g carbohydrate (51g sugars
- Cholesterol: 69mg cholesterol
- Protein: 7g protein.

- Total Fat: 28g fat (12g saturated fat)

440.   Coconut Trifle

Serving: 20 servings. | Prep: 20mins | Cook: 0mins | Ready in:

Ingredients

- 1 prepared angel food cake (8 to 10 ounces), cut into 1-inch cubes
- 2 cups cold whole milk
- 1 teaspoon coconut extract
- 2 packages (3.4 ounces each) instant vanilla pudding mix
- 1 quart vanilla ice cream, softened
- 1 cup sweetened shredded coconut, divided
- 1 carton (8 ounces) frozen whipped topping, thawed

Direction

- Put cake cubes in a big bowl. Whisk pudding mixes, extract and milk for 2 minutes in a bowl (it will be thick). Mix 3/4 cup coconut and ice cream in till blended; put on cake cubes. Mix till just combined.
- Put into a 5-qt. trifle bowl; spread with whipped topping. Toast leftover coconut; sprinkle on top. Cover; refrigerate before serving for 30 minutes minimum.

Nutrition Information

- Calories:
- Sodium:
- Fiber:
- Total Carbohydrate:
- Cholesterol:
- Protein:
- Total Fat:

441. Coffee Cream Tortilla Cups

Serving: 2 servings. | Prep: 15mins | Cook: 10mins | Ready in:

Ingredients

- 2 flour tortillas (8 inches), warmed
- 1 tablespoon butter, melted
- 1 tablespoon sugar
- 1/2 teaspoon ground cinnamon
- 1/2 cup half-and-half cream
- 2 teaspoons instant coffee granules
- 5 tablespoons instant French vanilla pudding mix
- 1 cup whipped topping
- 1-1/2 cups fresh blueberries, raspberries and sliced strawberries

Direction

- Use butter to brush one side of tortillas. Press each tortilla gently into a 10-ounce custard cup with buttered side facing up, then pleat edges. Mix cinnamon and sugar together and sprinkle over tortillas. Bake at 400 degrees until brown slightly and crispy, about 8 to 10 minutes. Allow to cool on a wire rack.
- Mix together coffee granules and cream in a small bowl until dissolved. Put in pudding mix and whisk about 2 minutes. Allow to stand until soft-set, about 2 minutes, then fold in whipped topping. Place a cover and chill for an hour. Scoop into tortilla cups and put berries on top.

Nutrition Information

- Calories: 548 calories
- Fiber: 3g fiber)
- Total Carbohydrate: 79g carbohydrate (39g sugars
- Cholesterol: 45mg cholesterol
- Protein: 7g protein.
- Total Fat: 21g fat (14g saturated fat)
- Sodium: 638mg sodium

442. Coffee Nut Torte

Serving: 12 servings. | Prep: 30mins | Cook: 30mins | Ready in:

Ingredients

- 1/2 cup butter, softened
- 1 cup sugar
- 3 large eggs, separated
- 1/2 cup all-purpose flour
- 2 teaspoons baking powder
- 2 cups fine graham cracker crumbs
- 1 cup cold strong coffee
- 1 teaspoon vanilla extract
- 3/4 cup chopped nuts
- FILLING:
- 1 package (3.4 ounces) instant vanilla pudding mix
- 1-1/4 cups whole milk
- 1 teaspoon instant coffee granules
- 1/2 cup heavy whipping cream, whipped

Direction

- Cream sugar and butter till fluffy and light in big mixing bowl. Add egg yolks; beat till light. Sift baking powder and flour; add cracker crumbs. Add to creamed mixture, alternately with coffee, beating well till smooth. Mix nuts and vanilla in.
- Beat egg whites till stiff in another bowl; fold into batter. Put in 2 round 8-in. waxed paper-lined baking pans then bake for 30-35 at 350°; completely cool.
- Filling: Prep pudding with coffee and milk; chill. Fold cream in; split every cake layer. Spread with filling.

Nutrition Information

- Calories: 340 calories
- Sodium: 373mg sodium

- Fiber: 1g fiber)
- Total Carbohydrate: 41g carbohydrate (26g sugars
- Cholesterol: 84mg cholesterol
- Protein: 6g protein.
- Total Fat: 17g fat (7g saturated fat)

443. Cookie Pudding Pots

Serving: 6 servings. | Prep: 15mins | Cook: 0mins | Ready in:

Ingredients

- 6 new terra-cotta flowerpots (3-1/2-inch diameter)
- 4 cups cold whole milk
- 2 packages (3.9 ounces each) instant chocolate fudge pudding mix
- 7 Oreo cookies, crushed, divided
- 6 medium fresh strawberries
- 12 mint sprigs

Direction

- Line plastic wrap on flowerpots; put aside. Whisk pudding mixes and milk for 2 minutes in a big bowl; stand till soft set for 2 minutes.
- In each flowerpot, sprinkle 2 tsp. cookie crumbs; top each using 2/3 cup pudding. Sprinkle leftover crumbs. To resemble a rose, cut each strawberry.
- Use mint sprigs and a strawberry rose to garnish each pot; refrigerate till serving.

Nutrition Information

- Calories: 232 calories
- Sodium: 416mg sodium
- Fiber: 1g fiber)
- Total Carbohydrate: 34g carbohydrate (25g sugars
- Cholesterol: 22mg cholesterol
- Protein: 6g protein.

- Total Fat: 8g fat (4g saturated fat)

444. Cool Chocolate Mousse

Serving: 6 servings. | Prep: 10mins | Cook: 0mins | Ready in:

Ingredients

- 2 cups cold 2% milk
- 1 package (5.9 ounces) instant chocolate pudding mix
- 1 carton (8 ounces) frozen whipped topping, thawed
- 1/2 cup sour cream
- Additional whipped topping, optional

Direction

- Whisk pudding mix and milk for 2 minutes in big bowl; stand till soft set for 2 minutes. Fold sour cream and whipped topping in; put in individual dessert dishes. If desired, dollop with whipped topping.

Nutrition Information

- Calories: 293 calories
- Sodium: 451mg sodium
- Fiber: 1g fiber)
- Total Carbohydrate: 38g carbohydrate (27g sugars
- Cholesterol: 21mg cholesterol
- Protein: 4g protein.
- Total Fat: 13g fat (10g saturated fat)

445. Country Poppy Seed Cake

Serving: 12-16 servings. | Prep: 15mins | Cook: 60mins | Ready in:

Ingredients

- 1/4 cup poppy seeds
- 1 package (5.1 ounces) instant vanilla pudding mix
- 1 package white cake mix (regular size)
- 1/2 cup vegetable oil
- 4 large eggs
- 1 cup water
- 1 teaspoon almond extract
- 2 tablespoons sugar
- 1/2 teaspoon ground cinnamon
- GLAZE:
- 1/2 cup confectioners' sugar
- 1/4 teaspoon vanilla extract
- 1 to 2 teaspoons whole milk

Direction

- Combine the cake mix, pudding and poppy seeds in a large bowl. Add the almond extract, eggs, water and oil into the mixture. On low speed, beat till the dry ingredients are moistened. Raise the speed to medium and beat for another 2 minutes. Mix together sugar and cinnamon; sprinkle the mixture into a greased 10-in. fluted tube pan.
- Transfer batter into the prepared pan and bake at 325° for 1 hour or till tested done with a toothpick. Let the cake cool down for 10 minutes, then take out to a wire rack. Mix together ingredients for the glaze and drizzle atop the cooled cake.

Nutrition Information

- Calories: 284 calories
- Sodium: 353mg sodium
- Fiber: 1g fiber)
- Total Carbohydrate: 40g carbohydrate (26g sugars
- Cholesterol: 53mg cholesterol
- Protein: 3g protein.
- Total Fat: 12g fat (2g saturated fat)

446. Country Style Vanilla Ice Cream

Serving: 2-1/2 quarts. | Prep: 30mins | Cook: 20mins | Ready in:

Ingredients

- 6 cups cold 2% milk, divided
- 2 cups sugar
- 4 eggs, lightly beaten
- 1 teaspoon vanilla extract
- 2 packages (3.4 ounces each) instant vanilla pudding mix
- 1 carton (8 ounces) frozen whipped topping, thawed

Direction

- Heat 2-1/2 cups milk to 175° in a large saucepan; stir the sugar into the mix until dissolved. Whisk a small portion of the hot mixture into the eggs. Pour it all back into the pan, whisk continuously. Cook and stir on low heat till the mixture is no less than 160° and can coat a metal spoon's back. Turn off heat. Place the pan in a bowl of ice water to let it cool down quickly; stir for 2 minutes. Stir vanilla into the mix.
- Add the remaining milk into a large bowl; whisk pudding mixes into the milk for 2 minutes. Let sit until soft set for about 2 minutes. Stir the mix into the egg mixture. Stir whipped topping into the mix. Press waxed paper onto the custard's surface. Refrigerate for a few hours or overnight.
- Fill into the cylinder of ice cream freezer until two-thirds full; freeze following the manufacturer's directions. Refrigerate the rest of the mixture till ready to freeze. Pour into a freezer container; freeze for about 2-4 hours before serving.

Nutrition Information

- Calories: 313 calories
- Fiber: 0 fiber)

- Total Carbohydrate: 54g carbohydrate (49g sugars
- Cholesterol: 76mg cholesterol
- Protein: 6g protein.
- Total Fat: 8g fat (6g saturated fat)
- Sodium: 276mg sodium

447. Cran Orange Delight

Serving: 10-14 servings. | Prep: 15mins | Cook: 25mins | Ready in:

Ingredients

- 1 package yellow cake mix (regular size)
- 1-1/3 cups orange juice
- 3 eggs
- 1/3 cup vegetable oil
- 1 teaspoon rum flavoring, optional
- FROSTING:
- 1 carton (12 ounces) cranberry-orange sauce
- 1 package (3.4 ounces) instant vanilla pudding mix
- 2/3 cup orange juice
- 1 carton (8 ounces) frozen whipped topping, thawed

Direction

- Beat initial 5 ingredients for 30 seconds on low speed in a big bowl; beat for 2 minutes on medium.
- Put in 2 9-in. round greased and floured baking pans; bake it at 350° till inserted toothpick in middle exits clean for 25-30 minutes. Cool for 10 minutes in pans. Transfer onto wire racks; fully cool.
- Frosting: Mix orange juice, pudding mix and cranberry-orange sauce in a big bowl; fold in whipped topping.
- Horizontally cut each cake to 2 layers; spread frosting on sides and top of cake and between layers. Keep refrigerated.

Nutrition Information

- Calories: 350 calories
- Sodium: 357mg sodium
- Fiber: 1g fiber)
- Total Carbohydrate: 55g carbohydrate (38g sugars
- Cholesterol: 46mg cholesterol
- Protein: 3g protein.
- Total Fat: 13g fat (5g saturated fat)

448. Cranberry Bliss Cookies

Serving: 10 dozen. | Prep: 60mins | Cook: 10mins | Ready in:

Ingredients

- 1-1/2 cups butter, softened
- 1 cup sugar
- 1 cup packed brown sugar
- 3 large eggs
- 3 tablespoons grated orange zest
- 1 teaspoon vanilla extract
- 1/2 teaspoon orange extract
- 4 cups all-purpose flour
- 1 package (5.1 ounces) instant vanilla pudding mix
- 1-1/2 teaspoons baking soda
- 3/4 teaspoon salt
- 2 cups dried cranberries
- 1 package (10 to 12 ounces) vanilla or white chips
- 1 cup coarsely chopped macadamia nuts

Direction

- Cream together butter and sugars in a large bowl till fluffy and light. Beat the eggs, orange zest and extracts into the mixture. Mix together the salt, baking soda, pudding mix and flour; add them slowly into the creamed mixture and combine thoroughly. Stir the cranberries, chips and nuts into the mixture.

- On ungreased baking sheets, drop tablespoonfuls of the dough 2 in. apart; slightly flatten them out. Bake until light brown at 375° or for 8-10 minutes. Transfer to wire racks. Keep in an airtight container.

Nutrition Information

- Calories: 85 calories
- Total Fat: 4g fat (2g saturated fat)
- Sodium: 72mg sodium
- Fiber: 0 fiber)
- Total Carbohydrate: 11g carbohydrate (7g sugars
- Cholesterol: 12mg cholesterol
- Protein: 1g protein. Diabetic Exchanges: 1 fat

449. Cranberry Ice Cream Pie

Serving: 8 servings. | Prep: 25mins | Cook: 0mins | Ready in:

Ingredients

- Pastry for single-crust pie (9 inches)
- 3/4 cup cold 2% milk
- 1 package (3.4 ounces) instant vanilla pudding mix
- 3 cups vanilla ice cream, softened
- 1 can (14 ounces) jellied cranberry sauce, cut into slices
- 2 cups whipped topping
- Red food coloring, optional

Direction

- Line pastry on a 9-in. pie plate. Trim then flute edges. Line a double thickness of heavy-duty foil onto unpricked pastry. Bake for 8 minutes at 450°F. Remove foil. Bake till golden brown for 5-7 more minutes. On a wire rack, cool.
- Whisk pudding mix and milk for 2 minutes in a big bowl. Let stand till soft set for 2 minutes. Fold ice cream in. In the crust, put 1/2

cranberry slices. Spread 1/2 ice cream mixture on top. Repeat the layers.
- Freeze, covered, till firm for 2 hours minimum. Tint whipped topping, if desired, with red food coloring in a small bowl. Prior to serving, spread it on the pie.

Nutrition Information

- Calories: 397 calories
- Total Carbohydrate: 59g carbohydrate (34g sugars
- Cholesterol: 28mg cholesterol
- Protein: 4g protein.
- Total Fat: 16g fat (10g saturated fat)
- Sodium: 332mg sodium
- Fiber: 1g fiber)

450. Cream Puff Dessert

Serving: 12 | Prep: 20mins | Cook: 30mins | Ready in:

Ingredients

- PUFF
- 1 cup water
- 1/2 cup butter
- 1 cup all-purpose flour
- 4 eggs
- FILLING
- 1 (8 ounce) package cream cheese, softened
- 3 1/2 cups cold milk
- 2 (3.9 ounce) packages instant chocolate pudding mix
- TOPPING
- 1 (8 ounce) container frozen whipped topping, thawed
- 1/4 cup milk chocolate flavored topping
- 1/4 cup caramel topping
- 1/3 cup slivered almonds

Direction

- Set oven to 400°F (200°C) to preheat. Lightly oil a 9x13-inch baking dish.
- Melt butter in water over medium heat in a medium saucepan until bubbly. Stir all of the flour into butter mixture in one time until a ball has formed. Take off the heat; allow to sit or 5 minutes. Whisk in eggs, one by one, until glossy and smooth. Transfer mixture to the prepared dish, spreading evenly.
- Bake for 30 to 35 minutes in the preheated oven until puffed and golden. Allow to cool entirely on a wire rack.
- Meanwhile, whisk pudding mix, milk, and cream cheese together. Distribute pudding mixture over the cooled puff. Refrigerate for 20 minutes.
- Spread whipped topping over the chilled filling; drizzle with caramel and chocolate sauces. Scatter top with almond. Place in the freezer for 1 hour before serving.

Nutrition Information

- Calories: 355 calories;
- Protein: 8.7
- Total Fat: 22.3
- Sodium: 243
- Total Carbohydrate: 29.2
- Cholesterol: 110

---

451.   Cream Puff Monsters

Serving: 2 dozen. | Prep: 40mins | Cook: 25mins |Ready in:

Ingredients

- 3/4 cup plus 2 tablespoons all-purpose flour
- 2 tablespoons sugar
- 2 tablespoons baking cocoa
- 1 cup water
- 1/2 cup butter, cubed
- 4 eggs
- 1 package (3.9 ounces) instant chocolate pudding mix
- 2 cups cold milk
- Yellow, red, blue and green food coloring
- 1 can (16 ounces) vanilla frosting
- Sprinkles, small candies and slivered almonds

Direction

- Mix the cocoa, sugar, and flour, then put aside. Add butter and water to a saucepan and bring to a boil over medium heat; lower the heat to low. Put in all of the flour mixture at once; whisk until a smooth ball forms. Take away from heat and let it sit for 5 minutes. Put in 1 egg at a time, whisk well after each addition. Whisk until smooth. Use greased foil to cover the baking sheets. Drop the batter by tablespoonfuls, at least 2 inches apart, onto the prepared sheets. Bake for 25-30 minutes at 400° until a bit browned. Lift the foil and move to a wire rack. Slice a slit in each puff right away to let the steam out, then cool. Follow the directions on the package to whisk the milk and pudding mix together, then refrigerate. Once the puffs are cool, divide and remove soft dough from inside. Scoop the pudding into the puffs, then replace the tops. Follow the directions on the food coloring package to mix yellow with red to make orange, blue with red to create purple. Split the frosting among 3 microwave-safe bowls; tint with green, purple, and orange food coloring. Microwave the frosting until thin but not runny. Spoon one or more colors onto puffs. Place the sprinkles and candy on top for eyes and almond for whiskers or teeth. Refrigerate.

Nutrition Information

- Calories: 180 calories
- Fiber: 0 fiber)
- Total Carbohydrate: 23g carbohydrate (17g sugars
- Cholesterol: 48mg cholesterol
- Protein: 2g protein.

- Total Fat: 9g fat (4g saturated fat)
- Sodium: 166mg sodium

452. Cream Puff Swans

Serving: 3 dozen. | Prep: 40mins | Cook: 40mins | Ready in:

Ingredients

- 1 cup water
- 1/2 cup butter
- 1 cup all-purpose flour
- 1/4 teaspoon salt
- 4 eggs
- Pastry bag or heavy-duty resealable plastic bag
- #5 round pastry tip
- 2 packages (3.4 ounces each) instant vanilla pudding mix
- Confectioners' sugar, optional

Direction

- Add butter and water to a heavy saucepan and bring the mixture to a boil over medium heat. Put in all of the salt and flour at once, whisk until a smooth ball forms. Take away from heat and let it sit for 5 minutes. Put in 1 egg at a time, whisk well after each addition; whisk until smooth. Slice a small hole in the corner of a plastic or pastry bag, then insert round tip. Put in half a cup of the batter.
- Pipe thirty-six 2-in. long S shapes on a greased baking sheet for necks, creating a small dollop at the end of each for heat. Bake for 10 minutes at 400° until golden. Transfer to wire racks to cool.
- Drop the remaining batter by level tablespoons, 2 inches apart, onto greased baking sheets. Form the batter into 2x1 1/2-inch teardrops using a small icing knife. Bake for 30-35 minutes at 400° until golden. Transfer to wire racks to cool.

- Follow the directions on the package to prepare the pudding, then refrigerate. Just before serving, slice off the top third of the bodies of the swan and put aside. Scoop the pudding into the puff bottoms. Slice the reserve top in half lengthwise to shape wings and put into the pudding. Arrange the necks in the pudding. You can sprinkle confectioners' sugar over the swans if you want.

Nutrition Information

- Calories:
- Total Fat:
- Sodium:
- Fiber:
- Total Carbohydrate:
- Cholesterol:
- Protein:

453. Cream Filled Strawberries

Serving: 18 strawberries. | Prep: 30mins | Cook: 0mins | Ready in:

Ingredients

- 18 large fresh strawberries
- 1 cup cold fat-free milk
- 1 package (1 ounce) sugar-free instant vanilla pudding mix
- 2 cups reduced-fat whipped topping
- 1/4 teaspoon almond extract

Direction

- Get rid of the stems from strawberries. Cut in top of each berry a deep X shape, then spread the berries apart.
- Whisk together pudding mix and milk in a big bowl about 2 minutes; fold in whipped topping and almond extract. Pipe or scoop into each berry with about 5 tsp. mixture. Refrigerate until ready to serve.

Nutrition Information

- Calories: 36 calories
- Total Carbohydrate: 6g carbohydrate (0 sugars
- Cholesterol: 1mg cholesterol
- Protein: 1g protein. Diabetic Exchanges: 1/2 fruit.
- Total Fat: 1g fat (1g saturated fat)
- Sodium: 73mg sodium
- Fiber: 1g fiber)

454. Creamy Banana Berry Pie

Serving: 8 servings. | Prep: 15mins | Cook: 15mins | Ready in:

Ingredients

- 1 sheet refrigerated pie pastry
- 1/4 cup chopped pecans
- 1-1/4 cups cold fat-free milk
- 1/2 cup reduced-fat sour cream
- Sugar substitute equivalent to 1/4 cup sugar
- 1 package (.9 ounce) sugar-free instant banana pudding mix
- 2 cups reduced-fat whipped topping
- 1 tablespoon lemon juice
- 2 medium bananas
- 1/3 cup fresh blueberries

Direction

- Unfold pastry on a lightly floured surface. Scatter with pecans; roll pecans into pastry lightly. Place on a 9-in. pie dish. Line pastry shell, unpricked, with a double thickness of heavy-duty foil. Bake for 8 minutes at 450°. Discard foil; bake for 5 minutes more. Let cool on a wire rack.
- Mix the sugar substitute, sour cream and milk in a small bowl. Mix in dry pudding mix slowly. Fold in whipped topping.

- In a small bowl, put in lemon juice. Cut bananas into juice and lightly mix to coat. Put aside 1/3 cup; scoop leftover banana slices into the shell. Garnish with saved banana slices, blueberries and pudding mixture. Cover and chill for half an hour before serving.

Nutrition Information

- Calories: 263 calories
- Fiber: 1g fiber)
- Total Carbohydrate: 31g carbohydrate (12g sugars
- Cholesterol: 11mg cholesterol
- Protein: 4g protein. Diabetic Exchanges: 2 starch
- Total Fat: 13g fat (6g saturated fat)
- Sodium: 266mg sodium

455. Creamy Cappuccino Mousse

Serving: 8 servings, 1/2 cup each | Prep: 20mins | Cook: | Ready in:

Ingredients

- 4 oz. (1/2 of 8-oz. pkg.) PHILADELPHIA Cream Cheese , softened
- 3/4 cup brewed strong GEVALIA Bold Dark Gold Roast , cooled
- 1/2 cup milk
- 1 pkg. (3.4 oz.) JELL-O Vanilla Flavor Instant Pudding
- 2-1/2 cups thawed COOL WHIP Whipped Topping , divided

Direction

- Use mixer to beat cream cheese till creamy in big bowl. Beat coffee in slowly then milk till blended. Add dry pudding mix; beat for 2 minutes. Let stand till thick for 5 minutes. Mix 2 cups cool whip in gently.

- Put in 8 dessert dishes.
- Refrigerate till chilled for a few hours; right before serving, garnish with leftover cool whip.

Nutrition Information

- Calories: 170
- Total Fat: 9 g
- Saturated Fat: 7 g
- Fiber: 0 g
- Cholesterol: 20 mg
- Sodium: 240 mg
- Sugar: 14 g
- Total Carbohydrate: 19 g
- Protein: 2 g

456. Creamy Chocolate Cake Roll

Serving: 10 servings. | Prep: 55mins | Cook: 15mins | Ready in:

Ingredients

- 5 large eggs, separated
- 1 cup confectioners' sugar
- 1 teaspoon vanilla extract
- 1/4 cup all-purpose flour
- 1/4 cup baking cocoa
- 2 tablespoons sugar
- CREAM FILLING/FROSTING:
- 1 package (8 ounces) cream cheese, softened
- 1/3 cup sugar
- 1 package (3.4 ounces) instant vanilla pudding mix
- 1 teaspoon vanilla extract
- 4 cups heavy whipping cream
- CHOCOLATE RASPBERRY SAUCE:
- 1-1/2 cups semisweet chocolate chips
- 1/2 cup seedless raspberry jam
- 1/4 cup heavy whipping cream
- 1 teaspoon almond extract

Direction

- Let egg whites stand at room temperature for half an hour in a bowl. Apply waxed paper to the bottom of a 15x10x1-inch baking pan. Grease paper and pan. Set aside.
- Beat yolks for 5 minutes on high speed, until lemon-colored and thick.
- Slowly add in confectioners' sugar. Add vanilla. Sift cocoa and flour together two times, then add to the mixture and mix well. Batter will be thick.
- Mix egg whites on medium speed. Wait for soft peaks to form. Add one tablespoon of sugar at a time, beating on high to form stiff peaks. Slowly fold into the batter mix. Pour to the pan.
- Bake for 12-15 minutes at 375°. It should spring back after touching. Let it cool for 5 minutes. Flip over a kitchen towel that's dusted with baking cocoa. Remove waxed paper slowly. Roll towel jelly-roll style. Start with a short side. Let it cool on a rack.
- Beat sugar, cream cheese and dry pudding mix in a bowl until smooth. Add vanilla. Stir in cream slowly until thick.
- Unroll cake. Apply 2 1/2 cups of the filling to within half an inch of the edges of the cake. Reroll. Place on a platter, seam-side down. Add frosting to sides, edges and top with the rest of the filling. Put cover on and chill for an hour.
- Mix jam, chips and cream in a microwave-safe bowl. Microwave with no lid for 1-2 minutes, on high heat, until smooth. Stir every half minute. Add extract. Serve with the cake. Chill leftovers.

Nutrition Information

- Calories: 766 calories
- Sodium: 276mg sodium
- Fiber: 2g fiber)
- Total Carbohydrate: 64g carbohydrate (55g sugars
- Cholesterol: 270mg cholesterol

- Protein: 9g protein.
- Total Fat: 56g fat (34g saturated fat)

457. Creamy Coconut Dessert

Serving: 15 servings. | Prep: 20mins | Cook: 20mins | Ready in:

Ingredients

- 1 cup all-purpose flour
- 2 tablespoons sugar
- 1/2 cup cold butter, cubed
- 1/2 cup chopped pecans
- FILLING:
- 1 package (8 ounces) cream cheese, softened
- 1 cup confectioners' sugar
- 1 carton (12 ounces) frozen whipped topping, thawed, divided
- 4 cups cold 2% milk
- 1-1/2 teaspoons coconut extract
- 3 packages (3.4 ounces each) instant vanilla pudding mix
- 2 cups sweetened shredded coconut, divided

Direction

- Mix sugar and flour together in a small mixing bowl; cut butter into mixture until crumbly. Fold in pecans. Pat mixture into a greased 13x9-inch baking dish. Bake for 20 to 25 minutes at 325° until edges turn brown lightly. Allow to cool on a wire rack.
- Beat cream cheese and confectioners' sugar in a large mixing bowl until smooth; add 1 cup whipped topping and fold gently. Spread cream cheese mixture over the crust.
- Beat pudding mixes, extract, and milk in a separate bowl for 2 minutes; allow mixture to sit until soft-set, about 2 minutes. Mix in 1 1/2 cups coconut. Spread over cream cheese layer. Spread the remaining whipped topping over top. Toast the rest of coconut; scatter over top. Chill overnight.

Nutrition Information

- Calories: 0
- Total Carbohydrate: 40 g carbohydrate
- Cholesterol: 52 mg cholesterol
- Protein: 6 g protein.
- Total Fat: 27 g fat (17 g saturated fat)
- Sodium: 267 mg sodium
- Fiber: 1 g fiber

458. Creamy Cranberry Ice Cream Pie

Serving: 8 servings. | Prep: 20mins | Cook: 15mins | Ready in:

Ingredients

- Pastry for single-crust pie (9 inches)
- 1-1/4 cups jellied cranberry sauce
- 2 cups vanilla ice cream, softened
- 1/4 cup thawed orange juice concentrate
- 1 package (3.4 ounces) instant vanilla pudding mix
- 1/2 cup heavy whipping cream
- Ground nutmeg

Direction

- Line pastry on a 9-in. pie plate. Trim then flute edges. Line a double thickness of heavy-duty foil on unpricked pastry. Bake for 8 minutes at 450°. Bake till lightly browned for 5-7 more minutes. On a wire rack, cool.
- On bottom of pie crust, spread cranberry sauce; put aside. Mix pudding mix, juice concentrate and ice cream in a big bowl. Beat cream till you make soft peaks in a small bowl. Fold it into the ice cream mixture. Over cranberry sauce, pour. Sprinkle nutmeg on. Freeze till firm. 15 minutes before slicing, remove from freezer.

Nutrition Information

- Calories: 359 calories
- Protein: 3g protein.
- Total Fat: 16g fat (9g saturated fat)
- Sodium: 312mg sodium
- Fiber: 1g fiber)
- Total Carbohydrate: 52g carbohydrate (30g sugars
- Cholesterol: 40mg cholesterol

---

459. Creamy Mango Loaf Cake

Serving: 6 servings. | Prep: 15mins | Cook: 0mins | Ready in:

Ingredients

- 1-1/4 cups cold fat-free half-and-half
- 1 package (1 ounce) sugar-free instant vanilla pudding mix
- 1 medium mango, peeled and diced
- 1 loaf-shaped angel food cake (10-1/2 ounces)
- 1 medium kiwifruit, peeled and sliced

Direction

- Add half & half and pudding mix into a large bowl and whisk together for 2 minutes. Add mango by folding in.
- Slice cake into 3 horizontal layers, apply pudding mixture between the layers and all over the cake's top. Use kiwi as a topping. Keep refrigerated for a minimum of 4 hours before consumption.

Nutrition Information

- Calories: 207 calories
- Sodium: 611mg sodium
- Fiber: 2g fiber)
- Total Carbohydrate: 45g carbohydrate (33g sugars
- Cholesterol: 0 cholesterol
- Protein: 5g protein.

- Total Fat: 1g fat (0 saturated fat)

---

460. Creamy Peach Pudding

Serving: 9 servings. | Prep: 20mins | Cook: 0mins | Ready in:

Ingredients

- 1 cup uncooked acini di pepe or orzo pasta
- 1 can (29 ounces) sliced peaches
- 1-3/4 cups cold milk
- 1 package (3.4 ounces) instant vanilla pudding mix
- 1/4 cup sugar
- 3 cups miniature marshmallows
- 2 cups whipped topping

Direction

- Following package directions to cook pasta, then drain and rinse under cold water. Drain peaches and save 1/4 cup of syrup, then put peaches aside.
- Whisk together reserved syrup, sugar, pudding mix and milk in a big bowl about 2 minutes. Allow to stand until soft-set, about 2 minutes, then stir in pasta and peaches. Fold in whipped topping and marshmallows, then cover and chill until ready to serve.

Nutrition Information

- Calories:
- Total Carbohydrate:
- Cholesterol:
- Protein:
- Total Fat:
- Sodium:
- Fiber:

461. Creamy Pineapple Cake

Serving: 6-8 servings. | Prep: 20mins | Cook: 0mins | Ready in:

Ingredients

- 5 individual cream-filled sponge cakes, split in half lengthwise or 7 slices pound cake (about 3/4 inch thick)
- 1 can (20 ounces) crushed pineapple, drained
- 1-1/2 cups cold milk
- 1 package (3.4 ounces) instant vanilla pudding mix
- 2 cups whipped topping, divided
- 1/2 cup chopped walnuts

Direction

- Arrange the cake in an ungreased 11x7-inch dish. Add pineapple on top; cover and put aside.
- Beat the pudding mix with milk in a bowl until smooth. Fold in half a cup of whipped topping; spread over the pineapple. Pour the remaining whipped topping over the pudding. Add nuts on top. Refrigerate until serving.

Nutrition Information

- Calories: 310 calories
- Sodium: 290mg sodium
- Fiber: 1g fiber)
- Total Carbohydrate: 46g carbohydrate (38g sugars
- Cholesterol: 10mg cholesterol
- Protein: 5g protein.
- Total Fat: 12g fat (5g saturated fat)

462. Creamy Rhubarb Dessert

Serving: 15 servings. | Prep: 25mins | Cook: 20mins | Ready in:

Ingredients

- 1-1/2 cups sugar
- 1/4 cup cornstarch
- 3/4 cup water
- 6 cups sliced fresh or frozen rhubarb
- CRUST:
- 2 cups all-purpose flour
- 2 tablespoons confectioners' sugar
- 1/2 cup chopped nuts, toasted
- 1 cup cold butter, cubed
- TOPPING:
- 2 cups heavy whipping cream
- 1-1/2 cups miniature marshmallows
- 1 package (3.4 ounces) instant vanilla pudding mix
- 1-2/3 cups cold milk
- 1/2 cup chopped nuts, toasted, optional

Direction

- Mix cornstarch and sugar together in a big saucepan; whisk in water until smooth. Put in rhubarb, then cook and stir for about 10 minutes until softened. Let it cool.
- In the meantime, blend nuts, sugar and flour together in a big bowl to make crust. Cut in butter until mixture looks like coarse crumbs. Press mixture onto an unoiled 13x9" baking dish. Bake for 20 minutes at 350 degrees or until browned slightly. Place on a wire rack to cool.
- Transfer cooled filling onto the crust. Beat cream until stiff peaks form in a bowl; fold in marshmallows. Spread atop filling. Stir milk and pudding mix together for 2 minutes in a bowl; let it rest until soft-set, or for 5 minutes. Spread on top of marshmallow topping. Add nuts to scatter over if preferred. Chill, covered, for a few hours.

Nutrition Information

- Calories: 459 calories
- Cholesterol: 80mg cholesterol
- Protein: 5g protein.
- Total Fat: 27g fat (16g saturated fat)
- Sodium: 244mg sodium

- Fiber: 2g fiber)
- Total Carbohydrate: 51g carbohydrate (32g sugars

463. Crisp Butter Pecan Cookies

Serving: about 2 dozen. | Prep: 20mins | Cook: 10mins | Ready in:

Ingredients

- 3/4 cup butter, softened
- 1 package (3.4 ounces) instant butterscotch pudding mix
- 1-1/4 cups all-purpose flour
- 1/2 cup chopped pecans

Direction

- Beat the pudding mix with butter in a small bowl until smooth. Slowly whisk in flour. Fold in pecans. Roll the dough into one and a half-inch balls.
- Arrange the balls 2 inches apart on the greased baking sheets; flatten the balls to half an inch using the bottom of a glass greased with cooking spray.
- Bake for 10-13 min. at 375° until light golden brown. Transfer from pans to wire racks.

Nutrition Information

- Calories: 211 calories
- Protein: 2g protein.
- Total Fat: 15g fat (7g saturated fat)
- Sodium: 241mg sodium
- Fiber: 1g fiber)
- Total Carbohydrate: 18g carbohydrate (6g sugars
- Cholesterol: 31mg cholesterol

464. Crunchy Chocolate Pudding Squares

Serving: 12-15 servings. | Prep: 30mins | Cook: 0mins | Ready in:

Ingredients

- 2 cups self-rising flour
- 1-1/2 cups finely chopped pecans
- 2/3 cup packed brown sugar
- 1 cup butter, melted
- 1 package (8 ounces) cream cheese, softened
- 1 cup confectioners' sugar
- 1 carton (8 ounces) frozen whipped topping, thawed, divided
- 3 cups cold milk
- 1 package (5.9 ounces) instant chocolate pudding mix
- Colored sprinkles, optional

Direction

- Combine the brown sugar, pecans and flour in a bowl. Mix butter into the mixture. Press into a 13-in. x 9-in. ungreased baking dish. Bake to a light brown, at 375° for 15-20 minutes. Let it cool down on a wire rack.
- Beat together cream cheese and confectioners' sugar in a bowl till smooth. Fold 1 cup whipped topping into the mixture. Spread atop the crust. In a different bowl, whisk together pudding mix and milk for 2 minutes. Spoon this mixture onto the cream cheese layer. Chill in refrigerator until set, for 15 minutes. Spread the remaining whipped topping on top. Chill till set. Garnish with sprinkles if you wish. Slice into squares.

Nutrition Information

- Calories: 475 calories
- Sodium: 553mg sodium
- Fiber: 2g fiber)
- Total Carbohydrate: 47g carbohydrate (29g sugars
- Cholesterol: 56mg cholesterol

- Protein: 6g protein.
- Total Fat: 30g fat (15g saturated fat)

Serving: 16 servings. | Prep: 20mins | Cook: 25mins | Ready in:

Ingredients

- 1 package dark chocolate cake mix (regular size)
- 4 ounces cream cheese, softened
- 1 package (3.9 ounces) instant chocolate pudding mix
- 1 cup 2% milk
- 3 large eggs
- 1 teaspoon ground cinnamon
- 3 cups shredded carrots
- 1 cup chopped walnuts, toasted, divided
- 2 cans (16 ounces each) cream cheese frosting

Direction

- In a large bowl, mix cinnamon, eggs, milk, pudding mix, cream cheese and cake mix together; beat for 30 seconds on low speed. Beat for 2 minutes on medium. Mix in 1/2 cup of walnuts and carrots. Transfer into three 8-inch round baking pans coated with grease and flour.
- Bake at 350° till a toothpick comes out clean when inserted into the center, 25-30 minutes. Allow to cool for 10 minutes then take out of pans and place on wire racks to cool completely.
- Spread the frosting between layers and over the top and sides of the cake. Sprinkle the remaining walnuts on top. Keep in a refrigerator.

Nutrition Information

- Calories: 504 calories
- Total Fat: 24g fat (8g saturated fat)
- Sodium: 570mg sodium
- Fiber: 2g fiber)
- Total Carbohydrate: 71g carbohydrate (52g sugars
- Cholesterol: 49mg cholesterol
- Protein: 5g protein.

Serving: 3 dozen. | Prep: 30mins | Cook: 10mins | Ready in:

Ingredients

- 2 tablespoons finely chopped crystallized ginger
- 1 tablespoon rum
- 3/4 cup butter, cubed
- 1/3 cup baking cocoa
- 1/4 cup sugar
- 1 egg, lightly beaten
- 1 teaspoon vanilla extract
- 1-1/2 cups graham cracker crumbs
- 1 cup sweetened shredded coconut
- 1/2 cup chopped walnuts
- 1/2 cup finely chopped red and green candied cherries
- FILLING:
- 1/4 cup butter, softened
- 3 tablespoons 2% milk
- 2 tablespoons instant vanilla pudding mix
- 2-1/2 cups confectioners' sugar
- TOPPING:
- 4 ounces semisweet chocolate, chopped
- 1 tablespoon butter
- 1/2 cup confectioners' sugar
- 2 teaspoons 2% milk

Direction

- Mix rum and ginger together in a small mixing bowl; put to one side.

- Combine sugar, cocoa, and butter in a large heavy saucepan, cook over medium-low heat, stirring, until melted. Stir a small amount of hot mixture into egg. Pour back into the pan, stirring continuously. Cook over medium-low heat, stirring, until mixture achieves 160°.
- Turn off the heat and whisk in vanilla. Whisk in ginger mixture, cherries, walnuts, coconut, and cracker crumbs. Pat mixture into a 9x9-inch baking pan lined with foil.
- To make filling, whisk pudding mix, milk, and butter together in a large mixing bowl until incorporated. Slowly whisk in confectioners' sugar until smooth; spread over crust. Place in the freezer until set, about 15 minutes.
- Melt butter and chocolate in a microwave; whisk until smooth. Distribute over top. Mix milk and confectioners' sugar together; sprinkle over top. Chill in the fridge until set, about 1 hour. Slice into bars to serve.

Nutrition Information

- Calories:
- Fiber:
- Total Carbohydrate:
- Cholesterol:
- Protein:
- Total Fat:
- Sodium:

---

467. Delightful Brownies

Serving: 1 dozen. | Prep: 15mins | Cook: 30mins |Ready in:

Ingredients

- 3 tablespoons butter, softened
- 2 egg whites
- 1 jar (4 ounces) prune baby food
- 1 teaspoon vanilla extract
- 2/3 cup sugar
- 1/2 cup all-purpose flour

- 1 package (1.4 ounces) sugar-free instant chocolate pudding mix
- 1/2 teaspoon baking powder
- 1/4 teaspoon salt
- 3/4 cup miniature semisweet chocolate chips

Direction

- Beat egg whites and butter till blended in a bowl; beat in vanilla and baby food. Mix salt, baking powder, pudding mix, flour and sugar; add to egg mixture. Mix in chocolate chips.
- Spread into 8-in. square baking pan that's coated in cooking spray; bake it at 350° till inserted toothpick in middle exits clean for 30-35 minutes. Cool on wire rack.

Nutrition Information

- Calories: 176 calories
- Total Fat: 6g fat (4g saturated fat)
- Sodium: 338mg sodium
- Fiber: 2g fiber)
- Total Carbohydrate: 30g carbohydrate (0 sugars
- Cholesterol: 8mg cholesterol
- Protein: 2g protein. Diabetic Exchanges: 2 starch

---

468. Deluxe Chocolate Pudding

Serving: 4 servings. | Prep: 10mins | Cook: 0mins | Ready in:

Ingredients

- 1-3/4 cups cold milk
- 1 package (3.9 ounces) instant chocolate pudding mix
- 1/4 cup sour cream
- 1/2 teaspoon almond or rum extract
- 1/4 cup chopped pecans, optional
- 4 pecan halves, optional

Direction

- Mix together extract, sour cream, pudding mix and milk in a bowl. Stir for about 2 to 3 minutes, until the mixture becomes a little thicker. Mix in pecans (optional). Divide into 4 bowls. Place pecan halves on top (optional).

Nutrition Information

- Calories: 140 calories
- Cholesterol: 7mg cholesterol
- Protein: 7g protein. Diabetic Exchanges: 1-1/2 starch
- Total Fat: 1g fat (0 saturated fat)
- Sodium: 369mg sodium
- Fiber: 0 fiber)
- Total Carbohydrate: 27g carbohydrate (0 sugars

---

469.   Dirt Dessert

Serving: 20 servings. | Prep: 30mins | Cook: 0mins | Ready in:

Ingredients

- 1 package (8 ounces) cream cheese, softened
- 1/4 cup butter, softened
- 1 cup confectioners' sugar
- 3-1/2 cups cold 2% milk
- 2 packages (3.4 ounces each) instant vanilla pudding mix
- 1 carton (12 ounces) frozen whipped topping, thawed
- 1 package (15-1/2 ounces) Oreo cookies, crushed
- Shaved white chocolate, optional

Direction

- Beat butter, cream cheese, and confectioners' sugar in a large mixing bowl until no lumps remain. Beat pudding mixes and milk together in another large mixing bowl for 2 minutes;

allow to sit until soft-set, for 2 minutes. Slowly mix into cream cheese mixture. Add whipped topping and fold gently.

- Distribute 1 1/3 cups of crushed cookies in an ungreased 13x9-inch dish. Spread half of pudding mixture over cookie and top with 1/2 of the rest of the cookies. Repeat layering process with remaining ingredients. Chill for a minimum of 1 hour prior to serving. Sprinkle top with shaved white chocolate, if desired.

Nutrition Information

- Calories: 278 calories
- Total Fat: 13g fat (7g saturated fat)
- Sodium: 316mg sodium
- Fiber: 1g fiber)
- Total Carbohydrate: 38g carbohydrate (26g sugars
- Cholesterol: 16mg cholesterol
- Protein: 3g protein.

---

470.   Double Berry Lemon Dessert

Serving: 8 servings. | Prep: 25mins | Cook: 20mins | Ready in:

Ingredients

- 1-1/3 cups angel food cake mix
- 2/3 cup cold water
- 1 cup cold 2% milk
- 1 package (1 ounce) sugar-free instant lemon pudding mix
- 1 package (8 ounces) reduced-fat cream cheese
- 1/2 cup fresh or frozen raspberries
- 1/2 cup fresh or frozen blackberries
- 1 teaspoon sugar

Direction

- Combine together in a small bowl the water and cake mix; whisk for 30 seconds on low speed. Whisk for 1 minute on medium speed. Place into an 11x7 inches baking pan that is not greased. Place inside the oven and bake for 20-25 minutes at 350 degrees F or until golden brown in color and whole top looks dry. Let it fully cool for about 40 minutes. Whisk pudding mix and milk in a small bowl. Beat cream cheese in small bowl until turns to smooth; add in pudding mixture until well combined. Use knife to run around sides of pan. Get the cake and slice into two layers horizontally. Place bottom layer on a serving plate: spread with half of pudding mixture Top with remaining cake layer and pudding mixture. Combine together in a small bowl the sugar, blackberries and raspberries. Present with cake. Keep the leftovers inside the refrigerator.

Nutrition Information

- Calories: 212 calories
- Protein: 7g protein. Diabetic Exchanges: 2 starch
- Total Fat: 7g fat (4g saturated fat)
- Sodium: 491mg sodium
- Fiber: 1g fiber)
- Total Carbohydrate: 32g carbohydrate (16g sugars
- Cholesterol: 22mg cholesterol

471. Double Chocolate Bundt Cakes

Serving: 12-14 servings. | Prep: 15mins | Cook: 60mins | Ready in:

Ingredients

- 1 package yellow cake mix (regular size)
- 1 package (3.4 ounces) instant vanilla pudding mix
- 1 cup (8 ounces) sour cream
- 3 large eggs
- 1/2 cup canola oil
- 1/2 cup water
- 4 ounces German sweet chocolate, grated
- 1 cup (6 ounces) semisweet chocolate chips
- 1/2 cup chopped pecans
- 1/2 cup chocolate frosting, melted
- Pecan halves

Direction

- Set oven to 350° to preheat. Mix the cake with water, oil, eggs, sour cream and pudding mixes in a big bowl; whip on low for half a minute. Whip on medium for 2 minutes. Fold in the pecans, chocolate chips and shredded chocolate. Remove to a greased and floured 10-inch fluted tube pan.
- Bake for 60-65 minutes or until a toothpick inserted in the middle comes out clean. Let cool for 10 minutes before taking out from pan to a wire rack. Sprinkle with frosting; top with pecan halves.

Nutrition Information

- Calories: 463 calories
- Sodium: 375mg sodium
- Fiber: 2g fiber)
- Total Carbohydrate: 56g carbohydrate (39g sugars
- Cholesterol: 56mg cholesterol
- Protein: 5g protein.
- Total Fat: 26g fat (9g saturated fat)

472. Double Chocolate Pie

Serving: 8 | Prep: 10mins | Cook: 40mins | Ready in:

Ingredients

- 1 (9 inch) pie crust, baked
- 1 1/2 cups white sugar
- 1/3 cup cornstarch
- 1/2 teaspoon salt

- 3 cups milk
- 3/4 cup semisweet chocolate chips
- 2 (1 ounce) squares unsweetened chocolate, chopped
- 4 egg yolks, beaten
- 1 tablespoon vanilla extract

Direction

- Mix together salt, cornstarch, and sugar in a 2-quart saucepan. Stir milk gradually into the mixture. Add chocolate chips and unsweetened chocolate into this mixture. Put on medium heat, stir continuously, until mixture boils and thickens. Boil and stir for about 1 minute.
- Add the egg yolks into a medium heatproof bowl. Pour 1/2 the mixture of chocolate into egg yolks slowly, whisk continuously.
- To the mixture inside the saucepan, whisk in the egg yolk mixture back. Put on medium heat and heat until boiling, stir continuously. Boil and stir for 1 minute. Take off from heat; stir vanilla extract into the mixture.
- Add the mixture into the baked pie shell. Press a plastic wrap layer onto the filling. Chill in refrigerator for no less than 4 hours but no longer than 48 hours. Take off the plastic wrap before serving and put whipped topping on top.

Nutrition Information

- Calories: 434 calories;
- Protein: 6.6
- Total Fat: 17.6
- Sodium: 293
- Total Carbohydrate: 67
- Cholesterol: 110

---

473.   Double Frosted Brownies

Serving: 3 dozen. | Prep: 15mins | Cook: 25mins | Ready in:

Ingredients

- 1 package fudge brownie mix (13-inch x 9-inch pan size)
- 1/2 cup butter, softened
- 1-1/2 cups confectioners' sugar
- 2 tablespoons instant vanilla pudding mix
- 2 to 3 tablespoons 2% milk
- 1 can (16 ounces) chocolate fudge frosting

Direction

- Follow instructions on the brownie mix package and prepare batter. Grease a 13x9-inch baking pan and spread with brownie batter. Bake in 350-degree oven until a toothpick exits clean when pierced into the cake, 2 inches from the pan's side, about 25 to 30 minutes. Place on a wire rack to cool entirely.
- Beat pudding mix, sugar and butter in a big bowl until incorporated. Put in enough milk until the consistency is spreadable. Spread onto brownies. Chill while covered for half an hour.
- Layer fudge frosting on top. Slice into bars. Keep in the refrigerator to store.

Nutrition Information

- Calories:
- Total Fat:
- Sodium:
- Fiber:
- Total Carbohydrate:
- Cholesterol:
- Protein:

---

474.   Double Chocolate Cream Roll

Serving: 12 servings. | Prep: 50mins | Cook: 0mins | Ready in:

Ingredients

- 1-1/2 teaspoons shortening
- 5 large eggs, separated
- 1 teaspoon vanilla extract
- 1 cup plus 2 teaspoons confectioners' sugar, divided
- 3 tablespoons baking cocoa
- 1/8 teaspoon salt
- 1-1/2 cups cold fat-free milk
- 2 packages (3.3 ounces each) instant white chocolate pudding mix or 2 packages (3.4 ounces) instant vanilla pudding mix
- 1 carton (8 ounces) frozen reduced-fat whipped topping, thawed
- 3 tablespoons fat-free caramel ice cream topping, divided
- 1/2 cup chopped walnuts, divided
- 1 tablespoon fat-free hot fudge ice cream topping, warmed

Direction

- Spray some oil on a 15x10x1-in baking sheet. Grease some shortening on a paraffin paper and line it in the baking sheet then set aside. Using high speed, whisk egg yolks in a big mixing bowl until the texture becomes thick and yellowish in color. Mix in vanilla. Using another mixing bowl, mix cocoa, salt and 1 cup confectioners' sugar; add the dry mixture gradually into the egg yolk mixture. Prepare a small mixing bowl and whisk egg whites until it forms a stiff peak. Add it and mix gently into egg yolk mixture. Pour the batter into prepared baking sheet. Place it in the oven and bake the cake for 14-16 minutes at 350 degrees. Once cooked, the cake will bounce back when pressed lightly. Prepare a linen towel and dust it off with some confectioners' sugar. Flip the cake immediately in the towel. Carefully remove the paraffin paper from the cake. Jelly-roll the cake in the towel and place on a wire shelve to cool thoroughly. Prepare a small mixing bowl and pour the pudding mix and milk. Mix for 2 minutes using a low speed and gently combine in whipped topping. Scoop out 1 cup and set aside. Unroll the cooled cake and evenly spread the filling within 1/2 inside of the edges. Topped with 2 tablespoons of caramel and drizzle with 6 tablespoons of walnuts. Roll the cake up again and evenly spread the filling into the cake. Garnish with warm fudge sauce and top with caramel. Drizzle again with some walnuts. Put a cake cover and keep refrigerated for 1 hour. Serve chilled. Keep all leftovers refrigerated.

Nutrition Information

- Calories: 227 calories
- Sodium: 301mg sodium
- Fiber: 1g fiber)
- Total Carbohydrate: 33g carbohydrate (0 sugars
- Cholesterol: 89mg cholesterol
- Protein: 5g protein. Diabetic Exchanges: 2 starch
- Total Fat: 8g fat (3g saturated fat)

---

475.   Double Decker Banana Cups

Serving: Makes 4 servings. | Prep: 5mins | Cook: | Ready in:

Ingredients

- 1-1/2 cups cold fat-free milk
- 1 pkg. (4-serving size) JELL-O Vanilla Flavor Sugar Free Fat Free Instant Pudding
- 1 cup thawed COOL WHIP LITE Whipped Topping
- 2 Tbsp. graham cracker crumbs
- 2 medium banana s, sliced

Direction

- 1. Add to a big bowl with milk. Put in dry pudding mix and use a wire whisk to beat until well-mixed, about 2 minutes. Stir in the

whipped topping gently. Allow to stand about 5 minutes.
- 2. Layer in 4 separate dessert dishes with 1/2 each of the pudding mixture, graham crumbs and bananas, then repeat all layers.
- 3. Chill until serving, for a minimum of an hour. Keep the leftovers dessert in the fridge for storage.

Nutrition Information

- Calories: 170
- Sodium: 380 mg
- Total Fat: 3 g
- Saturated Fat: 2.5 g
- Cholesterol: 0 mg
- Protein: 4 g
- Fiber: 2 g
- Sugar: 17 g
- Total Carbohydrate: 32 g

476. Double Layer Pumpkin Pie

Serving: 6-8 servings. | Prep: 20mins | Cook: 0mins | Ready in:

Ingredients

- 4 ounces cream cheese, softened
- 1 tablespoon sugar
- 1 tablespoon milk
- 1 carton (8 ounces) frozen whipped topping, thawed, divided
- 1 graham cracker crust (9 inches)
- 1 cup cold milk
- 2 packages (3.4 ounces each) instant vanilla pudding mix
- 1 can (15 ounces) solid-pack pumpkin
- 1 teaspoon ground cinnamon
- 1/2 teaspoon ground ginger
- 1/4 teaspoon ground cloves

Direction

- Mix milk, sugar and cream cheese in a small bowl. Fold in 1 and a half cups whipped topping. Scoop into the crust.
- Blend pudding mixes and cold milk for 2 minutes in a big bowl. Let sit for 2 minutes till soft-set. Mix in cloves, ginger, cinnamon and pumpkin.
- Scatter on top of cream cheese layer. Scatter leftover whipped topping over. Chill for a minimum of 3 hours prior to cutting.

Nutrition Information

- Calories: 369 calories
- Fiber: 3g fiber)
- Total Carbohydrate: 51g carbohydrate (36g sugars
- Cholesterol: 20mg cholesterol
- Protein: 4g protein.
- Total Fat: 16g fat (10g saturated fat)
- Sodium: 522mg sodium

477. Doughnut Parfaits

Serving: 4 servings. | Prep: 20mins | Cook: 0mins | Ready in:

Ingredients

- 2 cups cold milk
- 1 package (3.4 ounces) instant vanilla pudding mix
- 16 powdered sugar doughnut holes, halved
- 1 to 2 medium firm bananas, cut into 1/4-inch slices
- 2 cups whipped topping
- Chopped nuts and maraschino cherries

Direction

- Beat pudding mix and milk for 2 minutes in a large bowl. Allow it to stand for 2 minutes or until set to soft. In each of 4 parfait glasses, put four doughnut hole halves. Place half of the pudding, bananas, and whipped topping on top. Continue layers. Decorate with cherries and nuts.

Nutrition Information

- Calories: 528 calories
- Sodium: 706mg sodium
- Fiber: 2g fiber)
- Total Carbohydrate: 71g carbohydrate (42g sugars
- Cholesterol: 37mg cholesterol
- Protein: 7g protein.
- Total Fat: 23g fat (11g saturated fat)

---

478.   Down South Sweet Tea Cake

Serving: 12 servings. | Prep: 20mins | Cook: 45mins | Ready in:

Ingredients

- 1 package yellow cake mix (regular size)
- 1 package (3.4 ounces) instant vanilla pudding mix
- 1 cup strong brewed tea, cooled, divided
- 4 large eggs
- 3/4 cup canola oil
- 1 teaspoon vanilla extract
- 1/2 teaspoon lemon extract
- 1 cup chopped pecans, toasted
- 2 cups confectioners' sugar
- 1/3 cup unsalted butter, melted

Direction

- Set oven to 350 degrees and start preheating. Prepare a fluted tube pan of 10 inches by greasing and flouring. Mix together lemon extract, vanilla, oil, eggs, 3/4 cup tea, pudding mix and cake mix in a big bowl; beat the mixture for half a minute on low speed. Increase the speed to medium and beat for 2 minutes. Mix in pecans. Pour into the greased

and floured pan. Bake in preheated oven until a toothpick is clean when coming out of the center, about 45 to 50 minutes.
- Allow to cool in pan for 10 minutes, then transfer to a wire rack to cool entirely. Combine butter, confectioners' sugar and enough remaining tea in a small bowl to achieve wanted consistency. Glaze onto the cake, letting some drip over the sides.

Nutrition Information

- Calories:
- Total Fat:
- Sodium:
- Fiber:
- Total Carbohydrate:
- Cholesterol:
- Protein:

---

479.   Dr Pepper Cake

Serving: 12 servings. | Prep: 30mins | Cook: 20mins | Ready in:

Ingredients

- 1 package German chocolate cake mix, regular size
- 1 package (3.4 ounces) instant chocolate pudding mix
- 4 large eggs
- 1 can (12 ounces) Dr Pepper
- 1 teaspoon vanilla extract
- FROSTING:
- 1 container (12 ounces) whipped cream cheese, room temperature
- 1/3 cup butter, softened
- 1/3 cup baking cocoa
- 3-1/2 cups confectioners' sugar
- 1-1/2 teaspoons vanilla extract

Direction

- Start preheating the oven to 350°. Line the parchment paper onto the bottoms of 3 greased 9-inch round baking pans; grease the paper.
- Mix the pudding mix and cake mix in a big bowl. Put in 1 egg at a time, whisk well after each addition. Whisk in vanilla and Dr Pepper in a slow stream.
- Pour the batter into the prepared pans. Bake until the top springs back when you touch it slightly, 20-25 minutes. Let cool in pans for 10 minutes, then transfer to wire racks; discard the paper. Allow to cool completely.
- To make frosting, beat the butter and cream cheese in a big bowl until smooth. Whisk in cocoa. Put in vanilla and confectioners' sugar; whisk until creamy.
- Arrange 1 cake layer on a serving plate, then spread half a cup of frosting on top. Repeat the layers. Add the last cake layer on top. Spread the remaining frosting over the sides and top of the cake.

Nutrition Information

- Calories:
- Protein:
- Total Fat:
- Sodium:
- Fiber:
- Total Carbohydrate:
- Cholesterol:

---

480. Dreamy Creamy Peanut Butter Pie

Serving: 8 servings. | Prep: 30mins | Cook: 10mins | Ready in:

Ingredients

- 24 Nutter Butter cookies, crushed
- 1/3 cup butter, melted
- 1 cup cold 2% milk
- 1 package (3.4 ounces) instant vanilla pudding mix
- 1 cup creamy peanut butter
- 4 ounces cream cheese, softened
- 1/2 cup sweetened condensed milk
- 1/4 cup hot fudge ice cream topping, warmed
- 1 cup heavy whipping cream
- 2 tablespoons sugar
- Chocolate curls

Direction

- Mix together butter and cookie crumbs together until combined; pat onto the bottom and up the sides of an ungreased 9-inch pie plate. Bake for 6 to 8 minutes at 350° until crust turns brown lightly. Allow crust to cool on a wire rack.
- Combine pudding mix and milk in a small mixing bowl for 2 minutes until thickened. Beat cream cheese, condensed milk, and peanut butter in a large mixing bowl until smooth; mix in pudding. Put to one side.
- Gently distribute ice cream topping into the baked crust. Beat cream cheese in a large mixing bowl until starting to thicken. Beat in sugar until stiff peaks form. Mix 1 1/2 cups into pudding mixture; transfer mixture to the crust. Top with the rest of whipped cream; sprinkle with chocolate curls. Chill until ready to serve.

Nutrition Information

- Calories: 745 calories
- Total Fat: 51g fat (22g saturated fat)
- Sodium: 604mg sodium
- Fiber: 3g fiber)
- Total Carbohydrate: 63g carbohydrate (42g sugars
- Cholesterol: 86mg cholesterol
- Protein: 16g protein.

481. Easy Banana Cream Pie

Serving: Makes 8 servings. | Prep: 15mins | Cook: | Ready in:

Ingredients

- 2 medium ripe banana s, sliced
- 1 ready-to-use reduced-fat graham cracker crumb crust (6 oz.)
- 2-1/2 cups cold fat-free milk
- 2 pkg. (4-serving size each) JELL-O Vanilla Flavor Sugar Free Fat Free Instant Pudding
- 2 cups thawed COOL WHIP FREE Whipped Topping , divided

Direction

- 1. Arrange 1/2 of banana slices onto the bottom of crust. Put aside the remaining banana slices.
- 2. Add milk to a big bowl. Put in dry pudding mixes. Use a wire whisk to beat the mixture until well blended, 2 minutes. Whisk in 1 cup of the whipped topping gently. Scoop 1/2 the pudding mixture into the crust. Add the rest of the banana slices on top, then pour the remaining pudding mixture over.
- 3. Put into the refrigerator until set, 3 hrs. Add the remaining 1 cup of whipped topping on top, then serve. Refrigerate the leftover pie to store.

Nutrition Information

- Calories: 200
- Sodium: 440 mg
- Fiber: 1 g
- Sugar: 17 g
- Protein: 4 g
- Total Fat: 4.5 g
- Saturated Fat: 1.5 g
- Total Carbohydrate: 37 g
- Cholesterol: 0 mg

482. Easy Boston Cream Cake

Serving: 4-6 servings. | Prep: 25mins | Cook: 0mins | Ready in:

Ingredients

- 1-1/2 cups cold half-and-half cream
- 1 package (3.4 ounces) instant vanilla pudding mix
- 1 loaf (10-3/4 ounces) frozen pound cake, thawed
- 3/4 cup confectioners' sugar
- 2 tablespoons baking cocoa
- 4 to 5 teaspoons hot water

Direction

- Beat pudding mix and cream in a big bowl for 2 minutes. Allow to sit until the mixture is soft-set, or about 2 minutes.
- Slice cake horizontally into 3 layers. On a serving plate, put the bottom slice and spread 1/2 pudding on top. Repeat another cake and pudding layer. Finish with the third cake slice on top.
- Mix together cocoa, confectioners' sugar and enough water in a small bowl until the consistency is spreadable. Spread onto the cake, allowing to run down the sides.

Nutrition Information

- Calories: 395 calories
- Total Carbohydrate: 59g carbohydrate (42g sugars
- Cholesterol: 103mg cholesterol
- Protein: 6g protein.
- Total Fat: 15g fat (9g saturated fat)
- Sodium: 442mg sodium
- Fiber: 1g fiber)

483. Easy Chocolate Pound Cake

Serving: 12-14 servings. | Prep: 10mins | Cook: 55mins | Ready in:

Ingredients

- 1 package devil's food cake mix (regular size)
- 1 package (3.9 ounces) instant chocolate pudding mix
- 4 large eggs
- 1-1/4 cups water
- 1/2 cup vegetable oil
- 3/4 cup vanilla frosting

Direction

- Stir together oil, water, eggs, pudding and cake mixes in a big bowl. On low speed, blend until the mixture becomes moist. Increase the speed to medium and blend for 2 minutes. In a greased and floured 10-in fluted tube pan, put the batter. Bake at 350 degrees until a toothpick comes out clean when inserted in the cake's middle, or about 50 minutes to 1 hour. Let the cake cool for 10 minutes; transfer to a wire rack, then cool entirely.
- Into the microwave on high power, heat frosting in a microwaveable bowl until it becomes thin, or about 10 to 15 seconds. Once the cake is cooled, pour the heated frosting over.

Nutrition Information

- Calories: 337 calories
- Total Carbohydrate: 45g carbohydrate (29g sugars
- Cholesterol: 61mg cholesterol
- Protein: 4g protein.
- Total Fat: 15g fat (3g saturated fat)
- Sodium: 448mg sodium
- Fiber: 1g fiber)

484. Easy Chocolate Rice Pudding

Serving: 4 servings. | Prep: 10mins | Cook: 0mins | Ready in:

Ingredients

- 4 cups cold whole milk
- 1 package (3.9 ounces) instant chocolate pudding mix
- 1/4 cup raisins
- 1/4 teaspoon ground cinnamon
- 1 cup quick-cooking rice
- 1 large egg, well beaten
- 1/8 teaspoon ground nutmeg

Direction

- Mix all ingredients in a medium saucepan. Bring the mixture to a boil over medium heat. Let cool for 5 minutes, whisking two times. Refrigerate until serving.

Nutrition Information

- Calories: 385 calories
- Sodium: 546mg sodium
- Fiber: 1g fiber)
- Total Carbohydrate: 63g carbohydrate (36g sugars
- Cholesterol: 86mg cholesterol
- Protein: 12g protein.
- Total Fat: 10g fat (6g saturated fat)

485. Easy Grasshopper Pie

Serving: 8 servings | Prep: 15mins | Cook: | Ready in:

Ingredients

- 1 cup boiling water
- 1 pkg. (3 oz.) JELL-O Lime Flavor Gelatin
- 1/4 cup cold water
- 2 Tbsp. green creme de menthe

- 2 Tbsp. white creme de cacao liqueur
- 2 cups thawed COOL WHIP Whipped Topping
- 1 OREO Pie Crust (6 oz.)
- 1 oz. BAKER'S Semi-Sweet Chocolate, made into curls

Direction

- 1. In a big bowl, whisk the gelatin mix with boiling water for 2 minutes until completely dissolved. Whisk in liqueurs and cold water. Chill until a bit thickened, 1 1/2 hrs. Slowly whisk in COOL WHIP.
- 2. Scoop the mixture into pie crust.
- 3. Chill until firm for 3 hours. Add the chocolate curls on top just before serving.

Nutrition Information

- Calories: 240
- Protein: 2 g
- Fiber: 1 g
- Sugar: 22 g
- Total Carbohydrate: 34 g
- Cholesterol: 0 mg
- Total Fat: 10 g
- Saturated Fat: 6 g
- Sodium: 170 mg

486. Easy Pineapple Coconut Cake

Serving: 12-15 servings. | Prep: 15mins | Cook: 30mins | Ready in:

Ingredients

- 1 package yellow cake mix (regular size)
- 1-1/4 cups cold 2% milk
- 1 package (3.4 ounces) instant vanilla pudding mix
- 1 can (20 ounces) crushed pineapple, drained

- 1 envelope whipped topping mix (Dream Whip)
- 3 ounces cream cheese, softened
- 1/4 cup sugar
- 1/2 teaspoon vanilla extract
- 1/2 cup sweetened shredded coconut, toasted

Direction

- Prepare and bake the cake as directed on package, baking it in a buttered 13x9-inch baking pan. Allow cake to cool on a wire rack.
- Beat pudding mix and milk in a large mixing bowl for 2 minutes. Fold in pineapple. Spread pudding mixture over cake. Prepare whipped topping mix as directed on package; put to one side.
- Whisk cream cheese, vanilla, and sugar in a small mixing bowl until incorporated. Whisk in 1 cup whipped topping. Add the remaining topping and fold gently. Spread mixture over pudding layer. Scatter top with coconut. Chill, covered, for 3 hours or overnight.

Nutrition Information

- Calories:
- Sodium:
- Fiber:
- Total Carbohydrate:
- Cholesterol:
- Protein:
- Total Fat:

487. Easy Pistachio Bundt Cake

Serving: 12 servings. | Prep: 15mins | Cook: 35mins | Ready in:

Ingredients

- 1 package yellow cake mix (regular size)

- 1 package (3.4 ounces) instant pistachio pudding mix
- 4 large eggs
- 1-1/2 cups water
- 1/4 cup canola oil
- 1/2 teaspoon almond extract
- Confectioners' sugar
- Finely chopped pistachios, optional

Direction

- Set oven to 350 degrees. Grease a fluted tube pan of 10 inches and dust with flour.
- Mix together the first 6 ingredients in a big bowl; blend the mixture for half a minute on low. Increase to medium speed and beat for 2 minutes. Pour batter into the cake pan. Bake in preheated oven until a toothpick is clean when coming out of the middle of the cake, about 35 to 40 minutes. Let the cake cool for 10 minutes in the pan, then transfer to a wire rack and cool fully.
- Sprinkle confectioners' sugar over the cake. Top with pistachios (optional).

Nutrition Information

- Calories: 266 calories
- Fiber: 0 fiber)
- Total Carbohydrate: 41g carbohydrate (24g sugars
- Cholesterol: 62mg cholesterol
- Protein: 4g protein.
- Total Fat: 10g fat (2g saturated fat)
- Sodium: 416mg sodium

488.　　　Easy Strawberry Napoleons

Serving: 6 servings. | Prep: 20mins | Cook: 10mins | Ready in:

Ingredients

- 1 sheet puff pastry, thawed according to package directions
- 1 quart fresh strawberries, sliced
- 2 tablespoons sugar
- 1/4 teaspoon vanilla extract
- 1 cup cold whole milk
- 1 package (3.4 ounces) instant vanilla pudding mix
- 2 cups whipped topping
- 1/2 cup semisweet chocolate chips

Direction

- Start preheating the oven to 400°. Roll out the thawed puff pastry on a cutting board. Slice the pastry into 9 squares using a sharp knife. Grease a baking sheet with cooking spray and place the pastry in the prepared pan. Bake until golden brown, 10-15 minutes. Transfer from the pan to a wire rack to cool completely.
- Mix the vanilla, sugar and strawberries in a big bowl and put aside. Stir the pudding mix and milk in a different bowl for 2 minutes. Let it sit until partially set, 2 minutes. Whisk in whipped topping until thoroughly combined. Cover and put into the refrigerator.
- To assemble, horizontally divide puff pastry squares into 18 squares in total. Put aside 6 tops. Arrange 6 of the remaining pieces on individual serving plates. Spread each piece with approximately a quarter cup of pudding mixture. Add a spoonful of strawberries and another puff pastry piece on top. Spread the pastry pieces with the remaining pudding mixture. Add the remaining strawberries and reserved pastry tops on top.
- Microwave the chocolate chips until melted, whisk until smooth. Let it cool a bit. Move the chocolate to a small heavy-duty plastic bag. Slice off a tiny corner from the bag and squeeze the chocolate over the napoleons.

Nutrition Information

- Calories: 464 calories
- Protein: 6g protein.
- Total Fat: 21g fat (10g saturated fat)

- Sodium: 384mg sodium
- Fiber: 6g fiber)
- Total Carbohydrate: 65g carbohydrate (33g sugars
- Cholesterol: 6mg cholesterol

489. Easy Trifle For Two

Serving: 2 servings. | Prep: 15mins | Cook: 0mins | Ready in:

Ingredients

- 16 vanilla wafers
- 2 tablespoons raspberry preserves
- 1/2 cup prepared vanilla pudding
- 2 tablespoons sweetened shredded coconut, toasted
- 1/3 cup prepared tapioca pudding

Direction

- Spread 1/2 tsp. raspberry preserves each on flat side of 12 wafers; crumble leftover wafers. Put aside.
- Put 5 wafers, preserves side facing in, each around edges of 2 single 4-6-oz. dishes. Put 1 wafer, preserves side up, on bottom of each dish. Put vanilla pudding in center; sprinkle 1/2 coconut and wafer crumbs. Put leftover coconut and tapioca pudding over. Cover; refrigerate for 3 hours minimum.

Nutrition Information

- Calories:
- Protein:
- Total Fat:
- Sodium:
- Fiber:
- Total Carbohydrate:
- Cholesterol:

490. Easy Vanilla Ice Cream

Serving: 7 servings. | Prep: 10mins | Cook: 20mins | Ready in:

Ingredients

- 2 cups cold fat-free milk
- 1 can (14 ounces) fat-free sweetened condensed milk
- 1 package (1 ounce) sugar-free instant vanilla pudding mix

Direction

- Whisk all the ingredients in large bowl until the mixture is thickened and blended. Place in the ice cream freezer to freeze following the manufacturer's instructions.
- Move to the freezer container. Freeze, covered, until firm, about 60 mins.

Nutrition Information

- Calories: 196 calories
- Sodium: 264mg sodium
- Fiber: 0 fiber)
- Total Carbohydrate: 41g carbohydrate (38g sugars
- Cholesterol: 5mg cholesterol
- Protein: 7g protein. Diabetic Exchanges: 2-1/2 starch.
- Total Fat: 0 fat (0 saturated fat)

491. Eclair Torte

Serving: 12 servings. | Prep: 20mins | Cook: 30mins | Ready in:

Ingredients

- 1 cup water
- 1/2 cup butter
- 1/4 teaspoon salt
- 1 cup all-purpose flour

- 4 eggs
- 1 package (8 ounces) cream cheese, softened
- 3 cups cold milk
- 2 packages (3.4 ounces each) instant vanilla pudding mix
- 1 carton (12 ounces) frozen whipped topping, thawed
- 2 to 3 tablespoons chocolate syrup

Direction

- Bring butter, salt, and water in a small saucepan to a boil over medium heat. Put in all of the flour and whisk until mixture forms a ball. Turn off the heat; allow to sit for 5 minutes. Put in eggs, one by one, beating well between additions. Keep beating until mixture is shiny and smooth.
- Spread mixture into a greased 13x9-inch baking pan. Bake for 30 to 35 minutes at 400° until puffy and golden brown. Allow to cool entirely on a wire rack. Transfer from the baking pan to a serving platter, if desired.
- Whisk cream cheese in a large mixing bowl until light. Add pudding mix and milk; whisk until smooth. Spoon into puff; chill for 20 minutes. Spread whipped topping over cream cheese layer; chill in the fridge. Drizzle chocolate syrup over top right before serving. Chill leftovers.

Nutrition Information

- Calories: 350 calories
- Sodium: 348mg sodium
- Fiber: 0 fiber)
- Total Carbohydrate: 27g carbohydrate (14g sugars
- Cholesterol: 120mg cholesterol
- Protein: 7g protein.
- Total Fat: 23g fat (15g saturated fat)

492.   Eggnog Banana Cream Pies

Serving: 3 servings. | Prep: 20mins | Cook: 0mins | Ready in:

Ingredients

- 39 to 42 reduced-fat vanilla wafers
- 1 small banana, sliced
- 1/4 teaspoon ground nutmeg
- 1 cup fat-free milk
- 2 tablespoons plus 1 teaspoon sugar-free instant vanilla pudding mix
- 4 ounces fat-free cream cheese
- 1/4 teaspoon rum extract
- 1/2 cup fat-free whipped topping, thawed
- TOPPING:
- 1 small banana, sliced
- 1/8 teaspoon ground nutmeg

Direction

- Pack vanilla wafers onto bottoms and around the sides of 3 ungreased 5-inch pie plates. Place slices of banana on bottom wafers. Scatter with 1/4 teaspoon nutmeg. Put to one side.
- Beat pudding mix and milk together for 2 minutes. Whisk cream cheese in a separate bowl until smooth. Add extract and pudding mixture to cream cheese; beat on low speed until incorporated. Add whipped topping and fold gently. Spread cream cheese mixture over banana slices.
- Chill, covered, for 1 hour. Top with banana slices and sprinkle with 1/8 teaspoon nutmeg right before serving.

Nutrition Information

- Calories: 361 calories
- Total Carbohydrate: 67g carbohydrate (35g sugars
- Cholesterol: 6mg cholesterol
- Protein: 11g protein.
- Total Fat: 4g fat (trace saturated fat)

- Sodium: 549mg sodium
- Fiber: 2g fiber)

- Fiber: 1g fiber)
- Total Carbohydrate: 44g carbohydrate (33g sugars

493. Eggnog Ladyfinger Dessert

Serving: 12 servings. | Prep: 20mins | Cook: 0mins | Ready in:

Ingredients

- 2 packages (3 ounces each) ladyfingers, split
- 1 pint raspberry or cranberry sorbet
- 3 cups eggnog
- 1 cup evaporated milk
- 1/2 cup sour cream
- 2 packages (3.4 ounces each) instant vanilla pudding mix
- Fresh raspberries or cranberries and fresh mint leaves

Direction

- Around the edge of a non-oiled 9-inch springform pan, place 24 ladyfingers; place onto the bottom with 16 ladyfingers (keep the leftover to use later). Put sorbet on the ladyfingers. Put a cover on and freeze for 30 minutes.
- Whisk pudding mix, sour cream, evaporated milk, and eggnog together in a big bowl until thickened, about 2 minutes. Add to the sorbet. Put a cover on and freeze for 8 hours or overnight. Take out of the freezer before cutting, about 5-10 minutes. Use mint and raspberries to garnish.

Nutrition Information

- Calories: 275 calories
- Cholesterol: 76mg cholesterol
- Protein: 5g protein.
- Total Fat: 8g fat (5g saturated fat)
- Sodium: 367mg sodium

494. Eggnog Pudding

Serving: 6 | Prep: 10mins | Cook: 2hours | Ready in:

Ingredients

- 1 (5.1 ounce) package instant vanilla pudding mix
- 4 dashes ground cinnamon
- 2 dashes ground nutmeg
- 2 dashes ground cloves
- 1 pinch ground ginger
- 3 cups cold milk

Direction

- In a bowl, mix together cloves, ginger, nutmeg, cinnamon and dry pudding mix until well-combined. Whisk in milk while stirring for 2 minutes, until there are no lumps anymore.
- Transfer the pudding into serving dishes and chill until set, about 2 hours.

Nutrition Information

- Calories: 154 calories;
- Sodium: 394
- Total Carbohydrate: 28.8
- Cholesterol: 10
- Protein: 4.1
- Total Fat: 2.8

495. Eggnog Tube Cake

Serving: 12 servings. | Prep: 15mins | Cook: 40mins | Ready in:

Ingredients

- 1 package white cake mix (regular size)
- 1 package (3.9 ounces) instant vanilla pudding mix
- 4 large eggs
- 1 cup eggnog
- 1/4 cup canola oil
- 2 teaspoons rum extract
- 1-1/2 teaspoons ground nutmeg
- GLAZE:
- 1 cup confectioners' sugar
- 1/4 teaspoon rum extract
- 3 to 4 teaspoons eggnog

Direction

- Mix together nutmeg, extract, oil, eggnog, eggs, pudding mix and cake mix in a big bowl. On medium speed, beat the mixture for 2 minutes.
- Transfer batter to a thoroughly greased fluted tube pan of 10 inches. Bake in 350-degree oven until a toothpick is clean when coming out of the middle, about 38 to 41 minutes. Allow to cool in pan for 10 minutes, then transfer to a wire rack to cool entirely.
- Mix together extract, confectioners' sugar and enough eggnog in a small bowl until the mixture can be drizzled. Drizzle on top of the cake when cooled.

Nutrition Information

- Calories: 355 calories
- Protein: 5g protein.
- Total Fat: 12g fat (3g saturated fat)
- Sodium: 456mg sodium
- Fiber: 0 fiber)
- Total Carbohydrate: 56g carbohydrate (37g sugars
- Cholesterol: 84mg cholesterol

496.   Elegant Eggnog Dessert

Serving: 12 servings. | Prep: 30mins | Cook: 0mins |Ready in:

Ingredients

- 1 can (13-1/2 ounces) Pirouette cookies
- 1/2 cup graham cracker crumbs
- 1/4 cup butter, melted
- 2 packages (8 ounces each) cream cheese, softened
- 2 cups cold eggnog
- 1-1/3 cups cold whole milk
- 2 packages (3.4 ounces each) instant vanilla pudding mix
- 1/2 teaspoon rum extract
- 1/8 teaspoon ground nutmeg
- 1 cup heavy whipping cream

Direction

- Slice every cookie into 2 2-1/2-inch portions; reserve. Crush leftover an-inch portions. Mix butter, cracker crumbs and cookie crumbs in small bowl; force onto base of an oiled 9-inch springform pan.
- Whip cream cheese in a big bowl till smooth. Whip in nutmeg, extract, dry pudding mixes, milk and eggnog till smooth. Beat cream till firm peaks create. Into mixture of pudding, fold the whipped cream. Scoop on top of crust. Place cover and chill for 6 hours to overnight.
- Barely prior to serving, take pan sides off. Surround the dessert with reserved cookies and gently press into the sides. Chill remaining.

Nutrition Information

- Calories: 521 calories
- Cholesterol: 110mg cholesterol
- Protein: 7g protein.
- Total Fat: 34g fat (22g saturated fat)
- Sodium: 381mg sodium
- Fiber: 1g fiber)

- Total Carbohydrate: 48g carbohydrate (33g sugars

- Cholesterol: 29
- Protein: 9.5

497. English Trifle

Serving: 14 | Prep: | Cook: | Ready in:

Ingredients

- 2 (8 or 9 inch) white cake layers, baked and cooled
- 2 pints fresh strawberries
- 1/4 cup white sugar
- 1 pint fresh blueberries
- 2 bananas
- 1/4 cup orange juice
- 1 (3.5 ounce) package instant vanilla pudding mix
- 2 cups milk
- 1 cup heavy whipping cream
- 1/4 cup blanched slivered almonds
- 12 maraschino cherries

Direction

- Slice strawberries; sprinkle sugar. Cut bananas to slices; toss with orange juice. Mix milk and pudding mix till smooth; cut cake to 1-in. cubes.
- Line 1/2 cake cubes on bottom of big glass bowl; layer 1/2 strawberries then 1/2 blueberries then 1/2 bananas. Spread 1/2 pudding on fruit; repeat layers using the same order.
- Whip cream to stiff peaks in medium bowl; spread over trifle. Garnish with slivered almonds and maraschino cherries.

Nutrition Information

- Calories: 633 calories;
- Total Fat: 24
- Sodium: 537
- Total Carbohydrate: 98.4

498. Fancy Mousse Towers

Serving: 2 servings. | Prep: 15mins | Cook: 0mins | Ready in:

Ingredients

- 1/3 cup cold heavy whipping cream
- 2 tablespoons cold 2% milk
- 2 tablespoons instant chocolate fudge pudding mix
- 2 tablespoons chocolate syrup
- 6 chocolate wafers
- Whipped cream, chocolate garnish and fresh mint, optional

Direction

- Beat pudding mix, milk and cream till stiff peaks form in small bowl; put in small resealable plastic bag then cut small hole in corner of bag.
- Drizzle chocolate syrup on 2 serving plates. Put chocolate wafer in middle of every plate; pipe some pudding mixture on. Repeat layers 2 times; garnish with mint, chocolate and whipped cream (optional).

Nutrition Information

- Calories: 311 calories
- Protein: 3g protein.
- Total Fat: 18g fat (10g saturated fat)
- Sodium: 281mg sodium
- Fiber: 1g fiber)
- Total Carbohydrate: 36g carbohydrate (19g sugars
- Cholesterol: 56mg cholesterol

Serving: 8 servings. | Prep: 25mins | Cook: 15mins | Ready in:

Ingredients

- 1/2 cup butter, softened
- 3 tablespoons confectioners' sugar
- 1 cup all-purpose flour
- FILLING:
- 3/4 cup cold milk
- 1 package (3.4 ounces) instant lemon pudding mix
- 1 package (8 ounces) cream cheese, softened
- 1/4 cup confectioners' sugar
- 3 tablespoons lemon juice, divided
- 1/2 cup heavy whipping cream, whipped
- 2 cans (15 ounces each) apricot halves, well drained
- 1/3 cup apricot jam

Direction

- Beat butter with confectioners' sugar together in a small mixing bowl. Beat in flour until well combined. Pat dough onto the bottom and 1/2 inch up the sides of a 9-inch springform pan. Pierce the dough using a fork. Refrigerate for half an hour.
- Set the springform pan on a baking sheet. Bake for 12 to 15 minutes at 425° until golden brown. Allow to cool on a wire rack.
- To make filling; stir pudding mix and milk together in a mixing bowl until thickened, about 2 minutes. Whisk cream cheese, 2 tablespoons lemon juice, and confectioners' sugar together in a small mixing bowl until smooth. Whisk in pudding until well combined. Add whipped cream and fold gently. Spread filling over crust.
- Place apricots over the filling. Stir the rest of lemon juice and jam together; brush over apricot layer. Refrigerate, covered, for a minimum of 3 hours or overnight.

Nutrition Information

- Calories: 443 calories
- Total Carbohydrate: 53g carbohydrate (36g sugars
- Cholesterol: 75mg cholesterol
- Protein: 5g protein.
- Total Fat: 25g fat (16g saturated fat)
- Sodium: 366mg sodium
- Fiber: 1g fiber)

Serving: 12 servings. | Prep: 20mins | Cook: 0mins | Ready in:

Ingredients

- 1 package (15-1/2 ounces) Oreo cookies
- 1 package (8 ounces) cream cheese, softened
- 4 tablespoons butter, softened
- 1 cup confectioners' sugar
- 2 packages (3.4 ounces each) instant vanilla pudding mix
- 3-1/2 cups cold whole milk
- 1 carton (12 ounces) frozen whipped topping, thawed
- 1 new flowerpot (8 x 10 inches)
- Silk flowers
- Candy gummy worms

Direction

- Crush cookies in a blender or food processor until fine. Put to one side. Whisk butter, cream cheese, and sugar in a mixing bowl until smooth. Combine milk and pudding in a separate bowl until incorporated. Mix in cream cheese mixture; add whipped topping and fold gently. Layer cookie crumbs and pudding mixture, alternately, in the flowerpot, finishing with crumbs. Refrigerate for a couple of hours or overnight. Garnish with gummy worms and silk flower.

Nutrition Information

- Calories:
- Protein:
- Total Fat:
- Sodium:
- Fiber:
- Total Carbohydrate:
- Cholesterol:

501. Fluffy Chocolate Mousse Frosting

Serving: 3-1/2 cups. | Prep: 10mins | Cook: 0mins | Ready in:

Ingredients

- 1 cup cold 2% milk
- 1 package (3.9 ounces) instant chocolate fudge pudding mix
- 1 carton (8 ounces) frozen whipped topping, thawed

Direction

- Whisk together pudding mix and milk in a big bowl about 2 minutes, then fold in whipped topping. Keep in the fridge for storage.

Nutrition Information

- Calories: 78 calories
- Fiber: 0 fiber)
- Total Carbohydrate: 11g carbohydrate (7g sugars
- Cholesterol: 2mg cholesterol
- Protein: 1g protein.
- Total Fat: 3g fat (3g saturated fat)
- Sodium: 108mg sodium

502. French Vanilla Cream Puffs

Serving: about 2-1/2 dozen. | Prep: 30mins | Cook: 20mins |Ready in:

Ingredients

- 1 cup water
- 1/2 cup butter
- 1 cup all-purpose flour
- 1/4 teaspoon salt
- 4 eggs
- FILLING:
- 1-1/2 cups cold milk
- 1 package (3.4 ounces) instant French vanilla pudding mix
- 1 cup whipped topping
- 1 package (12 ounces) miniature semisweet chocolate chips
- Confectioners' sugar

Direction

- Bring butter and water in a saucepan to a boil. Pour salt and flour all at once; whisk until mixture forms a smooth ball. Turn off the heat; allow to sit for 5 minutes. Put in eggs, one by one, beating well between additions. Beat until mixture is shiny and smooth.
- Drop mixture onto greased baking sheets by rounded tablespoonfuls, separating them 2 inches apart. Bake for 20 to 25 minutes at 400° until golden brown. Transfer puffs to wire rack. Instantly make a slit in each puff to release steam. Allow puffs to cool. Split puffs and take out soft dough.
- To make filling, beat pudding mix and milk in a mixing bowl for 2 minutes on low speed. Chill for 5 minutes. Fold in chips and whipped topping. Fill cream into puffs right before serving; replace tops. Dust confectioners' sugar on top.

Nutrition Information

- Calories: 132 calories

- Total Carbohydrate: 14g carbohydrate (10g sugars
- Cholesterol: 38mg cholesterol
- Protein: 2g protein.
- Total Fat: 8g fat (5g saturated fat)
- Sodium: 111mg sodium
- Fiber: 1g fiber)

503. Frosted Butter Cutouts

Serving: 5-1/2 dozen. | Prep: 30mins | Cook: 40mins | Ready in:

Ingredients

- 1/2 cup butter, softened
- 1 cup sugar
- 1 egg
- 1/2 cup sour cream
- 1 teaspoon vanilla extract
- 3-1/2 cups all-purpose flour
- 1 teaspoon baking soda
- 1/2 teaspoon salt
- FROSTING:
- 1/4 cup cold milk
- 3 tablespoons instant vanilla pudding mix
- 1/4 cup butter, softened
- 2-1/2 cups confectioners' sugar
- 1 teaspoon vanilla extract
- Food coloring, optional

Direction

- Cream sugar and butter together in a big bowl, then beat in vanilla, sour cream and egg. Mix together salt, baking soda and flour, then put into the creamed mixture gradually. Place on a cover and refrigerate for an hour, or until handle easily.
- Roll out the dough on a work surface coated heavily with confectioners' sugar to the thickness of 1/8 inch. Use a 2 1/2 inch cookie cutter to cut the dough, then arrange on baking sheets coated with grease by 1 inch apart. Bake at 375 degrees until browned

slightly, or for 8 to 10 minutes. Transfer to wire racks instantly to cool.
- To make frosting, mix together pudding mix and milk until smooth, then put aside. Cream butter in a big bowl, then beat in pudding mixture. Put in food coloring, if wished, vanilla and confectioners' sugar gradually, then beat on high speed until fluffy and light. Use the frosting to frost cookies.

Nutrition Information

- Calories:
- Total Fat:
- Sodium:
- Fiber:
- Total Carbohydrate:
- Cholesterol:
- Protein:

504. Frosted Cinnamon Rolls

Serving: 21 rolls. | Prep: 35mins | Cook: 20mins | Ready in:

Ingredients

- 1 cup warm milk (70° to 80°)
- 1/4 cup water (70° to 80°)
- 1/4 cup butter, softened
- 1 large egg
- 1 teaspoon salt
- 4 cups bread flour
- 1/4 cup instant vanilla pudding mix
- 1 tablespoon sugar
- 1 tablespoon active dry yeast
- FILLING:
- 1/4 cup butter, softened
- 1 cup packed brown sugar
- 2 teaspoons ground cinnamon
- FROSTING:
- 4 ounces cream cheese, softened
- 1/4 cup butter, softened
- 1-1/2 cups confectioners' sugar

- 1-1/2 teaspoons milk
- 1/2 teaspoon vanilla extract

Direction

- Put initial 9 ingredients in order recommended by manufacturer in bread machine pan. Choose dough setting. After 5 minutes of mixing, check dough. If needed, add 1-2 tablespoons flour/water.
- Turn dough on lightly floured surface when cycle is complete. Roll to 17x10-in. rectangle. Spread butter on. Sprinkle cinnamon and brown sugar. Roll up, starting from long side, jelly-roll style. To seal, pinch seam. Slice to 21 slices.
- Put 12 slices in 13x9-in. greased baking pan, cut side down then 9 rolls in 9-in. square baking pan. Cover. Rise for 45 minutes till doubled in warm place.
- Bake for 20-25 minutes or till golden brown at 350°. On wire racks, cool for 10 minutes.
- Beat frosting ingredients till smooth in big bowl. Frost warm rolls. Keep in fridge.

Nutrition Information

- Calories: 266 calories
- Fiber: 1g fiber)
- Total Carbohydrate: 41g carbohydrate (21g sugars
- Cholesterol: 33mg cholesterol
- Protein: 4g protein.
- Total Fat: 10g fat (6g saturated fat)
- Sodium: 208mg sodium

505.   Frosty Coffee Pie

Serving: 8 servings. | Prep: 15mins | Cook: 0mins | Ready in:

Ingredients

- 1/4 cup hot fudge ice cream topping, warmed
- 1 chocolate crumb crust (9 inches)

- 3 cups coffee ice cream, softened
- 1 package (5.9 ounces) instant chocolate pudding mix
- 1/2 cup cold strong brewed coffee
- 1/4 cup cold 2% milk
- 1-3/4 cups whipped topping
- 1 cup marshmallow creme
- 1/4 cup miniature semisweet chocolate chips

Direction

- Spread ice cream topping on crust. Beat milk, coffee, dry pudding mix and ice cream in a big bowl till blended. Spoon onto crust.
- Mix marshmallow crème and whipped topping in another bowl. Spread on the top. Sprinkle chocolate chips on top. Freeze, covered, till firm.

Nutrition Information

- Calories: 429 calories
- Total Carbohydrate: 67g carbohydrate (48g sugars
- Cholesterol: 20mg cholesterol
- Protein: 5g protein.
- Total Fat: 17g fat (9g saturated fat)
- Sodium: 463mg sodium
- Fiber: 2g fiber)

506.   Frosty Peanut Butter Cups

Serving: 1 dozen. | Prep: 15mins | Cook: 0mins | Ready in:

Ingredients

- 1 cup reduced-fat graham cracker crumbs (about 5 whole crackers)
- 2 tablespoons butter, softened
- 1 cup cold 1% milk
- 1/2 cup reduced-fat creamy peanut butter

- 1 package (3.4 ounces) instant vanilla pudding mix
- 2 cups fat-free whipped topping

Direction

- Toss cracker crumbs with butter in a small mixing bowl. Pat about 1 tablespoon each into 12 muffin cups lined with paper.
- Beat peanut butter and milk together in a large mixing bowl until incorporated. Beat in pudding mix until well combined. Add whipped topping and fold gently. Place in the freezer until set. Peel off liners; allow to sit for 5 minutes at room temperature before serving.

Nutrition Information

- Calories: 154 calories
- Protein: 4g protein. Diabetic Exchanges: 1-1/2 starch
- Total Fat: 6g fat (1g saturated fat)
- Sodium: 277mg sodium
- Fiber: 1g fiber)
- Total Carbohydrate: 23g carbohydrate (0 sugars
- Cholesterol: 1mg cholesterol

507. Frosty Pistachio Delight

Serving: 15 servings. | Prep: 15mins | Cook: 10mins | Ready in:

Ingredients

- 2-1/2 cups chocolate graham cracker crumbs
- 2/3 cup butter, melted
- 1 carton (1-1/2 quarts) vanilla ice cream, softened
- 2 packages (3.4 ounces each) instant pistachio pudding mix
- 1 cup plus 2 tablespoons pistachios, chopped, divided
- 3 drops green food coloring, optional

- 1 carton (8 ounces) frozen whipped topping, thawed
- 1 jar (11-3/4 ounces) hot fudge ice cream topping, warmed

Direction

- Mix together the butter and cracker crumbs in a small bowl, then press it on a 13x9-inch baking dish that's greased. Let it bake for 7 to 9 minutes at 350 degrees or until it becomes set. Let it cool on a wire rack.
- Mix together the food coloring (if preferred), 1 cup pistachios, pudding mixes and ice cream in a big bowl, then fold in the whipped topping. Spread on top of the crust. Put cover and let it freeze for a minimum of 4 hours.
- Take it out of the freezer 10 minutes prior to serving. Drizzle fudge topping on top and sprinkle it with the leftover pistachios.

Nutrition Information

- Calories: 476 calories
- Protein: 6g protein.
- Total Fat: 25g fat (13g saturated fat)
- Sodium: 444mg sodium
- Fiber: 2g fiber)
- Total Carbohydrate: 57g carbohydrate (35g sugars
- Cholesterol: 49mg cholesterol

508. Frozen Cranberry Pie With Candied Almonds

Serving: 8 servings. | Prep: 30mins | Cook: 0mins | Ready in:

Ingredients

- 24 gingersnap cookies
- 3/4 cup milk
- 2 packages (3.4 ounces each) instant French vanilla pudding mix

- 1 can (14 ounces) whole-berry cranberry sauce
- 1 carton (8 ounces) frozen French vanilla whipped topping, thawed, divided
- 1/2 cup slivered almonds, divided
- 1 teaspoon chopped crystallized ginger
- 1 teaspoon almond extract
- 2 teaspoons butter
- 2 tablespoons brown sugar

Direction

- Place the cookies around the sides and bottom of an ungreased 9-inch pie plate; trim the cookies to fit into the dish if necessary.
- Mix the pudding mixes and milk in a small bowl. Whisk in the almond extract, ginger, 1/3 cup of almonds, half a cup of whipped topping, and the cranberry sauce. Spread over the prepared pie plate and refrigerate for an hour.
- At the same time, melt the butter in a small heavy skillet. Put in the remaining almonds and cook over medium heat for 4 minutes until the nuts are toasted. Drizzle sugar over the nuts. Cook while stirring until the sugar melts for 2-4 minutes. Spread on foil to cool.
- Spread the filling with the remaining whipped topping, then sprinkle almonds on top. Freeze, covered, overnight.

Nutrition Information

- Calories: 413 calories
- Protein: 3g protein.
- Total Fat: 12g fat (7g saturated fat)
- Sodium: 504mg sodium
- Fiber: 2g fiber)
- Total Carbohydrate: 72g carbohydrate (43g sugars
- Cholesterol: 5mg cholesterol

509.   Frozen Lemon Pie

Serving: 6-8 servings. | Prep: 5mins | Cook: 0mins | Ready in:

Ingredients

- 1-3/4 cups cold milk
- 2 packages (3.4 ounces each) instant vanilla pudding mix
- 3/4 cup thawed lemonade concentrate
- 1 carton (8 ounces) frozen whipped topping, thawed
- 1 graham cracker crust (9 inches)

Direction

- Stir pudding mixes and milk in a large bowl for two minutes. Allow to sit until the mixture is soft-set, about 2 minutes. Put in lemonade concentrate and stir for half a minute. Fold whipped topping into the mixture right away. Scoop mixture into the cracker crust. Put into the freezer for 25 minutes until the mixture sets.

Nutrition Information

- Calories: 300 calories
- Total Fat: 12g fat (7g saturated fat)
- Sodium: 318mg sodium
- Fiber: 0 fiber)
- Total Carbohydrate: 44g carbohydrate (34g sugars
- Cholesterol: 7mg cholesterol
- Protein: 3g protein.

510.   Frozen Mousse Brownie Sandwiches

Serving: 15 servings. | Prep: 30mins | Cook: 15mins | Ready in:

Ingredients

- 1 package reduced-fat brownie mix (13-inch x 9-inch pan size)
- 2 cups cold fat-free milk
- 2 packages (1 ounce each) sugar-free instant vanilla pudding mix
- 3 tablespoons vanilla or white chips, melted and cooled
- 1/2 cup reduced-fat whipped topping

Direction

- Use parchment paper to line sides and bottom of 2 13x9-inch baking pans. Use cooking spray to coat the liners. Follow directions on package to make brownie mix; distribute evenly between 2 pans.
- Bake in 350-degree oven until a toothpick has moist crumbs when coming out from the center of a cake and edges start to pull away from sides of the pans, about 15 to 18 minutes. Place on wire racks to cool.
- Beat pudding mixes and milk together in a bowl for 2 minutes to make mousse. Mix a little amount of pudding into melted chips, then put all back into the pudding. Fold in whipped topping.
- Use plastic wrap to cover 2 upturned 15x10x1-inch baking pans or big cutting boards. Turn upside down 1 brownie pan onto a prepped pan or board. Lightly remove parchment paper. Spread to within half inch of edges with mousse. Gently turn upside down the other brownie layer onto the second pan or board. Lightly remove parchment paper and place over mousse layer, right side down.
- Keep frozen while covered until filling is firm, about 4 hours. Take out of the freezer 10 minutes before cutting into sandwiches. Wrap remaining sandwiches separately and freeze to store.

Nutrition Information

- Calories: 206 calories
- Fiber: 1g fiber)
- Total Carbohydrate: 40g carbohydrate (0 sugars

- Cholesterol: 1mg cholesterol
- Protein: 4g protein. Diabetic Exchanges: 2-1/2 starch.
- Total Fat: 5g fat (2g saturated fat)
- Sodium: 199mg sodium

511.   Frozen Pistachio Dessert With Raspberry Sauce

Serving: 12 servings. | Prep: 25mins | Cook: 10mins | Ready in:

Ingredients

- 1-1/2 cups crushed vanilla wafers (about 45 wafers)
- 1/4 cup finely chopped pistachios
- 1/4 cup reduced-fat butter, melted
- 1-1/4 cups fat-free milk
- 1 package (1 ounce) sugar-free instant pistachio pudding mix
- 6 ounces reduced-fat cream cheese
- 1 carton (8 ounces) frozen fat-free whipped topping, thawed, divided
- 1 package (12 ounces) frozen unsweetened raspberries, thawed
- 2 tablespoons sugar
- 2 tablespoons orange liqueur or orange juice
- 2 tablespoons chopped pistachios

Direction

- Combine butter, wafers and finely chopped pistachios in a small bowl. Press onto bottom a 9-in. springform pan coated with the cooking spray. Put the pan on baking sheet. Bake for 10 mins at 350°, until lightly browned. Place on a wire rack to cool.
- In the meantime, whisk pudding mix and milk in a small bowl for 2 mins. Allow to stand until soft-set, about 2 mins. Beat the cream cheese in large bowl until smooth. Then beat in pudding.
- For garnish, put aside 3/4 cup of the whipped topping. Fold the remaining whipped topping

into the cream cheese mixture. Add the filling over the crust. Put in freezer 5 hours or up to overnight. Place the remaining whipped topping in refrigerator, covered.

- To make sauce: in a food processor, put liqueur, sugar and raspberries. Cover, process until smooth, about 1 to 2 mins. Strain and remove the pulp and seeds. Place in the refrigerator until serving.
- Discard the dessert from freezer 15 mins before using. Discard the sides of the pan. Add the remaining whipped topping and chopped pistachios for garnish. Enjoy with sauce.

Nutrition Information

- Calories: 214 calories
- Sodium: 268mg sodium
- Fiber: 2g fiber)
- Total Carbohydrate: 28g carbohydrate (14g sugars
- Cholesterol: 18mg cholesterol
- Protein: 4g protein. Diabetic Exchanges: 2 starch
- Total Fat: 9g fat (4g saturated fat)

512.   Fruit 'n' Pudding Dessert

Serving: 15 servings. | Prep: 30mins | Cook: 0mins | Ready in:

Ingredients

- 1 cup graham cracker crumbs
- 1/2 cup ground pecans
- 1/3 cup butter, melted
- 1/4 cup sugar
- 1 can (8 ounces) crushed pineapple
- 3 medium firm bananas, peeled and cut into 1/4-inch slices
- 1 package (8 ounces) cream cheese, softened
- 3-1/2 cups cold milk
- 2 packages (3.4 ounces each) instant lemon pudding mix

- TOPPING:
- 1 carton (8 ounces) frozen whipped topping, thawed
- 1/2 cup finely chopped pecans

Direction

- Mix the sugar, butter, pecans, and graham cracker crumbs in a small bowl. Press the crust into an ungreased 13x9-inch dish.
- Strain the pineapple, save the juice; put aside the pineapple. Add bananas to a small bowl and put in the reserve juice. Let it sit for 5-10 minutes, then strain. Place the bananas in 1 layer over the crust.
- Beat the cream cheese in a big bowl until smooth. Whisk in milk in a slow stream. Put in pudding mixes and beat until blended on low speed. Pour over the bananas, then add the pineapple on top. Spread the top with whipped topping; add the chopped pecans over. Cover and chill for a minimum of 2 hrs, then serve.

Nutrition Information

- Calories:
- Cholesterol:
- Protein:
- Total Fat:
- Sodium:
- Fiber:
- Total Carbohydrate:

513.   Fruit Fluff

Serving: 12 servings. | Prep: 10mins | Cook: 0mins | Ready in:

Ingredients

- 2 cups (16 ounces) fat-free reduced-sugar vanilla yogurt
- 1 package (1 ounce) sugar-free instant white chocolate or vanilla pudding mix

- 1 carton (8 ounces) frozen reduced-fat whipped topping, thawed
- 1 can (20 ounces) unsweetened pineapple tidbits, drained
- 1 can (11 ounces) mandarin oranges, drained
- 1/2 cup halved seedless red grapes

Direction

- Beat pudding mix and yogurt for 2 minutes in a large mixing bowl until thickened. Add whipped topping and fold gently. Mix in the fruit. Chill until ready to serve.

Nutrition Information

- Calories: 95 calories
- Protein: 1g protein. Diabetic Exchanges: 1/2 starch
- Total Fat: 2g fat (2g saturated fat)
- Sodium: 93mg sodium
- Fiber: 1g fiber)
- Total Carbohydrate: 17g carbohydrate (11g sugars
- Cholesterol: 1mg cholesterol

514.   Fruit Topped Almond Cream

Serving: 8 servings. | Prep: 15mins | Cook: 0mins | Ready in:

Ingredients

- 1 package (3.4 ounces) instant French vanilla pudding mix
- 2-1/2 cups cold milk
- 1 cup heavy whipping cream
- 1/2 to 3/4 teaspoon almond extract
- 3 cups assorted fruit (strawberries, grapes, raspberries, blueberries, mandarin oranges)

Direction

- Mix the milk and pudding mix in a big bowl. Whisk for 2 minutes on low speed, then put aside.
- Whisk the extract and cream in a small bowl until stiff peaks form. Fold into the pudding. Scoop the mixture into a shallow 2-quart serving dish. Refrigerate. Add fruit on top prior to serving.

Nutrition Information

- Calories: 222 calories
- Total Carbohydrate: 23g carbohydrate (19g sugars
- Cholesterol: 51mg cholesterol
- Protein: 3g protein.
- Total Fat: 14g fat (8g saturated fat)
- Sodium: 220mg sodium
- Fiber: 1g fiber)

515.   Fruity Angel Food Trifle

Serving: 16-20 servings. | Prep: 20mins | Cook: 0mins | Ready in:

Ingredients

- 4 cups cold milk
- 2 packages (3.4 ounces each) instant vanilla pudding mix
- 1 prepared angel food cake (8 to 10 ounces)
- 1 carton (8 ounces) frozen whipped topping, thawed
- 1 can (20 ounces) pineapple tidbits, drained
- 1 can (15-1/4 ounces) sliced pears, drained
- 1 pint strawberries, sliced
- 4 kiwifruit, peeled, halved and thinly sliced
- 1 cup fresh or frozen blueberries, thawed

Direction

- Beat pudding mix and milk for 2 minutes on low speed in big bowl; put aside.

- Horizontally split cake to thirds; put 1 layer in 5-qt. trifle/serving bowl 9-in. in diameter. Put 1/3 pudding, whipped topping then fruit over; repeat layers 2 times. Cover; chill for a minimum of 3 hours.

Nutrition Information

- Calories:
- Protein:
- Total Fat:
- Sodium:
- Fiber:
- Total Carbohydrate:
- Cholesterol:

---

516. Fruity Hazelnut Trifle

Serving: 12-14. | Prep: 15mins | Cook: 0mins | Ready in:

Ingredients

- 1-1/2 cups cold milk
- 2 tablespoons refrigerated hazelnut nondairy creamer
- 1 package (3.4 ounces) instant vanilla pudding mix
- 1 can (21 ounces) apple pie filling
- 1 can (14 ounces) whole-berry cranberry sauce
- 1 loaf (10-3/4 ounces) frozen pound cake, thawed and cubed
- 2 cups whipped topping

Direction

- Whisk pudding mix, creamer and milk for 2 minutes in big bowl; stand till soft set for 2 minutes. Mix cranberry sauce and pie filling in another bowl.
- Put 1/3 cake cubes in 3-qt. trifle bowl; layer using 1/4 cranberry mixture then 1/3 pudding mixture. Repeat the layers two times.

- Put leftover cranberry mixture over; garnish with whipped topping. Cover; refrigerate till serving.

Nutrition Information

- Calories: 247 calories
- Total Carbohydrate: 45g carbohydrate (31g sugars
- Cholesterol: 35mg cholesterol
- Protein: 2g protein.
- Total Fat: 7g fat (4g saturated fat)
- Sodium: 215mg sodium
- Fiber: 1g fiber)

---

517. Fudgy Almond Pops

Serving: 8 pops. | Prep: 10mins | Cook: 0mins | Ready in:

Ingredients

- 2 cups whole milk
- 1 package (3.9 ounces) instant chocolate fudge pudding mix
- 1/2 cup sugar
- 1/2 cup amaretto-flavored refrigerated nondairy creamer
- 1/8 teaspoon almond extract
- 8 freezer pop molds or 8 paper cups (3 ounces each) and wooden pop sticks

Direction

- Whisk extract, creamer, sugar, pudding mix and milk till creamy in big bowl or for 2 minutes. Put into cups/molds. Put holders on molds. Top with foil then insert sticks through foil if using cups. Freeze till firm.

Nutrition Information

- Calories:
- Cholesterol:
- Protein:

- Total Fat:
- Sodium:
- Fiber:
- Total Carbohydrate:

518.   Fudgy Chocolate Dessert

Serving: 20 servings. | Prep: 25mins | Cook: 20mins | Ready in:

Ingredients

- 1 package chocolate cake mix (regular size)
- 1 can (15 ounces) solid-pack pumpkin
- 3 cups cold fat-free milk
- 2 packages (1.4 ounces each) sugar-free instant chocolate pudding mix
- 1 package (8 ounces) fat-free cream cheese
- 1 carton (8 ounces) frozen reduced-fat whipped topping, thawed
- 1/4 cup fat-free hot fudge ice cream topping
- 1/4 cup fat-free caramel ice cream topping
- 1/4 cup sliced almonds, toasted

Direction

- Mix pumpkin and cake mix in a large bowl (the mixture should be thick). Transfer to a 13x9-in. baking dish coated with cooking spray and evenly spread.
- Bake at 375° until the inserted toothpick in the center is clean when coming out or for 20-25 minutes. Completely cool on a wire rack.
- Beat pudding mixes and milk for 2 minutes in a large bowl. Rest until soft-set or for 2 minutes.
- Whisk cream cheese until smooth in a small bowl. Add pudding; whisk until well blended. Spread over cake. Keep in the fridge with a cover for at least 2 hours.
- Spread whipped topping over dessert right before serving. Drizzle with caramel toppings and fudge; top with almonds. Keep leftovers in the fridge.

Nutrition Information

- Calories: 200 calories
- Total Carbohydrate: 35g carbohydrate (19g sugars
- Cholesterol: 2mg cholesterol
- Protein: 5g protein. Diabetic Exchanges: 2 starch
- Total Fat: 5g fat (2g saturated fat)
- Sodium: 376mg sodium
- Fiber: 2g fiber)

519.   Fudgy Raspberry Torte

Serving: 12 servings. | Prep: 20mins | Cook: 15mins | Ready in:

Ingredients

- 1 package chocolate fudge cake mix (regular size)
- 1-1/3 cups water
- 3 eggs
- 1/3 cup vegetable oil
- 3/4 cup ground pecans
- 1-1/2 cups cold milk
- 1 package (3.9 ounces) instant chocolate fudge or chocolate pudding mix
- 1/2 cup seedless raspberry jam
- 1-1/2 cups whipped topping
- 1/4 cup finely chopped pecans
- Fresh raspberries

Direction

- Mix oil, eggs, water, and cake mix in a large bowl; whisk for half a minute at low speed. Whisk for 2 minutes at medium speed. Add ground pecans and stir.
- Add into 3 floured and greased 9-inch round baking pans. Bake at 350 degrees until a toothpick comes out clean when inserted into the center, for 15-20 minutes. Let cool for 10 minutes, then transfer from pans onto wire racks to completely cool.

- Beat pudding mix and milk in a large bowl for 2 minutes. Allow to stand until soft-set, for 2 minutes. Melt the jam in a saucepan. Brush over the top of each cake.
- On a serving plate, arrange a cake layer; spread 1/2 of the pudding over. Repeat the layers. Place the third cake layer on top; spread the whipped topping over the top. Dust with the chopped pecans. Add raspberries to decorate. Keep in the fridge.

Nutrition Information

- Calories: 415 calories
- Total Fat: 19g fat (5g saturated fat)
- Sodium: 413mg sodium
- Fiber: 2g fiber)
- Total Carbohydrate: 55g carbohydrate (36g sugars
- Cholesterol: 57mg cholesterol
- Protein: 5g protein.

---

little thicker, 2 minutes. Fold 1/2 whipped topping into the mixture. Spread onto crust.
- In a separate bowl, beat white chocolate pudding mix and remaining milk until they become a little thicker, 2 minutes. Fold the rest of whipped topping into mixture; lather on top of the fudge pudding layer. Chill in the refrigerator to set for 4 hours. Sprinkle shaved chocolate on top to decorate.

Nutrition Information

- Calories: 208 calories
- Fiber: 1g fiber)
- Total Carbohydrate: 28g carbohydrate (0 sugars
- Cholesterol: 1mg cholesterol
- Protein: 4g protein. Diabetic Exchanges: 2 starch
- Total Fat: 7g fat (5g saturated fat)
- Sodium: 154mg sodium

---

520.   Fudgy White Chocolate Pudding Pie

Serving: 8 servings. | Prep: 20mins | Cook: 0mins | Ready in:

Ingredients

- 2 cups cold-fat-free milk, divided
- 1 package (1.4 ounces) sugar-free instant chocolate fudge pudding mix
- 1 carton (8 ounces) frozen reduced-fat whipped topping, thawed, divided
- 1 reduced-fat graham cracker crust (8 inches)
- 1 package (1 ounce) sugar-free instant white chocolate or vanilla pudding mix
- 1/2 ounce semisweet chocolate, shaved

Direction

- Beat chocolate fudge pudding mix and one cup milk in a small bowl until they become a

---

521.   Gift Box Wedding Cake

Serving: 50 servings. | Prep: 01hours35mins | Cook: 60mins | Ready in:

Ingredients

- 1-1/3 cups poppy seeds, divided
- 4 packages white cake mix (regular size)
- 1 package (3.4 ounces) instant lemon pudding mix
- FROSTING:
- 1-1/2 cups butter, softened
- 15 cups confectioners' sugar
- 3/4 cup half-and-half cream
- 1-1/2 teaspoons vanilla extract
- 1/2 teaspoon salt
- Pink liquid or paste food coloring

Direction

- In each of the 4 small bowls, put 1/3 cup poppy seeds; as mentioned in cake mix directions, add water to each bowl and soak for an hour.
- Follow package directions to prep cake batters, using poppy seed water then bake in 2 8-in. square pans and 3 13x9-in. greased and floured baking pans. Cool for 10 minutes. Transfer from pans onto wire racks; fully cool. Follow package directions to prep pudding; refrigerate.
- Frosting: Cream confectioners' sugar and butter in a big bowl. Add salt, vanilla and cream; beat at medium speed for 3 minutes till fluffy and light. Might need to be done in batches. To 4 1/2 cups of frosting, add food coloring.
- Cut small hole in corner of 2 pastry/plastic bags; insert #5 pastry tip in one bag then #3 in other. Put 1/2 cup pink frosting in the bag with #5 tip then 1/2 cup white frosting into other. Use a damp cloth to cover leftover frosting till needed.
- Trim 2 13x9-inch cakes to 12x8-inch rectangles; level tops. Off each, cut 8x2-inch strip, leaving 2 pieces called A. Halve each strip, making 4 4x2-inch pieces. Lengthwise attach 2 4x2-inch pieces using white frosting to make 4x4-inch pieces called B. Repeat using 2 leftover pieces; put aside.
- Trim leftover 13x9-inch cake to 12x7-inch rectangle; level top. Halve cake to make 2 7x6-inch pieces called C; put aside.
- Level tops of the 8-inch square cakes.
- There are 2 cake pieces including a lemon pudding filling between in each frosted cake layer. Put 1 piece A onto covered board; within 1/2-in. from edge, spread pudding. Put 2nd piece A over; put aside. Repeat the filling process for leftover layers including pieces 8-in. square, B and C; put onto covered boards.
- Bottom layer: Use 3 1/2 cups white frosting to frost piece A. Attach ribbon across piece A's corner, if desired.
- 2nd layer: Use 2 1/2 cups of pink frosting to frost 8-inch cake. Pipe continuous string, down and around, curving up, with prepped

bag of white frosting so strings don't cross or touch cake.
- 3rd layer: Use 2 cups white frosting to frost piece C; pipe dots on entire cake with prepped bag of pink frosting, 1/2-in. apart.
- Use leftover pink frosting to frost piece B; put bow over.
- Cut 1/4-inch dowel to 5 pieces height of every layer for bottom 3 layers; insert dowels in middle of every cake, 1-2-in. apart to support following layer. Stack layers onto serving platter carefully, working from biggest to smallest cake. Decorate as desired with silk flowers and ribbon. Before cutting each layer, remove dowels.

Nutrition Information

- Calories:
- Total Carbohydrate:
- Cholesterol:
- Protein:
- Total Fat:
- Sodium:
- Fiber:

---

522.   Gingerbread Pumpkin Trifle

Serving: 16 servings. | Prep: 35mins | Cook: 25mins | Ready in:

Ingredients

- 1/2 cup shortening
- 1/3 cup sugar
- 1 cup molasses
- 1 egg
- 2-1/3 cups all-purpose flour
- 1 teaspoon baking soda
- 1 teaspoon ground ginger
- 1 teaspoon ground cinnamon
- 3/4 teaspoon salt
- 3/4 cup hot water

- FILLING/TOPPING:
- 2 cups cold milk
- 1 package (3.4 ounces) instant vanilla pudding mix
- 1 can (15 ounces) solid-pack pumpkin
- 1/2 cup packed brown sugar
- 1 teaspoon vanilla extract
- 1/2 teaspoon ground cinnamon
- 2 cups heavy whipping cream
- 1/3 cup sugar
- 1 teaspoon rum extract

Direction

- Cream sugar and shortening till fluffy and light in big bowl; beat egg and molasses in. Mix salt, flour, cinnamon, ginger and baking soda; alternately with water, add to creamed mixture. Beat well after each addition.
- Put in 13x9-in. greased baking pan. Bake for 25-30 minutes at 350° till inserted toothpick in middle exits clean; cool on wire rack. Cut gingerbread to 1/2-1-in. cubes; put aside.
- Whisk pudding mix and milk for 2 minutes in big bowl; stand till soft set for 2 minutes. Mix cinnamon, vanilla, brown sugar and pumpkin; mix into pudding. Beat cream till it starts to thicken in another bowl. Add extract and sugar; beat till stiff peaks form.
- Put 1/4 cup gingerbread cubes aside. Layer 1/3 leftover gingerbread cubes in glass serving bowl/4-qt. trifle bowl. Put 1/3 pumpkin mixture then whipped cream over. Repeat layers two times. Crumble leftover gingerbread; sprinkle on top. Cover; refrigerate before serving for 1 hour minimum.

Nutrition Information

- Calories: 400 calories
- Protein: 4g protein.
- Total Fat: 19g fat (9g saturated fat)
- Sodium: 314mg sodium
- Fiber: 2g fiber)
- Total Carbohydrate: 55g carbohydrate (34g sugars

- Cholesterol: 57mg cholesterol

---

523.   Gingerbread Trifle

Serving: 15 servings, 2/3 cup each | Prep: 15mins | Cook: | Ready in:

Ingredients

- 1 pkg. (14.5 oz.) gingerbread mix
- 2 pkg. (3.4 oz. each) JELL-O Butterscotch Flavor Instant Pudding
- 1 tsp. each ground cinnamon and ground ginger
- 1/4 tsp. ground nutmeg
- 3 cups cold milk
- 1 tub (8 oz.) COOL WHIP Whipped Topping, thawed, divided
- 1 pkg. (4 oz.) BAKER'S White Chocolate
- 6 gingerbread men cookies (3 inch)
- 1/2 cup JET-PUFFED GINGERBREAD MALLOWS Marshmallows

Direction

- Follow package directions to prep gingerbread batter; put in 12 muffin pan cups coated in cooking spray using spoon.
- Bake for 25 minutes or till inserted toothpick in middle exits clean; cool for 10 minutes in pan. Transfer onto wire rack; completely cool.
- Meanwhile, use whisk to beat milk, spices and pudding mixes for 2 minutes in medium bowl; mix 1 cup COOL WHIP in. Refrigerate till needed.
- As direction on package, melt chocolate. Horizontally cut cupcakes in half. For next step, keep bottom cupcake halves for later. Put melted chocolate in piping bag with spoon and use to pipe some chocolate on cupcake tops in a swirl pattern. Decorate as desired with leftover melted chocolate, marshmallows and gingerbread cookies. Refrigerate the decorated marshmallows, cookies and cupcake tops till chocolate is firm.

- Cut leftover cupcake bottoms to quarters; put 1/2 in trifle bowl. Stand 1 cupcake layer tops along trifle bowl's side, decorated sides out. Some cupcake tops may not fit depending on trifle bowl size. Cut to quarters; keep for the following step.
- Put pudding mixture in trifle bowl; put leftover cupcake bottoms then unused cupcake tops over. Put marshmallows, leftover COOL WHIP then gingerbread cookies over.

Nutrition Information

- Calories: 330
- Saturated Fat: 7 g
- Sodium: 460 mg
- Sugar: 38 g
- Total Carbohydrate: 52 g
- Protein: 4 g
- Total Fat: 12 g
- Fiber: 0.6807 g
- Cholesterol: 20 mg

524.   Gingersnap Ice Cream Torte

Serving: 16-20 servings. | Prep: 20mins | Cook: 10mins | Ready in:

Ingredients

- 2 cups finely crushed gingersnaps (about 40 cookies)
- 1/2 cup packed brown sugar
- 1/2 cup butter, melted
- 1 package (14 ounces) caramels
- 1/3 cup half-and-half cream or milk
- 1-1/2 cups cold milk
- 2 packages (3.4 ounces each) instant vanilla pudding mix
- 1/2 gallon vanilla ice cream, softened
- 1/2 cup chopped pecans

Direction

- Mix the butter, brown sugar and gingersnaps in a bowl, then put aside half. Press the remaining half onto the bottom of a greased 9-inch springform pan. Bake for 10 minutes at 350°. Let cool completely. Melt the caramels in a heavy saucepan or in a microwave. Whisk in cream until smooth, then put aside.
- Beat the pudding mixes and milk in a bowl for 2 minutes on low speed. Whisk in ice cream until combined. Scoop half of the mixture into the crust. Add 1/2 of the reserved gingersnap mixture on top. Sprinkle with 1/2 of the caramel sauce, then drizzle 1/2 of the pecans on top. Repeat the layers. Freeze, covered, until firm for a minimum of 4 hrs. Take out of the freezer 15 minutes prior to serving.

Nutrition Information

- Calories: 356 calories
- Cholesterol: 41mg cholesterol
- Protein: 5g protein.
- Total Fat: 17g fat (9g saturated fat)
- Sodium: 310mg sodium
- Fiber: 1g fiber)
- Total Carbohydrate: 50g carbohydrate (37g sugars

525.   Gingersnap Pumpkin Pie

Serving: 8 | Prep: 30mins | Cook: 1hours | Ready in:

Ingredients

- 1 3/4 cups gingersnap cookie crumbs
- 2 1/2 tablespoons butter, melted
- 2 tablespoons white sugar
- 1 1/2 cups canned pumpkin
- 3/4 cup packed brown sugar
- 1 tablespoon cornstarch
- 1 teaspoon ground cinnamon
- 1/4 teaspoon ground nutmeg
- 1/4 teaspoon salt
- 1 teaspoon vanilla extract

- 2 eggs
- 1 (12 fluid ounce) can evaporated milk

Direction

- Preheat the oven to 165 °C or 325 °F.
- In a 9-inch pie pan, mix melted butter, granulated sugar and cookie crumbs. Force into the sides. Allow to bake for 5 minutes. Cool fully.
- Put together the milk, eggs, vanilla, salt, nutmeg, cinnamon, cornstarch, brown sugar and pumpkin. Mix using wire whisk till incorporated.
- Put into the crust. Allow to bake for an hour at 165 °C or 325 °F. Cool down. Chill.

Nutrition Information

- Calories: 315 calories;
- Total Fat: 11.9
- Sodium: 356
- Total Carbohydrate: 47.4
- Cholesterol: 70
- Protein: 6.2

526. Glazed Lemon Cake

Serving: 12 servings. | Prep: 10mins | Cook: 40mins | Ready in:

Ingredients

- 1 package white cake mix (regular size)
- 1 package (3.4 ounces) instant lemon pudding mix
- 3/4 cup canola oil
- 3 eggs
- 1 cup lemon-lime soda
- 1 cup confectioners' sugar
- 2 tablespoons lemon juice

Direction

- In the big bowl, mix eggs, oil, pudding mix, and cake mix; whip on low speed or for half a minute. Whip on medium for 2 minutes. Slowly whip in soda till just blended.
- Add to greased 13x9-inch baking plate. Bake at 350 degrees till the toothpick inserted into middle gets out clean or for 40 to 45 minutes.
- In the small-sized bowl, mix lemon juice and confectioner' sugar till becoming smooth; gently spread on the warm cake. Let cool down on wire rack.

Nutrition Information

- Calories: 398 calories
- Protein: 3g protein.
- Total Fat: 19g fat (3g saturated fat)
- Sodium: 388mg sodium
- Fiber: 1g fiber)
- Total Carbohydrate: 54g carbohydrate (36g sugars
- Cholesterol: 53mg cholesterol

527. Golden Chocolate Cake

Serving: 12 servings. | Prep: 15mins | Cook: 60mins | Ready in:

Ingredients

- 1 package yellow cake mix (regular size)
- 1 package (3.4 ounces) instant vanilla pudding mix
- 4 eggs
- 1 cup sour cream
- 1/2 cup canola oil
- 1/2 cup water
- 3 milk chocolate candy bars (1.55 ounces each), chopped
- 1 cup (6 ounces) semisweet chocolate chips
- 1 cup chopped pecans
- 1 cup sweetened shredded coconut
- Confectioners' sugar, optional

Direction

- Mix water, oil, sour cream, eggs, pudding mix and cake mix together in a big bowl; whisk for 30 seconds on low speed. Whisk for 2 minutes on medium speed. Mix in coconut, nuts, chocolate chips and candy bars.
- Add to a floured and lightly oiled 10-inch fluted tube pan. Bake at 350° until a toothpick will come out clean when you insert it into the middle, or for 60-65 minutes.
- Leave in the pan to cool for 15 minutes, and then transfer to a wire rack to fully cool. Refrigerate before cutting. If you want, dust confectioners' sugar over.

Nutrition Information

- Calories: 412 calories
- Fiber: 2g fiber)
- Total Carbohydrate: 44g carbohydrate (29g sugars
- Cholesterol: 64mg cholesterol
- Protein: 5g protein.
- Total Fat: 25g fat (9g saturated fat)
- Sodium: 330mg sodium

528.　　Golden Pound Cake

Serving: 12 servings. | Prep: 10mins | Cook: 45mins | Ready in:

Ingredients

- 1 package lemon cake mix (regular size)
- 1 package (3.4 ounces) instant vanilla pudding mix
- 4 eggs
- 3/4 cup canola oil
- 1 can (12 ounces) Mountain Dew
- Confectioners' sugar, optional

Direction

- Set oven to preheat at 350°. Combine the cake mix, soda, oil, eggs and pudding mix in a large bowl; beat for 30 seconds on low speed. Beat for another 2 minutes on medium.
- Transfer into a 10-in. fluted tube pan that is greased and floured. Bake till tested done with a toothpick for about 45-50 minutes. Let it cool down for 10 minutes, then transfer from pan to a wire rack to cool thoroughly. If you wish, sprinkle confectioner's sugar on top.

Nutrition Information

- Calories: 363 calories
- Cholesterol: 71mg cholesterol
- Protein: 4g protein.
- Total Fat: 19g fat (4g saturated fat)
- Sodium: 413mg sodium
- Fiber: 1g fiber)
- Total Carbohydrate: 46g carbohydrate (29g sugars

529.　　Gooey Butterscotch Bars

Serving: about 3 dozen. | Prep: 20mins | Cook: 20mins | Ready in:

Ingredients

- 1 package (17-1/2 ounces) sugar cookie mix
- 1 package (3.4 ounces) instant butterscotch pudding mix
- 1/2 cup butter, softened
- 1 large egg
- 1 package (14 ounces) caramels
- 1/2 cup evaporated milk
- 2 cups mixed nuts
- 1 teaspoon vanilla extract
- 1 cup butterscotch chips

Direction

- Mix the egg, butter, pudding mix, and the sugar cookie mix in a big bowl. Press the crust into an ungreased 13x9-inch baking pan. Bake for 20-25 minutes at 350° until set.

- Mix the milk and caramels in a big saucepan. Cook while stirring until melted over medium-low heat. Take away from heat. Whisk in vanilla and nuts. Spread over the crust. Add the butterscotch chips on top.
- Let cool completely. Slice into bars. Keep in an airtight container.

Nutrition Information

- Calories: 199 calories
- Protein: 3g protein.
- Total Fat: 10g fat (4g saturated fat)
- Sodium: 161mg sodium
- Fiber: 1g fiber)
- Total Carbohydrate: 26g carbohydrate (15g sugars
- Cholesterol: 13mg cholesterol

---

530.   Graham Cracker Banana Split Dessert

Serving: 15 servings. | Prep: 25mins | Cook: 0mins | Ready in:

Ingredients

- 2 cups reduced-fat graham cracker crumbs (about 10 whole crackers)
- 5 tablespoons reduced-fat margarine, melted
- 1 can (12 ounces) cold reduced-fat evaporated milk
- 3/4 cup cold fat-free milk
- 2 packages (1 ounce each) sugar-free instant vanilla pudding mix
- 2 medium firm bananas,sliced
- 1 can (20 ounces) unsweetened crushed pineapple, drained
- 1 carton (8 ounces) frozen reduced-fat whipped topping, thawed
- 3 tablespoons chopped walnuts
- 2 tablespoons chocolate syrup

- 5 maraschino cherries, quartered

Direction

- Mix together margarine and cracker crumbs; pat into a 13-in. x 9-in. dish sprayed with cooking spray.
- Whisk together the evaporated milk, fat-free milk and pudding mixes in a large bowl for 2 minutes (mixture will thicken).
- Evenly spread the pudding over the crust. Layer in the bananas, then pineapple and whipped topping. Sprinkle nuts on top and drizzle the top with chocolate syrup. Place cherries on top. Chill in refrigerator for no less than 1 hour before cutting.

Nutrition Information

- Calories: 194 calories
- Total Carbohydrate: 33g carbohydrate (0 sugars
- Cholesterol: 4mg cholesterol
- Protein: 3g protein. Diabetic Exchanges: 1-1/2 starch
- Total Fat: 6g fat (3g saturated fat)
- Sodium: 312mg sodium
- Fiber: 1g fiber)

---

531.   Graham Cracker Butterscotch Pie

Serving: 9 servings. | Prep: 20mins | Cook: 0mins | Ready in:

Ingredients

- 7-1/2 whole reduced-fat graham crackers
- 2 cups cold fat-free milk
- 1 package (1 ounce) sugar-free instant vanilla pudding mix
- 1 package (1/4 ounces) sugar-free instant butterscotch pudding mix
- 2 cups (16 ounces) reduced-fat sour cream

- 1 large ripe banana, cut into 1/4-inch slices
- 1 cup reduced-fat whipped topping

Direction

- Cut or break whole crackers into half. Place 9 graham cracker halves in a 9-inch square dish. Halve the rest of crackers once more; stand them up around the sides of the dish. Blend pudding mixes and milk in a bowl until slightly thicken, about 2 minutes. Put in sour cream; stir well. Place slices of banana over graham crackers; add pudding mixture on top. Refrigerate with a cover for at least 5-6 hours. Serve pie with whipped topping.

Nutrition Information

- Calories: 216 calories
- Cholesterol: 20mg cholesterol
- Protein: 7g protein. Diabetic Exchanges: 1-1/2 starch
- Total Fat: 6g fat (5g saturated fat)
- Sodium: 516mg sodium
- Fiber: 1g fiber)
- Total Carbohydrate: 31g carbohydrate (0 sugars

532. Grandma's Chewy Oatmeal Cookies

Serving: 7 dozen. | Prep: 15mins | Cook: 15mins | Ready in:

Ingredients

- 2 cups butter, softened
- 1-1/2 cups packed brown sugar
- 1/2 cup sugar
- 4 eggs
- 7 cups quick-cooking oats
- 2-1/2 cups all-purpose flour
- 1 package (5.1 ounces) instant vanilla pudding mix

- 2 teaspoons baking soda

Direction

- Cream the sugars and butter in a big bowl until fluffy and light. Put in 1 egg at a time, whisk well after each addition. Mix the baking soda, dry pudding mix, flour and the oats; slowly put into the cream mixture and whisk well.
- Onto lightly coated baking sheets, drop the mixture by heaping tablespoonfuls 2 inches apart. Bake for 12-14 minutes at 375° until golden brown. Transfer to wire racks to cool.

Nutrition Information

- Calories: 214 calories
- Sodium: 206mg sodium
- Fiber: 1g fiber)
- Total Carbohydrate: 28g carbohydrate (13g sugars
- Cholesterol: 44mg cholesterol
- Protein: 4g protein.
- Total Fat: 10g fat (6g saturated fat)

533. Grandma's English Trifle

Serving: 10 servings. | Prep: 30mins | Cook: 0mins | Ready in:

Ingredients

- 1 prepared loaf pound cake or 1 package (10-3/4 ounces) frozen pound cake, thawed
- 1/4 to 1/2 cup raspberry jam
- 1 package (3 to 3-1/2 ounces) regular or instant vanilla pudding mix
- 2-1/2 cups 2% milk
- 1 cup chilled heavy whipping cream
- 3 tablespoons confectioners' sugar
- Slivered almonds
- Maraschino cherries, halved

Direction

- Horizontally cut pound cake in half; spread jam. Put over cake top. Cut cake to 9 pieces; line cake pieces on sides and to fill middle of 2-qt. glass serving bowl. Prep pudding with milk; put on cake. Chill. Beat sugar and cream till soft peaks form; spread on pudding and cake. Chill for minimum of 4 hours; garnish with cherries and almonds.

Nutrition Information

- Calories: 292 calories
- Sodium: 176mg sodium
- Fiber: 0 fiber)
- Total Carbohydrate: 31g carbohydrate (24g sugars
- Cholesterol: 76mg cholesterol
- Protein: 4g protein.
- Total Fat: 16g fat (10g saturated fat)

534.   Hawaiian Cake

Serving: 14 | Prep: | Cook: |Ready in:

Ingredients

- 1 1/2 cups butter
- 2 cups white sugar
- 4 eggs
- 1/2 teaspoon salt
- 2 teaspoons baking soda
- 1 (20 ounce) can crushed pineapple, drained
- 1/4 cup unsweetened pineapple juice
- 1 (3.5 ounce) package flaked coconut
- 1 cup chopped walnuts
- 2 teaspoons vanilla extract
- 1 (16 ounce) package graham crackers, crushed

Direction

- Set oven temperature to 350 degrees F (175 degrees C) and preheat. Cover a tube pan measuring 10-inches with parchment paper and grease.

- Beat together sugar, eggs, and butter or margarine. Mix in baking soda, salt, pineapple juice, and mashed pineapples. Add in vanilla, walnuts, and coconut. Pour in graham cracker crumbs. Fill the pan with the batter until spread evenly.
- Bake for 1 hour and 30 minutes at 350 degrees F (175 degrees C).

Nutrition Information

- Calories: 566 calories;
- Total Fat: 32.5
- Sodium: 644
- Total Carbohydrate: 66.1
- Cholesterol: 105
- Protein: 6

535.   Hawaiian Dessert

Serving: 24 servings. | Prep: 20mins | Cook: 15mins | Ready in:

Ingredients

- 1 package yellow cake mix (regular size)
- 3 packages (3.4 ounces each) instant vanilla pudding mix
- 4 cups cold whole milk
- 1-1/2 teaspoons coconut extract
- 1 package (8 ounces) cream cheese, softened
- 1 can (20 ounces) crushed pineapple, well drained
- 2 cups heavy whipping cream, whipped and sweetened
- 2 cups sweetened shredded coconut, toasted

Direction

- Mix cake batter following the instructions on the package. Pour into two greased 13x9-inch baking pans. Bake at 350° for 15 minutes till the cakes test done. Allow to completely cool.
- In a large bowl, combine coconut extract, milk and pudding mixes; beat for approximately 2

minutes. Add the cream cheese and well beat. Stir in pineapple.

- Spread over the cooled cakes. Add whipped cream on top; sprinkle with coconut. Let chill for at least 2 hours.

Nutrition Information

- Calories:
- Total Fat:
- Sodium:
- Fiber:
- Total Carbohydrate:
- Cholesterol:
- Protein:

536.   Hawaiian Wedding Cake

Serving: 18 servings. | Prep: 20mins | Cook: 25mins | Ready in:

Ingredients

- 1 package yellow cake mix (regular size)
- 1-1/4 cups buttermilk
- 4 large egg whites
- 1 large egg
- 1 package (8 ounces) reduced-fat cream cheese, cubed
- 1 cup cold 2% milk
- 1 package (1 ounce) sugar-free instant vanilla pudding mix
- 2 cans (one 20 ounces, one 8 ounces) unsweetened crushed pineapple, drained
- 1 carton (8 ounces) frozen fat-free whipped topping, thawed
- 1/2 cup sweetened shredded coconut, toasted

Direction

- Mix the egg, egg whites, buttermilk, and the cake mix in a big bowl and beat for half a minute on low speed. Beat for 2 minutes on medium speed.

- Pour into a 13x9-inch baking pan greased with cooking spray. Bake for 25-30 minutes at 350° until the toothpick inserted into the middle comes out clean. Transfer to a wire rack to cool.
- Beat the cream cheese in a small bowl until fluffy. Whisk in pudding mix and milk gradually until well combined. Pour over the cake. Add whipped topping and pineapple on top. Add coconut over. Keep in a refrigerator.

Nutrition Information

- Calories: 221 calories
- Sodium: 378mg sodium
- Fiber: 1g fiber)
- Total Carbohydrate: 38g carbohydrate (0 sugars
- Cholesterol: 17mg cholesterol
- Protein: 6g protein. Diabetic Exchanges: 2 starch
- Total Fat: 5g fat (2g saturated fat)

537.   Holiday Cheesecake Pie

Serving: 2 pies (8 servings each). | Prep: 30mins | Cook: 45mins | Ready in:

Ingredients

- 1 can (15 ounces) solid-pack pumpkin
- 1 can (12 ounces) evaporated milk
- 3/4 cup sugar
- 4 ounces cream cheese, softened
- 1/2 teaspoon pumpkin pie spice
- 1/4 teaspoon salt
- 2 eggs, lightly beaten
- 2 graham cracker crusts (9 inches)
- 1-1/2 cups cold eggnog
- 1 package (3.4 ounces) instant vanilla pudding mix
- 1 cup whipped topping
- Additional whipped topping, optional

Direction

- Whisk salt, pumpkin pie spice, cream cheese, sugar, milk, and pumpkin together in a big bowl. Add eggs, whisk on low speed until just blended. Evenly distribute among the graham cracker crusts.
- Bake at 350° until a knife will come out clean when you insert it into the middle, about 45-55 minutes. Put on a wire rack to cool.
- Beat pudding mix and eggnog in a small bowl for 2 minutes. Fold in whipped topping. Spread onto the pies. Put a cover on and chill for 60 minutes. Use more whipped topping to garnish if you want.

Nutrition Information

- Calories: 266 calories
- Fiber: 1g fiber)
- Total Carbohydrate: 37g carbohydrate (29g sugars
- Cholesterol: 51mg cholesterol
- Protein: 5g protein.
- Total Fat: 11g fat (5g saturated fat)
- Sodium: 297mg sodium

---

538.   Holiday English Trifles

Serving: 15 servings. | Prep: 35mins | Cook: 35mins | Ready in:

Ingredients

- 1 package yellow cake mix (regular size)
- 1/3 cup orange juice or orange liqueur
- 1/3 cup sherry or additional orange juice
- 1 jar (18 ounces) seedless raspberry jam
- 1-1/2 cups cold 2% milk
- 1 package (3.4 ounces) instant vanilla pudding mix
- 1 cup (8 ounces) reduced-fat sour cream
- 2 cups heavy whipping cream
- 3 tablespoons confectioners' sugar

- 1-1/2 cups fresh raspberries

Direction

- Follow package directions to prep and bake cake with 13x9-in. greased baking pan. Cool; slice to 1-in. cubes.
- Mix sherry and orange juice in small bowl. Whisk jam in another bowl. Whisk pudding mix and milk for 2 minutes in big bowl; whisk sour cream in. Stand till soft set for 2 minutes.
- Divide 1/2 cake cubes to 15 dessert dishes/parfait glasses; drizzle 1/2 orange juice mixture. Layer each using pudding mixture and jam. Put leftover cake cubes over; drizzle leftover orange juice mixture. Cover; refrigerate for 4 hours minimum – overnight.
- Before serving, beat cream till it starts to thicken in big bowl. Add confectioners' sugar; beat till stiff peaks form. Dollop on trifles; garnish with raspberries.

Nutrition Information

- Calories: 506 calories
- Total Fat: 24g fat (10g saturated fat)
- Sodium: 364mg sodium
- Fiber: 1g fiber)
- Total Carbohydrate: 68g carbohydrate (51g sugars
- Cholesterol: 92mg cholesterol
- Protein: 5g protein.

---

539.   Holiday Fig Torte

Serving: 12-16 servings. | Prep: 20mins | Cook: 0mins | Ready in:

Ingredients

- 30 to 35 Fig Newton cookies (about 1 pound)
- 1 package (8 ounces) cream cheese, softened
- 1 cup confectioners' sugar
- 2 large bananas, sliced
- 2 tablespoons lemon juice

- 3 cups cold milk
- 1 package (5.1 ounces) instant vanilla pudding mix
- 1 carton (12 ounces) frozen whipped topping, thawed, divided
- 1/2 cup chopped pecans
- Red and green maraschino cherries, well drained

Direction

- Arrange cookies over the bottom of a 13x9-inch dish to cover. Whisk cream cheese and sugar in a large mixing bowl until fluffy; spread cream cheese mixture over cookies.
- Combine bananas with lemon juice; place over the layer of cream cheese. Beat pudding mix and milk together in a separate bowl for 2 minutes. Allow to sit until soft-set, about 2 minutes.
- Add half of the whipped topping and fold gently. Spread over banana layer. Top pudding layer with the rest of whipped topping. Scatter top with pecans. Garnish with cherries. Refrigerate overnight, covered.

Nutrition Information

- Calories: 354 calories
- Protein: 5g protein.
- Total Fat: 16g fat (9g saturated fat)
- Sodium: 305mg sodium
- Fiber: 3g fiber)
- Total Carbohydrate: 47g carbohydrate (35g sugars
- Cholesterol: 22mg cholesterol

540. Homemade Chocolate Easter Eggs

Serving: 20 | Prep: 25mins | Cook: 5mins | Ready in:

Ingredients

- 9 ounces 85% dark chocolate, chopped
- 1/4 cup heavy whipping cream
- 3 tablespoons unsalted butter
- 1 tablespoon rum
- 1/4 cup confectioners' sugar, or to taste
- 1/4 cup unsweetened cocoa powder, or as needed
- 1/4 cup coconut flakes, or as needed

Direction

- Put butter, cream and chocolate in top of double boiler above simmering water. Frequently mix, scraping sides down with rubber spatula to prevent scorching, for about 5 minutes till chocolate melts.
- Take off heat; mix rum in then confectioners' sugar. Briefly cool; cover. Cool till firm for about 5 hours in the fridge.
- Form chocolate mixture to oval eggs. Put coconut flakes and cocoa powder to different small bowls. Roll 1/2 chocolate eggs in cocoa powder and other 1/2 into coconut flakes. Put into fridge.

Nutrition Information

- Calories: 111 calories;
- Sodium: 3
- Total Carbohydrate: 10.1
- Cholesterol: 9
- Protein: 1.1
- Total Fat: 7.9

541. Honey Gingerbread Trifle

Serving: 12 servings. | Prep: 25mins | Cook: 25mins | Ready in:

Ingredients

- 1 cup sour cream
- 1 cup honey
- 1 large egg

- 1/4 cup canola oil
- 2-1/2 cups all-purpose flour
- 1/2 teaspoon salt
- 1 teaspoon baking soda
- 1 teaspoon baking powder
- 2 teaspoons ground ginger
- 1/2 teaspoon ground cinnamon
- PUDDING LAYER:
- 2 cups 2% milk
- 1 package (3.3 ounces) instant white chocolate pudding mix
- PUMPKIN MOUSSE LAYER:
- 1 cup 2% milk
- 1 package (3.4 ounces) instant pumpkin spice pudding mix
- 1 carton (8 ounces) frozen whipped topping, thawed

Direction

- Preheat an oven to 350°. Beat oil, egg, honey and sour cream till blended well. Whisk next 6 ingredients in another bowl; beat into sour cream mixture slowly. Put in 9-in. square greased baking pan; bake for 25-30 minutes till inserted toothpick in middle exits clean. Cool for 5 minutes in pan; transfer to wire rack to completely cool.
- Meanwhile, for pudding layer: whisk white chocolate pudding mix and milk for 2 minutes; stand for 5 minutes till soft set. Refrigerate. Mousse layer: whisk pumpkin spice pudding mix and milk for 2 minutes in another bowl; fold whipped topping in. Refrigerate.
- Assemble: Slice cake to 1-in. cubes. Layer 1/3 cake cubes, pumpkin mousse and white chocolate pudding in 3-qt. trifle bowl/other glass serving dish; repeat layers two times. Refrigerate for 4 hours – overnight, covered.

Nutrition Information

- Calories: 413 calories
- Total Carbohydrate: 64g carbohydrate (44g sugars
- Cholesterol: 25mg cholesterol

- Protein: 6g protein.
- Total Fat: 14g fat (7g saturated fat)
- Sodium: 514mg sodium
- Fiber: 1g fiber)

542.　　Ice Cream Pudding

Serving: 6 servings. | Prep: 5mins | Cook: 0mins | Ready in:

Ingredients

- 1 package (3.4 to 3.9 ounces) instant pudding mix, any flavor
- 1 cup cold milk
- 2 cups softened ice cream, any flavor
- Fresh fruit, optional

Direction

- Beat milk and pudding mix together in a mixing bowl on low for 1 minute. Add ice scream; fold gently until smooth. Spoon mixture into dishes. Refrigerate for a minimum of 1 hour. Decorate with fruit, if desired.

Nutrition Information

- Calories: 174 calories
- Fiber: 0 fiber)
- Total Carbohydrate: 27g carbohydrate (22g sugars
- Cholesterol: 25mg cholesterol
- Protein: 3g protein.
- Total Fat: 6g fat (4g saturated fat)
- Sodium: 282mg sodium

543. Irish Creme Chocolate Trifle

Serving: 16 servings. | Prep: 20mins | Cook: 30mins | Ready in:

Ingredients

- 1 package devil's food cake mix (regular size)
- 1 cup refrigerated Irish creme nondairy creamer
- 3-1/2 cups 2% milk
- 2 packages (3.9 ounces each) instant chocolate pudding mix
- 3 cups whipped topping
- 12 mint Andes candies, chopped

Direction

- Follow package directions to prep and bake cake mix with 13x9-in. pan. Cool for 1 hour in pan on wire rack.
- Poke holes in cake with meat fork/wooden skewer, 2-in. apart. Put creamer on cake slowly; refrigerate for 1 hour, covered.
- Whisk pudding mixes and milk for 2 minutes in a big bowl; stand for 2 minutes till soft set.
- Cut cake to 1 1/2-in. cubes. Layer a third of each of following in 3-qt. trifle/glass bowl: cake cubes, pudding, whipped topping and candies. Repeat twice; refrigerate till serving.

Nutrition Information

- Calories: 343 calories
- Sodium: 363mg sodium
- Fiber: 1g fiber)
- Total Carbohydrate: 49g carbohydrate (32g sugars
- Cholesterol: 39mg cholesterol
- Protein: 5g protein.
- Total Fat: 14g fat (5g saturated fat)

544. Island Swim Dessert

Serving: 1 centerpiece and 18 cookies. | Prep: 60mins | Cook: 45mins | Ready in:

Ingredients

- CREAM PUFF LAYER:
- 1 cup water
- 1/2 cup butter, cubed
- 1 cup all-purpose flour
- 4 large eggs
- COOKIES:
- 1 tube (16-1/2 ounces) refrigerated sugar cookie dough
- 2 cups confectioners' sugar
- 1/4 cup water
- 2 tablespoons light corn syrup
- Food coloring
- Red, blue and yellow writing icing
- Assorted jumbo nonpareils
- FILLING:
- 1 package (8 ounces) cream cheese, softened
- 3-1/2 cups cold milk
- 2 packages (3.9 ounces each) instant chocolate pudding mix
- 1 carton (8 ounces) frozen whipped topping, thawed
- Blue food coloring
- ISLAND:
- 3 Pirouette cookies
- Granulated sugar
- Spearmint leaf candies
- 2 tablespoons graham cracker crumbs

Direction

- Place butter and water in a large saucepan then make it boil over medium heat. All at once add flour; mix until forms a smooth ball. Separate from heat; for 5 minutes, let it stand. One at a time, add eggs, whisking well after every addition. Keep on beating until mixture turns shiny and smooth. Put into 3-qt. baking dish that is greased. Place inside the oven and bake for 30-35 minutes at 400°F or until golden brown in color and puffy. Fully cool on a wire rack. Lower heat to 350° F. Turn out cookie dough into a thickness of 1/4-inch. Cut out 12 swimmers using a floured 3 inch and 4 1/2 inch gingerbread boy cookie cutters. Then reroll scraps; for beach balls, slice out 1-1/2-inch circles. Then put on baking sheets that are not greased. Place inside of the oven and bake for 11 to 13 minutes at 350°F or until edges are light brown in color. Put on wire racks to fully cool. To make the glaze, mix together the corn syrup, water and confectioners' sugar until turns smooth. Split glaze among small bowls; use food coloring if desired to tint. While frequently stirring the glaze, use a small brush to put glaze over cookies. Let glazed cookies to set up for 1 or more hours. If desired, you can add designs with writing icing and nonpareils. To make filling, beat together in a large bowl the pudding mixes, milk and cream cheese until turns smooth. Put over a layer of puff; place inside the refrigerator for 20 minutes. Reserve 2 tablespoons whipped topping for crest of waves; mix blue food coloring into left topping. Scatter over filling, spin, making waves. Use the reserved topping to make crests. Cover and place in refrigerator to chill. In the meantime, to make palm trees, cut or break 1 inch from one Pirouette cookie and 1-1/2-inch from another Pirouette. Then keep left Pirouette full length. On a work surface, drizzle sugar, place three spearmint leaves on sugar surface for each palm tree. Roll each into an oval using a rolling pin; then shape into a palm leaf by cutting out. Attach three palm leaves to each pirouette cookie using spearmint leaf scraps; place flat. Let it stand until set without cover. Drizzle corner of dessert with cracker crumbs for an island just before serving; in the sand, position trees. Add a beach ball and swimmers to the water. Add additional cookies when served.

Nutrition Information

- Calories:
- Protein:
- Total Fat:
- Sodium:
- Fiber:
- Total Carbohydrate:
- Cholesterol:

---

545. Layered Banana Chocolate Pudding

Serving: 6 servings. | Prep: 25mins | Cook: 0mins | Ready in:

Ingredients

- 1-3/4 cups cold milk
- 1 package (3.9 ounces) instant chocolate pudding mix
- 24 vanilla wafers
- 2 large firm bananas
- 1 carton (8 ounces) frozen whipped topping, thawed
- Grated chocolate, optional

Direction

- Beat the pudding mix and milk for 2 minutes in a big bowl; let sit for 2 minutes or until soft-set. Put 1/2 of the vanilla wafers in a 1-quart bowl.
- Put whipped topping, bananas and half of the pudding on top. Keep layering. Cover and chill for 3 hours. Top with grated chocolate (optional).

Nutrition Information

- Calories: 326 calories
- Protein: 4g protein.
- Total Fat: 12g fat (8g saturated fat)
- Sodium: 357mg sodium
- Fiber: 2g fiber)
- Total Carbohydrate: 51g carbohydrate (34g sugars
- Cholesterol: 11mg cholesterol

546. Layered Brownie Dessert

Serving: 12-15 servings. | *Prep: 20mins* | *Cook: 20mins* | *Ready in:*

Ingredients

- 1 cup butter, softened
- 2 cups sugar
- 4 large eggs
- 1 teaspoon vanilla extract
- 1-1/2 cups all-purpose flour
- 1/2 cup baking cocoa
- 1/2 teaspoon salt
- 1/2 teaspoon baking powder
- 1 cup chopped walnuts
- FILLING:
- 11 ounces cream cheese, softened
- 2 cups confectioners' sugar
- 2 cups whipped topping
- TOPPING:
- 2 cups cold whole milk
- 1 package (3.9 ounces) instant chocolate pudding mix
- Whipped topping and chopped walnuts

Direction

- Start preheating the oven to 350°. Cream sugar and butter in a big bowl until fluffy and light. Add eggs, 1 egg each time, whisking thoroughly between each addition. Whisk in vanilla. Beat baking powder, salt, cocoa, and flour in a separate bowl; add to the creamed mixture just until moistened. Fold in nuts.
- Remove into an oil-coated 13x9-inch baking pan. Bake for 20-25 minutes until a toothpick will come out with moist crumbs when you insert it into the middle. Put the pan on a wire rack to fully cool.
- Whisk confectioners' sugar and cream cheese together in a small bowl until smooth. Fold in the whipped topping, spread onto the brownies.
- Beat pudding mix and milk in a big bowl for 2 minutes. Allow to sit for 2 minutes until soft-

set. Spread onto the filling. Chill in the fridge until eating, or about 60 minutes.
- Slice into squares, use nuts and whipped topping to garnish.

Nutrition Information

- Calories: 545 calories
- Total Carbohydrate: 67g carbohydrate (50g sugars
- Cholesterol: 106mg cholesterol
- Protein: 7g protein.
- Total Fat: 29g fat (15g saturated fat)
- Sodium: 327mg sodium
- Fiber: 2g fiber)

547. Layered Candy Cane Dessert

Serving: 24 servings. | *Prep: 25mins* | *Cook: 0mins* | *Ready in:*

Ingredients

- 1 package (14.3 ounces) Oreo cookies
- 6 tablespoons butter, melted
- 1 package (8 ounces) cream cheese, softened
- 1/4 cup sugar
- 2 tablespoons 2% milk
- 1 carton (12 ounces) frozen whipped topping, thawed, divided
- 3/4 cup crushed candy canes (about 7 regular size), divided
- 2 packages (3.3 ounces each) instant white chocolate pudding mix
- 2-3/4 cups cold 2% milk

Direction

- In a food processor, pulse cookies until finely crumbled. Put in melted butter; process just until incorporated. Pat mixture onto the bottom of a 13x9-inch dish. Chill while making filling.

- Whisk milk, sugar, and cream cheese together until no lumps remain. Fold in 1/2 cup crushed candies and 1 cup whipped topping. Spoon mixture into crust, spreading evenly.
- Beat milk and pudding mix for 2 minutes; distribute over cream cheese layer. Top with the rest of whipped topping. Cover and chill for 4 hours. Scatter top with the rest of candies right before serving.

Nutrition Information

- Calories: 251 calories
- Protein: 2g protein.
- Total Fat: 13g fat (7g saturated fat)
- Sodium: 250mg sodium
- Fiber: 1g fiber)
- Total Carbohydrate: 32g carbohydrate (25g sugars
- Cholesterol: 20mg cholesterol

548. Layered Carrot Cake

Serving: 12-14 servings. | Prep: 50mins | Cook: 35mins | Ready in:

Ingredients

- 1 package yellow cake mix (regular size)
- 1 package (3.4 ounces) instant vanilla pudding mix
- 2 teaspoons ground cinnamon
- 4 large eggs
- 2/3 cup orange juice
- 1/2 cup vegetable oil
- 3 cups grated carrots
- 1/2 cup raisins
- 1/2 cup chopped walnuts
- ORANGE CREAM CHEESE FROSTING:
- 1 package (8 ounces) cream cheese, softened
- 1/2 cup butter, softened
- 3 cups confectioners' sugar
- 1 to 2 tablespoons orange juice
- 1 tablespoon grated orange zest

Direction

- Mix cinnamon, pudding mix and cake mix in a large bowl. Whisk oil, orange juice and eggs; pour into dry ingredients. Beat till well blended. Mix in nuts, raisins and carrots. (The batter should be thick.)
- Transfer into 2 a 9-inch baking pans coated with grease and flour. Bake at 350° till a toothpick comes out clean when inserted into the center, 30-35 minutes. Allow to cool for 10 minutes; take out of the pans and place on wire racks and cool completely.
- For frosting, beat butter and cream cheese in a large bowl, till fluffy. Include in zest, orange juice and confectioners' sugar; beat till smooth. Spread the frosting between layers and over the top and sides of the cake. Keep in a refrigerator.

Nutrition Information

- Calories: 544 calories
- Total Fat: 27g fat (11g saturated fat)
- Sodium: 471mg sodium
- Fiber: 2g fiber)
- Total Carbohydrate: 71g carbohydrate (52g sugars
- Cholesterol: 96mg cholesterol
- Protein: 6g protein.

549. Layered Chocolate Peanut Butter Pie

Serving: 8 servings. | Prep: 10mins | Cook: 0mins | Ready in:

Ingredients

- 1/3 cup nonfat dry milk powder
- 1-1/4 cups cold water
- 1 package (1 ounce) sugar-free instant vanilla pudding mix
- 1/2 cup reduced-fat chunky peanut butter

- 1 reduced-fat graham cracker crust (8 inches)
- CHOCOLATE LAYER:
- 1/3 cup nonfat dry milk powder
- 1-1/4 cups cold water
- 1 package (1.4 ounces) sugar-free instant chocolate pudding mix
- 1 cup reduced-fat whipped topping
- 1/2 ounce semisweet chocolate, shaved into curls

Direction

- Beat water and milk powder for 20 seconds on low speed in a bowl. Add vanilla pudding mix and beat for 1 1/2 minutes on low. Add peanut butter; beat for 30 seconds on low; put into crust.
- Chocolate layer: Beat water and milk powder for 20 seconds on low in a bowl. Add chocolate pudding mix and beat for 2 minutes on low. Spread on peanut butter layer carefully; top with chocolate curls and whipped topping. Cover; refrigerate for 2 hours minimum.

Nutrition Information

- Calories: 257 calories
- Total Carbohydrate: 34g carbohydrate (0 sugars
- Cholesterol: 1mg cholesterol
- Protein: 8g protein. Diabetic Exchanges: 2 starch
- Total Fat: 10g fat (3g saturated fat)
- Sodium: 505mg sodium
- Fiber: 2g fiber)

550.   Layered Chocolate Pudding Dessert

Serving: 2 servings. | Prep: 20mins | Cook: 10mins | Ready in:

Ingredients

- 1/3 cup all-purpose flour
- 3 tablespoons chopped pecans
- 3 tablespoons butter, melted
- 3 ounces cream cheese, softened
- 1/3 cup confectioners' sugar
- 1 cup whipped topping, divided
- 2/3 cup cold 2% milk
- 3 tablespoons instant chocolate pudding mix

Direction

- Mix the butter, pecans and flour in a small bowl; push into a 5-3/4x3x2-in. loaf pan that's ungreased. Bake for 10-12 mins at 350° or until crust is slightly browned. Let cool on a wire rack.
- Whip confectioners' sugar and cream cheese in a small bowl until smooth; fold in half cup whipped topping. Put on top of shell.
- Beat pudding mix and milk in a small bowl for 2 minutes. Let sit for 2 minutes or until soft-set. Put on top of cream cheese mixture. Spread with leftover whipped topping. Put in the fridge until serving.

Nutrition Information

- Calories: 692 calories
- Total Carbohydrate: 67g carbohydrate (41g sugars
- Cholesterol: 81mg cholesterol
- Protein: 11g protein.
- Total Fat: 42g fat (25g saturated fat)
- Sodium: 614mg sodium
- Fiber: 2g fiber)

551.   Layered Ice Box Dessert

Serving: 16-20 servings. | Prep: 30mins | Cook: 15mins | Ready in:

Ingredients

- CRUST:

- 1 package German chocolate cake mix (regular size)
- 1 egg
- 1/2 cup butter, melted
- 1/2 cup chopped pecans
- FILLING/TOPPING:
- 1 package (8 ounces) cream cheese, softened
- 1 cup sugar
- 1 carton (12 ounces) frozen whipped topping, thawed, divided
- 3 cups cold milk
- 2 packages (3.4 ounces each) instant French vanilla pudding mix
- 1/4 teaspoon ground nutmeg
- 1/4 teaspoon rum extract
- 2 tablespoons chopped pecans, toasted

Direction

- Stir butter, dry cake mix, pecans and egg in a large bowl. Place it into a 13x9 inches greased baking pan and bake at 350 degrees F. Let it bake until a toothpick poked in the middle comes out clean, 15 to 20 minutes. Let it completely cool. The crust will fall in the middle to form shell once it is completely cooled.
- In a big bowl, mix for two minutes sugar and cream cheese. By folding add 1 cup of whipped topping; spread mixture over the crust. Place in refrigerator for 10 minutes.
- In a separate large bowl, beat pudding mix and milk for two minutes. Let it rest for two minutes until it is soft set. Add the extract and nutmeg; then place over the cream cheese layer. Drizzle it with the remaining whipped topping and pecans. Let it cool in the refrigerator, 2 or more hours.

Nutrition Information

- Calories: 344 calories
- Cholesterol: 40mg cholesterol
- Protein: 4g protein.
- Total Fat: 18g fat (10g saturated fat)
- Sodium: 331mg sodium

- Fiber: 1g fiber)
- Total Carbohydrate: 41g carbohydrate (28g sugars

552.   Layered Lemon Pies

Serving: 2 pies (10 servings each). | Prep: 40mins | Cook: 15mins | Ready in:

Ingredients

- Pastry for two single-crust pies (9 inches)
- 1-1/2 cups sugar
- 6 tablespoons cornstarch
- 1/4 teaspoon salt
- 2 cups cold water
- 3 large egg yolks, lightly beaten
- 1/3 cup lemon juice
- 1/4 cup butter, cubed
- 1 teaspoon grated lemon peel
- 1 teaspoon lemon extract
- 3 drops yellow food coloring, optional
- SECOND LAYER:
- 1 package (8 ounces) cream cheese, softened
- 1 cup confectioners' sugar
- 1-1/2 cups cold 2% milk
- 2 packages (3.4 ounces each) instant lemon pudding mix
- TOPPING:
- 1 package (8 ounces) cream cheese, softened
- 1 cup confectioners' sugar
- 1 carton (16 ounces) frozen whipped topping, thawed

Direction

- Set oven to 450° to preheat. Place pastry onto two 9-inch pie plates. Cut off excess pastry and flute edges. Place a double thickness of heavy-duty foil over unpricked pastry. Bake crust in the preheated oven for 8 minutes. Take off the foil; keep baking until golden brown, about 5 to 7 minutes more. Allow to cool on wire racks.

- Combine salt, cornstarch, and sugar in a large saucepan. Whisk in water until smooth. Cook over medium-high heat, stirring, until bubbly and thickened. Lower heat; cook for 2 more minutes, stirring while cooking. Take away from the heat.
- Whisk a small amount of hot filling into egg yolks; pour all back into the pan, stirring continuously. Heat mixture to a gentle boil; cook for 2 more minutes, stirring well. Turn off the heat. Gently whisk in extract, lemon peel, butter, lemon juice, and food coloring (if using). Allow mixture to cool to room temperature, undisturbed. Pour lemon mixture into crust, spreading evenly. Chill until firm, about half an hour.
- Beat cream cheese with confectioners' sugar in a large mixing bowl until smooth. Slowly whisk in milk. Beat in pudding mix for 2 more minutes. Allow to sit until soft-set, about 2 minutes. Pour over pies, spreading gently. Chill until set, about half an hour.
- To make topping, beat cream cheese with confectioners' sugar in a large mixing bowl until smooth. Add whipped topping and fold gently. Frost over tops of pies. Chill until set then serve.

Nutrition Information

- Calories: 428 calories
- Fiber: 0 fiber)
- Total Carbohydrate: 56g carbohydrate (38g sugars
- Cholesterol: 68mg cholesterol
- Protein: 4g protein.
- Total Fat: 21g fat (13g saturated fat)
- Sodium: 321mg sodium

553. Lemon Bundt Cake

Serving: 12 | Prep: 15mins | Cook: 45mins | Ready in:

Ingredients

- 1 (18.25 ounce) package lemon cake mix
- 1 (3.4 ounce) package instant lemon pudding mix
- 3/4 cup vegetable oil
- 4 eggs
- 1 cup lemon-lime flavored carbonated beverage

Direction

- Set oven to preheat at 165°C (325°F). Grease a 10-inch Bundt pan and dust with flour.
- Combine cake mix and pudding mix in a large bowl, then stir the oil into the mixture. Beat the eggs into the mixture, one by one, then mix in the lemon-lime soda.
- Transfer the batter into the prepared pan. In the preheated oven, bake until an inserted toothpick in the middle of cake exits clean, or for 45 to 50 minutes. Let it cool down.

Nutrition Information

- Calories: 364 calories;
- Total Fat: 20.4
- Sodium: 440
- Total Carbohydrate: 41.5
- Cholesterol: 73
- Protein: 4.7

554. Lemon Butterfly Cupcakes

Serving: 14 cupcakes. | Prep: 35mins | Cook: 20mins | Ready in:

Ingredients

- 1/2 cup butter, softened
- 1 cup sugar
- 2 eggs
- 1 teaspoon vanilla extract
- 1-3/4 cups cake flour
- 1-3/4 teaspoons baking powder

- 1/2 teaspoon salt
- 1/2 cup milk
- FILLING:
- 1-3/4 cups cold milk
- 1 package (3.4 ounces) instant lemon pudding mix
- 28 pieces shoestring licorice (2 inches), optional
- 1 teaspoon confectioners' sugar

Direction

- Beat butter with sugar in a large mixing bowl until fluffy and light. Put in eggs, one by one, beating well between additions. Whisk in vanilla. Mix salt, baking powder, and flour together; pour alternately with milk into creamed mixture, beating well between additions.
- Pour batter into paper-lined muffin cups to 2/3 full. Bake for 18 to 22 minutes at 350° until a toothpick comes out clean from the center. Allow to cool in pans for 10 minutes before transferring to wire racks to cool entirely.
- In the meantime, prepare filling. Beat pudding mix and milk in a small mixing bowl for 2 minutes. Allow to sit until soft-set, about 2 minutes.
- Cut a 1-inch cone-shaped piece with 1 inch deep from the middle of each cupcake using a sharp knife. Remove carefully and put to one side. Fill pudding mixture into cavity.
- To make wings, cut the reserved cone pieces in half vertically; place over the filling with points touching. Insert licorice for antennae, if desired. Sprinkle with confectioners' sugar. Chill leftovers.

Nutrition Information

- Calories: 235 calories
- Sodium: 292mg sodium
- Fiber: 0 fiber)
- Total Carbohydrate: 36g carbohydrate (22g sugars
- Cholesterol: 51mg cholesterol
- Protein: 4g protein.

- Total Fat: 9g fat (5g saturated fat)

555.   Lemon Cream Cheese Pie

Serving: 12-16 servings. | Prep: 45mins | Cook: 0mins | Ready in:

Ingredients

- 1 cup sugar
- 1/2 cup cornstarch
- 2-1/2 cups cold water
- 1/8 teaspoon salt
- 3 large eggs yolks, lightly beaten
- 3 tablespoons butter
- 2/3 cup lemon juice, divided
- 1 package (8 ounces) cream cheese, softened
- 1 can (14 ounces) sweetened condensed milk
- 1 package (3.4 ounces) lemon-flavored instant pudding mix
- 2 pie shells (9 inches), baked
- Whipped cream
- Lemon slices

Direction

- Combine salt, cornstarch, and sugar in a large saucepan; whisk in water until no lumps remain. Cook over medium-high heat, stirring, until bubbly and thickened. Lower heat, cook for 2 more minutes, stirring while cooking. Take off the heat. Whisk a small amount of hot filling into egg yolks; pour all back into the pan, stirring continuously. Heat to a gentle boil; cook for 2 more minutes, stirring.
- Put off the heat. Whisk in butter. Gently whisk in 1/3 cup lemon juice. Allow mixture to cool for a couple of hours or overnight.
- Whisk cream cheese and condensed milk together in a large mixing bowl until smooth. Whisk in the remaining lemon juice and pudding mix.
- Mix into chilled lemon filling. Divide and fill into baked pie shells. Chill for a couple of

hours. Pipe whipped cream on top and garnish with lemon slices.

Nutrition Information

- Calories: 378 calories
- Cholesterol: 77mg cholesterol
- Protein: 5g protein.
- Total Fat: 18g fat (10g saturated fat)
- Sodium: 293mg sodium
- Fiber: 0 fiber)
- Total Carbohydrate: 51g carbohydrate (32g sugars

556.   Lemon Cream Torte

Serving: 16 servings. | Prep: 10mins | Cook: 20mins | Ready in:

Ingredients

- 1/2 cup butter, softened
- 1-1/4 cups all-purpose flour
- 1 package (8 ounces) cream cheese, softened
- 1 cup confectioners' sugar
- 1 carton (8 ounces) frozen whipped topping, thawed, divided
- 2 packages (3.4 ounces each) instant lemon pudding mix
- 2-1/2 cups cold whole milk
- 1/2 cup chopped pecans, optional

Direction

- Mix flour and butter; pat into 13x9-in. baking pan. Bake for 20-25 minutes at 350° or till lightly browned; cool. Blend sugar and cream cheese at medium speed till smooth in big bowl. Add 1/2 whipped topping; beat on low. Spread on crust. Beat milk and pudding mixes on low speed for 2 minutes in another bowl; set for 10 minutes. Spread on cream cheese layer; set for 10-15 minutes. Use leftover whipped topping to cover. If desired, top with pecans. Refrigerate overnight.

Nutrition Information

- Calories: 249 calories
- Protein: 3g protein.
- Total Fat: 14g fat (10g saturated fat)
- Sodium: 191mg sodium
- Fiber: 0 fiber)
- Total Carbohydrate: 26g carbohydrate (15g sugars
- Cholesterol: 36mg cholesterol

557.   Lemon Custard Cake

Serving: 12-16 servings. | Prep: 15mins | Cook: 0mins | Ready in:

Ingredients

- 1 prepared angel food cake (8 to 10 ounces)
- 1 package (3.4 ounces) instant lemon pudding mix
- 1-1/2 cups cold whole milk
- 1 cup sour cream
- 1 can (21 ounces) cherry or strawberry pie filling

Direction

- Crumble the angel food cake into bite-size pieces. Put the cake pieces in a 9x13-inch baking pan. Mix the milk, pudding mix and sour cream together in a bowl. Beat the mixture for about two minutes until it becomes thick. Pour the pudding mixture over the cake. Use a spoon to top each cake piece with pie filling. Refrigerate until ready to serve.

Nutrition Information

- Calories: 143 calories
- Total Carbohydrate: 26g carbohydrate (15g sugars

- Cholesterol: 12mg cholesterol
- Protein: 2g protein.
- Total Fat: 3g fat (2g saturated fat)
- Sodium: 201mg sodium
- Fiber: 0 fiber)

- Sodium: 479mg sodium
- Fiber: 0 fiber)
- Total Carbohydrate: 54g carbohydrate (34g sugars
- Cholesterol: 46mg cholesterol
- Protein: 5g protein.

558.   Lemon Delight Trifle

Serving: 12 servings (1 cup each). | Prep: 30mins | Cook: 0mins | Ready in:

Ingredients

- 3-1/2 cups cold 2% milk
- 2 packages (3.4 ounces each) instant lemon pudding mix
- 1 package (8 ounces) cream cheese, softened
- 1/2 cup butter, softened
- 1/2 cup confectioners' sugar
- 1 carton (12 ounces) frozen whipped topping, thawed, divided
- 1 package (12 to 14 ounces) lemon cream-filled sandwich cookies, crushed

Direction

- Whisk pudding mixes and milk for 2 minutes in big bowl; stand till soft-set or for 2 minutes.
- Beat confectioners' sugar, butter and cream cheese till smooth in another bowl; mix pudding in slowly till blended.
- Put 1/4 cup each crushed cookies and whipped topping aside for garnish. Fold leftover whipped topping into the pudding mixture.
- Put 1/2 leftover cookies in 3-qt. glass bowl; top using 1/2 pudding mixture. Repeat layers; garnish using crushed cookies and reserved whipped topping. Refrigerate till serving.

Nutrition Information

- Calories: 476 calories
- Total Fat: 26g fat (16g saturated fat)

559.   Lemon Poppy Seed Cake

Serving: 12-16 servings. | Prep: 15mins | Cook: 50mins | Ready in:

Ingredients

- 1 package lemon cake mix (regular size)
- 1 package (3.4 ounces) instant lemon pudding mix
- 3/4 cup warm water
- 1/2 cup canola oil
- 4 eggs
- 1 teaspoon lemon extract
- 1 teaspoon almond extract
- 1/3 cup poppy seeds
- 1/2 cup confectioners' sugar
- Juice of 1 lemon
- Additional confectioners' sugar, optional

Direction

- Mix pudding mix and cake in a big bowl. Add extracts, eggs, oil and water; beat on low speed for 30 seconds; beat on medium speed for 2 minutes. Mix in poppy seeds; put into 12-cup greased fluted tube pan.
- Bake it at 350° till inserted toothpick in middle exits clean for 50-60 minutes; cool for 10 minutes in pan. Invert onto serving plate.
- Mix lemon juice and confectioner's sugar; brush on warm cake. Cool. If desired, dust with extra confectioners' sugar.

Nutrition Information

- Calories: 264 calories

- Fiber: 1g fiber)
- Total Carbohydrate: 37g carbohydrate (23g sugars
- Cholesterol: 53mg cholesterol
- Protein: 3g protein.
- Total Fat: 12g fat (2g saturated fat)
- Sodium: 294mg sodium

- Fiber: 0 fiber)
- Total Carbohydrate: 35g carbohydrate (22g sugars
- Cholesterol: 49mg cholesterol
- Protein: 4g protein.
- Total Fat: 20g fat (13g saturated fat)
- Sodium: 305mg sodium

560.   Lemon Pudding Dessert

Serving: 16 servings. | Prep: 20mins | Cook: 20mins | Ready in:

Ingredients

- 1 cup cold butter, cubed
- 2 cups all-purpose flour
- 1 package (8 ounces) cream cheese, softened
- 1 cup confectioners' sugar
- 1 carton (8 ounces) frozen whipped topping, thawed, divided
- 3 cups cold whole milk
- 2 packages (3.4 ounces each) instant lemon pudding mix

Direction

- Preheat the oven to 350 degrees. Chop the butter to the flour till crumbly. Press into the ungreased 13x9-inch baking plate. Bake for 18 to 22 minutes or till turning brown a bit. Let cool down on the wire rack.
- At the same time, whip the sugar and cream cheese till becoming smooth. Fold in 1 cup of the whipped topping. Spread on top of the cooled crust.
- Whip the pudding mix and milk on low speed for 2 minutes. Gently spread on the cream cheese layer. Add the rest of the whipped topping on top. Keep in the refrigerator for no less than 60 minutes.

Nutrition Information

- Calories: 348 calories

561.   Lemon Rice Pudding

Serving: 7 servings. | Prep: 15mins | Cook: 15mins | Ready in:

Ingredients

- 1-1/2 cups water
- 1/2 cup uncooked long grain rice
- 1/3 cup raisins
- 1/4 teaspoon ground nutmeg
- 1 package (1 ounce) sugar-free instant vanilla pudding mix
- 2 teaspoons grated lemon zest

Direction

- Boil nutmeg, raisins, rice and water in a saucepan. Lower heat; cover. Simmer till liquid is absorbed for 15-20 minutes. Cool. Follow package directions to prep pudding mix. Mix in lemon zest and rice mixture. Immediately serve or refrigerate.

Nutrition Information

- Calories: 0g saturated fat (0 sugars
- Total Fat: 0 fiber). Diabetic Exchanges: 1 starch.

562. Lemon Slice Sugar Cookies

Serving: about 2 dozen. | Prep: 15mins | Cook: 10mins | Ready in:

Ingredients

- 1/2 cup unsalted butter, softened
- 1 package (3.4 ounces) instant lemon pudding mix
- 1/2 cup sugar
- 1 large egg
- 2 tablespoons 2% milk
- 1-1/2 cups all-purpose flour
- 1 teaspoon baking powder
- 1/4 teaspoon salt
- ICING:
- 2/3 cup confectioners' sugar
- 2 to 4 teaspoons lemon juice

Direction

- Cream together sugar, pudding mix and butter in a big bowl until fluffy and light. Beat in milk and egg. Whisk together salt, baking powder and flour in a separate bowl, then beat into creamed mixture gradually.
- Split dough in half. Form each dough portion into a roll with the length of 6 inches on a work surface coated lightly with flour. Use plastic to wrap and chill until firm, or about 3 hours.
- Set the oven to 375 degrees to preheat. Unwrap dough and cut crosswise into slices, 1/2 inch each. Arrange onto ungreased baking sheets, 1 inch apart. Bake for 8 to 10 minutes, until edges are browned slightly. Allow to cool on pans for 2 minutes. Transfer to wire racks to cool thoroughly.
- Combine enough amount of lemon juice and confectioners' sugar in a small bowl to get a drizzling consistency, then drizzle over cookies. Allow to stand until set.
- For Making Ahead: You can make dough 2 days ahead of time; use plastic to wrap dough and put into a resealable bag. Keep in the fridge.
- Freeze option: Put wrapped logs into a resealable plastic freezer bag and freeze them. To use, unwrap frozen logs and cut them into slices. Follow directions to bake plus time by 1 to 2 minutes.

Nutrition Information

- Calories: 110 calories
- Fiber: 0 fiber)
- Total Carbohydrate: 17g carbohydrate (11g sugars
- Cholesterol: 18mg cholesterol
- Protein: 1g protein.
- Total Fat: 4g fat (2g saturated fat)
- Sodium: 99mg sodium

563. Light Lemon Cake

Serving: 20 servings. | Prep: 15mins | Cook: 25mins | Ready in:

Ingredients

- 1 package yellow cake mix (regular size)
- 1 package (3.4 ounces) instant lemon pudding mix
- 1-3/4 cups water
- 2 egg whites
- 3/4 cup cold fat-free milk
- 1/2 teaspoon lemon extract
- 1 package (1 ounce) instant sugar-free vanilla pudding mix
- 1 carton (8 ounces) frozen reduced-fat whipped topping, thawed

Direction

- Mix the egg whites, water, lemon pudding mix and cake mix in a big bowl. Whisk for half a minute on low speed. Whisk for 2 minutes on medium.

- Spread the batter into a 13x9-inch baking pan greased with cooking spray. Bake for 23-28 minutes at 350° until the toothpick inserted into the middle comes out clean. Let cool on a wire rack.
- At the same time, stir the vanilla pudding mix, extract and milk in a big bowl for 2 minutes. Let it sit for 2 minutes longer until partially set. Fold in whipped topping. Pour over the cake. Keep in the refrigerator.

Nutrition Information

- Calories: 161 calories
- Sodium: 289mg sodium
- Fiber: 1g fiber)
- Total Carbohydrate: 29g carbohydrate (17g sugars
- Cholesterol: 0 cholesterol
- Protein: 2g protein.
- Total Fat: 4g fat (2g saturated fat)

---

564. Lighter Boston Cream Pie

Serving: 12 servings. | Prep: 35mins | Cook: 15mins | Ready in:

Ingredients

- 1/3 cup butter, softened
- 3/4 cup sugar
- 2 large eggs, lightly beaten
- 1/3 cup unsweetened applesauce
- 1-1/2 teaspoons vanilla extract
- 2-1/4 cups cake flour
- 2 teaspoons baking powder
- 1/2 teaspoon salt
- 1/2 cup fat-free milk
- FILLING:
- 1-1/4 cups cold fat-free milk
- 1 package (1 ounce) sugar-free instant vanilla pudding mix
- GLAZE:
- 1-1/4 cups confectioners' sugar
- 2 tablespoons baking cocoa
- 1/2 teaspoon vanilla extract
- 1 to 2 tablespoons fat-free milk

Direction

- Whisk butter with sugar for about 2 minutes in a large mixing bowl until crumbly. Mix in eggs until combined. Whisk in vanilla and applesauce. Mix salt, baking powder, and flour together; mix alternately with milk into butter mixture until incorporated.
- Apply cooking spray to the inside of two 9-inch round baking pans; scatter with flour; pour in batter. Bake for 12 to 15 minutes at 350° until a toothpick comes out clean from the center. Allow cakes to cool in pans for 10 minutes before transferring to wire racks to cool entirely.
- To make filling, combine pudding mix and milk for 2 minutes in a small mixing bowl until thickened. Lay one layer of cake on a serving plate; spread filling over cake layer; place the remaining cake layer on top.
- To make glaze, mix vanilla, cocoa, and confectioners' sugar together in a small mixing bowl. Pour in enough milk until desired consistency is reached. Distribute glaze over top of cake, letting it run down the sides.

Nutrition Information

- Calories: 275 calories
- Sodium: 345mg sodium
- Fiber: 1g fiber)
- Total Carbohydrate: 50g carbohydrate (27g sugars
- Cholesterol: 50mg cholesterol
- Protein: 5g protein.
- Total Fat: 6g fat (3g saturated fat)

565. Low Fat Strawberry Cream Dessert

Serving: 8 servings. | *Prep: 20mins* | *Cook: 0mins* | *Ready in:*

Ingredients

- 1 package (8 ounces) reduced-fat cream cheese, softened
- 1 carton (8 ounces) reduced-fat whipped topping, thawed
- 3 cups cold fat-free milk
- 2 packages (1 ounce each) sugar-free instant vanilla pudding mix
- 2 pints fresh strawberries, halved

Direction

- Beat cream cheese in a big bowl until it becomes smooth. On low speed, mix in whipped topping until smooth then put aside. Mix together pudding mixes and milk in a separate big bowl. On low speed, mix for 2 minutes. Allow to sit for 5 minutes. Mix in cream cheese mixture until smooth. Reserve one cup strawberries. Fold the rest of strawberries into the pudding mixture. Pour into separate dessert dishes or a serving bowl. Chill while covered for no less than two hours. Top with the rest of strawberries.

Nutrition Information

- Calories: 216 calories
- Cholesterol: 18mg cholesterol
- Protein: 7g protein. Diabetic Exchanges: 1-1/2 starch
- Total Fat: 9g fat (7g saturated fat)
- Sodium: 428mg sodium
- Fiber: 2g fiber)
- Total Carbohydrate: 25g carbohydrate (0 sugars

566. Low Fat Vanilla Pudding

Serving: 6 servings. | *Prep: 10mins* | *Cook: 0mins* | *Ready in:*

Ingredients

- 1 cup fat-free milk
- 1 cup fat-free plain yogurt
- 1 cup fat-free sugar-free vanilla yogurt
- 1 package (.9 ounce) sugar-free instant vanilla pudding mix
- 1/2 teaspoon vanilla extract
- Maraschino cherries, optional
- Mint leaves, optional

Direction

- Beat vanilla, pudding mix, yogurt and milk for 2 minutes on high speed in a mixing bowl. Put into serving dishes; chill. Garnish with mint and cherries if desired.

Nutrition Information

- Calories: 88 calories
- Sodium: 261mg sodium
- Fiber: 0 fiber)
- Total Carbohydrate: 15g carbohydrate (0 sugars
- Cholesterol: 3mg cholesterol
- Protein: 5g protein. Diabetic Exchanges: 1/2 starch
- Total Fat: 1g fat (0 saturated fat)

567. Luscious Apple Trifle

Serving: 12-14 servings. | *Prep: 20mins* | *Cook: 0mins* | *Ready in:*

Ingredients

- 2 cups cold milk
- 1 package (3.4 ounces) instant vanilla pudding mix

- 1 package (8 ounces) cream cheese, softened
- 1 carton (8 ounces) frozen whipped topping, thawed, divided
- 1 loaf-shaped angel food cake (10-1/2 ounces), cut into 1-inch cubes
- 1 jar (12-1/4 ounces) butterscotch ice cream topping
- 3 medium red apples, chopped
- 1-1/2 teaspoons ground cinnamon

Direction

- Whisk pudding mix and milk for 2 minutes in a bowl; stand till soft set for 2 minutes. Beat cream cheese till smooth in a big bowl; beat pudding in. Fold 1 cup whipping topping in.
- Layer 1/3 cake cubes, 1/3 apples, 1/3 cup butterscotch topping, 1/2 tsp. cinnamon and 1/3 cream cheese mixture in a 3-qt. glass bowl; repeat layers twice. Garnish using leftover whipped topping; chill till serving.

Nutrition Information

- Calories:
- Protein:
- Total Fat:
- Sodium:
- Fiber:
- Total Carbohydrate:
- Cholesterol:

568.   Macadamia Chip Cookies

Serving: 5-1/2 dozen. | Prep: 15mins | Cook: 15mins | Ready in:

Ingredients

- 1 cup butter, softened
- 3/4 cup packed brown sugar
- 1/4 cup sugar
- 2 eggs
- 1 teaspoon vanilla extract

- 2-1/4 cups all-purpose flour
- 1 package (3.4 ounces) instant vanilla pudding mix
- 1 teaspoon baking soda
- 1/4 teaspoon salt
- 1 package (10 to 12 ounces) white baking chips
- 2 jars (3-1/4 ounces each) macadamia nuts, chopped
- 1/2 cup finely crushed peanut brittle

Direction

- Beat butter with sugars in a big bowl until light and fluffy. Add one egg at a time, whisking well before adding another. Mix in vanilla. Mix the salt, baking soda, dry pudding mix and flour together and add them to the creamed mixture, little by little and combine together. Mix in peanut brittle, nuts and chips.
- Grease baking trays. Take rounded tablespoonfuls of the batter and put each 2 inches apart from another on the prepared baking trays. Set oven at 375°F and start baking until they turn golden brown, about 10 to 12 minutes. Take the cookies to a wire rack and let cool.

Nutrition Information

- Calories:
- Cholesterol:
- Protein:
- Total Fat:
- Sodium:
- Fiber:
- Total Carbohydrate:

569.   Makeover Cherry Almond Mousse Pie

Serving: 8 servings. | Prep: 25mins | Cook: 0mins | Ready in:

Ingredients

- 1 can (14 ounces) fat-free sweetened condensed milk, divided
- 1 ounce unsweetened chocolate, chopped
- 1/2 teaspoon almond extract, divided
- 1 frozen pie shell, baked
- 1 jar (10 ounces) maraschino cherries, drained
- 1 package (8 ounces) fat-free cream cheese
- 3/4 cup cold water
- 1 package (1 ounce) sugar-free instant vanilla pudding mix
- 2 cups reduced-fat whipped topping
- 1/4 cup chopped almonds, toasted
- Chocolate curls, optional

Direction

- Cook and stir the chocolate and 1/2 cup milk in a small saucepan on low heat for 4-5 minutes or until the chocolate melts. Mix in 1/4 tsp of extract. Pour it into the pie shell, then put aside.
- For garnish, reserve 8 whole cherries. Chop the leftover cherries, then put aside. Beat the cream cheese in a big bowl until it becomes smooth. Slowly beat in the leftover milk and water, then add the leftover extract and pudding mix; stir well. Fold in whipped topping, then stir in reserved chopped cherries and almonds.
- Pour on top of the pie. Let chill in the fridge for 4 hours or until set. If preferred, put chocolate curls and whole cherries on top to garnish.

Nutrition Information

- Calories: 426 calories
- Sodium: 453mg sodium
- Fiber: 1g fiber
- Total Carbohydrate: 69g carbohydrate (47g sugars
- Cholesterol: 14mg cholesterol
- Protein: 10g protein.
- Total Fat: 13g fat (7g saturated fat)

570. Makeover Coconut Supreme Torte

Serving: 16 servings. | Prep: 25mins | Cook: 25mins | Ready in:

Ingredients

- 1 package yellow cake mix (regular size)
- 1-1/3 cups water
- 2 large eggs
- 4 large egg whites
- 1/2 cup unsweetened applesauce
- 1 package (1 ounce) sugar-free instant vanilla pudding mix
- 1 cup sweetened shredded coconut, toasted
- 1/2 cup chopped walnuts, toasted
- FROSTING:
- 1 package (8 ounces) reduced-fat cream cheese
- 2 teaspoons fat-free milk
- 1 teaspoon vanilla extract
- 2-3/4 cups confectioners' sugar
- 1 cup sweetened shredded coconut, toasted, divided

Direction

- Use cooking spray to coat 3 round 9-in. cake pans; dust with flour. Put aside. Mix pudding mix, eggs, applesauce, egg whites, water and cake mix in a big bowl; beat for 4 minutes on medium speed, occasionally scraping bowl sides. Mix walnuts and coconut in.
- Put in prepped pans; bake for 23-27 minutes at 350° till inserted toothpick in middle exits clean. Cool for 10 minutes. Transfer from pans onto wire racks; completely cool.
- Frosting: Beat vanilla, milk and cream cheese till smooth in a big bowl; beat confectioners' sugar in slowly. Mix 1/2 cup coconut in.
- Put bottom cake layer on serving plate; spread 2/3 cup frosting then repeat layers. Put leftover layer and frosting on top; sprinkle leftover coconut. Keep in fridge.

Nutrition Information

- Calories: 350 calories
- Protein: 6g protein.
- Total Fat: 13g fat (7g saturated fat)
- Sodium: 316mg sodium
- Fiber: 2g fiber)
- Total Carbohydrate: 54g carbohydrate (39g sugars
- Cholesterol: 37mg cholesterol

- Protein: 3g protein. Diabetic Exchanges: 2 starch
- Total Fat: 3g fat (2g saturated fat)
- Sodium: 255mg sodium
- Fiber: 1g fiber)
- Total Carbohydrate: 33g carbohydrate (12g sugars
- Cholesterol: 0 cholesterol

571. Makeover Toffee Crunch Dessert

Serving: 15 servings. | Prep: 20mins | Cook: 0mins | Ready in:

Ingredients

- 1-1/2 cups cold fat-free milk
- 1 package (1 ounce) sugar-free instant vanilla pudding mix
- 2 cartons (8 ounces each) frozen fat-free whipped topping, thawed
- 1 prepared angel food cake (8 to 10 ounces), cut into 1-inch cubes
- 4 Butterfinger candy bars (2.1 ounces each), crushed

Direction

- Whisk the pudding mix and milk in a big bowl for 2 minutes. Allow to stand for 2 minutes or until soft-set. Mix in 2 cups of the whipped topping, then fold in the leftover whipped topping.
- In a cooking spray coated 13x9-inch dish, layer 1/2 of the cake cubes, pudding mixture and crushed candy bars. Redo the layers. Put cover on and chill in the fridge for a minimum of 2 hours prior to serving.

Nutrition Information

- Calories: 177 calories

572. Mandarin Orange Cake

Serving: 12 servings. | Prep: 15mins | Cook: 30mins | Ready in:

Ingredients

- 1 package white cake mix (regular size)
- 2 eggs
- 1/3 cup unsweetened applesauce
- 1 can (11 ounces) mandarin oranges, undrained
- 1 carton (8 ounces) frozen whipped topping, thawed
- 1 can (8 ounces) crushed pineapple, undrained
- 1 package (3.4 ounces) instant vanilla pudding mix

Direction

- Mix together oranges, applesauce, eggs and cake mix in a big bowl, then beat on low speed about half a minute. Beat for 2 more minutes on medium speed.
- Transfer the mixture into 2 9-inch round baking pans coated with grease and flour. Bake at 325 degrees until a toothpick pricked in the center exits clean, about half an hour. Allow to cool in pans about 10 minutes, then transfer to wire racks to cool fully.
- Beat together pudding mix, pineapple and whipped topping in a separate bowl, then spread between layers, over top and sides of cake. Refrigerate.

Nutrition Information

- Calories: 308 calories
- Fiber: 1g fiber)
- Total Carbohydrate: 54g carbohydrate (33g sugars
- Cholesterol: 35mg cholesterol
- Protein: 3g protein.
- Total Fat: 8g fat (5g saturated fat)
- Sodium: 399mg sodium

---

573.   Milky Way Ice Cream

Serving: about 3 quarts. | Prep: 15mins | Cook: 20mins | Ready in:

Ingredients

- 16 ounces Milky Way candy bars
- 1 quart heavy whipping cream, divided
- 4 large eggs
- 6 cups cold whole milk
- 1 package (3.9 ounces) instant chocolate fudge pudding mix
- 1 package (3.4 ounces) instant vanilla pudding mix

Direction

- Melt the candy bars in large saucepan with 2 cups of cream. Beat remaining cream and eggs. Whisk into the chocolate mixture. Over low heat, cook while stirring the mixture until coating back of the spoon and achieving minimum of 160 degrees. Take away from heat.
- Place the pan into a bowl of the ice water to cool quickly; stir for 2 mins. Whisk pudding mixes and milk in a bowl for 2 mins. Allow to stand until soft-set, about 2 mins. Fold into the chocolate mixture. Press the plastic wrap onto the custard surface. Place in the fridge for several hours up to overnight. Fill 2/3 full cylinder of the ice cream freezer and freeze following the manufacturer's instructions.

- Place the remaining mixture in refrigerator until it is ready to freeze. Place the ice cream in freezer container once it is frozen; freeze about 2 to 4 hours. Then serve.

Nutrition Information

- Calories: 298 calories
- Sodium: 220mg sodium
- Fiber: 0 fiber)
- Total Carbohydrate: 25g carbohydrate (21g sugars
- Cholesterol: 101mg cholesterol
- Protein: 5g protein.
- Total Fat: 21g fat (12g saturated fat)

---

574.   Mini Coffee Cakes

Serving: about 1 dozen. | Prep: 10mins | Cook: 20mins | Ready in:

Ingredients

- 1/3 cup butter, softened
- 1/4 cup sugar
- 1 egg
- 1-1/2 cups all-purpose flour
- 1 package (3.4 ounces) instant vanilla pudding mix
- 1 tablespoon baking powder
- 1/4 teaspoon salt
- 1-1/4 cups 2% milk
- 1/2 cup chopped walnuts
- TOPPING:
- 1/2 cup chopped walnuts
- 1/3 cup packed brown sugar
- 2 tablespoons butter, melted
- 1/4 teaspoon ground cinnamon

Direction

- Cream sugar and butter in a big bowl till fluffy and light. Whisk in the egg. Mix salt, baking powder, pudding mix and flour; gently put

into creamed mixture alternating with the milk, whipping thoroughly after each addition. Mix in the walnuts.
- Fill muffin cups lined with paper 2/3 full. Mix ingredients for topping; scatter on top of batter. Bake for 20 to 25 minutes at 375° till a toothpick pricked in the middle gets out clean. Let cool for 10 minutes; transfer from the pan to the wire rack.

Nutrition Information

- Calories: 273 calories
- Protein: 6g protein.
- Total Fat: 14g fat (5g saturated fat)
- Sodium: 354mg sodium
- Fiber: 1g fiber)
- Total Carbohydrate: 32g carbohydrate (17g sugars
- Cholesterol: 40mg cholesterol

575.   Mini Rum Cakes

Serving: 6 servings. | Prep: 10mins | Cook: 0mins |Ready in:

Ingredients

- 2 cups cold 2% milk
- 1 package (3.4 ounces) instant vanilla pudding mix
- 1 teaspoon rum extract
- 6 individual round sponge cakes
- 1-1/2 cups whipped topping
- Fresh or frozen raspberries

Direction

- Beat the pudding mix and milk in a small bowl for 2 minutes; add the extract and stir. Allow to stand until soft-set, for 2 minutes.
- On the dessert plates, arrange sponge cakes; add the pudding on top. Add the raspberries and whipped topping to decorate.

Nutrition Information

- Calories: 238 calories
- Sodium: 320mg sodium
- Fiber: 0 fiber)
- Total Carbohydrate: 37g carbohydrate (27g sugars
- Cholesterol: 34mg cholesterol
- Protein: 4g protein.
- Total Fat: 7g fat (5g saturated fat)

576.   Mint Cake

Serving: 15 servings. | Prep: 25mins | Cook: 25mins |Ready in:

Ingredients

- 1 package yellow cake mix (regular size)
- 1/2 teaspoon mint extract, divided
- 1-1/2 cups cold whole milk
- 1 package (3.9 ounces) instant chocolate pudding mix
- 1 carton (8 ounces) frozen whipped topping, thawed
- 4 to 5 drops green food coloring

Direction

- Following package directions to prepare cake mix, then put into batter with 1/4 tsp. of mint extract, beating well.
- Transfer into a 13"x9" baking pan coated with grease, then bake at 350 degrees until a toothpick exits clean after being inserted into the center, about 25 to 30 minutes. Allow to cool thoroughly on a wire rack.
- Whisk together pudding mix and milk in a big bowl about 2 minutes. Allow to stand until soft-set, about 2 minutes. Poke in the cake with 24 holes using the end of a wooden spoon handle, then spread over cake evenly with pudding. Mix leftover extract, food coloring and whipped topping together, then spread

mixture over pudding. Place a cover and chill for a minimum of 2 hours.

Nutrition Information

- Calories: 0g sugar total. Diabetic Exchanges: 1-1/2 fruit
- Cholesterol: 1 fat.
- Total Fat: 1 starch

577.   Mocha Angel Food Torte

Serving: 10-12 servings. | Prep: 20mins | Cook: 0mins | Ready in:

Ingredients

- 1-1/3 cups cold whole milk
- 1 package (3.9 ounces) instant chocolate pudding mix
- 1 tablespoon instant coffee granules
- 1 cup heavy whipping cream, whipped, divided
- 1 prepared angel food cake (8 to 10 ounces)
- 2 Heath candy bars (1.4 ounces each), crushed

Direction

- Beat coffee, pudding mix and milk for 2 minutes at low speed till thick in a big bowl; fold 1/2 whipped topping in.
- Horizontally cut cake in half; put bottom layer on a serving plate. Spread with 1/2 pudding mixture; put leftover cake over the top.
- Fold leftover whipped cream into the leftover pudding mixture; spread on sides and top of cake. Sprinkle with crushed candy bars; before serving, chill for 2 hours.

Nutrition Information

- Calories:
- Fiber:
- Total Carbohydrate:

- Cholesterol:
- Protein:
- Total Fat:
- Sodium:

578.   Mocha Java Pie With Kahlua Cream

Serving: 8 servings. | Prep: 25mins | Cook: 0mins | Ready in:

Ingredients

- 1 teaspoon instant coffee granules
- 1 tablespoon hot water
- 1 package (8 ounces) cream cheese, softened
- 1/2 cup confectioners' sugar
- 1 teaspoon vanilla extract
- 2 cups whipped topping
- 1 chocolate graham cracker crust (9 inches)
- PUDDING LAYER:
- 1 teaspoon instant coffee granules
- 1 cup 2% milk
- 1 package (3.9 ounces) instant chocolate pudding mix
- 1-1/2 cups whipped topping
- KAHLUA CREAM:
- 1 cup heavy whipping cream
- 3 tablespoons confectioners' sugar
- 1 tablespoon Kahlua (coffee liqueur)
- Chocolate curls, optional

Direction

- Mix coffee granules with hot water to dissolve. In a large bowl, whip confectioners' sugar and cream cheese until fluffy. Put in coffee mixture and vanilla. Fold in whipped topping. Scoop into shell.
- Mix coffee granules with milk in a small bowl to dissolve. Mix milk mixture and pudding mix in a big bowl. Whip on high speed until mixture is thick. Fold in whipped topping. Put on top of cream cheese layer carefully.

- Whip cream in a small bowl until it starts to thicken. Put Kahlua and confectioners' sugar; whip until it holds soft peaks. Put on top of pudding layer. Top with chocolate shredding (optional). Chill for two hours or until firm.

Nutrition Information

- Calories: 507 calories
- Total Carbohydrate: 47g carbohydrate (35g sugars
- Cholesterol: 74mg cholesterol
- Protein: 5g protein.
- Total Fat: 32g fat (20g saturated fat)
- Sodium: 436mg sodium
- Fiber: 1g fiber)

579. Mocha Parfaits

Serving: 4-6 servings. | Prep: 15mins | Cook: 0mins | Ready in:

Ingredients

- 1-3/4 cups cold milk, divided
- 1 teaspoon instant coffee granules
- 1 package (8 ounces) cream cheese, softened
- 1 package (3.9 ounces) instant chocolate pudding mix
- 1 carton (8 ounces) frozen whipped topping, thawed
- 8 cream-filled chocolate sandwich cookies, crushed
- Additional cream-filled chocolate sandwich cookies, optional

Direction

- Place coffee granules and 1/4 cup milk in a microwave-safe dish and heat for about 30 seconds; mix until coffee is melted. Mix in remaining milk; blend well. Whisk milk mixture, pudding mix, and cream cheese in a small bowl until thickened.

- Layer half of the pudding mixture, whipped topping and crushed cookies in parfait glasses. Continue with the layers. Put whole cookies on top if wished.

Nutrition Information

- Calories:
- Fiber:
- Total Carbohydrate:
- Cholesterol:
- Protein:
- Total Fat:
- Sodium:

580. Mom's Chocolate Chip Cookies

Serving: 24 | Prep: | Cook: | Ready in:

Ingredients

- 1 cup butter, softened
- 3/4 cup packed brown sugar
- 1/4 cup white sugar
- 1 (3.5 ounce) package instant vanilla pudding mix
- 2 eggs
- 1 teaspoon vanilla extract
- 2 1/4 cups all-purpose flour
- 1 teaspoon baking soda
- 2 cups semisweet chocolate chips

Direction

- Heat oven beforehand to 190°C (375°F).
- Cream together butter and sugars in a mixing bowl. Add in the vanilla, eggs and pudding mix. Mix together the flour and baking soda; add them into the creamed mixture and combine well. Fold chocolate chips into the mix.
- Onto ungreased baking sheets, drop

teaspoonfuls of the dough. Bake to a light brown, for about 10 to 12 minutes.

Nutrition Information

- Calories: 233 calories;
- Total Fat: 12.4
- Sodium: 175
- Total Carbohydrate: 30.5
- Cholesterol: 36
- Protein: 2.4

581.　　Moon Cake

Serving: 35 | Prep: 30mins | Cook: 30mins | Ready in:

Ingredients

- 1 cup water
- 1/2 cup margarine
- 1 cup all-purpose flour
- 4 eggs
- 2 (3.4 ounce) packages instant vanilla pudding mix
- 3 cups milk
- 1 (8 ounce) package cream cheese
- 1 (8 ounce) container frozen whipped topping, thawed
- 1/4 cup chocolate syrup

Direction

- Prepare the oven by preheating top 400°F (200°C) and grease lightly a jelly roll pan.
- Place margarine and water in a large saucepan and make it boil. Separate from heat and stir in flour using an electric mixer. One at a time, add eggs, whisking well after every addition. Equally spread in the prepared pan.
- Place inside the preheated oven and bake for 20-25 minutes. Reserve and fully cool.
- Mix together in a large bowl the cream cheese, milk and pudding mix. Beat using an electric mixer until turns smooth. Equally spread over

cooled crust. Place whipped topping on top and drizzle on chocolate syrup. Let it chill inside the refrigerator and present cold.

Nutrition Information

- Calories: 133 calories;
- Total Fat: 8.1
- Sodium: 140
- Total Carbohydrate: 11.9
- Cholesterol: 82
- Protein: 2.6

582.　　Napoleon Cremes

Serving: 4 dozen. | Prep: 15mins | Cook: 0mins | Ready in:

Ingredients

- 2 cups finely crushed graham cracker crumbs
- 1 cup sweetened shredded coconut
- 1/4 cup granulated sugar
- 1/4 cup baking cocoa
- 1/2 cup plus 2 tablespoons butter, melted
- 1 teaspoon vanilla extract
- FILLING:
- 1/2 cup butter, softened
- 2 cups confectioners' sugar
- 1 package (3.4 ounces) instant pistachio or lemon pudding mix
- 3 tablespoons whole milk
- TOPPING:
- 1 cup semisweet chocolate chips
- 3 tablespoons butter

Direction

- Mix the coconut, sugar, graham cracker crumbs and cocoa, and combine in melted butter with vanilla. Even or flatten the bottom of a 9-inch greased square baking pan and press on it.

- To make the filling, soften butter and beat until smooth then add pudding mix, confectioners' sugar and milk, and beat until the mixture is fluffy. Pour mixture over the crust and place in refrigerator until firm for about 1.5 to 2 hours.
- For the topping, melt chocolate chips and butter in microwave on high setting while stirring every after 30 seconds until fully melted and smooth. After cooling, spread it over the pudding. Put in refrigerator until firm and slice it into bars.

Nutrition Information

- Calories:
- Sodium:
- Fiber:
- Total Carbohydrate:
- Cholesterol:
- Protein:
- Total Fat:

---

583. No Bake Pineapple Sour Cream Pie

Serving: 6-8 servings. | Prep: 5mins | Cook: 0mins | Ready in:

Ingredients

- 1 package (3.4 ounces) instant vanilla pudding mix
- 2 cups (16 ounces) sour cream
- 1 can (8 ounces) crushed pineapple, undrained
- 1 graham cracker crust (9 inches)
- Whipped cream, optional

Direction

- Mix sour cream and dry pudding mix together in a small mixing bowl. Fold in pineapple. Spread mixture into crust. Chill for 3 hours,

covered, until firm. Serve topped with whipped, if desired.

Nutrition Information

- Calories: 292 calories
- Cholesterol: 40mg cholesterol
- Protein: 3g protein.
- Total Fat: 15g fat (8g saturated fat)
- Sodium: 322mg sodium
- Fiber: 1g fiber)
- Total Carbohydrate: 33g carbohydrate (27g sugars

---

584. Nutty Butterscotch Bites

Serving: about 12 dozen. | Prep: 35mins | Cook: 20mins | Ready in:

Ingredients

- 1 cup butter, softened
- 3/4 cup packed brown sugar
- 1/4 cup sugar
- 2 large eggs
- 1 teaspoon vanilla extract
- 2-1/4 cups all-purpose flour
- 1 package (3.4 ounces) instant butterscotch pudding mix
- 1 teaspoon baking soda
- 1-1/3 cups butterscotch chips
- FILLING:
- 1/4 cup butter, cubed
- 1 cup sugar
- 1/4 cup evaporated milk
- 1 jar (7 ounces) marshmallow creme
- 1/4 cup peanut butter
- 1 teaspoon vanilla extract
- 1-1/2 cups salted peanuts
- CARAMEL LAYER:
- 1 package (14 ounces) caramels
- 1/4 cup heavy whipping cream
- TOPPING:
- 1 cup semisweet chocolate chips

- 1 cup butterscotch chips
- 1 teaspoon shortening
- 1/4 cup peanut butter

Direction

- Whisk butter with sugars in a big bowl. Put in eggs, 1 by 1, whipping well after each increment. Whisk in vanilla. Mix the baking soda, pudding mix and flour; put into creamed mixture gradually. Mix in butterscotch chips. Scatter into a greased 15x10x1-inch baking dish. Bake for 20-25 minutes at 350° or until a toothpick inserted in the middle exists clean. Let cool on a wire rack.
- In a heavy saucepan over medium heat, melt the butter for the filling. Put in milk and sugar; heat up to a gentle boil. Turn down heat to medium-low; boil and mix for 5 minutes. Take off from the heat. Mix in vanilla, peanut butter and marshmallow creme until combined and smooth. Mix in peanuts. Spread on crust. Chill until firm.
- Cook and mix the caramels with cream in a saucepan over low heat until melted and smooth; cook and mix for 4 minutes more. Spread on top of filling. Chill until firm.
- Melt the shortening, butterscotch chips and chocolate chips. Mix in peanut butter. Scatter over caramel layer. Chill for 4 hours or overnight. Take out from the fridge 20 minutes before slicing. Slice into 1-inch squares.

Nutrition Information

- Calories:
- Total Fat:
- Sodium:
- Fiber:
- Total Carbohydrate:
- Cholesterol:
- Protein:

585.   Old Fashioned Banana Cream Pie

Serving: 8 servings. | Prep: 10mins | Cook: 0mins | Ready in:

Ingredients

- 1 cup cold 2% milk
- 1/2 teaspoon vanilla extract
- 1 package (3.4 ounces) instant vanilla pudding mix
- 1 carton (12 ounces) frozen whipped topping, thawed, divided
- 1 graham cracker crust (9 inches)
- 2 medium firm bananas, sliced
- Additional banana slices, optional

Direction

- Beat pudding mix, vanilla, and milk for 2 minutes in a large mixing bowl until thickened. Add 3 cups whipped topping and fold gently.
- Transfer 1 1/3 cups pudding mixture to the pie crust. Place banana slices over pudding mixture; spread the rest of pudding mixture over banana slices. Spread the remaining whipped topping over top. Decorate with extra banana slices, if desired. Chill until ready to serve.

Nutrition Information

- Calories: 311 calories
- Cholesterol: 2mg cholesterol
- Protein: 2g protein.
- Total Fat: 13g fat (9g saturated fat)
- Sodium: 213mg sodium
- Fiber: 1g fiber)
- Total Carbohydrate: 43g carbohydrate (29g sugars

586. On The Green Cake

Serving: 12-15 servings. | Prep: 20mins | Cook: 30mins | Ready in:

Ingredients

- 1 package yellow cake mix (regular size)
- 1 can (11 ounces) mandarin oranges
- 1 can (20 ounces) crushed pineapple
- 1 carton (8 ounces) frozen whipped topping, thawed
- 1 package (3.4 ounces) instant vanilla pudding mix
- 3 to 6 drops green food coloring
- 1 wooden skewer (about 6 inches)
- 1 Chuckles candy
- 1 miniature white marshmallow

Direction

- Prepare cake batter as directed on package. Strain oranges, saving 2 tablespoons juice; put juice to one side. Fold oranges into the batter. Transfer mixture to a buttered 13x9-inch baking dish. Bake for 30 to 35 minutes at 350° until a toothpick comes out clean from the center. Allow cake to cool on a wire rack.
- Prick holes into the cake with a toothpick, separate holes 1 inch apart. Strain pineapple, saving 2 tablespoons juice; put pineapple to one side. Mix pineapple juices and the reserved orange together; stream over the cake. Chill until deep cold.
- Mix together pudding mix and whipped topping in a mixing bowl. Measure 1 cup and set into a small bowl; mix in food coloring. Pipe in a kidney bean shape onto the cake to make a putting green. Add pineapple to the remaining whipped topping mixture and fold gently; distribute over unfrosted part of the cake.
- Press wooden skewer into putting green for the pin. Trim candy into a triangle; stick to top of the skewer for flag. Slice marshmallow in half and shape into a ball; lay on the green. Chill until ready to serve.

Nutrition Information

- Calories:
- Protein:
- Total Fat:
- Sodium:
- Fiber:
- Total Carbohydrate:
- Cholesterol:

587. Orange Creme Squares

Serving: 9 servings. | Prep: 20mins | Cook: 0mins | Ready in:

Ingredients

- CRUST:
- 3/4 cup graham cracker crumbs
- 1/4 cup lightly packed brown sugar
- 1/4 cup butter, melted
- FILLING:
- 3/4 cup cold whole milk
- 1 pint vanilla ice cream, softened
- 2 teaspoons grated orange zest
- 1 package (3.4 ounces) instant vanilla pudding mix
- GLAZE:
- 4 teaspoons cornstarch
- 1/4 cup sugar
- 1/2 cup orange juice
- 2 tablespoons lemon juice
- 1 can (11 ounces) mandarin oranges, juice drained and reserved

Direction

- Mix crust ingredients together and pat into an 8-inch square pan. Refrigerate. To make filling, mix orange zest, ice cream, and milk together in a mixing bowl. Put in pudding mix, beating gradually using a mixer on lowest speed or with rotary beater until incorporated. Pour mixture into the crust. Refrigerate for about 1 hour or until set. In the meantime, prepare glaze. Combine reserved mandarin orange juice, lemon juice, orange juice, sugar, and cornstarch in a saucepan. Bring to a boil. Lower heat. Cook for about 2 minutes, stirring continuously, until thickened. Put off the heat and allow to cool. Top filing with oranges. Spread glaze over top. Refrigerate until firm.

Nutrition Information

- Calories: 263 calories
- Total Carbohydrate: 43g carbohydrate (33g sugars
- Cholesterol: 29mg cholesterol
- Protein: 2g protein.
- Total Fat: 10g fat (6g saturated fat)
- Sodium: 283mg sodium
- Fiber: 1g fiber)

588.　Orange Pineapple Torte

Serving: 12 servings. | Prep: 25mins | Cook: 25mins | Ready in:

Ingredients

- 1 package yellow cake mix (regular size)
- 2 packages (1 ounce each) sugar-free instant vanilla pudding mix, divided
- 4 egg whites
- 1 cup water
- 1/4 cup canola oil
- 1/4 teaspoon baking soda
- 1 cup cold fat-free milk
- 1 carton (8 ounces) frozen reduced-fat whipped topping, thawed
- 1 can (20 ounces) unsweetened crushed pineapple, well drained
- 1 can (11 ounces) mandarin oranges, drained, divided
- Fresh mint, optional

Direction

- Beat baking soda, oil, water, egg whites, 1 pudding mix package and cake mix for 30 seconds on low speed in big bowl; beat for 2 minutes on medium.
- Put in 2 9-in. greased and floured round baking pans; bake for 25-30 minutes at 350° till inserted toothpick in middle exits clean. Cool for 10 minutes. Transfer from pans to wire racks; completely cool.
- Filling: Whisk leftover pudding mix and milk for 2 minutes; stand for 2 minutes, it will be thick. Fold whipped topping in. Mix pineapple, 1/2 oranges and 1 1/2 cups pudding mixture in small bowl.
- Horizontally, cut every cake to 2 layers; top with 1/3 pineapple mixture. Repeat layers 2 times. Top with leftover layer; use leftover pudding mixture to frost sides and top of cake. Keep in the fridge; if desired, garnish with mint and leftover oranges.

Nutrition Information

- Calories: 335 calories
- Protein: 4g protein. Diabetic Exchanges: 2 starch
- Total Fat: 9g fat (0 saturated fat)
- Sodium: 516mg sodium
- Fiber: 0 fiber)
- Total Carbohydrate: 58g carbohydrate (0 sugars
- Cholesterol: 0 cholesterol

589.　Paradise Parfaits

Serving: 6 servings, about 1/2 cup each | Prep: 10mins | Cook: | Ready in:

Ingredients

- 1/4 cup MAXWELL HOUSE INTERNATIONAL CAFÉ Sugar Free French Vanilla Café
- 1 Tbsp. hot water

- 2 cups cold fat-free milk
- 1 pkg. (1 oz.) JELL-O Vanilla Flavor Sugar Free Fat Free Instant Pudding
- 1/2 cup thawed COOL WHIP FREE Whipped Topping
- 1 cup sliced fresh strawberries

Direction

- 1. In a medium bowl with hot water, add flavored instant coffee and melt. Stir in pudding mix and milk; use whisk to blend for 2 minutes. Mix in COOL WHIP.
- 2. Onto each of 6 dessert glasses, put half the pudding mixture; layer and cover with strawberries. Place the rest of the pudding mixture on top.
- 3. Store in the refrigerator for at least 1 hour prior to serving.

Nutrition Information

- Calories: 90
- Fiber: 1 g
- Total Carbohydrate: 15 g
- Saturated Fat: 1.5 g
- Sodium: 270 mg
- Sugar: 6 g
- Cholesterol: 0 mg
- Protein: 3 g
- Total Fat: 1.5 g

590. Patriotic Dessert

Serving: 12-15 servings. | Prep: 40mins | Cook: 0mins | Ready in:

Ingredients

- 1 cup all-purpose flour
- 1 cup finely chopped pecans
- 1/2 cup butter, softened
- 1 package (8 ounces) cream cheese, softened
- 1 cup confectioners' sugar

- 1 carton (8 ounces) frozen whipped topping, thawed, divided
- 1-1/2 cups cold milk
- 1 package (5.1 ounces) instant vanilla pudding mix
- 3 cups fresh strawberries, halved
- 1/2 cup fresh blueberries

Direction

- In a bowl, mix butter, pecans and flour together. Press into a clean and dry baking dish of 13x9 inches. Bake for 18-20 minutes at 350°. Let cool on a wire rack.
- Beat confectioners' sugar and cream cheese together in a bowl. Fold in 1/2 whipped topping; spread on top of the crust. In a separate bowl, whisk pudding mix and milk together for 2 minutes. Allow to rest until soft-set, about 2 minutes.
- Spread over the cream cheese layer. Add the remaining whipped topping on top to cover. Decorate with blueberries and strawberries to make a flag. Keep chilled for at least 1 hour before serving.

Nutrition Information

- Calories: 335 calories
- Sodium: 255mg sodium
- Fiber: 2g fiber)
- Total Carbohydrate: 34g carbohydrate (22g sugars
- Cholesterol: 36mg cholesterol
- Protein: 4g protein.
- Total Fat: 21g fat (11g saturated fat)

591. Patriotic Trifle

Serving: 16 servings, about 2/3 cup each | Prep: 30mins | Cook: | Ready in:

Ingredients

- 1 pkg. (1 oz.) JELL-O Vanilla Flavor Sugar Free Fat Free Instant Pudding
- 1-1/2 cups cold fat-free milk
- 1 tub (8 oz.) COOL WHIP LITE Whipped Topping , thawed, divided
- 1 pkg. (13 oz.) angel food cake , cut into 1/2-inch cubes (about 6-1/2 cups)
- 2 cups fresh strawberries , sliced
- 1 cup blueberries

Direction

- Use whisk to beat milk and pudding mix for 2 minutes in medium bowl; mix 1 1/2 cups COOL WHIP in.
- Layer 1/2 each of berries and cake in big serving bowl; use pudding mixture to cover. Put layers of leftover cake, berries then COOL WHIP over.
- Refrigerate for 1 hour.

Nutrition Information

- Calories: 120
- Saturated Fat: 2 g
- Sugar: 18 g
- Total Carbohydrate: 23 g
- Cholesterol: 0 mg
- Total Fat: 2 g
- Sodium: 250 mg
- Fiber: 1 g
- Protein: 2 g

592. Pay Dirt Cake

Serving: 8-10 servings. | Prep: 15mins | Cook: 0mins | Ready in:

Ingredients

- 28 Oreo cookies
- 1 package (8 ounces) cream cheese, softened
- 1/4 cup butter, softened
- 1 cup confectioners' sugar

- 3-1/3 cups cold milk
- 2 packages (3.4 ounces each) instant French vanilla pudding mix
- 1 carton (8 ounces) frozen whipped topping, thawed

Direction

- Process cookies till finely crushed in blender/food processor; put 2 tbsp. crumbs aside for topping.
- Beat sugar, butter and crema cheese in big bowl. Whisk pudding mix and milk for 2 minutes then add to cream cheese mixture; stir well. Fold whipped topping in.
- In 2 1/2-qt. container/bowl, put 1/2 cookie crumbs. Put 1/2 pudding mixture over; repeat layers. Sprinkle leftover crumbs; refrigerate till serving.

Nutrition Information

- Calories: 463 calories
- Cholesterol: 48mg cholesterol
- Protein: 6g protein.
- Total Fat: 25g fat (15g saturated fat)
- Sodium: 494mg sodium
- Fiber: 1g fiber)
- Total Carbohydrate: 52g carbohydrate (37g sugars

593. Peach Ice Cream

Serving: 32 | Prep: 20mins | Cook: | Ready in:

Ingredients

- 6 eggs, beaten
- 3 1/2 cups white sugar
- 10 fresh peaches, pitted and chopped
- 4 cups heavy cream
- 2 cups half-and-half cream
- 2 teaspoons vanilla extract
- 3/4 teaspoon salt

Direction

- Mix sugar and eggs till smooth in big bowl; puree peaches in food processor/blender. Mix 5 cups puree into egg mixture then mix salt, vanilla, half and half and cream in well.
- Put mixture in ice cream maker's freezer canister; follow manufacturer's instructions to freeze.

Nutrition Information

- Calories: 229 calories;
- Total Carbohydrate: 25.3
- Cholesterol: 81
- Protein: 2.2
- Total Fat: 13.7
- Sodium: 86

---

594.   Peach Pudding

Serving: 4 servings. | Prep: 10mins | Cook: 0mins | Ready in:

Ingredients

- 1/4 cup peach or apricot gelatin
- 1/2 cup hot milk
- 1-1/2 cups cold milk
- 1 package (3.4 ounces) instant vanilla pudding mix
- Sliced fresh peaches and whipped topping, optional

Direction

- Dissolve gelatin powder in a big bowl with hot milk then put aside. In the meantime, beat dry pudding mix and cold milk together in a big bowl on low speed about 2 minutes. Beat in gelatin mixture and allow to stand about 5 minutes. Scoop into separate dishes. Use peaches and whipped topping to decorate if you want.

Nutrition Information

- Calories: 217 calories
- Protein: 5g protein.
- Total Fat: 4g fat (3g saturated fat)
- Sodium: 432mg sodium
- Fiber: 0 fiber)
- Total Carbohydrate: 40g carbohydrate (36g sugars
- Cholesterol: 17mg cholesterol

---

595.   Peanut Butter Brownie Trifle

Serving: 20 servings (1 cup each). | Prep: 40mins | Cook: 20mins | Ready in:

Ingredients

- 1 fudge brownie mix (13-inch x 9-inch pan size)
- 1 package (10 ounces) peanut butter chips
- 2 packages (13 ounces each) miniature peanut butter cups
- 4 cups cold 2% milk
- 2 packages (5.1 ounces each) instant vanilla pudding mix
- 1 cup creamy peanut butter
- 4 teaspoons vanilla extract
- 3 cartons (8 ounces each) frozen whipped topping, thawed

Direction

- Preheat an oven to 350°. Follow package directions to prep brownie batter; mix peanut butter chips in. Bake for 20-25 minutes in 13x9-in. greased baking pan till inserted toothpick in middle exits with moist crumbs but don't overbake. On wire rack, cool; cut to 3/4-in. pieces.
- Halve peanut butter cups; put 1/3 cup aside for garnish. Whisk pudding mixes and milk for 2 minutes till thick in big bowl. Add vanilla

and peanut butter; stir well. Fold 1 1/2 cartons whipped topping in.

- Put 1/3 brownies in 5-qt. glass bowl; put 1/3 leftover peanut butter cups over. Put 1/3 pudding mixture on top. Repeat layers 2 times. Use leftover whipped topping to cover; garnish using leftover peanut butter cups. Refrigerate till chilled.

Nutrition Information

- Calories: 680 calories
- Cholesterol: 28mg cholesterol
- Protein: 13g protein.
- Total Fat: 38g fat (15g saturated fat)
- Sodium: 547mg sodium
- Fiber: 3g fiber)
- Total Carbohydrate: 73g carbohydrate (54g sugars

596. Peanut Butter Chocolate Dessert

Serving: 16 servings. | Prep: 20mins | Cook: 0mins | Ready in:

Ingredients

- 20 chocolate cream-filled chocolate sandwich cookies, divided
- 2 tablespoons butter, softened
- 1 package (8 ounces) cream cheese, softened
- 1/2 cup peanut butter
- 1-1/2 cups confectioners' sugar, divided
- 1 carton (16 ounces) frozen whipped topping, thawed, divided
- 15 miniature peanut butter cups, chopped
- 1 cup cold whole milk
- 1 package (3.9 ounces) instant chocolate fudge pudding mix

Direction

- Crumble 16 cookies; combine them with butter. Pat cookie mixture into an ungreased 9-inch dish; put to one side.
- Beat cream cheese with 1 cup confectioners' sugar and peanut butter in a large mixing bowl until smooth. Add half of the whipped topping and fold gently. Distribute mixture over the crust. Scatter top with peanut butter cups.
- Whisk pudding mix, the rest of confectioners' sugar and milk in a separate large bowl for 2 minutes on low speed. Allow to sit until soft-set, for 2 minutes. Add the rest of whipped topping to the mixture and fold gently.
- Distribute over peanut butter cups. Crumble the rest of cookies; scatter over top. Chill, covered, for a minimum of 3 hours.

Nutrition Information

- Calories: 366 calories
- Fiber: 1g fiber)
- Total Carbohydrate: 40g carbohydrate (28g sugars
- Cholesterol: 22mg cholesterol
- Protein: 5g protein.
- Total Fat: 21g fat (11g saturated fat)
- Sodium: 307mg sodium

597. Peanut Butter Chocolate Pie

Serving: 8 servings. | Prep: 10mins | Cook: 0mins | Ready in:

Ingredients

- 1 package (6 ounces) peanut butter cups
- 1 cup cold 2% milk
- 1 package (3.9 ounces) instant chocolate pudding mix
- 1 carton (8 ounces) frozen whipped topping, thawed
- 1 chocolate crumb crust (8 inches)

Direction

- Slice four peanut butter cups into halves; chop up the rest of the cups roughly and put aside. Whisk together milk and pudding mix in a large bowl for 2 minutes (the mixture will get thick). Fold the whipped topping into this mixture.
- Fold the chopped peanut butter cups into the mixture. Spoon it into crust. Decorate the top with halved peanut butter cups. Chill in refrigerator for no less than 15 minutes before serving.

Nutrition Information

- Calories: 364 calories
- Sodium: 388mg sodium
- Fiber: 2g fiber)
- Total Carbohydrate: 46g carbohydrate (31g sugars
- Cholesterol: 5mg cholesterol
- Protein: 5g protein.
- Total Fat: 17g fat (9g saturated fat)

598.   Peanut Butter Chocolate Pudding

Serving: 6 servings. | Prep: 25mins | Cook: 0mins | Ready in:

Ingredients

- 2 cups cold fat-free milk, divided
- 2 tablespoons reduced-fat chunky peanut butter
- 1 cup reduced-fat whipped topping, divided
- 1 package (1.4 ounces) sugar-free instant chocolate (fudge) pudding mix

Direction

- Mix together 2 tablespoons milk and peanut butter in a small bowl till smooth. Fold 3/4 cup whipped topping into the mixture; put

aside. Beat together the pudding mix and remaining milk in a bowl for about 2 minutes until blended. Let sit for 5 minutes.
- Into six parfait bowls or glasses, spoon half of the pudding; add the remaining pudding and peanut butter mixture on top. Garnish with the rest of the whipped topping.

Nutrition Information

- Calories: 102 calories
- Total Fat: 3g fat (0 saturated fat)
- Sodium: 144mg sodium
- Fiber: 0 fiber)
- Total Carbohydrate: 13g carbohydrate (0 sugars
- Cholesterol: 1mg cholesterol
- Protein: 5g protein. Diabetic Exchanges: 1 starch

599.   Peanut Butter Chocolate Tarts

Serving: 6 servings. | Prep: 15mins | Cook: 0mins | Ready in:

Ingredients

- 1 cup peanut butter chips
- 1 tablespoon vegetable oil
- 1 package (3.9 ounces) instant chocolate pudding mix
- 1-3/4 cups cold milk
- 1 package (6 count) individual graham cracker tart shells
- Whipped topping
- Halloween candy, sprinkles and/or cake decorations

Direction

- Heat oil and chips in a microwave until melted; whisk until no lumps remain. Allow mixture to cool for 5 minutes. In the meantime, whisk milk and pudding in a large mixing bowl until thickened. Add peanut butter mixture and fold gently. Put mixture into tart shells. Refrigerate for 15 minutes. Place a dollop of whipped topping on top and garnish as desired.

Nutrition Information

- Calories: 411 calories
- Fiber: 3g fiber)
- Total Carbohydrate: 53g carbohydrate (34g sugars
- Cholesterol: 10mg cholesterol
- Protein: 9g protein.
- Total Fat: 19g fat (7g saturated fat)
- Sodium: 521mg sodium

600. Peanut Butter Icebox Dessert

Serving: 12-15 servings. | Prep: 20mins | Cook: 0mins | Ready in:

Ingredients

- 1 package (8 ounces) Girl Scout Peanut Butter Sandwich Cookies, crushed, divided
- 1/4 cup sugar
- 1/4 cup butter, melted
- 1 package (8 ounces) cream cheese, softened
- 1-1/3 cups confectioners' sugar
- 1 carton (8 ounces) frozen whipped topping, thawed, divided
- 2-1/2 cups cold 2% milk
- 2 packages (3.9 ounces each) instant chocolate pudding mix
- Additional peanut butter cookies, broken into pieces

Direction

- Mix together butter, sugar and 1 3/4 cups of crushed cookies in a big bowl, then press the

mixture into a grease-free 9"x13" baking dish. Bake at 350 degrees until turn golden brown, about 6 to 8 minutes, then allow to cool on a wire rack.
- Beat confectioners' sugar and cream cheese together in a big bowl until smooth, then fold in 1 1/2 cups of whipped topping. Spread the cream cheese mixture over cooled crust.
- Beat pudding mix and milk in a separate big bowl on low speed until thickened, about 2 minutes. Spread this mixture over the cream cheese layer. Put leftover whipped topping on top and use 1/4 cup of crushed cookie pieces to sprinkle over top. Cover and chill for a minimum of an hour prior to serving.

Nutrition Information

- Calories:
- Protein:
- Total Fat:
- Sodium:
- Fiber:
- Total Carbohydrate:
- Cholesterol:

601. Peanut Butter Puddingwiches

Serving: 32 sandwiches. | Prep: 30mins | Cook: 0mins | Ready in:

Ingredients

- 1-1/2 cups peanut butter, divided
- 3 cups cold milk, divided
- 1 package (3.9 ounces) instant chocolate pudding mix
- 2 cups whipped topping, divided
- 1 package (3.4 ounces) instant vanilla pudding mix
- 32 whole graham crackers

Direction

- Line foil on 2 13x9-in. pans; put aside. Mix 1 1/2 cups milk and 3/4 cup peanut butter till smooth in big bowl. Beat in chocolate pudding mix till blended slowly; fold in 1 cup of whipped topping.
- Transfer into prepped pan; freeze till firm. Do the same with vanilla pudding and leftover peanut butter, whipped topping and milk. Remove into 2nd pan, freeze till firm.
- Cut/break graham crackers to square. Slice frozen pudding mixture to 32 2 1/2x2 1/4-in. squares; put every square between 2 crackers. In plastic, wrap; freeze overnight.

Nutrition Information

- Calories: 216 calories
- Total Carbohydrate: 28g carbohydrate (0 sugars
- Cholesterol: 0 cholesterol
- Protein: 6g protein. Diabetic Exchanges: 2 starch
- Total Fat: 9g fat (2g saturated fat)
- Sodium: 324mg sodium
- Fiber: 2g fiber)

602. Peanut Butter Tarts

Serving: 6 | Prep: | Cook: | Ready in:

Ingredients

- 1/2 cup shortening
- 1/2 cup white sugar
- 1/2 cup packed brown sugar
- 1 egg
- 1/2 cup peanut butter
- 1 1/4 cups all-purpose flour
- 1/2 teaspoon baking powder
- 3/4 teaspoon baking soda
- 1/4 teaspoon salt
- 12 miniature chocolate covered peanut butter cups, unwrapped
- 1 cup frozen whipped topping, thawed

Direction

- Cream white sugar, brown sugar, and shortening in a medium bowl. Stirring in the egg, then the peanut butter. Sifting salt, baking soda, baking powder and flour together; stirring this into the creamed mixture. Let dough sit for an hour in the refrigerator.
- Heat oven to 190°C (375°F) beforehand. Greasing a mini muffin pan lightly.
- Rolling the dough into balls with the size of walnuts and lay into mini muffin cups; slightly flatten. In preheated oven, allow to bake till cookies turn brown lightly for 8-10 minutes.
- During the time the cookies are baking, unwrapping the mini peanut butter cups. While mini peanut butter cups are still hot from the oven, in the center of the cookie tarts, pressing down mini peanut butter cups. Before removing cookies from the pan, let them cool down slightly. To decorate cookies for special occasions, use a spatula or small knifes to smooth off the top of the mini peanut butter cup, and pipe onto the center of each tart by piping a small star of whipped topping with a pastry bag.

Nutrition Information

- Calories: 639 calories;
- Protein: 10.9
- Total Fat: 36.9
- Sodium: 463
- Total Carbohydrate: 70.4
- Cholesterol: 32

603. Peanut Pudding Dessert

Serving: 15-18 servings. | Prep: 20mins | Cook: 20mins | Ready in:

Ingredients

- 1/2 cup cold butter, cubed
- 1 cup all-purpose flour
- 2/3 cup chopped dry roasted peanuts
- 1 package (8 ounces) cream cheese, softened
- 1 cup confectioners' sugar
- 1/3 cup peanut butter
- 1 carton (8 ounces) frozen whipped topping, thawed, divided
- 2-3/4 cups cold milk
- 1 package (3.9 ounces) instant chocolate pudding mix
- 1 package (3.4 ounces) instant vanilla pudding mix
- Chocolate curls and additional chopped peanuts, optional

Direction

- Cut butter into flour in a small mixing bowl until crumbly. Mix in peanuts. Pat mixture into an ungreased 13x9-inch baking dish. Bake for 16 to 20 minutes at 350° until lightly brown. Allow to cool on a wire rack.
- Whisk cream cheese, peanut butter, and confectioners' sugar together in a large mixing bowl until smooth. Fold in 1 1/2 cups whipped topping. Gently distribute over crust.
- Beat pudding mixes and milk in a large mixing bowl until thickened, about 2 minutes. Gently spread over the layer of cream cheese. Spread the remaining whipped topping over pudding mixture. Decorate with more peanuts and chocolate curls, if desired. Chill until ready to serve.

Nutrition Information

- Calories: 299 calories
- Sodium: 339mg sodium
- Fiber: 1g fiber)
- Total Carbohydrate: 29g carbohydrate (18g sugars
- Cholesterol: 33mg cholesterol
- Protein: 6g protein.
- Total Fat: 18g fat (10g saturated fat)

604. Pecan Butterscotch Cookies

Serving: about 1-1/2 dozen. | Prep: 10mins | Cook: 10mins | Ready in:

Ingredients

- 1 cup complete buttermilk pancake mix
- 1 package (3.4 ounces) instant butterscotch pudding mix
- 1/3 cup butter, melted
- 1 large egg
- 1/2 cup chopped pecans, toasted

Direction

- Beat together egg, butter, dry pudding mix and pancake mix in a big bowl until mixed, then stir in pecans.
- Roll the mixture into balls with 1 1/2 inches in size, then arrange balls on baking sheets coated with grease with 2 inches apart. Use the bottom of a glass to flatten balls. Bake at 350 degrees until edges start to brown, about 8 to 10 minutes. Transfer to wire racks to cool.

Nutrition Information

- Calories: 85 calories
- Total Fat: 5g fat (2g saturated fat)
- Sodium: 178mg sodium
- Fiber: 0 fiber)
- Total Carbohydrate: 9g carbohydrate (4g sugars
- Cholesterol: 17mg cholesterol
- Protein: 1g protein.

605. Pecan Chip Tube Cake

Serving: 12 servings. | Prep: 15mins | Cook: 55mins | Ready in:

Ingredients

- 1 package yellow cake mix (regular size)
- 1 package (3.4 ounces) instant vanilla pudding mix
- 4 eggs
- 1 cup vegetable oil
- 1 cup (8 ounces) sour cream
- 1 cup chopped pecans
- 1 cup (6 ounces) semisweet chocolate chips
- 1 cup miniature marshmallows

Direction

- Mix together the first 5 ingredients in a big bowl. Beat the mixture for half a minute on low speed. Increase to medium speed and beat for 2 minutes.
- Transfer 1/2 batter to a 10-inch tube pan already greased and dusted with flour. Mix together chocolate chips and pecans; scatter 1/2 mixture on top of the batter. Layer marshmallows and the rest of batter on top and scatter with the rest of pecan mixture.
- Bake in 350-degree oven until a toothpick is clean when coming out of the middle, about 55 to 60 minutes. Allow to cool in pan for 10 minutes, then turn up-side down onto a plate and serve.

Nutrition Information

- Calories: 438 calories
- Fiber: 2g fiber)
- Total Carbohydrate: 42g carbohydrate (27g sugars
- Cholesterol: 63mg cholesterol
- Protein: 5g protein.
- Total Fat: 29g fat (7g saturated fat)
- Sodium: 314mg sodium

606.   Pilgrim Pudding

Serving: 2 servings. | Prep: 10mins | Cook: 0mins | Ready in:

Ingredients

- 3/4 cup cold fat-free milk
- 1/3 cup canned pumpkin
- 2 tablespoons sugar-free instant vanilla pudding mix
- 1/2 cup plus 1 tablespoon fat-free whipped topping, divided
- 1-1/2 teaspoons fat-free caramel ice cream topping
- 1 teaspoon sliced almonds, toasted

Direction

- Mix pumpkins and milk in a large bowl. Add pudding mix; beat until slightly thickened or for 2 minutes. Allow to rest until soft-set or for 2 minutes. Fold in half cup of whipped topping.
- Scoop into 2 dessert dishes. Decorate with the rest of the whipped topping; drizzle with caramel topping and top with almonds.

Nutrition Information

- Calories: 117 calories
- Sodium: 362mg sodium
- Fiber: 2g fiber)
- Total Carbohydrate: 22g carbohydrate (9g sugars
- Cholesterol: 2mg cholesterol
- Protein: 4g protein. Diabetic Exchanges: 1 starch
- Total Fat: 1g fat (0 saturated fat)

607.   Pina Colada Bundt Cake

Serving: 12 servings. | Prep: 15mins | Cook: 45mins | Ready in:

Ingredients

- 1 package white cake mix (regular size)
- 1 package (3.4 ounces) instant coconut cream pudding mix
- 1 cup canola oil
- 3/4 cup water
- 2 large eggs
- 1/4 cup rum
- 1 cup drained crushed pineapple
- GLAZE:
- 2 cups confectioners' sugar, divided
- 2 tablespoons unsweetened pineapple juice
- 1/4 cup cream of coconut
- 1 tablespoon rum
- 1/4 cup sweetened shredded coconut

Direction

- Set oven to 350 degrees and start preheating. Grease a fluted tube pan of 10 inches and dust with flour.
- Whisk together rum, eggs, water, oil, pudding mix and cake mix in a big bowl; beat the mixture for half a minute on low speed. Increase the speed to medium and beat for 2 minutes. Mix pineapples into the batter. Pour into the cake pan. Bake at 350 degrees until a toothpick is clean when coming out of the middle, about 45 to 50 minutes. Let the cake cool for 15 minutes in the pan, then transfer to a wire rack.
- Combine pineapple juice and a cup of confectioners' sugar in a small bowl; brush on top of the cake while still warm. Allow cake to fully cool.
- Combine the rest of confectioners' sugar, rum and cream of coconut; pour onto the cake. Scatter coconut on top.

Nutrition Information

- Calories: 495 calories
- Protein: 3g protein.
- Total Fat: 25g fat (5g saturated fat)
- Sodium: 357mg sodium
- Fiber: 1g fiber)
- Total Carbohydrate: 64g carbohydrate (47g sugars
- Cholesterol: 31mg cholesterol

608. Pineapple Angel Food Torte

Serving: 12 servings. | Prep: 10mins | Cook: 0mins | Ready in:

Ingredients

- 1/2 cup cold whole milk
- 1 package (3.4 ounces) instant vanilla pudding mix
- 1 can (8 ounces) crushed pineapple, undrained
- 1 carton (8 ounces) frozen whipped topping, thawed
- 1 prepared angel food cake (8 to 10 ounces)
- 1/2 cup sweetened shredded coconut
- Maraschino cherries

Direction

- Stir pudding mix and milk together in a large mixing bowl for 2 minutes until thickened. Mix in pineapple. Add whipped topping and fold gently.
- Horizontally slice cake into 3 layers. Lay the bottom layer on a serving plate. Smear 1 1/3 cups pineapple mixture over the bottom layer. Repeat layering process. Set top layer on cake; spread the rest of pineapple mixture over top; scatter with coconut; decorate cake with cherries.

Nutrition Information

- Calories:
- Total Fat:
- Sodium:
- Fiber:
- Total Carbohydrate:
- Cholesterol:

- Protein:

609. Pineapple Coconut Pie

Serving: 8 | Prep: | Cook: | Ready in:

Ingredients

- 1 (9 inch) pie shell, baked
- 2 1/2 cups unsweetened pineapple juice
- 1/3 cup all-purpose flour
- 1 cup white sugar
- 1 teaspoon salt
- 1 egg
- 1 cup flaked coconut
- 1 tablespoon butter
- 1 teaspoon vanilla extract

Direction

- In a blender, combine egg, salt, sugar, flour, and pineapple juice. Blend till smooth.
- In medium saucepan, cook while stirring over medium heat until thick. Take away from heat. Whisk in vanilla, butter and coconut. Blend well. Spoon into baked pie shell. Let cool until set.

Nutrition Information

- Calories: 341 calories;
- Cholesterol: 27
- Protein: 3.4
- Total Fat: 12.6
- Sodium: 460
- Total Carbohydrate: 54.6

610. Pineapple Fluff Pie

Serving: 8 servings. | Prep: 10mins | Cook: 0mins | Ready in:

Ingredients

- 1 can (20 ounces) unsweetened crushed pineapple, drained
- 1 package (3.4 ounces) instant lemon pudding mix
- 1 carton (8 ounces) frozen whipped topping, thawed
- 1 graham cracker crust (9 inches)

Direction

- Combine pudding mix and pineapple in a large mixing bowl until thickened; add whipped topping and fold gently. Spread mixture into crust. Chill until ready to serve.

Nutrition Information

- Calories: 190 calories
- Protein: 2g protein. Diabetic Exchanges: 1-1/2 fat
- Total Fat: 7g fat (0 saturated fat)
- Sodium: 125mg sodium
- Fiber: 1g fiber)
- Total Carbohydrate: 28g carbohydrate (0 sugars
- Cholesterol: 0 cholesterol

611. Pineapple Icebox Dessert

Serving: 15 servings. | Prep: 10mins | Cook: 0mins | Ready in:

Ingredients

- 2 cups cold fat-free milk
- 1 package (1 ounce) sugar-free instant vanilla pudding mix
- 1 cup reduced-fat whipped topping
- 1 can (20 ounces) pineapple tidbits
- 2 packages (3 ounces each) ladyfingers

Direction

- Mix together pudding mix and milk for 2 minutes in a big bowl. Rest for 2 minutes. Mix in whipped topping and put the mixture aside.
- Drain the pineapple rings, leaving quarter cup of pineapple juice. Place half of the ladyfingers in 11x7-inch dish (ungreased).
- Brush the ladyfingers with 2 tablespoons of the leftover pineapple juice. Spread half of the pudding mixture and half of the pineapple. Repeat making the same layers. Cover and store in the fridge overnight. Cut into equal squares and serve.

Nutrition Information

- Calories: 183 calories
- Total Fat: 4g fat (2g saturated fat)
- Sodium: 234mg sodium
- Fiber: 1g fiber)
- Total Carbohydrate: 31g carbohydrate (0 sugars
- Cholesterol: 99mg cholesterol
- Protein: 5g protein. Diabetic Exchanges: 1 starch

---

612. Pineapple Orange Cake

Serving: 15 servings. | Prep: 15mins | Cook: 25mins | Ready in:

Ingredients

- 1 package yellow cake mix (regular size)
- 1 can (11 ounces) mandarin oranges, undrained
- 4 large egg whites
- 1/2 cup unsweetened applesauce
- TOPPING:
- 1 can (20 ounces) crushed pineapple, undrained
- 1 package (1 ounce) sugar-free instant vanilla pudding mix
- 1 carton (8 ounces) reduced-fat whipped topping

Direction

- Beat applesauce, egg whites, oranges and cake mix for 2 minutes on low speed in a big bowl; put into 13x9-in. baking dish that's coated in cooking spray.
- Bake it at 350° till inserted toothpick in middle exits clean for 25-30 minutes; cool on wire rack.
- Mix pudding mix and pineapple in a bowl; fold in whipped topping till just blended. Spread on cake; refrigerate before serving for a minimum of 1 hour.

Nutrition Information

- Calories: 231 calories
- Fiber: 1g fiber)
- Total Carbohydrate: 43g carbohydrate (27g sugars
- Cholesterol: 0 cholesterol
- Protein: 3g protein.
- Total Fat: 5g fat (3g saturated fat)
- Sodium: 310mg sodium

---

613. Pineapple Orange Trifle

Serving: 12 servings. | Prep: 20mins | Cook: 0mins | Ready in:

Ingredients

- 1 can (14 ounces) pineapple tidbits
- 2 cups cold 2% milk
- 2 packages (3.4 ounces each) instant vanilla pudding mix
- 1 cup (8 ounces) sour cream
- 1 can (11 ounces) mandarin oranges, drained
- 1 prepared angel food cake (8 to 10 ounces), cut into 1-inch cubes
- 1 carton (8 ounces) frozen whipped topping, thawed
- 1/2 teaspoon orange extract
- 1/3 cup sweetened shredded coconut, toasted

Direction

- Drain pineapple; keep 2/3 cup juice. Put aside pineapple. Whisk pudding mixes, pineapple juice and milk for 2 minutes in big bowl; stand till soft set for 2 minutes. Whisk sour cream in; fold pineapple and oranges in.
- Put 1/3 cake cubes in 3-qt. trifle bowl; put 1/3 pudding mixture over. Repeat layers twice. Cover; refrigerate for 3 hours. Mix extract and whipped topping; spread on top. Sprinkle coconut.

Nutrition Information

- Calories: 269 calories
- Protein: 3g protein.
- Total Fat: 9g fat (7g saturated fat)
- Sodium: 404mg sodium
- Fiber: 1g fiber)
- Total Carbohydrate: 43g carbohydrate (26g sugars
- Cholesterol: 16mg cholesterol

614.   Pineapple Pudding

Serving: 6 servings. | Prep: 5mins | Cook: 0mins |Ready in:

Ingredients

- 2 cups (16 ounces) fat-free sour cream
- 2 cans (8 ounces each) unsweetened crushed pineapple, undrained
- 1 package (1 ounces) sugar-free instant vanilla pudding mix
- 6 vanilla wafers

Direction

- Whisk the pudding mix, pineapple and sour cream in a bowl until it becomes thick and combined. Serve right away together with vanilla wafers. Put the leftovers in the fridge.

Nutrition Information

- Calories: 159 calories
- Total Carbohydrate: 31g carbohydrate (0 sugars
- Cholesterol: 0 cholesterol
- Protein: 5g protein. Diabetic Exchanges: 1 fruit
- Total Fat: 1g fat (0 saturated fat)
- Sodium: 274mg sodium
- Fiber: 1g fiber)

615.   Pistachio Bundt Cake

Serving: 12 servings. | Prep: 10mins | Cook: 60mins |Ready in:

Ingredients

- 1 package yellow cake mix (regular size)
- 2 packages (3.4 ounces each) instant pistachio pudding mix
- 1 cup water
- 4 large eggs
- 3/4 cup vegetable oil
- GLAZE:
- 1 cup confectioners' sugar
- 1 tablespoon butter, softened
- 2 to 3 tablespoons whole milk

Direction

- Mix together oil, eggs, water, pudding mixes and cake mix in a big bowl; on low speed, beat the mixture for half a minute. Beat for 2 minutes on medium speed.
- Transfer batter to a 10-inch fluted tube pan greased and dusted with flour. Bake in 350-degree oven until a toothpick is clean when coming out of the middle, about 1 hour to 1 hour and 10 minutes. Allow to cool in pan for 10 minutes, then turn out onto a wire rack and let cool fully.
- Mix together the ingredients for glaze in a small bowl, pouring in enough milk to achieve

the preferred texture. Spread the glaze over the cake.

Nutrition Information

- Calories: 406 calories
- Total Fat: 20g fat (4g saturated fat)
- Sodium: 415mg sodium
- Fiber: 1g fiber)
- Total Carbohydrate: 52g carbohydrate (34g sugars
- Cholesterol: 74mg cholesterol
- Protein: 4g protein.

616.   Pistachio Cheesecake

Serving: 12 -14 servings. | Prep: 15mins | Cook: 01hours05mins | Ready in:

Ingredients

- 2 cups all-purpose flour
- 1/2 cup ground almonds
- 1/2 cup cold butter
- 6 packages (8 ounces each) cream cheese, softened
- 1 can (14 ounces) sweetened condensed milk
- 2 packages (3.4 ounces each) instant pistachio pudding mix
- 5 eggs, lightly beaten
- Chocolate syrup
- Whipped cream and chopped pistachios, optional

Direction

- Mix in a small bowl the almond and flour; add in butter until crumbly. Then press onto the bottom and 1-1/4 inch up the sides of a 10-inch springform pan that is greased. Place in the oven and bake for 10 minutes at 400°F. In the meantime, beat pudding mixed, milk and cream cheese in a large bowl until smooth. Put in eggs; whisk on low speed just until mixed. Place over crust. Put the pan on a baking

sheet. Lower heat to 350°F. Then bake for 55-60 minutes or until middle is just set. Put on a wire rack to cool for 10 minutes. Gently run a knife around edge of pan to loosen; cool for 1 more hour. Put in the refrigerator overnight. Cut cheesecake; drizzle slices with chocolate syrup. Decorate with pistachios and whipped cream if you want.

Nutrition Information

- Calories: 344 calories
- Protein: 8g protein.
- Total Fat: 18g fat (10g saturated fat)
- Sodium: 269mg sodium
- Fiber: 1g fiber)
- Total Carbohydrate: 37g carbohydrate (21g sugars
- Cholesterol: 121mg cholesterol

617.   Pistachio Cherry Squares

Serving: 12-15 servings. | Prep: 20mins | Cook: 0mins | Ready in:

Ingredients

- 2 cups graham cracker crumbs (about 32 squares)
- 1/2 cup butter, melted
- 1/4 cup sugar
- CREAM CHEESE LAYER:
- 1 package (8 ounces) cream cheese, softened
- 2/3 cup confectioners' sugar
- 1 carton (8 ounces) frozen whipped topping, thawed
- PUDDING LAYER:
- 2-1/2 cups cold milk
- 2 packages (3.4 ounces each) instant pistachio pudding mix
- TOPPING:
- 1 carton (8 ounces) frozen whipped topping, thawed
- 2 cans (21 ounces each) cherry pie filling

Direction

- Mix sugar, butter, and cracker crumbs together; pat into a grease-free 13x9-inch dish. Chill in the fridge. Beat cream cheese with sugar in a mixing bowl; add whipped topping and fold gently. Distribute cream mixture over the prepared crust. Beat pudding mixes and milk in a mixing bowl for 2 minutes on low speed. Smear over the layer of cream cheese; refrigerate for about 1 hour or until set.
- Top pudding layer with whipped topping. Spread pie filling over top. Chill overnight. Slice into squares to serve.

Nutrition Information

- Calories: 368 calories
- Fiber: 1g fiber)
- Total Carbohydrate: 43g carbohydrate (30g sugars
- Cholesterol: 39mg cholesterol
- Protein: 3g protein.
- Total Fat: 19g fat (13g saturated fat)
- Sodium: 291mg sodium

618.   Pistachio Coconut Cake

Serving: 12-15 servings. | Prep: 15mins | Cook: 40mins | Ready in:

Ingredients

- 1 package white cake mix (regular size)
- 3/4 cup canola oil
- 3 eggs
- 1 cup lemon-lime or club soda
- 1 package (3/4 ounce) instant pistachio pudding mix
- 1 cup chopped pecans
- 1/2 cup sweetened shredded coconut
- ICING:
- 1-1/2 cups milk

- 2 envelopes whipped topping mix (Dream Whip)
- 1 package (3/4 ounce) instant pistachio pudding mix
- 3/4 cup chopped pecans
- 1/2 cup sweetened shredded coconut

Direction

- Mix dry pudding mix, soda, eggs, oil, and dry cake mix together in a large mixing bowl until well combined. Mix in coconut and pecans. Transfer mixture to a greased 13x9-inch baking pan. Bake for 40 to 45 minutes at 350° until a toothpick comes out clean from the center. Allow to cool entirely on a wire cooling rack.
- To make icing, mix dry pudding mix, topping mix, and milk together in a large mixing bowl; beat for about 4 minutes or until thickened. Spread pudding mixture over the cake. Scatter top with coconut and pecans. Keep the cake chilled in the fridge.

Nutrition Information

- Calories: 446 calories
- Total Fat: 29g fat (7g saturated fat)
- Sodium: 301mg sodium
- Fiber: 2g fiber)
- Total Carbohydrate: 42g carbohydrate (26g sugars
- Cholesterol: 46mg cholesterol
- Protein: 5g protein.

619.   Pistachio Cookie Dessert

Serving: 12-15 servings. | Prep: 20mins | Cook: 0mins | Ready in:

Ingredients

- 1 package (15-1/2 ounces) Oreo cookies
- 1/2 cup plus 2 tablespoons butter, melted
- 1-1/2 cups cold 2% milk

- 2 packages (3.4 ounces each) instant pistachio pudding mix
- 1 quart vanilla ice cream, softened
- 1 carton (16 ounces) frozen whipped topping, thawed

Direction

- Add cookies to a blender, process with the cover on until fine crumbs form. Whisk in butter. Put aside 1 cup for topping. Press the remaining crumb mixture into an ungreased 13x9-inch dish.
- Beat the pudding mix with milk in a big bowl for 2 minutes on low speed. Put in ice cream gradually. Fold in whipped topping.
- Pour over the crust. Drizzle reserved crumb mixture on top and slightly press down. Freeze with a cover overnight or for 4 hrs. Take out of the freezer 20 min prior to slicing.

Nutrition Information

- Calories: 446 calories
- Sodium: 459mg sodium
- Fiber: 1g fiber)
- Total Carbohydrate: 48g carbohydrate (30g sugars
- Cholesterol: 39mg cholesterol
- Protein: 4g protein.
- Total Fat: 25g fat (14g saturated fat)

620. Pistachio Cookies

Serving: Makes about 40 (1 1/2-inch) cookies | Prep: | Cook: | Ready in:

Ingredients

- 3 cups unsalted shelled natural pistachios (15 oz)
- 1 2/3 cups confectioners sugar
- 1 whole large egg
- 2 large egg yolks
- 1 tablespoon unsalted butter, melted
- 1 teaspoon rose water (preferably French)

Direction

- Preheat an oven to 300°F.
- In boiling water, blanch pistachios for 1 minute. Drain. Peel; use your fingers to slip off skins. Use paper towels to dry. Spread in shallow baking pan; bake in center of oven for 10 minutes till dry. Fully cool.
- Pulse confectioners' sugar and nuts till finely ground, not a paste, in a food processor.
- Mix yolks and whole egg with a fork in a big bowl; little by little, mix in ground pistachios till slightly sticky dough forms. Add rose water and butter; knead to mix. Shape dough to 2 disks.
- Roll 1 disk, keeping a disk covered in plastic wrap, on well-floured surface to 3/4-in. thick. Use floured cookie cutters to cut out various shapes.
- On ungreased big baking sheet, bake in center of oven for 20-25 minutes till bottoms are golden and crisp. Put cookies onto rack with a metal spatula; cool. While warm, dust with confectioners' sugar. Make extra cookies with leftover dough, rerolling scraps.
- Cookies keep for 2 days in airtight container in room temperature.

Nutrition Information

- Calories: 86
- Saturated Fat: 1 g(4%)
- Sodium: 3 mg(0%)
- Fiber: 1 g(4%)
- Total Carbohydrate: 8 g(3%)
- Cholesterol: 15 mg(5%)
- Protein: 2 g(5%)
- Total Fat: 5 g(8%)

621. Pistachio Cream Dessert

Serving: 18 | Prep: 20mins | Cook: | Ready in:

Ingredients

- 1 (3.4 ounce) package instant pistachio pudding mix
- 2 cups cold milk
- 1 pint heavy cream
- 2 tablespoons white sugar
- 1 (9 ounce) package chocolate wafers
- 10 chocolate-covered almond buttercrunch candies, crushed

Direction

- Prepare the pudding and milk as instructed on the package and let it chill in the fridge.
- Whip the sugar and cream until it forms stiff peaks. Fold a quarter of whipped cream into the pudding.
- Spread a thin layer of the pudding mixture in a 9x13-inch dish and put a layer of wafers on top. Spread 1/3 of whipped cream on top of the wafers, then sprinkle 1/3 of the crushed candy on top of the whipped cream. Redo the layers until you used up all the ingredients. Let it chill for 2 hours in the fridge prior to serving.

Nutrition Information

- Calories: 219 calories;
- Total Fat: 13.5
- Sodium: 190
- Total Carbohydrate: 22.5
- Cholesterol: 39
- Protein: 2.8

---
622.   Pistachio Fluff

Serving: 14 servings. | Prep: 15mins | Cook: 0mins | Ready in:

Ingredients

- 2 cups (16 ounces) 1% cottage cheese

- 4 cups (32 ounces) fat-free reduced-sugar vanilla yogurt, divided
- 1 package (1 ounce) sugar-free instant pistachio pudding mix
- 1 carton (8 ounces) frozen reduced-fat whipped topping, thawed
- 1 can (20 ounces) unsweetened crushed pineapple, drained
- 1 can (11 ounces) mandarin oranges, drained
- 1/2 cup halved maraschino cherries

Direction

- Process 1 cup yogurt and cottage cheese, covered, till smooth in a food processor.
- Whisk leftover yogurt and pudding mix for 2 minutes till slightly thick in a big bowl. Add cottage cheese mixture; stir well. Mix in leftover ingredients; refrigerate till serving.

Nutrition Information

- Calories: 137 calories
- Cholesterol: 3mg cholesterol
- Protein: 7g protein. Diabetic Exchanges: 1/2 starch
- Total Fat: 2g fat (2g saturated fat)
- Sodium: 249mg sodium
- Fiber: 0 fiber)
- Total Carbohydrate: 21g carbohydrate (0 sugars

---
623.   Pistachio Ice Cream Dessert

Serving: 12 | Prep: 15mins | Cook: 15mins | Ready in:

Ingredients

- Crust:
- 2 sleeves buttery round crackers, crushed
- 1/2 cup melted butter
- Topping:
- 1/2 gallon vanilla ice cream, softened

- 2 (3 ounce) packages instant pistachio pudding mix
- 1 1/2 cups milk
- 1 (12 ounce) container frozen whipped topping (such as Cool Whip®), thawed
- 1/4 cup chocolate-covered toffee bits (such as Heath®), or to taste

Direction

- Preheat an oven to 175°C/350°F.
- Mix melted butter and cracker crumbs till evenly moistened in a bowl; press onto sides and bottom of 9x13-in. baking dish.
- In preheated oven, bake for 15 minutes till crust smells toasted and lightly browned. Remove from oven; cool.
- Mix milk, pudding mix and ice cream till combined in a bowl; evenly spread on prepped crust. Spread whipping topping on ice cream mixture; put toffee bits over. Put into freezer for 1 hour till hardened.

Nutrition Information

- Calories: 539 calories;
- Total Carbohydrate: 57.7
- Cholesterol: 66
- Protein: 5.7
- Total Fat: 32.4
- Sodium: 574

624.   Pistachio Pudding Parfaits

Serving: 8 servings. | Prep: 20mins | Cook: 0mins | Ready in:

Ingredients

- 1 package (8 ounces) cream cheese, softened
- 1 cup confectioners' sugar
- 1-1/2 cups whipped topping

- 1 package (3.4 ounces) instant pistachio pudding mix
- 10 pecan shortbread cookies, coarsely crushed

Direction

- Mix confectioner's sugar and cream cheese in a small bowl. Add and fold in whipped topping; reserve. Prepare the pudding based on the package directions; reserve.
- Into each of 8 parfait glasses, scoop 1 tablespoon cookie crumbs. Followed with half of the pudding and whipped topping mixture. Continue layers. Then put the rest of the cookie crumbs on top. Let chill until serving time.

Nutrition Information

- Calories: 374 calories
- Sodium: 367mg sodium
- Fiber: 0 fiber)
- Total Carbohydrate: 45g carbohydrate (27g sugars
- Cholesterol: 41mg cholesterol
- Protein: 5g protein.
- Total Fat: 19g fat (11g saturated fat)

625.   Pistachio Pudding Tarts

Serving: 4 dozen. | Prep: 30mins | Cook: 15mins | Ready in:

Ingredients

- 1 cup butter, softened
- 1 package (8 ounces) cream cheese, softened
- 2 cups all-purpose flour
- 1-3/4 cups cold 2% milk
- 1 package (3.4 ounces) instant pistachio pudding mix

Direction

- Mix together cream cheese and butter in a big bowl until smooth. Put in flour, little by little until combined.
- Form mixture into 48 balls with 1-inch diameter; in each ungreased mini-muffin cup, press one ball onto the bottom and up the sides. Bake in 400-degree oven until crusts turn light brown, about 12 to 15 minutes. Allow to cool for 5 minutes; gently transfer from pans to a wire rack and let cool entirely.
- To make the filling, mix pudding and milk for two minutes. Allow to sit until the mixture sets, about two minutes. Chill while covered for 5 minutes. Spoon filling into the crusts.

Nutrition Information

- Calories: 165 calories
- Total Fat: 12g fat (7g saturated fat)
- Sodium: 170mg sodium
- Fiber: 0 fiber)
- Total Carbohydrate: 13g carbohydrate (4g sugars
- Cholesterol: 33mg cholesterol
- Protein: 2g protein.

---

626.   Pistachio Puffs

Serving: about 2 dozen. | Prep: 20mins | Cook: 15mins | Ready in:

Ingredients

- 1 cup water
- 1/2 cup butter, softened
- 1 teaspoon sugar
- 1/4 teaspoon salt
- 1 cup all-purpose flour
- 4 eggs
- 1 package (3.4 ounces) instant pistachio pudding mix
- 1-3/4 cups whipped topping

Direction

- Bring together salt, sugar, butter and water in a big saucepan to a boil. Put in all of flour at a time and stir until it forms into a smooth ball. Take away from the heat and allow to stand about 5 minutes.
- Put in 1 egg at a time while beating well between additions. Beat the mixture until shiny and smooth. Drop on grease-free baking sheets with rounded teaspoonfuls of mixture, spacing 2 inches apart.
- Bake at 400 degrees until golden brown, about 15 to 20 minutes. Transfer to wire racks. Cut a slit in each puff instantly to let steam escape then let it cool. Divide puffs, use a fork to take out soft dough from the inside. Follow package directions for pie to prepare pudding then fold in whipped topping. Scoop mixture into cream puffs.

Nutrition Information

- Calories:
- Sodium:
- Fiber:
- Total Carbohydrate:
- Cholesterol:
- Protein:
- Total Fat:

---

627.   Pistachio And Coconut Cake

Serving: 16 servings. | Prep: 20mins | Cook: 40mins | Ready in:

Ingredients

- 1 white cake mix (regular size)
- 1 package (3.4 ounces) instant pistachio pudding mix
- 1 cup lemon-lime soda
- 3/4 cup canola oil
- 3 large eggs
- 1/2 cup flaked coconut

- 1/2 cup toasted shelled pistachios, chopped
- FROSTING:
- 1-1/4 cups cold 2% milk
- 1 package (3.4 ounces) instant pistachio pudding mix
- 1 carton (8 ounces) frozen whipped topping, thawed
- TOPPINGS:
- 1/4 cup flaked coconut, toasted
- 1/4 cup toasted shelled pistachios, chopped

Direction

- Preheat an oven to 350°. Beat initial 5 ingredients on low speed for 30 seconds till moist; beat for 2 minutes on medium. Mix in toasted pistachios and coconut.
- Put into 13x9-in. greased baking pan/2 8-in. greased round baking pans; bake for 40-45 minutes till inserted toothpick in middle exits clean. On a wire rack, cool.
- Frosting: Beat pudding mix and milk for 2 minutes on low speed; fold in whipped topping. On top of cake, spread frosting and between layers, if using round pans. Put pistachios and toasted coconut over; refrigerate till serving.

Nutrition Information

- Calories: 380 calories
- Sodium: 431mg sodium
- Fiber: 1g fiber)
- Total Carbohydrate: 41g carbohydrate (28g sugars
- Cholesterol: 36mg cholesterol
- Protein: 5g protein.
- Total Fat: 21g fat (6g saturated fat)

---

628.   Possum Pie

Serving: 8 | Prep: | Cook: | Ready in:

Ingredients

- 3 egg whites
- 30 butter crackers, crushed
- 1 teaspoon vanilla extract
- 3/4 cup white sugar
- 1 cup chopped walnuts
- 1 (12 ounce) container frozen whipped topping, thawed
- 2 tablespoons flaked coconut

Direction

- Start preheating the oven to 165°C (325°F).
- Beat the egg whites in a big bowl until stiff peaks form. Fold in nuts, sugar, vanilla, and crackers.
- Pour the mixture into a 9-inch pie pan, spread evenly. Bake for 20 minutes in the preheated oven. Let cool completely.
- Spread the pie with whipped topping, then drizzle coconut on top.

Nutrition Information

- Calories: 380 calories;
- Total Carbohydrate: 40.6
- Cholesterol: 9
- Protein: 5.1
- Total Fat: 23.3
- Sodium: 124

---

629.   Puddin' Cones

Serving: 8 servings. | Prep: 15mins | Cook: 0mins | Ready in:

Ingredients

- 1-1/2 cups cold milk
- 1 package (3.4 ounces) instant vanilla pudding mix
- 3 envelopes whipped topping mix (Dream Whip)
- 8 cake ice cream cones (about 3 inches)

- Chopped nuts, jimmies and miniature colored-coated baking chips or topping of your choice

Direction

- Beat the pudding mix and milk in a big bowl for 2 minutes on low speed. Fold in whipped topping mix; cover and chill for a minimum of 1 hour. Scoop 1/4 cup of the mixture into each cone, then drizzle the toppings on top.

Nutrition Information

- Calories: 173 calories
- Fiber: 0 fiber)
- Total Carbohydrate: 28g carbohydrate (22g sugars
- Cholesterol: 6mg cholesterol
- Protein: 2g protein.
- Total Fat: 5g fat (4g saturated fat)
- Sodium: 198mg sodium

630.   Pudding Pumpkin Pie

Serving: 8 servings. | Prep: 15mins | Cook: 0mins | Ready in:

Ingredients

- 1 egg white, beaten
- 1 reduced-fat graham cracker crust (8 inches)
- 1 cup cold fat-free milk
- 1 package (1-1/2 ounces) sugar-free instant vanilla pudding mix
- 1 can (15 ounces) solid-pack pumpkin
- 1 teaspoon pumpkin pie spice
- 1/2 teaspoon ground cinnamon
- 1/2 teaspoon ground nutmeg
- 1-1/2 cups reduced-fat whipped topping, divided

Direction

- Brush egg white on crust; bake for 5 minutes till lightly browned at 375°. On wire rack, cool.

- Whisk pudding mix and milk in big bowl; mix nutmeg, cinnamon, pumpkin pie spice and pumpkin in. Fold 1 cup whipped topping in; put in crust. Refrigerate for 4 hours – overnight.
- Cut to slices; dollop using leftover whipped topping then refrigerate leftovers.

Nutrition Information

- Calories: 180 calories
- Sodium: 341mg sodium
- Fiber: 2g fiber)
- Total Carbohydrate: 29g carbohydrate (12g sugars
- Cholesterol: 1mg cholesterol
- Protein: 3g protein. Diabetic Exchanges: 2 starch
- Total Fat: 5g fat (3g saturated fat)

631.   Pudding Sugar Cookies

Serving: 7 dozen. | Prep: 15mins | Cook: 15mins | Ready in:

Ingredients

- 1 cup butter, softened
- 1 cup canola oil
- 1 cup sugar
- 1 cup confectioners' sugar
- 2 eggs
- 1 teaspoon vanilla extract
- 1 package (3.4 ounces) instant lemon pudding mix or instant pudding mix of your choice
- 4 cups all-purpose flour
- 1 teaspoon cream of tartar
- 1 teaspoon baking soda

Direction

- Whisk butter with sugars and oil in a large mixing bowl until fluffy and light. Whisk in dry pudding mix, vanilla, and eggs. Mix baking soda, cream of tartar, and flour together; slowly mix into creamed mixture until incorporated.

- Drop batter onto ungreased baking sheets by tablespoonfuls, separating them 2 inches apart. Press each mound with a glass dipped in sugar.
- Bake cookies for 12 to 15 minutes at 350° until lightly browned. Transfer cookies to wire racks.

Nutrition Information

- Calories: 169 calories
- Protein: 2g protein.
- Total Fat: 10g fat (3g saturated fat)
- Sodium: 105mg sodium
- Fiber: 0 fiber)
- Total Carbohydrate: 19g carbohydrate (9g sugars
- Cholesterol: 22mg cholesterol

---

632. Pudding Topped Fruit Salad

Serving: 12-14 servings. | Prep: 10mins | Cook: 0mins | Ready in:

Ingredients

- 1 can (20 ounces) pineapple chunks
- 1 can (8 ounces) crushed pineapple, undrained
- 1 cup (8 ounces) sour cream
- 1 package (3.4 ounces) instant vanilla pudding mix
- 2 medium ripe bananas, sliced
- 2 cups fresh or frozen blueberries, thawed
- 2 medium ripe peaches, peeled and sliced
- 2 cups sliced fresh strawberries
- 1 cup green grapes
- 1 cup seedless red grapes
- Fresh mint, optional

Direction

- Strain pineapple chunks, setting aside the juice; keep the pineapple in the refrigerator. Add water to juice if needed to measure 3/4 cup. Mix the pudding mix, sour cream, crushed pineapple, and the juice in a large bowl until combined. Refrigerate for at least 3 hours, covered, or until mixture becomes thick.
- Mix pineapple chunks, grapes, strawberries, peaches, blueberries, and bananas in a large bowl. Scatter the pudding mixture over the top. Decorate with mint if preferred.

Nutrition Information

- Calories: 149 calories
- Total Carbohydrate: 30g carbohydrate (24g sugars
- Cholesterol: 11mg cholesterol
- Protein: 2g protein.
- Total Fat: 3g fat (2g saturated fat)
- Sodium: 107mg sodium
- Fiber: 2g fiber)

---

633. Pumpkin Bundt Cake

Serving: 12 servings. | Prep: 10mins | Cook: 50mins | Ready in:

Ingredients

- 1 package yellow cake mix (regular size)
- 1 package (3.4 ounces) instant butterscotch pudding mix
- 4 eggs
- 1/4 cup water
- 1/4 cup canola oil
- 1 cup canned pumpkin
- 2 teaspoons pumpkin pie spice
- Whipped cream, optional

Direction

- Mix the first 7 ingredients together in a large mixing bowl. Beat for half a minute on low speed; raise speed to medium and beat for 2 more minutes.

- Transfer mixture to a buttered and floured 10-inch fluted tube pan. Bake for 50 to 55 minutes at 350° until a toothpick comes out clean from the center. Allow to cool in pan for 10 minutes before transferring to a wire rack to cool entirely. Serve cake with whipped cream, if desired.

Nutrition Information

- Calories: 215 calories
- Sodium: 319mg sodium
- Fiber: 1g fiber)
- Total Carbohydrate: 33g carbohydrate (20g sugars
- Cholesterol: 53mg cholesterol
- Protein: 3g protein.
- Total Fat: 8g fat (2g saturated fat)

634. Pumpkin Charlotte

Serving: 12 servings. | Prep: 30mins | Cook: 0mins | Ready in:

Ingredients

- 2 packages (3 ounces each) ladyfingers, split
- 6 ounces cream cheese, softened
- 2 tablespoons sugar
- 2-1/4 cups heavy whipping cream, divided
- 3 tablespoons confectioners' sugar, divided
- 1 cup cold whole milk
- 2 packages (3.4 ounces each) instant vanilla pudding mix
- 1/2 teaspoon ground cinnamon
- 1/4 teaspoon ground ginger
- 1/4 teaspoon pumpkin pie spice
- 1 can (15 ounces) solid-pack pumpkin
- Additional ground cinnamon

Direction

- Break ladyfingers; place on the bottom and upright around the sides of an unbuttered 9-inch springform pan, cutting off excess to fit, if needed. Put to one side.
- Whisk cream cheese and sugar together in a large mixing bowl until smooth. Whisk 1 3/4 cups whipping cream with 2 tablespoons confectioners' sugar in a small mixing bowl until stiff peaks form. Measure 1/2 cup whipped cream and set to one side. Add the remaining whipped cream to cream cheese mixture and fold gently. Transfer mixture to the prepared pan.
- Combine spices, pudding mixes, and milk in a mixing bowl. Beat for 1 minute on low speed. Put in pumpkin; beat for 1 more minute. Add the reserved whipped cream and fold gently. Spread over cream cheese layer. Chill, covered, for 8 hours or overnight.
- Whisk the remaining cream and confectioners' sugar until forming stiff peaks right before serving. Spread over the layer of pumpkin. Scatter with cinnamon. Take off the sides of the pan. Chill leftovers in the fridge.

Nutrition Information

- Calories: 275 calories
- Sodium: 173mg sodium
- Fiber: 2g fiber)
- Total Carbohydrate: 21g carbohydrate (16g sugars
- Cholesterol: 98mg cholesterol
- Protein: 3g protein.
- Total Fat: 21g fat (13g saturated fat)

635. Pumpkin Chiffon Pie

Serving: 8 | Prep: 30mins | Cook: 20mins | Ready in:

Ingredients

- 1 envelope (1 tablespoon) unflavored gelatin
- 1/4 cup water

- 4 eggs, separated
- 1 1/4 cups white sugar
- 1 1/4 cups pumpkin
- 2/3 cup evaporated milk
- 1/4 teaspoon salt
- 1/2 teaspoon ground cinnamon
- 1/2 teaspoon ground allspice
- 1/2 teaspoon ground nutmeg
- 1/4 teaspoon ground ginger
- 1 recipe pastry for a 9 inch single crust pie

Direction

- In a small bowl, combine water and gelatin, and reserve.
- Whisk egg yolks in a medium bowl till thick. Add in ginger, nutmeg, allspice, cinnamon, salt, evaporated milk, pumpkin and 3/4 cup sugar.
- Let the cook mixture in a double-broiler over boiling water, mixing continuously till thick. Put in gelatin. Mix to dissolve. Take off from heat and let mixture thicken till it coat the spoonful when dropped.
- Whisk egg whites in a dry, clean medium bowl till soft peaks create. Slowly add in the leftover half cup sugar, and keep whisking till firm. Fold in pumpkin mixture. Put to pie crust. Refrigerate for an hour till firm.

Nutrition Information

- Calories: 317 calories;
- Sodium: 251
- Total Carbohydrate: 47.1
- Cholesterol: 99
- Protein: 7.4
- Total Fat: 11.8

636.   Pumpkin Chip Cream Pie

Serving: 8 servings. | Prep: 20mins | Cook: 0mins | Ready in:

Ingredients

- 3/4 cup cold 2% milk
- 1 package (3.4 ounces) instant vanilla pudding mix
- 2/3 cup miniature semisweet chocolate chips
- 1/2 cup canned pumpkin
- 3/4 teaspoon pumpkin pie spice
- 1 carton (8 ounces) frozen whipped topping, thawed, divided
- 1 graham cracker crust (9 inches)
- Slivered almonds and chocolate curls, optional

Direction

- Beat pudding mix and milk in a big bowl for 2 minutes, mixture will become thick. Mix in pie spice, pumpkin and chocolate chips. Fold in 2 cups of whipped topping. Scoop into crust. Chill for 4 hours till set.
- Scatter the rest of whipped topping over; jazz up with chocolate curls and almonds if wished.

Nutrition Information

- Calories: 315 calories
- Sodium: 305mg sodium
- Fiber: 2g fiber)
- Total Carbohydrate: 43g carbohydrate (32g sugars
- Cholesterol: 2mg cholesterol
- Protein: 3g protein.
- Total Fat: 15g fat (9g saturated fat)

637.   Pumpkin Cream Trifle

Serving: 15-20 servings. | Prep: 30mins | Cook: 45mins | Ready in:

Ingredients

- 1 package spice cake mix (regular size)
- 1 package (3.4 ounces) instant vanilla pudding mix

- 1 cup canned pumpkin
- 1/2 cup water
- 1/2 cup vegetable oil
- 3 eggs
- 1 teaspoon ground cinnamon
- 1/2 teaspoon ground ginger
- 2 cups cold milk
- 2 packages (3.4 ounces each) instant cheesecake pudding mix
- 2 cups whipped topping
- 1 cup chopped pecans, toasted
- 3/4 cup English toffee bits or almond brickle chips

Direction

- Mix initial 8 ingredients in big bowl; put in 13x9-in. greased baking pan. Bake for 45-50 minutes at 350° till inserted toothpick in middle exits clean; on wire rack, cool.
- Whisk pudding mixes and milk for 2 minutes in big bowl; stand till soft set for 2 minutes. Fold whipped topping in.
- Cut cake to 1-in. cubes. Layer 1/3 cake cubes, pudding mixture, the pecans then toffee bits in trifle bowl or 3-qt. glass serving bowl. Repeat layers two times; refrigerate till serving.

Nutrition Information

- Calories: 333 calories
- Sodium: 406mg sodium
- Fiber: 1g fiber)
- Total Carbohydrate: 38g carbohydrate (27g sugars
- Cholesterol: 45mg cholesterol
- Protein: 4g protein.
- Total Fat: 19g fat (5g saturated fat)

638.   Pumpkin Crunch Parfaits

Serving: 6 servings. | Prep: 20mins | Cook: 0mins |Ready in:

Ingredients

- 3/4 cup cold whole milk
- 1 package (3.4 ounces) instant vanilla pudding mix
- 2 cups whipped topping
- 1 cup canned pumpkin
- 1/2 teaspoon pumpkin pie spice
- 1 cup chopped pecans
- 32 gingersnap cookies, crushed (about 1-1/2 cups)
- Additional whipped topping

Direction

- Beat milk and pudding mix in a big bowl for2 minutes on low speed. Add in pumpkin, pie spice and whipped topping. Fold in pecans.
- Scoop 1/2 pudding mixture into 6 parfait glasses; place 1/2 of the gingersnap crumbs on top of pudding mixture. Repeat pudding mixture and gingersnap crumb layers once more. Top with more whipped topping. Keep leftovers in the fridge.

Nutrition Information

- Calories: 447 calories
- Sodium: 486mg sodium
- Fiber: 3g fiber)
- Total Carbohydrate: 55g carbohydrate (31g sugars
- Cholesterol: 4mg cholesterol
- Protein: 5g protein.
- Total Fat: 23g fat (7g saturated fat)

639.   Pumpkin Gingersnap Dessert

Serving: 16 servings. | Prep: 20mins | Cook: 10mins |Ready in:

Ingredients

- 1-1/2 cups finely crushed gingersnaps (about 32 cookies)
- 1/4 cup butter, melted
- 1/2 teaspoon ground cinnamon
- 1/4 teaspoon ground nutmeg
- FILLING:
- 2 packages (3.4 ounces each) instant vanilla pudding mix
- 1-1/3 cups cold milk
- 1 can (15 ounces) solid-pack pumpkin
- 1-1/2 teaspoons ground cinnamon
- 1/2 teaspoon each ground ginger, cloves and nutmeg
- 2 cups whipped topping
- TOPPING:
- 1-1/2 cups evaporated milk
- 1 cup packed brown sugar
- 1 cup chopped pecans
- 2 teaspoons vanilla extract

Direction

- Mix together the first 4 ingredients, press onto the bottom of an oil-coated 13x9-inch baking pan. Bake for 8 minutes at 350°, let fully cool. To prepare the filling, in a bowl, whisk together milk and pudding mixes. Add nutmeg, cloves, ginger, cinnamon, and pumpkin; stir thoroughly. Fold in the whipped topping. Add to the crust. Refrigerate for a minimum of 4 hours. To prepare the topping, boil brown sugar and milk in a heavy saucepan over low heat, whisking sometimes. Keep whisking and cooking over low heat until the mixture has thickened, about 6-8 minutes. Take away from heat, mix in vanilla and pecans. Let cool to room temperature. Slice the dessert into squares, drizzle the topping over.

Nutrition Information

- Calories: 288 calories
- Total Fat: 13g fat (6g saturated fat)
- Sodium: 245mg sodium
- Fiber: 2g fiber)

- Total Carbohydrate: 38g carbohydrate (28g sugars
- Cholesterol: 18mg cholesterol
- Protein: 4g protein.

---

640.   Pumpkin Layered Angel Cake

Serving: 12 servings. | Prep: 15mins | Cook: 0mins | Ready in:

Ingredients

- 1-1/2 cups canned pumpkin
- 1-1/4 cups heavy whipping cream
- 1 package (5.1 ounces) instant vanilla pudding mix
- 1 teaspoon ground cinnamon
- 1/2 teaspoon ground allspice
- 1 prepared angel food cake (16 ounces), split twice horizontally
- 1/4 cup gingersnap cookies (about 5 cookies)

Direction

- Mix cream and pumpkin in a bowl. Add spices and pudding mix. Then beat for 2 minutes on low speed or until thickened.
- Put the bottom layer of cake onto a serving plate and then smear with 3/4 cup of the pudding mixture. Repeat this once. Add the remaining cake layer on top and then smear with the remaining pudding mixture. Scatter with the crushed cookies. Chill until serving. Keep in the fridge.

Nutrition Information

- Calories:
- Sodium:
- Fiber:
- Total Carbohydrate:
- Cholesterol:
- Protein:

- Total Fat:

641.　　Pumpkin Mousse

Serving: 7 | Prep: | Cook: |Ready in:

Ingredients

- 3 eggs
- 1 cup milk
- 3/4 cup honey
- 1/2 cup milk
- 1 (.25 ounce) package unflavored gelatin
- 1 1/2 cups pumpkin puree
- 3 tablespoons white sugar
- 1 teaspoon ground cinnamon
- 1/2 teaspoon ground cloves
- 1/2 teaspoon ground mace
- 1/2 teaspoon ground nutmeg
- 1/2 teaspoon ground ginger
- 1 teaspoon vanilla extract
- 2 tablespoons chopped crystallized ginger

Direction

- In a little bowl, Pour half cup of milk or water and pour gelatin to soften.
- Prepare eggs. Separate the egg yolks by putting into a microwavable bowl that measures 2 cups. Put the egg whites into electric mixer bowl.
- In a heavy bottomed saucepan, mix together the honey, milk and spices; heat until mixture is steaming hot or until the honey dissolves. Blend the gelatin with its liquid, stir continuously until completely dissolved.
- Whisk more hot milk mixture into egg yolks, beat continuously. Transfer the egg yolk mixture back into the pot; continue to heat until consistency is thick and nearly boiling. Add in pumpkin, stirring until big bubbles stop appearing when not stirred for a few seconds. Take from the heat and beat in vanilla.

- Whisk egg whites until frothy. Gradually add the sugar and continue beating until stiff peaks form. Add the whites using a large spatula and fold into pumpkin custard; fold in the rest of the egg whites. Wash six metal cup molds with cold water, and then pour mousse into molds. Store in the fridge overnight. To remove mold, dip the metal cup molds 30 seconds in hot water then turn onto a serving platter. Alternatively, scoop the mousse in each wine glasses or ramekins with 1-2 tbsp. of gingersnap crumbs chopped crystalized ginger on the bottom. Serve with whipped cream.

Nutrition Information

- Calories: 212 calories;
- Sodium: 57
- Total Carbohydrate: 42.6
- Cholesterol: 84
- Protein: 5.8
- Total Fat: 3.4

642.　　Pumpkin Pie Dessert

Serving: 12-15 servings. | Prep: 20mins | Cook: 0mins | Ready in:

Ingredients

- 2-1/4 cups crushed butter-flavored crackers (about 50 crackers)
- 1/2 cup sugar
- 3/4 cup butter, melted
- 2 cups cold milk
- 2 packages (3.4 ounces each) instant vanilla pudding mix
- 1 can (15 ounces) solid-pack pumpkin
- 1 teaspoon pumpkin pie spice
- 1/2 teaspoon ground cinnamon
- 1/4 teaspoon ground ginger
- 1/4 teaspoon ground nutmeg
- Whipped topping and chopped pecans

Direction

- Mix together butter, sugar and cracker crumbs in a small bowl. Grease a 13x9-inch dish and pat in the mixture; put aside.
- Beat pudding mix and milk in a large bowl for 2 minutes. Let sit until soft-set, about 2 minutes. Mix in spices and pumpkin. Pour onto crust. Chill in the refrigerator until firm, about 3 hours. Sprinkle with nuts and whipped topping.

Nutrition Information

- Calories: 232 calories
- Sodium: 312mg sodium
- Fiber: 2g fiber)
- Total Carbohydrate: 26g carbohydrate (15g sugars
- Cholesterol: 29mg cholesterol
- Protein: 3g protein.
- Total Fat: 14g fat (7g saturated fat)

643. Pumpkin Pudding

Serving: 9-12 servings. | Prep: 15mins | Cook: 0mins | Ready in:

Ingredients

- 1 cup solid-pack pumpkin
- 1 tablespoon molasses
- 1/2 teaspoon ground cinnamon
- 1/8 teaspoon ground cloves
- 1/4 teaspoon salt
- 1-1/2 cups cold milk
- 1 package (3.4 ounces) instant vanilla pudding mix
- 1/2 cup heavy whipping cream, whipped
- Additional whipped cream, optional
- Additional ground cinnamon, optional

Direction

- Mix spices, molasses and pumpkin in a bowl; add milk slowly. Add pudding mix; slowly beat with electric mixer for 1 minute till thick. Fold in whipped cream.
- Put into individual serving dishes/serving bowl; chill for 1 hour. Top each serving with dollop of whipped cream and a sprinkling of cinnamon, if desired.

Nutrition Information

- Calories: 95 calories
- Fiber: 1g fiber)
- Total Carbohydrate: 12g carbohydrate (9g sugars
- Cholesterol: 18mg cholesterol
- Protein: 2g protein.
- Total Fat: 5g fat (3g saturated fat)
- Sodium: 183mg sodium

644. Pumpkin Pudding Dessert

Serving: 2 servings. | Prep: 30mins | Cook: 0mins | Ready in:

Ingredients

- 1 cup vanilla soy milk
- 1 package (1 ounce) sugar-free instant vanilla pudding mix
- 3/4 cup canned pumpkin
- 1/4 teaspoon ground cinnamon
- 1/8 teaspoon ground nutmeg
- 1/8 teaspoon ground cloves
- 4 vanilla wafers

Direction

- Beat pudding mix and milk until thickened or for 2 minutes in a small bowl. Beat in cloves, nutmeg, cinnamon and pumpkin.
- Scoop into 2 dessert dishes. Keep in the fridge,

covered, for at least 20 minutes. Decorate with vanilla wafers right before serving.

Nutrition Information

- Calories: 164 calories
- Fiber: 4g fiber)
- Total Carbohydrate: 29g carbohydrate (9g sugars
- Cholesterol: 1mg cholesterol
- Protein: 5g protein. Diabetic Exchanges: 2 starch.
- Total Fat: 4g fat (0 saturated fat)
- Sodium: 665mg sodium

---

645. Pumpkin Pudding Desserts

Serving: 2 servings. | Prep: 10mins | Cook: 0mins | Ready in:

Ingredients

- 3/4 cup canned pumpkin
- 1/2 teaspoon ground cinnamon
- 1/4 teaspoon ground ginger
- 3/4 cup cold 2% milk
- 1 package (3.3 ounces) instant white chocolate pudding mix
- 1/4 cup whipped topping

Direction

- Beat ginger, cinnamon, and pumpkin together in a small bowl. Add pudding mix and milk, beat for 2 minute (the mixture should be thick).
- Remove into separate serving plates. Chill until eating. Use whipped topping to garnish each serving.

Nutrition Information

- Calories: 279 calories

- Protein: 5g protein.
- Total Fat: 4g fat (3g saturated fat)
- Sodium: 724mg sodium
- Fiber: 4g fiber)
- Total Carbohydrate: 57g carbohydrate (52g sugars
- Cholesterol: 7mg cholesterol

---

646. Pumpkin Spice Cake

Serving: 24 servings | Prep: 30mins | Cook: | Ready in:

Ingredients

- 1 pkg. (2-layer size) yellow cake mix
- 1 pkg. (3.4 oz.) JELL-O Vanilla Flavor Instant Pudding
- 1 cup mashed cooked fresh pumpkin
- 1/2 cup oil
- 1/2 cup water
- 3 egg s
- 1 Tbsp. pumpkin pie spice
- 1/2 cup chopped toasted PLANTERS Pecans

Direction

- 1. Use a mixer to beat the first 7 ingredients until blended. Pour the mixture into 13x9-inch pan coated with cooking spray.
- 2. Bake for 32 to 35 minutes or until when you insert a toothpick in the center, it should come out clean. Let cool down completely.
- 3. Use PHILADELPHIA Cream Cheese Frosting to spread over the cake; sprinkle with nuts. Store in the refrigerator.

Nutrition Information

- Calories: 270
- Sodium: 250 mg
- Saturated Fat: 4.5 g
- Sugar: 31 g
- Total Carbohydrate: 39 g
- Cholesterol: 40 mg

- Protein: 2 g
- Total Fat: 13 g
- Fiber: 1 g

647. Pumpkin Spiced Pudding

Serving: 4-6 servings. | Prep: 10mins | Cook: 0mins | Ready in:

Ingredients

- 1-1/2 cups cold milk
- 1 cup heavy whipping cream, divided
- 1 package (3.4 ounces) instant vanilla pudding mix
- 1 teaspoon pumpkin pie spice
- 1 cup canned pumpkin
- Additional pumpkin pie spice for garnish
- Gingersnaps, optional

Direction

- Mix pie spice, pudding mix, 1/2 cup cream, and milk together in a bowl; beat for 2 minutes until smooth and thick. Mix in pumpkin. Put into pumpkin dishes.
- Whip the leftover cream until forming stiff peaks. On each pudding serving, put a dollop of the whipped cream. Sprinkle pie spice over. Enjoy with gingersnaps if you want.

Nutrition Information

- Calories: 249 calories
- Sodium: 273mg sodium
- Fiber: 2g fiber)
- Total Carbohydrate: 22g carbohydrate (17g sugars
- Cholesterol: 63mg cholesterol
- Protein: 4g protein.
- Total Fat: 17g fat (10g saturated fat)

648. Pumpkin Trifle

Serving: 12-15 servings. | Prep: 20mins | Cook: 0mins | Ready in:

Ingredients

- 2 to 3 cups leftover crumbled unfrosted spice cake, muffins or gingerbread
- 2-1/2 cups cold milk
- 1 can (15 ounces) solid-pack pumpkin
- 4 packages (3.4 ounces each) instant butterscotch pudding mix
- 1 teaspoon ground cinnamon
- 1/4 teaspoon ground nutmeg
- 1/4 teaspoon ground ginger
- 1/4 teaspoon ground allspice
- 2 cups heavy whipping cream
- Maraschino cherries, optional

Direction

- Put 1/4 cup cake crumbs aside for topping. Divide leftover crumbs to 4 portions; sprinkle 1 portion in 3-qt. serving bowl/trifle bowls.
- Beat spices, pudding mixes, pumpkin and milk till smooth in big bowl; put 1/2 in serving bowl. Sprinkle 2nd crumbs portion. Beat cream till stiff peaks form in small bowl; put 1/2 in bowl.
- Sprinkle 3rd crumbs portion; put leftover pumpkin mixture over then leftover crumbs portion and whipped cream. Sprinkle reserved crumbs around bowl edge; if desired, garnish with cherries. Cover; chill before serving for 2 hours minimum.

Nutrition Information

- Calories: 186 calories
- Protein: 3g protein.
- Total Fat: 14g fat (8g saturated fat)
- Sodium: 163mg sodium
- Fiber: 1g fiber)
- Total Carbohydrate: 14g carbohydrate (10g sugars
- Cholesterol: 49mg cholesterol

Serving: 20-24 servings. | Prep: 60mins | Cook: 20mins | Ready in:

Ingredients

- 1 package white cake mix (regular size)
- 3-1/2 cups cold milk
- 2 packages (3.4 ounces each) instant vanilla pudding mix
- 1 can (20 ounces) crushed pineapple, drained
- 1-1/2 cups sweetened shredded coconut
- 1/3 cup chopped pecans
- 1 carton (8 ounces) frozen whipped topping, thawed
- Additional chopped pecans, optional

Direction

- Follow package direction to bake cake with a 13x9-in. greased baking pan. Completely cool cake on a wire rack. Whisk pudding mixes and milk for 2 minutes in a big bowl; stand till soft set for 2 minutes. Fold pineapple in. Cover; refrigerate. Fold nuts and coconut into whipped topping.
- Assemble: Cut the cake into 1-in. cubes; put 1/2 in a 5-qt. punch bowl. Put 1/2 pudding mixture then 1/2 whipped topping mixture over the top. Repeat layers. Sprinkle with extra pecans (optional). Cover; refrigerate till serving.

Nutrition Information

- Calories:
- Total Carbohydrate:
- Cholesterol:
- Protein:
- Total Fat:
- Sodium:
- Fiber:

Serving: 55 (1/2-cup) servings. | Prep: 25mins | Cook: 30mins | Ready in:

Ingredients

- 2 cans (20 ounces each) unsweetened crushed pineapple
- 1 package yellow cake mix (regular size)
- 1 package (5.1 ounces) instant vanilla pudding mix
- 2 cans (21 ounces each) cherry pie filling
- 4 medium ripe bananas, sliced
- 2 cans (15-1/4 ounces each) fruit cocktail, drained
- 2 cans (11 ounces each) mandarin oranges
- 1 carton (16 ounces) frozen whipped topping, thawed
- 1 package (7 ounces) sweetened shredded coconut, toasted

Direction

- Drain pineapple, keep juice; put aside pineapple. Follow package title_direction to prep cake batter; use pineapple juice for water. If needed, add water to get the right measurement. Bake as directions in 13x9-in. greased pan; cool.
- Meanwhile, follow package directions to prep pudding. Cut cake to 1-in. cubes; put 1/2 in 6-qt. punch bowl. Put 1/2 pudding, coconut, whipped topping, oranges, fruit cocktail, bananas, pineapple and pie filling; repeat layers. Cover; chill trifle for 6 hours – overnight.

Nutrition Information

- Calories:
- Sodium:
- Fiber:
- Total Carbohydrate:
- Cholesterol:

- Protein:
- Total Fat:

651.   Quick Apple Cream Pie

Serving: 6-8 servings. | Prep: 30mins | Cook: 0mins | Ready in:

Ingredients

- 4 cups thinly sliced peeled tart apples
- 2 tablespoons sugar
- 2 tablespoons lemon juice
- 1/4 cup butter
- 1 package (8 ounces) cream cheese, softened
- 1-1/2 cups cold whole milk, divided
- 1 package (3.4 ounces) instant vanilla pudding mix
- 1 teaspoon grated lemon zest
- 1 pastry shell (9 inches), baked
- 1/4 cup apricot preserves or strawberry jelly, melted

Direction

- Add butter into a large skillet and sauté lemon juice, sugar and apples in it until the apples turn softened. Let it cool.
- Beat the cream cheese in a bowl until smoothened. Add in lemon zest, dry pudding mix and 1 cup milk while slowly beating. Beat in the remaining milk until the mixture becomes thick. Add onto the pastry shell and spread out. Place apple on top of the filling. Use preserves to brush on.
- Put on the refrigerator until ready to serve for 1 hour. Brush more preserves on top to your interest.

Nutrition Information

- Calories:
- Fiber:
- Total Carbohydrate:

- Cholesterol:
- Protein:
- Total Fat:
- Sodium:

652.   Quick Chocolate Mousse

Serving: 4 | Prep: 5mins | Cook: 1mins | Ready in:

Ingredients

- 1 (1.5 ounce) bar milk chocolate candy bar
- 1 tablespoon milk
- 1 1/2 cups plain fat-free Greek yogurt

Direction

- In microwave-safe bowl, put milk and chocolate bar; microwave for 30 seconds till chocolate is melted and soft. Mix Greek yogurt into chocolate mixture till smooth.

Nutrition Information

- Calories: 104 calories;
- Protein: 8
- Total Fat: 3.4
- Sodium: 39
- Total Carbohydrate: 10.2
- Cholesterol: 3

653.   Quick Coconut Cream Pie

Serving: 6-8 servings. | Prep: 15mins | Cook: 0mins | Ready in:

Ingredients

- 1-1/2 cups cold 2% milk
- 1 package (5.1 ounces) instant vanilla pudding mix

- 1 carton (8 ounces) frozen whipped topping, thawed, divided
- 3/4 to 1 cup sweetened shredded coconut, toasted, divided
- 1 pastry shell, baked or graham cracker crust (8 or 9 inches)

Direction

- Beat pudding and milk together in a big bowl on low speed about 2 minutes. Fold in half of the whipped topping and 1/2 to 3/4 cup of coconut.
- Pour into crust then spread leftover whipped topping over and sprinkle with leftover coconut. Refrigerate.

Nutrition Information

- Calories: 338 calories
- Protein: 3g protein.
- Total Fat: 16g fat (11g saturated fat)
- Sodium: 400mg sodium
- Fiber: 0 fiber)
- Total Carbohydrate: 42g carbohydrate (23g sugars
- Cholesterol: 11mg cholesterol

654. Quick Creamy Banana Pie

Serving: 8 servings. | Prep: 15mins | Cook: 0mins | Ready in:

Ingredients

- 1 package (8 ounces) reduced-fat cream cheese
- Sugar substitute equivalent to 1/2 cup sugar
- 1 carton (8 ounces) frozen reduced-fat whipped topping, thawed, divided
- 1 reduced-fat graham cracker crust (8 inches)
- 3 medium firm bananas, sliced
- 1-1/3 cups cold 2% milk

- 1 package (1 ounce) sugar-free instant vanilla pudding mix

Direction

- Beat sugar substitute and cream cheese together in a bowl until smooth. Fold in 1 cup of whipped topping and scoop into crust. Put on top with banana slices. Whisk together pudding mix and milk in a bowl about 2 minutes. Pour the mixture over bananas. Use the leftover whipped topping to spread over mixture. Chill for a minimum of 4 hours to overnight.

Nutrition Information

- Calories: 302 calories
- Sodium: 347mg sodium
- Fiber: 1g fiber)
- Total Carbohydrate: 43g carbohydrate (0 sugars
- Cholesterol: 19mg cholesterol
- Protein: 6g protein. Diabetic Exchanges: 2 starch
- Total Fat: 11g fat (7g saturated fat)

655. Quick Dirt Cake

Serving: 16-20 servings. | Prep: 30mins | Cook: 0mins | Ready in:

Ingredients

- 2 packages (8 ounces each) cream cheese, softened
- 1/4 cup butter, softened
- 1 cup confectioners' sugar
- 2 packages (3.9 ounces each) instant chocolate fudge pudding mix
- 3-1/2 cups cold milk
- 1 carton (12 ounces) frozen whipped topping, thawed
- 1 plastic flowerpot (8-inch diameter)

- 1 package (20 ounces) chocolate sandwich cookies, crushed
- Artificial flowers, gummy worms and plastic shovel, optional

Direction

- Cream butter and cream cheese in a big bowl. Add sugar; put aside. Mix whipped topping, pudding and mix till smooth in another bowl. Add creamed mixture. Line plastic wrap inside of flowerpot, covering the whole on bottom of pot. Put 1/3 crushed cookies in pot; top with 1/2 pudding/cream cheese mixture. Repeat layers; finish with cookies. Refrigerate it overnight. Decorate cake with a plastic shovel, gummy worms and flowers, if desired.

Nutrition Information

- Calories: 314 calories
- Protein: 4g protein.
- Total Fat: 17g fat (9g saturated fat)
- Sodium: 342mg sodium
- Fiber: 1g fiber)
- Total Carbohydrate: 37g carbohydrate (24g sugars
- Cholesterol: 24mg cholesterol

656. Quick Icebox Sandwiches

Serving: 2 dozen. | Prep: 20mins | Cook: 0mins | Ready in:

Ingredients

- 1 package (3.4 ounces) instant vanilla pudding mix
- 2 cups cold milk
- 2 cups whipped topping
- 1 cup miniature semisweet chocolate chips
- 24 whole graham crackers, halved

Direction

- Combine milk and pudding as directed on package; chill until firm. Fold in chocolate chips and whipped topping.
- Arrange 24 graham cracker halves on a baking sheet; place about 3 tablespoons filling on top of each cracker half. Replace top with another cracker half. Wrap separately in plastic wrap; keep frozen until set, for 1 hour. Enjoy sandwiches frozen.

Nutrition Information

- Calories: 144 calories
- Total Fat: 5g fat (3g saturated fat)
- Sodium: 162mg sodium
- Fiber: 1g fiber)
- Total Carbohydrate: 23g carbohydrate (13g sugars
- Cholesterol: 3mg cholesterol
- Protein: 2g protein.

657. Quick Peanut Butter Pudding

Serving: 4 servings. | Prep: 15mins | Cook: 0mins | Ready in:

Ingredients

- 1-3/4 cups fat-free milk
- 2 tablespoons reduced-fat creamy peanut butter
- 1 package (1 ounce) sugar-free instant vanilla pudding mix
- 1/4 cup reduced-fat whipped topping
- 4 teaspoons chocolate syrup

Direction

- Stir the peanut butter and milk in a bowl until combined. Put in pudding mix and stir until thickened a bit for 2 min. Scoop the mixture into dessert dishes. Chill for a minimum of 5 min. until set. Just before serving, dollop with whipped topping and sprinkle chocolate syrup on top.

Nutrition Information

- Calories: 112 calories
- Protein: 6g protein. Diabetic Exchanges: 1/2 starch
- Total Fat: 3g fat (1g saturated fat)
- Sodium: 186mg sodium
- Fiber: 1g fiber)
- Total Carbohydrate: 14g carbohydrate (0 sugars
- Cholesterol: 2mg cholesterol

658.   Quick Rice Pudding

Serving: 6 servings. | Prep: 10mins | Cook: 0mins | Ready in:

Ingredients

- 1 package (3.4 ounces) instant vanilla pudding mix
- 2 cups cold milk
- 1 cup cold cooked rice
- 1/2 cup raisins
- Whipped topping
- Maraschino cherries

Direction

- Beat milk and pudding mix till well blended for 1-2 minutes in a bowl; mix in raisins and rice. Put pudding into individual bowls then chill. Garnish with a cherry and whipped topping.

Nutrition Information

- Calories: 181 calories
- Sodium: 268mg sodium
- Fiber: 1g fiber)

- Total Carbohydrate: 36g carbohydrate (24g sugars
- Cholesterol: 11mg cholesterol
- Protein: 4g protein.
- Total Fat: 3g fat (2g saturated fat)

659.   Raisin Butterscotch Pie

Serving: 6-8 servings. | Prep: 10mins | Cook: 0mins | Ready in:

Ingredients

- 2 cups cold milk
- 1 package (3.4 ounces) instant vanilla pudding mix
- 1 package (3.4 ounces) instant butterscotch pudding mix
- 2 cups sour cream
- 1 cup raisins
- 1 medium firm banana, sliced into 1/4-inch pieces
- 1 pastry shell (9 inches), baked
- Whipped topping

Direction

- Whisk dry pudding mixes and milk together in a large mixing bowl until thickened, about 3 minutes. Add sour cream and fold gently. Mix in raisins.
- Arrange banana slice in a pastry shell; spread pudding mixture over top. Refrigerate until ready to serve. Decorate with whipped topping.

Nutrition Information

- Calories: 434 calories
- Fiber: 1g fiber)
- Total Carbohydrate: 58g carbohydrate (38g sugars
- Cholesterol: 53mg cholesterol
- Protein: 6g protein.

- Total Fat: 19g fat (11g saturated fat)
- Sodium: 520mg sodium

660. Raspberry Brownie Dessert

Serving: 18 servings. | Prep: 20mins | Cook: 25mins | Ready in:

Ingredients

- 1 package fudge brownie mix (13-inch x 9-inch pan size)
- 2 cups heavy whipping cream, divided
- 1 package (3.3 ounces) instant white chocolate pudding mix
- 1 can (21 ounces) raspberry pie filling

Direction

- In a greased 13x9" baking pan, bake brownies following the instructions on brownie mix package. Leave on a wire rack to cool completely.
- Blend pudding mix and 1 cup of cream together in a small bowl, then stir for 2 minutes or until thickened. Beat remaining cream in a small bowl until it forms stiff peaks, then fold into pudding. Spread this cream gently over the brownies and spread pie filling on top. Leave in the fridge, covered, for at least 2 hours prior to slicing.

Nutrition Information

- Calories: 333 calories
- Sodium: 225mg sodium
- Fiber: 2g fiber)
- Total Carbohydrate: 37g carbohydrate (26g sugars
- Cholesterol: 52mg cholesterol
- Protein: 3g protein.
- Total Fat: 20g fat (8g saturated fat)

661. Raspberry Chocolate Trifle

Serving: 4-6 servings. | Prep: 15mins | Cook: 0mins | Ready in:

Ingredients

- 2 cups cold milk
- 1 package (3.9 ounces) instant chocolate pudding mix
- 1 loaf (10-3/4 ounces) frozen pound cake, thawed
- 2 cups fresh or frozen raspberries, thawed
- 1 cup raspberry preserves
- Whipped topping
- Additional raspberries, optional

Direction

- Follow package directions to mix pudding and milk; chill. Slice cake into 1-in. cubes; put 1/2 in a 2-qt. glass bowl. Mix preserves and raspberries together gently in a small bowl; put 1/2 on cake.
- Put 1/2 pudding on raspberries; cover with leftover cake cubes. Layer with leftover berries then pudding. Chill till serving time. If desired, garnish with raspberries and whipped topping.

Nutrition Information

- Calories: 493 calories
- Protein: 7g protein.
- Total Fat: 14g fat (8g saturated fat)
- Sodium: 497mg sodium
- Fiber: 4g fiber)
- Total Carbohydrate: 88g carbohydrate (65g sugars
- Cholesterol: 84mg cholesterol

662.   Raspberry Cream Cake

Serving: 14 slices. | Prep: 20mins | Cook: 30mins | Ready in:

Ingredients

- 1 package yellow cake mix (regular size)
- 1/4 teaspoon baking soda
- 1-1/3 cups water
- 4 large egg whites
- 2 tablespoons unsweetened applesauce
- 1-1/3 cups cold fat-free milk
- 1 package (1 ounce) sugar-free instant vanilla pudding mix
- 3/4 teaspoon vanilla extract
- 1-1/2 cups fresh raspberries, divided
- 1/2 cup fat-free hot fudge ice cream topping
- 1 tablespoon light corn syrup

Direction

- Mix baking soda and cake mix in a large bowl. Add applesauce, egg whites, and water; whisk for half a minute at low speed. Whisk for 2 minutes at medium speed.
- Add into 2 greased 9-inch round baking pans. Bake at 350 degrees until a toothpick comes out clean when inserted into the center, for 28-32 minutes. Allow to cool for 10 minutes, then transfer from the pans onto wire racks to cool completely.
- For the filling: Beat vanilla, pudding mix, and milk for 2 minutes in a large bowl; allow to stand until soft-set, for 2 minutes.
- On a serving plate, arrange 1 cake layer. Spread the pudding mixture over; dust with 3/4 cup of the raspberries. Add the rest of the cake layer on top. Mix corn syrup and ice cream topping; whisk until smooth. Spread over the top of the cake and allow the glaze to drip over the sides. Top with the rest of berries.

Nutrition Information

- Calories: 215 calories

- Total Carbohydrate: 42g carbohydrate (24g sugars
- Cholesterol: 0 cholesterol
- Protein: 4g protein. Diabetic Exchanges: 3 starch
- Total Fat: 4g fat (1g saturated fat)
- Sodium: 388mg sodium
- Fiber: 2g fiber)

663.   Raspberry Cream Trifle

Serving: 14-16 servings. | Prep: 30mins | Cook: 0mins | Ready in:

Ingredients

- 1 can (14 ounces) sweetened condensed milk
- 1 cup cold water
- 1 teaspoon almond extract
- 1 package (3.4 ounces) instant vanilla pudding mix
- 2 cups heavy whipping cream, whipped
- 1 prepared angel food cake (8 to 10 ounces), cut into 1-inch cubes
- 2 tablespoons seedless raspberry jam
- 2 cups fresh raspberries
- Chocolate curls and fresh mint

Direction

- Beat extract, water and milk till blended in big bowl. Add pudding mix then whisk for 2 minutes; stand till soft set for 2 minutes. Cover; chill till mixture sets partially. Fold whipped cream in.
- Put 1/2 cake cubes in 2-qt. glass serving bowl; put 1/2 cream mixture over. Spread jam carefully; sprinkle 1 cup raspberries. Layer leftover cake cubes, cream mixture then raspberries; garnish with mint and chocolate curls.

Nutrition Information

- Calories:

- Total Fat:
- Sodium:
- Fiber:
- Total Carbohydrate:
- Cholesterol:
- Protein:

- Fiber: 1g fiber)
- Total Carbohydrate: 47g carbohydrate (33g sugars
- Cholesterol: 6mg cholesterol
- Protein: 3g protein.
- Total Fat: 11g fat (7g saturated fat)

664. Raspberry Mousse Pie

Serving: 6-8 servings. | Prep: 10mins | Cook: 0mins | Ready in:

Ingredients

- 1-1/2 cups cold milk
- 1 package (3.4 ounces) instant cheesecake or vanilla pudding mix
- 1 chocolate crumb crust (9 inches)
- 1-1/2 teaspoons unflavored gelatin
- 2 tablespoons cold water
- 1/2 cup seedless raspberry jam
- 1 teaspoon lemon juice
- 1 carton (8 ounces) frozen whipped topping, thawed
- Fresh raspberries and mint, optional

Direction

- Whisk pudding mix and milk for 2 minutes in big bowl; stand till soft set for 2 minutes. Put into crust. Cover; refrigerate.
- Sprinkle gelatin on cold water; stand for a minute. Microwave for 20-30 seconds on high; mix. Let stand till gelatin melts completely for a minute. Whisk lemon juice and jam in slowly; chill for 10 minutes. Fold whipped topping in; spread on pudding.
- Refrigerate till set for 2 hours; if desired, garnish with mint and raspberries.

Nutrition Information

- Calories: 305 calories
- Sodium: 294mg sodium

665. Raspberry Peach Delight

Serving: 15 servings. | Prep: 20mins | Cook: 0mins | Ready in:

Ingredients

- 1 prepared angel food cake (8 to 10 ounces), cut into 1-inch cubes
- 1 package (.3 ounce) sugar-free raspberry gelatin
- 1 cup boiling water
- 1 cup cold water
- 1 can (15 ounces) sliced peaches in juice, well drained and halved
- 3 cups cold fat-free milk
- 1 package (1.5 ounces) sugar-free instant vanilla pudding mix
- 1 carton (8 ounces) frozen reduced-fat whipped topping, thawed

Direction

- Place the cake cubes in a 13x 9-inch dish.
- Dissolve the gelatin in a small bowl with the boiling water; then stir in the cold water. Add over the cake. Place peaches over the gelatin.
- Whisk pudding mix and milk in large bowl about 2 mins. Allow to stand until soft-set, about 2 mins. Spoon over the peaches. Add the whipped topping over top. Place in the refrigerator, covered, at least 120 mins, then cut.

Nutrition Information

- Calories:
- Sodium:

- Fiber:
- Total Carbohydrate:
- Cholesterol:
- Protein:
- Total Fat:

666. Raspberry Pudding Parfaits

Serving: 4 servings. | Prep: 10mins | Cook: 0mins | Ready in:

Ingredients

- 1-1/2 cups cold milk
- 1 package (5.1 ounces) instant vanilla pudding mix
- 1 package (12 ounces) frozen unsweetened raspberries, thawed
- Whipped topping, optional

Direction

- Beat pudding mix and milk in a large bowl; whisk for 2 minutes or until thickened. Put half into four parfait glasses. Place half of the raspberries on top. Continue layers. Decorate with whipped topping if preferred.

Nutrition Information

- Calories: 230 calories
- Protein: 4g protein.
- Total Fat: 3g fat (2g saturated fat)
- Sodium: 556mg sodium
- Fiber: 2g fiber)
- Total Carbohydrate: 46g carbohydrate (36g sugars
- Cholesterol: 12mg cholesterol

667. Raspberry Trifle

Serving: 18 | Prep: 20mins | Cook: | Ready in:

Ingredients

- 1 1/2 cups heavy cream
- 1/4 cup white sugar
- 2 (8 ounce) packages cream cheese, softened
- 2 teaspoons lemon juice
- 1 1/2 teaspoons vanilla extract
- 1/2 cup white sugar
- 1 (10.75 ounce) package prepared pound cake
- 2 (10 ounce) packages frozen raspberries, thawed
- 2 tablespoons unsweetened cocoa powder, for dusting

Direction

- Beat 1/4 cup sugar and cream till stiff peaks form in medium bowl. Cream 1/2 cup sugar, vanilla, lemon juice and cream cheese in another bowl; fold 2 cups whipped cream into cream cheese mixture. Keep leftover whipped cream.
- Cut pound cake to 18 1/2-in. slices. Drain raspberries; keep juice. Line bottom of trifle bowl/3-qt. glass bowl with 1/3 cake slices. Drizzle some raspberry juice; spread 1/4 cream cheese mixture on cake. Sift 1/4 cocoa over it. Sprinkle 1/3 raspberries; repeat layers 2 times. Put leftover cream cheese mixture, the whipped cream then sifted cocoa over. Cover; refrigerate before serving for 4 hours.

Nutrition Information

- Calories: 287 calories;
- Sodium: 148
- Total Carbohydrate: 26.4
- Cholesterol: 92
- Protein: 3.5
- Total Fat: 19.5

668. Raspberry Vanilla Pudding Parfaits

Serving: 6 servings. | Prep: 10mins | Cook: 0mins | Ready in:

Ingredients

- 2 cups cold 2% milk
- 1 package (3.4 ounces) instant vanilla or French vanilla pudding mix
- 1 cup whipped topping
- 1 pint fresh raspberries

Direction

- Blend pudding mix and milk for two minutes in a big bowl. Leave to sit for two minutes until set to soft. Fold in one cup whipped topping. Scoop 1/3 pudding into 6 parfait glasses.
- Reserve 6 raspberries for garnishing; place 1/2 of remaining berries on top of pudding. Repeat layers once more and ending with the rest of the pudding. Garnish reserved berries on top.

Nutrition Information

- Calories: 158 calories
- Total Fat: 5g fat (4g saturated fat)
- Sodium: 267mg sodium
- Fiber: 1g fiber)
- Total Carbohydrate: 25g carbohydrate (19g sugars
- Cholesterol: 11mg cholesterol
- Protein: 3g protein.

669. Rave Review Coconut Cake

Serving: 16-20 servings. | Prep: 25mins | Cook: 25mins | Ready in:

Ingredients

- CAKE:
- 1 package yellow cake mix (regular size)
- 1 package (3-1/2 ounces) instant vanilla pudding mix
- 1-1/3 cups water
- 4 large eggs, room temperature
- 1/4 cup vegetable oil
- 2 cups sweetened shredded coconut
- 1 cup chopped pecans
- FROSTING:
- 4 tablespoons butter, divided
- 2 cups sweetened shredded coconut
- 1 package (8 ounces) cream cheese
- 2 teaspoons milk
- 1/2 teaspoon vanilla
- 3-1/2 cups confectioners' sugar

Direction

- Beat oil, eggs, water and pudding for 3 minutes at medium speed in a big bowl; mix in nuts and coconut. Put into 3 8-in. round greased and floured baking pans; bake it at 350° till cake springs back when you touch the center for 25-30 minutes. Cool for 10 minutes in pans. Transfer to rack; fully cool.
- Frosting: In skillet, melt 2 tbsp. butter. Add coconut; constantly mix on low heat till golden brown. On absorbent paper towel, spread coconut; cool. Cream vanilla, milk, cream cheese and leftover 2 tbsp. butter. Add sugar; beat well to blend. Mix in 1 1/2 cups of toasted coconut; spread on sides and top of cake. Sprinkle leftover coconut on cake.

Nutrition Information

- Calories: 442 calories
- Sodium: 351mg sodium
- Fiber: 2g fiber)
- Total Carbohydrate: 56g carbohydrate (42g sugars
- Cholesterol: 61mg cholesterol
- Protein: 4g protein.
- Total Fat: 23g fat (12g saturated fat)

670. Rawhide's Whiskey Cake

Serving: 16 slices. | Prep: 15mins | Cook: 60mins |Ready in:

Ingredients

- 1 package spice cake mix with pudding (regular size)
- 1 package (3.4 ounces) instant vanilla pudding mix
- 3/4 cup 2% milk
- 3/4 cup whiskey
- 1/2 cup canola oil
- 4 large eggs
- 1-1/3 cups coarsely chopped walnuts, divided
- GLAZE:
- 1 cup sugar
- 1/2 cup butter, cubed
- 1/2 cup whiskey
- 1 teaspoon water

Direction

- Set oven to preheat at 300°. Grease a 10-in. tube pan, then dust with flour.
- Mix together the first six ingredients; beat for 30 seconds on low speed. On medium speed, beat for 2 minutes; fold 1 cup nuts into the mixture. Transfer the batter into the prepared pan; sprinkle the remaining nuts on top. Bake for 60-65 minutes till tested done with a toothpick. Let it cool down in pan.
- To make the glaze, in a small saucepan, mix together all ingredients; cook on medium-high heat till boiling. Lower the heat and simmer 10 minutes. Let it cool for 3 minutes. Pour 1/3 glaze atop the cake, let some flow down the sides. Let sit for 1 hour. Take out of the pan to cool thoroughly; cover.
- On the next day, reheat glaze; brush half of it atop the cake, cool it down before covering. Repeat the following day with the remaining glaze.

Nutrition Information

- Calories: 400 calories
- Cholesterol: 63mg cholesterol
- Protein: 5g protein.
- Total Fat: 23g fat (6g saturated fat)
- Sodium: 298mg sodium
- Fiber: 1g fiber)
- Total Carbohydrate: 43g carbohydrate (30g sugars

671. Red, White And Blueberry Pie

Serving: 8 servings. | Prep: 20mins | Cook: 0mins |Ready in:

Ingredients

- 2 ounces white baking chocolate, melted
- One 9-inch graham cracker crust (about 6 ounces)
- 3/4 cup sliced fresh strawberries
- 1 package (8 ounces) cream cheese, softened
- 3/4 cup confectioners' sugar
- 3/4 cup 2% milk
- 1 package (3.3 ounces) instant white chocolate pudding mix
- 1 cup whipped topping
- 8 fresh strawberries, halved lengthwise
- 1 cup fresh blueberries

Direction

- Arrange melted chocolate onto the bottom and sides of the crust; spread. Cover with sliced strawberries.
- Beat confectioners' sugar and cream cheese in a bowl, till smooth; slowly beat in milk. Include in pudding mix; whisk on low speed for around 2 minutes, till thickened. Arrange over the strawberries and spread out.

- Garnish the pie with halved strawberries, blueberries and whipped topping. Keep in a refrigerator till serving.

Nutrition Information

- Calories: 383 calories
- Protein: 4g protein.
- Total Fat: 19g fat (10g saturated fat)
- Sodium: 395mg sodium
- Fiber: 1g fiber)
- Total Carbohydrate: 50g carbohydrate (44g sugars
- Cholesterol: 30mg cholesterol

672.   Rich Chocolate Cream Bars

Serving: about 3 dozen. | Prep: 25mins | Cook: 0mins | Ready in:

Ingredients

- 1/2 cup butter
- 5 tablespoons baking cocoa
- 1/4 cup sugar
- 1 egg, lightly beaten
- 1 teaspoon vanilla extract
- 1-1/2 cups graham cracker crumbs (about 24 squares)
- 1 cup sweetened shredded coconut
- 1/2 cup chopped walnuts
- FILLING:
- 1/4 cup butter, softened
- 3 tablespoons milk
- 2 tablespoons instant vanilla pudding mix
- 2 cups confectioners' sugar
- 1 teaspoon vanilla extract
- GLAZE:
- 4 ounces semisweet chocolate, chopped
- 1 tablespoon butter

Direction

- Mix and cook vanilla, egg, sugar, cocoa and butter in small saucepan on medium low heat till mixture reads 160°.
- Mix walnuts, coconut and graham cracker crumbs in big bowl. Mix cocoa mixture in till blended; press in 9-in. greased square pan. Put aside.
- Filling: Beat pudding mix, milk and butter till blended in big bowl. Beat vanilla and confectioners' sugar in till smooth; spread on crust.
- Glaze: Melt butter and chocolate in microwave; mix till smooth. Spread on filling; cover. Chill till set; cut to bars.

Nutrition Information

- Calories:
- Total Fat:
- Sodium:
- Fiber:
- Total Carbohydrate:
- Cholesterol:
- Protein:

673.   Rich Peach Ice Cream

Serving: 4 quarts. | Prep: 15mins | Cook: 20mins | Ready in:

Ingredients

- 2 cups cold fat-free milk
- 1 package (3.4 ounces) instant vanilla pudding mix
- 4 medium peaches, peeled and chopped
- 2 cans (12 ounces each) fat-free evaporated milk
- 1 can (14 ounces) sweetened condensed milk
- 1/2 cup sugar
- 1/4 cup lemon juice
- 1 teaspoon vanilla extract
- 1/2 teaspoon almond extract
- 1/8 teaspoon salt

- 1 carton (8 ounces) fat-free frozen whipped topping, thawed

Direction

- Whip pudding mix and milk in a big bowl about 2 minutes on low speed. Whip in salt, extracts, lemon juice, sugar, condensed milk, evaporated milk and peaches. Whip in whipped topping just till combined.
- Pour into the ice cream freezer cylinder, filling 2/3 full; freeze following directions of manufacturer. Chill the rest of the mixture till ready to freeze. Remove into freezer containers and freeze prior to serving, about 2 to 4 hours.

Nutrition Information

- Calories: 140 calories
- Sodium: 139mg sodium
- Fiber: 0 fiber)
- Total Carbohydrate: 27g carbohydrate (23g sugars
- Cholesterol: 7mg cholesterol
- Protein: 4g protein. Diabetic Exchanges: 2 starch.
- Total Fat: 2g fat (1g saturated fat)

674. Rocky Road Freezer Pie

Serving: 16 servings. | Prep: 15mins | Cook: 0mins | Ready in:

Ingredients

- 1-1/2 cups half-and-half cream
- 1 package (3.9 ounces) instant chocolate pudding mix
- 1 carton (8 ounces) frozen whipped topping, thawed
- 1/3 cup semisweet chocolate chips
- 1/3 cup miniature marshmallows
- 1/3 cup chopped pecans
- 1 graham cracker crust (9 inches)

- Miniature marshmallows, chopped pecans and chocolate sauce, optional

Direction

- Beat pudding mix and cream in a big bowl for 2 minutes. Fold whipped topping into the mixture. Mix in pecans, marshmallows and chocolate chips. Pour into the pie shell. Put in the freezer for 6 hours until firm. Take out of the freezer for 10 minutes then serve.

Nutrition Information

- Calories: 184 calories
- Total Fat: 10g fat (5g saturated fat)
- Sodium: 175mg sodium
- Fiber: 1g fiber)
- Total Carbohydrate: 20g carbohydrate (15g sugars
- Cholesterol: 11mg cholesterol
- Protein: 2g protein.

675. Root Beer Float Pie

Serving: 8 servings. | Prep: 15mins | Cook: 0mins | Ready in:

Ingredients

- 1 carton (8 ounces) frozen reduced-fat whipped topping, thawed, divided
- 3/4 cup cold diet root beer
- 1/2 cup fat-free milk
- 1 package (1 ounce) sugar-free instant vanilla pudding mix
- 1 graham cracker crust (9 inches)
- Maraschino cherries, optional

Direction

- Measure 1/2 cup whipped topping and chill for garnish later. Beat pudding mix, milk, and root beer together in a large mixing bowl for 2 minutes. Add half of the remaining whipped topping and fold in gently. Spoon mixture into graham cracker crust, spreading evenly.

- Top pie with the rest of whipped topping. Place in the freezer for a minimum of 8 hours or overnight.
- Top each serving with dollop of reserved whipped topping; place a maraschino cherry on top of each portion, if desired.

Nutrition Information

- Calories: 185 calories
- Protein: 1g protein. Diabetic Exchanges: 2 starch
- Total Fat: 8g fat (4g saturated fat)
- Sodium: 275mg sodium
- Fiber: 0 fiber)
- Total Carbohydrate: 27g carbohydrate (14g sugars
- Cholesterol: 0 cholesterol

676. S'more Parfaits

Serving: 4 servings. | Prep: 10mins | Cook: 0mins | Ready in:

Ingredients

- 2 cups cold milk
- 1 package (3.9 ounces) instant chocolate fudge or chocolate pudding mix
- 2 cups coarsely crushed graham crackers (about 24 squares)
- 1 cup miniature marshmallows
- 4 tablespoons miniature semisweet chocolate chips

Direction

- Beat pudding mix and milk in a bowl for 2 minutes. Allow it to stand for 2 minutes or until soft-set.
- Into four parfait glasses, put 3 tablespoons each of the pudding mixture. Then layer each with 1/4 cup cracker crumbs, then 3

tablespoons pudding, 1/4 cup marshmallows and 1 tablespoon chocolate chips. Put the remaining pudding and crumbs on top. Keep for 1 hour in the refrigerator prior to serving.

Nutrition Information

- Calories: 218 calories
- Protein: 6g protein. Diabetic Exchanges: 2-1/2 starch
- Total Fat: 5g fat (2g saturated fat)
- Sodium: 361mg sodium
- Fiber: 2g fiber)
- Total Carbohydrate: 40g carbohydrate (0 sugars
- Cholesterol: 3mg cholesterol

677. Sacher Torte Cookies

Serving: about 2-1/2 dozen. | Prep: 20mins | Cook: 15mins | Ready in:

Ingredients

- 1 cup butter, softened
- 1 package (3.9 ounces) instant chocolate pudding mix
- 1 large egg
- 2 cups all-purpose flour
- 1/4 cup sugar
- 1/2 cup raspberry, strawberry or apricot preserves
- GLAZE:
- 1/3 cup semisweet chocolate chips
- 2 teaspoons shortening

Direction

- Set oven to 325° to preheat. Beat pudding mix and butter together until fluffy and light. Add egg and beat well. Slowly beat flour into creamed mixture. Form dough into balls, about 1 1/4 inches in diameter. Roll balls in sugar to coat. Arrange cookies 2 inches apart on unbuttered baking sheets. Press a deep

- indentation in the middle of each cookie with your thumb or a wooden spoon handle.
- Bake for 15 to 18 minutes in the preheated oven until set. Allow to cool for 2 minutes in pans before transferring to wire racks. Fill preserves into each indentation. Allow to cool entirely.
- To make glaze, melt shortening and chocolate chips in a microwave oven; whisk until smooth. Allow to cool briefly. Drizzle chocolate syrup over cookies. Allow to cool thoroughly.

Nutrition Information

- Calories: 133 calories
- Total Carbohydrate: 16g carbohydrate (8g sugars
- Cholesterol: 24mg cholesterol
- Protein: 1g protein.
- Total Fat: 7g fat (5g saturated fat)
- Sodium: 72mg sodium
- Fiber: 1g fiber)

678. Salted Butterscotch & Pecan No Bakes

Serving: 4 dozen. | Prep: 25mins | Cook: 0mins | Ready in:

Ingredients

- 1-3/4 cups pecans, toasted
- 1-1/2 teaspoons kosher salt
- 1 can (14 ounces) sweetened condensed milk
- 1-1/2 cups unsweetened finely shredded coconut
- 1 package (3.4 ounces) instant butterscotch pudding mix
- 1/2 cup sugar
- 48 pecan halves, toasted

Direction

- Put salt and 1 3/4 cups pecans into a food processor; process until pecans are ground very finely. Pour into a large mixing bowl. Whisk in pudding mix, coconut, and milk until incorporated. Cover and chill until mixture is hard enough to roll, about half an hour.
- Form mixture into 48 balls about 1 inch in diameter, then roll balls in sugar to coat. Place a pecan half onto each ball, gently pressing to flatten slightly. Keep cookies in airtight containers in the fridge.

Nutrition Information

- Calories:
- Total Fat:
- Sodium:
- Fiber:
- Total Carbohydrate:
- Cholesterol:
- Protein:

679. Shortcut Shortcake

Serving: 12-15 servings. | Prep: 20mins | Cook: 0mins | Ready in:

Ingredients

- 2 cups cold milk
- 1 package (5.1 ounces) instant vanilla pudding mix
- 1 package (15 ounces) cream-filled sponge cakes
- 4 cups sliced fresh strawberries
- 1 carton (8 ounces) frozen whipped topping, thawed
- Additional strawberries, halved, optional

Direction

- Beat pudding mix and milk in a big bowl for 2 minutes. Allow to stand for 2 minutes till soft-set; reserve. Halve sponge cakes lengthwise; in a 13x9-inch ungreased dish, put filling side facing up. Scatter pudding over top.

- Set sliced strawberries on top of pudding. Scatter whipped topping on top of berries. Put cover and chill for a minimum of an hour prior slicing. Jazz up with strawberry halves if wished. Chill the rest.

Nutrition Information

- Calories: 215 calories
- Protein: 2g protein.
- Total Fat: 7g fat (4g saturated fat)
- Sodium: 256mg sodium
- Fiber: 1g fiber)
- Total Carbohydrate: 35g carbohydrate (30g sugars
- Cholesterol: 9mg cholesterol

---

680. Shortcut Strawberry Vanilla Dessert

Serving: 7 servings. | Prep: 15mins | Cook: 0mins | Ready in:

Ingredients

- 2 cups fresh strawberries, sliced
- 1 teaspoon sugar
- 1-1/2 cups cold 2% milk
- 1 package (3.4 ounces) instant vanilla pudding mix
- 2 cups whipped topping, divided
- 1 loaf (10-3/4 ounces) frozen pound cake, thawed

Direction

- Mix together sugar and strawberries in a small bowl; allow to sit for half an hour. In the meantime, stir pudding mix and milk in a big bowl for 2 minutes. Allow to sit until the mixture is soft-set, about 2 minutes. Fold a cup

of whipped topping into the mixture and put aside.

- Slice cake into 14 slices. Spread 7 cake slices with two tablespoons of strawberries, one-third cup of pudding mixture and layer another cake slice on top. Garnish with whipped topping and the rest of strawberries.

Nutrition Information

- Calories: 314 calories
- Protein: 5g protein.
- Total Fat: 12g fat (8g saturated fat)
- Sodium: 379mg sodium
- Fiber: 1g fiber)
- Total Carbohydrate: 46g carbohydrate (30g sugars
- Cholesterol: 66mg cholesterol

---

681. Six Fruit Trifle

Serving: 12-14 servings. | Prep: 20mins | Cook: 20mins | Ready in:

Ingredients

- 1 package (9 ounces) yellow cake mix
- 1 can (20 ounces) pineapple tidbits, drained
- 2 medium firm bananas, sliced
- 2 medium peach or nectarines, peeled and sliced
- 2 cups sliced fresh strawberries, divided
- 2 cups cold milk
- 1 package (3.4 ounces) instant vanilla pudding mix
- 1 cup heavy whipping cream
- 1 tablespoon sugar
- 1/2 cup fresh blueberries
- 2 kiwifruit, peeled and sliced

Direction

- Follow package directions to prep and bake cake with round 9-in. baking pan. Cool then cut to 1-in. cubes. Mix 1/2 cup strawberries, peaches, bananas and pineapple in big bowl.

- Whisk pudding mix and milk for 2 minutes in another bowl; stand till soft set for 2 minutes.
- Beat cream till soft peaks form in small bowl. Add sugar; beat till stiff peaks form.
- Layer 1/2 cake cubes, pudding, fruit mixture and whipped cream in 3-qt. trifle bowl; repeat layers. Put leftover strawberries, kiwi and blueberries over. Cover; refrigerate it for 4 hours – overnight.

Nutrition Information

- Calories:
- Total Carbohydrate:
- Cholesterol:
- Protein:
- Total Fat:
- Sodium:
- Fiber:

---

682. Skinny Mint Chip Ice Cream

Serving: 1-1/2 quarts. | Prep: 15mins | Cook: 20mins | Ready in:

Ingredients

- 4 cups fat-free half-and-half
- 1 package (3.4 ounces) instant vanilla pudding mix
- 1 can (14 ounces) fat-free sweetened condensed milk
- 2 teaspoons mint extract
- 3 to 4 drops green food coloring, optional
- 1-1/2 cups semisweet chocolate chunks

Direction

- Beat pudding mix and half-and-half in large bowl for 2 mins on low speed. Beat in extract, condensed milk and if desired, food coloring.

- Fill the cylinder of the ice cream freezer; then freeze following the manufacturer's instructions. If desired, chop chocolate chunks coarsely; mix into the ice cream. Put into freezer containers. Freeze about 2 to 4 hours. Then serve.

Nutrition Information

- Calories: 289 calories
- Total Fat: 7g fat (4g saturated fat)
- Sodium: 216mg sodium
- Fiber: 1g fiber)
- Total Carbohydrate: 50g carbohydrate (44g sugars
- Cholesterol: 4mg cholesterol
- Protein: 6g protein.

---

683. Slow Cooker Chocolate Lava Cake

Serving: 8 servings | Prep: 10mins | Cook: | Ready in:

Ingredients

- 2 cups sugar
- 2 cups all-purpose flour
- 6 Tbsp. plus 1/2 cup unsweetened cocoa powder
- 4 tsp. CALUMET Baking Powder
- 1 tsp. salt
- 1 cup milk
- 4 Tbsp. butter, melted
- 1 tsp. vanilla extract
- 1 pkg. (4 oz.) BAKER'S White Chocolate, coarsely chopped
- 1 pkg. (4 oz.) BAKER'S GERMAN'S Sweet Chocolate, coarsely chopped
- 1-1/2 cups brown sugar
- 3 cups boiling water
- COOL WHIP Whipped Topping

Direction

- On the stove, put 3 cups of water; start heating to boiling.
- Use a liner to line a slow cooker or lightly coat it with cooking spray. In the slow cooker, mix together salt, baking powder, 6 tablespoons of cocoa powder, flour and sugar; stir properly.
- Mix in baker's chocolate, vanilla, melted butter and milk till combined; spread the batter evenly onto the bottom of the slow cooker.
- Combine 1/2 cup of cocoa powder ad brown sugar; pour it over the batter.
- Transfer boiling water over the top; allow to soak in (do not combine).
- Cook with a cover on high for approximately 2 1/2 hours.
- Turn off the heat; take the lid away; before serving, allow to stand for 20-30 minutes. Scoop out a serving; place COOL WHIP whipped topping on top.

Nutrition Information

---

684.   Snappy Pumpkin Dessert

Serving: 12 servings. | Prep: 20mins | Cook: 10mins | Ready in:

Ingredients

- 2-1/2 cups finely crushed gingersnaps (about 40 cookies)
- 1/2 cup butter, melted
- 1 package (8 ounces) cream cheese, softened
- 1/2 cup confectioners' sugar
- 2 tablespoons milk
- TOPPING:
- 3 cups cold milk
- 2 packages (3.4 ounces each) instant vanilla pudding mix
- 1 can (15 ounces) solid-pack pumpkin
- 2-1/2 teaspoons pumpkin pie spice
- 2 cups whipped topping
- Additional whipped topping, optional

Direction

- Mix butter and gingersnap crumbs in a large bowl; press into a clean and dry 13-in. x 9-in. baking dish. Bake for 10 minutes at 325°. Cool.
- Beat milk, confectioners' sugar and cream cheese until smooth in a large bowl. Spread over the crust. Whisk pudding mix and milk for a minute in another large bowl. Add pie spice and pumpkin; beat until blended well.
- Fold in whipped topping. Place on top of cream cheese layer and spread. Keep in the fridge for at least 3 hours. Cut into squares; decorate with whipped topping if preferred.

Nutrition Information

- Calories: 397 calories
- Total Carbohydrate: 48g carbohydrate (30g sugars
- Cholesterol: 46mg cholesterol
- Protein: 5g protein.
- Total Fat: 21g fat (13g saturated fat)
- Sodium: 369mg sodium
- Fiber: 2g fiber)

---

685.   Snowflake Bar Cookies

Serving: 3-4 dozen. | Prep: 10mins | Cook: 15mins | Ready in:

Ingredients

- 1 cup butter, softened
- 3/4 cup packed brown sugar
- 1/4 cup sugar
- 1 package (3.9 ounces) instant chocolate pudding mix
- 2 large eggs
- 1-1/2 teaspoons vanilla extract
- 1-3/4 cups quick-cooking oats
- 1-1/2 cups all-purpose flour
- 1 teaspoon baking soda
- 1 cup white baking chips

- 1/2 cup semisweet chocolate chips

Direction

- Beat sugars and butter in a large bowl until fluffy and light. Pour in vanilla, eggs and pudding mix; stir thoroughly. Mix together baking soda, flour and oats; slowly pour into beaten mixture. Mix until smooth. Mix in chips.
- Grease a 15x10x1-inch baking pan and pour in mixture. Bake in the oven at 350 degrees until a toothpick is clean when coming out of the center, about 15 – 20 minutes. Place on a wire rack to cool.

Nutrition Information

- Calories:
- Sodium:
- Fiber:
- Total Carbohydrate:
- Cholesterol:
- Protein:
- Total Fat:

686.   Southern Chocolate Torte

Serving: 12 servings. | Prep: 25mins | Cook: 20mins | Ready in:

Ingredients

- 1 package Swiss chocolate or devil's food cake mix (regular size)
- 1 package (3.4 ounces) instant vanilla pudding mix
- 3 large eggs
- 1-1/4 cups milk
- 1/2 cup canola oil
- FROSTING:
- 1 package (8 ounces) cream cheese, softened
- 1 cup sugar
- 1 cup confectioners' sugar

- 10 milk chocolate candy bars with almonds (1.45 ounces each), divided
- 1 carton (16 ounces) frozen whipped topping, thawed

Direction

- Sift cake and pudding mixes in big bowl. Whisk oil, milk and eggs in another bowl. Add to dry ingredients; beat till blended well.
- Put in 3 9-in. round greased and floured baking pans; bake for 20-25 minutes at 350° or till inserted toothpick in middle exits clean. Cool for 10 minutes. Transfer from pans to wire racks; completely cool.
- Beat sugars and cream cheese till smooth in big bowl. Chop 8 candy bars finely; mix into cream cheese mixture. Fold whipped topping in.
- Spread frosting onto cake plate, on top and sides and between layers of cake. Chop leftover candy bars; sprinkle along the bottom cake edge and over the top. Cover; refrigerate overnight. Keep in the fridge.

Nutrition Information

- Calories: 617 calories
- Fiber: 1g fiber)
- Total Carbohydrate: 79g carbohydrate (56g sugars
- Cholesterol: 78mg cholesterol
- Protein: 6g protein.
- Total Fat: 29g fat (15g saturated fat)
- Sodium: 531mg sodium

687.   Special Chocolate Ice Cream

Serving: 12 servings. | Prep: 10mins | Cook: 0mins | Ready in:

Ingredients

- 1 package (1.5 ounces) sugar-free instant chocolate pudding mix
- 6 packets aspartame sweetener (equivalent to 1/4 cup sugar)
- 2 tablespoons baking cocoa
- 4 cups fat-free evaporated milk
- 1 teaspoon vanilla extract
- 4 ounces light frozen whipped topping, thawed

Direction

- Mix together vanilla, milk, cocoa, sweetener and pudding mix in a blender; blend on low until the mixture is smooth. Fold whipped topping into mixture until smooth. Transfer to a shallow freezer container of 2 quarts. Freeze while covered for half an hour. Use a wire whisk to mix and put back to the freezer until serving.

Nutrition Information

- Calories: 140 calories
- Fiber: 0 fiber)
- Total Carbohydrate: 20g carbohydrate (0 sugars
- Cholesterol: 4mg cholesterol
- Protein: 10g protein. Diabetic Exchanges: 1 fat-free milk
- Total Fat: 3g fat (0 saturated fat)
- Sodium: 257mg sodium

---

688.   Spiced Sherry Cake

Serving: 12 servings. | Prep: 15mins | Cook: 35mins | Ready in:

Ingredients

- 1 package yellow cake mix (regular size)
- 1 package (3.4 ounces) instant vanilla pudding mix
- 1 tablespoon grated orange zest
- 1 teaspoon ground cinnamon

- 1/2 teaspoon ground allspice
- 1/2 teaspoon ground nutmeg
- 4 large eggs
- 3/4 cup canola oil
- 3/4 cup sherry
- Confectioners' sugar

Direction

- Set oven to 350° to preheat. Butter and flour a 10-inch fluted tube pan.
- Combine the first 6 ingredients in a large mixing bowl; add sherry, oil, and eggs. Beat for half a minute on low speed, then raise speed to medium and beat for 2 more minutes. Pour batter into the prepared pan. Bake in the preheated oven until a toothpick comes out clean from the center, for 35 to 40 minutes.
- Allow to cool in pans for 10 minutes before transferring to wire rack to cool entirely. Dust top with confectioners' sugar.

Nutrition Information

- Calories:
- Fiber:
- Total Carbohydrate:
- Cholesterol:
- Protein:
- Total Fat:
- Sodium:

---

689.   St. Patrick's Day Cupcakes

Serving: 1 dozen. | Prep: 15mins | Cook: 20mins | Ready in:

Ingredients

- 1-3/4 cups all-purpose flour
- 2/3 cup sugar
- 1 package (3.4 ounces) instant pistachio pudding mix

- 2 teaspoons baking powder
- 1/2 teaspoon salt
- 2 eggs
- 1-1/4 cups 2% milk
- 1/2 cup canola oil
- 1 teaspoon vanilla extract
- Green food coloring, optional
- Cream cheese frosting

Direction

- Mix together salt, baking powder, pudding mix, sugar and flour in a big bowl. Beat together vanilla, oil, milk and eggs in a small bowl, then put into dry mixture and mix until combined.
- Fill batter into muffin cups lined with paper until 3/4 full, then bake at 375 degrees until a toothpick exits clean after being inserted into the center, about 18 to 22 minutes. Allow to cool about 10 minutes prior to transferring from pan to a wire rack to cool thoroughly. Put into frosting with food coloring if wanted, then frost cupcakes.

Nutrition Information

- Calories: 250 calories
- Total Fat: 11g fat (2g saturated fat)
- Sodium: 301mg sodium
- Fiber: 0 fiber)
- Total Carbohydrate: 34g carbohydrate (18g sugars
- Cholesterol: 39mg cholesterol
- Protein: 4g protein.

---

690. St. Patrick's Day Pistachio Cupcakes

Serving: about 1-1/2 dozen. | Prep: 15mins | Cook: 20mins | Ready in:

Ingredients

- 1-3/4 cups all-purpose flour
- 2/3 cup sugar
- 1 package (3.4 ounces) instant pistachio pudding mix
- 2-1/2 teaspoons baking powder
- 1/2 teaspoon salt
- 2 eggs
- 1-1/2 cups milk
- 1/2 cup vegetable oil
- 1 teaspoon vanilla extract
- 3/4 cup miniature semisweet chocolate chips
- 1 cup cream cheese frosting
- Green sprinkles and/or chocolate jimmies

Direction

- Mix together salt, baking powder, pudding mix, sugar and flour in a big bowl. Mix together vanilla, oil, milk and eggs in a separate bowl, then stir into dry mixture until blended. Fold in chocolate chips.
- Fill the mixture into muffin cups lined with paper or foil until 2/3 full. Bake at 375 degrees until a toothpick exits clean, about 18 to 20 minutes. Allow to cool about 5 minutes prior to transferring from pans to wire racks to cool thoroughly. Frost cake and garnish as preferred.

Nutrition Information

- Calories: 270 calories
- Fiber: 1g fiber)
- Total Carbohydrate: 38g carbohydrate (26g sugars
- Cholesterol: 26mg cholesterol
- Protein: 3g protein.
- Total Fat: 12g fat (3g saturated fat)
- Sodium: 245mg sodium

---

691. Stars And Stripes Torte

Serving: 10-14 servings. | Prep: 20mins | Cook: 30mins | Ready in:

Ingredients

- 1 package white cake mix (regular size)
- 1-1/2 cups cold milk
- 1 package (3.3 ounces) instant white chocolate pudding mix
- 1/2 teaspoon almond extract
- 1 cup heavy whipping cream, whipped
- 1-2/3 cups raspberry pie filling
- 1-2/3 cups blueberry pie filling
- Fresh blueberries and raspberries, optional

Direction

- Follow package directions to prep and bake cake with 2 9-in. round greased and floured baking pans; cool for 10 minutes. Transfer from pans onto wire racks; completely cool.
- Beat vanilla, pudding mix and milk for 2 minutes on low speed in small bowl; stand till set or for 2 minutes. Cover; refrigerate till thick or for 10 minutes. Fold whipped cream in.
- Horizontally cut each cake to 2 layers; put bottom layer on serving plate. Spread raspberry pie filling. Put 2nd cake layer over; spread 1 2/3 cups pudding mixture. Put 3rd cake layer over; spread blueberry pie filing. Put leftover cake layer over and pudding mixture.
- Put blueberries around top cake edge; create a star with raspberries and blueberries if desired.

Nutrition Information

- Calories:
- Sodium:
- Fiber:
- Total Carbohydrate:
- Cholesterol:
- Protein:
- Total Fat:

692.   Strawberries 'n' Cream Trifle

Serving: 12 servings. | Prep: 20mins | Cook: 0mins | Ready in:

Ingredients

- 1/2 cup sweetened condensed milk
- 1-1/2 cups cold water
- 1 package (1 ounce) sugar-free instant vanilla pudding mix
- 1 carton (8 ounces) frozen reduced-fat whipped topping, thawed
- 1 prepared angel food cake (8 to 10 ounces)
- 4 cups sliced fresh strawberries
- 3 whole fresh strawberries

Direction

- Whisk water and milk in bowl; whisk pudding mix in for 2 minutes. Stand till soft set for 2 minutes; fold whipped topping in. Cut cake to 1/2-in. cubes.
- Put 1/3 pudding mixture in 4-qt. trifle/glass bowl. Put 1/2 cake cubes then sliced strawberries over; repeat layers 1 time. Put leftover pudding mixture over; use whole strawberries to garnish.

Nutrition Information

- Calories: 156 calories
- Cholesterol: 4mg cholesterol
- Protein: 3g protein. Diabetic Exchanges: 2 starch
- Total Fat: 3g fat (3g saturated fat)
- Sodium: 223mg sodium
- Fiber: 1g fiber)
- Total Carbohydrate: 28g carbohydrate (0 sugars

693. Strawberry Banana Trifle

Serving: 14 servings. | Prep: 20mins | Cook: 0mins | Ready in:

Ingredients

- 1 cup sugar
- 1/4 cup cornstarch
- 3 tablespoons strawberry gelatin powder
- 1 cup cold water
- 1 pint fresh strawberries, sliced
- 1-3/4 cups cold milk
- 1 package (3.4 ounces) instant vanilla pudding mix
- 3 medium firm bananas, sliced
- 1 tablespoon lemon juice
- 6 cups cubed angel food cake
- 2 cups heavy whipping cream, whipped
- Additional strawberries or banana slices, optional

Direction

- Mix gelatin, cornstarch and sugar in a saucepan; mix water in till smooth. Boil; mix and cook till thick for 2 minutes. Take off from heat. Mix strawberries in; put aside.
- Beat pudding mix and milk for 2 minutes on low speed in a big bowl; put aside. Toss lemon juice and bananas; drain. Put aside.
- Put 1/2 cake cubes in a 3-qt. serving bowl/trifle bowl; layer with 1/2 pudding, whipped cream, strawberry sauce and bananas. Repeat layers. Cover; refrigerate for 2 hours minimum. Garnish with extra fruit (optional).

Nutrition Information

- Calories: 315 calories
- Sodium: 217mg sodium
- Fiber: 1g fiber)
- Total Carbohydrate: 46g carbohydrate (38g sugars
- Cholesterol: 42mg cholesterol
- Protein: 4g protein.

- Total Fat: 14g fat (9g saturated fat)

694. Strawberry Bliss

Serving: 12 servings. | Prep: 30mins | Cook: 20mins | Ready in:

Ingredients

- 1 cup water
- 1/2 cup butter, cubed
- 1 cup all-purpose flour
- 4 large eggs
- 1 package (8 ounces) cream cheese, softened
- 1/2 cup sugar
- 5 tablespoons seedless strawberry jam
- 3 cups cold milk
- 1 package (5.1 ounces) instant vanilla pudding mix
- 1/2 cup heavy whipping cream
- 3 cups quartered fresh strawberries

Direction

- Set the oven at 400° to preheat. Bring butter and water to a rolling boil in a large saucepan. Put in flour, all at once, beating until combined. Over medium heat, cook and vigorously stir until the mixture separates from the sides of the pan and forms a ball. Remove from the heat; allow to sit for 5 minutes.
- Put in the eggs, 1 at a time; after each addition, beat well. Keep beating until the mixture is shiny and smooth.
- Spread into a greased 15x10x1-in. baking pan. Then bake until puffed and golden brown, for 20-25 minutes (the surface will be uneven). Allow to cool thoroughly in the pan on a wire rack.
- Beat jam, sugar, and cream cheese in a large bowl until smooth. Continue to beat in pudding mix and milk until smooth. Beat cream in a small bowl until it forms stiff peaks,

then fold into the pudding mixture. Spread onto the crust. Chill for at least 1 hour.
- Put strawberries on top just before serving.

Nutrition Information

- Calories: 377 calories
- Total Carbohydrate: 40g carbohydrate (27g sugars
- Cholesterol: 131mg cholesterol
- Protein: 7g protein.
- Total Fat: 22g fat (13g saturated fat)
- Sodium: 332mg sodium
- Fiber: 1g fiber)

---

695. Strawberry Cheesecake Pie

Serving: 10 servings | Prep: 35mins | Cook: | Ready in:

Ingredients

- 2 cups fresh strawberries, divided
- 1 env. (1/4 oz.) KNOX Unflavored Gelatine
- 1/4 cup cold water
- 1-1/2 pkg. (8 oz. each) PHILADELPHIA Cream Cheese (12 oz.), softened
- 1/2 cup sugar
- 1/4 cup milk
- 1 cup thawed COOL WHIP Whipped Topping, divided
- 1 ready-to-use chocolate flavor crumb crust (6 oz.)

Direction

- Save 5 strawberries to decorate; finely chop the rest of the strawberries.
- In small saucepan, sprinkle gelatine on top of the cold water; let sit for 1 minute. Cook for 3 minutes on low heat or till the gelatine dissolves fully, stir continuously. Take off from heat.

- Use mixer to beat together the cream cheese, sugar and milk in medium bowl till blended. Add in the chopped strawberries; combine thoroughly. Gradually whisk the gelatin into the mix. Refrigerate for 5 minutes, or until slightly thicken. Whisk 1/2 cup COOL WHIP into the mixture; transfer it into the crust.
- Refrigerate till firm, for 3 hours.
- Halve the reserved strawberries. Use them and the remaining COOL WHIP to garnish pie.

Nutrition Information

- Calories: 270
- Sodium: 220 mg
- Sugar: 18 g
- Protein: 4 g
- Cholesterol: 45 mg
- Total Fat: 17 g
- Saturated Fat: 9 g
- Fiber: 1 g
- Total Carbohydrate: 27 g

---

696. Strawberry Ice Cream Dessert

Serving: 16 | Prep: 15mins | Cook: | Ready in:

Ingredients

- 1 cup butter
- 4 cups crispy rice cereal (such as Rice Krispies®)
- 1 cup brown sugar
- 1 cup shredded coconut
- 1 cup chopped pecans
- 1/2 gallon strawberry ice cream, softened

Direction

- In a large saucepan, melt butter over medium-low heat; take off the heat. Put in pecans, coconut, brown sugar, and rice cereal; mix thoroughly. Press 1/2 the cereal mixture down to the bottom of a 9x13-inch baking pan.

- Slice ice cream and spread evenly over cereal mixture, layer the leftover cereal mixture over ice cream layer.
- Chill in the freezer at least an hour until firm up. Slice into squares before serving.

Nutrition Information

- Calories: 285 calories;
- Protein: 2.3
- Total Fat: 20.2
- Sodium: 168
- Total Carbohydrate: 26.2
- Cholesterol: 39

697.   Strawberry Lemon Trifle

Serving: 14 servings. | Prep: 20mins | Cook: 0mins |Ready in:

Ingredients

- 4 ounces fat-free cream cheese, softened
- 1 cup fat-free vanilla yogurt
- 2 cups fat-free milk
- 1 package (3.4 ounces) instant lemon pudding mix
- 2 teaspoons grated lemon zest
- 2-1/2 cups sliced fresh strawberries, divided
- 1 tablespoon white grape juice or water
- 1 prepared angel food cake (8 to 10 ounces)

Direction

- Beat yogurt and cream cheese in big bowl. Add lemon zest, dry pudding mix and milk; beat till smooth. Process grape juice and 1/2 cup strawberries till blended in blender.
- Tear cake to 1-in. cubes; put 1/3 in 3-qt. serving bowl/trifle bowl. Put 1/3 pudding mixture then 1/2 leftover strawberries over. Drizzle 1/2 strawberry sauce; repeat. Put

leftover cake then pudding mixture over. Cover; refrigerate for a minimum of 2 hours.

Nutrition Information

- Calories: 0g saturated fat (0 sugars
- Cholesterol: 1/2 fruit.
- Total Fat: 0 fiber). Diabetic Exchanges: 2 starch

698.   Strawberry Peach Trifle

Serving: 14 servings. | Prep: 15mins | Cook: 0mins |Ready in:

Ingredients

- 3 cups cold fat-free milk
- 2 packages (1 ounce each) instant sugar-free white chocolate pudding mix
- 1 prepared angel food cake (8 to 10 ounces), cut into 1-inch cubes
- 3 cups sliced fresh strawberries
- 2 cups fresh or frozen sliced unsweetened peaches
- 1 carton (8 ounces) frozen reduced-fat whipped topping, thawed
- Additional sliced fresh strawberries

Direction

- Beat pudding mixes and milk for 2 minutes at low speed in mixing bowl. Put 1/3 cake cubes in 2 1/2-qt. glass serving bowl/trifle bowl. Put 1/3 pudding, 1 cup of strawberries, 1 cup of peaches then 1/3 whipped topping over. Put leftover cake, the pudding, the strawberries, the peaches then whipped topping over; garnish using extra sliced strawberries.

Nutrition Information

- Calories:
- Sodium:

- Fiber:
- Total Carbohydrate:
- Cholesterol:
- Protein:
- Total Fat:

699. Strawberry Raspberry Trifle

Serving: 14 servings. | Prep: 20mins | Cook: 0mins | Ready in:

Ingredients

- 3 cups cold fat-free milk
- 2 packages (1 ounce each) sugar-free instant white chocolate pudding mix
- 1 prepared angel food cake (8 to 10 ounces), cut into 1-inch cubes
- 3 cups sliced fresh strawberries
- 3 cups fresh raspberries
- 1 carton (8 ounces) frozen reduced-fat whipped topping, thawed
- 3 whole strawberries, quartered

Direction

- Whisk pudding mix and milk for 2 minutes in big bowl; it will be thick.
- Put 1/3 cake cubes in 3 1/2-qt. glass serving bowl/trifle bowl. Put 1/3 pudding, 1 cup sliced strawberries, 1 1/2 cups raspberries then 1/3 whipped topping. Layer with 1/3 pudding and cake, 1 cup strawberries then 1/3 whipped topping.
- Put leftover cake, pudding, raspberries, strawberries then whipped topping over; garnish using quartered strawberries. Immediately serve/cover then chill till serving.

Nutrition Information

- Calories: 0g sugar total.

700. Strawberry Shortcake Trifle

Serving: 12 | Prep: 15mins | Cook: 5mins | Ready in:

Ingredients

- 2 1/2 cups water
- 2 cups white sugar
- 5 tablespoons cornstarch
- 1 (3 ounce) package strawberry-flavored gelatin mix (such as Jell-O®)
- 2 pints strawberries, sliced
- 1 1/2 (8 ounce) containers fat-free whipped topping (such as Cool Whip®), or more to taste
- 1 (16 ounce) prepared pound cake (such as Sara Lee®), cut into cubes

Direction

- In a saucepan, mix cornstarch, sugar and water together; cook for 5 to 10 minutes over medium-high heat, mixing continuously, till mixture is thickened and boiling. Take off saucepan from the stove and add gelatin mix into the sugar mixture till dissolved. Reserve strawberry glaze to cool.
- In the bottom of glass bowl or trifle, arrange 1/2 the strawberries. On top of strawberry layer, sprinkle 1/2 strawberry glaze till equally coated. On top of strawberry layer, scatter 1/2 whipped topping; put pound cake on top. Layer the rest of the strawberries, the strawberry glaze, and the whipped topping, accordingly, on top of pound cake.

Nutrition Information

- Calories: 380 calories;
- Sodium: 197
- Total Carbohydrate: 74.8
- Cholesterol: 84

- Protein: 3.1
- Total Fat: 7.7

---

701. Strawberry Sorbet Sensation

Serving: 8 servings. | Prep: 20mins | Cook: 0mins | Ready in:

Ingredients

- 2 cups strawberry sorbet, softened if necessary
- 1 cup cold fat-free milk
- 1 package (1 ounce) sugar-free instant vanilla pudding mix
- 1 carton (8 ounces) frozen reduced-fat whipped topping, thawed
- Sliced fresh strawberries

Direction

- Take plastic wrap and line an 8x4-inch loaf pan. Pour sorbet onto the pan, spreading evenly across the bottom. Freeze for 15 minutes.
- Meanwhile, combine pudding mix and milk in a bowl and whisk for 2 minutes. Set aside for 2 minutes until it sets lightly. Fold in the whipped topping and spread mixture on top of the sorbet. Return in the freeze, covered, and freeze overnight or for at least 4 hours.
- About 10-15 minutes before serving, remove the sorbet from the freezer. Turn the dessert over onto a serving plate and remove the plastic wrap. Slice and garnish with strawberries.

Nutrition Information

- Calories: 153 calories
- Total Carbohydrate: 27g carbohydrate (18g sugars
- Cholesterol: 1mg cholesterol

- Protein: 1g protein. Diabetic Exchanges: 2 starch
- Total Fat: 3g fat (3g saturated fat)
- Sodium: 163mg sodium
- Fiber: 2g fiber)

---

702. Strawberry Swirl Mousse Tarts

Serving: 6 servings. | Prep: 10mins | Cook: 0mins | Ready in:

Ingredients

- 1-1/2 cups cold milk
- 1 package (3.3 ounces) instant white chocolate pudding mix
- 1 cup whipped topping
- 1 package (6 count) individual graham cracker tart shells
- 1/4 cup strawberry ice cream topping
- 6 fresh strawberries

Direction

- Whisk pudding and milk slowly for 2 minutes in small bowl; stand till soft-set or for 2 minutes. Fold whipped topping in gently; put in tart shells using spoon. Drizzle strawberry topping; refrigerate for 30 minutes minimum. Garnish using strawberries.

Nutrition Information

- Calories: 282 calories
- Total Fat: 10g fat (4g saturated fat)
- Sodium: 402mg sodium
- Fiber: 1g fiber)
- Total Carbohydrate: 46g carbohydrate (30g sugars
- Cholesterol: 9mg cholesterol
- Protein: 3g protein.

703. Strawberry Trifle

Serving: 12 | Prep: 15mins | Cook: | Ready in:

Ingredients

- 1 (5 ounce) package instant vanilla pudding mix
- 3 cups cold milk
- 1 (9 inch) angel food cake, cut in cubes
- 4 bananas, sliced
- 1 (16 ounce) package frozen strawberries, thawed
- 1 (12 ounce) container frozen whipped topping, thawed

Direction

- Follow package directions to prep pudding with milk. Layer 1/2 cake pieces, 1/2 pudding, 1/2 bananas, 1/2 strawberries and 1/2 whipped topping in trifle bowl/other glass dish; repeat layers. Cover; refrigerate for 4 hours. Serve.

Nutrition Information

- Calories: 242 calories;
- Total Fat: 6.5
- Sodium: 272
- Total Carbohydrate: 40.2
- Cholesterol: 6
- Protein: 4.6

704. Strawberry Banana Graham Pudding

Serving: 12 servings. | Prep: 20mins | Cook: 0mins | Ready in:

Ingredients

- 9 whole reduced-fat cinnamon graham crackers
- 1-3/4 cups cold fat-free milk
- 1 package (1 ounce) sugar-free instant cheesecake or vanilla pudding mix
- 1 large firm banana, sliced
- 1/2 teaspoon lemon juice
- 2 cups sliced fresh strawberries, divided
- 2-1/2 cups reduced-fat whipped topping, divided
- Mint sprigs, optional

Direction

- Use 4-1/2 graham crackers to line the bottom of a 9x9-inch square pan and put aside.
- Beat pudding mix and milk in a small bowl for two minutes. Allow to sit until the mixture is soft-set, about two minutes. In a separate bowl, add sliced bananas and stir with lemon juice. Mix one cup of strawberries and bananas into the pudding mixture. Fold 1-3/4 cups of whipped topping into the mixture.
- Spread 1/2 pudding onto the cracker layer and repeat making layers. Chill while covered overnight. Chill the rest of whipped topping and berries. Add the rest of whipped topping and berries on top immediately prior to serving. Top with mint (optional).

Nutrition Information

- Calories: 117 calories
- Sodium: 171mg sodium
- Fiber: 1g fiber)
- Total Carbohydrate: 23g carbohydrate (11g sugars
- Cholesterol: 1mg cholesterol
- Protein: 2g protein. Diabetic Exchanges: 1 starch
- Total Fat: 2g fat (2g saturated fat)

705. Strudel Pudding Dessert

Serving: 9 servings. | Prep: 30mins | Cook: 0mins | Ready in:

Ingredients

- 4 frozen strawberry-filled strudel pastries
- 2 cups cold milk
- 1 package (5.9 ounces) instant chocolate pudding mix
- 1 carton (8 ounces) frozen whipped topping, thawed, divided

Direction

- Toast pastries as directed on package; allow to cool for 5 minutes. In the meantime, mix pudding mix and milk together in a large mixing bowl for 2 minutes. Allow to sit until soft-set, about 2 minutes; add 2 cups whipped topping and fold gently.
- Arrange pastries in an ungreased 8x8-inch dish. Top with pudding. Chill, covered, for a minimum of 20 minutes. Slice into squares to serve. Spread the remaining whipped topping over top.

Nutrition Information

- Calories: 258 calories
- Protein: 3g protein.
- Total Fat: 10g fat (6g saturated fat)
- Sodium: 386mg sodium
- Fiber: 1g fiber)
- Total Carbohydrate: 36g carbohydrate (22g sugars
- Cholesterol: 10mg cholesterol

706. Sugar Free Pineapple Pie

Serving: 8 servings. | Prep: 10mins | Cook: 10mins | Ready in:

Ingredients

- 1 cup crushed graham cracker crumbs
- 1/2 cup butter, melted
- 1 package (1 ounce) sugar-free instant vanilla pudding mix
- 1 cup fat-free sour cream
- 1 can (20 ounces) unsweetened crushed pineapple, drained
- Sugar substitute equivalent to 2 teaspoons sugar

Direction

- Mix butter and crumbs; pat into base and up sides of pie plate, a 9-inch in size. Allow to bake for 8 to 10 minutes at 350°; let cool. Mix sour cream and pudding mix in a bowl; combine thoroughly. Mix in sweetener and pineapple. Spread into the crust. Refrigerate for a minimum of 3 hours.

Nutrition Information

- Calories: 212 calories
- Total Fat: 9g fat (0 saturated fat)
- Sodium: 322mg sodium
- Fiber: 0 fiber)
- Total Carbohydrate: 24g carbohydrate (0 sugars
- Cholesterol: 0 cholesterol
- Protein: 3g protein. Diabetic Exchanges: 2 fat

707. Sugar Free Pumpkin Chiffon Pie

Serving: 8 servings. | Prep: 10mins | Cook: 0mins | Ready in:

Ingredients

- 2-1/2 cups cold fat-free milk
- 2 packages (1.5 ounces each) sugar-free instant vanilla pudding mix
- 1 can (15 ounces) solid-pack pumpkin
- 1 teaspoon ground cinnamon

- 1/2 teaspoon ground ginger
- 1/4 teaspoon ground cloves
- 1 reduced-fat graham cracker crust (9 inches)
- Reduced-fat whipped topping and additional cinnamon, optional

Direction

- Mix pudding mix and milk in a large bowl. Beat for a minute (the mixture should be thick). Add spices and pumpkin; whisk 1 more minutes. Transfer to pie crust.
- Keep in the fridge with a cover for 2 hours until firm. If preferred, decorate with whipped topping and top with cinnamon.

Nutrition Information

- Calories: 217 calories
- Total Fat: 3g fat (0 saturated fat)
- Sodium: 684mg sodium
- Fiber: 0 fiber)
- Total Carbohydrate: 42g carbohydrate (0 sugars
- Cholesterol: 1mg cholesterol
- Protein: 4g protein. Diabetic Exchanges: 2-1/2 starch

708.   Sugar Free Chocolate Eclairs

Serving: 8 eclairs. | Prep: 25mins | Cook: 25mins |Ready in:

Ingredients

- 1/2 cup water
- 1/4 cup butter
- 1/2 cup all-purpose flour
- 2 eggs
- VANILLA FILLING:
- 1-1/4 cups cold fat-free milk
- 1/4 teaspoon vanilla extract

- 1 package (1 ounce) sugar-free instant vanilla pudding mix
- 1 cup fat-free whipped topping
- CHOCOLATE TOPPING:
- 1-1/2 cups cold fat-free milk
- 1 package (1.4 ounces) sugar-free instant chocolate pudding mix

Direction

- In a large saucepan, heat water and butter until boiling. Add all the flour in at once, mix until it forms a smooth ball. Take off heat; let sit for 5 minutes. Add 1 egg in at a time, beating well after each addition. Keep on beating till smooth and shiny. Pour into a resealable plastic bag; seal up.
- In one corner of the bag, cut a 1-in. hole. Onto an ungreased baking sheet, pipe out eight 3-1/2-in. logs. Bake for 10 minutes at 450°. Lower the heat to 400°; bake to a golden brown or for 15-20 minutes more. Put them onto a wire rack. Cut a slit in each right away to vent stream; cool down. Split them up and put the tops aside. Throw out the soft dough inside.
- To make the filling, in a large bowl, whisk together pudding mix, vanilla and milk for 2 minutes. Let stand until soft-set, for 2 minutes. Fold whipped topping into the mixture; put aside.
- In a different large bowl, whisk chocolate pudding mix and milk together for 2 minutes. Let sit until soft-set, for 2 minutes. Use a spoon to add vanilla filling into éclairs; place the tops back on. Spread chocolate topping on top.

Nutrition Information

- Calories: 170 calories
- Fiber: 0 fiber)
- Total Carbohydrate: 19g carbohydrate (0 sugars
- Cholesterol: 70mg cholesterol
- Protein: 6g protein. Diabetic Exchanges: 1-1/2 starch
- Total Fat: 7g fat (4g saturated fat)

- Sodium: 418mg sodium

709.   Sugarless Rice Pudding

Serving: 6 servings. | Prep: 10mins | Cook: 0mins | Ready in:

Ingredients

- 2 cups cold 2% milk
- 1 package (1 ounce) sugar-free instant vanilla pudding mix
- 1/4 teaspoon vanilla extract
- 2 cups cold cooked rice

Direction

- Stir pudding mix and milk together in a mixing bowl until slightly thickened, about 2 minutes. Mix in vanilla until well combined. Mix in rice. Serve right away or chill, covered.

Nutrition Information

- Calories: 115 calories
- Total Fat: 2g fat (1g saturated fat)
- Sodium: 241mg sodium
- Fiber: 0 fiber)
- Total Carbohydrate: 20g carbohydrate (0 sugars
- Cholesterol: 7mg cholesterol
- Protein: 4g protein. Diabetic Exchanges: 1-1/2 starch.

710.   Swedish Cream

Serving: 6 | Prep: 10mins | Cook: 10mins | Ready in:

Ingredients

- 1 cup heavy cream
- 3 tablespoons water

- 1/2 cup sugar
- 1 (.25 ounce) envelope unflavored gelatin
- 1 cup sour cream
- 1/2 teaspoon vanilla extract
- 1/2 teaspoon almond extract
- 1 cup frozen lingonberries, thawed

Direction

- Mix the water, gelatin, sugar and cream in a saucepan placed over low heat. Continuously stir until the gelatin has dissolved. Turn off the heat, and leave it to cool slightly for about 10 minutes, until it becomes thick; ensure its consistency is like that of beaten eggs. Add the almond extract, sour cream and vanilla extract. Transfer into a mold, chill covered for at least 4 hours, preferably overnight, until it sets.
- Dip into hot water to loosen from the mold. To unmold, invert to a serving plate. Top with lingonberries

Nutrition Information

- Calories: 298 calories;
- Total Fat: 22.7
- Sodium: 38
- Total Carbohydrate: 21.7
- Cholesterol: 71
- Protein: 3.1

711.   Sweetheart Trifle

Serving: 12-15 servings. | Prep: 20mins | Cook: 30mins | Ready in:

Ingredients

- 1 package chocolate cake mix (regular size)
- 1 package (10 ounces) peanut butter chips
- 4-1/4 cups cold milk, divided
- 1/2 cup heavy whipping cream
- 1/4 teaspoon vanilla extract

- 2 packages (5.9 ounces each) instant chocolate pudding mix
- 1 carton (12 ounces) frozen whipped topping, thawed
- 4 Nestlé Crunch candy bars (1.55 ounces each), crumbled

Direction

- Follow package directions to prep cake mix; put batter in 13x9-in. greased baking pan.
- Bake for 30-35 minutes at 350° or till inserted toothpick in middle exits clean; on wire rack, cool.
- Mix and cook cream, 1/4 cup milk and chips in heavy saucepan on low heat till chips melt. Take off heat; mix vanilla in. Cool it to room temperature; whisk pudding mixes and leftover milk for 2 minutes in big bowl; it will be thick.
- Assemble: Crumble 1/2 cake into big bowl/4-qt. trifle bowl. Layer 1/2 peanut butter sauce, pudding, the whipped topping then candy bars; repeat layers then cover. Refrigerate before serving for a minimum of 3 hours.

Nutrition Information

- Calories:
- Protein:
- Total Fat:
- Sodium:
- Fiber:
- Total Carbohydrate:
- Cholesterol:

712.   Tempting Caramel Apple Pudding With Gingersnap Crust

Serving: 15 servings. | Prep: 30mins | Cook: 0mins | Ready in:

Ingredients

- 2 cups crushed gingersnap cookies (about 40 cookies)
- 1/3 cup butter, melted
- 1 package (8 ounces) cream cheese, softened
- 1/4 cup sugar
- 3-1/4 cups cold 2% milk, divided
- 1 carton (8 ounces) frozen whipped topping, thawed, divided
- 2 packages (3.4 ounces each) instant butterscotch pudding mix
- 1/2 cup hot caramel ice cream topping, divided
- 1 medium Red Delicious, Gala or Cortland apple, chopped
- 1 medium Granny Smith apple, chopped
- 1/3 cup dry roasted peanuts, chopped

Direction

- Combine butter and crushed cookies in a small bowl until incorporated; in a greased 13x9-inch baking dish, press mixture into the bottom. Chill for no less than 15 minutes.
- In the meantime, beat one-fourth cup of milk, sugar and cream cheese in a big bowl until smooth. Fold one cup of whipped topping into the mixture and layer onto the crust.
- Mix pudding mixes and the rest of milk in a big bowl for two minutes; allow to sit until soft-set, about 2 minutes. Mix in one-fourth cup of caramel topping. Scoop onto the previous layer in the dish. Chill while covered for 15 minutes.
- Layer the rest whipped topping over top. Chill while covered for a minimum of four hours until the filling firms up.
- Immediately prior to serving, top with apples; drizzle with the rest of caramel topping. Scatter peanuts over top.

Nutrition Information

- Calories: 347 calories
- Cholesterol: 30mg cholesterol
- Protein: 5g protein.
- Total Fat: 16g fat (10g saturated fat)

- Sodium: 467mg sodium
- Fiber: 1g fiber)
- Total Carbohydrate: 43g carbohydrate (31g sugars

- -
713.   Tiny Tim Trifle
- -

Serving: 16 servings. | Prep: 35mins | Cook: 20mins | Ready in:

Ingredients

- 1/2 cup plus 2 tablespoons butter, softened
- 1-1/3 cups sugar
- 2 large eggs, lightly beaten
- 4 large egg whites
- 1/2 cup reduced-fat sour cream
- 1/3 cup fat-free evaporated milk
- 1 teaspoon vanilla extract
- 1/4 teaspoon peppermint extract, optional
- 1-1/3 cups all-purpose flour
- 2/3 cup baking cocoa
- 1 teaspoon baking powder
- 1/4 teaspoon salt
- PUDDING:
- 3-1/2 cups cold fat-free milk
- 2 packages (1.4 ounces each) sugar-free instant chocolate pudding mix
- 1 carton (8 ounces) frozen fat-free whipped topping, thawed
- 1 candy cane, crushed

Direction

- Beat butter in big bowl. Add sugar slowly; beat for 2 minutes. Add peppermint extract (optional), vanilla, milk, sour cream, egg whites and eggs. Mix salt, baking powder, cocoa and flour; add to butter mixture till just blended.
- Put in 13x9-in. baking pan coated in cooking spray. Bake for 20-25 minutes at 350° till inserted toothpick in middle exits clean; on wire rack, cool.

- Pudding: Whisk pudding mixes and milk for 2 minutes in big bowl; stand till soft set for 2 minutes. Crumble brownies; put 1/2 crumbs in trifle dish/3-qt. bowl. Put 1/2 pudding and whipped topping over; repeat layers. Sprinkle crushed candy cane. Cover; refrigerate before serving for 1 hour.

Nutrition Information

- Calories: 267 calories
- Total Carbohydrate: 40g carbohydrate (23g sugars
- Cholesterol: 50mg cholesterol
- Protein: 7g protein. Diabetic Exchanges: 2-1/2 starch
- Total Fat: 9g fat (5g saturated fat)
- Sodium: 352mg sodium
- Fiber: 1g fiber)

- -
714.   Tiramisu Parfaits
- -

Serving: Serves 4 | Prep: | Cook: |Ready in:

Ingredients

- 1/2 cup chilled whipping cream
- 8 large egg yolks
- 1/3 cup plus 1/4 cup sugar
- 3 tablespoons water
- 3 tablespoons coffee liqueur
- 2 tablespoons instant espresso powder
- 2 8-ounce containers mascarpone cheese*
- 1/2 cup orange juice
- 3 tablespoons Grand Marnier or other orange liqueur
- 1 tablespoon grated orange peel
- 1/2 cup water
- 2 tablespoons sugar
- 4 teaspoons instant espresso powder
- 4 purchased biscotti
- Cocoa powder
- *Italian cream cheese available at Italian markets and many supermarkets. If

unavailable, blend 3/4 pound cream cheese with 6 tablespoons whipping cream and 1/4 cup sour cream.

Direction

- Preparation: For parfaits: whisk the cream in a small bowl until it forms stiff peaks. Then cover; let it chill. In a medium metal bowl, mix the espresso powder, liqueur, 3 tablespoons water, 1/3 cup sugar and 4 yolks. Place the bowl over the saucepan of simmering water (Keep the bowl from touching the water). Whisk mixture using a handheld mixer for about 5 minutes, until thickened and a thermometer reads 175°F. Separate from water; whisk for about 6 minutes, until mixture cools. Add in one 8-ounce container mascarpone then fold, next half of whipped cream. Keep the espresso cream mixture in the refrigerator.
- In another medium metal bowl, mix the orange peel, Grand Marnier, remaining 1/4 cup sugar, orange juice and 4 yolks. Place the bowl over a saucepan of simmering water (keep the bowl from touching the water). Whisk yolk mixture using a hand-held mixer fitted with clean dry beaters for about 7 minutes, until thickened and a thermometer reads 175°F. Separate from the water; keep on whisking for about 6 minutes until mixture cools. Add in second container of mascarpone then fold, next the remaining whipped cream.
- Scoop 1/4 cup espresso mousse, next 1/4 cup orange mousse into each of four 10-ounce goblets. Continue layering with remaining mousse mixtures. Keep in the refrigerator overnight, covered.
- For espresso syrup: In a small saucepan over medium heat, mix espresso powder, sugar and 1/2 cup water until sugar dissolves. Store in the refrigerator until chilled.
- Submerge 1 biscotti halfway into espresso syrup. Put the syrup-coated section into 1 parfait. Continue with remaining biscotti and syrup. Dust cocoa over parfaits.

Nutrition Information

---

715.   Toasted Pecan Pudding

Serving: 10-12 servings. | Prep: 15mins | Cook: 30mins | Ready in:

Ingredients

- 1/2 cup butter, melted
- 1-1/2 cups sweetened shredded coconut
- 1 cup all-purpose flour
- 1 cup chopped pecans
- 1/4 cup packed brown sugar
- 2 packages (3.4 ounces each) instant vanilla pudding mix
- 3 cups cold milk
- 1 carton (8 ounces) frozen whipped topping, thawed

Direction

- Combine sugar, pecans, flour, coconut, and butter in a medium mixing bowl. Spread over the bottom of an ungreased 15x10x1-inch baking pan. Bake for 30 minutes at 325° until lightly browned, stirring sometimes. Allow to cool.
- In the meantime, beat milk and pudding mix together on low speed in a large mixing bowl, for 2 minutes. Refrigerate for 5 minutes. Add whipped topping and fold gently. Spread half of the pecan mixture into a 13x9-inch dish. Top pecan mixture with pudding mixture then spread the rest of pecan mixture over top. Refrigerate until ready to serve.

Nutrition Information

- Calories:
- Protein:
- Total Fat:
- Sodium:
- Fiber:

- Total Carbohydrate:
- Cholesterol:

- Sodium: 329mg sodium

Serving: 16 servings. | Prep: 20mins | Cook: 25mins
| Ready in:

Ingredients

- 1 package fudge brownie mix (13x9-in. pan size)
- 2-1/2 cups cold whole milk
- 1 package (3.4 ounces) instant cheesecake or vanilla pudding mix
- 1 package (3.3 ounces) instant white chocolate pudding mix
- 1 carton (8 ounces) frozen whipped topping, thawed
- 2 to 3 Heath candy bars (1.4 ounces each), chopped

Direction

- Follow package directions to get cake-like brownies to prep and bake brownies in 13x9-in. greased baking pan; on wire rack, completely cool.
- Beat pudding mixes and milk for 2 minutes on low speed in big bowl; stand till soft set or for 2 minutes. Fold whipped topping in.
- Cut brownies to 1-in. cubes; put 1/2 in serving dish/3-qt. glass trifle bowl. Use 1/2 pudding to cover; repeat layers. Sprinkle chopped candy bars then refrigerate leftovers.

Nutrition Information

- Calories: 265 calories
- Fiber: 1g fiber
- Total Carbohydrate: 45g carbohydrate (31g sugars
- Cholesterol: 7mg cholesterol
- Protein: 3g protein.
- Total Fat: 8g fat (4g saturated fat)

Serving: 8 servings. | Prep: 15mins | Cook: 0mins
| Ready in:

Ingredients

- 1-1/2 cups half-and-half cream
- 1 package (3.4 ounces) instant vanilla pudding mix
- 6 Heath candy bars (1.4 ounces each), chopped
- 1 carton (8 ounces) frozen whipped topping, thawed, divided
- 1 chocolate crumb crust (9 inches)

Direction

- Stir the pudding mix with cream in a big bowl for 2 minutes. Let it sit for 2 min. until partially set. Whisk in 1 cup of chopped candy. Fold in 2 cups of whipped topping. Pour over the crust.
- Spread the top with the remaining whipped topping and drizzle with the remaining candy. Freeze, covered, until firm for a minimum of 4 hrs.

Nutrition Information

- Calories: 445 calories
- Protein: 4g protein.
- Total Fat: 23g fat (13g saturated fat)
- Sodium: 367mg sodium
- Fiber: 1g fiber)
- Total Carbohydrate: 52g carbohydrate (38g sugars
- Cholesterol: 28mg cholesterol

718. Toffee Ice Cream Dessert

Serving: 12-15 servings. | Prep: 15mins | Cook: 0mins | Ready in:

Ingredients

- 1 package (10 ounces) butter cookies, crushed (3 cups crumbs)
- 1/2 cup butter, melted
- 1 cup cold milk
- 2 packages (3.4 ounces each) instant vanilla pudding mix
- 1 quart vanilla ice cream, softened
- 1 carton (8 ounces) frozen whipped topping, thawed
- 2 Heath candy bars (1.4 ounces each), crushed

Direction

- Mix butter and cookie crumbs together in a small mixing bowl. Pat into a 13x9-inch dish. Chill in the fridge.
- Combine pudding mixes and milk in a mixing bowl for 2 minutes. Mix in ice cream. Spoon into crust, spreading evenly. Spread whipped topping over top. Chill, covered, for a minimum of 2 hours. Scatter with crushed candy bars before serving.

Nutrition Information

- Calories: 309 calories
- Cholesterol: 38mg cholesterol
- Protein: 3g protein.
- Total Fat: 18g fat (11g saturated fat)
- Sodium: 281mg sodium
- Fiber: 0 fiber)
- Total Carbohydrate: 32g carbohydrate (15g sugars

719. Triple Fudge Brownies

Serving: 24 | Prep: | Cook: | Ready in:

Ingredients

- 1 (3.9 ounce) package instant chocolate pudding mix
- 2 cups milk
- 1 (18.25 ounce) package chocolate cake mix
- 2 cups semisweet chocolate chips
- 1/3 cup confectioners' sugar for decoration

Direction

- Start preheating oven to 175°C (or 350°F). Prepare a greased 15x10 inch baking pan.
- Using 2 cups of milk, make pudding mix following the instructions on the package. Whip in the cake mix. Add in chocolate chips. Cover the prepared pan with the batter.
- Bake for 30-35 minutes at 350°F (175°C) or until the top is springy at the touch of hand. Slightly sprinkle confectioners' sugar on top. If preferred, have this dish with ice cream.

Nutrition Information

- Calories: 193 calories;
- Total Carbohydrate: 31.2
- Cholesterol: 2
- Protein: 2.6
- Total Fat: 8
- Sodium: 253

720. Triple Layer Mud Pie

Serving: 10 servings. | Prep: 20mins | Cook: 0mins | Ready in:

Ingredients

- 18 cream-filled chocolate sandwich cookies, finely crushed
- 3 tablespoons butter, melted
- 3 squares (1 ounce each) semisweet chocolate, melted
- 1/4 cup sweetened condensed milk
- 1/2 cup chopped pecans, optional

- 2 cups cold milk
- 2 packages (3.9 ounces each) JELL-O® Chocolate Flavor Instant Pudding
- 1 carton (8 ounces) Cool Whip® Whipped Topping, thawed
- Chocolate curls, optional

Direction

- Combine crumbs and butter in a small bowl; press the mixture onto an ungreased 9-in. pie plate's bottom and sides. Mix together the condensed milk and chocolate till well blended. Transfer it into crust; sprinkle the top with pecans if you wish.
- Whisk together milk and pudding mixes in a large bowl for 2 minutes. Let it sit for 2 minutes or till soft-set. Use a spoon to transfer 1-1/2 cups of pudding into the crust. Mix 1/2 the whipped topping into the rest of the pudding till well blended. Spread atop the pudding; layer the rest of the whipped topping on top. Chill in refrigerator for 3 hours. Garnish the top with chocolate curls if you wish.

Nutrition Information

- Calories:
- Sodium:
- Fiber:
- Total Carbohydrate:
- Cholesterol:
- Protein:
- Total Fat:

721. Triple Chocolate Cake With Raspberry Sauce

Serving: 12 servings (2-2/3 cups sauce). | Prep: 20mins | Cook: 60mins | Ready in:

Ingredients

- 1 package chocolate cake mix (regular size)
- 1 package (3.4 ounces) instant vanilla pudding mix
- 1 package (3.4 ounces) instant chocolate pudding mix
- 4 large eggs
- 1-1/2 cups water
- 1/2 cup canola oil
- 1 cup (6 ounces) semisweet chocolate chips
- RASPBERRY SAUCE:
- 1 cup water
- 2 packages (10 ounces each) frozen sweetened raspberries, thawed
- 1 tablespoon sugar
- 3 tablespoons cornstarch
- 2 tablespoons lemon juice
- Confectioners' sugar

Direction

- Set the oven at 325 to preheat. Mix oil, water, eggs, pudding mixes and cake mix in a big bowl; beat for 30 seconds on low speed. Switch to medium speed and beat for 2 more minutes. Fold in chocolate chips.
- Pour the mixture into a 10-inch fluted tube pan coated well with cooking spray. Bake for 60-65 minutes or until a toothpick comes out clean when inserted in the center. Let it cool for 10 minutes before transferring from pan to wire rack to cool completely.
- Meanwhile, put sugar, raspberries and water into a blender; blend with a cover until well mixed. Combine lemon juice and cornstarch in a small saucepan; stir in raspberry puree. Boil. Cook while stirring for 2 minutes or until the mixture is thickened. Put in the fridge until serving.
- Sprinkle cake with confectioners' sugar. Serve the cake with sauce.

Nutrition Information

- Calories: 466 calories
- Fiber: 4g fiber)

- Total Carbohydrate: 74g carbohydrate (52g sugars
- Cholesterol: 71mg cholesterol
- Protein: 5g protein.
- Total Fat: 19g fat (5g saturated fat)
- Sodium: 548mg sodium

722. Tropical Fruit Cream Pie

Serving: 6-8 servings. | Prep: 10mins | Cook: 0mins | Ready in:

Ingredients

- 2 cups cold 2% milk
- 1/2 teaspoon coconut extract
- 1 package (3.4 ounces) instant vanilla pudding mix
- 1 can (15-1/4 ounces) mixed tropical fruit, drained
- 1/2 cup sweetened shredded coconut, toasted
- 1 graham cracker crust (9 inches)

Direction

- Beat pudding mix, extract, and milk in a large mixing bowl for 2 minutes. Allow to sit until soft-set, about 2 minutes. Fold in coconut and fruit. Spread over the crust. Chill until ready to serve.

Nutrition Information

- Calories: 0
- Total Carbohydrate: 42 g carbohydrate
- Cholesterol: 8 mg cholesterol
- Protein: 3 g protein.
- Total Fat: 10 g fat (5 g saturated fat)
- Sodium: 293 mg sodium
- Fiber: 2 g fiber

723. Tropical Meringue Tarts

Serving: 10 servings. | Prep: 30mins | Cook: 50mins | Ready in:

Ingredients

- 4 egg whites
- 1 teaspoon white vinegar
- 1 teaspoon vanilla extract
- 1 teaspoon cornstarch
- 1 cup sugar
- 1-1/4 cups cold fat-free milk
- 1 package (1 ounce) sugar-free instant vanilla pudding mix
- 1 cup reduced-fat whipped topping
- 1 cup cubed fresh pineapple
- 2 medium kiwifruit, peeled and sliced
- 2 tablespoons sweetened shredded coconut, toasted

Direction

- Put egg whites in a large mixing bowl; allow to sit for half an hour at room temperature. In the meantime, prepare a baking sheet lined with foil or parchment paper. Trace 10 circles (about 3 inches in diameter) on the paper; put to one side.
- Add vanilla and vinegar to the bowl of egg whites; beat on medium speed until soft peaks are formed. Add cornstarch and beat well. Slowly beat in sugar on high speed, 2 tablespoons at a time, until sugar is dissolved and stiff glossy peaks form.
- Snip a tiny hole in the corner of plastic or pastry bag; insert a large star pastry tip (#6B). Fill meringue into the bag. Pipe meringue in a spiral fashion to fill in circles on the paper-lined pan. Pipe meringue twice around each shell's base in a spiral fashion to form the sides.
- Bake for 50 to 60 minutes at 275° until dry and set. Turn off the oven and leave the door closed; allow meringues to stay for 1 hour in the oven.
- To make filling, beat pudding mix and milk in a large bowl for 2 minutes. Add whipped

topping and fold gently. Fill mixture into meringue shells. Top with coconut, kiwi, and pineapple.

Nutrition Information

- Calories: 145 calories
- Sodium: 157mg sodium
- Fiber: 1g fiber)
- Total Carbohydrate: 30g carbohydrate (0 sugars
- Cholesterol: 1mg cholesterol
- Protein: 3g protein. Diabetic Exchanges: 2 starch.
- Total Fat: 2g fat (1g saturated fat)

724. Two Layer Silk Pie

Serving: 2 pies (6-8 servings each). | Prep: 30mins | Cook: 0mins | Ready in:

Ingredients

- 2 unbaked pastry shells (9 inches)
- 2-1/2 cups cold 2% milk
- 1 package (5.9 ounces) instant chocolate pudding mix
- 1 can (14 ounces) sweetened condensed milk
- 1/2 cup creamy peanut butter
- 1 carton (12 ounces) frozen whipped topping, thawed
- Chocolate curls and chopped peanuts, optional

Direction

- Line a double thickness heavy-duty foil onto unpricked pastry shells. Bake for 8 minutes at 450°. Discard the foil and bake for 5 more minutes. Let cool on wire racks.
- Stir the pudding mix with milk in a big bowl for 2 minutes. Let it sit until partially set. Pour the mixture over crusts.
- Beat the peanut butter and condensed milk in a different big bowl until smooth. Put aside 2

cups of whipped topping for decoration; cover and put into the refrigerator.

- Fold the remaining whipped topping into the peanut butter mixture. Spread the mixture over the pudding layer. Put into the refrigerator until set, 6 hrs.
- Use the reserved whipped topping to garnish; you can also add the peanuts and chocolate curls on top if you want.

Nutrition Information

- Calories: 367 calories
- Sodium: 342mg sodium
- Fiber: 1g fiber)
- Total Carbohydrate: 44g carbohydrate (26g sugars
- Cholesterol: 19mg cholesterol
- Protein: 6g protein.
- Total Fat: 18g fat (10g saturated fat)

725. Vanilla Chocolate Chip Cake

Serving: 12 servings. | Prep: 15mins | Cook: 55mins | Ready in:

Ingredients

- 1 package yellow cake mix (regular size)
- 1 package (3.4 ounces) instant vanilla pudding mix
- 1 cup 2% milk
- 1 cup canola oil
- 4 eggs
- 1 cup miniature semisweet chocolate chips
- 5 tablespoons grated German sweet chocolate, divided
- 2 tablespoons confectioners' sugar

Direction

- Mix together eggs, oil, milk, pudding and cake mixes in a large bowl. Beat for 30 seconds on low speed. Beat for 2 minutes on medium. Mix in 3 tablespoons of grated chocolate and chocolate chips. Transfer into a 10-in. fluted tube pan coated with grease and flour.

- Bake at 350° till a toothpick turns out clean when inserted into the center, about 55-65 minutes. Allow to cool for 10 minutes; take away from the pan and place on a wire rack; cool completely.
- Mix together the remaining grated chocolate and confectioners' sugar; sprinkle over the cake.

Nutrition Information

- Calories: 498 calories
- Fiber: 2g fiber)
- Total Carbohydrate: 55g carbohydrate (38g sugars
- Cholesterol: 74mg cholesterol
- Protein: 6g protein.
- Total Fat: 30g fat (8g saturated fat)
- Sodium: 417mg sodium

726.   Vanilla Cream Puffs

Serving: 1 dozen. | Prep: 40mins | Cook: 30mins | Ready in:

Ingredients

- 1 cup water
- 1/2 cup butter
- 1/4 teaspoon salt
- 1 cup all-purpose flour
- 4 eggs
- FILLING:
- 1-1/2 cups cold milk
- 1 package (5.1 ounces) instant vanilla pudding mix
- 1/2 to 1 teaspoon almond extract
- 2 cups heavy whipping cream, whipped
- CHOCOLATE GLAZE:
- 6 tablespoons semisweet chocolate chips

- 1-1/2 teaspoons shortening
- 3/4 teaspoon corn syrup
- 1/4 teaspoon ground cinnamon

Direction

- Boil salt, butter and water in a big saucepan. Add all flour at once; mix to make a smooth ball. Take off from heat; stand for about 5 minutes.
- Add eggs one by one; beat well after each. Beat till mixture is shiny and smooth.
- Drop onto greased baking sheet by 1/4 cupfuls, 3-in. apart; bake at 400° till golden brown for 30-35 minutes. Transfer to wire rack. Split puffs open immediately; remove tops. Put aside. Discard the soft dough inside and cool the puffs.
- Beat extract, pudding mix and milk for 2 minutes on low speed in a bowl; stand for about 5 minutes. Fold in the whipped cream. Fill the cream puffs then put the tops back on.
- Mix glaze ingredients in a heavy saucepan; mix and cook on low heat till it is smooth and chocolate melts. Drizzle on cream puffs; chill before serving for 1 hour minimum. Refrigerate leftovers.

Nutrition Information

- Calories: 362 calories
- Sodium: 349mg sodium
- Fiber: 1g fiber)
- Total Carbohydrate: 26g carbohydrate (15g sugars
- Cholesterol: 150mg cholesterol
- Protein: 5g protein.
- Total Fat: 27g fat (16g saturated fat)

727.   Vanilla Fruit Dessert

Serving: 4-6 servings (1-3/4 cups topping). | Prep: 5mins | Cook: 0mins | Ready in:

Ingredients

- 1/2 cup cold 2% milk
- 1 package (3.4 ounces) instant vanilla pudding mix
- 1 cup (8 ounces) vanilla yogurt
- 1/2 cup thawed orange juice concentrate
- 4 to 6 cups assorted fruit (apples, grapes, mandarin oranges, etc.)

Direction

- Mix orange juice concentrate, yogurt, pudding mix and milk in a large bowl. Beat for 2 minutes over low speed. Pour atop fruit and serve. Leave the remaining topping in the fridge.

Nutrition Information

- Calories: 169 calories
- Protein: 3g protein.
- Total Fat: 2g fat (1g saturated fat)
- Sodium: 266mg sodium
- Fiber: 2g fiber)
- Total Carbohydrate: 36g carbohydrate (31g sugars
- Cholesterol: 6mg cholesterol

728. Vanilla Pudding Dessert

Serving: 12-14 servings. | Prep: 30mins | Cook: 0mins | Ready in:

Ingredients

- 2-3/4 cups cold milk
- 1 package (5.1 ounces) instant vanilla pudding mix
- 1 can (14 ounces) sweetened condensed milk
- 1 carton (12 ounces) frozen whipped topping, thawed
- 4 cups crushed vanilla wafers (about 120 wafers)
- 3 cups sliced fresh strawberries

Direction

- Whisk pudding mix and milk for 2 minutes in big bowl; stand for 15 minutes. Fold condensed milk in. Put 2 tbsp. wafer crumbs and 1 tbsp. whipped topping aside. Fold leftover whipped topping into pudding.
- Layer 1/3 strawberries, wafer crumbs then pudding mixture in 3-qt. serving bowl; repeat layers 2 times. Sprinkle leftover wafer crumbs; put leftover whipped topping over. Refrigerate till serving.

Nutrition Information

- Calories: 382 calories
- Protein: 5g protein.
- Total Fat: 14g fat (8g saturated fat)
- Sodium: 309mg sodium
- Fiber: 1g fiber)
- Total Carbohydrate: 60g carbohydrate (42g sugars
- Cholesterol: 19mg cholesterol

729. Very Berry Cream Pie

Serving: 8 servings. | Prep: 20mins | Cook: 0mins | Ready in:

Ingredients

- 1-1/2 cups reduced-fat graham cracker crumbs
- 1 tablespoon sugar
- 1 egg white
- 1/4 cup butter, melted
- 2 cups reduced-fat whipped topping, divided
- 1 cup fresh raspberries
- 1 cup fresh blueberries
- Sugar substitute equivalent to 1 tablespoon sugar, optional
- 1-1/2 cups cold fat-free milk
- 1 package (1-1/2 ounces) sugar-free instant vanilla pudding mix

Direction

- In a small bowl, mix sugar and cracker crumbs; beat in butter and egg white. Press onto the bottom and up the sides of a 9-inch pie plate. Bake at 375°, about 8 to 10 minutes, until set. Let cool fully on a wire rack.
- Spread the crust with 1/2 cup of whipped topping. Blend sugar substitute and berries if wanted; spoon 1/2 cup over topping.
- In a bowl, blend pudding mix and milk for 2 minutes; allow to stand about 2 minutes, until soft-set. Spoon over berries. Spread with the whipped topping left. Garnish with berries left. Put in the refrigerator for 45 minutes, until set.

Nutrition Information

- Calories: 206 calories
- Sodium: 377mg sodium
- Fiber: 2g fiber)
- Total Carbohydrate: 30g carbohydrate (12g sugars
- Cholesterol: 16mg cholesterol
- Protein: 3g protein. Diabetic Exchanges: 2 starch
- Total Fat: 9g fat (6g saturated fat)

730. Very Berry Parfaits

Serving: Makes 6 servings, 2/3 cup each. | Prep: 15mins | Cook: | Ready in:

Ingredients

- 2 cups assorted fresh berries (sliced strawberries, raspberries and blueberries)
- 2 cups vanilla low-fat yogurt
- 1/4 cup BAKER'S ANGEL FLAKE Coconut
- 12 OREO Cookies , coarsely chopped, divided

Direction

- 1. Toss berries with coconut and yogurt until coated evenly.
- 2. Set aside 1/2 cup of the chopped cookies for decorating. In six 6-8-ounce parfait glasses or dessert dishes, layer the rest of the chopped cookies and yogurt mixture.
- 3. Serve right away. Alternately, store in the refrigerator, covered, for 1 hour. Dust evenly with the reserved chopped cookies just prior to serving.

Nutrition Information

- Calories: 230
- Total Carbohydrate: 36 g
- Cholesterol: 5 mg
- Protein: 5 g
- Total Fat: 8 g
- Saturated Fat: 3 g
- Fiber: 3 g
- Sodium: 190 mg
- Sugar: 26 g

731. Walnut Carrot Bundt Cake

Serving: 12-16 servings. | Prep: 15mins | Cook: 50mins | Ready in:

Ingredients

- 1 cup butter, softened
- 1-2/3 cups sugar
- 4 large eggs
- 1 teaspoon vanilla extract
- 1 teaspoon grated lemon peel
- 2-1/2 cups all-purpose flour
- 1 package (3.4 ounces) instant lemon pudding mix
- 1-1/2 teaspoons baking powder
- 1 teaspoon baking soda
- 1 teaspoon ground cinnamon
- 1/2 teaspoon salt
- 1 cup (8 ounces) plain yogurt

- 2-1/2 cups grated carrots
- 3/4 cup chopped walnuts
- 1 can (16 ounces) cream cheese frosting

Direction

- Cream sugar and butter in a large bowl, till fluffy and light. Put in eggs, one each time, beating well after each. Whisk in lemon peel and vanilla. Mix together salt, cinnamon, baking soda, baking powder, pudding mix and flour; slowly put into the creamed mixture alternately with yogurt, beating well after each addition. Mix in nuts and carrots.
- Transfer onto a 10-inch fluted tube pan coated with grease and flour. Bake at 350° till a toothpick comes out clean when inserted into the center, 50-55 minutes.
- Allow to cool for 10 minutes; take out of pan and place on a wire rack. Let it cool completely before frosting. Keep in a refrigerator.

Nutrition Information

- Calories: 467 calories
- Cholesterol: 86mg cholesterol
- Protein: 6g protein.
- Total Fat: 22g fat (9g saturated fat)
- Sodium: 464mg sodium
- Fiber: 1g fiber)
- Total Carbohydrate: 64g carbohydrate (45g sugars

732. Watergate Cake

Serving: Makes 16 servings. | Prep: 10mins | Cook: | Ready in:

Ingredients

- 1 pkg. (2-layer size) yellow cake mix
- 1 pkg. (4-serving size) JELL-O Pistachio Flavor Instant Pudding
- 1 cup club soda
- 1/2 cup oil

- 4 eggs
- 1/2 cup chopped PLANTERS Walnuts
- 2 Tbsp. powdered sugar

Direction

- Preheat an oven to 350°F. Beat eggs, oil, soda, dry pudding mix and cake mix with electric mixer at low speed till just moist in a big bowl; beat, scraping bowl's sides occasionally, for 2 minutes at medium speed. Mix in walnuts gently.
- Put batter into greased then floured 10-in. tube pan/fluted tube pan.
- Bake till inserted toothpick near center exits clean for 40-45 minutes; cool for 10 minutes in pan. Remove cake from pan; fully cool on wire rack. Before serving, sprinkle powdered sugar.

Nutrition Information

- Calories: 320
- Protein: 4 g
- Total Fat: 20 g
- Sodium: 340 mg
- Fiber: 1 g
- Total Carbohydrate: 33 g
- Cholesterol: 95 mg
- Saturated Fat: 3 g
- Sugar: 23 g

733. Wedding Swan Cream Puffs

Serving: 3 dozen. | Prep: 01hours30mins | Cook: 35mins | Ready in:

Ingredients

- 1 cup water
- 1/2 cup butter, cubed
- 1/4 teaspoon salt
- 1 cup all-purpose flour
- 4 eggs

- 2 packages (3.4 ounces each) instant vanilla pudding mix
- 2 tablespoons seedless raspberry jam, optional
- Confectioners' sugar

Direction

- Place a heavy saucepan on the stove and turn on medium heat, put in salt, butter and water and make it boil. Stir in flour all at once; mix until forms a smooth ball. Take saucepan off heat; for 5 minutes, let it stand. One at a time, add eggs, whisking well after every addition. Mix well until shiny and smooth. Slice a small circle in the corner of pastry bag or heavy-duty resealable plastic bag; insert pastry tip # 7. Pack bag with batter. Pipe 3 dozen 2-in-long "S" shapes for the swan necks, making a small dollop at the end of each for the head, on a baking sheet that is greased. Place inside the oven and bake for 5-8 minutes at 400 degrees F or until golden brown in color. Put on wire racks to cool. On a greased baking sheets, put left butter by 36 level tablespoonfuls 2 in. apart, to create swan bodies. Form batter into 2-in x 1-1/2 in teardrops using a spatula or small icing knife. Place inside the oven and bake for 30-35 minutes at 400 degrees F or until golden brown in color. Let it cool on wire racks. In the meantime, ready pudding based on package directions for pie filling; let it chill. Prior to serving, slice off top third of swan bodies; reserve tops. Discard any soft dough inside. Into the bottoms of puffs, spoon filling. If desired, put a bit amount of jam on top. To form wings, slice reserved tops in half lengthwise; put wings in filling. Put necks in filling. Sprinkle with confectioner's sugar.

Nutrition Information

- Calories:
- Sodium:
- Fiber:
- Total Carbohydrate:
- Cholesterol:
- Protein:

- Total Fat:

734.   Whipped Chocolate Dessert

Serving: 12 servings. | Prep: 15mins | Cook: 15mins | Ready in:

Ingredients

- 3/4 cup cold butter, cubed
- 1 package chocolate cake mix (regular size)
- 1 egg, lightly beaten
- 1 package (8 ounces) cream cheese, softened
- 1 cup confectioners' sugar
- 4 cups whipped topping, divided
- 3 cups cold milk
- 2 packages (3.9 ounces each) instant chocolate pudding mix
- 2 tablespoons chocolate curls

Direction

- In the bowl, cut butter into the cake mix till crumbly. Put in egg and combine well. Press to the greased 13x9-inch baking plate. Bake at 350 degrees till set or for 15 to 18 minutes. Let cool down totally on the wire rack.
- In small-sized bowl, whip confectioners' sugar and cream cheese till becoming smooth. Fold in 1 cup whipped topping. Gently spread on crust; keep in the refrigerator.
- In the big bowl, stir pudding mix and milk for 2 minutes. Spread on cream cheese layer. Add the rest of the whipped topping on top. Keep in the refrigerator for 2 hours prior to cutting. Use chocolate curls to decorate. Keep the remaining in the refrigerator.

Nutrition Information

- Calories: 553 calories
- Fiber: 1g fiber)

- Total Carbohydrate: 65g carbohydrate (44g sugars
- Cholesterol: 78mg cholesterol
- Protein: 7g protein.
- Total Fat: 30g fat (19g saturated fat)
- Sodium: 618mg sodium

735. White Chocolate Berry Parfaits

Serving: 4 servings. | Prep: 15mins | Cook: 0mins | Ready in:

Ingredients

- 1 package (3.3 ounces) instant white chocolate pudding mix
- 1 cup sliced fresh strawberries
- 1/2 cup Oreo cookie crumbs
- 1/2 cup whipped topping

Direction

- Assemble pudding following the package instructions.
- Scoop pudding; 1/4 cup each, into 4 parfait glasses. Arrange cookie crumbs and half of the strawberries on top of the pudding. Repeat layering once more. Top with whipped topping. Store in refrigerator to chill before serving.

Nutrition Information

- Calories: 308 calories
- Fiber: 2g fiber)
- Total Carbohydrate: 50g carbohydrate (42g sugars
- Cholesterol: 12mg cholesterol
- Protein: 5g protein.
- Total Fat: 10g fat (5g saturated fat)
- Sodium: 553mg sodium

736. White Chocolate Pie

Serving: 6-8 servings. | Prep: 20mins | Cook: 0mins | Ready in:

Ingredients

- 1 package (8 ounces) cream cheese, softened
- 3/4 cup confectioners' sugar
- 1 carton (8 ounces) frozen whipped toping, thawed, divided
- 1 chocolate crumb crust (8 inches)
- 1-1/4 cups cold milk
- 1 package (3.3 ounces) instant white chocolate pudding mix
- Red food coloring

Direction

- Beat the cream cheese, confectioners' sugar and 1/4 cup whipped topping together in a large bowl till smooth. Spread it atop the crust.
- On low speed, beat milk and pudding mix in a small bowl for 2 minutes (the mixture will thicken). Put it over the cream cheese layer. Chill in refrigerator for 2 hours or until firm.
- Use red food coloring to tint the rest of the whipped topping pink. Spread it on top of the pie right before serving. Chill leftovers in refrigerator.

Nutrition Information

- Calories: 391 calories
- Total Fat: 21g fat (13g saturated fat)
- Sodium: 373mg sodium
- Fiber: 1g fiber)
- Total Carbohydrate: 45g carbohydrate (31g sugars
- Cholesterol: 37mg cholesterol
- Protein: 5g protein.

737. White Chocolate Tarts

Serving: 12 servings. | Prep: 30mins | Cook: 0mins | Ready in:

Ingredients

- 1 can (14 ounces) sweetened condensed milk
- 1 cup cold water
- 1 package (3.4 ounces) instant white chocolate pudding mix
- 2 cups whipped topping
- 2 packages (6 count each) individual graham cracker tart shells

Direction

- Mix together pudding mix, water and milk in a big bowl for two minutes. Allow to sit until soft-set, about another two minutes. Chill while covered for 10 minutes.
- Fold whipped topping into the mixture. In each tart crust, add one third cup of mixture. Chill until ready to serve.

Nutrition Information

- Calories: 226 calories
- Sodium: 229mg sodium
- Fiber: 0 fiber)
- Total Carbohydrate: 36g carbohydrate (28g sugars
- Cholesterol: 11mg cholesterol
- Protein: 3g protein.
- Total Fat: 8g fat (4g saturated fat)

Chapter 4: Jello Salad Recipes

***

738. 7 Layer Gelatin Salad

Serving: 20 servings. | Prep: 30mins | Cook: 0mins | Ready in:

Ingredients

- 4-1/2 cups boiling water, divided
- 7 packages (3 ounces each) assorted flavored gelatin
- 4-1/2 cups cold water, divided
- 1 can (12 ounces) evaporated milk, divided
- 1 carton (8 ounces) frozen whipped topping, thawed
- Sliced strawberries and kiwifruit, optional

Direction

- Add 1 gelatin package with 3/4 cup of boiling water in a small bowl. Stir for 2 minutes till dissolve completely. Add in 3/4 cup of cold water then stir. Transfer into a glass bowl or a 3 quart trifle. Store in the fridge for 40 minutes till set but not firm.
- Let another gelatin package dissolve into 1/2 cup of boiling water in a clean bowl. Add 1/2 cup of milk and 1/2 cup of cold water; stir. Pour over the first layer the store in the fridge till set but not firm.
- Do the same for 5 more times, alternate creamy and plain gelatin layers. Store each layer in the fridge till set but not firm then add the next layer. Cover and keep in the fridge overnight. Add whipped topping and, if preferred, fruit to serve.

Nutrition Information

- Calories: 163 calories
- Sodium: 85mg sodium
- Fiber: 0 fiber)
- Total Carbohydrate: 30g carbohydrate (30g sugars
- Cholesterol: 6mg cholesterol
- Protein: 4g protein.
- Total Fat: 3g fat (3g saturated fat)

739. Angler's Gelatin Delight

Serving: 6 servings. | Prep: 15mins | Cook: 0mins | Ready in:

Ingredients

- 1 medium cucumber, peeled
- 1 package (3 ounces) lime gelatin
- 1 cup boiling water
- 1 cup chopped celery
- 1 small onion, chopped
- 1 cup (8 ounces) 4% cottage cheese
- 3/4 cup mayonnaise
- 1 tablespoon lemon juice
- 1 raisin
- 1 sweet red pepper strip
- Lemon and lime slices, green grapes and celery leaves, optional

Direction

- To make the fish's eye, cut 1 slice from the middle of a cucumber; chill. Peel off the skin and cut the rest of the cucumber. Melt the gelatin in water in a big bowl. Add the cut cucumber, onion, and celery. Mix in lemon juice, mayonnaise, and cottage cheese. Put in an 8-in. round pan and an 8-in. square pan (or a 6-cup lobster and fish mold) that are coated in cooking spray. Chill until set or overnight.
- Remove from the round pan onto a 14-in. round serving dish. Remove from the square pan onto a cutting board; slice in half diagonally to create 2 triangles. Place one triangle on the dish with the tip touching the circle, creating the tail. Cut the other triangle into two. Put each piece on top of the circle and the other on the bottom to make the fins; carefully curve fins towards the tail.
- For the eye, on the opposite circle side of the tail, put the saved cucumber slice, put raisin in the middle. Add red pepper strip to make the mouth. Use celery leaves, grapes, lemon, and lime slices to garnish if you want. Refrigerate until eating.

Nutrition Information

- Calories: 307 calories
- Protein: 6g protein.
- Total Fat: 24g fat (4g saturated fat)
- Sodium: 333mg sodium
- Fiber: 1g fiber)
- Total Carbohydrate: 17g carbohydrate (16g sugars
- Cholesterol: 18mg cholesterol

740. Apple Cherry Salad

Serving: 8-10 servings. | Prep: 20mins | Cook: 0mins | Ready in:

Ingredients

- 1 package (3 ounces) cherry gelatin
- 1 cup boiling water
- 1 can (21 ounces) cherry pie filling
- 4 medium apples, chopped
- 1 cup chopped celery

Direction

- Melt the gelatin in boiling water in a big bowl. Mix in celery, apples, and pie filling. Put in the fridge until chilled, about 30 minutes.

Nutrition Information

- Calories: 134 calories
- Protein: 1g protein. Diabetic Exchanges: 2 fruit.
- Total Fat: 0 fat (0 saturated fat)
- Sodium: 40mg sodium
- Fiber: 2g fiber)
- Total Carbohydrate: 33g carbohydrate (28g sugars
- Cholesterol: 0 cholesterol

741.   Apple Cider Gelatin Salad

Serving: 6 servings. | Prep: 20mins | Cook: 0mins | Ready in:

Ingredients

- 2 envelopes unflavored gelatin
- 1/2 cup cold water
- 2 cups apple cider or juice
- 1/2 cup sugar
- 1/3 cup lemon juice
- 1/4 teaspoon ground cloves
- Dash salt
- 1 cup diced unpeeled apples
- 1/2 cup chopped walnuts
- 1/2 cup chopped celery
- TOPPING:
- 3/4 cup sour cream
- 1/4 cup mayonnaise
- 1 tablespoon sugar
- Ground cinnamon
- Cinnamon sticks, optional

Direction

- Sprinkle gelatin over a small bowl of cold water. Let it sit for 1 minute.
- Boil cider in a big saucepan, mix in sugar and the gelatin mixture until dissolved. Mix in salt, cloves, and lemon juice. Put in a big bowl. Put into the fridge for 1 hour until slightly thickened.
- Tuck in celery, walnuts, and apples. Put on separate dishes or 1-qt.dish. Put into the fridge for 2 hours until set.
- To make the topping, mix sugar, mayonnaise, and sour cream together in a small bowl until combined. Put on the salad, use cinnamon to sprinkle. Eat with cinnamon sticks if you want.

Nutrition Information

- Calories: 328 calories
- Protein: 6g protein.
- Total Fat: 18g fat (5g saturated fat)
- Sodium: 112mg sodium
- Fiber: 1g fiber)
- Total Carbohydrate: 36g carbohydrate (31g sugars
- Cholesterol: 23mg cholesterol

742.   Apple Cider Salad

Serving: 6-8 servings. | Prep: 25mins | Cook: 0mins | Ready in:

Ingredients

- 1-3/4 cups apple cider or juice, divided
- 1 package (3 ounces) cherry gelatin
- 1 cup chopped peeled apple
- 1 envelope unflavored gelatin
- 1/4 cup cold water
- 1 cup applesauce
- 3 ounces cream cheese, softened
- 1 can (5 ounces) evaporated milk
- Red or green food coloring, optional

Direction

- Boil a cup of apple cider in a small saucepan. Take away from heat, mix in cherry gelatin until melted. Mix in the rest of the cider. Let chill until the mixture starts to become thick. Mix in apples. Put into a grease coated 6-cup mold, refrigerate until firm.
- In the meantime, put unflavored gelatin in cold water to soften. Mix together cream cheese and applesauce in a saucepan until creamy. Add unflavored gelatin and milk; stir and cook until the gelatin is completely melted on low heat, about 4 minutes. If you want, add food coloring.
- Refrigerate until the mixture starts to become thick. Put on the first layer. Refrigerate until firm. Take off the mold and put on a serving dish.

Nutrition Information

- Calories: 148 calories
- Cholesterol: 17mg cholesterol
- Protein: 4g protein.
- Total Fat: 5g fat (3g saturated fat)
- Sodium: 80mg sodium
- Fiber: 1g fiber)
- Total Carbohydrate: 23g carbohydrate (21g sugars

---

743. Apple Cranberry Delight

Serving: 6 servings. | Prep: 20mins | Cook: 5mins |Ready in:

Ingredients

- 1-1/2 cups fresh or frozen cranberries
- 1-3/4 cups unsweetened apple juice, divided
- 1 package (.3 ounce) sugar-free cranberry gelatin
- 2 cups chopped peeled Golden Delicious apples

Direction

- Mix 1 cup apple juice with cranberries in a small saucepan. Boil it. Decrease the heat, put a cover on and simmer until the berries pop, about 10-15 minutes. Mix in gelatin until dissolved. Take away from heat, mix in the rest of the apple juice and apples.
- Put into a 4-cup mold sprayed with cooking spray. Put into the fridge until set, about 4 hours. Take out of the mold and serve onto a serving dish.

Nutrition Information

- Calories: 70 calories
- Total Carbohydrate: 16g carbohydrate (13g sugars
- Cholesterol: 0 cholesterol

- Protein: 1g protein. Diabetic Exchanges: 1 fruit.
- Total Fat: 0 fat (0 saturated fat)
- Sodium: 42mg sodium
- Fiber: 2g fiber)

---

744. Apple Cinnamon Gelatin

Serving: 8 servings. | Prep: 30mins | Cook: 0mins |Ready in:

Ingredients

- 2 packages (3 ounces each) cranberry gelatin
- 1-1/2 cups water
- 3 tablespoons red-hot candies
- 1-1/2 cups cold water
- 2 medium tart apples, peeled and chopped
- 1 package (8 ounces) cream cheese, softened

Direction

- In a large bowl, put gelatin. Combine candies and water in a small pan. Stir and cook until candies are dissolved and the mixture begins to boil. Mix into gelatin and mix in cold water.
- Reserve 1 cup of gelatin mixture, let it cool at room temperature. Put the rest of the gelatin in the fridge until set but not firm. Grease a 6-cup mold with cooking spray. Fold the firm gelatin with apples and pour into the prepared mold. Put the mold into the fridge until firm, about half an hour.
- Beat cream cheese until smooth in a small bowl. Whisk in reserved gelatin little by little, gently spoon over apple layer. Cover and put in the fridge for at least 6 hours. Take out of the mold and move to a serving platter.

Nutrition Information

- Calories: 212 calories
- Fiber: 1g fiber)
- Total Carbohydrate: 28g carbohydrate (26g sugars

- Cholesterol: 31mg cholesterol
- Protein: 4g protein.
- Total Fat: 10g fat (6g saturated fat)
- Sodium: 132mg sodium

745.   Applesauce Gelatin Squares

Serving: 16 servings. | Prep: 5mins | Cook: 0mins | Ready in:

Ingredients

- 4 packages (.3 ounce each) sugar-free raspberry gelatin or flavor of your choice
- 4 cups boiling water
- 2 cups cold water
- 1 jar (46 ounces) unsweetened applesauce

Direction

- In a bowl containing boiling water, dissolve the gelatin. Mix in applesauce and cold water. Add into a 13x9-in. plate coated using cooking spray. Keep chilled in the refrigerator for 8 hours or overnight. Chop into square pieces.

Nutrition Information

- Calories: 42 calories
- Fiber: 0 fiber)
- Total Carbohydrate: 10g carbohydrate (0 sugars
- Cholesterol: 0 cholesterol
- Protein: 1g protein. Diabetic Exchanges: 1/2 fruit.
- Total Fat: 0 fat (0 saturated fat)
- Sodium: 48mg sodium

746.   Applesauce Berry Gelatin Mold

Serving: 12 servings. | Prep: 10mins | Cook: 0mins | Ready in:

Ingredients

- 2 packages (3 ounces each) strawberry gelatin
- 2 cups boiling water
- 1 can (14 ounces) whole-berry cranberry sauce
- 1-3/4 cups chunky applesauce

Direction

- In a big bowl with boiling water, dissolve the gelatin. Mix in applesauce and cranberry sauce. Add to a 6-cup ring mold coated using cooking spray. Keep it covered and let chill in the refrigerator overnight. Unmold to a serving platter.

Nutrition Information

- Calories: 134 calories
- Protein: 1g protein. Diabetic Exchanges: 1-1/2 starch
- Total Fat: 0 fat (0 saturated fat)
- Sodium: 41mg sodium
- Fiber: 1g fiber)
- Total Carbohydrate: 34g carbohydrate (28g sugars
- Cholesterol: 0 cholesterol

747.   Applesauce Raspberry Gelatin Mold

Serving: 10 servings. | Prep: 10mins | Cook: 5mins | Ready in:

Ingredients

- 3 cups unsweetened applesauce
- 1/4 cup orange juice
- 2 packages (3 ounces each) raspberry gelatin

- 1-1/2 cups lemon-lime soda

Direction

- Boil orange juice and applesauce in a big saucepan. Take out of the heat; mix in gelatin till dissolved. Gradually pour in soda.
- Add to a 6-cup mold coated using cooking spray. Keep chilled in the refrigerator till firm. Unmold to a serving platter.

Nutrition Information

- Calories: 111 calories
- Total Carbohydrate: 27g carbohydrate (26g sugars
- Cholesterol: 0 cholesterol
- Protein: 2g protein. Diabetic Exchanges: 1 starch
- Total Fat: 0 fat (0 saturated fat)
- Sodium: 44mg sodium
- Fiber: 1g fiber)

748.   Apricot Aspic

Serving: 10 servings. | Prep: 15mins | Cook: 0mins | Ready in:

Ingredients

- 2 cans (16 ounces each) apricot halves
- Pinch salt
- 2 packages (3 ounces each) orange gelatin
- 1 can (6 ounces) frozen orange juice concentrate, thawed
- 1 tablespoon lemon juice
- 1 cup lemon-lime soda

Direction

- Strain apricots, saving 1-1/2 cup syrup; put apricots to one side. Bring apricot syrup and salt in a small saucepan to a boil over medium heat. Turn off the heat; stir in gelatin until completely dissolved.

- Combine lemon juice, orange juice concentrate, and apricots in a blender, pulse until smooth. Pour soda with gelatin mixture, stir well. Transfer into an oiled 6-cup mold. Refrigerate until entirely set.

Nutrition Information

- Calories: 93 calories
- Sodium: 55mg sodium
- Fiber: 0 fiber)
- Total Carbohydrate: 21g carbohydrate (0 sugars
- Cholesterol: 0 cholesterol
- Protein: 1g protein. Diabetic Exchanges: 1-1/2 fruit.
- Total Fat: 0 fat (0 saturated fat)

749.   Apricot Gelatin Mold

Serving: 12 servings (1/2 cup each). | Prep: 20mins | Cook: 5mins | Ready in:

Ingredients

- 1 can (8 ounces) unsweetened crushed pineapple
- 2 packages (3 ounces each) apricot or peach gelatin
- 1 package (8 ounces) reduced-fat cream cheese
- 3/4 cup grated carrots
- 1 carton (8 ounces) frozen fat-free whipped topping, thawed

Direction

- Drain pineapple, saving the juice in a 2-cup measuring cup; pour enough water in to measure 2 cups. Put pineapple aside. Add juice mixture to a small-sized saucepan. Boil; take out of the heat. In juice mixture, dissolve the gelatin. Let it cool down for 10 minutes.
- Whip cream cheese till creamy in a big bowl. Slowly put in gelatin mixture, whipping till smooth in consistency. Keep chilled in the

refrigerator till thickened a bit or for 30 to 40 minutes.

- Fold in carrots and pineapple, then whipped topping. Add into an 8-cup ring mold coated using cooking spray. Keep chilled in the refrigerator till set. Unmold to a serving platter.

Nutrition Information

- Calories: 144 calories
- Protein: 3g protein. Diabetic Exchanges: 1-1/2 starch
- Total Fat: 4g fat (3g saturated fat)
- Sodium: 128mg sodium
- Fiber: 0 fiber)
- Total Carbohydrate: 23g carbohydrate (18g sugars
- Cholesterol: 13mg cholesterol

---

750. Apricot Gelatin Salad

Serving: 8 | Prep: 10mins | Cook: 10mins | Ready in:

Ingredients

- 2 (3 ounce) packages apricot-flavored gelatin (such as Jell-O®)
- 1 cup miniature marshmallows
- 4 cups boiling water
- 1 (20 ounce) can crushed pineapple, drained and juice reserved
- 2 ripe bananas, mashed
- Topping:
- 3/4 cup white sugar
- 1 egg, beaten
- 2 tablespoons butter
- 1 tablespoon all-purpose flour
- 1 (8 ounce) package cream cheese, softened
- 1 (8 ounce) tub frozen whipped topping (such as Cool Whip®), thawed

Direction

- In a bowl, mix marshmallows and gelatin; pour in boiling water and put aside till marshmallows and gelatin are both dissolved. Mix bananas and pineapple into gelatin mixture and add to a 9x13-inch casserole dish. Keep chilled in the refrigerator for no less than 2 hours till set and firm.
- On low heat, mix flour, butter, egg and sugar in a saucepan; cook and stir for roughly 10 minutes till thickened. Take the saucepan out of heat and whip cream cheese into mixture using an electric mixer till smooth in consistency. Keep the topping chilled in the refrigerator for no less than 15 minutes till totally cooled down. Fold whipped topping into topping and spread on top of gelatin mixture; keep in the refrigerator for 8 hours to overnight.

Nutrition Information

- Calories: 465 calories;
- Cholesterol: 62
- Protein: 5.9
- Total Fat: 20.6
- Sodium: 208
- Total Carbohydrate: 67.8

---

751. Apricot Orange Gelatin Salad

Serving: 10 servings. | Prep: 15mins | Cook: 0mins | Ready in:

Ingredients

- 2 cans (16 ounces each) apricot halves
- Dash salt
- 2 packages (3 ounces each) orange gelatin
- 1 can (6 ounces) frozen orange juice concentrate, thawed
- 1 tablespoon lemon juice
- 1 cup lemon-lime soda

Direction

- Drain apricots, saving one and a half cups of juice; put apricots aside. On medium heat, boil salt and apricot juice in a small-sized saucepan. Take out of the heat; put in gelatin, mixing till gelatin dissolves.
- Mix reserved apricots, lemon juice and orange juice concentrate in a blender; keep it covered and process till smooth in texture. Add to gelatin mixture with soda; stir well. Add to a 6-cup mold coated using cooking spray. Keep it covered and let chill in the refrigerator till firm. Unmold and place onto a serving dish.

Nutrition Information

- Calories: 181 calories
- Protein: 3g protein.
- Total Fat: 0 fat (0 saturated fat)
- Sodium: 60mg sodium
- Fiber: 2g fiber)
- Total Carbohydrate: 45g carbohydrate (43g sugars
- Cholesterol: 0 cholesterol

---

752. Asian Veggie Gelatin

Serving: 4 servings. | Prep: 15mins | Cook: 0mins | Ready in:

Ingredients

- 1 package (.3 ounce) sugar-free orange gelatin
- 3/4 cup boiling water
- 1 cup cold water
- 4-1/2 teaspoons reduced-sodium soy sauce
- 1 tablespoon lemon juice
- 1/2 cup canned bean sprouts
- 1/2 cup sliced celery
- 1/2 cup shredded carrots
- 1/4 cup sliced water chestnuts, halved
- 1 tablespoon chopped green onion

Direction

- In boiling water, dissolve the gelatin in a big bowl. Mix in the lemon juice, soy sauce and cold water. Put in onion, water chestnuts, carrots, celery, and bean sprouts; stir the mixture well.
- Scoop into four 6-oz. bowls coated using cooking spray. Keep chilled in the refrigerator till set for 60 minutes. Invert to salad dishes.

Nutrition Information

- Calories: 30 calories
- Protein: 2g protein.
- Total Fat: 0 fat (0 saturated fat)
- Sodium: 307mg sodium
- Fiber: 1g fiber)
- Total Carbohydrate: 5g carbohydrate (1g sugars
- Cholesterol: 0 cholesterol

---

753. Beet Salad

Serving: 16 | Prep: 20mins | Cook: 45mins | Ready in:

Ingredients

- 4 bunches fresh small beets, stems removed
- 2 tablespoons olive oil
- 1 tablespoon lemon juice
- 2 tablespoons white wine vinegar
- 1 tablespoon honey
- 2 tablespoons Dijon mustard
- 1 teaspoon dried thyme, crushed
- 1/2 cup vegetable oil
- salt and pepper to taste
- 2 medium heads Belgian endive
- 1 pound spring lettuce mix
- 1 cup crumbled feta cheese

Direction

- Preheat your oven to 230°C/450°F. Lightly oil the beets until coated and roast until tender or for about 45 minutes. Set aside to cool thoroughly. Once cooled, peel the beet and dice them.

- To make the dressing, in a blender, add thyme, mustard, honey, vinegar and lemon. Add in 1/2 cup of oil gradually while the blender is running. Add salt and pepper to taste. In a salad bowl, put the spring lettuce mix and pour the amount of dressing to your liking over the greens; toss until coated.
- Rinse the endive, tear whole leaves off, then pat leaves dry. Place 3 leaves on each serving plate. Split the dressed salad greens among the plates and add the feta cheese and diced beets on top.

Nutrition Information

- Calories: 166 calories;
- Protein: 4.2
- Total Fat: 10.8
- Sodium: 254
- Total Carbohydrate: 14.9
- Cholesterol: 8

754. Berry Gelatin Mold

Serving: 8 servings. | Prep: 15mins | Cook: 0mins | Ready in:

Ingredients

- 2 packages (3 ounces each) strawberry gelatin
- 2 cups boiling cranberry juice
- 1-1/2 cups club soda, chilled
- 1 teaspoon lemon juice
- 1 cup each fresh blueberries, raspberries and sliced strawberries
- Lettuce leaves
- Additional mixed fresh berries, optional

Direction

- Dissolve gelatin in boiling cranberry syrup in a large bowl. Allow to sit for 10 minutes. Pour

lemon juice and club soda into the bowl, stir. Chill until partly firm for 45 minutes.

- Add berries and fold. Transfer the mixture into a 6-cup ring mold greased with cooking spray. Chill in the fridge until entirely firm for 4 hours. Remove the mold and place the jello onto a platter lined with lettuce leaves. Add more berries into the mold's center if desired.

Nutrition Information

- Calories: 131 calories
- Cholesterol: 0 cholesterol
- Protein: 3g protein. Diabetic Exchanges: 1 starch
- Total Fat: 0 fat (0 saturated fat)
- Sodium: 59mg sodium
- Fiber: 2g fiber)
- Total Carbohydrate: 32g carbohydrate (30g sugars

755. Berry Gelatin Ring

Serving: 8 servings. | Prep: 15mins | Cook: 0mins | Ready in:

Ingredients

- 1 package (6 ounces) raspberry gelatin
- 2 cups boiling water
- 1 can (14 ounces) whole-berry cranberry sauce
- 1 can (8 ounces) crushed pineapple, undrained
- 1/2 cup red wine or grape juice
- 1/3 cup chopped walnuts
- 1 package (8 ounces) cream cheese, softened
- 1/4 cup mayonnaise
- 1 teaspoon grated orange zest

Direction

- Melt the gelatin in water in a big bowl. Add walnuts, wine, pineapple, and cranberry sauce. Refrigerate for 2 hours until partly set.

- Put in a grease-coated 6-cup ring mold. Chill until set. Remove from the mold onto a serving dish. Mix orange zest, mayonnaise, and cream cheese together in a small bowl. Enjoy with the salad.

Nutrition Information

- Calories: 367 calories
- Total Carbohydrate: 46g carbohydrate (36g sugars
- Cholesterol: 34mg cholesterol
- Protein: 5g protein.
- Total Fat: 18g fat (7g saturated fat)
- Sodium: 183mg sodium
- Fiber: 1g fiber)

756. Best Rosy Rhubarb Mold

Serving: 12 servings. | Prep: 25mins | Cook: 0mins | Ready in:

Ingredients

- 4 cups chopped fresh or frozen rhubarb
- 1 cup water
- 2/3 cup sugar
- 1/4 teaspoon salt
- 1 package (6 ounces) strawberry gelatin
- 1-1/2 cups cold water
- 1/4 cup lemon juice
- 2 cans (11 ounces each) mandarin oranges, drained
- 1 cup chopped celery
- Optional garnishes: lettuce leaves, sliced strawberries, green grapes, sour cream and ground nutmeg

Direction

- Mix salt, sugar, water and rhubarb in a saucepan; boil on medium heat. Boil till rhubarb turns soft or for 1 to 2 minutes; take out of the heat. Mix in gelatin till dissolved.

Mix in lemon juice and cold water. Keep chilled till set partly. Fold in celery and oranges. Add to a 6-cup mold or an 8-in. square dish that's coated using cooking spray. Keep chilled till it becomes set. Chop into square pieces or unmold to lettuce leaves. If you wish, decorate with fruit and serve alongside sour cream scattered with nutmeg.

Nutrition Information

- Calories: 79 calories
- Protein: 2g protein. Diabetic Exchanges: 1 fruit.
- Total Fat: 0 fat (0 saturated fat)
- Sodium: 98mg sodium
- Fiber: 0 fiber)
- Total Carbohydrate: 19g carbohydrate (0 sugars
- Cholesterol: 0 cholesterol

757. Best Rosy Rhubarb Salad

Serving: 8 servings. | Prep: 20mins | Cook: 0mins | Ready in:

Ingredients

- 3 cups sliced fresh or frozen rhubarb (1-inch pieces)
- 1 tablespoon sugar
- 1 package (3 ounces) raspberry gelatin
- 1 cup unsweetened pineapple juice
- 1 teaspoon lemon juice
- 1 cup diced peeled apples
- 1 cup diced celery
- 1/4 cup chopped pecans

Direction

- Cook rhubarb with sugar over medium-low heat in a medium saucepan, stir until the rhubarb is soft and tender. Turn off heat, stir in gelatin until completely dissolved. Add lemon juice and pineapple, still. Refrigerate until partly firm.

- Add pecans, celery, and apples, stir to combine. Transfer into a glass bowl or a 4-1/2 cup mold greased with cooking spray. Refrigerate for a couple of hours or overnight.

Nutrition Information

- Calories: 108 calories
- Cholesterol: 0 cholesterol
- Protein: 2g protein.
- Total Fat: 3g fat (0 saturated fat)
- Sodium: 39mg sodium
- Fiber: 2g fiber)
- Total Carbohydrate: 20g carbohydrate (18g sugars

758.   Blueberry Gelatin Salad

Serving: 8 | Prep: 5mins | Cook: 5mins | Ready in:

Ingredients

- 2 (3 ounce) packages grape flavored Jell-O® mix
- 2 cups boiling water
- 1 (8 ounce) can crushed pineapple, undrained
- 1 (21 ounce) can blueberry pie filling
- Topping:
- 1 (8 ounce) package cream cheese, softened
- 1 cup sour cream
- 1/2 cup white sugar
- 1 teaspoon vanilla extract

Direction

- Combine pie filling, pineapple, boiling water, and gelatin powder in a big bowl. Put in a glass baking dish or a mold and chill for a minimum of 2 hours until set.
- Combine vanilla, sugar, sour cream, and cream cheese in a medium-sized bowl until creamy. Spread over the top of the gelatin. If

you use a mold, remove the gelatin from the mold before adding the topping.

Nutrition Information

- Calories: 440 calories;
- Sodium: 163
- Total Carbohydrate: 70.8
- Cholesterol: 43
- Protein: 5.1
- Total Fat: 15.8

759.   Blueberry Raspberry Gelatin

Serving: 6 servings. | Prep: 20mins | Cook: 0mins | Ready in:

Ingredients

- 1 package (.3 ounce) sugar-free raspberry gelatin
- 1 cup boiling water
- 3/4 cup cold water
- 1 cup fresh or frozen unsweetened blueberries, thawed
- TOPPING:
- 2 ounces reduced-fat cream cheese
- 1/4 cup fat-free sour cream
- Sugar substitute equivalent to 2 teaspoons sugar
- 1/2 teaspoon vanilla extract
- 2 tablespoons chopped pecans, toasted

Direction

- In a small bowl with boiling water, dissolve gelatin. Mix in cold water. Keep it covered and let chill in the refrigerator till partially set. Fold in blueberries. Place into an 8x4-in. loaf pan coated using cooking spray. Keep it covered and let chill in the refrigerator till set or for 60 minutes.

- To make topping, whip sour cream, and cream cheese in a small-sized bowl till smooth in consistency. Mix in the vanilla and sugar substitute. Unmold gelatin; chop into 6 slices. Add pecans and topping on top of each slice.

Nutrition Information

- Calories: 72 calories
- Fiber: 1g fiber)
- Total Carbohydrate: 6g carbohydrate (4g sugars
- Cholesterol: 8mg cholesterol
- Protein: 3g protein. Diabetic Exchanges: 1 fat
- Total Fat: 4g fat (2g saturated fat)
- Sodium: 80mg sodium

---

760. Broken Glass Gelatin

Serving: 15 servings. | Prep: 30mins | Cook: 10mins | Ready in:

Ingredients

- 1-1/2 cups reduced-fat graham cracker crumbs (about 8 whole crackers)
- 7 tablespoons sugar, divided
- 5 tablespoons reduced-fat butter, melted
- 1 cup unsweetened pineapple juice
- 1 envelope unflavored gelatin
- 1 package (.3 ounce) sugar-free orange gelatin
- 4-1/2 cups boiling water, divided
- 1 package (.3 ounce) sugar-free lime gelatin
- 1 package (.3 ounce) sugar-free strawberry gelatin
- 1 carton (8 ounces) frozen reduced-fat whipped topping, thawed

Direction

- Mix butter, 5 tbsp. of sugar and cracker crumbs in a big bowl; push into one ungreased 13x9-in. plate. Let chill.

- Mix the leftover sugar and pineapple juice in a small-sized saucepan. Drizzle unflavored gelatin on top of juice mixture; let rest for 60 seconds. Heat on low heat while keep stirring till the gelatin dissolves totally. Add into a big bowl; let cool.
- In one and a half cups of boiling water, dissolve the orange gelatin; add to one 8x4-in. loaf pan coated using cooking spray. Keep chilled in the refrigerator till firm. Repeat with leftover boiling water, lime and strawberry gelatins, using extra loaf pans.
- Mix whipped topping into pineapple juice mixture lightly; keep it covered and let chill in the refrigerator. Chop flavored gelatins into 1-in. cubes; lightly mix into whipped topping mixture. Scoop on top of crust. Keep chilled in the refrigerator for a few hours or overnight.

Nutrition Information

- Calories: 98 calories
- Protein: 2g protein. Diabetic Exchanges: 1 starch
- Total Fat: 4g fat (3g saturated fat)
- Sodium: 78mg sodium
- Fiber: 0 fiber)
- Total Carbohydrate: 13g carbohydrate (10g sugars
- Cholesterol: 7mg cholesterol

---

761. Buttermilk Orange Salad

Serving: 6-8 servings. | Prep: 25mins | Cook: 0mins | Ready in:

Ingredients

- 1 can (8-1/2 ounces) crushed pineapple in syrup
- 1 package (6 ounces) orange gelatin
- 2 cups buttermilk
- 1 carton (8 ounces) frozen whipped topping, thawed

- 1/4 cup chopped pecans

Direction

- Boil syrup and pineapple in a big saucepan. Take out of the heat; mix in gelatin. Let it cool down to room temperature. Mix in the buttermilk. Fold in pecans and whipped topping. Add to an 8-cup mold; keep chilled for 4 hours or overnight.

Nutrition Information

- Calories: 230 calories
- Sodium: 113mg sodium
- Fiber: 1g fiber)
- Total Carbohydrate: 34g carbohydrate (30g sugars
- Cholesterol: 2mg cholesterol
- Protein: 4g protein.
- Total Fat: 8g fat (5g saturated fat)

762.　　Cabbage Cucumber Gelatin Cups

Serving: 4 servings. | Prep: 10mins | Cook: 0mins | Ready in:

Ingredients

- 1 package (3 ounces) lime gelatin
- 1 cup boiling water
- 1/2 cup mayonnaise
- 1 cup shredded cabbage
- 1/2 cup chopped cucumber
- 2 tablespoons chopped green pepper

Direction

- Melt the gelatin in boiling water in a bowl. Mix in mayonnaise until smooth. Mix in green pepper, cucumber, and cabbage. Put in 4 custard cups. Put a cover on and chill until set.

Nutrition Information

- Calories: 284 calories
- Cholesterol: 10mg cholesterol
- Protein: 2g protein.
- Total Fat: 22g fat (3g saturated fat)
- Sodium: 202mg sodium
- Fiber: 1g fiber)
- Total Carbohydrate: 20g carbohydrate (19g sugars

763.　　Cherry Coke Salad

Serving: 10-12 servings. | Prep: 10mins | Cook: 0mins | Ready in:

Ingredients

- 1 can (20 ounces) crushed pineapple
- 1/2 cup water
- 2 packages (3 ounces each) cherry gelatin
- 1 can (21 ounces) cherry pie filling
- 3/4 cup cola

Direction

- Drain pineapple, saving the juice; put fruit aside. Boil water and pineapple juice in a microwave or saucepan. Put in gelatin; mix till dissolved. Mix in cola and pie filling.
- Add to a serving bowl. Keep chilled in the refrigerator till thickened a bit. Fold in reserved pineapple. Keep chilled in the refrigerator till firm.

Nutrition Information

- Calories: 118 calories
- Sodium: 26mg sodium
- Fiber: 1g fiber)
- Total Carbohydrate: 29g carbohydrate (26g sugars
- Cholesterol: 0 cholesterol
- Protein: 1g protein.
- Total Fat: 0 fat (0 saturated fat)

764.　　Cherry Cola Salad

Serving: 8-10 servings. | Prep: 10mins | Cook: 0mins | Ready in:

Ingredients

- 1 package (6 ounces) cherry gelatin
- 1-1/2 cups boiling water
- 1-1/2 cups carbonated cola beverage
- 1 can (21 ounces) cherry pie filling
- Whipped topping, optional

Direction

- Melt gelatin in water. Add pie filling and cola; toss thoroughly. Put in an 8-in. square baking plate. Chill until firm. Use whipped topping to garnish if you want.

Nutrition Information

- Calories: 146 calories
- Cholesterol: 0 cholesterol
- Protein: 2g protein.
- Total Fat: 0 fat (0 saturated fat)
- Sodium: 51mg sodium
- Fiber: 0 fiber)
- Total Carbohydrate: 35g carbohydrate (33g sugars

765.　　Cherry Cranberry Salad

Serving: 16 | Prep: 10mins | Cook: 10mins | Ready in:

Ingredients

- 3 cups cranberries
- 2 cups water
- 1 cup white sugar

- 1 (6 ounce) package cherry-flavored gelatin mix (such as Jell-O®)
- 1 (20 ounce) can crushed pineapple, undrained
- 1 1/2 cups diced apples
- 1 cup chopped walnuts

Direction

- In a saucepan, mix water and cranberries. Bring water to a boil, then lower heat to medium and cook about 5 to 7 minutes until all cranberries have popped and softened; take away from heat to cool a bit.
- Into the cranberry mixture, stir gelatin and sugar until totally dissolved. Put in walnuts, apples and pineapple with juice, then transfer mixture into a 2-qt. serving bowl.
- Use plastic wrap to cover bowl and chill until firm and cold, 3-4 hours.

Nutrition Information

- Calories: 170 calories;
- Total Fat: 4.8
- Sodium: 50
- Total Carbohydrate: 31.9
- Cholesterol: 0
- Protein: 2.3

766.　　Cherry Gelatin Fruit Salad

Serving: 8 servings. | Prep: 10mins | Cook: 0mins | Ready in:

Ingredients

- 1 cup applesauce
- 2 packages (3 ounces each) cherry gelatin
- 1 can (12 ounces) lemon-lime soda
- 1 can (8 ounces) crushed pineapple, undrained

Direction

- Boil applesauce in a large saucepan. Take away from the heat; add gelatin and stir to dissolve. Gradually place in pineapple and soda. Transfer into a 1 1/2-quart serving bowl. Store in the fridge till firm.

Nutrition Information

- Calories: 102 calories
- Protein: 1g protein.
- Total Fat: 0 fat (0 saturated fat)
- Sodium: 30mg sodium
- Fiber: 1g fiber)
- Total Carbohydrate: 26g carbohydrate (25g sugars
- Cholesterol: 0 cholesterol

767.   Cherry Gelatin Salad With Bananas

Serving: 6 servings. | Prep: 15mins | Cook: 0mins | Ready in:

Ingredients

- 1 can (15 ounces) pitted dark sweet cherries
- 1 package (3 ounces) cherry gelatin
- 1 cup cold water
- 1 tablespoon lemon juice
- 2 medium bananas, sliced
- 1/4 cup chopped pecans
- Additonal sliced banana and chopped pecans, optional

Direction

- Drain cherries and save their liquid in a 1-cup measuring cup. Put in enough amount of water to measure 1 cup. Bring the mixture in a small saucepan to a boil. Take away from the heat and stir in gelatin until it is dissolved. Stir in lemon juice and cold water.
- Cover and chill for 40 minutes, until syrupy. Fold in cherries, pecans and bananas. Transfer the mixture temperature a 6-cup mold greased with cooking spray, then chill until firm.

- Unmold dessert onto a serving platter, then use more banana and pecans to decorate if you want.

Nutrition Information

- Calories: 169 calories
- Protein: 3g protein. Diabetic Exchanges: 1 starch
- Total Fat: 4g fat (0 saturated fat)
- Sodium: 35mg sodium
- Fiber: 3g fiber)
- Total Carbohydrate: 34g carbohydrate (29g sugars
- Cholesterol: 0 cholesterol

768.   Cherry Gelatin Squares

Serving: 9 servings. | Prep: 15mins | Cook: 0mins | Ready in:

Ingredients

- 2 packages (3 ounces each) cherry gelatin
- 1-1/2 cups boiling water
- 1 can (21 ounces) cherry pie filling
- 1-1/4 cups lemon-lime soda, chilled
- Whipped topping, optional

Direction

- Dissolve gelatin in a big bowl of water. Mix in pie filling and stir well. Slowly mix in soda (mixture will foam).
- Pour into an 8 inch square plate. Put a cover on and put in the fridge until firm. Slice into squares. Use whipped topping to garnish if you want.

Nutrition Information

- Calories: 68 calories
- Sodium: 115mg sodium
- Fiber: 0 fiber)

- Total Carbohydrate: 13g carbohydrate (11g sugars
- Cholesterol: 0 cholesterol
- Protein: 2g protein. Diabetic Exchanges: 1 fruit.
- Total Fat: 1g fat (0 saturated fat)

769.   Cherry Pineapple Salad

Serving: 12-16 servings. | Prep: 20mins | Cook: 0mins | Ready in:

Ingredients

- 3 packages (3 ounces each) cherry gelatin
- 2-1/3 cups boiling water
- 2 cans (16-1/2 ounces each) pitted dark sweet cherries
- 1 can (20 ounces) pineapple tidbits
- 1/3 cup lemon juice
- 1/3 cup heavy whipping cream
- 1/3 cup mayonnaise
- 6 ounces cream cheese, softened
- Dash salt
- 1/2 cup coarsely chopped nuts

Direction

- In a big bowl with water, dissolve gelatin. Drain off fruits, saving enough cherry and pineapple juices to measure 2-1/2 cups; pour to gelatin along with lemon juice. Put fruits aside.
- Separate gelatin mixture into 2 equal portions. Put aside one portion of gelatin to rest at room temperature; chill the other portion till partially set. Fold pineapple into chilled gelatin; add to a 13x9-in. plate. Keep chilled till nearly firm.
- Whip salt, cream cheese, mayonnaise, and cream in a small-sized bowl till light and fluffy. Spread on top of chilled gelatin layer. Keep in the refrigerator till firm. Let chill the reserved gelatin mixture till partially set. Fold in nuts and cherries; spread on top of cream

cheese layer. Keep chilled for no less than 3 hours.

Nutrition Information

- Calories: 151 calories
- Fiber: 1g fiber)
- Total Carbohydrate: 16g carbohydrate (14g sugars
- Cholesterol: 14mg cholesterol
- Protein: 2g protein.
- Total Fat: 10g fat (3g saturated fat)
- Sodium: 65mg sodium

770.   Cherry Ribbon Salad

Serving: 12 servings. | Prep: 10mins | Cook: 0mins | Ready in:

Ingredients

- 1 package (3 ounces) cherry gelatin
- 2-1/4 cups boiling water, divided
- 1 can (21 ounces) cherry pie filling
- 1 package (3 ounces) orange gelatin
- 1 can (8 ounces) crushed pineapple, undrained
- 1 cup whipped topping
- 1/3 cup mayonnaise
- 1/4 cup chopped pecans, optional

Direction

- Dissolve cherry gelatin in 1-1/4 cups boiling water in a large bowl. Add pie filling, stir. Transfer into a 7-cup ring mold covered with cooking spray; chill until thickened but not totally firm, about 1 hour.
- Mix orange gelatin in unused boiling water in a large bowl. Add pineapple, and stir. Chill until thickened but not totally firm for 1 hour.
- Mix mayonnaise, whipped topping together and pecans if desired; and fold in orange mixture. Spoon mayonnaise mixture over the cherry layer. Chill until completely set for 1

hour or more. Remove the mold and serve in a plate.

Nutrition Information

- Calories: 184 calories
- Protein: 2g protein.
- Total Fat: 6g fat (2g saturated fat)
- Sodium: 75mg sodium
- Fiber: 0 fiber)
- Total Carbohydrate: 31g carbohydrate (28g sugars
- Cholesterol: 2mg cholesterol

771. Christmas Cranberry Salad

Serving: 6 | Prep: | Cook: | Ready in:

Ingredients

- 1 pound cranberries, finely ground
- 2 cups white sugar
- 1 (20 ounce) can crushed pineapple, drained
- 1 (16 ounce) package miniature marshmallows
- 1 cup chopped pecans (optional)
- 1 pint whipped cream, beaten stiff

Direction

- Combine sugar and cranberries together; keep it covered and let chill in the refrigerator overnight.
- Whisk whipped cream, pecans, marshmallows and pineapple with the cranberry mixture on the following day. Stir them well.
- Add to a 3-quart dish, keep it covered and let chill in the refrigerator or keep frozen till ready to serve.

Nutrition Information

- Calories: 771 calories;
- Total Fat: 18.5

- Sodium: 92
- Total Carbohydrate: 156.6
- Cholesterol: 18
- Protein: 4.4

772. Christmas Gelatin Ring

Serving: 12 servings. | Prep: 30mins | Cook: 0mins | Ready in:

Ingredients

- 1 package (3 ounces) cherry gelatin
- 3 cups boiling water, divided
- 1 can (29 ounces) sliced pears, undrained
- 1 package (3 ounces) lemon gelatin
- 1 package (8 ounces) cream cheese, cubed and softened
- 1 package (3 ounces) lime gelatin
- 1 can (20 ounces) crushed pineapple

Direction

- Dissolve cherry gelatin in 1 cup of boiling water in a bowl. Strain pears, saving 1 cup syrup (get rid of the remaining syrup or reserve for the next use). Add reserved syrup and pears into cherry gelatin and mix. Transfer mixture into a 3-qt ring mold greased with cooking spray or 10-inch fluted tube pan. Chill in the fridge for about 1 and 1/4 hours until almost firm.
- Dissolve lemon gelatin in 1 cup of boiling water in a bowl; chill until partially thickened. Whisk cream cheese until combined then pour over the cherry layer.
- Dissolve lime gelatin in remaining boiling water in another bowl. Drain pineapple, saving syrup. Add water to pineapple syrup to equal 3/4 cup. Add reserved syrup and pineapple into the lime gelatin, mix; pour over the lemon layer. Chill until completely set. Remove the mold and place the finished salad onto a plate to serve.

Nutrition Information

- Calories: 215 calories
- Protein: 4g protein.
- Total Fat: 7g fat (4g saturated fat)
- Sodium: 110mg sodium
- Fiber: 1g fiber)
- Total Carbohydrate: 37g carbohydrate (35g sugars
- Cholesterol: 21mg cholesterol

773. Christmas Ribbon Salad

Serving: 15 servings. | Prep: 20mins | Cook: 0mins | Ready in:

Ingredients

- 2 packages (.3 ounce each) sugar-free lime gelatin
- 5 cups boiling water, divided
- 4 cups cold water, divided
- 2 packages (.3 ounce each) sugar-free lemon gelatin
- 1 package (8 ounces) reduced-fat cream cheese, cubed
- 1 can (8 ounces) crushed pineapple, undrained
- 1/4 cup chopped pecans
- 2 cups reduced-fat whipped topping
- 2 packages (.3 ounce each) sugar-free cherry gelatin

Direction

- In a bowl containing 2 cups of boiling water, dissolve lime gelatin. Pour in 2 cups of cold water; mix. Add to a 13x9-in. plate coated using cooking spray. Keep chilled in the refrigerator for roughly 2 hours till nearly set.
- In a bowl with 1 cup of boiling water, dissolve lemon gelatin; mix in cream cheese till smooth in consistency. Mix in pecans and pineapple. Fold in whipped topping. Scoop on top of first layer. Keep chilled in the refrigerator for roughly 60 minutes till firm.

- In a bowl containing the leftover boiling water, dissolve cherry gelatin. Pour in leftover cold water; mix. Keep chilled till it becomes a bit thickened and syrupy. Gently scoop on top of second layer. Keep chilled in the refrigerator for roughly 4 hours till set.

Nutrition Information

- Calories: 92 calories
- Fiber: 1g fiber)
- Total Carbohydrate: 5g carbohydrate (0 sugars
- Cholesterol: 8mg cholesterol
- Protein: 3g protein. Diabetic Exchanges: 1 fat
- Total Fat: 5g fat (3g saturated fat)
- Sodium: 140mg sodium

774. Christmas Wreath Salad

Serving: 6 servings. | Prep: 10mins | Cook: 0mins | Ready in:

Ingredients

- 1 package (6 ounces) strawberry gelatin
- 1 cup boiling water
- 1 can (20 ounces) crushed pineapple
- 1 cup (8 ounces) plain yogurt
- 1 cup chopped pecans, optional
- 1/2 cup red maraschino cherries, halved
- Lettuce leaves and additional cherries, optional

Direction

- In a big bowl with boiling water, dissolve gelatin. Keep chilled in the refrigerator for roughly half an hour till partially set. Drain pineapple, saving the juice; put pineapple aside. Pour enough cold water into juice to measure 1-3/4 cups; mix into gelatin mixture. Mix in yogurt till smooth in consistency. Fold in the reserved pineapple, cherries and nuts if you want.

- Add to a 2-qt. ring mold coated using cooking spray. Keep chilled in the refrigerator till set. Unmold to a serving dish lined with lettuce and use extra cherries for decoration if you want.

Nutrition Information

- Calories: 212 calories
- Total Fat: 1g fat (1g saturated fat)
- Sodium: 93mg sodium
- Fiber: 1g fiber)
- Total Carbohydrate: 48g carbohydrate (42g sugars
- Cholesterol: 5mg cholesterol
- Protein: 4g protein.

---

775.   Chunky Cranberry Salad

Serving: 12 servings. | Prep: 10mins | Cook: 15mins | Ready in:

Ingredients

- 4 cups fresh or frozen cranberries
- 3-1/2 cups unsweetened pineapple juice
- 2 envelopes unflavored gelatin
- 1/2 cup cold water
- 2 cups sugar
- 1 can (20 ounces) unsweetened pineapple tidbits, drained
- 1 cup chopped pecans
- 1 cup green grapes, chopped
- 1/2 cup finely chopped celery
- 2 teaspoons grated orange zest

Direction

- Mix pineapple juice and cranberries together in a big saucepan. Cook over medium heat for 15 minutes until the berries pop.
- In the meantime, drizzle gelatin over cold water in a small bowl. Let it sit for 5 minutes. Mix softened gelatin, sugar, and the berry

mixture in a big bowl. Refrigerate until partly set.
- Tuck in orange zest, celery, grapes, pecans, and pineapple. Put into individual serving plates. Refrigerate until firm.

Nutrition Information

- Calories: 288 calories
- Sodium: 9mg sodium
- Fiber: 3g fiber)
- Total Carbohydrate: 57g carbohydrate (52g sugars
- Cholesterol: 0 cholesterol
- Protein: 3g protein.
- Total Fat: 7g fat (1g saturated fat)

---

776.   Cider Cranberry Salad

Serving: 6-8 servings. | Prep: 5mins | Cook: 0mins | Ready in:

Ingredients

- 1 package (3 ounces) orange gelatin
- 3/4 cup boiling apple cider
- 3/4 cup cold apple cider
- 1 can (14 ounces) whole-berry cranberry sauce

Direction

- In a bowl with boiling cider, dissolve gelatin. Mix in cranberry sauce and cold cider. Add to separate plates. Keep chilled till firm.

Nutrition Information

- Calories: 142 calories
- Protein: 1g protein.
- Total Fat: 0 fat (0 saturated fat)
- Sodium: 41mg sodium
- Fiber: 1g fiber)
- Total Carbohydrate: 36g carbohydrate (28g sugars

- Cholesterol: 0 cholesterol

777. Cinnamon Apple Salad

Serving: 9 servings. | Prep: 15mins | Cook: 0mins | Ready in:

Ingredients

- 1/2 cup red-hot candies
- 1 cup boiling water
- 1 package (3 ounces) lemon gelatin
- 1 cup applesauce
- 1 package (8 ounces) cream cheese, softened
- 1/2 cup Miracle Whip
- 1/2 cup chopped pecans
- 1/4 cup chopped celery

Direction

- Melt the candies in water in a bowl (reheat if needed). Add gelatin; toss to melt. Mix in applesauce. Lightly grease an 8-in. square pan with cooking spray and put half in. Chill until firm. Put a cover on and set the rest of the gelatin mixture aside at room temperature.
- In the meantime, mix together celery, pecans, Miracle Whip, and cream cheese and spread over the cold gelatin mixture. Gently put the rest of the gelatin mixture on the cream cheese layer. Refrigerate overnight.

Nutrition Information

- Calories:
- Fiber:
- Total Carbohydrate:
- Cholesterol:
- Protein:
- Total Fat:
- Sodium:

778. Cinnamon Gelatin Salad

Serving: 4 | Prep: 5mins | Cook: |Ready in:

Ingredients

- 1 (3 ounce) package raspberry flavored Jell-O® mix
- 1 cup boiling water
- 1 (2.25 ounce) package cinnamon red hot candies
- 1 cup applesauce

Direction

- Combine boiling water and gelatin in a small serving bowl until the gelatin is fully melted. Mix in cinnamon candies until dissolved, and then stir in the applesauce. Refrigerate for 3 hours until set.

Nutrition Information

- Calories: 165 calories;
- Total Carbohydrate: 40.5
- Cholesterol: 0
- Protein: 2
- Total Fat: 0
- Sodium: 85

779. Circus Peanut Gelatin

Serving: 12 servings. | Prep: 10mins | Cook: 0mins | Ready in:

Ingredients

- 44 circus peanut candies, divided
- 1 cup boiling water, divided
- 2 packages (3 ounces each) orange gelatin
- 2 cans (8 ounces each) crushed pineapple, undrained
- 1 carton (8 ounces) frozen whipped topping, thawed

Direction

- In a microwave-safe bowl, place 32 candies chopped into small pieces. Pour 1/4 cup of boiling water into the bowl. Microwave with cover for 45 seconds on high setting; stir. But back in the microwave oven and cook for 45 seconds more. Take the bowl out and stir until smooth. Dissolve gelatin in unused boiling water in a large bowl. Add pineapple and melted candies and mix. Chill until soft-set.
- Add whipped topping and fold. Transfer into a 13x9-inch dish oiled with cooking spray. Chill until completely firm. Divide the candy Jell-O into squares; garnish each with a circus peanut on top.

Nutrition Information

- Calories: 189 calories
- Total Fat: 3g fat (3g saturated fat)
- Sodium: 16mg sodium
- Fiber: 0 fiber)
- Total Carbohydrate: 38g carbohydrate (34g sugars
- Cholesterol: 0 cholesterol
- Protein: 1g protein.

780.   Citrus Chiffon Salad

Serving: 8 servings. | Prep: 10mins | Cook: 0mins | Ready in:

Ingredients

- 1 cup orange juice
- 1 tablespoon lemon juice
- 1 package (.3 ounce) sugar-free lemon or orange gelatin
- 1 package (8 ounces) fat-free cream cheese, cubed
- 1 cup reduced-fat whipped topping
- 1 can (8 ounces) unsweetened crushed pineapple, undrained

- 1/3 cup reduced-fat mayonnaise

Direction

- Boil lemon and orange juices in a small saucepan; mix in gelatin until melted. Put mayonnaise, pineapple, whipped topping, cream cheese in a blender and start blending until creamy. Add gelatin mixture, put the lid on and blend until combined.
- Put in a cooking spray-coated 4-cup mold. Chill until firm, about a few hours or overnight.

Nutrition Information

- Calories: 153 calories
- Total Fat: 9g fat (5g saturated fat)
- Sodium: 193mg sodium
- Fiber: 0 fiber)
- Total Carbohydrate: 12g carbohydrate (0 sugars
- Cholesterol: 19mg cholesterol
- Protein: 4g protein. Diabetic Exchanges: 2 fat

781.   Citrus Gelatin Salad

Serving: 16 servings. | Prep: 30mins | Cook: 0mins | Ready in:

Ingredients

- 2 envelopes unflavored gelatin
- 1/4 cup cold water
- 1 cup sugar
- 1-3/4 cups boiling water
- 3 tablespoons lemon juice
- 1 drop yellow food coloring, optional
- 1 can (20 ounces) unsweetened pineapple tidbits, drained
- 1/2 cup sliced firm banana
- 1-1/2 cups miniature marshmallows
- TOPPING:
- 1/2 cup sugar

- 3 tablespoons cornstarch
- 2/3 cup orange juice
- 1/4 cup lemon juice
- 1-1/2 cups reduced-fat whipped topping

Direction

- Mix cold water and gelatin in a bowl; let it rest for 60 seconds. Put in boiling water and sugar; mix till gelatin and sugar are dissolved. If you want, mix in food coloring and lemon juice; put aside. In a 13 x 9-in. plate, layer pineapple, banana and marshmallows. Add gelatin mixture on top. Keep it covered and chilled in the refrigerator overnight.
- Mix cornstarch and sugar in a saucepan. Slowly mix in juices till smooth in consistency. Boil; cook and stir till thickened or for 2 minutes. Take out of the heat; let it cool down to room temperature. Add into a bowl; put in whipped topping. Whip till blended. Spread on top of gelatin layer. Keep it covered and chilled till serving or for 60 minutes. Chop into square pieces.

Nutrition Information

- Calories: 132 calories
- Cholesterol: 0 cholesterol
- Protein: 1g protein. Diabetic Exchanges: 2 fruit.
- Total Fat: 1g fat (1g saturated fat)
- Sodium: 5mg sodium
- Fiber: 0 fiber)
- Total Carbohydrate: 31g carbohydrate (0 sugars

782. Cool Cucumber Salad

Serving: 4 | Prep: 15mins | Cook: |Ready in:

Ingredients

- 2 large cucumbers, peeled and thinly sliced
- 1/2 (8 ounce) carton sour cream

- 1 green onion, chopped
- 2 tablespoons chopped fresh dill
- 1/2 teaspoon kosher salt
- 1/2 teaspoon cracked black pepper

Direction

- In a salad bowl, put cucumbers and mix with pepper, kosher salt, dill, green onion, and sour cream. Put a cover on the bowl with plastic wrap and chill the salad for 30 minutes before serving.

Nutrition Information

- Calories: 80 calories;
- Total Fat: 6.2
- Sodium: 260
- Total Carbohydrate: 5.3
- Cholesterol: 12
- Protein: 1.9

783. Cool Lime Salad

Serving: 1 serving. | Prep: 20mins | Cook: 0mins |Ready in:

Ingredients

- 1/2 cup undrained canned crushed pineapple
- 2 tablespoons lime gelatin
- 1/4 cup 4% cottage cheese
- 1/4 cup whipped topping

Direction

- Boil pineapple in a small saucepan. Turn the heat off, add gelatin and stir until completely dissolved. Allow to cool to room temperature. Add whipped topping and cottage cheese into the pan, stir. Refrigerate until firm.

Nutrition Information

- Calories: 312 calories

- Protein: 10g protein.
- Total Fat: 6g fat (5g saturated fat)
- Sodium: 266mg sodium
- Fiber: 1g fiber)
- Total Carbohydrate: 57g carbohydrate (53g sugars
- Cholesterol: 13mg cholesterol

784. Cottage Cheese Fluff

Serving: 6 | Prep: 5mins | Cook: | Ready in:

Ingredients

- 3 cups low-fat cottage cheese
- 2 (0.3 ounce) packages sugar-free lemon flavored Jell-O® mix
- 1 (8 ounce) container lite frozen whipped topping, thawed

Direction

- In a food processor, put cottage cheese and process until smooth. Mix in the flavored gelatin powder, and then fold in the thawed whipped topping. Chill until serving.

Nutrition Information

- Calories: 183 calories;
- Sodium: 519
- Total Carbohydrate: 18.2
- Cholesterol: 5
- Protein: 15.8
- Total Fat: 4.1

785. Cran Blueberry Mold

Serving: 6 servings. | Prep: 20mins | Cook: 0mins | Ready in:

Ingredients

- 2 envelopes unflavored gelatin
- 1-1/2 cups cold water
- Sugar substitute equivalent to 1/4 cup sugar
- 2 cups reduced-calorie reduced-sugar cranberry juice, chilled
- 2 cups fresh peaches, peeled and cut into chunks
- 1-1/2 cups fresh blueberries

Direction

- Drizzle gelatin over water in a saucepan and let it sit for 1 minute. Add sugar substitute. Stir and cook until gelatin and sugar substitute are melted and the mixture is warm (do not boil it). Move to a bowl. Mix in cranberry juice. Put a cover on and chill until slightly firm. Tuck in blueberries and peaches. Move to a grease-coated 2-qt. bowl or a 7-cup mold. Chill until firm. Remove from the mold onto a serving platter or a dish.

Nutrition Information

- Calories: 71 calories
- Sodium: 9mg sodium
- Fiber: 2g fiber)
- Total Carbohydrate: 16g carbohydrate (0 sugars
- Cholesterol: 0 cholesterol
- Protein: 3g protein. Diabetic Exchanges: 1 fruit.
- Total Fat: 0 fat (0 saturated fat)

786. Cran Orange Gelatin Salad

Serving: 15 servings. | Prep: 45mins | Cook: 0mins | Ready in:

Ingredients

- 1 can (15 ounces) mandarin oranges

- 2 packages (.3 ounce each) sugar-free cranberry gelatin
- 1-1/2 cups boiling water
- 1 can (14 ounces) whole-berry cranberry sauce
- 1-1/2 cups crushed salt-free pretzels
- 6 tablespoons butter, melted
- Sugar substitute equivalent to 5 tablespoons sugar, divided
- 1 package (8 ounces) fat-free cream cheese
- 1 carton (8 ounces) frozen reduced-fat whipped topping, thawed

Direction

- Drain oranges, saving juice in a 2-cup measuring cup; put oranges and juice aside.
- In boiling water, dissolve gelatin in a big bowl. Mix in cranberry sauce till melted. Pour in enough cold water to the reserved juice to measure one and a half cups; pour into gelatin mixture. Mix in oranges. Keep chilled till set partially.
- At the same time, mix 2 tbsp. of sugar substitute, butter and pretzels in a big bowl. Push into 1 ungreased 13x9-in. plate; keep chilled.
- Whip leftover sugar substitute and cream cheese in a small-sized bowl till smooth in texture. Fold in whipped topping. Spread on top of crust. Scoop gelatin mixture on top of cream cheese layer. Keep chilled for no less than 3 hours till set.

Nutrition Information

- Calories: 183 calories
- Sodium: 185mg sodium
- Fiber: 1g fiber)
- Total Carbohydrate: 26g carbohydrate (12g sugars
- Cholesterol: 13mg cholesterol
- Protein: 4g protein. Diabetic Exchanges: 2 starch
- Total Fat: 7g fat (5g saturated fat)

Serving: 8 servings. | Prep: 15mins | Cook: 0mins | Ready in:

Ingredients

- 1 package (3 ounces) raspberry gelatin
- 1-1/2 cups boiling water
- 1 cup fresh cranberries or frozen cranberries
- 1/2 cup raspberry jam or spreadable fruit
- 1 can (8 ounces) crushed pineapple, undrained

Direction

- In a bowl containing water, dissolve gelatin. In a food processor or blender, put in gelatin mixture, jam and cranberries; keep it covered and process till cranberries are chopped roughly. Add into a bowl; mix in pineapple. Keep chilled in the refrigerator till set.

Nutrition Information

- Calories: 58 calories
- Total Fat: 1g fat (0 saturated fat)
- Sodium: 30mg sodium
- Fiber: 0 fiber)
- Total Carbohydrate: 14g carbohydrate (0 sugars
- Cholesterol: 0 cholesterol
- Protein: 1g protein. Diabetic Exchanges: 1 fruit.

788. Cran Raspberry Gelatin Salad

Serving: 10 servings. | Prep: 15mins | Cook: 0mins | Ready in:

Ingredients

- 2 packages (3 ounces each) raspberry gelatin
- 1 cup boiling water
- 1 can (14 ounces) whole-berry cranberry sauce

- 1 can (8 ounces) crushed pineapple, undrained
- 1 cup orange juice

Direction

- In a big bowl with boiling water, dissolve gelatin. Whisk in orange juice, pineapple, and cranberry sauce. Add to a 6-cup ring mold coated using cooking spray.
- Keep it covered and let chill in the refrigerator till set or for 4 hours. Unmold to a serving platter.

Nutrition Information

- Calories: 155 calories
- Sodium: 49mg sodium
- Fiber: 1g fiber)
- Total Carbohydrate: 39g carbohydrate (32g sugars
- Cholesterol: 0 cholesterol
- Protein: 2g protein.
- Total Fat: 0 fat (0 saturated fat)

789.   Cran Raspberry Sherbet Mold

Serving: 10-12 servings. | Prep: 10mins | Cook: 0mins | Ready in:

Ingredients

- 2 packages (3 ounces each) raspberry gelatin
- 1-1/2 cups boiling water
- 1 can (14 ounces) jellied cranberry sauce
- 2 cups raspberry sherbet, softened
- 1 tablespoon lemon juice
- Cranberries, raspberries, orange segments and fresh mint, optional

Direction

- In a big bowl with boiling water, dissolve gelatin. Mix in cranberry sauce till smooth in

consistency. Keep chilled in the refrigerator till thickened a bit or for half an hour.

- Fold in lemon juice and sherbet. Add into a 6-cup ring mold coated using cooking spray. Keep chilled in the refrigerator till firm.
- Unmold to a serving platter. Fill the middle with raspberries and cranberries, and enjoy with mint and oranges if you want.

Nutrition Information

- Calories: 114 calories
- Cholesterol: 1mg cholesterol
- Protein: 1g protein.
- Total Fat: 0 fat (0 saturated fat)
- Sodium: 36mg sodium
- Fiber: 1g fiber)
- Total Carbohydrate: 28g carbohydrate (21g sugars

790.   Cranberry Cherry Salad

Serving: 10 servings. | Prep: 20mins | Cook: 0mins | Ready in:

Ingredients

- 1 can (14-1/2 ounces) pitted tart red cherries
- 1 package (3 ounces) cherry gelatin
- 1 can (8 ounces) jellied cranberry sauce
- 1 package (3 ounces) lemon gelatin
- 1 cup boiling water
- 3 ounces cream cheese, softened
- 1/3 cup mayonnaise
- 1 can (8 ounces) crushed pineapple, undrained
- 1/2 cup heavy whipping cream, whipped
- 1 cup miniature marshmallows

Direction

- Strain cherries; reserve syrup, put cherries to one side. Pour cherry juice into a measuring cup and add enough water to reach 1 cup. Pour mixture into a saucepan, and boil.

Dissolve cherry gelatin by stirring in boiling juice mixture. Combine with cranberry sauce and whisk until smooth. Add cherries. Transfer the mixture into an 11x7-inch dish. Chill until completely set.

- Dissolve lemon gelatin in boiling water in a bowl. Whip mayonnaise together with cream cheese in a small bowl. Add lemon gelatin slowly and beat until incorporated, add pineapple and stir.
- Chill until nearly firm. Fold in marshmallows and whipped cream. Pour over the cherry layer. Chill until firm, and enjoy.

Nutrition Information

- Calories: 279 calories
- Total Fat: 13g fat (5g saturated fat)
- Sodium: 119mg sodium
- Fiber: 1g fiber)
- Total Carbohydrate: 39g carbohydrate (34g sugars
- Cholesterol: 28mg cholesterol
- Protein: 3g protein.

Direction

- In a 2-qt saucepan, mix water and pineapple juice together, bring to a boil. Turn off the heat; put gelatin in and stir to dissolve. Add nutmeg, zest, lemon juice, cranberry sauce then stir. Refrigerate until partly thickened. Pour sour cream and mix until completely combined. Add pecans and pineapple, fold. Transfer into an 8-cup mold, refrigerate until totally set. Remove the mold and place onto a plate to serve. Decorate with fresh strawberries if you like.

Nutrition Information

- Calories: 254 calories
- Sodium: 60mg sodium
- Fiber: 1g fiber)
- Total Carbohydrate: 38g carbohydrate (32g sugars
- Cholesterol: 25mg cholesterol
- Protein: 3g protein.
- Total Fat: 10g fat (5g saturated fat)

---

791. Cranberry Delight

Serving: 12 servings. | Prep: 20mins | Cook: 0mins | Ready in:

Ingredients

- 1 can (20 ounces) crushed pineapple, juice drained and reserved
- 1 cup water
- 1 package (6 ounces) strawberry gelatin
- 1 can (14 ounces) whole-berry cranberry sauce
- 3 tablespoons lemon juice
- 1 teaspoon grated lemon zest
- 1/2 teaspoon ground nutmeg
- 2 cups sour cream
- 1/2 cup chopped pecans
- Fresh strawberries, optional

---

792. Cranberry Eggnog Salad

Serving: 12 servings. | Prep: 10mins | Cook: 5mins | Ready in:

Ingredients

- 2-1/2 cups boiling water
- 2 packages (3 ounces each) cranberry or raspberry gelatin
- 1 can (14 ounces) whole-berry cranberry sauce
- 1 can (20 ounces) crushed pineapple, undrained
- 2 envelopes unflavored gelatin
- 1-1/2 cups eggnog
- 2 tablespoons lime juice

Direction

- Melt cranberry gelatin in boiling water in a big bowl, toss for 2 minutes until fully melted. Chill until slightly thickened, about 40-50 minutes.
- In a small bowl, put cranberry sauce, toss to break up. Fold in the gelatin mixture. Put in a grease-coated 8-cup ring mold, chill until set but not firm, about another 15-20 minutes.
- In the meantime, strain crushed pineapple thoroughly, saving the juice in a small saucepan. Use unflavored gelatin to drizzle over the pineapple juice, let it sit for 1 minute. Heat and toss over low heat until the gelatin is fully melted. Mix in lime juice and eggnog. Chill until slightly thickened, about 12-15 minutes.
- Fold the pineapple into the eggnog mixture. Gently put on the gelatin in the mold. Chill until firm. Remove from the mold onto a dish.

Nutrition Information

- Calories: 180 calories
- Sodium: 66mg sodium
- Fiber: 1g fiber)
- Total Carbohydrate: 37g carbohydrate (31g sugars
- Cholesterol: 19mg cholesterol
- Protein: 7g protein.
- Total Fat: 1g fat (1g saturated fat)

793.　　Cranberry Fruit Mold

Serving: Makes 9 servings, about 2/3 cup each. | Prep: 15mins | Cook: |Ready in:

Ingredients

- 2 cups boiling water
- 1-1/2 cups cold diet ginger ale or water
- 2 cups green and/or red seedless grapes halves
- 1 can (11 oz.) mandarin oranges, drained

Direction

- 1. In a big bowl, mix boiling water into gelatin for no less than 2 minutes till dissolved totally. Mix in cold diet ginger ale. Keep chilled in the refrigerator till thickened, about one and a half hours (spoon drawn through leaves definite impression).
- 2. Mix in oranges and grapes. Add to 6-cup mold sprayed using cooking spray.
- 3. Keep chilled in the refrigerator till firm, about 4 hours. Unmold. Keep the remaining gelatin mold in the fridge.

Nutrition Information

- Calories: 45
- Total Carbohydrate: 9 g
- Saturated Fat: 0 g
- Fiber: 1 g
- Sugar: 8 g
- Cholesterol: 0 mg
- Protein: 2 g
- Total Fat: 0 g
- Sodium: 75 mg

794.　　Cranberry Gelatin Mold

Serving: 12 | Prep: | Cook: |Ready in:

Ingredients

- 1 (6 ounce) package cranberry flavored Jell-O® mix
- 1 (16 ounce) can whole cranberry sauce
- 1 (6 ounce) package lime flavored Jell-O® mix
- 8 ounces cream cheese, softened
- 1 (8 ounce) can crushed pineapple, drained
- 1 (8 ounce) container frozen whipped topping, thawed
- 1 cup chopped walnuts

Direction

- Assemble cranberry gelatin as directed. Transfer the gelatin mixture into a 9x13-in. dish. Add cranberries and mix well. Chill for at least 4 hours in the fridge until firm.
- Make lime gelatin by following the directions. Set aside to cool a bit, then combine with cream cheese. Add pineapple and mix. Gradually pour over the cranberry gelatin layer. Stand for at least 4 hours to set.
- Distribute the whipped topping on top and garnish with chopped walnuts just before serving.

Nutrition Information

- Calories: 355 calories;
- Total Fat: 17.7
- Sodium: 180
- Total Carbohydrate: 47.1
- Cholesterol: 21
- Protein: 5.8

795.   Cranberry Gelatin Salad

Serving: 12 | Prep: 15mins | Cook: 10mins | Ready in:

Ingredients

- 1 (16 ounce) can jellied cranberry sauce
- 1 (16.5 ounce) can pitted dark sweet cherries, drained
- 10 1/2 ounces crushed pineapple with juice
- 1 (6 ounce) package cherry Jell-O®
- 2 cups boiling water
- 1 cup chopped pecans (optional)

Direction

- On low heat, melt the cranberry sauce in a medium-sized saucepan.
- Chop the cherries into pieces and place them into the melted sauce. Mix in the pineapple juice and pineapple. Take mixture out of heat.

- Add boiling water on the gelatin in a medium-sized bowl. Mix till all gelatin has dissolved.
- Pour the gelatin mixture into the cranberry mixture and mix. Mix in the optional nuts. Add to one 9x13-inch pan and keep chilled till set.

Nutrition Information

- Calories: 206 calories;
- Total Carbohydrate: 37
- Cholesterol: 0
- Protein: 2.6
- Total Fat: 6.6
- Sodium: 77

796.   Cranberry Gelatin Salad Mold

Serving: 10-12 servings. | Prep: 20mins | Cook: 0mins | Ready in:

Ingredients

- 1 package (12 ounces) cranberries
- 3/4 cup plus 2 tablespoons sugar, divided
- 1-1/2 cups water, divided
- 3/4 cup pineapple tidbits, drained
- 1 medium tart apple, peeled and diced
- 1/4 cup chopped walnuts
- 1 envelope unflavored gelatin
- 1/4 teaspoon salt
- 1/2 cup mayonnaise
- 2 tablespoons lemon juice
- 1 teaspoon grated lemon zest

Direction

- Mix half a cup of water, three quarters cup of sugar and cranberries in a saucepan. Boil; boil till berries pop or for 3 to 4 minutes. Take out of the heat; mix in nuts, apple and pineapple. Keep chilled till cooled.

- In a different saucepan, add leftover water and gelatin; let it rest for 60 seconds. Put in the leftover sugar and salt; cook and stir on low heat till dissolved. Take out of the heat; mix in zest, lemon juice and mayonnaise.
- Add into a bowl; chill for roughly 60 minutes till partially set. Whip till it becomes fluffy. Fold in the cranberry mixture. Add to a 6-cup mold coated using cooking spray. Keep chilled for roughly 8 hours till firm.

Nutrition Information

- Calories:
- Fiber:
- Total Carbohydrate:
- Cholesterol:
- Protein:
- Total Fat:
- Sodium:

---

797. Cranberry Gelatin Squares

Serving: 12 servings. | Prep: 30mins | Cook: 0mins | Ready in:

Ingredients

- 2 cans (8 ounces each) crushed pineapple
- 2 packages (3 ounces each) strawberry gelatin
- 3/4 cup cold water
- 1 can (14 ounces) jellied cranberry sauce
- 1/3 cup chopped pecans
- 1 tablespoon butter
- 1/2 cup cold whole milk
- 1/2 cup heavy whipping cream
- 1 package (3.4 ounces) instant vanilla pudding mix
- 3 ounces cream cheese, softened

Direction

- Preheat oven to 350 degrees. Drain pineapple, saving the juice in a 1-cup measuring cup. Pour in enough water to measure 1 cup. Put pineapple aside.
- Boil apple juice mixture in a small-sized saucepan on medium heat. Take out of the heat; mix in gelatin till dissolved. Mix in cold water; place into a bowl. Keep it covered and let chill in the refrigerator till partially set.
- Mix reserved pineapple and cranberry sauce in a small-sized bowl; mix into gelatin mixture. Add to a 9-in. square plate; keep it covered and let chill in the refrigerator till it becomes firm.
- Into a shallow baking pan, add butter and pecans. Bake till golden brown while mixing once in a while or for 8 minutes; let it cool down.
- Mix pudding mix, cream and milk in a small-sized bowl for 2 minutes. Whip cream cheese in a different small-sized bowl till smooth in consistency. Put in pudding mixture; whip on low speed till just combined. Spread on top of gelatin. Drizzle with toasted pecans. Keep chilled till firm.

Nutrition Information

- Calories: 255 calories
- Protein: 3g protein.
- Total Fat: 10g fat (5g saturated fat)
- Sodium: 189mg sodium
- Fiber: 1g fiber)
- Total Carbohydrate: 41g carbohydrate (34g sugars
- Cholesterol: 25mg cholesterol

---

798. Cranberry Luncheon Salad

Serving: 10 servings. | Prep: 25mins | Cook: 0mins | Ready in:

Ingredients

- 2 cups orange juice, divided
- 1 cup water
- 2 packages (3 ounces each) cranberry gelatin
- 1 can (14 ounces) whole-berry cranberry sauce
- 1 can (15-1/4 ounces) sliced peaches, drained
- 3 cups cubed cooked chicken
- 2 celery ribs, chopped
- 1/2 cup mayonnaise
- 1 tablespoon cider vinegar
- 1/2 teaspoon salt
- 1/8 teaspoon pepper
- Lettuce leaves
- 1/4 cup coarsely chopped pecans

Direction

- Boil water and 1 cup of orange juice in a small-sized saucepan. Add gelatin into a big bowl; pour juice mixture and stir till dissolved. Mix in the leftover orange juice. Keep chilled for roughly one and a half hours till set partially.
- Mix in cranberry sauce. Add to a 6-cup ring mold coated using cooking spray. Keep it covered and let chill in the refrigerator for 6 hours or overnight.
- Put aside several slices of peach for decoration; cube the leftover peaches. Mix pepper, salt, vinegar, mayonnaise, celery, chicken and cubed peaches in a big bowl. Keep it covered and place in the refrigerator till chilled or for 60 minutes.
- To a serving dish, invert the gelatin mold; line ring middle using lettuce leaves. Mix pecans into chicken salad; scoop into the middle of the gelatin. Add reserved peach slices on top.

Nutrition Information

- Calories:
- Fiber:
- Total Carbohydrate:
- Cholesterol:
- Protein:
- Total Fat:
- Sodium:

799.   Cranberry Mousse Salad

Serving: 10-12 servings. | Prep: 15mins | Cook: 0mins | Ready in:

Ingredients

- 2 packages (3 ounces each) strawberry gelatin
- 3/4 cup boiling water
- 1 can (14 ounces) whole-berry cranberry sauce
- 2 tablespoons lemon juice
- 1 teaspoon grated lemon zest
- 1/4 teaspoon ground nutmeg
- 1 can (20 ounces) crushed pineapple
- 2 cups sour cream
- 1/2 cup chopped pecans

Direction

- Melt the gelatin in water in a bowl. Add nutmeg, zest, lemon juice, and cranberry sauce, toss thoroughly. Strain pineapple, add the juice to the gelatin and set the pineapple aside. Chill until syrupy.
- Mix in sour cream. Add pecans and the pineapple. Put in a nonstick oiled 8-cup mold. Refrigerate until firm.

Nutrition Information

- Calories: 249 calories
- Sodium: 61mg sodium
- Fiber: 1g fiber)
- Total Carbohydrate: 36g carbohydrate (29g sugars
- Cholesterol: 27mg cholesterol
- Protein: 3g protein.
- Total Fat: 10g fat (5g saturated fat)

800.   Cranberry Pecan Salad

Serving: 6 | Prep: 15mins | Cook: 10mins | Ready in:

Ingredients

- 1 cup pecan halves
- 2 tablespoons raspberry vinegar
- 1/2 teaspoon Dijon mustard
- 1/2 teaspoon sugar
- 1/2 teaspoon salt
- freshly ground black pepper to taste (optional)
- 6 tablespoons olive oil
- 6 cups mixed salad greens, rinsed and dried
- 3/4 cup dried cranberries
- 1/2 medium red onion, thinly sliced
- crumbled feta cheese

Direction

- Set oven at 400°F (200°C) and start preheating. On a baking sheet, spread pecans evenly.
- Put pecans in the oven and toast for 8 to 10 minutes or until turn lightly brown and scented.
- Stir salt, pepper, sugar, mustard and vinegar together in a small bowl; mix well until salt and sugar dissolve fully in the liquid. Add in olive oil, whisk properly.
- Toss cheese, onions, pecans, cranberries and the greens together in a salad bowl. Pour in vinaigrette, toss lightly to coat salad with vinaigrette.

Nutrition Information

- Calories: 456 calories;
- Total Fat: 38.6
- Sodium: 780
- Total Carbohydrate: 21
- Cholesterol: 45
- Protein: 10

801.   Cranberry Relish Salad

Serving: 12 servings. | Prep: 10mins | Cook: 0mins | Ready in:

Ingredients

- 1 package (3 ounces) cherry gelatin
- 1 package (3 ounces) raspberry gelatin
- 1/4 cup sugar
- 1-1/2 cups boiling water
- 1 can (12 ounces) lemon-lime soda
- 1 can (8 ounce) crushed pineapple, undrained
- 2 packages (10 ounces each) frozen cranberry-orange sauce

Direction

- Melt sugar and gelatins in boiling water in a big bowl. Add cranberry-orange sauce, pineapple, and soda, refrigerate until partly set. Put in an 11x7-in. dish or individual dishes. Chill until firm or overnight.

Nutrition Information

- Calories: 133 calories
- Fiber: 0 fiber)
- Total Carbohydrate: 33g carbohydrate (32g sugars
- Cholesterol: 0 cholesterol
- Protein: 1g protein.
- Total Fat: 0 fat (0 saturated fat)
- Sodium: 43mg sodium

802.   Cranberry Salad

Serving: 12 | Prep: 15mins | Cook: | Ready in:

Ingredients

- 2 (12 ounce) packages cranberries
- 4 cups white sugar
- 1 cup diced celery
- 1 cup chopped walnuts
- 2 (12 ounce) containers frozen whipped topping, thawed
- 1 (10.5 ounce) package miniature marshmallows

Direction

- In a food processor or a blender, chop cranberries finely. Add into a non-reactive bowl, cover with sugar, and let stand for 4 hours.
- Mix marshmallows, whipped topping, walnuts, and celery with sugared cranberries; completely coat by mixing. Keep chilled in the refrigerator till serving.

Nutrition Information

- Calories: 595 calories;
- Total Fat: 15.9
- Sodium: 40
- Total Carbohydrate: 108
- Cholesterol: 0
- Protein: 1.8

803. Cranberry Salad Mold

Serving: 12 servings. | Prep: 30mins | Cook: 0mins | Ready in:

Ingredients

- 8 cups fresh cranberries
- 2-1/2 cups sugar
- 2 tablespoons unflavored gelatin
- 1/3 cup orange juice
- 2 cups diced apples
- 1 cup chopped nuts
- Leaf lettuce and mayonnaise for garnish

Direction

- In a food chopper, finely crush cranberries. Add sugar and stir well. Let it sit for 15 minutes, tossing sometimes. (If you use frozen berries, let the mixture sit to room temperature). In the top of a double boiler over hot water, put orange juice and gelatin and toss until the gelatin is melted. Add to the cranberries along with nuts and apples. Use

cold water to rinse a 7-cup mold and put the mixture in. Refrigerate until set. Remove from the mold onto leaf lettuce. Use mayonnaise to garnish.

Nutrition Information

- Calories: 275 calories
- Cholesterol: 0 cholesterol
- Protein: 4g protein.
- Total Fat: 6g fat (0 saturated fat)
- Sodium: 3mg sodium
- Fiber: 4g fiber)
- Total Carbohydrate: 55g carbohydrate (49g sugars

804. Cranberry Turkey Salad

Serving: 12-15 servings. | Prep: 20mins | Cook: 0mins | Ready in:

Ingredients

- 1 package (3 ounces) lemon gelatin
- 2 cups boiling water, divided
- 2 cups cubed cooked turkey or chicken
- 4 celery ribs, chopped
- 8 ounces process cheese (Velveeta), cubed
- 1 cup chopped almonds
- 3 hard-boiled large eggs, chopped, optional
- 1 cup Miracle Whip
- 1 cup heavy whipping cream, whipped
- 1/2 teaspoon salt
- 1/2 teaspoon onion salt
- 1 package (3 ounces) raspberry gelatin
- 1 can (14 ounces) whole-berry cranberry sauce

Direction

- In 1 cup of boiling water in a bowl, dissolve lemon gelatin; keep it chilled in the refrigerator till lightly thickened for 60 minutes. Beat on high speed for 60 seconds. Mix in eggs if desired, onion salt, salt, cream,

Miracle Whip, almonds, cheese, celery and turkey. Spread equally into a 13x9-in. dish. Keep it covered and chilled in the refrigerator till firm for about 2 hours.

- In the leftover boiling water, dissolve the raspberry gelatin; mix in cranberry sauce till blended and melted. Scoop on top of turkey mixture. Keep chilled in the refrigerator until set for 2 hours. Cut into squares.

Nutrition Information

- Calories: 379 calories
- Sodium: 460mg sodium
- Fiber: 2g fiber)
- Total Carbohydrate: 25g carbohydrate (19g sugars
- Cholesterol: 51mg cholesterol
- Protein: 12g protein.
- Total Fat: 27g fat (8g saturated fat)

---

805. Cranberry Waldorf Gelatin

Serving: 12 servings. | Prep: 15mins | Cook: 0mins | Ready in:

Ingredients

- 1 envelope unflavored gelatin
- 1 cup cold water, divided
- 1 package (3 ounces) cranberry gelatin
- 2 cups boiling water
- 1 can (14 ounces) whole-berry cranberry sauce
- 1/2 to 1 teaspoon ground cinnamon
- 1/4 teaspoon ground ginger
- 1/8 to 1/4 teaspoon salt
- 2 medium tart apples, peeled and diced
- 1 cup chopped walnuts

Direction

- Drizzle unflavored gelatin on top of a quarter cup of cold water; let it rest for 5 minutes. In a

bowl with boiling water, dissolve cranberry gelatin and softened gelatin. Mix in cranberry sauce till blended. Put in the leftover cold water, salt, ginger and cinnamon. Keep it covered and let chill in the refrigerator till nearly set. Fold in walnuts and apples. Add to an ungreased 2-1/2-qt. serving bowl. Keep chilled in the refrigerator till firm.

Nutrition Information

- Calories: 156 calories
- Protein: 4g protein.
- Total Fat: 6g fat (0 saturated fat)
- Sodium: 50mg sodium
- Fiber: 1g fiber)
- Total Carbohydrate: 24g carbohydrate (18g sugars
- Cholesterol: 0 cholesterol

---

806. Cranberry Eggnog Gelatin Salad

Serving: 16 servings. | Prep: 30mins | Cook: 5mins | Ready in:

Ingredients

- 2 packages (3 ounces each) raspberry gelatin
- 2 cups boiling water
- 1 cup cold water
- 1 can (14 ounces) whole-berry cranberry sauce
- 1 medium navel orange, peeled and chopped
- 1 tablespoon grated orange zest
- 1 can (20 ounces) unsweetened crushed pineapple, undrained
- 2 envelopes unflavored gelatin
- 1-1/2 cups eggnog
- 3 tablespoons lime juice

Direction

- Melt raspberry gelatin in boiling water in a large bowl. Mix with cold water then orange zest, orange and cranberry sauce. Transfer in to a 12-cup ring mold or 10-inch fluted tube pan coated with cooking spray. Chill until firm for 40 minutes.

- In the meantime, juice pineapple then pour into a saucepan. Combine unflavored gelatin with pineapple juice, let sit for 1 minute. Cook with low heat until gelatin is totally dissolved, stirring.
- Mix lime juice and eggnog together in a large bowl. Pour into gelatin mixture and stir slowly. Refrigerate until partly firm. Add pineapple and fold. Pour over raspberry layer. Chill in the fridge overnight. Remove the mold and serve in a platter.

Nutrition Information

- Calories:
- Fiber:
- Total Carbohydrate:
- Cholesterol:
- Protein:
- Total Fat:
- Sodium:

---

807. Cranberry Pineapple Gelatin Mold

Serving: 10 servings. | Prep: 15mins | Cook: 5mins | Ready in:

Ingredients

- 1 can (20 ounces) unsweetened crushed pineapple
- 2 envelopes unflavored gelatin
- 1 package (12 ounces) fresh or frozen cranberries
- 3 medium navel oranges, peeled and cut into segments
- 1/2 cup honey
- Whipped cream, optional

Direction

- Drain pineapple, saving the juice; put pineapple aside. Into a small-sized saucepan, add reserved juice. Drizzle with gelatin; let it rest till tender or for 60 seconds. Heat on low heat, while stirring till gelatin has dissolved totally. Take out of the heat.
- Mix oranges and cranberries in a food processor; keep it covered and pulse till chunky. Pour in pineapple and honey; keep it covered and pulse till just blended. Mix in juice mixture. Add into a 6-cup mold coated using cooking spray. Keep chilled in the refrigerator till firm.
- Unmold to a serving platter. Serve with whipped cream if you want.

Nutrition Information

- Calories: 126 calories
- Total Carbohydrate: 32g carbohydrate (26g sugars
- Cholesterol: 0 cholesterol
- Protein: 2g protein.
- Total Fat: 0 fat (0 saturated fat)
- Sodium: 5mg sodium
- Fiber: 3g fiber)

---

808. Cranberry/Orange Molded Salad

Serving: 8-10 servings. | Prep: 10mins | Cook: 0mins | Ready in:

Ingredients

- 1 package (6 ounces) raspberry gelatin
- 2 cups boiling water
- 1 can (14 ounces) whole-berry cranberry sauce
- 1/4 teaspoon ground cinnamon
- Dash ground cloves
- 2 cups diced orange sections
- Lettuce leaves, optional

Direction

- Dissolve gelatin in a big bowl with boiling water. Fold in cloves, cinnamon and cranberry sauce. Refrigerate until partly set. Put in orange sections. Transfer into an oiled 6-cup mold. Refrigerate for 3 hours until set. Unmold and serve on a platter lined with lettuce, if wanted.

Nutrition Information

- Calories: 144 calories
- Total Fat: 0 fat (0 saturated fat)
- Sodium: 48mg sodium
- Fiber: 2g fiber)
- Total Carbohydrate: 36g carbohydrate (29g sugars
- Cholesterol: 0 cholesterol
- Protein: 2g protein.

809. Creamy 'n' Fruity Gelatin Salad

Serving: 10 servings. | Prep: 15mins | Cook: 0mins | Ready in:

Ingredients

- 2 packages (3 ounces each) orange gelatin
- 1 cup boiling water
- 1 pint orange or pineapple sherbet
- 1 can (11 ounces) mandarin oranges, drained
- 1 can (8 ounces) crushed pineapple, drained
- 1 cup miniature marshmallows
- 1 cup heavy whipping cream, whipped

Direction

- Let gelatin dissolve in a large bowl of boiling water. Stir in sherbet till smooth. Add marshmallows, pineapple and oranges; stir. Add whipped cream and fold.
- Transfer into a 6-cup serving bowl with. Store in the fridge, covered, till set for 3-4 hours.

Nutrition Information

- Calories: 158 calories
- Sodium: 42mg sodium
- Fiber: 0 fiber)
- Total Carbohydrate: 28g carbohydrate (25g sugars
- Cholesterol: 18mg cholesterol
- Protein: 2g protein.
- Total Fat: 5g fat (3g saturated fat)

810. Creamy Blueberry Gelatin Salad

Serving: 15 servings. | Prep: 30mins | Cook: 0mins | Ready in:

Ingredients

- 2 packages (3 ounces each) grape gelatin
- 2 cups boiling water
- 1 can (21 ounces) blueberry pie filling
- 1 can (20 ounces) unsweetened crushed pineapple, undrained
- TOPPING:
- 1 package (8 ounces) cream cheese, softened
- 1 cup sour cream
- 1/2 cup sugar
- 1 teaspoon vanilla extract
- 1/2 cup chopped walnuts

Direction

- Dissolve gelatin in a big bowl with boiling water. Allow to cool for about 10 minutes. Stir in pineapple and pie filling until combined. Place onto a 13x9-in dish. Cover and chill for 1 hour until partly set.
- To make topping, whisk together vanilla, sugar, sour cream and cream cheese in a small bowl. Scatter over gelatin carefully, then sprinkle with walnuts. Cover and chill until firm.

Nutrition Information

- Calories: 221 calories
- Protein: 4g protein.
- Total Fat: 10g fat (5g saturated fat)
- Sodium: 76mg sodium
- Fiber: 1g fiber)
- Total Carbohydrate: 29g carbohydrate (26g sugars
- Cholesterol: 27mg cholesterol

---

811. Creamy Citrus Salad

Serving: 12-14 servings. | Prep: 20mins | Cook: 0mins | Ready in:

Ingredients

- 1 package (6 ounces) orange gelatin
- 2 cups boiling water
- 1 can (6 ounces) frozen orange juice concentrate, thawed
- 2 cans (11 ounces each) mandarin oranges, drained
- 1 can (20 ounces) crushed pineapple, undrained
- 1 cup cold milk
- 1 package (3.4 ounces) instant lemon pudding mix
- 1 cup heavy whipping cream, whipped

Direction

- In boiling water, dissolve gelatin in a big bowl; mix in orange juice concentrate. Keep cooled till set partially. Mix in pineapple and oranges. Add to 1 greased 13x9-in. plate. Keep chilled till firm.
- Whip pudding mix and milk for 2 minutes in a small-sized bowl; mix in cream. Spread on top of gelatin. Keep chilled for half an hour.

Nutrition Information

- Calories: 196 calories
- Sodium: 127mg sodium
- Fiber: 1g fiber)
- Total Carbohydrate: 33g carbohydrate (30g sugars
- Cholesterol: 26mg cholesterol
- Protein: 3g protein.
- Total Fat: 7g fat (4g saturated fat)

---

812. Creamy Cranberry Gelatin

Serving: 10 servings. | Prep: 20mins | Cook: 0mins | Ready in:

Ingredients

- 1 package (12 ounces) fresh or frozen cranberries, chopped
- 1 to 1-1/4 cups sugar
- 2 packages (3 ounces each) cherry gelatin
- 2 cups (16 ounces) plain yogurt
- 1 carton (8 ounces) frozen whipped topping, thawed
- 1/3 cup chopped pecans

Direction

- Mix sugar and cranberries in a bowl; keep it covered and let chill in refrigerator for 8 hours or overnight.
- Mix gelatin and cranberry mixture in a big saucepan. Cook and stir till gelatin dissolves totally; let it cool down. Mix in whipped topping and yogurt. Add to a 2-qt. serving bowl. Drizzle with pecans. Keep chilled in the refrigerator till firm, about 2 hours.

Nutrition Information

- Calories: 204 calories
- Total Fat: 6g fat (3g saturated fat)
- Sodium: 83mg sodium
- Fiber: 2g fiber)

- Total Carbohydrate: 33g carbohydrate (0 sugars
- Cholesterol: 1mg cholesterol
- Protein: 4g protein. Diabetic Exchanges: 2 fruit

813. Creamy Cranberry Pineapple Gelatin

Serving: 6 servings. | Prep: 15mins | Cook: 0mins | Ready in:

Ingredients

- 1 cup orange juice
- 1 package (3 ounces) pineapple gelatin
- 3 ounces cream cheese, softened
- 1 can (14 ounces) jellied cranberry sauce

Direction

- Boil orange juice in a small saucepan. In a small bowl, put gelatin, add the orange juice and mix until melted. Chill until slightly thickened.
- Whisk the cream cheese in a small bowl until fluffy. Add cranberry sauce and whisk until creamy. Whisk in the gelatin mixture. Put in 6 grease-coated 1/2-cup gelatin molds. Chill for a few hours or overnight. Remove from the mold onto serving dishes.

Nutrition Information

- Calories: 227 calories
- Total Carbohydrate: 45g carbohydrate (35g sugars
- Cholesterol: 16mg cholesterol
- Protein: 3g protein.
- Total Fat: 5g fat (3g saturated fat)
- Sodium: 90mg sodium
- Fiber: 1g fiber)

814. Creamy Fruit Mold

Serving: 6 servings. | Prep: 10mins | Cook: 0mins | Ready in:

Ingredients

- 3 ounces cream cheese, softened
- 1 package (3 ounces) lime gelatin
- 1 cup boiling water
- 1/4 cup mayonnaise
- 1 can (15-1/4 ounces) fruit cocktail, drained
- 1/2 cup chopped pecans

Direction

- Mix gelatin with cream cheese in a bowl. Add water; toss until the gelatin is melted. Chill for 1 hour until thickened, tossing regularly. Add mayonnaise, beat until creamy. Mix in pecans and fruit. Put in a grease-coated 1-quart mold. Refrigerate until firm. Remove from the mold onto a serving plate.

Nutrition Information

- Calories: 289 calories
- Fiber: 2g fiber)
- Total Carbohydrate: 28g carbohydrate (26g sugars
- Cholesterol: 19mg cholesterol
- Protein: 4g protein.
- Total Fat: 19g fat (5g saturated fat)
- Sodium: 129mg sodium

815. Creamy Orange Fluff

Serving: 15 servings. | Prep: 15mins | Cook: 0mins | Ready in:

Ingredients

- 1 package (6 ounces) orange gelatin
- 2-1/2 cups boiling water

- 2 cans (11 ounces each) mandarin oranges, drained
- 1 can (8 ounces) crushed pineapple, undrained
- 1 can (6 ounces) frozen orange juice concentrate, thawed
- TOPPING:
- 1 package (8 ounces) cream cheese, softened
- 1 cup cold 2% milk
- 1 package (3.4 ounces) instant vanilla pudding mix

Direction

- Dissolve gelatin in boiling water in a large bowl. Add orange juice concentrate, pineapple, and oranges into the bowl, mix. Grease a 13x9-in dish with cooking spray, and pour the gelatin mixture in; refrigerate until set.
- Whisk cream cheese until smooth in a large bowl. Slowly add pudding mix and milk, whisk until smooth. Pour over orange layer. Refrigerate until completely firm.

Nutrition Information

- Calories: 181 calories
- Sodium: 125mg sodium
- Fiber: 1g fiber)
- Total Carbohydrate: 31g carbohydrate (29g sugars
- Cholesterol: 17mg cholesterol
- Protein: 3g protein.
- Total Fat: 6g fat (3g saturated fat)

816. Creamy Orange Gelatin

Serving: 12 servings (3/4 cup each). | Prep: 20mins | Cook: 0mins | Ready in:

Ingredients

- 4 cups boiling water
- 4 packages (3 ounces each) orange gelatin

- 1 quart vanilla ice cream, softened
- 1-1/2 cups orange juice
- 2 cans (11 ounces each) mandarin oranges, drained
- Orange slices, optional

Direction

- Pour boiling water to gelatin; mix till totally dissolve for 2 minutes. Mix in orange juice and ice cream till blended. Keep chilled in the refrigerator till partially set.
- Fold in oranges. Add to two 6-cup ring molds coated using cooking spray. Keep chilled in the refrigerator till firm or overnight. Unmold to a serving plate. Serve alongside slices of orange if you want.

Nutrition Information

- Calories: 224 calories
- Fiber: 0 fiber)
- Total Carbohydrate: 43g carbohydrate (40g sugars
- Cholesterol: 19mg cholesterol
- Protein: 5g protein.
- Total Fat: 5g fat (3g saturated fat)
- Sodium: 102mg sodium

817. Creamy Orange Salad

Serving: Makes 4 servings. | Prep: 10mins | Cook: | Ready in:

Ingredients

- 2 seedless oranges , peeled, sectioned
- 1 large apple , cored, sliced
- 1/4 cup sliced celery
- 2 Tbsp. sliced black olives
- 1/2 cup KRAFT ROKA Blue Cheese Dressing

Direction

- In a medium bowl, toss olives, celery, apple and oranges.
- Lightly toss in dressing.
- Store in the fridge till ready to eat or for 1 hour. If preferred, place on a plate covered with lettuce to serve.

Nutrition Information

- Calories: 190
- Sugar: 13 g
- Protein: 1 g
- Saturated Fat: 2.5 g
- Fiber: 3 g
- Cholesterol: 5 mg
- Total Fat: 13 g
- Sodium: 340 mg
- Total Carbohydrate: 17 g

818.   Crisp Cranberry Gelatin

Serving: 12 servings. | Prep: 10mins | Cook: 10mins | Ready in:

Ingredients

- 2 cups fresh or frozen cranberries
- 1-1/2 cups water
- 1 cup sugar
- 1 package (3 ounces) orange gelatin
- 1 medium apple, chopped
- 1 celery rib, chopped
- 1/2 cup chopped walnuts
- 1/4 cup orange juice
- 2 teaspoons grated orange zest

Direction

- Boil water and cranberries in a big saucepan. Lower the heat; let it simmer till the berries pop while mixing once in a while or for 3 minutes. Mix in gelatin and sugar till dissolved. Add to an 11x7-in. plate; keep

chilled in the refrigerator till set yet not firm for roughly 60 minutes.
- Mix zest, orange juice, walnuts, celery and apple; mix into gelatin mixture. Keep chilled in the refrigerator till firm.

Nutrition Information

- Calories:
- Total Fat:
- Sodium:
- Fiber:
- Total Carbohydrate:
- Cholesterol:
- Protein:

819.   Cucumber & Grapefruit Mold

Serving: 6 servings. | Prep: 15mins | Cook: 10mins | Ready in:

Ingredients

- 3 large pink grapefruit
- 1 envelope unflavored gelatin
- 1/4 cup cold water
- 2 tablespoons sugar
- 1/8 teaspoon salt
- 1 tablespoon white balsamic vinegar
- 1 cup chopped seeded peeled cucumber
- Leaf lettuce leaves, optional

Direction

- Slice each grapefruit into two; take out the sections, and save the juice. Put the sections aside. Add 1-1/2 cups of water to the juice.
- Drizzle gelatin over cold water in a small bowl; let it sit for 1 minute.
- In the meantime, mix grapefruit juice mixture, salt, and sugar together in a small saucepan. Stir and cook until sugar is melted. Take away from heat; mix in gelatin until fully melted.

Mix in vinegar. Refrigerate for 1 hour until slightly firm.

- Put in grapefruit sections and cucumber. Move to a grease-coated 1-qt. mold. Chill until set.
- Remove from the mold onto a serving dish lined with lettuce if you want.

Nutrition Information

- Calories: 77 calories
- Protein: 2g protein. Diabetic Exchanges: 1 fruit.
- Total Fat: 0 fat (0 saturated fat)
- Sodium: 53mg sodium
- Fiber: 2g fiber)
- Total Carbohydrate: 19g carbohydrate (16g sugars
- Cholesterol: 0 cholesterol

820. Eggnog Molded Salad

Serving: 12 servings. | Prep: 35mins | Cook: 0mins | Ready in:

Ingredients

- 1 teaspoon unflavored gelatin
- 1 can (15-1/4 ounces) sliced pears
- 1 package (6 ounces) lemon gelatin
- 1 cup sour cream
- 3/4 cup eggnog
- 1 can (11 ounces) mandarin oranges, drained
- Orange slices, maraschino cherries and mint leaves, optional

Direction

- Drizzle unflavored gelatin on top of a quarter cup of cold water in a small-sized bowl; let it rest for 60 seconds.
- Drain pears on top of a 2-cup measuring cup, saving the syrup. Pour enough water into the syrup to measure 2 cups; add to a saucepan. Boil; take out of the heat. Put in unflavored gelatin mixture and lemon gelatin; mix till

totally dissolved for 2 minutes. Let it cool down for 15 minutes.

- Mix in eggnog and sour cream till blended well. Keep chilled in the refrigerator till partially set.
- Chop drained pears and oranges into chunks; mix into gelatin mixture. Add to a 6-cup ring mold coated using cooking spray. Keep chilled in the refrigerator while covered, till firm. Serve alongside mint, cherries, and oranges if you want.

Nutrition Information

- Calories:
- Sodium:
- Fiber:
- Total Carbohydrate:
- Cholesterol:
- Protein:
- Total Fat:

821. Festive Cranberry Relish Salad

Serving: 6-8 servings. | Prep: 10mins | Cook: 0mins | Ready in:

Ingredients

- 1 package (3 ounces) strawberry gelatin
- 1 cup boiling water
- 1/2 cup thawed orange juice concentrate
- 1 package (12 ounces) fresh or frozen cranberries, chopped
- 1 medium apple, peeled and chopped
- 1-1/2 cups sugar
- 1/2 cup chopped pecans

Direction

- Dissolve gelatin with boiling water in a large bowl. Stir until completely dissolved. Mix sugar, apple, and cranberries together and add to gelatin mixture. Add pecans and mix. Transfer everything into a 1-1/2-qt. Serving dish. Chill in the fridge overnight or for at least 4 hours before serving.

Nutrition Information

- Calories: 292 calories
- Total Carbohydrate: 62g carbohydrate (58g sugars
- Cholesterol: 0 cholesterol
- Protein: 2g protein.
- Total Fat: 6g fat (0 saturated fat)
- Sodium: 26mg sodium
- Fiber: 3g fiber)

822. Festive Fruit Gelatin

Serving: 12 servings. | Prep: 15mins | Cook: 0mins | Ready in:

Ingredients

- 1 package (.3 ounce) sugar-free lime gelatin
- 3 cups boiling water, divided
- 1 can (8 ounces) unsweetened crushed pineapple, undrained
- 1-1/2 teaspoons unflavored gelatin
- 2 tablespoons cold water
- 1 package (8 ounces) reduced-fat cream cheese
- 1/4 cup fat-free milk
- 2 packages (.3 ounce each) sugar-free strawberry gelatin
- 1 can (14 ounces) jellied cranberry sauce

Direction

- In a small bowl with 1 cup of boiling water, dissolve lime gelatin; mix in pineapple. Add to a 13x9-in. plate coated using cooking spray. Keep chilled in the refrigerator till set yet not firm.
- Drizzle gelatin on top of cold water; let it rest for 60 seconds. Microwave on high setting for

15 seconds. Mix and let rest till gelatin is dissolved totally or for 60 seconds.
- Whip cream cheese in a small-sized bowl till it becomes fluffy. Slowly pour in gelatin mixture and milk; whip till smooth in consistency. Carefully spread on top of lime layer. Keep in the refrigerator till set yet not firm.
- In a big bowl containing the leftover boiling water, dissolve strawberry gelatin. Mix in cranberry sauce till smooth in texture. Keep chilled in the refrigerator till partially set. Carefully spread on top of cream cheese layer. Keep in the refrigerator till firm.

Nutrition Information

- Calories: 122 calories
- Protein: 4g protein. Diabetic Exchanges: 1 starch
- Total Fat: 4g fat (3g saturated fat)
- Sodium: 139mg sodium
- Fiber: 1g fiber)
- Total Carbohydrate: 18g carbohydrate (12g sugars
- Cholesterol: 13mg cholesterol

823. Flavorful Cranberry Gelatin Mold

Serving: 8 servings. | Prep: 10mins | Cook: 0mins | Ready in:

Ingredients

- 2 packages (.3 ounce each) sugar-free raspberry gelatin
- 1-1/2 cups boiling water
- 1 can (20 ounces) unsweetened crushed pineapple, drained
- 1 can (14 ounces) whole-berry cranberry sauce
- 1/2 cup chopped walnuts
- 1/3 cup port wine or red grape juice
- Mint leaves for garnish, optional

Direction

- In boiling water, dissolve gelatin in a big bowl. Mix in wine, walnuts, cranberry sauce and pineapple.
- Add to one 5-cup mold coated using cooking spray. Run a knife through the gelatin mixture to equally distribute the fruit. Keep chilled in the refrigerator till firm, about two and a half hours.
- Unmold to a serving dish. If you want, use mint to decorate.

Nutrition Information

- Calories: 193 calories
- Fiber: 2g fiber)
- Total Carbohydrate: 33g carbohydrate (24g sugars
- Cholesterol: 0 cholesterol
- Protein: 3g protein. Diabetic Exchanges: 1 starch
- Total Fat: 4g fat (0 saturated fat)
- Sodium: 66mg sodium

824. Fluffy Cranberry Delight

Serving: 8-10 servings. | Prep: 20mins | Cook: 0mins | Ready in:

Ingredients

- 4 cups cranberries
- 1-1/2 cups sugar
- 3/4 cup water
- 1 envelope unflavored gelatin
- 1/4 cup lemon juice
- 2 tablespoons orange juice
- 1-1/2 cups heavy whipping cream
- 3 tablespoons confectioners' sugar
- 1 teaspoon vanilla extract

Direction

- Boil water, sugar, and cranberries in a saucepan. Lower the heat and cook until the berries pop. Drain through a sieve or a food mill into a big bowl.
- Mix in orange juice, lemon juice, and gelatin. Let it cool down until the mixture covers the back of a spoon.
- Beat cream until forming soft peaks in a small bowl. Add vanilla and confectioners' sugar, whisk until forming stiff peaks. Fold into the cranberry mixture. Refrigerate until set.

Nutrition Information

- Calories: 273 calories
- Protein: 2g protein.
- Total Fat: 13g fat (8g saturated fat)
- Sodium: 16mg sodium
- Fiber: 2g fiber)
- Total Carbohydrate: 39g carbohydrate (36g sugars
- Cholesterol: 49mg cholesterol

825. Fluffy Cranberry Mousse

Serving: 16-20 servings. | Prep: 15mins | Cook: 0mins | Ready in:

Ingredients

- 1 package (6 ounces) strawberry gelatin
- 1 cup boiling water
- 1 can (20 ounces) crushed pineapple
- 1 can (14 ounces) whole-berry cranberry sauce
- 3 tablespoons lemon juice
- 1 teaspoon grated lemon zest
- 1/2 teaspoon ground nutmeg
- 2 cups sour cream
- 1/2 cup chopped pecans

Direction

- Melt gelatin in boiling water in big bowl. Drain pineapple; put aside pineapple. Add juice into gelatin. Mix nutmeg, zest, lemon juice and cranberry sauce in; chill till mixture thickens. Fold pecans, pineapple and sour cream in; put in oiled 9-cup mold/glass serving bowl. Chill for 2 hours minimum till set.

Nutrition Information

- Calories: 150 calories
- Protein: 2g protein.
- Total Fat: 6g fat (3g saturated fat)
- Sodium: 37mg sodium
- Fiber: 1g fiber)
- Total Carbohydrate: 22g carbohydrate (17g sugars
- Cholesterol: 16mg cholesterol

826.   Fluffy Lime Salad

Serving: 9 servings. | Prep: 15mins | Cook: 0mins | Ready in:

Ingredients

- 1 can (8 ounces) crushed pineapple
- 1 package (3 ounces) lime gelatin
- 3 tablespoons water
- 2 packages (3 ounces each) cream cheese, softened
- 1 cup chopped walnuts
- 1 cup miniature marshmallows
- 1 cup heavy whipping cream, whipped

Direction

- Strain pineapple, saving the juice, and put the pineapple aside. Mix the saved juice, water, and gelatin together in a saucepan. Stir and cook on low heat until the gelatin is melted. Chill for 30 minutes until syrupy.
- Whisk cream cheese until fluffy in a small bowl. Mix in the saved pineapple, marshmallows, walnuts, and gelatin mixture. Tuck in the whipped cream.

- Move to a 1-qt. serving bowl. Put a cover on and chill until set, about 2 hours.

Nutrition Information

- Calories: 276 calories
- Cholesterol: 47mg cholesterol
- Protein: 6g protein.
- Total Fat: 21g fat (9g saturated fat)
- Sodium: 63mg sodium
- Fiber: 1g fiber)
- Total Carbohydrate: 19g carbohydrate (15g sugars

827.   Fluffy Raspberry Salad

Serving: 32-40 servings. | Prep: 10mins | Cook: 0mins | Ready in:

Ingredients

- 3 packages (3 ounces each) raspberry gelatin
- 2 packages (3 ounces each) orange gelatin
- 5 cups boiling water
- 4 packages (10 ounces each) frozen sweetened raspberries
- 1 jar (20 ounces) chunky applesauce
- 3 cups miniature marshmallows
- 2 cups heavy whipping cream, whipped

Direction

- In boiling water, dissolve gelatin. Put in raspberries; mix till thawed. Mix in applesauce. Keep chilled in the refrigerator till set partially.
- Mix in whipped cream and marshmallows. Add to two 13x9-in. plates. Keep in the refrigerator till firm.

Nutrition Information

- Calories: 87 calories
- Cholesterol: 16mg cholesterol

- Protein: 1g protein.
- Total Fat: 4g fat (3g saturated fat)
- Sodium: 16mg sodium
- Fiber: 0 fiber)
- Total Carbohydrate: 12g carbohydrate (10g sugars

828. For Goodness Sakes Salad

Serving: 12-16 servings. | Prep: 15mins | Cook: 0mins | Ready in:

Ingredients

- 1 package (3 ounces) lemon gelatin
- 1 package (3 ounces) lime gelatin
- 1 cup boiling water
- 1 cup evaporated milk
- 1 can (20 ounces) crushed pineapple, undrained
- 1 cup mayonnaise
- 1 cup (8 ounces) 4% cottage cheese
- 1 cup chopped nuts
- 1 tablespoon horseradish sauce

Direction

- Melt the gelatins in boiling water in a big bowl. Let it cool down slightly. Mix in horseradish sauce, nuts, cottage cheese, mayonnaise, pineapple with juice, and milk; toss thoroughly. Refrigerate until partly set. Put in a greased 8-cup mold. Refrigerate for 6 hours or overnight. Remove the mold.

Nutrition Information

- Calories: 252 calories
- Cholesterol: 14mg cholesterol
- Protein: 6g protein.
- Total Fat: 17g fat (3g saturated fat)
- Sodium: 171mg sodium
- Fiber: 1g fiber)

- Total Carbohydrate: 20g carbohydrate (18g sugars

829. Fourth Of July Jell O

Serving: 6-8 servings. | Prep: 15mins | Cook: 0mins | Ready in:

Ingredients

- 1 package (3 ounces) berry blue gelatin
- 2 cups boiling water, divided
- 1/2 cup cold water, divided
- 1 package (3 ounces) strawberry gelatin
- 1 can (15 ounces) pear halves, drained and cubed

Direction

- Melt berry gelatin in 1 cup of boiling water in a big bowl. Mix in 1/4 cup of cold water. Put in a 9x5-inch loaf pan, but do not grease it. Chill until firm. Do the same with the strawberry gelatin and the rest of the boiling and cold water.
- Once the gelatin is set, slice into cubes. In individual dishes or a big glass bowl, lightly mix pears with gelatin cubes right before serving.

Nutrition Information

- Calories: 117 calories
- Sodium: 51mg sodium
- Fiber: 1g fiber)
- Total Carbohydrate: 29g carbohydrate (27g sugars
- Cholesterol: 0 cholesterol
- Protein: 2g protein.
- Total Fat: 0 fat (0 saturated fat)

830. Frankenstein Salads

Serving: 6 servings. | Prep: 20mins | Cook: 0mins | Ready in:

Ingredients

- 2 packages (6 ounces each) lime gelatin
- 2-1/2 cups boiling water
- 3/4 cup bean sprouts
- 12 orange jelly beans
- 6 red jelly beans
- 3 tablespoons sour cream
- 12 miniature marshmallows
- Purple kale, optional

Direction

- Dissolve gelatin in water in a bowl. Transfer gelatin mixture into an 8-inch square pan oiled with cooking spray. Chill until firm for 4 hours. Divide into 6 separate rectangles and put them on a plate. Ornament with a red jelly bean for nose, orange jelly beans for eyes, and bean sprouts for hair. Fill sour cream into a small plastic bag; cut the corner of the bag to make a small hole. Start piping a jagged smile on face. Make bolts by putting marshmallows on side of the head. Decorate more with kale if desired.

Nutrition Information

- Calories:
- Sodium:
- Fiber:
- Total Carbohydrate:
- Cholesterol:
- Protein:
- Total Fat:

831. Frosted Cranberry Gelatin Salad

Serving: 9-12 servings. | Prep: 20mins | Cook: 10mins | Ready in:

Ingredients

- 1 can (8 ounces) crushed pineapple
- 2 packages (3 ounces each) lemon gelatin
- 1 cup ginger ale, chilled
- 1 can (14 ounces) jellied cranberry sauce
- 1/2 cup chopped peeled tart apple
- 1/2 cup chopped celery
- 1 package (8 ounces) cream cheese, softened
- 1/4 cup sugar
- 1 envelope whipped topping mix (Dream Whip)
- 1/2 cup chopped pecans, toasted

Direction

- Strain pineapple and reserve the liquid. Put pineapple to one side. Pour pineapple juice into a measuring cup and add enough water to reach 1 cup. Use a small saucepan to bring the pineapple mixture to a boil. Gradually pour into a large bowl. Add gelatin and stir until completely dissolved. Pour ginger ale in. chill for about 45 minutes until syrupy.
- Mix reserved pineapple, celery, apple, and the cranberry sauce together then fold into the gelatin mix. Pour the mixture into a 9-inch square dish. Chill in the fridge until complete firm.
- Whip cream cheese with sugar in a small bowl until fluffy. Follow the directions to make whipped topping mix; onto cream cheese mixture, fold. Pour over gelatin layer and spread over the surface. Garnish with pecans on top.

Nutrition Information

- Calories: 265 calories
- Sodium: 102mg sodium
- Fiber: 1g fiber)

- Total Carbohydrate: 41g carbohydrate (34g sugars
- Cholesterol: 21mg cholesterol
- Protein: 3g protein.
- Total Fat: 11g fat (5g saturated fat)

832. Frosted Cranberry Salad

Serving: 8 servings. | Prep: 30mins | Cook: 0mins | Ready in:

Ingredients

- 1 can (20 ounces) crushed pineapple
- 1 envelope unflavored gelatin
- 1 package (3 ounces) cherry gelatin
- 1 cup chilled ginger ale
- 1 can (14 ounces) jellied cranberry sauce
- 1 package (8 ounces) cream cheese, softened
- 1 envelope whipped topping mix (Dream Whip)
- 1/2 cup milk
- 1 teaspoon vanilla extract
- 8 pecan halves, toasted
- 8 fresh cranberries

Direction

- Drain pineapple, saving juice to measure 1 cup; put pineapple aside. Add enough water to measure one cup to the juice. Pour into a small-sized saucepan; put in the unflavored gelatin and let it rest for 60 seconds. Boil. Put in cherry gelatin; mix till dissolved. Mix in ginger ale. Add to a bowl. Keep chilled in the refrigerator for half an hour till set partially.
- Mix in the cranberry sauce and pineapple. Pour into one 11x7-in. plate coated using cooking spray. Keep chilled in the refrigerator till set.
- Whip cream cheese till smooth in texture in a big bowl. Whip vanilla, milk, and whipped topping mix on low speed in a small-sized bowl till blended. Whip on high speed till thickened or for 4 minutes. Put into cream

cheese; whip till blended. Spread on top of gelatin. Keep chilled in the refrigerator overnight. Chop into square pieces; use cranberry and a pecan half to decorate each.

Nutrition Information

- Calories:
- Total Fat:
- Sodium:
- Fiber:
- Total Carbohydrate:
- Cholesterol:
- Protein:

833. Frosted Fruit Gelatin Salad

Serving: 9 servings. | Prep: 20mins | Cook: 0mins | Ready in:

Ingredients

- 1 can (15 ounces) blueberries
- 1 can (8 ounces) unsweetened pineapple tidbits
- 1 package (.6 ounce) sugar-free raspberry gelatin
- 2 cups boiling water
- 1 package (8 ounces) fat-free cream cheese, softened
- 1/2 cup fat-free sour cream
- 1/3 cup sugar
- 1/2 teaspoon vanilla extract

Direction

- Strain pineapple and blueberries, saving the juice; set the fruit aside. Melt the gelatin in boiling water in a bowl. Add water to the saved fruit juices to measure 1-1/4 cups, mix into the gelatin. Refrigerate until set partly. Mix in the saved fruit. Put in an 8-inch square plate. Chill until firm.

- Mix sour cream with cream cheese in a bowl. Whisk vanilla with sugar. Gently spread over the gelatin. Chill until serving.

Nutrition Information

- Calories: 125 calories
- Sodium: 191mg sodium
- Fiber: 1g fiber)
- Total Carbohydrate: 25g carbohydrate (0 sugars
- Cholesterol: 3mg cholesterol
- Protein: 6g protein. Diabetic Exchanges: 1 starch
- Total Fat: 1g fat (0 saturated fat)

834. Frosted Gelatin Salad

Serving: 12 servings. | Prep: 20mins | Cook: 0mins | Ready in:

Ingredients

- 2 packages (3 ounces each) orange gelatin
- 2 cups boiling water
- 3/4 cup miniature marshmallows
- 2 cans (15-1/4 ounces each) apricot halves
- 1 can (20 ounces) crushed pineapple, drained
- 1/2 cup sugar
- 3 tablespoons all-purpose flour
- 1 egg, lightly beaten
- 1 teaspoon vanilla extract
- 2 envelopes whipped topping mix (Dream Whip)
- 1/4 cup finely shredded cheddar cheese

Direction

- In boiling water, dissolve gelatin in a big bowl. Put in marshmallows; mix till melted. Drain apricots, saving one cup of juice; put juice aside. Chop apricots; put into gelatin along with pineapple. Add to one 11x7-in. plate. Keep chilled till firm.

- At the same time, mix the flour and sugar in a small-sized saucepan. Mix reserved apricot juice, vanilla, and egg till smooth. Bring to a boil; boil while stirring for 2 minutes. Let it cool down totally.
- Based on the instruction on the package, prepare the whipped topping; mix in cooled juice mixture. Spread on top of gelatin. Drizzle with cheese. Keep chilled for 60 minutes.

Nutrition Information

- Calories:
- Protein:
- Total Fat:
- Sodium:
- Fiber:
- Total Carbohydrate:
- Cholesterol:

835. Frosted Orange Salad

Serving: 12 servings. | Prep: 35mins | Cook: 0mins | Ready in:

Ingredients

- 3 packages (3 ounces each) orange gelatin
- 3 cups boiling water
- 1 can (20 ounces) crushed pineapple
- 3 cups cold water
- 4 medium firm bananas, sliced
- 2-1/2 cups miniature marshmallows
- 1/2 cup sugar
- 1 tablespoon all-purpose flour
- 1 egg, lightly beaten
- 1 package (8 ounces) cream cheese, softened
- 1 cup heavy whipping cream, whipped
- 3/4 cup chopped pecans, toasted
- 1/2 cup sweetened shredded coconut, toasted

Direction

- Melt the gelatin in boiling water in a big bowl. Strain pineapple, saving the juice. Mix pineapple, marshmallows, bananas, and cold water into the gelatin.
- Put in a grease-coated 13x9-in. dish and chill until firm.
- In the meantime, mix flour with sugar in a big saucepan. Mix in the saved pineapple juice until smooth. Boil it over medium heat, stir and cook until bubbly and thickened, about 2 minutes. Lower the heat, stir and cook for another 2 minutes.
- Take away from heat. Mix a small amount of hot filling into the egg, put all back to the pan, tossing nonstop. Lightly boil it, stir and cook for another 2 minutes. Let it cool down.
- Whisk cream cheese until creamy in a big bowl. Mix in cooled filling. Tuck in the whipped cream. Spread over the gelatin (the dish will be full). Use coconut and nuts to drizzle.

Nutrition Information

- Calories: 369 calories
- Sodium: 101mg sodium
- Fiber: 2g fiber)
- Total Carbohydrate: 44g carbohydrate (36g sugars
- Cholesterol: 66mg cholesterol
- Protein: 5g protein.
- Total Fat: 21g fat (11g saturated fat)

---

836. Frosted Pineapple Lemon Gelatin

Serving: 12 servings. | Prep: 20mins | Cook: 10mins | Ready in:

Ingredients

- 1 can (20 ounces) crushed pineapple
- 2 packages (3 ounces each) lemon gelatin
- 2 cups boiling water
- 2 cups ginger ale, chilled
- 2 large firm bananas, sliced
- 1/2 cup sugar
- 2 tablespoons all-purpose flour
- 1 large egg, lightly beaten
- 2 tablespoons butter
- 1 cup heavy whipping cream

Direction

- Drain pineapple, saving the juice; put pineapple aside. In a big bowl containing boiling water, dissolve gelatin. Mix in crushed pineapple, bananas, and ginger ale. Place into a 13x9-in. plate. Keep chilled in the refrigerator till firm.
- To make topping, in a small-sized saucepan, mix flour and sugar. Slowly mix in reserved pineapple juice. Boil on medium heat; cook and stir till thickened or for 2 minutes.
- Take out of the heat. Mix a small amount into egg; bring all back to the pan, mixing continuously. Cook and stir till a thermometer reaches 160 degrees and mixture is thickened. Take out of the heat; mix in butter. Let it cool down to room temperature.
- Whip cream on high speed in a small-sized bowl till it forms stiff peaks. Carefully fold into custard. Spread on top of gelatin. Keep in the refrigerator till chilled or for 60 minutes.

Nutrition Information

- Calories: 250 calories
- Total Fat: 10g fat (6g saturated fat)
- Sodium: 63mg sodium
- Fiber: 1g fiber)
- Total Carbohydrate: 40g carbohydrate (36g sugars
- Cholesterol: 50mg cholesterol
- Protein: 3g protein.

837. Frosted Strawberry Salad

Serving: 16-20 servings. | Prep: 15mins | Cook: 0mins | Ready in:

Ingredients

- 2 packages (6 ounces each) strawberry gelatin
- 3 cups boiling water
- 2 packages (10 ounces each) frozen sweetened sliced strawberries, thawed
- 1 can (20 ounces) crushed pineapple, undrained
- 1 cup chopped pecans
- 1/2 cup chopped maraschino cherries
- TOPPING:
- 1 package (8 ounces) cream cheese, softened
- 1 jar (7 ounces) marshmallow creme
- 1 carton (8 ounces) frozen whipped topping, thawed
- Fresh strawberries and mint

Direction

- In a big bowl with boiling water, dissolve gelatin. Mix in pineapple and strawberries. Keep chilled in the refrigerator till set partially.
- Mix in cherries and pecans. Add into a 13x9-in. plate. Keep chilled for 2 hours or till firm.
- To make the topping, whip marshmallow crème and cream cheese in a small-sized bowl just till combined; fold in whipped topping. Spread on top of salad. Keep chilled for a few hours or overnight. Chop into square pieces. Use mint and strawberries for decoration.

Nutrition Information

- Calories: 216 calories
- Total Fat: 10g fat (5g saturated fat)
- Sodium: 65mg sodium
- Fiber: 1g fiber)
- Total Carbohydrate: 30g carbohydrate (24g sugars
- Cholesterol: 12mg cholesterol
- Protein: 2g protein.

838. Fruit Parfaits

Serving: 4 servings. | Prep: 25mins | Cook: 0mins | Ready in:

Ingredients

- 1 can (15 ounces) fruit cocktail
- 1 package (3 ounces) lemon gelatin
- 8 ice cubes (1-1/2 cups crushed ice)

Direction

- Drain fruit cocktail, saving syrup. Separate fruit between four parfait glasses and put aside. Pour water into the syrup to measure three quarters cup; add to a saucepan. Boil.
- In a blender, add gelatin; pour in syrup gently. Keep it covered and blend on low speed for roughly half a minute till gelatin dissolves. Put in ice; keep it covered and blend for roughly 60 seconds till dissolved. Add on top of the fruit. Keep it covered and let chill in the refrigerator for roughly 15 minutes till set.

Nutrition Information

- Calories: 69 calories
- Protein: 1g protein. Diabetic Exchanges: 1 fruit.
- Total Fat: 0 fat (0 saturated fat)
- Sodium: 53mg sodium
- Fiber: 0 fiber)
- Total Carbohydrate: 16g carbohydrate (0 sugars
- Cholesterol: 0 cholesterol

839. Fruit Filled Raspberry Ring

Serving: 12-16 servings. | Prep: 10mins | Cook: 0mins | Ready in:

Ingredients

- 2 packages (6 ounces each) raspberry gelatin
- 4 cups boiling water
- 1 quart raspberry sherbet
- 1 can (14 ounces) pineapple tidbits, drained
- 1 can (11 ounces) mandarin oranges, drained
- 1 cup sweetened shredded coconut
- 1 cup miniature marshmallows
- 1 cup (8 ounces) sour cream

Direction

- To dissolve gelatin, put it in a big bowl of boiling water. Add in sherbet and mix until melted. Use cooking spray to coat an 8-cup ring mold and pour it in. Let chill until firm or overnight.
- Mix sour cream, marshmallows, coconut, oranges, and pineapple in a big bowl. Put a cover on and let chill. Take gelatin out onto a dish when serving. Place the fruit mixture into the middle of the ring.

Nutrition Information

- Calories: 180 calories
- Total Carbohydrate: 32g carbohydrate (28g sugars
- Cholesterol: 12mg cholesterol
- Protein: 2g protein.
- Total Fat: 5g fat (4g saturated fat)
- Sodium: 68mg sodium
- Fiber: 1g fiber)

840. Fruit Packed Gelatin Salad

Serving: 15 servings. | Prep: 20mins | Cook: 0mins | Ready in:

Ingredients

- 2 packages (.3 ounce each) sugar-free strawberry gelatin
- 2 cups boiling water
- 2 packages (12 ounces each) frozen unsweetened strawberries, thawed and cut in half
- 1 can (20 ounces) unsweetened crushed pineapple
- 3 medium firm bananas, sliced
- 1 package (8 ounces) reduced-fat cream cheese
- 1 cup (8 ounces) fat-free sour cream
- 1/2 cup chopped walnuts, toasted

Direction

- Melt gelatin with boiling water in a large bowl. Add bananas, pineapple, and strawberries, mix. Pour into a 13x9-in. dish covered with cooking spray. Chill while covered until partly firm for about 1 hour.
- Combine sour cream and cream cheese in a small bowl till blended. Pour over gelatin mixture and spread carefully. Cover and chill until set. Garnish with some walnuts before serving.

Nutrition Information

- Calories: 142 calories
- Protein: 5g protein. Diabetic Exchanges: 1 fruit
- Total Fat: 6g fat (2g saturated fat)
- Sodium: 105mg sodium
- Fiber: 2g fiber)
- Total Carbohydrate: 19g carbohydrate (14g sugars
- Cholesterol: 13mg cholesterol

841. Fruited Cranberry Gelatin

Serving: 12-16 servings. | Prep: 20mins | Cook: 0mins | Ready in:

Ingredients

- 1 package (6 ounces) cranberry or raspberry gelatin
- 1/2 cup sugar
- 1-1/2 cups boiling water
- 1 package (12 ounces) cranberries
- 3 medium unpeeled green apples, cut into wedges
- 1 medium navel orange, peeled and quartered
- 1 cup diced celery
- 1 cup chopped pecans
- 1 cup cold water
- 1 tablespoon cider vinegar
- 2 teaspoons grated orange zest
- 1-1/2 teaspoons lemon juice
- 1/2 teaspoon salt
- 3/4 cup mayonnaise
- 2 tablespoons orange juice

Direction

- Melt sugar and gelatin in boiling water in a big bowl. Blend cranberries in a food processor or a blender until coarsely chopped and add to the gelatin mixture. Do the same with orange and apples. Mix in salt, lemon juice, orange zest, vinegar, water, pecans, and celery. Put in a 2 1/2-qt. bowl or 13x9-in. dish. Refrigerate for 3 hours until set.
- Combine orange juice and mayonnaise, serve along with the salad.

Nutrition Information

- Calories: 221 calories
- Sodium: 161mg sodium
- Fiber: 3g fiber)
- Total Carbohydrate: 25g carbohydrate (22g sugars
- Cholesterol: 4mg cholesterol
- Protein: 2g protein.

- Total Fat: 14g fat (2g saturated fat)

842. Fruited Cranberry Salad

Serving: 12 servings. | Prep: 45mins | Cook: 0mins | Ready in:

Ingredients

- 2 cups fresh or frozen cranberries
- 1 medium unpeeled orange, cut into wedges and seeds removed
- Sugar substitute equivalent to 3/4 cup sugar
- 1 package (.3 ounce) sugar-free cherry gelatin
- 1 cup boiling water
- 1 cup seedless red grapes, halved
- 1 cup unsweetened crushed pineapple, drained
- 1/2 cup diced celery
- 1/4 cup finely chopped pecans

Direction

- In a food processor or a blender, mix together the first 3 ingredients. Put the lid on and blend until the fruit is coarsely cut. Let it sit for 30 minutes.
- In the meantime, melt the gelatin in water in a big bowl. Chill until the mixture starts to firm, about 15-20 minutes. Add pecans, celery, pineapple, grapes, and the cranberry mixture. Put on individual plates or a 2-quart serving bowl. Chill for a few hours or overnight.

Nutrition Information

- Calories: 49 calories
- Fiber: 0 fiber)
- Total Carbohydrate: 9g carbohydrate (0 sugars
- Cholesterol: 0 cholesterol
- Protein: 1g protein. Diabetic Exchanges: 1/2 fruit
- Total Fat: 2g fat (0 saturated fat)
- Sodium: 5mg sodium

custard. Spread over the gelatin, use cheese to drizzle. Chill until cold, about 1 hour.

Nutrition Information

- Calories: 242 calories
- Fiber: 1g fiber)
- Total Carbohydrate: 38g carbohydrate (33g sugars
- Cholesterol: 46mg cholesterol
- Protein: 4g protein.
- Total Fat: 10g fat (6g saturated fat)
- Sodium: 91mg sodium

---

843. Fruited Gelatin Salad

Serving: 12-16 servings. | Prep: 30mins | Cook: 0mins | Ready in:

Ingredients

- 2 packages (3 ounces each) orange gelatin
- 2 cups boiling water
- 1 cup apricot nectar
- 1 cup pineapple juice
- 1 can (15 ounces) apricot halves, drained and mashed
- 1 can (8 ounces) crushed pineapple, drained
- 4 cups miniature marshmallows
- TOPPING:
- 1/2 cup sugar
- 2 tablespoons all-purpose flour
- 1/2 cup apricot nectar
- 1/2 cup pineapple juice
- 1 large egg, lightly beaten
- 2 tablespoons butter
- 1 cup heavy whipping cream
- 1 cup shredded cheddar cheese

Direction

- Melt the gelatin in boiling water in a big bowl. Mix in pineapple, apricots, and juices. Move to a cooking spray-coated 13x9-in. plate. Chill until partly set, about 30 minutes. Use marshmallows to drizzle and chill.
- To make the topping, mix flour and sugar together in a saucepan. Slowly stir in juices. Boil it over medium heat, stir and cook until thickened, about 2 minutes. Take away from heat. Mix a small amount into egg, put all back to the pan, tossing nonstop. Stir and cook until the mixture is thickened and a thermometer displays 160°. Take away from heat; mix in butter. Let it cool down to room temperature.
- Whisk cream on high speed in a small bowl until stiff peaks form. Carefully tuck into

---

844. Fruited Lemon Gelatin Salad

Serving: 15-18 servings. | Prep: 30mins | Cook: 0mins | Ready in:

Ingredients

- 1 package (6 ounces) lemon gelatin
- 2 cups boiling water
- 1 can (12 ounces) lemon-lime soda
- 1 can (20 ounces) crushed pineapple
- 1 can (15 ounces) mandarin oranges, drained
- 2 cups halved green grapes
- 1 egg
- 1/2 cup sugar
- 2 tablespoons all-purpose flour
- 1 tablespoon butter
- 1 cup heavy whipping cream, whipped
- Lettuce leaves, optional

Direction

- In boiling water, dissolve gelatin. Mix in soda. Keep chilled till partially set.
- Drain pineapple, saving the juice; put pineapple aside. Pour water into pineapple juice, if needed, to measure 1 cup; put aside. Mix the grapes, oranges and pineapple into

gelatin. Add to a greased 13x9-in. plate. Keep chilled till firm.

- At the same time, on medium heat, in a big saucepan, mix reserved pineapple juice, butter, flour, sugar and egg. Boil; cook and stir till thickened or for 2 minutes. Let it cool down totally. Fold in whipped cream. Spread on top of gelatin. Keep chilled till firm. Chop into square pieces; serve over lettuce if you want.

Nutrition Information

- Calories: 146 calories
- Protein: 2g protein.
- Total Fat: 4g fat (2g saturated fat)
- Sodium: 38mg sodium
- Fiber: 1g fiber)
- Total Carbohydrate: 29g carbohydrate (26g sugars
- Cholesterol: 23mg cholesterol

845.   Fruity Gelatin Salad

Serving: 7 | Prep: | Cook: |Ready in:

Ingredients

- 7 fluid ounces lemon-lime flavored carbonated beverage
- 2 cups miniature marshmallows
- 1 (3 ounce) package lime flavored Jell-O® mix
- 8 ounces cream cheese
- 1 (20 ounce) can crushed pineapple with juice
- 3/4 cup chopped pecans
- 1 teaspoon mayonnaise
- 1 cup frozen whipped topping, thawed

Direction

- Mix marshmallows and carbonated beverage together in a nonreactive saucepan. Heat the pan to dissolve everything, stirring frequently. Stir in gelatin until completely dissolved.

- Add cream cheese and whisk until smooth by hand or with an electric mixer.
- Add whipped topping, nuts, mayonnaise, juice, and pineapple. Transfer into a 7x11 dish. Refrigerate until entirely firm.

Nutrition Information

- Calories: 375 calories;
- Cholesterol: 36
- Protein: 5.2
- Total Fat: 21.9
- Sodium: 170
- Total Carbohydrate: 42.4

846.   Fruity Lime Salad Mold

Serving: 6-8 servings. | Prep: 10mins | Cook: 0mins | Ready in:

Ingredients

- 1 package (3 ounces) lime gelatin
- 1 cup boiling water
- 3 ounces cream cheese, softened
- 1 can (8 ounces) crushed pineapple, undrained
- 1 cup heavy whipping cream, whipped
- 1/4 cup chopped pecans
- 1/4 cup chopped maraschino cherries

Direction

- Melt the gelatin in boiling water in a big bowl and refrigerate until syrupy. Mix pineapple and cream cheese together in a small bowl, mix into the cooled gelatin.
- Put in cherries, pecans, and whipped cream. Put in a cooking spray-coated 4-cup mold. Chill for 3 hours or overnight.

Nutrition Information

- Calories:
- Sodium:

- Fiber:
- Total Carbohydrate:
- Cholesterol:
- Protein:
- Total Fat:

---

847. Fruity Orange Gelatin

Serving: 10-12 servings. | Prep: 20mins | Cook: 0mins | Ready in:

Ingredients

- 1 package (6 ounces) orange gelatin
- 2 cups boiling water
- 2 cups orange sherbet
- 1 can (20 ounces) crushed pineapple, undrained
- 1 can (11 ounces) mandarin oranges, drained

Direction

- Melt the gelatin in water in a bowl. Mix in sherbet until dissolved. Mix in oranges and pineapple. Put in a 2-qt. serving bowl. Refrigerate until firm.

Nutrition Information

- Calories: 77 calories
- Protein: 1g protein. Diabetic Exchanges: 1 fruit.
- Total Fat: 1g fat (0 saturated fat)
- Sodium: 17mg sodium
- Fiber: 0 fiber)
- Total Carbohydrate: 18g carbohydrate (0 sugars
- Cholesterol: 2mg cholesterol

---

848. Fruity Strawberry Gelatin Salad

Serving: 9 servings. | Prep: 10mins | Cook: 0mins | Ready in:

Ingredients

- 1 package (6 ounces) strawberry gelatin
- 1 cup boiling water
- 2 packages (12 ounces each) frozen unsweetened strawberries, thawed
- 2 cans (8 ounces each) unsweetened crushed pineapple, undrained
- 3 medium firm bananas, mashed

Direction

- In a bowl with boiling water, dissolve the gelatin. Mix in bananas, pineapple and strawberries; stir well. Add into a 2-qt. serving bowl. Keep chilled in the refrigerator till firm.

Nutrition Information

- Calories: 82 calories
- Sodium: 55mg sodium
- Fiber: 3g fiber)
- Total Carbohydrate: 19g carbohydrate (0 sugars
- Cholesterol: 0 cholesterol
- Protein: 2g protein. Diabetic Exchanges: 1 fruit.
- Total Fat: 0 fat (0 saturated fat)

---

849. Gelatin Christmas Ornaments

Serving: 1 dozen. | Prep: 20mins | Cook: 0mins | Ready in:

Ingredients

- 3-1/4 cups white grape juice
- 1 package (6 ounces) lime gelatin

- 1 package (6 ounces) raspberry gelatin
- 6 each red and green maraschino cherries with stems
- Mayonnaise, sour cream or whipped cream in a can

Direction

- Boil grape juice in a saucepan. Add lime gelatin to a bowl; pour in 1/2 of the juice and mix till totally dissolved. Repeat with raspberry gelatin. Add lime gelatin to 6 muffin cups (about one third cup in each) coated using cooking spray. Repeat the process, filling 6 more cups with raspberry gelatin. Keep chilled in the refrigerator till firm, about 4 hours.
- Use a sharp knife to loosen gelatin around the edges; invert muffin tin to waxed paper. Add to serving dishes using a metal spatula. Pour in mayonnaise to fill a small-sized plastic bag; cut a small hole in the bag corner. Pipe a small circle close to 1 edge of each ornament; add cherry into the middle. If you want, garnish the ornaments with extra mayonnaise.

Nutrition Information

- Calories: 153 calories
- Protein: 3g protein.
- Total Fat: 0 fat (0 saturated fat)
- Sodium: 68mg sodium
- Fiber: 0 fiber)
- Total Carbohydrate: 37g carbohydrate (37g sugars
- Cholesterol: 0 cholesterol

850.   Gelatin Fruit Salad

Serving: 8 servings. | Prep: 15mins | Cook: 0mins | Ready in:

Ingredients

- 1 cup unsweetened applesauce

- 1 package (.6 ounces) sugar-free cherry gelatin
- 1 can (12 ounces) or 1-1/2 cups diet ginger ale
- 1 can (8 ounces) unsweetened crushed pineapple, undrained
- Apple slices and fresh mint, optional

Direction

- Bring the applesauce in a saucepan to a boil, then take it away from heat.
- Stir in gelatin until dissolved. Put in pineapple and ginger ale gradually. Transfer the mixture into a 2-quart serving bowl. Refrigerate until set. Decorate with apples and mint if wanted.

Nutrition Information

- Calories: 39 calories
- Cholesterol: 0 cholesterol
- Protein: 1g protein. Diabetic Exchanges: 1/2 fruit.
- Total Fat: 0 fat (0 saturated fat)
- Sodium: 66mg sodium
- Fiber: 1g fiber)
- Total Carbohydrate: 8g carbohydrate (6g sugars

851.   Gelatin Ring With Cream Cheese Balls

Serving: 10-12 servings. | Prep: 15mins | Cook: 0mins | Ready in:

Ingredients

- 2 packages (3 ounces each) raspberry gelatin
- 2 cups boiling water
- 2 cans (16 ounces each) whole-berry cranberry sauce
- 1 package (8 ounces) cream cheese
- 1 cup ground walnuts

Direction

- Melt the gelatin in boiling water in a big bowl. Mix in cranberry sauce until well combined. Put in a grease-coated 6-cup ring mold. Chill until firm or overnight.
- Roll cream cheese into 3/4-inch balls and use walnuts to coat. Remove the gelatin from the mold onto a serving dish. Put the cream cheese balls in the middle of the ring.

Nutrition Information

- Calories: 189 calories
- Total Carbohydrate: 22g carbohydrate (16g sugars
- Cholesterol: 21mg cholesterol
- Protein: 3g protein.
- Total Fat: 11g fat (5g saturated fat)
- Sodium: 80mg sodium
- Fiber: 1g fiber)

852. Ginger Pear Gelatin

Serving: 6 servings. | Prep: 5mins | Cook: 0mins |Ready in:

Ingredients

- 1 package (3 ounces) lemon gelatin
- 1 cup boiling water
- 1 cup chilled ginger ale
- 1 can (15-1/4 ounces) pear halves, drained and cubed
- 1 cup halved green grapes

Direction

- In a bowl containing boiling water, dissolve gelatin. Mix in ginger ale. Keep it covered and let chill in the refrigerator till set partially. Mix in pears and grapes. Add to a serving bowl. Keep chilled till set.

Nutrition Information

- Calories: 138 calories
- Total Carbohydrate: 34g carbohydrate (31g sugars
- Cholesterol: 0 cholesterol
- Protein: 2g protein.
- Total Fat: 0 fat (0 saturated fat)
- Sodium: 39mg sodium
- Fiber: 1g fiber)

853. Gingered Lime Gelatin

Serving: 12 servings. | Prep: 10mins | Cook: 0mins | Ready in:

Ingredients

- 1 can (20 ounces) pineapple tidbits
- 1 package (6 ounces) lime gelatin
- 1-1/2 cups boiling water
- 1 cup ginger ale, chilled
- 1/4 teaspoon ground ginger

Direction

- Drain pineapple, saving the juice; put the pineapple aside. In a bowl containing water, dissolve the gelatin. Mix in the reserved juice, ginger and ginger ale. Keep chilled for roughly 45 minutes till it becomes syrupy. Fold in pineapple. Add into a 6-cup mold coated using cooking spray. Keep chilled in the refrigerator till firm. Unmold to a serving platter.

Nutrition Information

- Calories: 21 calories
- Sodium: 37mg sodium
- Fiber: 0 fiber)
- Total Carbohydrate: 4g carbohydrate (0 sugars
- Cholesterol: 0 cholesterol
- Protein: 1g protein.
- Total Fat: 1g fat (0 saturated fat)

854. Golden Gelatin Salad

Serving: 8 servings. | Prep: 10mins | Cook: 0mins | Ready in:

Ingredients

- 1 envelope unflavored gelatin
- 1/4 cup cold water
- 1 can (20 ounces) crushed pineapple
- 1/4 cup sugar
- 1/4 teaspoon salt
- 1/2 cup orange juice
- 1/4 cup vinegar
- 1 cup grated carrots

Direction

- Drizzle gelatin over cold water in a bowl; let it sit for 1 minute. Strain pineapple, saving 1 cup of juice (dispose the rest of juice or save for later use). Set the pineapple aside.
- Boil the saved juice in a saucepan. Take away from heat. Mix in gelatin mixture, salt, and sugar until melted. Add vinegar and orange juice. Chill until partly set, about 2 hours. Tuck in pineapple and carrots. Move to a cooking spray-coated 4-cup mold. Chill until firm. Remove from the mold onto a serving dish.

Nutrition Information

- Calories: 82 calories
- Protein: 1g protein.
- Total Fat: 0 fat (0 saturated fat)
- Sodium: 81mg sodium
- Fiber: 1g fiber)
- Total Carbohydrate: 20g carbohydrate (17g sugars
- Cholesterol: 0 cholesterol

855. Golden Glow Gelatin Mold

Serving: 12-16 servings. | Prep: 15mins | Cook: 0mins | Ready in:

Ingredients

- 2 cans (8 ounces each) crushed pineapple
- 30 large marshmallows
- 1 package (6 ounces) lemon gelatin
- 2 cups boiling water
- 3 ounces cream cheese, softened
- 1 cup cold water
- 1-1/2 cups shredded carrots
- Leaf lettuce and lemon slices, optional

Direction

- Drain pineapple, saving the juice; put the pineapple aside. Mix marshmallows and pineapple juice in a big saucepan; cook and stir on low heat till marshmallows melt. Take out of the heat.
- In boiling water, dissolve gelatin. Put in cream cheese; mix till the mixture is totally blended. Mix in marshmallow mixture and cold water. Keep chilled till partially set. Fold in pineapple and carrots.
- Add to a 6-cup mold coated using cooking spray. Keep chilled in the refrigerator till set. Unmold to a serving plate lined with lettuce if you want. If preferred, use slices of lemon to decorate.

Nutrition Information

- Calories: 113 calories
- Total Fat: 2g fat (1g saturated fat)
- Sodium: 50mg sodium
- Fiber: 0 fiber)
- Total Carbohydrate: 24g carbohydrate (19g sugars
- Cholesterol: 6mg cholesterol
- Protein: 2g protein.

856. Golden Glow Salad

Serving: 6 servings. | Prep: 15mins | Cook: 0mins | Ready in:

Ingredients

- 1 package (3 ounces) orange gelatin
- 1 cup boiling water
- 1 can (8 ounces) crushed pineapple
- 1 tablespoon lemon juice
- Cold water
- 1/4 teaspoon salt, optional
- 3/4 cup finely shredded carrots

Direction

- In a bowl with boiling water, dissolve gelatin. Drain pineapple, saving the juice. Pour in enough cold water and lemon juice to pineapple juice to make 1 cup; put in salt if you want. Mix into gelatin. Keep chilled till set a bit. Mix in carrots and pineapple. Add to an oiled 4-cup mold; keep it covered and chilled till firm. Unmold.

Nutrition Information

- Calories: 35 calories
- Total Fat: 0 fat (0 saturated fat)
- Sodium: 42mg sodium
- Fiber: 0 fiber)
- Total Carbohydrate: 8g carbohydrate (0 sugars)
- Cholesterol: 0 cholesterol
- Protein: 1g protein. Diabetic Exchanges: 1/2 fruit.

857. Grandma's Gelatin Fruit Salad

Serving: 12-15 servings. | Prep: 20mins | Cook: 5mins | Ready in:

Ingredients

- 2 cups boiling water, divided
- 1 package (3 ounces) lemon gelatin
- 2 cups ice cubes, divided
- 1 can (20 ounces) crushed pineapple, liquid drained and reserved
- 1 package (3 ounces) orange gelatin
- 2 cups miniature marshmallows
- 1/2 cup sugar
- 2 tablespoons cornstarch
- 1 cup reserved pineapple juice
- 1 large egg, lightly beaten
- 1 tablespoon butter
- 3 large bananas, sliced
- 1 cup whipped topping
- 1/2 cup finely shredded cheddar cheese

Direction

- Mix lemon gelatin and 1 cup of water in a big bowl. Put in 1 cup of ice cubes, mixing till melted. Mix in pineapple. Add to a 13x9-in. plate coated using cooking spray; keep chilled in the refrigerator till set yet not firm.
- Repeat with the ice, leftover water and orange gelatin. Mix in marshmallows. Add on top of lemon layer; keep chilled in the refrigerator till firm.
- At the same time, mix cornstarch and sugar in a small-sized saucepan. Mix in reserved pineapple juice till smooth in consistency. Cook and stir on medium-high heat till thickened and bubbly. Lower the heat; cook and stir 2 more minutes. Take out of the heat.
- Mix a small amount of hot filling into egg; bring all back to the pan, mixing continuously. Boil gently; cook and stir for 2 more minutes. Take out of the heat; mix in butter. Let it cool down to room temperature, no stirring. Keep in the refrigerator till chilled or for 60 minutes.
- Arrange bananas on top of gelatin. Mix whipped topping into dressing. Spread on top of bananas. Drizzle with cheese.

Nutrition Information

- Calories: 194 calories
- Total Carbohydrate: 40g carbohydrate (35g sugars
- Cholesterol: 20mg cholesterol
- Protein: 3g protein.
- Total Fat: 3g fat (2g saturated fat)
- Sodium: 64mg sodium
- Fiber: 1g fiber)

858. Grandmother's Orange Salad

Serving: 10 servings. | Prep: 20mins | Cook: 0mins | Ready in:

Ingredients

- 1 can (11 ounces) mandarin oranges
- 1 can (8 ounces) crushed pineapple
- Water
- 1 package (6 ounces) orange gelatin
- 1 pint orange sherbet, softened
- 2 bananas, sliced

Direction

- Drain pineapple and oranges, saving their juices. Put pineapple and oranges aside. Pour water into juices to measure 2 cups. Add into a saucepan and boil; add on top of gelatin in a big bowl. Mix till gelatin dissolves. Mix in sherbet till smooth in consistency.
- Keep chilled till set partially while watching carefully. Fold in bananas, pineapple and oranges. Add to an oiled 6-cup mold. Keep chilled till firm.

Nutrition Information

- Calories: 161 calories
- Total Fat: 1g fat (0 saturated fat)
- Sodium: 55mg sodium
- Fiber: 1g fiber)

- Total Carbohydrate: 39g carbohydrate (35g sugars
- Cholesterol: 2mg cholesterol
- Protein: 2g protein.

859. Grapefruit Gelatin

Serving: 30 servings. | Prep: 20mins | Cook: 0mins | Ready in:

Ingredients

- 8 jars (16 ounces each) grapefruit sections
- 1 cup water
- 8 envelopes unflavored gelatin
- 2 cups sugar
- 2 to 3 teaspoons salt
- 1/3 cup lemon juice

Direction

- Drain grapefruit, saving 6 cups of juice; put 4 cups of juice and fruit aside. Mix gelatin, water, and 2 cups of juice in a saucepan; let it rest for 60 seconds. Cook and stir on low heat till gelatin dissolves. Take out of the heat. Put in salt and sugar; mix till dissolved. Put in reserved grapefruit and juice and lemon juice. Add to two 13-in. x 9-in. pans. Keep it covered and let chill in the refrigerator till set.

Nutrition Information

- Calories: 63 calories
- Sodium: 161mg sodium
- Fiber: 0 fiber)
- Total Carbohydrate: 15g carbohydrate (14g sugars
- Cholesterol: 0 cholesterol
- Protein: 2g protein.
- Total Fat: 0 fat (0 saturated fat)

860. Grapefruit Gelatin Molds

Serving: 2-3 servings. | Prep: 10mins | Cook: 10mins | Ready in:

Ingredients

- 1 envelope unflavored gelatin
- 2 tablespoons cold water
- 1/3 cup sugar
- 1/3 cup water
- 1/2 cup grapefruit juice
- 3 tablespoons orange juice
- 4 teaspoons lemon juice

Direction

- Drizzle gelatin on top of cold water in a small-sized bowl; let it rest for 60 seconds. Mix water and sugar in a saucepan; boil. Lower the heat; mix in gelatin till dissolved. Mix in juices; add to three 1/2-cup or one 2-cup mold coated using cooking spray. Keep chilled in the refrigerator till set or for 4 to 5 hours.

Nutrition Information

- Calories: 118 calories
- Total Carbohydrate: 28g carbohydrate (27g sugars
- Cholesterol: 0 cholesterol
- Protein: 2g protein.
- Total Fat: 0 fat (0 saturated fat)
- Sodium: 5mg sodium
- Fiber: 0 fiber)

861. Green Flop Jell O

Serving: 16 servings (3/4 cup each). | Prep: 15mins | Cook: 0mins | Ready in:

Ingredients

- 2 cups lemon-lime soda
- 2 packages (3 ounces each) lime gelatin

- 6 ounces cream cheese, softened
- 2 cups lemon-lime soda, chilled
- 1 carton (12 ounces) frozen whipped topping, thawed

Direction

- Microwave 2 cups of soda on high heat till hot or for 1 to 2 minutes. Pour gelatin and hot soda into a blender; cover up and process till gelatin is dissolved. Put in cream cheese; process till blended.
- Add into a big bowl; mix in chilled soda. Stir in whipped topping. Add to a 3-qt. trifle bowl or glass bowl. Keep chilled in the refrigerator, while covered, till it becomes firm or for 4 hours.

Nutrition Information

- Calories: 159 calories
- Cholesterol: 12mg cholesterol
- Protein: 2g protein.
- Total Fat: 7g fat (6g saturated fat)
- Sodium: 62mg sodium
- Fiber: 0 fiber)
- Total Carbohydrate: 21g carbohydrate (18g sugars

862. Guacamole Mousse With Salsa

Serving: 18-24 servings. | Prep: 30mins | Cook: 0mins | Ready in:

Ingredients

- 3 medium ripe avocados, peeled and pitted
- 4 teaspoons lemon juice
- 3/4 teaspoon chili powder
- 1/4 teaspoon salt
- Pinch white pepper
- 3 plum tomatoes, peeled, seeded and chopped
- 1 cup sour cream

- 1 cup heavy whipping cream
- 1/3 cup mayonnaise
- 4 teaspoons finely chopped onion
- 2 envelopes unflavored gelatin
- 1/4 cup cold water
- 3 tablespoons minced fresh cilantro
- SALSA:
- 5 plum tomatoes, seeded and diced
- 2 medium sweet red peppers, diced
- 1 to 2 medium jalapeno peppers, seeded and minced
- 1/4 cup finely chopped onion
- 4 teaspoons lime juice
- 4 teaspoons olive oil
- 1/8 to 1/4 teaspoon salt

Direction

- Cover then process avocados, lemon juice, pepper, salt and chili powder in a food processor until smooth. Put in a bowl; pour tomatoes, onion, cream, sour cream and mayonnaise.
- Sprinkle gelatin on cold water in a small saucepan; allow to stand for 1 minute. Cook on low heat, and stir until gelatin is dissolved. Pour in avocado mixture, stir. Add the mixture in a 6-cup mold greased with cooking spray; sprinkle cilantro. Cool down until set.
- At the same time, mix salsa ingredients; keep chilled. When serving, unmold mousse onto a platter; best served with salsa.

Nutrition Information

- Calories: 132 calories
- Sodium: 69mg sodium
- Fiber: 2g fiber)
- Total Carbohydrate: 4g carbohydrate (2g sugars
- Cholesterol: 21mg cholesterol
- Protein: 2g protein.
- Total Fat: 12g fat (4g saturated fat)

863.   Hidden Pear Salad

Serving: 6-8 servings. | Prep: 15mins | Cook: 0mins | Ready in:

Ingredients

- 1 can (16 ounces) pears, liquid drained and reserved
- 1 package (3 ounces) lime gelatin
- 3 ounces cream cheese, softened
- 1/4 teaspoon lemon juice
- 1 envelope whipped topping mix (Dream Whip)
- Lettuce leaves

Direction

- Boil pear liquid in a saucepan. Mix in gelatin till dissolved. Take out of the heat; let it cool down at room temperature till it becomes syrupy. At the same time, in the blender, puree pears.
- Whip lemon juice and cream cheese in a bowl till fluffy and smooth in consistency. Put in pureed pears and stir well. Based on instruction on the package, prepare whipped topping; fold into pear mixture. Fold in cooled gelatin.
- Add to a 4-1/2-cup mold coated using cooking spray. Keep chilled overnight. Just prior to serving, unmold salad to a platter lined with lettuce.

Nutrition Information

- Calories: 139 calories
- Total Carbohydrate: 22g carbohydrate (22g sugars
- Cholesterol: 12mg cholesterol
- Protein: 2g protein.
- Total Fat: 5g fat (3g saturated fat)
- Sodium: 60mg sodium
- Fiber: 0 fiber)

864. Holiday Cranberry Gelatin Salad

Serving: 12 servings. | Prep: 30mins | Cook: 0mins | Ready in:

Ingredients

- 2 packages (3 ounces each) raspberry gelatin
- 2 cups boiling water, divided
- 1 can (14 ounces) whole-berry cranberry sauce
- 2 tablespoons lemon juice
- 1 cup heavy whipping cream
- 1 package (8 ounces) cream cheese, softened
- 1/2 cup chopped pecans

Direction

- In one cup of boiling water in a small bowl, dissolve gelatin. Mix leftover water, and cranberry sauce in a separate bowl; put in lemon juice and gelatin mixture. Add to a 13x9-in. plate coated using cooking spray; let chill in the refrigerator for roughly 60 minutes till firm.
- Whip cream in a big bowl till it forms stiff peaks. Whip cream cheese in a separate bowl till smooth in consistency. Mix in half cup of whipped cream; fold in the leftover whipped cream. Spread on top of gelatin mixture; drizzle with pecans. Keep chilled in the refrigerator for no less than 2 hours.

Nutrition Information

- Calories: 241 calories
- Total Carbohydrate: 28g carbohydrate (22g sugars
- Cholesterol: 34mg cholesterol
- Protein: 3g protein.
- Total Fat: 14g fat (7g saturated fat)
- Sodium: 100mg sodium
- Fiber: 1g fiber)

865. Holiday Cranberry Salad

Serving: 8 | Prep: 15mins | Cook: | Ready in:

Ingredients

- 1 (12 ounce) package fresh or frozen cranberries, coarsely chopped
- 1 (20 ounce) can crushed pineapple, with juice
- 2 cups white sugar
- 1/2 pint heavy whipping cream
- 1 cup chopped walnuts
- 2 cups miniature marshmallows

Direction

- Mix sugar, pineapple and its juice and cranberries in a big bowl. Let it rest for roughly 60 minutes, to let sugar dissolves, and then add the mixture to a strainer set over a bowl. Let drain, while covered, in the refrigerator for no less than 2 hours or overnight. The drippings mixed with lime-lemon soda can make the cranberry so great.
- Prior to serving, beat the cream till it forms soft peaks. If you want, sweeten the whipped cream by adding in a bit of sugar. Mix marshmallows, walnuts and cranberry mixture in a big bowl. Fold in the whipped cream and keep in the refrigerator till serving.

Nutrition Information

- Calories: 498 calories;
- Protein: 3.3
- Total Fat: 20.7
- Sodium: 29
- Total Carbohydrate: 79.2
- Cholesterol: 41

866. Holiday Gelatin Mold

Serving: 16 servings. | Prep: 02hours00mins | Cook: 0mins | Ready in:

Ingredients

- 1 can (8 ounces) sliced pineapple
- 1 package (3 ounces) lime gelatin
- 4 cups boiling water,divided
- 2 tablespoons lemon juice
- 1 package (3 ounces) lemon gelatin
- 6 ounces cream cheese, softened
- 1/3 cup mayonnaise
- 1 package (3 ounces) raspberry gelatin
- 2 medium firm bananas

Direction

- Drain pineapple, saving the juice. In one cup of boiling water in a bowl, dissolve the lime gelatin. Combine enough cold water, lemon juice and pineapple juice to measure 1 cup; pour into dissolved gelatin. Halve slices of pineapple; arrange over the bottom of a 12-cup ring mold coated using cooking spray.
- Add a small amount of lime gelatin on top of the pineapple; keep chilled in the refrigerator till set. Put in the leftover lime gelatin; keep chilled in the refrigerator till firm. In one cup of boiling water in a small bowl, dissolve lemon gelatin. Keep chilled in the refrigerator till set partially. Whip till it becomes fluffy and light.
- Whip cream cheese in a separate small bowl till fluffy. Mix in the mayonnaise. Fold in whipped gelatin; add on top of lime layer. Keep chilled in the refrigerator till firm.
- In the leftover boiling water, dissolve the raspberry gelatin. Slice bananas; add on top of lemon layer. Scoop gently the raspberry gelatin on top of bananas. Keep chilled in the refrigerator till firm or overnight.

Nutrition Information

- Calories: 131 calories
- Fiber: 0 fiber)
- Total Carbohydrate: 19g carbohydrate (18g sugars
- Cholesterol: 8mg cholesterol
- Protein: 2g protein.

- Total Fat: 6g fat (2g saturated fat)
- Sodium: 78mg sodium

867. Holiday Gelatin Salad

Serving: 12 servings (3/4 cup topping). | Prep: 25mins | Cook: 0mins |Ready in:

Ingredients

- 1 package (.3 ounce) sugar-free lemon gelatin
- 1 package (.3 ounce) sugar-free strawberry gelatin
- 1 package (.3 ounce) sugar-free cherry gelatin
- 1-3/4 cups boiling water
- 1 can (20 ounces) unsweetened crushed pineapple
- 1 can (14 ounces) whole-berry cranberry sauce
- 1 medium navel orange, peeled and sectioned
- 3/4 cup reduced-fat whipped topping
- 1/4 cup fat-free sour cream

Direction

- Melt the gelatins in boiling water in a big bowl. Strain the pineapple, use a 2-cup measuring cup to save the juice, add cold water to measure 2 cups. Mix in the gelatin mixture.
- In a food processor, add orange, cranberry sauce, and pineapple, put the lid on and pulse until combined. Mix into the gelatin mixture. Move to a grease-coated 8-cup ring mold. Chill until firm.
- Mix sour cream with whipped topping in a small bowl. Remove the gelatin from the mold and enjoy with topping.

Nutrition Information

- Calories: 105 calories
- Protein: 1g protein. Diabetic Exchanges: 1 fruit
- Total Fat: 1g fat (1g saturated fat)
- Sodium: 62mg sodium

- Fiber: 1g fiber)
- Total Carbohydrate: 24g carbohydrate (16g sugars
- Cholesterol: 1mg cholesterol

868.   Holiday Ribbon Gelatin

Serving: 12-15 servings. | Prep: 40mins | Cook: 0mins | Ready in:

Ingredients

- 2 packages (3 ounces each) lime gelatin
- 5 cups boiling water, divided
- 4 cups cold water, divided
- 1 package (3 ounces) lemon gelatin
- 1/2 cup miniature marshmallows
- 1 package (8 ounces) cream cheese, softened
- 1 cup mayonnaise
- 1 can (8 ounces) crushed pineapple, undrained
- 2 packages (3 ounces each) cherry gelatin

Direction

- Melt lime gelatin in 2 cups of boiling water in a big bowl. Add 2 cups of cold water and toss. Put in a 13-inch x 9-inch plate, chill for 1 hour until firm but not set.
- Melt lemon gelatin in 1 cup of boiling water in a big bowl. Mix in marshmallows until dissolved. Cool for 20 minutes. Whisk mayonnaise and cream cheese together in a small bowl until creamy. Slowly whisk in lemon gelatin. Mix in pineapple. Gently put on the lime layer. Refrigerate until firm but not set.
- Melt cherry gelatin in 2 cups of boiling water. Add the rest of the cold water and mix. Put on the lemon layer. Chill the whole gelatin salad overnight. For serving, slice into squares.

Nutrition Information

- Calories: 236 calories

- Total Carbohydrate: 19g carbohydrate (18g sugars
- Cholesterol: 22mg cholesterol
- Protein: 3g protein.
- Total Fat: 17g fat (5g saturated fat)
- Sodium: 164mg sodium
- Fiber: 0 fiber)

869.   Igloo Salad

Serving: 6 servings. | Prep: 30mins | Cook: 0mins | Ready in:

Ingredients

- 1 can (15-1/4 ounces) fruit cocktail, drained
- 1 can (11 ounces) mandarin oranges, drained
- 1/2 cup sweetened shredded coconut
- 1-3/4 cups whipped topping, divided
- 2-1/2 cups miniature marshmallows, divided

Direction

- Mix 1/2 cup marshmallows, 1 cup whipped topping, coconut, oranges, and the fruit cocktail together in a bowl. Use a spoon to form into 2 balls, one is 3-1/2 in, and the other one is 5-1/2 in.
- Place the smaller ball in front of the bigger one on a serving plate. Make a doorway by distributing some salad from the smaller ball. Cover with the remaining marshmallows and whipped topping.

Nutrition Information

- Calories: 248 calories
- Protein: 1g protein.
- Total Fat: 6g fat (6g saturated fat)
- Sodium: 38mg sodium
- Fiber: 1g fiber)
- Total Carbohydrate: 47g carbohydrate (38g sugars
- Cholesterol: 0 cholesterol

870. Jazzy Gelatin

Serving: 12 servings. | Prep: 10mins | Cook: 0mins | Ready in:

Ingredients

- 1 package (6 ounces) orange gelatin
- 2 cups boiling water
- 1 cup ice cubes
- 1 can (15 ounces) mandarin oranges, drained
- 1 can (8 ounces) unsweetened crushed pineapple, undrained
- 1 can (6 ounces) frozen orange juice concentrate, thawed
- Green grapes and fresh mint, optional

Direction

- Use boiling water to dissolve gelatin in a large bowl. Combine it with orange juice concentrate, pineapple, oranges and ice cubes. Coat with cooking-spray a 6-cup ring mold and pour in the mixture. Put it into the refrigerator until firm or overnight.
- Take it out of the mold and transfer to a plate before serving. Add grapes into the center and use mint to decorate if you want.

Nutrition Information

- Calories: 107 calories
- Fiber: 1g fiber)
- Total Carbohydrate: 26g carbohydrate (25g sugars
- Cholesterol: 0 cholesterol
- Protein: 2g protein.
- Total Fat: 0 fat (0 saturated fat)
- Sodium: 35mg sodium

871. Jiggly Applesauce

Serving: 8 servings. | Prep: 10mins | Cook: 0mins | Ready in:

Ingredients

- 2 cups boiling water
- 1/4 cup Red Hots, crushed
- 2 packages (3 ounces each) strawberry gelatin
- 2 cups cold unsweetened applesauce
- Finely chopped fresh strawberries, optional

Direction

- Put crushed Red Hots and boiling water into the gelatin. Stir to dissolve candy and gelatin completely, about 2 mins. Stir in the cold applesauce. Transfer to an 8 inches square dish or individual serving glasses. Place in the refrigerator for 120 mins or until firm. Enjoy with the finely chopped strawberries, if desired.

Nutrition Information

- Calories: 130 calories
- Sodium: 50mg sodium
- Fiber: 1g fiber)
- Total Carbohydrate: 32g carbohydrate (29g sugars
- Cholesterol: 0 cholesterol
- Protein: 2g protein.
- Total Fat: 0 fat (0 saturated fat)

872. Layered Berry Gelatin Salad

Serving: 15 servings. | Prep: 20mins | Cook: 5mins | Ready in:

Ingredients

- 1 package (.3 ounce) sugar-free raspberry gelatin

- 1 cup boiling water
- 1 can (14 ounces) jellied cranberry sauce
- CREAM LAYER:
- 1 envelope unflavored gelatin
- 1/2 cup cold water
- 2 cups (16 ounces) reduced-fat sour cream
- 1 teaspoon vanilla extract
- 1 cup reduced-fat whipped topping
- ORANGE LAYER:
- 2 cans (11 ounces each) mandarin oranges
- 1 package (.3 ounce) sugar-free orange gelatin
- 1 cup boiling water

Direction

- Let raspberry dissolve in a small bowl of boiling water. Add cranberry sauce then stir till blended. Coat a 13x9-inch dish with cooking spray then move the mixture into it. Store in the fridge for 45 minutes till set but not firm.
- To make cream layer: Drizzle gelatin over cold water in a small saucepan. Leave to stand for 1 minute. Heat and stir over low heat till gelatin dissolves completely. Let cool to room temperature.
- Combine vanilla and sour cream in a small bowl. Fold in the gelatin mixture first then whipped topping next. Gently spread over the cranberry layer. Store in the fridge for 45 minutes till set but not firm.
- Drain the oranges and save up 1 cup of syrup; put oranges aside. Let orange gelatin dissolve in a small bowl of boiling water. Add in the reserved syrup and stir. Store in fridge for 45 minutes till slightly thickened. Add in oranges and stir. Carefully place over the sour cream layer. Store in the fridge, covered for 8 hours or overnight.

Nutrition Information

- Calories: 129 calories
- Protein: 3g protein. Diabetic Exchanges: 1-1/2 starch
- Total Fat: 3g fat (3g saturated fat)
- Sodium: 58mg sodium

- Fiber: 1g fiber)
- Total Carbohydrate: 21g carbohydrate (16g sugars
- Cholesterol: 11mg cholesterol

873.   Layered Christmas Gelatin

Serving: 10 servings. | Prep: 30mins | Cook: 0mins | Ready in:

Ingredients

- 1 package (3 ounces) lime gelatin
- 1 cup boiling water
- 1/3 cup unsweetened pineapple juice
- 1 cup crushed pineapple, drained
- CREAM CHEESE LAYER:
- 1 teaspoon unflavored gelatin
- 2 tablespoons cold water
- 1 package (8 ounces) cream cheese, softened
- 1/3 cup milk
- BERRY LAYER:
- 2 packages (3 ounces each) strawberry gelatin
- 2 cups boiling water
- 1 can (14 ounces) whole-berry cranberry sauce
- Optional ingredients: thawed whipped topping, lime wedges and fresh strawberries

Direction

- Let lime gelatin dissolve in boiling water. Add in pineapple juice and stir. Transfer into an 11x7-inch dish then store in the fridge till set.
- Drizzle over cold water in a small saucepan with unflavored gelatin and allow to stand for 1 minute. Over low heat, heat and stir till gelatin completely dissolves. Move to a small bowl then beat in milk and cream cheese till smooth. Pour over lime layer then store in the fridge till set.
- Let strawberry gelatin dissolve in boiling water. Add in cranberry sauce and stir. Let cool for 10 minutes. Spread carefully over

cream cheese layer and store in the fridge till set.

- Slice into squares. Add fresh strawberries, lime wedges and whipped topping (if preferred). Serve.

Nutrition Information

- Calories: 267 calories
- Cholesterol: 26mg cholesterol
- Protein: 5g protein.
- Total Fat: 8g fat (5g saturated fat)
- Sodium: 139mg sodium
- Fiber: 1g fiber)
- Total Carbohydrate: 46g carbohydrate (39g sugars

874. Layered Cranberry Gelatin Salad

Serving: 12 servings. | Prep: 20mins | Cook: 0mins | Ready in:

Ingredients

- CRANBERRY LAYER:
- 1 package (3 ounces) cranberry or raspberry gelatin
- 1 cup boiling water
- 1 can (14 ounces) whole-berry cranberry sauce
- LEMON LAYER:
- 1 package (3 ounces) lemon gelatin
- 1 cup boiling water
- 3 ounces cream cheese, softened
- 1/3 cup mayonnaise
- 1 can (8 ounces) crushed pineapple, undrained
- 1/2 cup heavy whipping cream, whipped
- 1 cup miniature marshmallows
- 2 tablespoons chopped pecans

Direction

- Let cranberry gelatin dissolve in a small bowl of boiling water. Add in cranberry sauce and

stir till blended. Move to an 8-inch square dish. Store in the fridge till set.

- Let lemon gelatin dissolve in another bowl of boiling water. Beat mayonnaise and cream cheese till smooth. Add into lemon gelatin with pineapple then stir. Store in the fridge for 2 hours till slightly thickened.
- Fold pecans, marshmallows and cream into the cream cheese mixture. Pour over the cranberry layer. Store in the fridge till set for 4 hours.

Nutrition Information

- Calories: 239 calories
- Total Fat: 12g fat (5g saturated fat)
- Sodium: 100mg sodium
- Fiber: 1g fiber)
- Total Carbohydrate: 32g carbohydrate (26g sugars
- Cholesterol: 24mg cholesterol
- Protein: 2g protein.

875. Layered Gelatin Salad

Serving: 8-10 servings. | Prep: 15mins | Cook: 10mins | Ready in:

Ingredients

- 1 package (3 ounces) lemon gelatin
- 2-1/2 cups boiling water, divided
- 2 cans (8 ounces each) crushed pineapple
- 1 package (8 ounces) cream cheese, softened
- 1/4 cup mayonnaise
- 1/4 cup whipped topping
- 1 envelope envelope unflavored gelatin
- 3/4 cup cold water, divided
- 1 package (3 ounces) lime gelatin

Direction

- In a bowl with 1-1/2 cups of boiling water, let the lemon gelatin dissolve. Drain the pineapple; keep 2/3 cup of juice and put the juice aside. Add pineapple into gelatin; stir. Transfer to a 2 quart glass bowl. Store in the fridge till firm, covered.

- Combine whipped topping, mayonnaise and cream cheese in a small bowl then put aside. Drizzle 1/4 cup of cold water with unflavored gelatin. Leave to for 1 minute t stand. Boil the reserved pineapple juice in a small saucepan. Add in the dissolved unflavored gelatin then stir. Mix well into the cream cheese mixture. Pour over the chilled lemon layer carefully. Store in the fridge till firm.

- Let lime gelatin dissolve in the leftover boiling water in a small bowl. Add in the leftover cold water then stir. Chill till it sets partially. Use a portable mixer to beat till foamy. Spread over the layer of cream cheese. Store in the fridge for 3 hours or overnight till firm.

Nutrition Information

- Calories: 206 calories
- Sodium: 137mg sodium
- Fiber: 0 fiber)
- Total Carbohydrate: 20g carbohydrate (20g sugars
- Cholesterol: 27mg cholesterol
- Protein: 4g protein.
- Total Fat: 13g fat (6g saturated fat)

876. Layered Orange Gelatin

Serving: 10 servings. | Prep: 15mins | Cook: 0mins | Ready in:

Ingredients

- 2 packages (.3 ounce each) sugar-free orange gelatin
- 2 cups boiling water
- 1 can (15 ounces) mandarin oranges
- 3 ounces reduced-fat cream cheese, cubed
- 1 pint orange sherbet, softened

- 1-1/2 cups reduced-fat whipped topping

Direction

- Let gelatin dissolve in a bowl of boiling water. Drain and put oranges aside; reserve the juice. Add juice in to gelatin and stir. Beat in cream cheese till smooth. Add in whipped topping and sherbet; stir. Use cooking spray to coat a 6-cup ring mold then pour in the salad. Place oranges on top. Cover and store in the fridge overnight.

Nutrition Information

- Calories: 125 calories
- Fiber: 0 fiber)
- Total Carbohydrate: 20g carbohydrate (0 sugars
- Cholesterol: 20mg cholesterol
- Protein: 2g protein. Diabetic Exchanges: 1 starch
- Total Fat: 4g fat (3g saturated fat)
- Sodium: 90mg sodium

877. Lime Chiffon Jell O

Serving: 12 servings. | Prep: 25mins | Cook: 0mins | Ready in:

Ingredients

- 1 package (3 ounces) lime gelatin
- 1/4 cup sugar
- 1 cup boiling water
- 1 can (12 ounces) evaporated milk
- 3/4 cup graham cracker crumbs
- 3 tablespoons butter, melted

Direction

- Into a bowl, add sugar and gelatin. Pour boiling water into gelatin mixture; mix for 2 minutes to dissolve totally. Keep chilled in the refrigerator for roughly half an hour till it becomes very thick.

- At the same time, into a bowl, add mixer beaters and milk. Freeze for roughly half an hour till ice crystals form around bowl's edge. Whip milk on high speed till fluffy and light. During whipping process, add in thickened jello mixture; whip on high speed till it forms soft peak.
- Add to an 11x7-in. plate. Whisk butter and cracker crumbs; scatter over the top. Keep chilled in the refrigerator for no less than 4 hours prior to serving with the cover on.

Nutrition Information

- Calories:
- Protein:
- Total Fat:
- Sodium:
- Fiber:
- Total Carbohydrate:
- Cholesterol:

Nutrition Information

- Calories: 329 calories
- Sodium: 293mg sodium
- Fiber: 1g fiber)
- Total Carbohydrate: 52g carbohydrate (43g sugars
- Cholesterol: 8mg cholesterol
- Protein: 10g protein.
- Total Fat: 9g fat (8g saturated fat)

---

878. **Lime Delight**

Serving: 2 servings. | Prep: 10mins | Cook: 0mins | Ready in:

Ingredients

- 1 can (8 ounces) crushed pineapple, undrained
- 1/4 cup lime gelatin powder
- 1/2 cup cream-style cottage cheese
- 1 cup whipped topping

Direction

- Boil pineapple over medium heat in a small saucepan. Take away from heat, mix in gelatin until melted. Refrigerate for 30 minutes until slightly thickened. Mix in whipped topping and cottage cheese. Put a cover on and chill until thickened.

---

879. **Lime Gelatin Salad**

Serving: 9 | Prep: | Cook: | Ready in:

Ingredients

- 1 (6 ounce) package lime flavored Jell-O® mix
- 1 1/2 cups boiling water
- 1 (8 ounce) package cream cheese
- 1 (20 ounce) can crushed pineapple with juice
- 2 cups heavy whipping cream
- 1 cup chopped pecans

Direction

- In a big bowl, add 1 boiling water cup on the gelatin mix. Mix it till dissolved. Pour in half a cup of pineapple juice. Add it into the refrigerator to partially gel. It is essential that the gelatin is just partially gelled.
- At the same time, in a small saucepan, cook pineapple till it boils. Let it cook for roughly 5 minutes. Let it cool down to room temperature.
- Once the gelatin is partially gelled, mix the softened cream cheese into it till it becomes creamy. Mix in the cooled, cooked pineapple.
- Beat the cream till fluffy. Mix it into the gelatin-cream cheese mixture. Mix the nuts into the gelatin mixture. Add all of it to a pretty crystal bowl and put it in the fridge to gel totally.

Nutrition Information

- Calories: 458 calories;
- Total Fat: 37
- Sodium: 179
- Total Carbohydrate: 29.7
- Cholesterol: 100
- Protein: 6

---

880. Lime Pear Salad

Serving: 6-8 servings. | Prep: 20mins | Cook: 0mins | Ready in:

Ingredients

- 3 ounces cream cheese, softened
- 1 package (3 ounces) lime gelatin
- 1 can (16 ounces) pear halves
- 2 cups vanilla ice cream, softened

Direction

- Whip gelatin and cream cheese till smooth in texture in a bowl. Drain pears, saving syrup; put pears aside. Pour in enough water into syrup to measure 1 cup if needed.
- Boil syrup in a small saucepan. Slowly pour into gelatin mixture, whipping till smooth in consistency. Mix in ice cream till dissolved. Smash pears and fold into gelatin mixture. Add to one greased 6-cup mold. Keep chilled till firm.

Nutrition Information

- Calories: 184 calories
- Total Fat: 7g fat (5g saturated fat)
- Sodium: 85mg sodium
- Fiber: 1g fiber)
- Total Carbohydrate: 28g carbohydrate (24g sugars
- Cholesterol: 26mg cholesterol
- Protein: 3g protein.

---

881. Lime Sherbet Molded Salad

Serving: 16 servings. | Prep: 20mins | Cook: 0mins | Ready in:

Ingredients

- 2 packages (3 ounces each) lime gelatin
- 2 cups boiling water
- 2 pints lime sherbet, softened
- 1 carton (8 ounces) whipped topping, thawed

Direction

- In a big bowl with boiling water, dissolve gelatin. Mix in sherbet till well blended. Keep chilled till it becomes syrupy.
- Scoop whipped topping to a big bowl. Slowly whip in the gelatin mixture on low speed till well blended. Add to a 12-cup mold coated using cooking spray. Keep chilled in the refrigerator till set or for 6 to 8 hours.

Nutrition Information

- Calories: 110 calories
- Total Fat: 3g fat (3g saturated fat)
- Sodium: 29mg sodium
- Fiber: 0 fiber)
- Total Carbohydrate: 19g carbohydrate (15g sugars
- Cholesterol: 2mg cholesterol
- Protein: 1g protein.

---

882. Lime Strawberry Surprise

Serving: 8-10 servings. | Prep: 20mins | Cook: 0mins | Ready in:

Ingredients

- 1 package (3 ounces) lime gelatin

- 1 can (8 ounces) crushed pineapple, drained
- 1 package (8 ounces) cream cheese, softened
- 1/2 cup mayonnaise
- 1/2 cup chopped pecans
- 1 package (3 ounces) cherry or strawberry gelatin

Direction

- Based on the instructions on the package, prepare the lime gelatin. Keep chilled in the refrigerator for roughly 60 minutes till partially set. Mix in pineapple. Add to an 8-cup bowl or mold coated using cooking spray. Keep it covered and let chill in the refrigerator for roughly 3 hours till firm.
- Whip mayonnaise and cream cheese in a small-sized bowl till smooth in consistency; mix in pecans. Spread on top of lime gelatin. Keep chilled in the refrigerator for roughly 2 hours till firm.
- Based on the instructions on the package, prepare strawberry gelatin; let it cool down a bit. Gently scoop on top of cheese layer. Keep chilled in the refrigerator for roughly 3 hours or overnight, till firm.

Nutrition Information

- Calories: 276 calories
- Total Carbohydrate: 20g carbohydrate (18g sugars
- Cholesterol: 29mg cholesterol
- Protein: 4g protein.
- Total Fat: 21g fat (7g saturated fat)
- Sodium: 166mg sodium
- Fiber: 1g fiber)

883.   Lime Pear Gelatin Bells

Serving: 12 servings. | Prep: 15mins | Cook: 0mins | Ready in:

Ingredients

- 2 packages (3 ounces each) lime gelatin
- 2 cups boiling water
- 2 cans (15-1/4 ounces each) sliced or halved pears, drained
- 12 ounces whipped cream cheese
- 1 cup heavy whipping cream, whipped
- Leaf lettuce
- 6 maraschino cherries, halved

Direction

- In a bowl with boiling water, dissolve gelatin. Add pears into a food processor or a blender; keep it covered and process till smooth in consistency. Put in cream cheese; process till smooth in consistency. Put to gelatin and mix well. Keep chilled in the refrigerator for roughly 15 minutes till cool.
- Fold in the whipped cream. Add to 12 individual bell-shaped molds or other molds coated using cooking spray. Keep in the refrigerator till firm. Unmold to dishes lined with lettuce. Add a cherry piece at the end of each bell for clapper.

Nutrition Information

- Calories: 242 calories
- Cholesterol: 61mg cholesterol
- Protein: 3g protein.
- Total Fat: 17g fat (11g saturated fat)
- Sodium: 157mg sodium
- Fiber: 0 fiber)
- Total Carbohydrate: 21g carbohydrate (21g sugars

884.   Luau Centerpiece

Serving: 1 centerpiece. | Prep: 20mins | Cook: 0mins | Ready in:

Ingredients

- 4 packages (3 ounces each) berry blue gelatin
- 3 cups boiling water

- 3 cups cold water
- 2 medium unpeeled potatoes
- 4 medium carrots
- 4 medium green peppers
- Strawberries, grapes, and chunks of honeydew, cantaloupe, star fruit and pineapple
- 1 whole pineapple

Direction

- Dissolve gelatin in boiling water in a large bowl. Add cold water and stir. Pour the gelatin mixture into an 8-cup ring mold greased with cooking spray. Chill until firm for 2 hours.
- Cut each potato in half vertically to make the palm tree bases. In the uncut side of potato halves make a hole which is big enough to keep a carrot, put to one side. Use a sharp knife to cut on 1 side of each carrot toward the bottom to make thin petals-shaped for tree trunks, keeping slice attached. Turn carrot 1/4 round and do another cut. Repeat the process once to twice around the carrot. Make another cut series about 1-1/2 inch above the first set, and process the thirds sets about 1-1/2 inch above the second. Add carrots in potatoes.
- Cut green pepper's tops and remove all the seeds to make palm leaves (throw away the tops or reserve for another use). Cut the pepper around the bottom edge to form deep V shapes. Put a pepper part on top of each carrot to assemble palm trees; bond with toothpicks.
- Use wooden skewers to string fruit; insert the skewer into whole pineapple. Remove the ring and put on a 19x12-inch platter. Put the whole pineapple in the center of gelatin. Around the gelatin, place palm trees and the additional fruit chunks.

Nutrition Information

- Calories: 309 calories
- Protein: 8g protein.
- Total Fat: 0 fat (0 saturated fat)

- Sodium: 193mg sodium
- Fiber: 0 fiber)
- Total Carbohydrate: 73g carbohydrate (73g sugars
- Cholesterol: 0 cholesterol

---

885.   Luncheon Mold

Serving: 6-8 servings. | Prep: 15mins | Cook: 0mins | Ready in:

Ingredients

- 1 package (3 ounces) lemon gelatin
- 1-1/3 cups boiling water
- 1/2 cup Miracle Whip
- 2 tablespoons prepared horseradish
- 1 teaspoon prepared mustard
- 2 cups chopped cooked corned beef
- 1 cup chopped celery
- 1/4 cup chopped green pepper
- 3 hard-boiled large eggs, chopped
- 2 tablespoons finely chopped onion
- Lettuce leaves, optional

Direction

- Melt gelatin in boiling water in a bowl, mix in mustard, horseradish, and Miracle Whip. Refrigerate until partly set; whisk until frothy. Tuck in onion, eggs, green pepper, celery, and corned beef. Put in a grease-coated 4-cup mold. Refrigerate until firm. Remove from the mold onto a dish lined with lettuce leaves if you want.

Nutrition Information

- Calories:
- Protein:
- Total Fat:
- Sodium:
- Fiber:
- Total Carbohydrate:

- Cholesterol:

- Total Fat: 12g fat (7g saturated fat)
- Sodium: 125mg sodium

886.   Makeover Fluffy Lime Salad

Serving: 8 servings. | Prep: 10mins | Cook: 5mins | Ready in:

Ingredients

- 1 can (8 ounces) unsweetened crushed pineapple, undrained
- 1 package (.3 ounce) sugar-free lime gelatin
- 3 tablespoons water
- 6 ounces reduced-fat cream cheese
- 1 cup miniature marshmallows
- 1/2 cup chopped walnuts
- 1 carton (8 ounces) frozen reduced-fat whipped topping, thawed

Direction

- Drain pineapple, saving juice; put pineapple aside. Whisk reserved juice, water and gelatin in a small saucepan. Cook and stir on low heat till the gelatin dissolves. Keep chilled in the refrigerator for roughly half an hour till it becomes syrupy.
- Whip cream cheese in a small-sized bowl till fluffy. Mix in pineapple, walnuts, marshmallows and gelatin mixture. Mix in whipped topping.
- Add into a serving bowl. Keep it covered and let chill in the refrigerator till set, about 2 hours.

Nutrition Information

- Calories: 206 calories
- Fiber: 1g fiber)
- Total Carbohydrate: 21g carbohydrate (11g sugars
- Cholesterol: 15mg cholesterol
- Protein: 4g protein.

887.   Mango Delight Gelatin Mold

Serving: 10 servings. | Prep: 30mins | Cook: 5mins | Ready in:

Ingredients

- 5 medium ripe mangoes, peeled and pitted
- 1 cup evaporated milk
- 3/4 cup sugar
- 1 cup orange juice
- 3 envelopes unflavored gelatin
- 2 cups whipped topping

Direction

- Slice the mangoes into big chunks; add to a food processor. Keep it covered and run the machine till smooth in consistency; add into a big bowl. Mix in sugar and milk; put aside.
- In a small-sized saucepan, add orange juice; drizzle gelatin on top of juice. Let rest for 2 minutes. Heat on low heat, while mixing till = gelatin totally dissolves. Mix into mango mixture. Fold in whipped topping.
- Add into an 8-cup mold coated using cooking spray. Keep it covered and let chill in the refrigerator till firm or for 2 hours. Just prior to serving, unmold to a serving platter.

Nutrition Information

- Calories:
- Total Fat:
- Sodium:
- Fiber:
- Total Carbohydrate:
- Cholesterol:
- Protein:

Serving: 8 servings. | Prep: 30mins | Cook: 0mins | Ready in:

Ingredients

- 2 cans (15 ounces each) diced or sliced mangoes, drained
- 1 package (8 ounces) cream cheese, softened and cubed
- 2 cups boiling water
- 2 packages (3 ounces each) lemon gelatin
- 1 package (3 ounces) apricot gelatin
- 2 cups cold water
- Fresh mint leaves and cranberries, optional

Direction

- In a food processor, add cream cheese and mangoes; run the machine till blended.
- Put boiling water into gelatins in a big bowl; mix for 2 minutes till totally dissolved. Mix in cold water, then mango mixture. Add to an 8-cup ring mold coated using cooking spray or one 2-qt. serving bowl. Keep chilled in the refrigerator for roughly 4 hours till firm. Unmold onto a serving dish if you use a mold. It can be served with cranberries and mint if you want.

Nutrition Information

- Calories: 227 calories
- Cholesterol: 28mg cholesterol
- Protein: 4g protein.
- Total Fat: 9g fat (6g saturated fat)
- Sodium: 147mg sodium
- Fiber: 1g fiber)
- Total Carbohydrate: 35g carbohydrate (33g sugars

Serving: 9-12 servings. | Prep: 10mins | Cook: 0mins | Ready in:

Ingredients

- 1 package (3 ounces) lime gelatin
- 1 package (3 ounces) lemon gelatin
- 2 cups boiling water
- 2 cups miniature marshmallows
- 1 can (20 ounces) crushed pineapple, undrained
- 1 cup (8 ounces) 4% cottage cheese
- 1 cup mayonnaise

Direction

- In boiling water, dissolve 2 packages of gelatin in a bowl. Put in marshmallows and mix till dissolved. Keep chilled till set partially.
- Mix mayonnaise, cottage cheese and pineapple; mix into gelatin. Add to one 9-in. square plate. Keep chilled till firm.

Nutrition Information

- Calories: 259 calories
- Fiber: 0 fiber)
- Total Carbohydrate: 27g carbohydrate (23g sugars
- Cholesterol: 11mg cholesterol
- Protein: 4g protein.
- Total Fat: 16g fat (2g saturated fat)
- Sodium: 200mg sodium

Serving: 7 servings. | Prep: 30mins | Cook: 0mins | Ready in:

Ingredients

- 2 packages (3 ounces each) lemon gelatin
- 2 cups boiling water

- 3 ounces cream cheese, softened
- 1 cup heavy whipping cream, divided
- 1 cup thinly sliced celery
- 1 cup sliced pimiento-stuffed olives
- SHRIMP SAUCE:
- 2 hard-boiled large eggs, finely chopped
- 1 cup mayonnaise
- 1 can (4 ounces) tiny shrimp, rinsed and drained
- 1 jar (2 ounces) chopped pimientos, drained
- 1/4 cup minced fresh parsley
- 2 tablespoons finely chopped onion
- 1 tablespoon lemon juice
- 1/2 teaspoon salt
- 1/4 teaspoon pepper

Direction

- Dissolve gelatin into a bowl of boiling water. Let it chill for around 30 minutes to let it become syrupy. During which time, in a bowl, whisk cream cheese with 1 tbsp. of cream till the mixture gets smooth.
- Whisk the remaining cream in a different bowl to get soft peaks; carefully fold the cream into the cream cheese mixture. Fold in gelatin, olives and celery. Fill seven 6-ounce greased custard molds or cups with the mixture; let chill to firm up.
- Mix the sauce ingredients together. Let chill. Take the salads out of the mold and into individual servings. Serve with the sauce.

Nutrition Information

- Calories: 557 calories
- Sodium: 1094mg sodium
- Fiber: 1g fiber)
- Total Carbohydrate: 26g carbohydrate (23g sugars
- Cholesterol: 168mg cholesterol
- Protein: 9g protein.
- Total Fat: 47g fat (14g saturated fat)

891.   Minty Lime Gelatin

Serving: 10-12 servings. | Prep: 10mins | Cook: 0mins | Ready in:

Ingredients

- 1 can (20 ounces) crushed pineapple, undrained
- 1 package (3 ounces) lime gelatin
- 1 package (10-1/2 ounces) miniature marshmallows
- 1 package (8 ounces) butter mints, finely crushed
- 1 cup heavy whipping cream, whipped

Direction

- In a big bowl, add pineapple along with juice. Drizzle with gelatin; mix till dissolved. Put in marshmallows. Add to one 13x9-in. plate. Keep chilled till set, about 6 hours.
- Mix butter mints into whipped cream in a bowl. Spread on top of gelatin. Chop into square pieces.

Nutrition Information

- Calories: 277 calories
- Protein: 2g protein.
- Total Fat: 7g fat (5g saturated fat)
- Sodium: 67mg sodium
- Fiber: 0 fiber)
- Total Carbohydrate: 52g carbohydrate (44g sugars
- Cholesterol: 27mg cholesterol

892.   Missouri Peach And Applesauce Salad

Serving: 8-12 servings. | Prep: 20mins | Cook: 0mins | Ready in:

Ingredients

- 1 cup lemon-lime soda
- 1 package (3 ounces) peach or orange gelatin
- 1 cup applesauce
- 1 cup heavy whipping cream
- 1 tablespoon sugar
- 1/8 teaspoon ground nutmeg
- 1/8 teaspoon vanilla extract
- 1 cup chopped peeled ripe peaches
- Red grapes and mint leaves, optional

Direction

- Boil soda in a saucepan. Take out of the heat; mix in gelatin till dissolved. Pour in applesauce. Keep chilled till mixture mounds a bit when dropped from a spoon.
- Beat vanilla, nutmeg and sugar with cream in a bowl till stiff. Mix into gelatin mixture with the peaches. Add into a 1 1/2-qt. bowl. Keep chilled till firm. If you want, use mint and grapes to decorate.

Nutrition Information

- Calories: 121 calories
- Total Fat: 7g fat (5g saturated fat)
- Sodium: 26mg sodium
- Fiber: 1g fiber)
- Total Carbohydrate: 14g carbohydrate (13g sugars
- Cholesterol: 27mg cholesterol
- Protein: 1g protein.

893. Molded Asparagus Salad

Serving: 6-8 servings. | Prep: 20mins | Cook: 0mins | Ready in:

Ingredients

- 1 cup sliced fresh asparagus
- 1 can (10-3/4 ounces) condensed cream of asparagus soup, undiluted
- 1 package (8 ounces) cream cheese, cubed
- 1 package (3 ounces) lemon gelatin
- 1 cup boiling water
- 1/2 teaspoon lemon extract
- 1/2 cup diced celery
- 1/2 cup diced green pepper
- 2 teaspoons finely chopped onion
- 2 teaspoons diced pimientos
- 1/2 cup finely chopped pecans
- 1/2 cup mayonnaise
- Celery leaves
- Chopped pimientos
- Lemon slice

Direction

- In a small amount of water, cook asparagus. Drain and put aside to let cool down. On medium heat, in a small-sized saucepan, mix cream cheese and soup. Cook and stir till the mixture is blended and the cheese is melted.
- In boiling water, dissolve gelatin in a big bowl; pour in the extract. Let it cool down. Put in soup mixture, mayonnaise, pecans, diced pimientos, onion, green pepper, celery and asparagus. Add to 5-6 cup mold coated using nonstick cooking spray. Keep chilled for roughly 5 hours till firm.
- Unmold; use lemon slice, chopped pimientos and celery leaves to decorate.

Nutrition Information

- Calories: 320 calories
- Protein: 5g protein.
- Total Fat: 27g fat (9g saturated fat)
- Sodium: 421mg sodium
- Fiber: 2g fiber)
- Total Carbohydrate: 16g carbohydrate (12g sugars
- Cholesterol: 38mg cholesterol

894. Molded Cherry Pineapple Salad

Serving: 8-10 servings. | Prep: 15mins | Cook: 0mins | Ready in:

Ingredients

- 2 envelopes unflavored gelatin
- 1/4 cup cold water
- 1 can (20 ounces) crushed pineapple, undrained
- 1 package (8 ounces) cream cheese
- 1/2 cup sugar
- 2 tablespoons lemon juice
- 2 tablespoons maraschino cherry juice
- 1/2 pint heavy whipping cream, whipped
- 12 maraschino cherries, halved

Direction

- In cold water in a medium saucepan, dissolve gelatin. Put in juices, sugar, cream cheese and pineapple; cook on medium heat while mixing frequently till gelatin dissolves and cream cheese melts. Keep chilled till syrupy. Fold in cherries and cream. Add to an oiled 6-cup mold. Keep chilled till firm.

Nutrition Information

- Calories: 253 calories
- Total Fat: 17g fat (10g saturated fat)
- Sodium: 80mg sodium
- Fiber: 0 fiber)
- Total Carbohydrate: 24g carbohydrate (22g sugars
- Cholesterol: 58mg cholesterol
- Protein: 4g protein.

895. Molded Cranberry Fruit Salad

Serving: 16 servings. | Prep: 15mins | Cook: 0mins | Ready in:

Ingredients

- 2 packages (.6 ounce each) sugar-free cherry gelatin
- 2 cups boiling water
- 1 package (12 ounces) fresh or frozen cranberries
- 1 large apple, peeled and chopped
- 1 large orange, peeled, chopped and seeded
- 1 piece of orange peel (1 inch)
- 1 can (20 ounces) crushed unsweetened pineapple, undrained

Direction

- In a bowl containing water, dissolve the gelatin. Mix in all leftover ingredients. Process in small batches till chopped coarsely in a blender. Add to a 13x9-in. plate or a 3-qt. serving bowl. Keep chilled for roughly 2 to 3 hours till set.

Nutrition Information

- Calories: 47 calories
- Sodium: 46mg sodium
- Fiber: 0 fiber)
- Total Carbohydrate: 11g carbohydrate (0 sugars
- Cholesterol: 0 cholesterol
- Protein: 2g protein. Diabetic Exchanges: 1 fruit.
- Total Fat: 1g fat (0 saturated fat)

896.　　Molded Cranberry Gelatin Salad

Serving: 8-10 servings. | Prep: 15mins | Cook: 20mins | Ready in:

Ingredients

- 2 envelopes unflavored gelatin
- 2-1/2 cups chilled cranberry juice
- 1 cup sugar
- 3 cups Sugar 'n' Spice Cranberries
- 1 small apple, peeled and finely chopped
- 1 medium navel orange, peeled and chopped
- 1/2 cup halved red seedless grapes
- 1/2 cup chopped walnuts, optional
- 1/4 cup finely chopped celery, optional

Direction

- Drizzle gelatin on top of the cranberry juice in a big saucepan; let it rest for 60 seconds. Cook on low heat, while stirring till gelatin is totally dissolved. Mix in sugar till dissolved. Put in walnuts, grapes, orange, apple, cranberries and celery if you want.
- Add to an 8-cup ring mold coated using cooking spray. Keep in the refrigerator till set. Unmold to a serving dish.

Nutrition Information

- Calories:
- Total Carbohydrate:
- Cholesterol:
- Protein:
- Total Fat:
- Sodium:
- Fiber:

897.　　Molded Cranberry Nut Salad

Serving: 10-12 servings. | Prep: 10mins | Cook: 10mins | Ready in:

Ingredients

- 1 envelope unflavored gelatin
- 1-1/2 cups cold water, divided
- 4 cups (16 ounces) fresh or frozen cranberries
- 1-1/2 cups sugar
- 1-1/2 cups dry red wine or cranberry juice
- 1 package (6 ounces) lemon gelatin
- 1-1/2 cups diced celery
- 3/4 cup chopped walnuts
- 1 cup sour cream
- 3/4 cup mayonnaise
- Celery leaves

Direction

- In 1/2 cup of water, put unflavored gelatin to soften, put aside. Mix cranberry juice, wine, sugar, and cranberries together in a 3-quart saucepan; boil it, tossing sometimes. Lower the heat and simmer for 5 minutes, tossing regularly. Take away from heat. Add softened unflavored gelatin and lemon gelatin, toss until melted. Mix in the rest of the water. Refrigerate until the mixture is partly ser. Tuck in walnuts and celery. Put in a grease-coated 8-cup mold, put a cover on and refrigerate until set. In the meantime, mix mayonnaise with sour cream, chill until ready to enjoy. For serving, remove the gelatin from the mold and put a dollop of dressing on top of each serving. Use celery leaves to garnish.

Nutrition Information

- Calories: 377 calories
- Fiber: 2g fiber)
- Total Carbohydrate: 44g carbohydrate (40g sugars
- Cholesterol: 18mg cholesterol
- Protein: 5g protein.

- Total Fat: 19g fat (4g saturated fat)
- Sodium: 134mg sodium

---

898.   Molded Cranberry Salad

Serving: 100 servings. | Prep: 20mins | Cook: 0mins | Ready in:

Ingredients

- 10 packages (6 ounces each) strawberry gelatin
- 5 quarts boiling water
- 10 cans (16 ounces each) whole-berry cranberry sauce
- 5 cups cold water
- 5 cans (20 ounces each) crushed pineapple, undrained
- 5 cans (15 ounces each) mandarin oranges, drained

Direction

- In boiling water, dissolve gelatin. Break up and mix in cranberry sauce till blended. Mix in cold water. Keep chilled till set partially.
- Fold in oranges and pineapple with liquid. Coat five 13x9-in. pans using cooking spray; add roughly eleven and a half cups of gelatin mixture to each. Keep chilled for roughly 4 hours till it becomes firm.

Nutrition Information

- Calories: 19 calories
- Total Fat: 0 fat (0 saturated fat)
- Sodium: 5mg sodium
- Fiber: 0 fiber)
- Total Carbohydrate: 5g carbohydrate (4g sugars
- Cholesterol: 0 cholesterol
- Protein: 0 protein.

---

899.   Molded Cranberry Orange Salad

Serving: 12 servings. | Prep: 20mins | Cook: 0mins | Ready in:

Ingredients

- 1 teaspoon unflavored gelatin
- 1 tablespoon plus 1 cup cold water, divided
- 1 cup boiling water
- 1 package (3 ounces) raspberry gelatin
- 3 cups (12 ounces) fresh or thawed frozen cranberries, divided
- 2 medium apples, cut into wedges
- 1 medium navel orange, peeled
- 1 cup sugar
- 1/2 cup chopped walnuts
- 1/2 cup finely chopped celery

Direction

- Drizzle unflavored gelatin on top of 1 tbsp. of cold water; let it rest for 60 seconds. Pour in raspberry gelatin and boiling water; mix till gelatin dissolves for roughly 2 minutes. Mix in leftover cold water. Keep chilled in the refrigerator for roughly 45 minutes till thickened.
- In a food processor, process orange, apples and 2 and a third cups of cranberries till chopped. Add into a small-sized bowl; mix in sugar. Mix fruit mixture in the thickened gelatin. Fold in leftover whole cranberries, celery and walnuts.
- Coat a 10-in. fluted tube pan, or an 8-cup ring mold or two 4-cup molds using cooking spray; add in the gelatin mixture. Keep it covered and let chill in the refrigerator overnight or until firm. Unmold to a platter.

Nutrition Information

- Calories: 154 calories
- Sodium: 21mg sodium
- Fiber: 2g fiber)

- Total Carbohydrate: 32g carbohydrate (28g sugars
- Cholesterol: 0 cholesterol
- Protein: 2g protein.
- Total Fat: 3g fat (0 saturated fat)

- Total Carbohydrate: 6g carbohydrate (5g sugars
- Cholesterol: 270mg cholesterol
- Protein: 10g protein.
- Total Fat: 42g fat (7g saturated fat)
- Sodium: 660mg sodium

900. Molded Egg Salad

Serving: 8-10 servings. | Prep: 15mins | Cook: 0mins | Ready in:

Ingredients

- 3 packets unflavored gelatin
- 1 cup water
- 2 cups mayonnaise
- 12 hard-boiled large eggs, chopped
- 1/2 cup chopped celery
- 1/2 cup chopped sweet red pepper
- 1/2 cup sliced green onions
- 1/2 cup sweet pickle relish
- 1 teaspoon salt
- 1/4 teaspoon pepper
- Thinly sliced fully cooked ham, optional

Direction

- Soften gelatin in water in a medium-sized saucepan for 5 minutes. Mix on low heat till gelatin dissolves. Take out of the heat.
- Mix in mayonnaise. Mix in eggs. Put in pepper, salt, relish, onions, red pepper and celery then mix them well. Add to an 8-cup mold coated using cooking spray. Keep chilled overnight.
- Unmold to a serving platter. If using a ring mold, you can add a few pieces of ham in the middle or, use it to decorate around the mold's sides.

Nutrition Information

- Calories: 441 calories
- Fiber: 1g fiber)

901. Molded Lime Salad

Serving: 8-10 servings. | Prep: 30mins | Cook: 0mins | Ready in:

Ingredients

- 2 cups boiling water
- 1 package (6 ounces) lime gelatin
- 1 cup cold water
- 1 tablespoon vinegar
- Dash salt
- Dash white pepper, optional
- 3/4 cup mayonnaise
- 1/2 cup shredded carrots
- 1/2 cup finely chopped peeled cucumber
- 1/2 cup finely chopped celery
- 1/2 cup finely chopped green pepper
- 2 tablespoons finely chopped onion

Direction

- Add boiling water on top of gelatin in a bowl. Mix to dissolve. Pour in salt, vinegar, cold water and pepper if you want. Add 1 cup of the mixture to 6-cup mold; put aside. Keep chilled the leftover gelatin for half an hour, then put in mayonnaise and blend with a rotary beater till smooth in consistency. Keep chilled till nearly set. At the same time, chill gelatin in mold till nearly set. Turn gelatin/mayonnaise mixture into a bowl and beat till fluffy. Fold in vegetables. Scoop into mold. Keep chilled till firm. Unmold to serve.

Nutrition Information

- Calories:
- Sodium:
- Fiber:
- Total Carbohydrate:
- Cholesterol:
- Protein:
- Total Fat:

902.   Molded Peach Gelatin

Serving: 4-6 servings. | Prep: 20mins | Cook: 0mins | Ready in:

Ingredients

- 1 can (15-1/4 ounces) sliced peaches
- 1/2 cup sugar
- 1/4 to 1/2 teaspoon ground nutmeg
- 1 package (3 ounces) peach or orange gelatin

Direction

- Drain peaches, saving the juice; pour in enough water to juice to measure 1 cup. Add peaches into a blender. Cover up and process till smooth in consistency; put aside.
- Mix the reserved juice mixture, nutmeg and sugar in a big saucepan. Boil on medium heat; cook and stir till the sugar dissolves or for 60 seconds. Take out of the heat; mix in gelatin till dissolved. Mix in the peach puree.
- Add to a 3-cup mold coated using cooking spray. Keep chilled in the refrigerator till set. Just prior to serving, unmold to a serving dish.

Nutrition Information

- Calories: 173 calories
- Total Fat: 0 fat (0 saturated fat)
- Sodium: 38mg sodium
- Fiber: 1g fiber)
- Total Carbohydrate: 43g carbohydrate (41g sugars
- Cholesterol: 0 cholesterol

- Protein: 1g protein.

903.   Molded Rhubarb Salad

Serving: 10-12 servings. | Prep: 15mins | Cook: 0mins | Ready in:

Ingredients

- 3 cups diced rhubarb
- 2 cups water
- 1-2/3 cups sugar
- 1 package (6 ounces) strawberry gelatin
- 1 can (20 ounces) crushed pineapple, drained
- 1/2 cup chopped walnuts

Direction

- Cook rhubarb in water in a saucepan on moderate heat for about 5 minutes, until softened. Take away from the heat then whisk in gelatin and sugar until dissolved. Put in nuts and pineapple, then transfer into a greased 6-cup mold. Refrigerate until set.

Nutrition Information

- Calories: 225 calories
- Protein: 3g protein.
- Total Fat: 3g fat (0 saturated fat)
- Sodium: 34mg sodium
- Fiber: 1g fiber)
- Total Carbohydrate: 49g carbohydrate (46g sugars
- Cholesterol: 0 cholesterol

904.   Molded Strawberry Salad

Serving: 8 servings. | Prep: 10mins | Cook: 0mins | Ready in:

Ingredients

- 1 package (6 ounces) strawberry gelatin
- 1-1/2 cups boiling water
- 1 package (10 ounces) frozen sweetened sliced strawberries, thawed
- 1 can (8 ounces) unsweetened crushed pineapple
- 1 cup sour cream
- Leaf lettuce and fresh strawberries, optional

Direction

- In water, dissolve gelatin in a big bowl. Put in pineapple and strawberries. Strain, saving the fruit and liquid. Put aside 1 cup of the liquid to rest at room temperature.
- Add fruit and leftover liquid to one 5-cup ring mold or 9-in. square pan coated using cooking spray. Keep it covered and let chill in the refrigerator for roughly 60 minutes till set.
- Mix reserved liquid and sour cream; add on top of gelatin. Keep it covered and let chill in the refrigerator till set.
- Chop into square pieces and add onto separate dishes; or unmold to a serving platter. If you want, use strawberries and lettuce to decorate.

Nutrition Information

- Calories: 182 calories
- Protein: 3g protein.
- Total Fat: 5g fat (4g saturated fat)
- Sodium: 64mg sodium
- Fiber: 1g fiber)
- Total Carbohydrate: 31g carbohydrate (30g sugars
- Cholesterol: 20mg cholesterol

905. Molded Vegetable Salad

Serving: 8 servings. | Prep: 15mins | Cook: 0mins | Ready in:

Ingredients

- 1 package (6 ounces) lime gelatin

- 1/4 teaspoon salt, optional
- 1-1/2 cups boiling water
- 3/4 cup cold water
- 3 tablespoons vinegar
- 1 cup chopped celery
- 1 cup chopped tomato
- 1 cup thinly shredded lettuce
- 3/4 cup thinly sliced radishes
- 1/4 cup finely chopped green pepper
- 4 teaspoons grated onion
- Dash pepper

Direction

- Dissolve salt (if you want) and gelatin in boiling water in a bowl. Add vinegar and cold water. Refrigerate until partly set. Tuck in the rest of the ingredients. Put in a lightly grease-coated a 4-cup mold. Refrigerate until firm. Remove the mold onto a serving dish.

Nutrition Information

- Calories: 38 calories
- Protein: 2g protein. Diabetic Exchanges: 1-1/2 vegetable.
- Total Fat: 0 fat (0 saturated fat)
- Sodium: 77mg sodium
- Fiber: 0 fiber)
- Total Carbohydrate: 8g carbohydrate (0 sugars
- Cholesterol: 0 cholesterol

906. Mom's Orange Spice Gelatin

Serving: 10 servings. | Prep: 15mins | Cook: 10mins | Ready in:

Ingredients

- 1 can (15 ounces) sliced peaches in extra-light syrup
- 2 tablespoons cider vinegar
- 3 cinnamon sticks (3 inches)

- 12 whole cloves
- 3 cups boiling water
- 4 packages (.3 ounce each) sugar-free orange gelatin
- 2 cups cold water
- Sugar substitute equivalent to 1/3 cup sugar
- 1/4 cup finely chopped pecans

Direction

- Drain peaches, saving the syrup; put peaches aside. Mix reserved syrup, cloves, cinnamon sticks and vinegar in a small-sized saucepan. Boil; cook till decreased to roughly half a cup. Strain, getting rid of cloves and cinnamon.
- Pour boiling water into syrup mixture; mix in gelatin till dissolved. Mix in sugar substitute and cold water. Keep chilled in the refrigerator for roughly 35 minutes till thickened a bit.
- Coarsely chop the peaches. Mix pecans and peaches into gelatin mixture. Place into a 6-cup ring mold coated using cooking spray. The mold may be filled up full. Keep in the refrigerator till firm, or for 3-4 hours. Unmold to a serving dish.

Nutrition Information

- Calories: 62 calories
- Total Fat: 2g fat (0 saturated fat)
- Sodium: 91mg sodium
- Fiber: 1g fiber)
- Total Carbohydrate: 8g carbohydrate (6g sugars
- Cholesterol: 0 cholesterol
- Protein: 2g protein. Diabetic Exchanges: 1/2 starch

---

907. Orange Buttermilk Gelatin Salad

Serving: 10 servings. | Prep: 15mins | Cook: 0mins | Ready in:

Ingredients

- 1 can (20 ounces) crushed pineapple
- 1 package (6 ounces) orange gelatin
- 2 cups buttermilk
- 1 carton (8 ounces) frozen whipped topping, thawed

Direction

- Boil juice with pineapple in a saucepan. Mix in gelatin until melted. Take away from heat, mix in buttermilk. Let it cool down to room temperature. Tuck in whipped topping. Put in a 2-quart bowl or an 11x7-inch plate. Refrigerate for a minimum of 4 hours.

Nutrition Information

- Calories: 115 calories
- Cholesterol: 2mg cholesterol
- Protein: 3g protein. Diabetic Exchanges: 1/2 fruit
- Total Fat: 3g fat (0 saturated fat)
- Sodium: 93mg sodium
- Fiber: 0 fiber)
- Total Carbohydrate: 16g carbohydrate (0 sugars

---

908. Orange Buttermilk Gelatin Salad Mold

Serving: 12-16 servings. | Prep: 15mins | Cook: 0mins | Ready in:

Ingredients

- 1 can (20 ounces) unsweetened crushed pineapple, undrained
- 3 tablespoons sugar
- 1 package (6 ounces) orange gelatin
- 2 cups buttermilk
- 1 carton (8 ounces) frozen whipped topping, thawed
- 1 cup chopped nuts

Direction

- Mix sugar and pineapple in a saucepan; boil while mixing once in a while. Once mixture boils, put in and stir gelatin instantly till dissolved. Let it cool down a bit. Mix in buttermilk. Keep chilled till partially set. Fold in nuts and whipped topping. Keep chilled till mixture mounds a bit if needed. Add to a slightly oiled 8-1/2-cup mold. Keep chilled overnight.

Nutrition Information

- Calories: 168 calories
- Total Carbohydrate: 23g carbohydrate (19g sugars
- Cholesterol: 1mg cholesterol
- Protein: 4g protein.
- Total Fat: 7g fat (3g saturated fat)
- Sodium: 57mg sodium
- Fiber: 1g fiber)

909. Orange Buttermilk Salad

Serving: 10 | Prep: 15mins | Cook: 15mins |Ready in:

Ingredients

- 1 (20 ounce) can crushed pineapple, undrained
- 3 tablespoons white sugar
- 1 (6 ounce) package orange flavored Jell-O®
- 2 cups buttermilk
- 1 (8 ounce) container frozen whipped topping, thawed

Direction

- In a medium-sized saucepan, whisk sugar and pineapple, and bring to a low boil, mixing once in a while. Mix in gelatin till dissolved totally, take out of the heat, and let it cool down to room temperature. Pour in buttermilk, and keep chilled in the refrigerator till set partially, about 60 minutes.

- Mix lightly in whipped topping. Add mixture to a lightly oiled gelatin mold. Keep chilled in the refrigerator 8 hours till set totally.

Nutrition Information

- Calories: 203 calories;
- Total Carbohydrate: 35.3
- Cholesterol: 2
- Protein: 3.4
- Total Fat: 6.1
- Sodium: 100

910. Orange Gelatin Cups

Serving: 4 servings. | Prep: 5mins | Cook: 0mins |Ready in:

Ingredients

- 1 package (3 ounces) orange gelatin
- 1 cup boiling water
- 1 cup applesauce
- 1 can (11 ounces) mandarin oranges, drained

Direction

- Melt the gelatin in boiling water in a small bowl. Mix in applesauce. Put into 4 dessert plates. Add oranges. Put a cover on and chill until set, about 2 hours.

Nutrition Information

- Calories: 151 calories
- Sodium: 54mg sodium
- Fiber: 1g fiber)
- Total Carbohydrate: 38g carbohydrate (36g sugars
- Cholesterol: 0 cholesterol
- Protein: 2g protein.
- Total Fat: 0 fat (0 saturated fat)

911. Orange Gelatin Salad

Serving: 7 | Prep: 10mins | Cook: | Ready in:

Ingredients

- 1 (11 ounce) can mandarin oranges, drained
- 1 (8 ounce) can crushed pineapple, drained
- 1 (6 ounce) package orange flavored Jell-O® mix
- 16 ounces cottage cheese
- 8 ounces frozen whipped topping, thawed

Direction

- Mix together gelatin, pineapple and oranges in a mixing bowl. Combine thoroughly and refrigerate for 30 minutes.
- To fruit, put cottage cheese; mix to blend.
- Gently fold in the whipped topping; refrigerate and serve.

Nutrition Information

- Calories: 289 calories;
- Cholesterol: 10
- Protein: 10.3
- Total Fat: 8.2
- Sodium: 350
- Total Carbohydrate: 41.2

912. Overnight Fruit Cup

Serving: 15-20 servings. | Prep: 20mins | Cook: 0mins | Ready in:

Ingredients

- 1 package (3 ounces) lemon gelatin
- 2 cups boiling water
- 1 can (6 ounces) frozen orange juice concentrate, thawed
- 1 can (20 ounces) pineapple chunks, undrained
- 1 can (15-1/4 ounces) sliced peaches, drained
- 1 can (11 ounces) mandarin orange segments, undrained
- 1 cup sliced fresh strawberries
- 1 cup fresh blueberries
- 1 cup green grapes
- 1 firm banana, thinly sliced

Direction

- Dissolve the gelatin in water in a large bowl. Pour in orange juice concentrate and thoroughly mix. Add all the fruit and mix. Cover and chill in refrigerator overnight.

Nutrition Information

- Calories:
- Protein:
- Total Fat:
- Sodium:
- Fiber:
- Total Carbohydrate:
- Cholesterol:

913. Pastel Gelatin Salad

Serving: 15 servings. | Prep: 25mins | Cook: 0mins | Ready in:

Ingredients

- 1 package (3 ounces) lemon gelatin
- 1 package (3 ounces) lime gelatin
- 2 cups boiling water
- 1 package (8 ounces) cream cheese, cubed
- 1/2 cup evaporated milk
- 1/2 cup mayonnaise
- 1 can (8 ounces) unsweetened crushed pineapple, undrained
- 1/2 cup chopped walnuts
- 1 package (10-1/2 ounces) pastel miniature marshmallows

Direction

- Mix lime gelatin and lemon with boiling water in a big bowl, toss until dissolved. Add cream cheese and let sit for 10 minutes. Whisk on high speed until smooth. Add mayonnaise and milk and mix. Tuck into a pineapple.
- Pour into a 13-in. x 9-in. dish, but do not grease it. Use marshmallows and nuts to drizzle. Put a cover on and put in the fridge until set.

Nutrition Information

- Calories: 250 calories
- Total Fat: 14g fat (5g saturated fat)
- Sodium: 135mg sodium
- Fiber: 0 fiber)
- Total Carbohydrate: 30g carbohydrate (25g sugars
- Cholesterol: 18mg cholesterol
- Protein: 4g protein.

914.   Patriotic Gelatin Salad

Serving: 16 servings. | Prep: 20mins | Cook: 0mins | Ready in:

Ingredients

- 2 packages (3 ounces each) berry blue gelatin
- 2 packages (3 ounces each) strawberry gelatin
- 4 cups boiling water, divided
- 2-1/2 cups cold water, divided
- 2 envelopes unflavored gelatin
- 2 cups milk
- 1 cup sugar
- 2 cups sour cream
- 2 teaspoons vanilla extract

Direction

- Dissolve each package of gelatin in a cup of boiling water in 4 different bowls. Pour half a cup of cold water in each bowl; stir. Transfer a bowl of blue gelatin to a 10-in. fluted pan coated with cooking spray; chill for about half an hour till nearly set.
- Set aside the other 3 gelatin bowls, keep at room temperature. Use the remaining cold water to soften unflavored gelatin, allow to sit for 5 minutes.
- Pour milk in a saucepan then heat on medium heat just below boiling. Add sugar and softened gelatin then stir till the sugar is dissolved. Take the pan off heat, stir in vanilla and sour cream till smooth. When blue gelatin in pan nearly set, spoon carefully 1- 1/2 cups of sour cream mixture on top of the gelatin. Chill for about half an hour till almost set.
- Transfer carefully using spoon one bowl of strawberry gelatin over cream layer. Let chill till nearly set. Spoon carefully 1 1/2 cups of cream mixture on top of the strawberry layer. Let chill till almost set. Repeat the process. Add layers of blue gelatin, cream mixture and strawberry gelatin; remember to chill in between each. Let chill for a few hours or overnight.

Nutrition Information

- Calories: 69 calories
- Cholesterol: 11mg cholesterol
- Protein: 5g protein. Diabetic Exchanges: 1/2 starch
- Total Fat: 3g fat (2g saturated fat)
- Sodium: 84mg sodium
- Fiber: 0 fiber)
- Total Carbohydrate: 5g carbohydrate (4g sugars

915.   Peach Bavarian

Serving: 8 servings. | Prep: 15mins | Cook: 0mins | Ready in:

Ingredients

- 1 can (15-1/4 ounces) sliced peaches
- 2 packages (3 ounces each) peach or apricot gelatin
- 1/2 cup sugar
- 2 cups boiling water
- 1 teaspoon almond extract
- 1 carton (8 ounces) frozen whipped topping, thawed
- Additional sliced peaches, optional

Direction

- Drain peaches and reserve 2/3 cup syrup. Cut peaches into small pieces, then put to one side. Dissolve sugar and gelatin in boiling water in a large bowl. Add reserved juice and stir. Refrigerate until partly firm. Add extract into whipped topping, stir, then carefully fold in gelatin mixture. Add chopped peaches, fold.
- Transfer into a greased6-cup mold. Refrigerate overnight. Remove the mold and place the jello onto a platter to serve; top with extra peaches if desired.

Nutrition Information

- Calories: 249 calories
- Protein: 2g protein.
- Total Fat: 5g fat (5g saturated fat)
- Sodium: 53mg sodium
- Fiber: 0 fiber)
- Total Carbohydrate: 47g carbohydrate (47g sugars
- Cholesterol: 0 cholesterol

916. Peach Gelatin Salad

Serving: 8 servings. | Prep: 15mins | Cook: 0mins | Ready in:

Ingredients

- 1 can (29 ounces) sliced peaches, drained
- 1-1/2 cups boiling water

- 2 packages (3 ounces each) lemon gelatin
- 1 can (12 ounces) ginger ale, chilled
- 1/3 cup chopped walnuts, toasted

Direction

- Arrange 1/2 of the slices of peach on a 6-cup ring mold coated using cooking spray. Pour in boiling water to gelatin in a small-sized bowl; mix for 2 minutes to dissolve totally.
- Mix in ginger ale. Add 1/2 of the mixture on top of peaches; scatter with walnuts. Keep in the refrigerator till set yet not firm or for half an hour. Let leftover gelatin mixture rest at room temperature.
- Gently arrange leftover slices of peach on top of gelatin in mold. Scoop leftover gelatin mixture on top. Keep in the refrigerator till it becomes firm. Unmold to a serving dish.

Nutrition Information

- Calories:
- Sodium:
- Fiber:
- Total Carbohydrate:
- Cholesterol:
- Protein:
- Total Fat:

917. Peach Cranberry Gelatin Salad

Serving: 14-18 servings. | Prep: 20mins | Cook: 0mins | Ready in:

Ingredients

- 2 packages (3 ounces each) peach or orange gelatin
- 4 cups water, divided
- 1 cup orange juice
- 2 cans (15 ounces each) sliced peaches, drained

- 1 package (6 ounces) cranberry or raspberry gelatin
- 1 cup cranberry juice
- 2 large oranges, peeled
- 2 cups fresh or frozen cranberries
- 1 cup sugar

Direction

- Add peach gelatin into a large bowl. Boil 2 cups of water, then pour into the bowl to dissolve the gelatin, stirring. Pour orange juice in and mix well. Refrigerate the mixture until soft-set.
- Add peaches, fold. Transfer into a 3-qt serving bowl. Refrigerate until firm. In another bowl, put cranberry gelatin in. Boil the remaining water, then pour into the cranberry gelatin bowl, stir until dissolved. Pour the cranberry juice in and stir until well combined.
- Combine sugar, cranberries, and oranges in a food processor; pulse until the fruit is roughly crushed. Pour over the cranberry gelatin, slowly spoon the gelatin over. Refrigerate until completely firm.

Nutrition Information

- Calories:
- Fiber:
- Total Carbohydrate:
- Cholesterol:
- Protein:
- Total Fat:
- Sodium:

918.　　　Peaches 'n' Cream Salad

Serving: 9 servings. | Prep: 15mins | Cook: 0mins | Ready in:

Ingredients

- 1 package (3 ounces) lemon gelatin
- 3/4 cup boiling water

- 1 cup orange juice
- 1 envelope whipped topping mix (Dream Whip)
- 3 ounces cream cheese, softened
- 1/4 cup chopped pecans, optional
- PEACH LAYER:
- 1 package (3 ounces) lemon gelatin
- 1 cup boiling water
- 1 can (21 ounces) peach pie filling

Direction

- Melt gelatin in water in a bowl; add orange juice. Chill until partly set. Make the topping mix as the package instructions. Whisk cream cheese until creamy in a bowl, tuck in pecans and whipped topping if you want. Put into the gelatin mixture. Put into an 8-in. square platter that is ungreased. Chill until firm.
- To make the peach layer, melt the gelatin in water, mix in the pie filling. Refrigerate until partly set. Gently put on the creamy gelatin layer (the pan will be full). Refrigerate until firm.

Nutrition Information

- Calories: 198 calories
- Total Fat: 4g fat (3g saturated fat)
- Sodium: 82mg sodium
- Fiber: 1g fiber)
- Total Carbohydrate: 37g carbohydrate (35g sugars
- Cholesterol: 10mg cholesterol
- Protein: 3g protein.

919.　　　Peachy Applesauce Salad

Serving: 6 servings. | Prep: 15mins | Cook: 0mins | Ready in:

Ingredients

- 1 cup diet lemon-lime soda

- 1 package (.3 ounces) sugar-free peach or mixed fruit gelatin
- 1 cup unsweetened applesauce
- 2 cups reduced-fat whipped topping
- 1/8 teaspoon ground nutmeg
- 1/8 teaspoon vanilla extract
- 1 fresh peach, peeled and chopped

Direction

- Boil soda in a saucepan. Take out of the heat; mix in gelatin till dissolved. Pour in applesauce; keep chilled till partially set. Mix in vanilla, nutmeg and whipped topping. Mix in peach. Keep chilled till firm.

Nutrition Information

- Calories: 99 calories
- Protein: 0 protein. Diabetic Exchanges: 1 fruit
- Total Fat: 3g fat (0 saturated fat)
- Sodium: 6mg sodium
- Fiber: 0 fiber)
- Total Carbohydrate: 15g carbohydrate (0 sugars
- Cholesterol: 0 cholesterol

920. Pear Lime Gelatin

Serving: 6 servings. | Prep: 20mins | Cook: 0mins | Ready in:

Ingredients

- 1 can (29 ounces) pear halves in juice
- 1 package (3 ounces) lime gelatin
- 3 ounces cream cheese, cubed
- 1 cup whipped topping

Direction

- Drain pears, saving the juice; put pears aside. Measure the juice; pour in water if necessary to equal 1-1/2 cups. Add to a saucepan; boil. Put in gelatin; mix till dissolved. Slowly put in

cream cheese, mixing till smooth in consistency.
- Keep it covered and let chill in the refrigerator till cool. Smash reserved pears; fold into the gelatin mixture. Fold in the whipped topping. Add to a 6-cup serving bowl. Keep chilled in the refrigerator till set.

Nutrition Information

- Calories: 172 calories
- Total Fat: 3g fat (2g saturated fat)
- Sodium: 398mg sodium
- Fiber: 2g fiber)
- Total Carbohydrate: 21g carbohydrate (0 sugars
- Cholesterol: 5mg cholesterol
- Protein: 8g protein. Diabetic Exchanges: 2 fruit

921. Pear Lime Gelatin Salad

Serving: 8 servings. | Prep: 20mins | Cook: 0mins | Ready in:

Ingredients

- 1 can (15 ounces) pear halves
- 1 package (3 ounces) lime gelatin
- 1 package (8 ounces) cream cheese, cubed
- 1 can (20 ounces) unsweetened crushed pineapple, well drained
- 1 cup chopped pecans, toasted, divided
- 1 carton (8 ounces) frozen whipped topping, thawed

Direction

- Drain pears, saving the juice; put pears aside. Boil juice in a small-sized saucepan. Mix in gelatin till dissolved. Take out of the heat; let it cool down a bit.
- Mix cream cheese and pears in a food processor; keep it covered and run the processor till smooth in texture. Add to a big bowl; mix in gelatin mixture till blended. Mix

in three quarters cup of pecans and pineapple. Fold in whipped topping.

- Add to one ungreased 11x7-in. plate. Keep chilled in the refrigerator till set. Drizzle with leftover pecans. Chop into squares.

Nutrition Information

- Calories: 401 calories
- Protein: 5g protein.
- Total Fat: 25g fat (12g saturated fat)
- Sodium: 111mg sodium
- Fiber: 3g fiber)
- Total Carbohydrate: 40g carbohydrate (30g sugars
- Cholesterol: 31mg cholesterol

---

922. Picnic Potato Squares Salad

Serving: 9 servings. | Prep: 20mins | Cook: 0mins | Ready in:

Ingredients

- 2 envelopes unflavored gelatin
- 2-1/4 cups milk, divided
- 1 cup mayonnaise
- 1 tablespoon prepared mustard
- 2 teaspoons sugar
- 1/2 teaspoon salt
- 1/4 teaspoon pepper
- 2-1/2 cups cubed red potatoes, cooked and cooled
- 1/2 cup shredded carrot
- 1/2 cup thinly sliced celery
- 1/3 cup chopped dill pickle
- 2 tablespoons diced onion
- Lettuce leaves, optional

Direction

- In a saucepan, place gelatin and 1 cup milk; allow to sit for 1 minute. Cook over low-heat,

stirring until the gelatin is completely dissolved. Turn off the heat, mix in the remaining milk, pepper, salt, sugar, mustard, and mayonnaise until smooth. Refrigerate until partly set. Fold in onion, pickle, celery, carrot, and potatoes. Pour the mixture into an ungreased 8-in. square dish, refrigerate until completely firm. Slice into square-shaped pieces; these can be served on lettuce if desired.

Nutrition Information

- Calories: 261 calories
- Cholesterol: 17mg cholesterol
- Protein: 4g protein.
- Total Fat: 22g fat (4g saturated fat)
- Sodium: 394mg sodium
- Fiber: 1g fiber)
- Total Carbohydrate: 12g carbohydrate (5g sugars

---

923. Pina Colada Molded Salad

Serving: 8 servings. | Prep: 25mins | Cook: 0mins | Ready in:

Ingredients

- 1 can (20 ounces) unsweetened crushed pineapple
- 2 envelopes unflavored gelatin
- 1/2 cup cold water
- 1 cup cream of coconut
- 1 cup (8 ounces) sour cream
- 3/4 cup lemon-lime soda
- 3/4 cup sweetened shredded coconut
- 1/2 cup chopped macadamia nuts
- Pineapple chunks and freshly shredded coconut, optional

Direction

- Strain pineapple, keep the juice. Put pineapple to one side. Add gelatin into cold water, let sit for 1 minutes in a large saucepan. Bring to cook over low heat for about 2 minutes to dissolve the gelatin completely, stirring. Turn off the heat, combine with reserved pineapple juice, soda, sour cream, and cream of coconut. Pour into a large bowl. Cover and refrigerate until thickened for 30 minutes. Stirring sometimes.
- Add reserved pineapple, nuts, and coconut flakes, fold. Transfer into a 6-cup ring mold greased by cooking spray. Cover and chill until completely set, about 3 hours.
- Remove the mold and place the salad onto a platter to serve. Put pineapple chunks into the center of the salad, sprinkle with shredded coconut if desired.

Nutrition Information

- Calories: 331 calories
- Total Carbohydrate: 37g carbohydrate (33g sugars
- Cholesterol: 20mg cholesterol
- Protein: 4g protein.
- Total Fat: 20g fat (11g saturated fat)
- Sodium: 82mg sodium
- Fiber: 2g fiber)

924.   Pineapple Citrus Gelatin Salad

Serving: 6 servings. | Prep: 15mins | Cook: 0mins | Ready in:

Ingredients

- 1 package (3 ounces) lemon gelatin
- 1 cup boiling water
- 1 can (8 ounces) crushed pineapple
- 1/3 cup orange juice concentrate
- 1 can (11 ounces) mandarin oranges, drained

Direction

- In boiling water, dissolve gelatin in a bowl. Drain pineapple, saving juice. Put pineapple aside. Pour in enough water to the juice to equal 1 cup; mix into gelatin. Pour in orange juice concentrate. Keep chilled till partially set. Mix in oranges and pineapple. Add to a glass bowl or one 4-cup mold. Keep chilled till set.

Nutrition Information

- Calories: 112 calories
- Fiber: 1g fiber)
- Total Carbohydrate: 28g carbohydrate (26g sugars
- Cholesterol: 0 cholesterol
- Protein: 2g protein.
- Total Fat: 0 fat (0 saturated fat)
- Sodium: 36mg sodium

925.   Pineapple Gelatin Salad

Serving: 12-16 servings. | Prep: 25mins | Cook: 0mins | Ready in:

Ingredients

- 1 can (20 ounces) crushed pineapple
- 1 package (6 ounces) lemon gelatin
- 3 cups boiling water
- 1 package (8 ounces) cream cheese, softened
- 1 carton (16 ounces) frozen whipped topping, thawed
- 3/4 cup sugar
- 3 tablespoons lemon juice
- 3 tablespoons water
- 2 tablespoons all-purpose flour
- 2 large egg yolks, lightly beaten

Direction

- Drain pineapple, saving the juice. In water, dissolve the gelatin; put in pineapple. Add to a

13x9-in. plate; let chill for roughly 45 minutes till nearly set.

- Whip whipped topping and cream cheese in a bowl till smooth in texture. Gently spread on top of gelatin; let chill for half an hour. At the same time, mix reserved pineapple juice, egg yolks, flour, water, lemon juice and sugar on medium heat in a saucepan; boil, mixing continuously. Cook till thickened or for 60 seconds. Let it cool down. Gently spread on top of cream cheese layer. Keep chilled for no less than 60 minutes.

Nutrition Information

- Calories: 236 calories
- Protein: 3g protein.
- Total Fat: 10g fat (8g saturated fat)
- Sodium: 68mg sodium
- Fiber: 0 fiber)
- Total Carbohydrate: 32g carbohydrate (26g sugars
- Cholesterol: 42mg cholesterol

---

926. Pineapple Lime Molds

Serving: 6 servings. | Prep: 20mins | Cook: 0mins | Ready in:

Ingredients

- 1 can (8 ounces) unsweetened crushed pineapple
- 1 package (3 ounces) lime gelatin
- 1 package (8 ounces) cream cheese, softened
- 3/4 cup lemon-lime soda
- 1 teaspoon vanilla extract

Direction

- Strain pineapple; reserve syrup, put pineapple to one side. Measure pineapple juice and add enough water to the juice to reach 1 cup; pour the pineapple mixture into a saucepan, and boil. Add gelatin and stir until dissolved.

- Whip cream cheese until smooth in a small bowl. Pour the gelatin mixture and beat for 2 minutes on medium setting. Add vanilla and soda, then beat for one more minute. Put the reserved pineapple in and continue to whip for 1 minute on low speed. Divide into 6 separate dessert dishes or molds. Chill until firm for 4 hours.

Nutrition Information

- Calories: 220 calories
- Sodium: 148mg sodium
- Fiber: 0 fiber)
- Total Carbohydrate: 22g carbohydrate (21g sugars
- Cholesterol: 42mg cholesterol
- Protein: 4g protein.
- Total Fat: 13g fat (8g saturated fat)

---

927. Pineapple Blueberry Gelatin Salad

Serving: 8 servings. | Prep: 15mins | Cook: 0mins | Ready in:

Ingredients

- 2 packages (3 ounces each) grape gelatin
- 2 cups boiling water
- 1 can (20 ounces) crushed pineapple
- 2 cups fresh blueberries
- 1 package (8 ounces) cream cheese, softened
- 1/2 cup sour cream
- 1/2 cup sugar
- 1 teaspoon vanilla extract
- 1/2 cup chopped pecans

Direction

- Melt the gelatin in boiling water in a big bowl. Strain pineapple, saving juice in a measuring cup, add water to measure 1 cup. Mix in the gelatin. Add blueberries and pineapple. Move to an 11x7-inch dish, put a cover on and chill until firm.

- Whisk vanilla, sugar, sour cream, and cream cheese together in a small bowl. Spread over the gelatin. Put a cover on and chill until serving. Use pecans to drizzle right before eating.

Nutrition Information

- Calories: 344 calories
- Sodium: 117mg sodium
- Fiber: 2g fiber)
- Total Carbohydrate: 44g carbohydrate (40g sugars
- Cholesterol: 41mg cholesterol
- Protein: 5g protein.
- Total Fat: 18g fat (8g saturated fat)

928.   Pineapple Lime Gelatin Mold

Serving: 12 servings. | Prep: 10mins | Cook: 0mins | Ready in:

Ingredients

- 2 packages (3 ounces each) lime gelatin
- 2 cups boiling water
- 1 can (20 ounces) crushed pineapple, undrained
- 1 cup (8 ounces) sour cream
- 1/2 cup chopped pecans

Direction

- Dissolve gelatin in a big bowl with water. Stir in pineapple then cover and chill until syrupy.
- Stir in sour cream and then put in pecans. Remove the mixture to a 6-cup ring mold greased with cooking spray. Cover and chill until firm, then unmold onto a serving plate.

Nutrition Information

- Calories: 135 calories
- Protein: 2g protein.
- Total Fat: 7g fat (3g saturated fat)
- Sodium: 26mg sodium
- Fiber: 1g fiber)
- Total Carbohydrate: 17g carbohydrate (16g sugars
- Cholesterol: 13mg cholesterol

929.   Pomegranate Gelatin

Serving: 10 servings. | Prep: 15mins | Cook: 0mins | Ready in:

Ingredients

- 2 packages (3 ounces each) raspberry gelatin
- 2 cups boiling water
- 1 cup cold water
- 1-1/2 cups pomegranate seeds (about 2 pomegranates)
- 1 can (8 ounces) crushed pineapple, drained
- 1/2 cup sour cream
- 1/2 cup mayonnaise

Direction

- In a big bowl containing boiling water, dissolve gelatin. Mix in pineapple, pomegranate seeds and cold water. Add to an 11x7-in. plate. Keep chilled in the refrigerator till firm.
- Mix mayonnaise and sour cream; spread on top of gelatin. Keep chilled in the refrigerator till serving.

Nutrition Information

- Calories: 194 calories
- Fiber: 0 fiber)
- Total Carbohydrate: 22g carbohydrate (21g sugars
- Cholesterol: 12mg cholesterol

- Protein: 2g protein.
- Total Fat: 11g fat (3g saturated fat)
- Sodium: 106mg sodium

930. Pomegranate Cranberry Salad

Serving: 8 servings. | Prep: 15mins | Cook: 0mins | Ready in:

Ingredients

- 1 package (.3 ounce) sugar-free cranberry gelatin
- 1 cup boiling water
- 1/2 cup cold water
- 1-2/3 cups pomegranate seeds
- 1 can (14 ounces) whole-berry cranberry sauce
- 1 can (8 ounces) unsweetened crushed pineapple, drained
- 3/4 cup chopped pecans
- Frozen whipped topping, thawed, optional
- Additional chopped pecans, optional

Direction

- Melt the gelatin in boiling water in a big bowl. Add cold water and toss. Add pecans, pineapple, cranberry sauce, and pomegranate seeds. Put in a 1 1/2-qt. serving bowl. Chill until firm, about 4-5 hours. Put additional pecans and whipped topping on top if you want.

Nutrition Information

- Calories: 190 calories
- Protein: 2g protein. Diabetic Exchanges: 1-1/2 fat
- Total Fat: 8g fat (1g saturated fat)
- Sodium: 41mg sodium
- Fiber: 2g fiber)
- Total Carbohydrate: 30g carbohydrate (21g sugars

- Cholesterol: 0 cholesterol

931. Pretty Gelatin Molds

Serving: 4 servings. | Prep: 15mins | Cook: 0mins | Ready in:

Ingredients

- 1 package (3 ounces) orange gelatin
- 3/4 cup boiling water
- 3/4 cup whole-berry cranberry sauce
- 1 medium navel orange, peeled and finely chopped
- 4 lettuce leaves

Direction

- In big bowl containing boiling water, dissolve gelatin. Mix in orange and cranberry sauce. Add to flour 1/2-cup molds coated using cooking spray. Keep chilled till set or for 3 to 4 hours. Unmold to dishes lined with lettuce.

Nutrition Information

- Calories: 93 calories
- Sodium: 49mg sodium
- Fiber: 1g fiber)
- Total Carbohydrate: 22g carbohydrate (22g sugars
- Cholesterol: 0 cholesterol
- Protein: 2g protein.
- Total Fat: 0 fat (0 saturated fat)

932. Quick Cran Raspberry Gelatin

Serving: 12 servings. | Prep: 20mins | Cook: 0mins | Ready in:

Ingredients

- 3 packages (3 ounces each) raspberry gelatin
- 2 cups boiling water
- 1 can (14 ounces) jellied cranberry sauce
- 1 can (21 ounces) raspberry pie filling
- 1 carton (8 ounces) frozen whipped topping, thawed

Direction

- Melt the gelatin in boiling water in a big bowl. Beat cranberry sauce in a small bowl, mix into the gelatin mixture until combined. Chill for 1-1/2 hours until partly set.
- Fold in the pie filling. Move to a grease-coated 6-cup ring mold. Chill until set, about 4 hours.
- Remove from the mold onto a serving dish. Use whipped topping to pipe into the middle of the ring.

Nutrition Information

- Calories: 228 calories
- Cholesterol: 0 cholesterol
- Protein: 2g protein.
- Total Fat: 3g fat (3g saturated fat)
- Sodium: 77mg sodium
- Fiber: 2g fiber)
- Total Carbohydrate: 48g carbohydrate (37g sugars

933.   Quick Cranberry Gelatin Salad

Serving: 8-10 servings. | Prep: 10mins | Cook: 0mins | Ready in:

Ingredients

- 1 package (6 ounces) cherry gelatin
- 1-1/2 cups boiling water
- 1 can (20 ounces) crushed pineapple, undrained
- 1 can (14 ounces) whole-berry cranberry sauce
- 1-1/2 cups seedless red grapes, halved

- 1/4 cup chopped pecans

Direction

- Melt the gelatin in water in a big bowl. Mix in cranberry sauce and pineapple. Chill for 30 minutes. Mix in pecans and grapes. Put in a 2-quart serving bowl. Chill until firm.

Nutrition Information

- Calories: 146 calories
- Total Fat: 2g fat (0 saturated fat)
- Sodium: 62mg sodium
- Fiber: 0 fiber)
- Total Carbohydrate: 32g carbohydrate (0 sugars
- Cholesterol: 0 cholesterol
- Protein: 1g protein. Diabetic Exchanges: 2 fruit

934.   Rainbow Gelatin

Serving: 16-20 servings. | Prep: 25mins | Cook: 0mins | Ready in:

Ingredients

- 6 packages (3 ounces each) fruit-flavored gelatins of your choice
- 6 cups boiling water, divided
- 3 cups cold water, divided
- 1 package (8 ounces) cream cheese, cut into six cubes

Direction

- In a bowl with 1 cup of boiling water, dissolve one gelatin package. Pour half a cup of cold water; mix. Scoop 1/2 into an oiled 10-in. fluted tube pan. Keep chilled for roughly 40 minutes till nearly set. Let cool down the other 1/2 of gelatin mixture; add to a blender. Put in one cube of cream cheese and blend till smooth in consistency. Scoop on top of the first layer. Keep chilled till set. Repeat five times, alternating plain gelatin layer with creamed gelatin layer, and chilling between each step. Just prior to serving, unmold to a serving platter.

Nutrition Information

- Calories: 55 calories
- Total Fat: 4g fat (2g saturated fat)
- Sodium: 43mg sodium
- Fiber: 0 fiber)
- Total Carbohydrate: 4g carbohydrate (4g sugars
- Cholesterol: 12mg cholesterol
- Protein: 1g protein.

935. Rainbow Gelatin Cubes

Serving: about 9 dozen. | Prep: 30mins | Cook: 0mins | Ready in:

Ingredients

- 4 packages (3 ounces each) assorted flavored gelatin
- 6 envelopes unflavored gelatin, divided
- 5-3/4 cups boiling water, divided
- 1 can (14 ounces) sweetened condensed milk
- 1/4 cup cold water

Direction

- Mix 1 envelope of unflavored gelatin with 1 package of flavored gelatin in a small bowl. Mix in 1 cup of hot water until melted. Put in a grease-coated 13-inch x 9-inch plate. Chill for 20 minutes until set but not firm.
- Mix 1 cup of boiling water with condensed milk in a small bowl. Drizzle 2 envelopes of unflavored gelatin over cold water in another bowl; let it sit for 1 minute. Mix in 3/4 cup of boiling water. Add to the milk mixture. Put 1 cup of the creamy gelatin mixture on the first layer of flavored gelatin. Chill for 25 minutes until set but not firm.

- Repeat the whole process 2 times, switching between flavored gelatin and creamy gelatin layers. Chill each layer until set but not firm and add the next layer on top. Put the final layer of flavored gelatin on top. Once you have finished the last layer, chill for a minimum of 1 hour and slice into 1-inch squares.

Nutrition Information

- Calories: 26 calories
- Total Fat: 0 fat (0 saturated fat)
- Sodium: 27mg sodium
- Fiber: 0 fiber)
- Total Carbohydrate: 4g carbohydrate (0 sugars
- Cholesterol: 0 cholesterol
- Protein: 2g protein. Diabetic Exchanges: 1/2 fruit.

936. Rainbow Gelatin Salad

Serving: 16-20 servings. | Prep: 60mins | Cook: 0mins | Ready in:

Ingredients

- 7 packages (3 ounces each) assorted flavored gelatin
- 4-1/2 cups boiling water, divided
- 4-1/2 cups cold water, divided
- 1 can (12 ounces) evaporated milk, chilled, divided

Direction

- Melt one package of gelatin in 3/4 cup of boiling water in a small bowl. Mix in 3/4 cup of cold water. Put in a grease-coated 13-inch x 9-inch baking plate. Chill for 1 hour until firm.
- Melt another package of gelatin in 1/2 cup of boiling water. Mix in 1/2 cup of milk and 1/2 cup of cold water. Put on the first layer. Refrigerate until firm.

- Repeat 5 times, switching between creamy gelatin. Refrigerate until each layer is firm and add the next layer. Chill overnight. Slice into squares.

Nutrition Information

- Calories: 130 calories
- Fiber: 0 fiber)
- Total Carbohydrate: 27g carbohydrate (27g sugars
- Cholesterol: 5mg cholesterol
- Protein: 4g protein. Diabetic Exchanges: 1-1/2 starch.
- Total Fat: 1g fat (1g saturated fat)
- Sodium: 84mg sodium

---

937. Raspberry Congealed Salad

Serving: 6 servings. | Prep: 20mins | Cook: 0mins | Ready in:

Ingredients

- 1 can (8 ounces) crushed pineapple
- 1 package (12 ounces) frozen unsweetened raspberries, thawed
- 1 package (3 ounces) raspberry gelatin
- 1 cup applesauce
- 1/4 cup coarsely chopped pecans
- Mayonnaise, optional

Direction

- Drain off raspberries and pineapple, saving the juices. Add fruit into a big bowl; put aside. Pour enough water into the juice to measure 1 cup. Add to a saucepan; boil. Take away from the heat; mix in gelatin till dissolved.
- Add on top of fruit mixture. Put in pecans and applesauce. Add to a 1-qt. bowl. Chill till set. Scoop to separate dessert plates; if you want add a mayonnaise dollop on top.

Nutrition Information

- Calories: 151 calories
- Fiber: 3g fiber)
- Total Carbohydrate: 29g carbohydrate (24g sugars
- Cholesterol: 0 cholesterol
- Protein: 3g protein.
- Total Fat: 4g fat (0 saturated fat)
- Sodium: 34mg sodium

---

938. Raspberry Cranberry Gelatin Salad

Serving: 12-15 servings. | Prep: 30mins | Cook: 0mins | Ready in:

Ingredients

- 1 package (3 ounces) cranberry gelatin
- 1 package (3 ounces) cherry gelatin
- 1 package (3 ounces) raspberry gelatin
- 1 teaspoon ground cinnamon
- 1 can (8 ounces) crushed pineapple
- 3/4 cup each cherry, cranberry and orange juice
- 1 can (14 ounces) jellied cranberry sauce
- 1 cup red wine or grape juice
- 1 can (11 ounces) mandarin oranges, drained
- 1 package (10 ounces) frozen sweetened raspberries, thawed
- 1/2 cup finely chopped celery
- 1/2 cup chopped pecans or walnuts

Direction

- Mix cinnamon and gelatins in a big bowl; put aside. Drain pineapple, saving the juice; put pineapple aside.
- Mix orange juices, cranberry and cherry in a big saucepan; put in reserved pineapple juice. Boil. Add on top of gelatin mixture; whip till dissolved.

- Mix in grape juice or wine and cranberry sauce till smooth in consistency. Mix in pineapple, nuts, celery, raspberries and oranges. Add to a 13x9-in. plate. Keep chilled till firm or for 6 hours or overnight. Chop into square pieces.

Nutrition Information

- Calories: 206 calories
- Total Carbohydrate: 43g carbohydrate (36g sugars
- Cholesterol: 0 cholesterol
- Protein: 2g protein.
- Total Fat: 3g fat (0 saturated fat)
- Sodium: 52mg sodium
- Fiber: 2g fiber)

939. Raspberry Gelatin Jewels

Serving: 8 servings. | Prep: 10mins | Cook: 0mins | Ready in:

Ingredients

- 1 package (6 ounces) raspberry gelatin
- 1-1/2 cups boiling water
- 1 can (20 ounces) unsweetened crushed pineapple, drained
- 1 package (12 ounces) frozen unsweetened raspberries

Direction

- In a big bowl containing boiling water, dissolve the gelatin. Mix in fruit. Add to a greased 11x7-in. plate. Keep chilled in the refrigerator till firm or for 4 hours. Chop into square pieces.

Nutrition Information

- Calories: 139 calories
- Sodium: 50mg sodium
- Fiber: 2g fiber)

- Total Carbohydrate: 34g carbohydrate (29g sugars
- Cholesterol: 0 cholesterol
- Protein: 3g protein.
- Total Fat: 0 fat (0 saturated fat)

940. Raspberry Gelatin Salad

Serving: 15 servings. | Prep: 10mins | Cook: 0mins | Ready in:

Ingredients

- 3 packages (.3 ounce each) sugar-free raspberry gelatin
- 1-1/2 cups boiling water
- 1 package (12 ounces) frozen unsweetened raspberries
- 1 can (20 ounces) unsweetened pineapple, undrained
- 2 medium ripe bananas, mashed
- 1 cup fat-free sour cream

Direction

- Dissolve gelatin in water in a bowl. Put in bananas, pineapple and raspberries then stir. Pour half of the mixture into an 11x7-inch dish; keen in the fridge for half an hour or until firm. Set aside the remaining gelatin mixture at room temperature. Spread sour cream on top of the gelatin in pan; then put the remaining gelatin mixture on top. Keep in the fridge for an hour or until the mixture gets firm.

Nutrition Information

- Calories: 63 calories
- Total Carbohydrate: 14g carbohydrate (0 sugars
- Cholesterol: 1mg cholesterol
- Protein: 2g protein. Diabetic Exchanges: 1 fruit.
- Total Fat: 0 fat (0 saturated fat)

- Sodium: 50mg sodium
- Fiber: 0 fiber)

- Cholesterol: 10mg cholesterol

941. Raspberry Luscious Gelatin Salad

Serving: 16 servings. | Prep: 20mins | Cook: 0mins | Ready in:

Ingredients

- 2 packages (3 ounces each) raspberry gelatin
- 1 envelope unflavored gelatin
- 1 cup boiling water
- 2 cups cold water
- 1 can (20 ounces) crushed pineapple with juice
- 2 large ripe bananas, mashed
- 1 pint fresh or frozen whole unsweetened raspberries
- 1 cup sour cream

Direction

- Mix boiling water, unflavored gelatin, and raspberry gelatin in a big bowl; mix until dissolved. Mix in the raspberries, bananas, pineapple and cold water.
- Add 1/2 of gelatin mixture to a glass serving bowl or 13x9-in. plate; keep chilled till firm. Keep the leftover half stand at room temperature. Once gelatin becomes firm, spread sour cream equally on top, then scoop gently reserved mixture on the sour cream. Keep chilled till firm.

Nutrition Information

- Calories: 102 calories
- Protein: 2g protein.
- Total Fat: 3g fat (2g saturated fat)
- Sodium: 21mg sodium
- Fiber: 2g fiber)
- Total Carbohydrate: 18g carbohydrate (16g sugars

942. Raspberry Pineapple Gelatin Salad

Serving: 12-16 servings. | Prep: 25mins | Cook: 0mins | Ready in:

Ingredients

- 2 packages (3 ounces each) cranberry gelatin
- 1 cup boiling water
- 1 package (8 ounces) cream cheese, softened
- 1 package (12 ounces) frozen raspberries, thawed and drained
- 1 cup ginger ale
- 1 can (8 ounces) crushed pineapple, drained
- 1/3 cup chopped pecans
- 1/2 teaspoon vanilla extract
- 1 carton (8 ounces) frozen whipped topping, thawed
- 1-1/2 cups miniature marshmallows
- Additional whipped topping

Direction

- In a small bowl with boiling water, dissolve gelatin. Whip cream cheese till smooth in consistency in a big bowl. Slowly put in hot gelatin mixture and whip till smooth in consistency. Mix in vanilla, pecans, pineapple, ginger ale, and raspberries. Keep it covered and let chill in the refrigerator till set partly or for half an hour.
- Fold in marshmallows and whipped topping. Place into a 13x9-in. plate coated using cooking spray. Keep it covered and let chill in the refrigerator till firm or for 4 hours. Spread with extra whipped topping.

Nutrition Information

- Calories: 176 calories

- Total Carbohydrate: 21g carbohydrate (17g sugars
- Cholesterol: 16mg cholesterol
- Protein: 2g protein.
- Total Fat: 9g fat (6g saturated fat)
- Sodium: 58mg sodium
- Fiber: 1g fiber)

943. Red, White 'n' Blue Salad

Serving: 16 servings. | Prep: 30mins | Cook: 0mins | Ready in:

Ingredients

- 1 package (3 ounces) berry blue gelatin
- 2 cups boiling water, divided
- 2-1/2 cups cold water, divided
- 1 cup fresh blueberries
- 1 envelope unflavored gelatin
- 1 cup heavy whipping cream
- 6 tablespoons sugar
- 2 cups (16 ounces) sour cream
- 1 teaspoon vanilla extract
- 1 package (3 ounces) raspberry gelatin
- 1 cup fresh raspberries
- Whipped topping and additional berries, optional

Direction

- In 1 cup of boiling water, put berry blue gelatin to melt; mix in 1 cup of cold water. Add blueberries. Put in a 3-qt. serving bowl. Chill for 1 hour until firm.
- Drizzle unflavored gelatin over 1/2 cup of cold water in a saucepan; let it sit for 1 minute. Add sugar and cream, stir and cook on low heat until melted. Let it cool down to room temperature. Mix in vanilla and sour cream. Put on top of the blue layer. Chill until firm.
- Melt raspberry gelatin in the rest of the hot water, mix in the rest of the cold water. Add raspberries. Put on top of the cream layer.

Refrigerate until set. Put berries and whipped topping on top if you want.

Nutrition Information

- Calories: 179 calories
- Protein: 3g protein.
- Total Fat: 11g fat (7g saturated fat)
- Sodium: 46mg sodium
- Fiber: 1g fiber)
- Total Carbohydrate: 18g carbohydrate (16g sugars
- Cholesterol: 40mg cholesterol

944. Red, White And Blueberry Salad

Serving: 12-16 servings. | Prep: 30mins | Cook: 0mins | Ready in:

Ingredients

- 2 packages (3 ounces each) raspberry gelatin
- 2 cups boiling water, divided
- 1-1/2 cups cold water, divided
- 1 envelope unflavored gelatin
- 1 cup half-and-half cream
- 3/4 to 1 cup sugar
- 1 package (8 ounces) cream cheese, cubed
- 1/2 cup chopped pecans
- 1 teaspoon vanilla extract
- 1 can (15 ounces) blueberries in syrup, undrained

Direction

- In big bowl containing 1 cup of boiling water, dissolve one raspberry gelatin package. Mix in 1 cup of cold water. Add to a 13x9-in. plate; keep chilled till set. In a small bowl containing the leftover cold water, soften unflavored gelatin; put aside.
- Mix sugar and cream in a big saucepan; stir on medium heat till sugar dissolves. Put in

softened unflavored gelatin and cream cheese; cook and stir till smooth in consistency. Let it cool down. Mix in vanilla and pecans. Scoop on top of raspberry gelatin. Keep chilled in the refrigerator till set totally.

- In the leftover boiling water in a big bowl, dissolve second raspberry gelatin package. Mix in blueberries. Scoop gently on top of cream cheese layer. Keep chilled for a few hours or overnight.

Nutrition Information

- Calories:
- Total Carbohydrate:
- Cholesterol:
- Protein:
- Total Fat:
- Sodium:
- Fiber:

945.   Red Hot Gelatin Salad

Serving: 6 servings. | Prep: 15mins | Cook: 0mins | Ready in:

Ingredients

- 1 package (3 ounces) cherry gelatin
- 1-1/2 cups boiling water, divided
- 1/4 cup red-hot candies
- 1/4 cup plus 1-1/2 teaspoons cold water
- 1 cup chopped tart apples
- 1 cup chopped celery
- 1/2 cup chopped walnuts

Direction

- In 1 cup of boiling water in a small bowl, dissolve the gelatin. In a different bowl containing the leftover water, dissolve red hots; mix into gelatin. Mix in cold water. Keep chilled in the refrigerator for roughly 60 minutes till it becomes thickened a bit.

- Fold in the walnuts, celery, and apples. Transfer into a 4-cup mold greased with cooking spray. Place in the fridge for 2 hours or until firm.

Nutrition Information

- Calories:
- Total Carbohydrate:
- Cholesterol:
- Protein:
- Total Fat:
- Sodium:
- Fiber:

946.   Red Hot Molded Hearts

Serving: 10-12 servings. | Prep: 15mins | Cook: 0mins | Ready in:

Ingredients

- 1/4 cup red-hot candies
- 1 cup boiling water
- 1 package (3 ounces) strawberry gelatin
- 2-1/2 cups applesauce

Direction

- In a big bowl containing water, dissolve candies. Mix in gelatin till dissolved. Fold in applesauce. Add to 12 greased 1/3-cup separate molds, a 4-cup heart-shaped mold or a 1-qt. bowl. Keep chilled in the refrigerator till set or overnight.

Nutrition Information

- Calories:
- Total Fat:
- Sodium:
- Fiber:
- Total Carbohydrate:
- Cholesterol:

- Protein:

- Calories: 203 calories
- Sodium: 12mg sodium
- Fiber: 2g fiber)
- Total Carbohydrate: 38g carbohydrate (35g sugars
- Cholesterol: 20mg cholesterol
- Protein: 3g protein.
- Total Fat: 6g fat (3g saturated fat)

947. Red White And Blue Berry Delight

Serving: 8 servings. | Prep: 20mins | Cook: 5mins | Ready in:

Ingredients

- 1/2 cup sugar
- 2 envelopes unflavored gelatin
- 4 cups white cranberry-peach juice drink, divided
- 1 tablespoon lemon juice
- 2 cups fresh strawberries, halved
- 2 cups fresh blueberries
- CREAM:
- 1/2 cup heavy whipping cream
- 1 tablespoon sugar
- 1/4 teaspoon vanilla extract

Direction

- Mix gelatin with sugar in a big saucepan. Add 1 cup of cranberry-peach juice; stir and cook on low heat for 5 minutes until the gelatin is fully melted. Take away from heat; mix in the rest of the cranberry-peach juice and lemon juice.
- In an 8-cup ring mold that is coated in cooking spray, put the strawberries; add 2 cups of the gelatin mixture. Chill for 30 minutes until set but not firm. Put aside the rest of the gelatin mixture.
- Mix blueberries into the rest of gelatin mixture, put on the strawberry layer. Chill overnight. Remove from the mold onto a serving dish.
- Whisk the cream until it starts to thicken in a small bowl. Add vanilla and sugar, whisk until stiff peaks form. Serve along with gelatin.

Nutrition Information

948. Refreshing Rhubarb Salad

Serving: 12-14 servings. | Prep: 20mins | Cook: 0mins | Ready in:

Ingredients

- 4 cups diced fresh or frozen rhubarb
- 1-1/2 cups water
- 1/2 cup sugar
- 1 package (6 ounces) strawberry gelatin
- 1 cup orange juice
- 1 teaspoon grated orange zest
- 1 cup sliced fresh strawberries
- Mayonnaise, fresh mint and additional strawberries, optional

Direction

- Add sugar, water, and rhubarb to a saucepan and boil it over medium heat. Cook without a cover for 6-8 minutes until rhubarb is soft. Take away from heat; mix in gelatin until melted. Mix in zest and orange juice.
- Refrigerate until the mixture starts to firm. Tuck in strawberries. Put in a 2-qt. bowl and refrigerate until set. Use a dollop of strawberries, mint, and mayonnaise to garnish if you want.

Nutrition Information

- Calories: 91 calories
- Sodium: 29mg sodium

- Fiber: 1g fiber)
- Total Carbohydrate: 22g carbohydrate (21g sugars
- Cholesterol: 0 cholesterol
- Protein: 2g protein.
- Total Fat: 0 fat (0 saturated fat)

949. Rhubarb Berry Delight Salad

Serving: 12 servings. | Prep: 30mins | Cook: 0mins | Ready in:

Ingredients

- 4 cups diced fresh rhubarb or frozen rhubarb
- 2 cups fresh or frozen strawberries
- 1-1/2 cups sugar, divided
- 1 package (6 ounces) raspberry gelatin
- 2 cups boiling water
- 1 cup milk
- 1 envelope unflavored gelatin
- 1/4 cup cold water
- 1-1/2 teaspoons vanilla extract
- 2 cups sour cream

Direction

- Cook strawberries and rhubarb with 1 cup sugar in a large saucepan until the fruit is soft. Dissolve raspberry gelatin with boiling water in a large bowl. Add fruit, stir, and put to one side.
- Mix leftover sugar with milk in another saucepan and bring to low heat until sugar is dissolved. In the meantime, dissolve unflavored gelatin in cold water to soften. Add gelatin into hot milk mixture and stir until dissolved. Turn off the heat, stir in vanilla. Allow to cool to slightly warm; mix with sour cream. Put to one side at room temperature.
- Add 1/3 of fruit mixture into a 3-qt. bowl. Refrigerate until nearly firm. Spread 1/3 of sour cream mixture over the fruit layer; chill until nearly firm. Duplicate the process twice,

refrigerating between layers if needed. Chill for at least 3 hours until completely set, then serve

Nutrition Information

- Calories: 255 calories
- Total Fat: 7g fat (5g saturated fat)
- Sodium: 64mg sodium
- Fiber: 1g fiber)
- Total Carbohydrate: 43g carbohydrate (41g sugars
- Cholesterol: 28mg cholesterol
- Protein: 4g protein.

950. Rhubarb Pear Gelatin

Serving: 12 servings. | Prep: 15mins | Cook: 10mins | Ready in:

Ingredients

- 2 packages (6 ounces each) strawberry gelatin
- 2 cups miniature marshmallows, divided
- 4 cups sliced fresh or frozen rhubarb
- 2 cups water
- 2/3 cup sugar
- 2 cups cold water
- 1 can (15-1/4 ounces) sliced pears, drained and chopped

Direction

- In a big bowl, add 1 cup of marshmallows and gelatin; put aside.
- Mix sugar, water and rhubarb in a big saucepan. Boil. Lower the heat; keep it covered and let simmer till rhubarb becomes softened or for 3 to 4 minutes. Take out of the heat; add on top of marshmallow mixture, mixing to dissolve gelatin. Mix in the leftover marshmallows, pears and cold water.
- Add into a 13x9-in. plate. Keep chilled in the refrigerator till firm or for no less than 6 hours.

Nutrition Information

- Calories: 204 calories
- Sodium: 73mg sodium
- Fiber: 1g fiber)
- Total Carbohydrate: 50g carbohydrate (46g sugars
- Cholesterol: 0 cholesterol
- Protein: 3g protein.
- Total Fat: 0 fat (0 saturated fat)

---

951.   Rhubarb Salad

Serving: 8 servings. | Prep: 5mins | Cook: 10mins | Ready in:

Ingredients

- 4 cups diced fresh or frozen rhubarb
- 1-1/2 cups cold water, divided
- 3/4 cup sugar
- 1 package (6 ounces) raspberry or strawberry gelatin
- 1 tablespoon grated orange zest
- 1/2 cup finely chopped celery
- 1/2 cup chopped nuts, optional

Direction

- Cook sugar, 1/2 cup of water, and rhubarb in a saucepan for 8 minutes until forming a sauce. Take away from heat, add gelatin and toss until melted. Add the rest of the water, nuts if you want, celery, and orange peel, toss thoroughly. Put in a lightly grease-coated 4- to 5-1/2-cup mold. Put a cover on and chill until set.

Nutrition Information

- Calories: 165 calories
- Fiber: 1g fiber)
- Total Carbohydrate: 40g carbohydrate (38g sugars
- Cholesterol: 0 cholesterol

- Protein: 3g protein.
- Total Fat: 0 fat (0 saturated fat)
- Sodium: 58mg sodium

---

952.   Rhubarb Strawberry Gelatin Molds

Serving: 2 servings. | Prep: 15mins | Cook: 0mins | Ready in:

Ingredients

- 1 cup diced fresh or frozen rhubarb
- 1/4 cup water
- 1 tablespoon sugar
- 3 tablespoons plus 1 teaspoon strawberry gelatin
- 1/4 cup sliced fresh strawberries
- 1/4 cup orange juice
- 1/4 teaspoon grated orange zest
- Whipped cream, optional

Direction

- Boil sugar, water and rhubarb in a small-sized saucepan on medium heat. Lower the heat; let it simmer, while uncovered, till rhubarb has softened or for 3 to 5 minutes. Take out of the heat; mix in gelatin till dissolved. Put in zest, orange juice, and strawberries.
- Separate among two 4-in. mini fluted pans coated using cooking spray; keep chilled in the refrigerator till firm or for 4 hours. Just prior to serving, invert molds to serving dishes; if you want, use whipped cream to decorate.

Nutrition Information

- Calories: 143 calories
- Cholesterol: 0 cholesterol
- Protein: 3g protein. Diabetic Exchanges: 1-1/2 starch
- Total Fat: 0 fat (0 saturated fat)
- Sodium: 56mg sodium

- Fiber: 2g fiber)
- Total Carbohydrate: 34g carbohydrate (31g sugars

953.   Rosey Raspberry Salad

Serving: 12-14 servings. | Prep: 15mins | Cook: 0mins | Ready in:

Ingredients

- 3 packages (3 ounces each) raspberry gelatin
- 3 cups boiling water
- 3 cups raspberry sherbet
- 1 package (12 ounces) unsweetened frozen raspberries

Direction

- Melt the gelatin in boiling water in a big bowl. Add sherbet and mix until dissolved. Refrigerate until syrupy. Add raspberries. Put in a greased 8-cup mold. Refrigerate until firm.

Nutrition Information

- Calories: 77 calories
- Protein: 1g protein.
- Total Fat: 1g fat (0 saturated fat)
- Sodium: 29mg sodium
- Fiber: 1g fiber)
- Total Carbohydrate: 17g carbohydrate (14g sugars
- Cholesterol: 2mg cholesterol

954.   Rosy Rhubarb Mold

Serving: 50 servings. | Prep: 40mins | Cook: 0mins | Ready in:

Ingredients

- 24 cups chopped rhubarb
- 6 cups water
- 3 cups sugar
- 6 packages (6 ounces each) strawberry gelatin
- 3 cups orange juice
- 2 tablespoons grated orange zest
- 6 cups sliced fresh strawberries
- Leaf lettuce
- Additional strawberries
- DRESSING:
- 3 cups mayonnaise
- 3 cups whipped topping
- 6 to 7 tablespoons whole milk

Direction

- Stir and cook sugar, water, and rhubarb in a kettle over medium-low heat until rhubarb is tender and soft. Take away from heat; mix in gelatin until melted. Mix in orange juice and zest. Refrigerate for 2-3 hours until partly set. Mix in strawberries. Put into 6 grease-coated 5-cup ring molds. Chill overnight. Remove from the molds to dishes lined with lettuce, use berries to garnish.
- To make the dressing, mix whipped topping with mayonnaise, add enough milk to thin to the preferred consistency. Serve in a bowl in the middle of the mold.

Nutrition Information

- Calories: 193 calories
- Protein: 1g protein.
- Total Fat: 12g fat (2g saturated fat)
- Sodium: 83mg sodium
- Fiber: 2g fiber)
- Total Carbohydrate: 22g carbohydrate (19g sugars
- Cholesterol: 5mg cholesterol

955.   Rosy Rhubarb Salad

Serving: 8-10 servings. | Prep: 25mins | Cook: 0mins | Ready in:

Ingredients

- 4 cups diced raw or frozen rhubarb
- 1/2 cup water
- 1/2 cup sugar
- 2 packages (3 ounces each) strawberry gelatin
- 1 cup applesauce
- 1 cup orange juice
- 2 teaspoons grated orange zest
- 1 cup sliced fresh strawberries

Direction

- Mix sugar, water and rhubarb in a saucepan. Cook on medium heat till rhubarb softened. Mix gelatin and hot rhubarb in a big bowl. Mix till dissolved. Put in orange peel and juice and applesauce. Keep chilled till syrupy. Fold in the strawberries. Add to a slightly greased 5 to 6 cup mold. Keep chilled for roughly 4 hours or overnight till set.

Nutrition Information

- Calories: 107 calories
- Cholesterol: 0 cholesterol
- Protein: 1g protein.
- Total Fat: 0 fat (0 saturated fat)
- Sodium: 22mg sodium
- Fiber: 2g fiber)
- Total Carbohydrate: 26g carbohydrate (24g sugars

956.   Ruby Apple Salad

Serving: 6-8 servings. | Prep: 10mins | Cook: 0mins | Ready in:

Ingredients

- 1 package (3 ounces) cherry gelatin
- 2 tablespoons red-hot candies
- 1-3/4 cups boiling water
- 1-1/2 to 2 cups chopped apples
- 1/2 cup chopped celery
- 1/2 cup chopped walnuts

Direction

- Combine candies and gelatin in a bowl of boiling water until dissolved. Put into the fridge to chill until partly set. Tuck in walnuts, celery, and apples. Put into a 1-qt. serving bowl. Put into the fridge for a minimum of 4 hours until set.

Nutrition Information

- Calories:
- Fiber:
- Total Carbohydrate:
- Cholesterol:
- Protein:
- Total Fat:
- Sodium:

957.   Ruby Gelatin Salad

Serving: 8 servings. | Prep: 10mins | Cook: 0mins | Ready in:

Ingredients

- 1 package (3 ounces) cherry gelatin
- 1 cup boiling water
- 1 cup orange juice
- 1 cup diced peeled apple
- 1 cup chopped celery
- 1/2 cup chopped walnuts

Direction

- Melt the gelatin in water in a bowl. Add orange juice; chill until partly set. Mix in walnuts, celery, and apple. Chill until firm.

Nutrition Information

- Calories: 72 calories
- Cholesterol: 0 cholesterol

- Protein: 2g protein. Diabetic Exchanges: 1 fat
- Total Fat: 5g fat (0 saturated fat)
- Sodium: 13mg sodium
- Fiber: 0 fiber)
- Total Carbohydrate: 7g carbohydrate (0 sugars

- Cholesterol: 15mg cholesterol
- Protein: 2g protein.
- Total Fat: 4g fat (3g saturated fat)
- Sodium: 42mg sodium

958. Ruby Red Raspberry Salad

Serving: 12-16 servings. | Prep: 15mins | Cook: 0mins | Ready in:

Ingredients

- 1 package (3 ounces) raspberry gelatin
- 2 cups boiling water, divided
- 1 package (10 ounces) frozen sweetened raspberries
- 1-1/2 cups sour cream
- 1 package (3 ounces) cherry gelatin
- 1 can (20 ounces) crushed pineapple, drained
- 1 can (14 ounces) whole-berry cranberry sauce
- Mayonnaise and mint sprigs, optional

Direction

- In 1 cup of boiling water, dissolve raspberry gelatin. Put in raspberries and mix till berries become thawed and separated. Add to a 13x9-in. dish; keep chilled till set.
- Gently spread with sour cream; keep chilled. In the leftover boiling water, dissolve cherry gelatin. Put in pineapple and cranberry sauce; stir them well. Let it thicken a bit.
- Gently scoop on sour cream mixture; keep chilled. Use mint and mayonnaise to decorate if you want.

Nutrition Information

- Calories: 164 calories
- Fiber: 1g fiber)
- Total Carbohydrate: 31g carbohydrate (25g sugars

959. Ruby Red Beet Salad

Serving: 12-15 servings. | Prep: 15mins | Cook: 0mins | Ready in:

Ingredients

- 1 package (3 ounces) cherry gelatin
- 1 package (3 ounces) raspberry gelatin
- 1 package (3 ounces) strawberry gelatin
- 4 cups boiling water
- 1 can (20 ounces) crushed pineapple
- 1 can (15 ounces) diced beets, drained
- DRESSING:
- 1/2 cup mayonnaise
- 1/2 cup sour cream
- 3 tablespoons each chopped celery, green pepper and chives
- Leaf lettuce, optional

Direction

- Mix the gelatins in a big bowl; pour in boiling water and mix to dissolve. Drain pineapple, saving the juice; put pineapple aside. Mix juice into gelatin. Keep in the refrigerator till thickened a bit. Mix in pineapple and beets. Add to a 13x9-in. plate. Keep chilled in the refrigerator till it becomes firm.
- To make the dressing, in a small-sized bowl, mix chives, green pepper, celery, sour cream and mayonnaise. Chop gelatin into square pieces; serve over salad plates lined with lettuce if you want. Use dressing to dollop.

Nutrition Information

- Calories: 164 calories
- Protein: 2g protein.

- Total Fat: 7g fat (2g saturated fat)
- Sodium: 139mg sodium
- Fiber: 1g fiber)
- Total Carbohydrate: 23g carbohydrate (21g sugars
- Cholesterol: 8mg cholesterol

---

960. Sailboat Salads

Serving: 4 servings. | Prep: 15mins | Cook: 0mins | Ready in:

Ingredients

- 1 package (3 ounces) berry blue gelatin
- 1 cup boiling water
- 1 cup cold water
- 1 can (29 ounces) peach halves, drained
- 4 toothpicks
- 2 thick slices process American cheese
- 2 cups torn lettuce

Direction

- In a bowl, add gelatin then boiling water and toss until the gelatin is melted. Mix in cold water. Put the gelatin on 4 salad dishes and chill until firm. To make the boat, put a half of a peach with the cut side turning up in the middle of each dish (chill the rest of the peaches for later use). Cut cheese slices into two diagonally. To make the sail, gently install a toothpick into the top center of each cheese triangle. Lightly bend the cheese and force the toothpick through the bottom center of the cheese. Stick the toothpick into the edge of the peach. Put lettuce leaves around the dish.

Nutrition Information

- Calories: 264 calories
- Total Fat: 3g fat (2g saturated fat)
- Sodium: 190mg sodium
- Fiber: 3g fiber)

- Total Carbohydrate: 61g carbohydrate (57g sugars
- Cholesterol: 7mg cholesterol
- Protein: 5g protein.

---

961. School Colors Salad

Serving: 12-16 servings. | Prep: 30mins | Cook: 0mins | Ready in:

Ingredients

- 2 packages (3 ounces each) lime gelatin
- 1 package (3 ounces) lemon gelatin
- 4-1/2 cups boiling water, divided
- 1 envelope unflavored gelatin
- 1/4 cup cold water
- 1 cup heavy whipping cream
- 1/4 cup sugar
- 1 cup sour cream

Direction

- In three different bowls, dissolve each flavored gelatin package in one and a half cups boiling water. Add one lime gelatin bowl to 1 oiled 8-cup serving bowl or mold; keep chilled for roughly 60 minutes till nearly set. Put other two gelatin bowls aside at room temperature.
- In cold water, soften unflavored gelatin; let rest for 5 minutes. On medium heat, heat cream in a medium-sized saucepan just below boiling. Mix in sugar and softened gelatin till dissolved. Take out of the heat; mix in sour cream till smooth in consistency. Scoop gently 1/2 on top of chilled lime gelatin layer. Keep chilled for roughly half an hour till nearly set.
- Scoop gently lemon gelatin on top of cream layer. Keep chilled for roughly 60 minutes till nearly set.
- Mix the leftover cream mixture; gently scoop on top of lemon layer. Keep chilled for roughly half an hour till nearly set.
- Scoop gently the second bowl of lime gelatin on top of cream layer. Keep chilled for a few

hours or overnight. Unmold if a mold was used.

Nutrition Information

- Calories:
- Protein:
- Total Fat:
- Sodium:
- Fiber:
- Total Carbohydrate:
- Cholesterol:

962.   Seaside Gelatin Salad

Serving: 12-15 servings. | Prep: 15mins | Cook: 0mins | Ready in:

Ingredients

- 4 packages (3 ounces each) berry blue gelatin
- 3 cups boiling water
- 3 cups cold water
- 1 can (20 ounces) crushed pineapple, drained
- 1-3/4 cups graham cracker crumbs
- 6 tablespoons butter, melted
- 1/4 cup sugar
- Candies for decorating

Direction

- In a big bowl with boiling water, dissolve gelatin. Mix in pineapple and cold water. Add to a 13x9-in. plate. Keep chilled in the refrigerator till set. Mix sugar, butter, and cracker crumbs in a bowl; keep it covered and chilled in the refrigerator. Just prior to serving, drizzle cracker mixture on 1/2 of the gelatin to form a beach. Garnish as you want.

Nutrition Information

- Calories: 138 calories
- Cholesterol: 12mg cholesterol

- Protein: 1g protein.
- Total Fat: 6g fat (3g saturated fat)
- Sodium: 119mg sodium
- Fiber: 1g fiber)
- Total Carbohydrate: 22g carbohydrate (15g sugars

963.   Seven Layer Gelatin Salad

Serving: 12-15 servings. | Prep: 20mins | Cook: 10mins | Ready in:

Ingredients

- 1 package (3 ounces) cherry gelatin
- 4 cups boiling water, divided
- 2-1/2 cups cold water, divided
- 2 envelopes unflavored gelatin
- 2 cups milk
- 1 cup sugar
- 2 cups (16 ounces) sour cream
- 2 teaspoons vanilla extract
- 1 package (3 ounces) lemon gelatin
- 1 package (3 ounces) orange gelatin
- 1 package (3 ounces) lime gelatin

Direction

- Let cherry gelatin dissolve in 1 cup of boiling water in a bowl. Stir in 1/2 cup of cold water. Coat a 13x9-inch dish with cooking spray then pour in the mixture. Store in the fridge for about 30 minutes till set but not firm.
- Drizzle unflavored gelatin over 1/2 cup of cold water in a small saucepan. Leave to stand for 1 minute. Add in sugar and milk; stir. Cook while stirring till sugar and gelatin dissolve over medium heat.
- Take away from the heat. Add in vanilla and sour cream; whisk till smooth. Top the first flavored layer with 1-2/3 cups of creamy gelatin mixture. Let chill till set but not firm. Follow the direction for cherry gelatin to prepare the leftover flavored gelatin layers. Layer creamy gelatin alternately with flavored

gelatin layers. Only add the next layer when the previous one is set. Place lime gelatin on top and store in the fridge overnight. Slice into squares.

Nutrition Information

- Calories: 222 calories
- Fiber: 0 fiber)
- Total Carbohydrate: 36g carbohydrate (35g sugars
- Cholesterol: 26mg cholesterol
- Protein: 5g protein.
- Total Fat: 6g fat (4g saturated fat)
- Sodium: 85mg sodium

---

964.   Simple Lime Gelatin Salad

Serving: 10 servings. | Prep: 20mins | Cook: 0mins | Ready in:

Ingredients

- 2 packages (3 ounces each) lime gelatin
- 2 cups boiling water
- 1 quart lime sherbet
- 1 carton (8 ounces) frozen whipped topping, thawed

Direction

- In boiling water, dissolve gelatin in a big bowl. Whip in sherbet till melted. Pour in whipped topping; whip the mixture well.
- Add to one 8-cup ring mold coated using cooking spray. Keep chilled in the refrigerator till set, about 4 hours. Unmold to a serving platter.

Nutrition Information

- Calories: 210 calories
- Fiber: 2g fiber)

- Total Carbohydrate: 38g carbohydrate (32g sugars
- Cholesterol: 0 cholesterol
- Protein: 2g protein.
- Total Fat: 5g fat (4g saturated fat)
- Sodium: 66mg sodium

---

965.   Six Layer Gelatin Salad

Serving: 16-20 servings. | Prep: 40mins | Cook: 0mins | Ready in:

Ingredients

- 2 packages (3 ounces each) lime gelatin
- 4-1/2 cups boiling water, divided
- 4-1/2 cups cold water, divided
- 1 cup heavy whipping cream
- 3 tablespoons confectioners' sugar
- 2 packages (3 ounces each) orange gelatin
- 1 can (8 ounces) crushed pineapple, drained
- 1 package (3 ounces) strawberry gelatin
- 2 medium firm bananas, thinly sliced

Direction

- Let 1 package of lime gelatin dissolve in a bowl of 3/4 cup of boiling water. Add in 3/4 cup of cold water and stir. Store in the fridge till slightly thick. Beat cream in a small bowl till slightly thick. Beat in sugar till it forms soft peaks. Fold into the lime gelatin with 1/3 of whipped cream. Transfer into a 4-quart bowl. Store in the fridge till firm. Store the leftover whipped cream in the fridge.
- Let 1 package of orange gelatin dissolve in a bowl of 3/4 cup of boiling water. Add in 3/4 cup of cold water and stir. Store in the fridge till slightly thick. Fold in mandarin oranges then spread over the layer of creamy lime. Store in the fridge till firm.
- Let lemon gelatin dissolve in a bowl of 3/4 cup of boiling water. Add in 3/4 cup of cold water and stir. Store in the fridge till slightly thick. Fold in 1/3 of whipped cream then

spread over the layer of orange. Store in the fridge till firm.

- Let the leftover package of lime gelatin dissolve in a bowl of 3/4 cup of boiling water. Add in 3/4 cup of cold water and stir. Store in the fridge till slightly thick. Fold in pineapple then spread over the layer of creamy lemon. Store in the fridge till firm.
- Let the leftover package of orange gelatin dissolve in a bowl of 3/4 cup of boiling water. Add in 3/4 cup of cold water and stir. Store in the fridge till slightly thick. Fold in the leftover whipped cream then spread over the layer of lime. Store in the fridge till firm.
- Let strawberry gelatin dissolve in a bowl of the leftover boiling water. Add in the leftover cold water and stir. Store in the fridge till slightly thick. Fold in bananas. Spread over the layer of creamy orange. Store in the fridge overnight.

Nutrition Information

- Calories: 109 calories
- Protein: 2g protein.
- Total Fat: 4g fat (3g saturated fat)
- Sodium: 34mg sodium
- Fiber: 0 fiber)
- Total Carbohydrate: 17g carbohydrate (16g sugars
- Cholesterol: 16mg cholesterol

966.   Slimy Red Goop Salad

Serving: 8 servings. | Prep: 20mins | Cook: 0mins | Ready in:

Ingredients

- 1 can (15 ounces) mandarin oranges
- 1/2 cup water
- 2 packages (3 ounces each) cherry gelatin
- 1 can (21 ounces) cherry pie filling
- 3/4 cup cola

Direction

- Drain mandarin oranges, saving juice; put fruit aside. Boil water and mandarin orange juice in a big saucepan; take out of the heat. Mix in gelatin till dissolved. Mix in cola and pie filling.
- Add to one 1 1/2-qt. serving bowl. Keep chilled in the refrigerator till thickened a bit, about 50 minutes. Mix in reserved oranges. Keep chilled in the refrigerator till set, about 3 more hours.

Nutrition Information

- Calories: 166 calories
- Sodium: 42mg sodium
- Fiber: 1g fiber)
- Total Carbohydrate: 41g carbohydrate (38g sugars
- Cholesterol: 0 cholesterol
- Protein: 1g protein.
- Total Fat: 0 fat (0 saturated fat)

967.   Snow White Salad

Serving: 16 servings. | Prep: 25mins | Cook: 0mins | Ready in:

Ingredients

- 2 envelopes unflavored gelatin
- 1/2 cup cold water
- 1 can (20 ounces) crushed pineapple, undrained
- 1/4 cup sugar
- 2 packages (8 ounces each) cream cheese, softened
- 1 jar (7 ounces) marshmallow creme
- 2 envelopes whipped topping mix (Dream Whip)
- Red and green candied cherries, optional

Direction

- Mix water and gelatin in a small-sized bowl; put aside. Boil sugar and pineapple in saucepan. Take away from the heat; mix in gelatin mixture till dissolved totally.
- Whip cream cheese in a big bowl till fluffy. Mix in pineapple mixture and marshmallow crème. Keep in the refrigerator for half an hour.
- Based on the instruction on the package, prepare whipped topping; fold into pineapple mixture. Add to an ungreased 13x9-in. plate. Keep it covered and let chill in the refrigerator overnight. If you want, garnish with cherries.

Nutrition Information

- Calories: 141 calories
- Total Carbohydrate: 21g carbohydrate (18g sugars
- Cholesterol: 16mg cholesterol
- Protein: 2g protein.
- Total Fat: 5g fat (4g saturated fat)
- Sodium: 54mg sodium
- Fiber: 0 fiber)

968.   Snowy Raspberry Gelatin Mold

Serving: 8 servings. | Prep: 25mins | Cook: 5mins | Ready in:

Ingredients

- 1 envelope unflavored gelatin
- 1/2 cup cold water
- 1 cup half-and-half cream
- 1/2 cup sugar
- 1 package (8 ounces) cream cheese, softened
- 1 teaspoon vanilla extract
- 1 package (3 ounces) raspberry gelatin
- 1 cup boiling water
- 1 package (10 ounces) frozen sweetened raspberries, thawed
- Fresh raspberries, optional

Direction

- Drizzle unflavored gelatin over cold water in a small bowl and let it sit for 1 minute. Mix sugar and half-and-half together in a small saucepan. Stir and cook just until the mixture begins to simmer. Take away from heat then mix into gelatin until melted.
- Whisk cream cheese until creamy in a big bowl. Mix in gelatin mixture. Mix in vanilla. Put into a 6-cup mold that is coated in cooking spray. Chill for 45 minutes until set but not firm.
- Melt the raspberry gelatin in boiling water in a small bowl. Mix in raspberries until combined. Gently put on top of the cream cheese layer. Put a cover on and chill for a minimum of 4 hours.
- Remove from the mold onto a serving dish, use fresh berries to garnish if you want.

Nutrition Information

- Calories: 267 calories
- Fiber: 2g fiber)
- Total Carbohydrate: 33g carbohydrate (30g sugars
- Cholesterol: 46mg cholesterol
- Protein: 5g protein.
- Total Fat: 13g fat (8g saturated fat)
- Sodium: 125mg sodium

969.   Sparkling Gelatin Salad

Serving: 6 servings. | Prep: 15mins | Cook: 0mins | Ready in:

Ingredients

- 2 envelopes unflavored gelatin
- 1-1/2 cups white grape juice, divided
- 1-1/2 cups sweet white wine or additional white grape juice
- 1/4 cup sugar

- 1 can (15 ounces) mandarin oranges, drained
- 1 cup green grapes, halved
- 3/4 cup fresh raspberries

Direction

- Scatter gelatin on top of half a cup of juice in a small saucepan; let it rest for 60 seconds. Heat on low heat, mixing till gelatin dissolves totally. Mix in leftover juice, sugar and wine. Cook and stir till sugar dissolves.
- Add to a 1-1/2-qt. serving bowl. Keep in the refrigerator for roughly 60 minutes till set yet not firm. Fold in the raspberries, grapes and oranges. Keep in the refrigerator until firm.

Nutrition Information

- Calories: 179 calories
- Sodium: 15mg sodium
- Fiber: 2g fiber)
- Total Carbohydrate: 32g carbohydrate (29g sugars
- Cholesterol: 0 cholesterol
- Protein: 3g protein.
- Total Fat: 0 fat (0 saturated fat)

970.   Sparkling Rhubarb Salad

Serving: 8-10 servings. | Prep: 15mins | Cook: 0mins | Ready in:

Ingredients

- 4 cups diced fresh or frozen rhubarb
- 1-1/2 cups water
- 1/2 cup sugar
- 2 packages (3 ounces each) strawberry gelatin
- 1 cup orange juice
- 1 tablespoon grated orange zest
- 2 cups sliced fresh strawberries

Direction

- Mix sugar, water, and rhubarb together in a big saucepan. Cook over medium heat for 5 minutes until the rhubarb is soft. Take away from heat. Mix in gelatin until melted. Add zest and orange juice. Refrigerate until it's slightly thickened, about 2 to 2-1/2 hours.
- Mix in strawberries, put in a 2-quart bowl. Refrigerate until firm, about 2-3 hours.

Nutrition Information

- Calories:
- Sodium:
- Fiber:
- Total Carbohydrate:
- Cholesterol:
- Protein:
- Total Fat:

971.   Special Strawberry Salad

Serving: 10-12 servings. | Prep: 20mins | Cook: 0mins | Ready in:

Ingredients

- 1 envelope unflavored gelatin
- 1/4 cup cold water
- 1 cup half-and-half cream
- 2/3 cup sugar
- 2 cups sour cream
- 1 teaspoon vanilla extract
- 1 package (6 ounces) strawberry gelatin
- 2 cups boiling water
- 1 package (16 ounces) unsweetened frozen strawberries
- 1 can (11 ounces) mandarin oranges

Direction

- Melt unflavored gelatin in cold water. Heat sugar and cream over low heat in a medium-sized saucepan until the sugar is melted. Mix in the gelatin mixture until melted. Take away from heat; mix in vanilla and sour cream. Put in a 2-quart glass bowl, refrigerate until firm. Melt strawberry gelatin in boiling water. Strain the orange liquid into the strawberry gelatin, mix well. Carefully mix in strawberries until defrosted. Put on the cream layer and put oranges on top (let it settle) and refrigerate until firm.

Nutrition Information

- Calories: 233 calories
- Sodium: 66mg sodium
- Fiber: 1g fiber)
- Total Carbohydrate: 33g carbohydrate (32g sugars
- Cholesterol: 37mg cholesterol
- Protein: 4g protein.
- Total Fat: 9g fat (6g saturated fat)

972. Spiced Cranberry Gelatin Mold

Serving: 10 servings. | Prep: 15mins | Cook: 0mins | Ready in:

Ingredients

- 2 packages (3 ounces each) cranberry gelatin
- 2 cups boiling water
- 1-1/2 cups chilled cranberry juice
- 1 tablespoon lemon juice
- 3/4 teaspoon ground cinnamon
- 1/4 teaspoon ground cloves
- 1-1/2 cups finely chopped fresh or frozen cranberries, thawed
- 3/4 cup sugar
- 1 medium navel orange, peeled and finely chopped
- 1/2 cup chopped pecans
- Lettuce leaves

Direction

- Dissolve gelatin in boiling water in a large bowl. Let the gelatin sit for 10 minutes. Add cloves, cinnamon, lemon juice, and cranberry juice, stir; chill until partly firm for about 1 hour.
- Mix pecans, orange, sugar, and cranberries together and fold into the gelatin mix. Transfer into a 6-cup ring mold covered with cooking spray. Chill in the fridge until completely set for 4 hours. Remove the mold and place the salad on a lettuce-lined platter.

Nutrition Information

- Calories: 191 calories
- Total Fat: 4g fat (0 saturated fat)
- Sodium: 40mg sodium
- Fiber: 2g fiber)
- Total Carbohydrate: 38g carbohydrate (36g sugars
- Cholesterol: 0 cholesterol
- Protein: 2g protein.

973. Spiced Cranberry Chutney Gelatin Salad

Serving: 12 servings. | Prep: 25mins | Cook: 30mins | Ready in:

Ingredients

- 1 cup sugar
- 1 cup water
- 2 cups fresh or frozen cranberries
- 1/2 cup golden raisins
- 1/4 cup red wine vinegar
- 1 tablespoon molasses
- 1-1/2 teaspoons Worcestershire sauce
- 1 teaspoon ground ginger
- 1/2 teaspoon curry powder
- 1/4 teaspoon salt
- 1/4 teaspoon ground nutmeg
- 1/4 cup chopped salted roasted almonds
- GELATIN:

- 1 package (6 ounces) raspberry gelatin
- 1-1/2 cups boiling water
- 1/2 cup cold water
- 12 red lettuce leaves
- 3/4 cup sour cream
- 1/4 cup chopped salted roasted almonds

Direction

- Mix water and sugar in a big saucepan. Boil on medium heat. Lower the heat; let it simmer while uncovered for 5 minutes. Mix in cranberries; cook on medium heat for roughly 15 minutes till the berries pop.
- Mix in nutmeg, salt, curry, ginger, Worcestershire sauce, molasses, vinegar and raisins. Lower the heat; let it simmer while uncovered for 15 minutes, mixing once in a while. Add into a big bowl; let it cool down to room temperature. Mix in almonds.
- In the meantime, for gelatin, in a big bowl containing boiling water, dissolve gelatin. Mix in cold water. Put in the cranberry mixture. Add into an 11x7-in. plate coated using cooking spray. Keep it covered and let chill in the refrigerator till set or for no less than 4 hours.
- Serve over lettuce leaves. Add almonds and sour cream on top.

Nutrition Information

- Calories: 215 calories
- Total Carbohydrate: 39g carbohydrate (35g sugars
- Cholesterol: 10mg cholesterol
- Protein: 3g protein.
- Total Fat: 6g fat (2g saturated fat)
- Sodium: 117mg sodium
- Fiber: 2g fiber)

974. Spiced Orange Gelatin Salad

Serving: 8 servings. | Prep: 15mins | Cook: 0mins | Ready in:

Ingredients

- 2 packages (3 ounces each) orange gelatin, divided
- 1-3/4 cups boiling water, divided
- 3/4 cup cold water
- 1 cup sweetened applesauce
- 1 cup (8 ounces) sour cream
- 1/4 teaspoon ground cinnamon
- Lettuce leaves and sliced apples, optional

Direction

- In 1 cup of boiling water, dissolve 1 gelatin package in a big bowl. Mix in cold water. Add to one 6-cup ring mold coated using cooking spray. Keep chilled in the refrigerator for roughly 60 minutes till set yet not firm.
- At the same time, in the leftover boiling water, dissolve leftover gelatin package in a big bowl. Mix in cinnamon, sour cream and applesauce. Keep chilled in the refrigerator till thickened, 60 minutes. Spread lightly on top of gelatin in mold. Keep chilled in the refrigerator until firm.
- If you want, use lettuce to line one serving dish; unmold gelatin to the dish. If you want use extra lettuce and apples to decorate.

Nutrition Information

- Calories: 162 calories
- Sodium: 60mg sodium
- Fiber: 0 fiber)
- Total Carbohydrate: 26g carbohydrate (25g sugars
- Cholesterol: 20mg cholesterol
- Protein: 3g protein. Diabetic Exchanges: 1-1/2 starch
- Total Fat: 5g fat (4g saturated fat)

975. Spiced Peach Salad

Serving: 8-10 servings. | *Prep: 25mins* | *Cook: 0mins* | *Ready in:*

Ingredients

- 1/2 cup sugar
- 3 tablespoons white vinegar
- 2 cups water
- 1 tablespoon whole cloves
- 4 cinnamon sticks
- 2 packages (3 ounces each) peach or orange gelatin
- 1 can (29 ounces) peach halves

Direction

- Mix water, vinegar, and sugar in a large saucepan. Use a cheesecloth bag to tie cinnamon and cloves; put into the saucepan. Bring everything to a boil. Lower heat, simmer without a cover for 10 minutes.
- Turn the heat off and remove the spice bag. Stir in gelatin until completely dissolved. Drain peaches, reserving peach juice, put peaches to one side. Add enough water to the syrup to measure 2 cups. Pour into gelatin mixture, stir until incorporated.
- Refrigerate until partially thickened. Cut peaches into thin slices, put into gelatin mixture. Transfer into a 2-qt. glass bowl. Refrigerate until entirely set.

Nutrition Information

- Calories: 161 calories
- Total Fat: 0 fat (0 saturated fat)
- Sodium: 44mg sodium
- Fiber: 1g fiber)
- Total Carbohydrate: 41g carbohydrate (40g sugars
- Cholesterol: 0 cholesterol
- Protein: 2g protein.

976. Spicy Citrus Gelatin Mold

Serving: 8 servings. | *Prep: 30mins* | *Cook: 0mins* | *Ready in:*

Ingredients

- 2 cans (11 ounces each) mandarin oranges
- 1 cinnamon stick (3 inches)
- 8 whole cloves
- 1/8 teaspoon salt
- 1 package (.3 ounce) sugar-free lemon gelatin
- 1 package (.3 ounce) sugar-free orange gelatin
- 1 cup cranberry juice
- 1/4 cup lemon juice
- DRESSING:
- 1 cup (8 ounces) fat-free sour cream
- 1 tablespoon orange juice
- 1 tablespoon honey
- 2 teaspoons grated orange zest
- 1/8 teaspoon salt

Direction

- Drain oranges, saving the juice; put oranges aside. Pour enough water into juice to measure two and a half cups; add to a big saucepan. Put in salt, cloves and cinnamon stick. Boil. Lower the heat; keep it covered and let it simmer for 10 minutes. Let it cool down a bit. Strain off the liquid; get rid of spices.
- Bring liquid back to the pan and boil again. Mix orange and lemon gelatins in a big bowl; pour in boiling liquid and mix till dissolved. Mix in lemon juices and cranberry. Keep it covered and let chill in refrigerator for roughly 45 minutes till it becomes syrupy. Fold in mandarin oranges. Add into a 1-1/2-qt. mold coated using cooking spray. Keep it covered and let chill in the refrigerator till firm.
- Mix dressing ingredients in a small-sized bowl. Unmold gelatin to a serving platter; serve alongside the dressing.

Nutrition Information

- Calories: 113 calories
- Sodium: 154mg sodium
- Fiber: 1g fiber)
- Total Carbohydrate: 25g carbohydrate (20g sugars
- Cholesterol: 4mg cholesterol
- Protein: 3g protein. Diabetic Exchanges: 1 fruit
- Total Fat: 0 fat (0 saturated fat)

977.   Spinach Salad Ring

Serving: 10-12 servings. | Prep: 30mins | Cook: 0mins | Ready in:

Ingredients

- 2 envelopes unflavored gelatin
- 1 can (10-1/2 ounces) condensed beef broth, undiluted
- 1/4 cup water
- 2 tablespoons lemon juice
- 1/2 teaspoon salt
- 1 cup mayonnaise
- 1 package (10 ounces) frozen chopped spinach, thawed and squeezed dry
- 4 hard-boiled large eggs, chopped
- 1/4 pound sliced bacon, cooked and crumbled
- 1/4 cup thinly sliced green onions
- Cherry tomatoes, optional

Direction

- Add gelatin over broth in a saucepan; allow to sit for 5 minutes. Cook the broth over low heat until gelatin is totally dissolved. Stir well in salt, lemon juice, and water.
- In a bowl of mayonnaise, slowly pour the broth mixture, stirring continuously until incorporated. Refrigerate for about 40 minutes until partly thickened. Add onions, bacon, eggs, and spinach, gold. Transfer the mixture into an oiled 6-cup mold. Refrigerate until completely set.

- Once ready, remove the mold and place the Jell-O salad onto a platter. Serve with some additional tomatoes if desired.

Nutrition Information

- Calories: 192 calories
- Total Fat: 18g fat (3g saturated fat)
- Sodium: 480mg sodium
- Fiber: 1g fiber)
- Total Carbohydrate: 2g carbohydrate (0 sugars
- Cholesterol: 80mg cholesterol
- Protein: 5g protein.

978.   Spring Rhubarb Salad

Serving: 8-10 servings. | Prep: 10mins | Cook: 10mins | Ready in:

Ingredients

- 4 cups diced fresh rhubarb
- 1-1/2 cups water
- 1/2 cup sugar
- 1 package (6 ounces) strawberry gelatin
- 1 cup orange juice
- 1 teaspoon grated orange zest
- 1 cup sliced fresh strawberries

Direction

- In a saucepan, mix together sugar, water, and rhubarb. Stir and cook over medium heat until rhubarb is soft. Take away from heat, add gelatin and toss until the gelatin is melted. Add zest and orange juice. Refrigerate until syrupy. Add strawberries. Put in a 6-cup mold and refrigerate until set.

Nutrition Information

- Calories: 127 calories
- Cholesterol: 0 cholesterol
- Protein: 2g protein.

- Total Fat: 0 fat (0 saturated fat)
- Sodium: 41mg sodium
- Fiber: 1g fiber)
- Total Carbohydrate: 31g carbohydrate (29g sugars

---

979. Springtime Luncheon Salad

Serving: 8-10 servings. | Prep: 30mins | Cook: 0mins | Ready in:

Ingredients

- 2 envelopes unflavored gelatin
- 2-1/2 cups orange juice, divided
- 2 cups sugar
- Dash salt
- 4 large egg yolks, lightly beaten
- 3 medium navel oranges, peeled and sectioned
- 3 tablespoons lemon juice
- 1 teaspoon grated orange zest
- 1 teaspoon grated lemon zest
- 2 cups heavy whipping cream, whipped
- CHICKEN SALAD:
- 6 cups cubed cooked chicken
- 1 cup chopped celery
- 1 cup mayonnaise
- 1/8 teaspoon white vinegar
- Salt and pepper to taste
- 1/2 cup heavy whipping cream whipped
- 1/2 cup sliced almonds, toasted
- Orange peel strips and fresh thyme, optional

Direction

- Drizzle gelatin over 1 cup of orange juice in a big saucepan and let it sit for 1 minute. Mix in salt and sugar. Stir and cook on low heat until sugar and gelatin are fully melted. Take away from heat. Mix a small amount of the hot mixture into egg yolks, put all back into the pan, tossing nonstop. Boil it lightly, stir and cook for additional 2 minutes. Take away from heat.

- Mix the rest of the orange juice, grated zest, lemon juice, and orange sections in. Let it cool down.
- Tuck in whipped cream. Put into a cooking spray-coated 9-cup ring mold. Refrigerate until set.
- Mix celery with chicken in a big bowl. Mix pepper, salt, vinegar, and mayonnaise together in a small bowl; tuck in whipped cream. Tuck into the chicken mixture.
- Remove the gelatin from the mold onto a serving dish. Use the chicken salad to stuff the middle. Use almonds to drizzle. Enjoy with thyme and orange peel if you want.

Nutrition Information

- Calories: 786 calories
- Cholesterol: 249mg cholesterol
- Protein: 30g protein.
- Total Fat: 50g fat (19g saturated fat)
- Sodium: 246mg sodium
- Fiber: 2g fiber)
- Total Carbohydrate: 55g carbohydrate (50g sugars

---

980. Strawberry Apple Salad

Serving: 15 servings. | Prep: 20mins | Cook: 10mins | Ready in:

Ingredients

- 1 can (20 ounces) crushed pineapple
- 2 packages (3 ounces each) strawberry gelatin
- 2 cups boiling water
- 2 cups diced peeled apples
- 1/2 cup sugar
- 2 tablespoons all-purpose flour
- 1 large egg, beaten
- 2 tablespoons butter
- 4 ounces cream cheese, softened
- 1 envelope whipped topping mix (Dream Whip)

Direction

- Take water out of the pineapple, save the juice; set aside 1/2 cup. Add enough cold water to measure 2 cups to the rest of the juice.
- In a bowl, combine gelatin and boiling water until dissolved, mix in the juice mixture. Add apples and pineapple. Grease a 13x9 inch dish with cooking spray. Pour the mixture in the prepared dish, cover and let chill until firm.
- Mix flour and sugar together in a small saucepan. Mix in the reserved pineapple juice until smooth. Stir and cook over medium-high heat until thickened and bubbly. Lower heat to low, cook and stir for 2 more minutes. Take the saucepan away from the heat. Blend a small amount or give the amount of hot filling into egg, pour the mixture back to the pot, stirring constantly. Boil gently, stir while cooking for 2 minutes. Take away from the heat, mix in cream cheese gently until smooth. Let it cool down.
- Follow the package directions to make whipped topping mix. Fold whipped topping into cream cheese mixture. Scatter the mixture on top of the gelatin. Cover and let chill for about 3 hours, until topping is set.

Nutrition Information

- Calories: 161 calories
- Protein: 2g protein.
- Total Fat: 5g fat (3g saturated fat)
- Sodium: 68mg sodium
- Fiber: 1g fiber)
- Total Carbohydrate: 28g carbohydrate (25g sugars
- Cholesterol: 27mg cholesterol

981.   Strawberry Bavarian Salad

Serving: 6 servings. | Prep: 15mins | Cook: 0mins | Ready in:

Ingredients

- 1 package (3 ounces) strawberry gelatin
- 1 cup boiling water
- 2 packages (10 ounces each) frozen sweetened sliced strawberries
- 1 cup miniature marshmallows
- 1/2 cup heavy whipping cream, whipped

Direction

- In water in a big bowl, dissolve the gelatin. Mix in the strawberries; fold in whipped cream and marshmallows. Add into a 5-cup serving bowl. Keep it covered and let chill in the refrigerator overnight.

Nutrition Information

- Calories: 185 calories
- Total Carbohydrate: 39g carbohydrate (35g sugars
- Cholesterol: 14mg cholesterol
- Protein: 2g protein.
- Total Fat: 4g fat (2g saturated fat)
- Sodium: 42mg sodium
- Fiber: 1g fiber)

982.   Strawberry Gelatin Salad

Serving: 8 servings. | Prep: 10mins | Cook: 0mins | Ready in:

Ingredients

- 2 cups frozen unsweetened strawberries
- 2 medium ripe bananas
- Sugar substitute equivalent to 2 tablespoons sugar
- 1 package (.6 ounce) sugar-free strawberry gelatin
- 2 cups boiling water
- 1 can (8 ounces) unsweetened crushed pineapple, undrained
- 1 cup (8 ounces) reduced-fat plain yogurt

Direction

- Crush sugar substitute, bananas, and strawberries; put aside. Melt gelatin in boiling water. Mix in pineapple and the strawberry mixture.
- Put in a grease-coated 8-inch square plate. Refrigerate until firm. Mix the rest of the gelatin mixture with yogurt, put on the first layer. Refrigerate for 3 hours until firm.

Nutrition Information

- Calories: 86 calories
- Protein: 3g protein. Diabetic Exchanges: 1 fruit
- Total Fat: 1g fat (0 saturated fat)
- Sodium: 76mg sodium
- Fiber: 0 fiber)
- Total Carbohydrate: 18g carbohydrate (0 sugars
- Cholesterol: 2mg cholesterol

983. Strawberry Banana Gelatin Salad

Serving: 12-15 servings. | *Prep: 20mins* | *Cook: 0mins* | *Ready in:*

Ingredients

- 1 package (6 ounces) strawberry gelatin
- 1 cup boiling water
- 2 packages (10 ounces each) frozen sweetened sliced strawberries, partially thawed
- 1 can (20 ounces) crushed pineapple, drained
- 1 cup mashed firm bananas (about 3 medium)
- 1/2 to 3/4 cup chopped walnuts
- 2 cups (16 ounces) sour cream
- 2 teaspoons sugar
- 1/2 teaspoon vanilla extract

Direction

- In water in a big bowl, dissolve gelatin. Mix in nuts, bananas, pineapple, and strawberries.

Add 1/2 of the mixture into one 13x9-in. plate. Keep chilled in the refrigerator till set, about 60 minutes.
- Put the leftover gelatin mixture aside. Mix vanilla, sugar and sour cream. Spread on top of the chilled gelatin. Scoop the leftover gelatin mixture on top. Keep chilled overnight.

Nutrition Information

- Calories: 184 calories
- Sodium: 42mg sodium
- Fiber: 1g fiber)
- Total Carbohydrate: 26g carbohydrate (23g sugars
- Cholesterol: 20mg cholesterol
- Protein: 3g protein.
- Total Fat: 8g fat (4g saturated fat)

984. Strawberry Rhubarb Gelatin

Serving: 6 servings. | *Prep: 20mins* | *Cook: 0mins* | *Ready in:*

Ingredients

- 1 cup chopped fresh or frozen rhubarb
- 3/4 cup water
- 1 package (3 ounces) strawberry gelatin
- 1/3 cup sugar
- 1 tablespoon strawberry jam or strawberry spreadable fruit
- 1 cup unsweetened pineapple juice
- 1 medium tart apple, diced
- 1/2 cup chopped walnuts, optional
- Lettuce leaves and mayonnaise, optional

Direction

- Pour water over rhubarb in a saucepan and bring to a boil over medium heat. Lower heat, simmer, covered until the rhubarb is tender for 8 to 10 minutes. Turn off the heat. Add jam, sugar, and gelatin power, mix until the gelatin is completely dissolved. Pour pineapple juice in. refrigerate until partly firm.

- Stir in nuts and apple if desired. Transfer into a 1-qt bowl covered with cooking spray or six 1/2-cup molds. Refrigerate until complete firm. Remove the mold and place onto lettuce leaves if desired. Put a dollop of mayonnaise on top, then serve.

Nutrition Information

- Calories: 96 calories
- Sodium: 33mg sodium
- Fiber: 0 fiber)
- Total Carbohydrate: 24g carbohydrate (0 sugars
- Cholesterol: 0 cholesterol
- Protein: 1g protein. Diabetic Exchanges: 1-1/2 fruit.
- Total Fat: 0 fat (0 saturated fat)

---

985.   Sugar Free Cranberry Gelatin Salad

Serving: 12 servings. | Prep: 20mins | Cook: 0mins | Ready in:

Ingredients

- 1 package (12 ounces) fresh or frozen cranberries, thawed
- 1 can (12 ounces) frozen apple juice concentrate, thawed
- 2 packages (.3 ounce each) sugar-free raspberry gelatin
- 1 can (8 ounces) crushed pineapple, undrained
- 1 cup chopped celery
- 1 medium navel orange, peeled, sectioned and chopped
- 1/2 cup chopped walnuts

Direction

- Combine apple juice concentrate with cranberries in a 3-qt. microwave-safe dish; use waxed paper to cover. Microwave from 6 to 7.5 minutes on high setting until the most of berries have split. Instantly add gelatin powder and stir until completely dissolved. Allow to cool for 10 to 15 minutes. Add the rest of ingredients and mix properly. Transfer into a 2-qt. ring mold greased with cooking spray. Chill for about 3 hours until totally set. Remove the mold and place onto a serving plate. Enjoy right away.

Nutrition Information

- Calories: 115 calories
- Total Carbohydrate: 20g carbohydrate (0 sugars
- Cholesterol: 0 cholesterol
- Protein: 2g protein. Diabetic Exchanges: 1 fruit
- Total Fat: 3g fat (1g saturated fat)
- Sodium: 49mg sodium
- Fiber: 2g fiber)

---

986.   Summertime Strawberry Gelatin Salad

Serving: 12-16 servings. | Prep: 30mins | Cook: 0mins | Ready in:

Ingredients

- 1 package (3 ounces) strawberry gelatin
- 1 cup boiling water
- 1 cup cold water
- MIDDLE LAYER:
- 1 envelope unflavored gelatin
- 1/2 cup cold water
- 1 cup half-and-half cream
- 1 package (8 ounces) cream cheese, softened
- 1 cup sugar
- 1/2 teaspoon vanilla extract
- TOP LAYER:
- 1 package (6 ounces) strawberry gelatin

- 1 cup boiling water
- 1 cup cold water
- 3 to 4 cups sliced fresh strawberries

Direction

- In a bowl with boiling water, dissolve strawberry gelatin; mix in cold water. Add to a 13x9-in. plate coated using cooking spray; let chill in the refrigerator till set.
- At the same time, drizzle unflavored gelatin on top of cold water in a small-sized bowl; let it rest for 60 seconds. Heat cream but don't boil it in a saucepan on medium heat. Mix in softened gelatin and stir till gelatin dissolves. Let it cool down to room temperature.
- Whip vanilla, sugar and cream cheese in a bowl till smooth in consistency. Slowly pour in the unflavored gelatin mixture; stir well. Gently add on top of the bottom layer. Keep chilled in the refrigerator for roughly 60 minutes till set.
- In boiling water, dissolve strawberry gelatin for making top layer; mix in cold water. Let it cool down to room temperature. Mix in strawberries; gently scoop on top of middle layer. Keep chilled in the refrigerator overnight.

Nutrition Information

- Calories: 187 calories
- Protein: 4g protein.
- Total Fat: 7g fat (4g saturated fat)
- Sodium: 87mg sodium
- Fiber: 1g fiber)
- Total Carbohydrate: 29g carbohydrate (28g sugars
- Cholesterol: 23mg cholesterol

987.　　　Sunshine Gelatin Mold

Serving: 12 servings. | Prep: 15mins | Cook: 0mins | Ready in:

Ingredients

- 2 packages (3 ounces each) lemon gelatin
- 1 cup boiling water
- 1 quart vanilla ice cream, softened
- 1 can (11 ounces) mandarin oranges, drained
- 1 can (8 ounces) unsweetened crushed pineapple, drained

Direction

- Melt the gelatin in boiling water in a big bowl. Mix in ice cream until dissolved. Mix in pineapple and oranges. Put in a cooking spray-coated 6-cup ring mold. Chill until firm, about 2 hours. Remove from the mold onto a serving dish.

Nutrition Information

- Calories: 167 calories
- Total Carbohydrate: 30g carbohydrate (26g sugars
- Cholesterol: 19mg cholesterol
- Protein: 3g protein. Diabetic Exchanges: 2 starch
- Total Fat: 5g fat (3g saturated fat)
- Sodium: 69mg sodium
- Fiber: 0 fiber)

988.　　　Sunshine Gelatin Salad

Serving: 12 servings. | Prep: 30mins | Cook: 0mins | Ready in:

Ingredients

- 1 package (.3 ounce) sugar-free lemon gelatin
- 1 package (.3 ounce) sugar-free orange gelatin
- 2 cups boiling water
- 1-1/2 cups cold water
- 1 can (20 ounces) unsweetened crushed pineapple
- 3 medium firm bananas, chopped
- 1/3 cup miniature marshmallows

- Sugar substitute equivalent to 1/4 cup sugar
- 2 tablespoons all-purpose flour
- 1 egg, lightly beaten
- 2 tablespoons butter, cubed
- 2-1/2 cups whipped topping

Direction

- Melt orange and lemon gelatin in boiling water in a big bowl. Mix in cold water. Put a cover on and chill for 1 1/2 hours until partly set.
- Strain pineapple and save the juice. Add enough water to the juice to get 1 cup.
- Put pineapple, marshmallows, and bananas into the gelatin mixture. Move to a 13x9-in. plate. Put a cover on and chill until firm
- Mix flour and sugar substitute together in a small saucepan. Slowly mix in pineapple juice mixture. Stir and cook on medium-high heat until bubbly and thickened. Lower the heat, stir and cook for another 2 minutes. Take away from heat.
- Mix a small amount of boiling filling into egg and put all back to the pan, tossing nonstop. Boil it slightly, stir and cook for 2 minutes. Take away from heat; mix in butter until dissolved.
- Let cool to room temperature, do not toss. Tuck in whipped topping. Spread over the gelatin. Put a cover on and chill for a minimum of 1 hour before slicing.

Nutrition Information

- Calories: 109 calories
- Fiber: 1g fiber)
- Total Carbohydrate: 16g carbohydrate (11g sugars
- Cholesterol: 18mg cholesterol
- Protein: 2g protein. Diabetic Exchanges: 1 fruit
- Total Fat: 4g fat (3g saturated fat)
- Sodium: 49mg sodium

Serving: 8 servings. | Prep: 15mins | Cook: 0mins | Ready in:

Ingredients

- 1 package (3 ounces) lemon gelatin
- 1 cup boiling water
- 1 can (8 ounces) pineapple chunks, undrained
- 1 large grapefruit, peeled, sectioned and diced
- 1 medium apple, peeled and chopped
- 1/4 cup chopped pecans

Direction

- In boiling water, dissolve gelatin in a bowl. Drain pineapple, saving the juice; put pineapple aside. Pour cold water into juice to measure 1 cup; mix into gelatin mixture. Keep chilled till partially set. Mix in pineapple, pecans, apple, and grapefruit; add to one 1 1/2-qt. bowl. Keep chilled till firm.

Nutrition Information

- Calories: 65 calories
- Fiber: 0 fiber)
- Total Carbohydrate: 10g carbohydrate (0 sugars
- Cholesterol: 0 cholesterol
- Protein: 1g protein. Diabetic Exchanges: 1/2 fruit
- Total Fat: 3g fat (0 saturated fat)
- Sodium: 24mg sodium

---
990. **Sweetheart Jell O Salad**

Serving: 12-16 servings. | Prep: 20mins | Cook: 0mins | Ready in:

Ingredients

- 2 envelopes unflavored gelatin
- 1/4 cup cold water

- 1/2 cup sugar
- 1 can (20 ounces) crushed pineapple, undrained
- 2 tablespoons lemon juice
- 1/4 cup maraschino cherry juice
- 6 ounces cream cheese, softened
- 12 maraschino cherries, quartered
- 2 to 3 drops red food coloring, optional
- 1 carton (12 ounces) frozen whipped topping, thawed
- Lettuce leaves, optional

Direction

- Soak gelatin in cold water to soften. In the meantime, combine pineapple with syrup and sugar in a saucepan, and bring to a boil, stirring to dissolve the sugar completely. Turn the heat off. Add softened gelatin and mix until totally dissolved. Pour cherry and lemon juices into the saucepan. Allow to cool to slightly warm. Add cream cheese and whisk until perfectly combined. Mix cherries, and some food coloring if desired. Refrigerate until slightly set. Add whipped topping, fold. Pour mixture into a greased 8-1/2-cup mold or 13x9-inch pan; refrigerate until entirely set. Serve with the mold or divide into squares and place individually onto plates lined with lettuce leaves.

Nutrition Information

- Calories:
- Sodium:
- Fiber:
- Total Carbohydrate:
- Cholesterol:
- Protein:
- Total Fat:

991.   Tangy Cucumber Gelatin

Serving: 2 servings. | Prep: 10mins | Cook: 0mins | Ready in:

Ingredients

- 1 package (3 ounces) lemon gelatin
- 1/2 cup boiling water
- 1 medium cucumber, peeled and diced
- 4 green onions, chopped
- 1 cup (8 ounces) 4% cottage cheese
- 1/2 cup mayonnaise

Direction

- Put gelatin in boiling water to dissolve in a bowl. Mix in onions and cucumber. Add mayonnaise and cottage cheese; stir until blended. Pour into two 1-1/2-cup molds coated with cooking-spray. Put them into the refrigerator until set or overnight. Take it out of the mold when ready to serve.

Nutrition Information

- Calories: 707 calories
- Total Carbohydrate: 48g carbohydrate (45g sugars
- Cholesterol: 45mg cholesterol
- Protein: 19g protein.
- Total Fat: 49g fat (9g saturated fat)
- Sodium: 802mg sodium
- Fiber: 2g fiber)

992.   Tangy Lemon Gelatin

Serving: 8-10 servings. | Prep: 15mins | Cook: 0mins | Ready in:

Ingredients

- 1 package (6 ounces) orange gelatin or lemon gelatin
- 2 cups boiling water

- 3/4 cup thawed lemonade concentrate
- 1 to 3 tablespoons prepared horseradish
- 1 carton (8 ounces) frozen whipped topping, thawed
- 2 to 3 tablespoons orange marmalade

Direction

- In a big bowl with boiling water, dissolve gelatin. Mix in horseradish and lemonade concentrate. Keep it covered and let chill in the refrigerator for roughly 60 minutes till partially set. Mix in marmalade and whipped topping. Coat a 2-qt. ring mold using cooking spray; put in gelatin mixture. Keep chilled for no less than 4 hours, or till firm. Just prior to serving, invert to a serving platter.

Nutrition Information

- Calories: 175 calories
- Total Carbohydrate: 33g carbohydrate (29g sugars
- Cholesterol: 0 cholesterol
- Protein: 2g protein.
- Total Fat: 4g fat (4g saturated fat)
- Sodium: 47mg sodium
- Fiber: 0 fiber)

993. Tart Cherry Salad

Serving: 16-18 servings. | Prep: 15mins | Cook: 0mins | Ready in:

Ingredients

- 2 cans (16 ounces each) tart red cherries
- 2 cans (8 ounces each) crushed pineapple
- 1 cup sugar
- 2 packages (6 ounces each) cherry gelatin
- 3 cups ginger ale
- 3/4 cup sweetened shredded coconut
- 1 cup chopped nuts, optional

Direction

- Drain pineapple and cherries, saving the juices. Put fruit aside. Pour enough water into combined juices to make 3-1/4 cups; add to a saucepan. Put in sugar; boil. Take out of the heat; mix in gelatin till dissolved. Put in ginger ale, pineapple and cherries. Keep chilled till partially set. If you want, mix in nuts and coconut. Add to an oiled 3-qt. mold or 13x9-in. pan. Keep chilled for roughly 3 hours till firm.

Nutrition Information

- Calories: 137 calories
- Sodium: 36mg sodium
- Fiber: 0 fiber)
- Total Carbohydrate: 31g carbohydrate (30g sugars
- Cholesterol: 0 cholesterol
- Protein: 1g protein.
- Total Fat: 1g fat (1g saturated fat)

994. Thanksgiving Cranberry Gelatin

Serving: 16-20 servings. | Prep: 30mins | Cook: 0mins | Ready in:

Ingredients

- 1 package (6 ounces) cherry gelatin
- 1/3 to 1/2 cup sugar
- 2 cups boiling cranberry juice
- 1-1/2 cups ice cubes
- 2 celery ribs, finely chopped
- 1 medium pear, peeled and finely chopped
- 1 cup chopped fresh or frozen cranberries
- 3/4 cup ground walnuts, divided
- 1 package (3 ounces) lemon gelatin
- 1 cup boiling water
- 1 cup mayonnaise
- 1 carton (8 ounces) frozen whipped topping, thawed, divided

Direction

- Melt sugar and cherry gelatin in boiling cranberry juice in a big bowl. Add ice cubes, toss until melted. Chill for 45 minutes until thickened.
- Fold in 1/2 cup of walnuts, cranberries, pear, and celery. Move to a grease-coated 13-inch x 9-inch plate. Chill for 50 minutes until firm.
- In the meantime, melt lemon gelatin in water in another bowl. Chill for 35 minutes until slightly thickened. Mix in 1/4 cup of mayonnaise, put in the rest of the mayonnaise. Fold in half of the whipped topping. Gently put on the cherry layer. Chill until firm, about 45 minutes.
- Use the rest of the whipped topping to spread. Use the rest of the walnuts to drizzle. Chill for a minimum of 3 hours. Slice into squares.

Nutrition Information

- Calories: 210 calories
- Total Carbohydrate: 22g carbohydrate (20g sugars
- Cholesterol: 4mg cholesterol
- Protein: 2g protein.
- Total Fat: 13g fat (3g saturated fat)
- Sodium: 93mg sodium
- Fiber: 1g fiber)

---

995.   Three Layer Fruit Salad

Serving: 8 servings. | Prep: 15mins | Cook: 0mins | Ready in:

Ingredients

- 1 can (15 ounces) pear halves in extra-light syrup
- 2 cans (8-1/4 ounces each) reduced-sugar apricot halves
- 2 medium firm bananas, cut into 1/2-inch slices
- 2 packages (.3 ounce each) sugar-free lime gelatin
- 2 cups boiling water

Direction

- Drain apricots and pears; reserve 1-1/2 cup of syrup. Coat a 9x5-inch loaf pan with cooking spray then make layers of pears, apricots and bananas. Let gelatin dissolve in a big bowl of boiling water. Add in the reserved syrup and stir. Pour over bananas with gelatin mixture. Store in the fridge, covered, till firm. Unmold the gelatin and slice.

Nutrition Information

- Calories: 76 calories
- Total Fat: 0 fat (0 saturated fat)
- Sodium: 62mg sodium
- Fiber: 2g fiber)
- Total Carbohydrate: 17g carbohydrate (0 sugars
- Cholesterol: 0 cholesterol
- Protein: 2g protein. Diabetic Exchanges: 1 fruit.

---

996.   Three Layer Gelatin Salad

Serving: 12-16 servings. | Prep: 10mins | Cook: 20mins | Ready in:

Ingredients

- 1 package (3 ounces) raspberry gelatin
- 1 cup boiling water
- 1 package (10 ounces) frozen sweetened raspberries
- ORANGE LAYER:
- 1 can (11 ounces) mandarin oranges
- 1 package (3 ounces) orange gelatin
- 1 cup boiling water
- 1 package (8 ounces) cream cheese, softened
- LIME LAYER:
- 1 package (3 ounces) lime gelatin
- 1 cup boiling water

- 1 can (8-1/2 ounces) crushed pineapple

Direction

- Let gelatin dissolve in the boiling water in a big bowl. Add in raspberries and stir till thawed. Grease an 8-inch square dish then pour in the mixture. Store in the fridge till set.
- Let the orange drain and reserve the juice. Let orange gelatin dissolve in boiling water in a small bowl. Beat reserved juice and cream cheese in a big bowl till smooth. Mix in gelatin mixture. Fold in oranges. Spread over the raspberry layer then store in the fridge till set.
- Let lime gelatin dissolve in boiling water in a big bowl. Add in pineapple then cool for 10 minutes. Carefully pour over orange layer. Store in the fridge till set.

Nutrition Information

- Calories: 149 calories
- Total Carbohydrate: 25g carbohydrate (24g sugars
- Cholesterol: 16mg cholesterol
- Protein: 3g protein.
- Total Fat: 5g fat (3g saturated fat)
- Sodium: 80mg sodium
- Fiber: 1g fiber)

997.　　Three Ring Mold

Serving: 16-18 servings. | Prep: 30mins | Cook: 0mins | Ready in:

Ingredients

- FIRST LAYER:
- 2 cans (29 ounces each) pear halves
- 1 package (3 ounces) cherry gelatin
- 3/4 cup boiling water
- SECOND LAYER:
- 1 package (8 ounces) cream cheese, softened
- 1 package (3 ounces) lemon gelatin

- 3/4 cup boiling water
- 3/4 cup cold water
- 1 cup heavy whipping cream, whipped
- THIRD LAYER:
- 1 can (20 ounces) crushed pineapple
- 1 package (3 ounces) lime gelatin
- 3/4 cup boiling water

Direction

- Drain pears, saving three quarters cup of juice. Arrange pears into a 4-qt. glass bowl or trifle plate. In boiling water, dissolve cherry gelatin; pour in reserved juice. Add on top of pears. Keep chilled till firm.
- For second layer, whip cream cheese in a bowl till smooth and creamy in texture. In boiling water, dissolve lemon gelatin; slowly pour to cream cheese. Whip till smooth in consistency. Mix in cold water. Put in cream and blend till smooth in consistency. Add atop first layer. Keep chilled till firm.
- For third layer, drain pineapple, saving three quarters cup of juice. In boiling water, dissolve lime gelatin; pour in reserved juice and pineapple. Add atop second layer. Keep chilled till firm.

Nutrition Information

- Calories: 194 calories
- Protein: 3g protein.
- Total Fat: 9g fat (6g saturated fat)
- Sodium: 77mg sodium
- Fiber: 1g fiber)
- Total Carbohydrate: 27g carbohydrate (24g sugars
- Cholesterol: 32mg cholesterol

998.　　Triple Cranberry Salad Mold

Serving: 8-10 servings. | Prep: 20mins | Cook: 0mins | Ready in:

Ingredients

- 2 packages (3 ounces each) cranberry gelatin
- 3 cups boiling water
- 1 cup cranberry juice
- 2 packages (3 ounces each) cream cheese, softened
- 1 carton (8 ounces) frozen whipped topping, thawed
- 1 cup chopped walnuts
- 1 cup chopped celery
- 1 cup chopped fresh or frozen cranberries

Direction

- In a big bowl with boiling water, dissolve gelatin; mix in cranberry juice. Keep chilled in the refrigerator till thickened a bit. Whip cream cheese in a small-sized bowl till smooth in consistency. Put in the whipped topping till blended. Fold to the gelatin mixture. Fold in cranberries, celery, and walnuts.
- Add to a 3-qt. ring mold coated using cooking spray. Keep in the refrigerator till set. Unmold to a serving dish.

Nutrition Information

- Calories: 218 calories
- Sodium: 56mg sodium
- Fiber: 1g fiber)
- Total Carbohydrate: 19g carbohydrate (14g sugars
- Cholesterol: 9mg cholesterol
- Protein: 5g protein.
- Total Fat: 14g fat (6g saturated fat)

---

999.   Waldorf Orange Cinnamon Holiday Mold

Serving: 12 servings (1/2 cup each). | Prep: 30mins | Cook: 8mins |Ready in:

Ingredients

- 2 packages (3 ounces each) cherry gelatin
- 1/2 cup Red Hots
- 1/3 cup sugar
- 1-1/2 cups water
- 1-3/4 cups orange juice
- 1/3 cup sour cream
- 1-1/2 cups orange sections, chopped
- 1 medium apple, peeled and finely chopped
- 1/2 cup chopped pecans

Direction

- Add gelatin into a big bowl. Mix water, sugar and Red Hots in a small-sized saucepan. Cook and stir till candies are dissolved and the mixture boils. Mix into gelatin. Mix in sour cream and orange juice. Keep in the refrigerator till thickened or for 30 to 45 minutes. Mix in pecans, apple and oranges. Add to a 6-cup ring mold coated using cooking spray. Keep chilled in the refrigerator till firm or for 4 hours. Unmold to a platter.

Nutrition Information

- Calories:
- Protein:
- Total Fat:
- Sodium:
- Fiber:
- Total Carbohydrate:
- Cholesterol:

1000.   Waldorf Salad Mold

Serving: 12 servings. | Prep: 25mins | Cook: 0mins | Ready in:

Ingredients

- 2 packages (3 ounces each) strawberry gelatin
- 2 cups boiling water
- 1-1/2 cups cold water
- 2 medium apples, diced

- 1/2 cup chopped celery
- 1/4 cup chopped walnuts
- LEMON YOGURT DRESSING:
- 3/4 cup (6 ounces) lemon yogurt
- 1-1/2 teaspoons brown sugar
- 1/8 teaspoon salt
- Dash to 1/8 teaspoon ground cinnamon

Direction

- Melt the gelatin in boiling water in a big bowl. Mix in cold water. Put a cover on and chill for 1-1/2 hours until partly set. Fold in the walnuts, celery, and apples. Put in a grease-coated 6-cup ring mold. Put a cover on and chill until set, about 4 hours.
- To prepare the dressing, mix cinnamon, salt, brown sugar, and yogurt together; refrigerate until serving. For serving, remove the salad from the mold onto a dish. Enjoy with the dressing.

Nutrition Information

- Calories: 103 calories
- Sodium: 74mg sodium
- Fiber: 1g fiber)
- Total Carbohydrate: 19g carbohydrate (18g sugars
- Cholesterol: 2mg cholesterol
- Protein: 3g protein. Diabetic Exchanges: 1-1/2 fruit.
- Total Fat: 2g fat (1g saturated fat)

1001. Whipped Cream Gelatin Mosaic

Serving: 10 servings. | Prep: 50mins | Cook: 0mins | Ready in:

Ingredients

- 1 package (3 ounces) cherry gelatin
- 3-3/4 cups boiling water, divided
- 1-1/2 cups cold water, divided
- 1 package (3 ounces) lime gelatin
- 1 package (3 ounces) orange gelatin
- 1 package (3 ounces) lemon gelatin
- 1/4 cup sugar
- 1/2 cup lemonade
- 1-3/4 cups whipped topping
- Additional whipped topping, optional

Direction

- In 1 cup of boiling water in a small-sized bowl, dissolve the cherry gelatin; mix in half a cup of cold water. Add to an 8-in. square plate coated using cooking spray. Keep chilled in the refrigerator till set.
- Repeat with orange gelatin and lime, using different 8-in. square plates for each.
- In a big bowl containing the leftover boiling water, dissolve sugar and lemon gelatin; mix in lemonade. Keep it covered and let chill in the refrigerator till thickened a bit. Fold in the whipped topping.
- Chop the orange gelatin, lime and cherry into half-an-inch cubes. Fold into lemon gelatin mixture. Scoop to separate serving plates. Keep it covered and let chill in the refrigerator for no less than 2 hours. If you want, use extra whipped topping for decoration.

Nutrition Information

- Calories: 184 calories
- Cholesterol: 0 cholesterol
- Protein: 3g protein.
- Total Fat: 2g fat (2g saturated fat)
- Sodium: 78mg sodium
- Fiber: 0 fiber)
- Total Carbohydrate: 39g carbohydrate (37g sugars

Index

A

Almond 8,9,287,290,292,321

Amaretti 3,18

Apple
3,6,7,9,10,11,12,13,17,163,177,200,211,244,320,363,394,4
09,410,411,412,426,462,472,482,495,512,525

Apricot 3,8,11,15,282,412,413,414

Asparagus 12,482

B

Baking 118,164,379

Banana
3,4,6,7,8,9,10,11,13,16,45,96,97,169,178,179,180,181,182,
183,184,185,186,187,188,212,220,245,258,270,273,279,29
9,308,330,364,384,390,421,526

Beef 38

Beer 10,375

Berry
3,5,6,7,8,11,12,13,16,17,18,112,113,127,133,157,172,173,1
88,189,190,220,258,267,403,406,412,415,416,472,508,509

Blackberry 3,5,19,114,126

Blueberry
3,4,5,6,10,11,13,28,62,114,134,140,159,193,194,195,373,4
17,418,430,442,499,507

Bran 45,175

Bread 7,216

Brie 213,305

Butter
6,7,8,9,10,11,13,118,156,164,178,179,198,199,200,201,202
,203,204,205,206,209,219,220,223,238,263,272,284,286,29
6,299,300,310,313,322,329,335,336,337,338,340,366,367,3
76,382,419,489,490

C

Cabbage 11,419

Cake
3,4,5,6,7,8,9,10,11,27,57,75,82,83,112,113,114,115,116,11
7,118,119,120,121,122,123,124,125,126,127,128,129,130,1
31,132,133,134,135,136,137,139,140,147,148,149,150,152,
153,154,155,156,157,158,159,160,161,162,163,164,166,16
8,169,170,171,173,174,175,177,183,186,188,190,191,205,2
07,208,213,219,221,222,225,226,228,231,234,244,249,253,
259,261,262,264,267,271,272,274,275,276,280,283,294,29
7,298,301,302,309,312,315,316,318,323,324,325,327,330,3
33,340,341,343,345,346,351,354,358,361,362,365,368,372,
379,382,399,401,404,405

Caramel 5,7,10,110,116,211,212,394

Carrot 3,8,9,11,21,264,309,404

Celery 483,485

Cheese
3,4,5,6,7,9,10,11,12,32,56,69,112,124,133,134,135,140,141
,142,143,144,145,146,147,165,172,174,175,178,179,182,18
6,193,206,214,227,259,303,314,345,361,385,429,445,462

Cherry
3,4,5,7,9,11,12,13,18,22,23,24,25,80,116,117,119,142,214,
215,216,217,218,221,222,242,321,346,409,420,421,422,42
3,432,483,523,531

Chips 3,46

Chocolate
3,5,6,7,8,9,10,11,22,26,27,28,37,110,117,118,119,120,121,
123,143,161,174,180,181,190,192,196,208,209,218,220,22
1,222,223,224,225,226,227,228,229,230,231,232,233,234,2
35,236,237,238,239,240,241,242,244,245,252,259,263,264,
266,267,268,269,273,274,275,283,292,293,296,298,304,30
6,308,310,321,326,327,335,336,337,339,345,364,368,369,3
73,379,380,381,391,398,399,400,401,406,407

Chutney 13,521

Cider 11,409,410,426

Cinnamon 3,7,8,11,13,23,244,285,409,411,426,427,534

Citrus fruit 69

Cocoa powder 395

Coconut

6,7,8,9,10,125,171,180,213,226,245,246,247,248,249,250,2
60,275,322,342,346,351,364,372,404

Coffee 3,7,8,9,30,244,251,285,324

Cola 9,11,13,341,420,497

Corn syrup 33

Coulis 4,72

Cranberry

3,4,5,8,11,12,13,21,32,33,34,38,45,52,89,121,130,255,261,
287,410,420,423,425,426,432,433,434,435,436,437,438,43
9,440,441,443,445,447,448,449,452,457,458,468,469,473,4
84,485,486,494,500,501,504,520,521,527,532,534

Cream

3,4,5,6,7,8,9,10,11,12,13,14,17,18,26,28,31,32,35,36,43,63,
64,69,70,73,74,75,76,84,91,92,98,103,107,116,121,128,133
,144,148,157,161,164,171,172,173,175,180,181,182,183,18
4,185,187,193,195,196,199,206,212,213,215,216,221,227,2
32,234,239,245,246,251,252,253,255,256,257,258,259,260,
261,262,269,272,273,274,278,279,284,285,290,294,295,29
6,301,306,308,314,317,318,319,323,324,326,327,328,330,3
34,339,348,349,356,361,363,364,365,368,369,371,372,373,
374,378,381,382,384,385,386,393,397,399,401,403,404,40
5,441,442,443,444,445,462,494,535

Crumble 295,315,336,393,395

Cucumber 11,12,13,419,429,446,531

Custard 9,315

D

Date 5,122

Dijon mustard 415,437

E

Egg

3,8,9,11,12,38,39,40,164,279,280,281,304,433,440,446,486

F

Fat

9,15,16,17,18,19,20,21,22,23,24,25,26,27,28,29,30,31,32,3
3,34,35,36,37,38,39,40,41,42,43,44,45,46,47,48,49,50,51,5
2,53,54,55,56,57,58,59,60,61,62,63,64,65,66,67,68,69,70,7
1,72,73,74,75,76,77,78,79,80,81,82,83,84,85,86,87,88,89,9
0,91,92,93,94,95,96,97,98,99,100,101,102,103,104,105,106
,107,108,109,110,111,112,113,114,115,116,117,118,119,12
0,121,122,123,124,125,126,127,128,129,130,131,132,133,1
34,135,136,137,138,139,140,141,142,143,144,145,146,147,
148,149,150,151,152,153,154,155,156,157,158,159,160,16
1,162,163,164,166,167,168,169,170,171,172,173,174,175,1
76,177,178,179,180,181,182,183,184,185,186,187,188,189,
190,191,192,193,194,195,196,197,198,199,200,201,202,20
3,204,205,206,207,208,209,210,211,212,213,214,215,216,2
17,218,219,220,221,222,223,224,225,226,227,228,229,230,
231,232,233,234,235,236,237,238,239,240,241,242,243,24
4,245,246,247,248,249,250,251,252,253,254,255,256,257,2
58,259,260,261,262,263,264,265,266,267,268,269,270,271,
272,273,274,275,276,277,278,279,280,281,282,283,284,28
5,286,287,288,289,290,291,292,293,294,295,296,297,298,2
99,300,301,302,303,304,305,306,307,308,309,310,311,312,
313,314,315,316,317,318,319,320,321,322,323,324,325,32
6,327,328,329,330,331,332,333,334,335,336,337,338,339,3
40,341,342,343,344,345,346,347,348,349,350,351,352,353,
354,355,356,357,358,359,360,361,362,363,364,365,366,36
7,368,369,370,371,372,373,374,375,376,377,378,379,380,3
81,382,383,384,385,386,387,388,389,390,391,392,393,394,
395,396,397,398,399,400,401,402,403,404,405,406,407,40
8,409,410,411,412,413,414,415,416,417,418,419,420,421,4
22,423,424,425,426,427,428,429,430,431,432,433,434,435,
436,437,438,439,440,441,442,443,444,445,446,447,448,44
9,450,451,452,453,454,455,456,457,458,459,460,461,462,4
63,464,465,466,467,468,469,470,471,472,473,474,475,476,
477,478,479,480,481,482,483,484,485,486,487,488,489,49

0,491,492,493,494,495,496,497,498,499,500,501,502,503,5
04,505,506,507,508,509,510,511,512,513,514,515,516,517,
518,519,520,521,522,523,524,525,526,527,528,529,530,53
1,532,533,534,535,536

Fig 9,304

Fish 154,155

Flour 118,164

Fruit
3,4,6,8,10,11,12,13,35,44,45,67,79,200,289,290,291,353,37
8,399,402,421,433,441,444,447,453,456,457,458,459,460,4
61,464,484,491,532

Fudge 5,7,10,127,131,132,231,398

G

Game 3,46

Gelatine 385

Gin
4,5,6,7,8,9,10,12,82,128,202,243,295,296,297,305,357,361,
394,462,463

Grapefruit 12,446,466

Grapes 3,43

Guacamole 12,467

H

Hazelnut 7,8,232,291

Heart 4,6,13,93,166,508

Honey 9,305

I

Ice cream 118,127

J

Jelly 269

Jus 46,50,205,257,366,468,480,487,502,511,515,531

L

Lemon
3,4,5,6,7,8,9,10,12,13,41,42,52,53,54,55,56,57,58,100,124,
126,128,129,132,133,134,135,136,144,149,159,162,189,19

4,207,267,288,297,312,313,314,315,316,317,318,386,408,4
54,459,483,531

Lettuce
71,416,425,436,441,459,468,479,496,520,522,527,530

Lime
3,4,5,11,12,13,26,51,59,60,61,70,79,136,145,157,275,429,4
49,460,463,475,476,477,479,481,482,487,495,496,498,499,
516

M

Macadamia 9,320

Mandarin 3,4,9,31,63,323

Mango 8,12,261,480

Marmalade 5,139

Marshmallow 6,12,125,168,190,296,481

Mayonnaise 461,503,509,513

Melon 4,64

Meringue 11,400

Milk 9,118,143,164,323

Mince 3,25

Mint 7,9,10,12,234,235,236,320,325,378,390,448,482

Mustard 38

N

Nut
6,7,9,12,15,16,17,18,19,20,21,22,23,24,25,26,27,28,29,30,3
1,32,33,34,35,36,37,38,39,40,41,42,43,44,45,46,47,48,49,5
0,51,52,53,54,55,56,57,58,59,60,61,62,63,64,65,66,67,68,6
9,70,71,72,73,74,75,76,77,78,79,80,81,82,83,84,85,86,87,8
8,89,90,91,92,93,94,95,96,97,98,99,100,101,102,103,104,1
05,106,107,108,109,110,111,112,113,114,115,116,117,118,
119,120,121,122,123,124,125,126,127,128,129,130,131,13
2,133,134,135,136,137,138,139,140,141,142,143,144,145,1
46,147,148,149,150,151,152,153,154,155,156,157,158,159,
160,161,162,163,164,165,166,167,168,169,170,171,172,17
3,174,175,176,177,178,179,180,181,182,183,184,185,186,1
87,188,189,190,191,192,193,194,195,196,197,198,199,200,

201,202,203,204,205,206,207,208,209,210,211,212,213,21
4,215,216,217,218,219,220,221,222,223,224,225,226,227,2
28,229,230,231,232,233,234,235,236,237,238,239,240,241,
242,243,244,245,246,247,248,249,250,251,252,253,254,25
5,256,257,258,259,260,261,262,263,264,265,266,267,268,2
69,270,271,272,273,274,275,276,277,278,279,280,281,282,
283,284,285,286,287,288,289,290,291,292,293,294,295,29
6,297,298,299,300,301,302,303,304,305,306,307,308,309,3
10,311,312,313,314,315,316,317,318,319,320,321,322,323,
324,325,326,327,328,329,330,331,332,333,334,335,336,33
7,338,339,340,341,342,343,344,345,346,347,348,349,350,3
51,352,353,354,355,356,357,358,359,360,361,362,363,364,
365,366,367,368,369,370,371,372,373,374,375,376,377,37
8,379,380,381,382,383,384,385,386,387,388,389,390,391,3
92,393,394,395,396,397,398,399,400,401,402,403,404,405,
406,407,408,409,410,411,412,413,414,415,416,417,418,41
9,420,421,422,423,424,425,426,427,428,429,430,431,432,4
33,434,435,436,437,438,439,440,441,442,443,444,445,446,
447,448,449,450,451,452,453,454,455,456,457,458,459,46
0,461,462,463,464,465,466,467,468,469,470,471,472,473,4
74,475,476,477,478,479,480,481,482,483,484,485,486,487,
488,489,490,491,492,493,494,495,496,497,498,499,500,50
1,502,503,504,505,506,507,508,509,510,511,512,513,514,5
15,516,517,518,519,520,521,522,523,524,525,526,527,528,
529,530,531,532,533,534,535,536

O

Oatmeal 7,8,225,300

Octopus 155

Oil 153

Orange
3,4,5,6,7,8,9,11,12,13,42,63,65,68,69,70,71,105,106,121,13
0,148,149,157,171,208,254,323,331,343,344,414,419,430,4
41,444,445,446,454,460,465,474,486,489,490,491,522,524,
534

P

Papaya 4,72

Parfait
3,4,6,7,8,9,10,11,12,19,22,33,46,50,56,65,181,183,185,192,
203,210,214,220,232,236,271,326,332,349,357,370,371,37
5,395,403,406,456

Pastry 49,255,257,261,312

Peach
3,4,5,6,7,8,9,10,12,13,45,74,75,76,94,103,150,151,154,155,
195,247,261,334,370,374,387,482,487,493,494,495,522

Peanut butter 220

Pear 4,12,13,77,462,468,476,477,495,496,510

Pecan
5,6,7,8,9,10,11,120,202,212,263,268,340,361,376,396,437

Peel 165,184,286,348,408

Pepper 4,7,8,77,239,272

Pie
3,4,5,6,7,8,9,10,11,29,38,42,58,59,63,76,82,89,94,103,113,
130,135,142,144,147,160,179,180,187,188,195,196,204,20
9,212,214,219,220,227,232,233,238,245,246,247,248,255,2
58,261,268,270,272,273,275,279,282,285,287,288,293,297,
300,303,310,312,314,318,321,326,328,330,336,342,351,35
2,355,356,359,363,364,367,369,373,374,375,385,391,397,3
98,399,400,403,407

Pineapple
3,4,5,7,8,9,10,11,12,13,21,71,78,79,115,152,153,239,240,2
48,262,275,328,331,342,343,344,391,422,440,443,454,483,
497,498,499,506

Pistachio
5,7,8,9,10,154,216,248,276,286,289,345,346,347,348,349,3
50,351,383,405

Pizza 7,224,240

Pomegranate 13,500

Port 87,95

Potato 13,496

Pulse 348

Pumpkin

4,5,7,8,10,82,111,146,204,205,270,295,297,352,354,355,356,357,358,359,360,361,362,379,391

R

Raspberry
3,4,5,6,7,8,10,11,12,13,29,31,32,34,66,83,84,85,86,87,88,121,157,158,159,241,249,289,293,367,368,369,370,371,387,399,412,418,431,450,456,501,503,504,505,506,511,513,518

Rhubarb
4,5,6,8,11,12,13,90,91,113,147,160,167,170,262,416,417,488,509,510,511,512,519,524,527

Rice
3,4,6,7,8,9,10,25,43,101,104,161,217,275,317,366,386,392

Rosemary 6,162

Rum 4,7,9,90,213,324

S

Salad
3,4,10,11,12,13,14,21,24,34,45,60,67,77,105,353,408,409,410,413,414,415,417,419,420,421,422,423,424,425,426,427,428,429,430,431,432,433,434,435,436,437,438,439,440,441,442,445,446,447,449,450,451,452,453,454,455,457,458,459,460,461,463,464,465,468,469,470,471,472,473,474,476,477,479,480,481,482,483,484,485,486,487,488,489,490,491,492,493,494,495,496,497,498,499,500,501,503,504,505,506,507,509,510,511,512,513,514,515,516,517,518,519,520,521,522,523,524,525,526,527,528,529,530,531,532,533,534,535

Salsa 12,467

Salt 10,118,376,524

Sherry 10,382

Shortbread 4,90

Soda 3,16

Sorbet 10,388

Spinach 13,523

Strawberry

3,4,5,6,7,8,9,10,12,13,26,30,36,59,62,67,81,89,91,96,97,98,99,100,101,125,137,147,164,165,166,167,168,169,170,173,175,214,276,319,377,384,385,386,387,388,389,390,455,461,477,488,511,520,525,526,527,528

Sugar
3,4,5,6,9,10,13,15,43,58,62,72,78,87,96,98,102,105,115,118,126,131,133,143,144,146,154,158,162,164,166,167,168,170,185,201,211,237,258,259,270,273,275,296,317,332,333,353,361,365,386,391,392,403,404,405,418,430,434,445,458,484,489,526,527,529

Syrup 4,5,64,110

T

Tea 3,4,8,50,94,123,271,387

Terrine 5,110

Thyme 6,162

Toffee 6,7,9,10,197,206,322,396,397

Turkey 11,439

W

Walnut 11,404,405

Watermelon 5,6,108,109,174

Worcestershire sauce 521

Conclusion

Thank you again for downloading this book!

I hope you enjoyed reading about my book!

If you enjoyed this book, please take the time to share your thoughts and post a review on Amazon. It'd be greatly appreciated!

Write me an honest review about the book – I truly value your opinion and thoughts and I will incorporate them into my next book, which is already underway.

Thank you!

If you have any questions, **feel free to contact at:** _author@ashkenazirecipes.com_

Ellen Grubbs

ashkenazirecipes.com

Made in the USA
Las Vegas, NV
30 December 2024

15543057R00299